Safe Places for the 80s

David and Holly Franke

THE DIAL PRESS
DOUBLEDAY & COMPANY, INC.
GARDEN CITY, NEW YORK
1984

Published by The Dial Press

Manufactured in the United States of America
First printing

Library of Congress Cataloging in Publication Data

Franke, David.
Safe places for the 80s.

Includes index.
1. United States—Description and travel—1981–
—Guide-books. 2. Criminal statistics—United States.
3. Cities and towns—United States—Guide-books.
I. Franke, Holly. II. Title. III. Title: Safe places for
the eighties.
E158.F673 1984 973.927 83-45187
ISBN 0-385-27876-4

FOR MELISSA
AND
FOR OUR PARENTS,
WITH LOVE

Contents

Tables and Charts

Acknowledgments

We thank the wonderful people we met in each of our Safe Places who gave so freely of their time and knowledge. They are far too numerous to mention individually here, but you will find their names in our discussions of each town.

Special thanks to our agent, Lila Karpf, and to our editors at The Dial Press for their faith in the project and for their forbearance as the timetable proved rather more elastic than we had originally planned. Also our appreciation to Carmen Accashian and to our neighbors Kurt and Helga Freter for helping to keep our homestead a Safe Place while we were on the road, to Malcolm Wright for his editorial and stylistic advice, to Nancy Egbert for her assistance with the crime statistics, to John Bernick for his help in locating some Safe Places in Colorado, and to Robert Ritchie for the fascinating materials he supplied for our Texas chapter.

Holly wishes to give a special note of appreciation to her parents, Pascal and Mary Lambro, for their unending encouragement on this project, for giving her the early opportunity to see and appreciate the beauty of this country, and for their foresight in raising her in such a lovely Safe Place as Wellesley.

Above all, loving thanks to our daughter Melissa for being so understanding and selfless in giving up her time with us, so many days and so many evenings when we had to devote our attentions to this manuscript. She was a real trooper on our interesting and at times thrilling, but more often hectic and tiresome, trip across the United States. Her love of people, eye for beauty, and willingness to learn and take advantage of this rich opportunity made even the most tedious of days a joy when we turned to her.

Finally our thanks and love to each other for the time, patience, consideration, and stamina each of us put into doing our part for this book.

Introduction

Each year almost one out of every three households in the United States is hit by crime. Crime is more of a threat to you and your family than the possibility of an automobile accident or being stricken by cancer or heart disease.

A poll conducted by the ABC television network reveals that about half of the American people live in daily fear of becoming victims of crime. The statistics—and common-sense observation—indicate that they have every reason to be fearful.

The fear—and the reality—hits home at an early age. In New York City a routine statistical compilation by school officials shows assaults up 16 percent in the 1982–83 school year. That's in the *elementary* schools. Assaults increased 23 percent in the middle schools and 27 percent in the high schools.

The old nostrum "Crime does not pay" is so outdated as to be laughable. Only it hurts when we laugh. Crime pays handsomely and it's a growth field that is immune to the recessions that plague the rest of the economy. Today less than one out of seven burglaries, for example, is solved by an arrest. And you can imagine how many of those who are arrested ever pay for their crimes.

"Right now," says Georgia Supreme Court Justice Charles L. Weltner, "a person who has been through the system and is contemplating a crime probably views things as follows: (1) 'If I do it, I won't get caught'; (2) 'If I get caught, I won't get prosecuted'; (3) 'If I get prosecuted, I won't get convicted'; (4) 'If I get convicted, I won't go to prison'; (5) 'If I go to prison, it won't be for very long.' The fact of the matter is that these assumptions are strongly based on reality."

It shouldn't be any mystery why the cop shows on television are so popular. That's the only place in America where the criminals still get caught and put in jail.

In 1972 our book *Safe Places* was published. It was the first book to tell Americans *where* they could live without constantly looking over their shoulders in fear.

The response was dramatic and personally gratifying to us. We became pen pals with people we had never met, some of whom added us to their Christmas card list with a note of thanks for leading them to their new home.

Shortly after *Safe Places* was published, we made our own move—from decidedly unsafe Manhattan to a Safe Place in Connecticut. We followed our own advice and have never regretted it, though we will always have fond memories of New York and of the great place it *could* be.

When you move to the country, you tend to stop worrying about things like crime or congestion or whether a brick is going to fall down on you from the façade of the skyscraper you're passing by. But we aren't *that* far out in the country to where we could forget completely. We are still within range of the New York TV channels and, yes, we subscribe to New York and Washington newspapers, so we try to keep up with what's going on in the outside world, depressing as that may be.

One of the depressing stories that refuses to go away is, of course, crime. And we were repeatedly surprised by queries that arrived years after *Safe Places* was out of print. Even ten years after the book was published, an official with the chamber of commerce in one of our Safe Places informed us: "We received a great deal of written responses to your book and from time to time still get a letter or phone call referring to your book. An interesting fact that I noted about these calls and letters is that in many of the cases, the request came to us from someone who had been a recent victim of a crime (or crimes) and just felt that they couldn't bear to be victimized again."

We decided to take a closer look and even we were startled. In the decade that has passed since *Safe Places* was published, major crime in the United States has increased by an astounding 55 percent.

The *murder* rate is up 30 percent since 1971.

The incidence of *rape* has almost doubled, shooting upward by 94 percent.

Robbery is up 42 percent.

Aggravated assault has jumped 78 percent.

Burglary has increased by 57 percent.

Larceny-theft has zoomed up by 61 percent.

And while *motor vehicle theft* showed the smallest rate of increase, even that grew by 18 percent.

It's almost wishful thinking to say that the criminals are winning. In large areas of the nation, *they have won.* In this, the nation's second civil war, they control the turf in our areas of greatest population—the cities—and hold decent citizens hostage. They manipulate the judicial system to their advantage and have destroyed it as a system of "justice." What we are witnessing today is a mopping-up operation, a consolidation and expansion of their enterprises. "The city has probably been picked fairly clean," says Nassau County, New York,

District Attorney Denis E. Dillon, "and so these people have just found out that there are areas [in the suburbs] where they can practice their criminal endeavors very lucratively." Paramus, New Jersey, Police Chief Joseph J. Delaney agrees, asserting that "95 percent of all our violent criminals are transients, predominantly from New York." That's a pattern, moreover, that is repeated today in every metropolitan region across America.

Are there any Safe Places left? We decided to find out, and that's how *Safe Places for the 80s* was born.

SHOW AND TELL: "HOW WE SPENT OUR SUMMER"

We began as we had the first time around, a decade earlier, by consulting the FBI's annual report, *Crime in the United States.* It lists the *number* of crimes, in seven major categories, for all towns and cities in the United States with a population of 10,000 or more. In 1980 there were 2,613 of these communities that reported to the FBI, representing virtually all of the urban population of the United States.

So our first task was to take the bare crime statistics and population figures for 2,613 communities and determine their crime *rates.* We tell you how we did this in our next chapter, "When Is a Town 'Safe'?" We strongly urge you to read it before turning to the individual towns in this book. Otherwise you're going to be wondering how a town of 5,000 population can have 3,000 crimes in a year and be safe. That's not the situation at all, of course, so *read that chapter!*

Then we wrote to all of the towns that met our requirements for a low crime rate. We also wrote to numerous smaller communities we had encountered on our previous travels around the country, which weren't listed in the FBI report but would be nice places in which to live—*if* they were safe. Even as mounds of literature on these towns was coming back, making us very unpopular with the post office, we mapped out a travel route and schedule around the country. You have to take chamber of commerce promotional literature with a grain of salt and we knew the only way we could separate the dumpy Safe Places from the nice Safe Places was by personal inspection.

Then came the trip itself. When we made our research trip for 1972's *Safe Places,* we were able to schedule it for August through November—touring the North during August and saving the hot regions for the pleasant autumn months. This time around there was a difference—our seven-year-old daughter Melissa. The special joy of this trip was the opportunity it gave us to show her all the regions of the United States, but school schedules also made it necessary to do this during the summer.

So we sweated our way through the Humid Belt at the worst possible time and rushed to get everything done before school bells rang in September. The writing would have to wait until later. For now, we would be inspecting the towns that qualified statistically as Safe Places, interviewing people in them, gathering information, and recording our impressions and our notes.

It was worth it. Sandwiched in between all the work, we were able to act like typical tourists and gawk at Johnny Cash's house in our Safe Place of Hendersonville, Tennessee, watch the filming of a TV show at Old Tucson, briefly hit the tables and the one-armed bandits while staying at Caesars Palace (Holly actually came out ahead by $50—big stakes for us!), and take an evening carriage ride through the streets of Chicago.

Covering the entire nation in one swoop gives you a perspective that is impossible to obtain piecemeal. We were as spellbound as we previously had been, a decade earlier, by the sheer geographical magnitude, natural beauty, and kaleidoscopic variety of the American continent. This time around—due, no doubt, to economic circumstances—we faced very few crowds of tourists, even though it was summertime; and of the tourists we did see, it was equally noticeable how many were speaking in foreign tongues—French, Queen's English, various Scandinavian and Asian varieties. They all seemed to be appreciating the "bargains" while we were bemoaning how much more this trip was costing us than the previous one.

Another vivid and dramatic change between the two trips was in American eating habits. In the early seventies, we were still in the era of dining at home; public places were confined mostly to truck stops, diners, pallid hotel fare, and—in each small town—a steak-and-potatoes joint that passed as the high-class place to take your spouse or date on Saturday night. What a revolution in eating habits this past decade has seen! Today Americans seem to dine out more often than they eat at home, though that's cause for fear and trepidation when you consider a lot of what we're now eating. Nevertheless, the variety available to the traveler today is light-years beyond what existed ten years ago and enough of it is good enough to make the pit stops bearable. Unfortunately for us, we had been spoiled at home by the culinary perfection and tender loving care given us at Capriccio, a splendid *ristorante* down the road and across the state line from us, in Brewster, New York. Nino, Umberto, and Vittorio must have had red ears all summer long as we talked about them. "It's not Capriccio" was our usual complaint. On rare occasions, the accolade "Almost as good as Capriccio" was our equivalent of a four-star rating.

Most of all, the extracurricular activities on the trip were for Melissa. You couldn't ask a member of the E.T. generation to pass up the NASA Space Center in Houston or the McDonald Observatory or Devil's Tower, and Mount St. Helens was adventurous icing on the cake. This was also our opportunity to introduce her to the natural wonders of the West, from Grand Canyon to the paint pots and fumaroles of Yellowstone. Labor Day weekend found us in a hotel in Chicago, where somehow management had managed to find a room for us despite a convention of science fiction zanies dressed up as giant rats, wolfmen, Venusian slaves, or something a little more strange, and where the favorite pet was a vulture (stuffed, we *hope)* perched on one's shoulder. We knew it was time to get home—and quickly.

AT THE RAINBOW'S END: 110 SAFE PLACES

In a guide such as this, there is no avoiding the likes and dislikes of the authors. As much as is humanly possible, though, we have tried to avoid making this a scrapbook devoted solely to our favorites. Selecting a place to call "home" is a very personal matter and we realize that tastes vary widely when it comes to the climates our readers will desire, the geographical locations that are suitable for you, and the type of community you are seeking—whether it's a suburb close in to the central city, a more rustic suburb, a classic small town, or a retreat. So, in the best-intended sense of the phrase, we have attempted to find "something for (almost) everyone." With our 110 Safe Places, we think we have succeeded.

Due to time limitations, however, we were not able to cover all fifty of the United States. Even in the states we did cover, there are other havens waiting to be discovered. So if you don't find something here that you like, we urge you to use the methods we describe in "When Is a Town 'Safe'?" and look for your own. Half the fun is in the search.

You might also want to subscribe to our *Safe Places Report.* We finished writing this book knowing a lot more about the subject than when we started—particularly about how to find the statistics that will allow us to discover more havens. Each issue of our newsletter will keep you updated on the Safe Places in this book, will bring new ones to your attention, and will also give you tips on protecting your life and your property. So, if you're interested, drop us a line at *Safe Places Report,* P.O. Box 603, Ridgefield, CT 06877.

As we personally investigated the towns that were statistically safe, we found that a few were places we could discard without any qualms. They were dumps and we couldn't see directing you to them no matter *how* safe they were.

In most cases, however, we found that the Safe Places were also among the most desirable places in other ways as well. When you think about it, that shouldn't be too much of a surprise. If a town has the ability to keep a lid on crime in an era as overrun by crime as ours is, then it must be doing something right. Looking at the crime rate is a shorthand way of seeing how livable a community is.

Our own preferences are reflected in the Connecticut town we chose as our home. Ridgefield is a historic New England village that might now be called an exurb—an outer suburb. Many of its residents commute to jobs in corporate centers such as Stamford, Connecticut, or White Plains, New York, and a few hardy souls even commute 60 miles southwest to New York City. The features that attracted us were its historic charm, the compact downtown shopping area, its broad Main Street lined by stately elms and large white clapboard homes, the winding country roads, its hilly terrain (a surprise, this far south in New England), and everywhere the dense covering of trees and foliage and the undeveloped conservation areas that quite effectively hide the fact that 20,000 people live here.

Before we ever started house hunting, we spent dozens of weekends town hunting before we settled on Ridgefield. So perhaps it should come as no surprise that we found very few towns across the United States that came even close—in our biased estimation—to our home base in charm and livability. But while we had no desire or intention to limit ourselves to carbon copies of Ridgefield around the country, we *did* look, as much as possible, for towns that had a defined business area rather than one big mass of suburban sprawl, for neighborhoods that had some style and individuality, for settings that would be pleasant ones in which to spend a good part of your life—whether they be by the ocean, in the mountains, or conveniently close in to a vibrant metropolitan area. In short, we tried to find suburbs and towns that were not only safe but that also possess something we would call "character."

Sometimes we had to settle for what was available (though we never picked a town that we both positively disliked) and sometimes we couldn't get as wide a mix of communities as we would have liked. But overall we are delighted with the Safe Places we discovered. They prove that viable, attractive communities are available almost anywhere in the country—provided you take the time and put in the effort to find them.

In these pages, you will find pristine villages, all-American small towns, and vibrant small cities. You'll find picturesque fishing villages, alpine retreats, some that hug a romantic river, and towns set in the midst of some of the nation's most bounteous agricultural lands. Classic New England gems, dusty Western cow towns, college and university towns—they're all here. And in most of the major metropolitan areas of the United States, we have suburbs—close-in suburbs, outer-rim suburbs, suburbs that range economically from the posh to the solidly middle-class to havens that are poorer in wealth but not in pride or community spirit. They range in color from virtually all-white to virtually all-black and their ethnic diversity is as rich as that of the nation-at-large.

At the beginning of this introduction, we noted that crime poses more of a threat to you and your family than the possibility of an automobile accident or cancer or heart disease. In seeking to minimize those other dangers, we now realize it's not enough to rely on others to protect us. We practice defensive driving, wear seat belts, and seek to develop a lifestyle that actively encourages the maintenance of good health rather than merely responding to illness once it occurs. So, too, in regard to crime. You can no longer rely on others to protect you and your family. You must act to defend yourself, and one of your most significant decisions is the choice of the community in which you live. We hope this book helps you to make that choice more wisely and with years of happy—and safe—living as your reward.

When Is a Town "Safe"?

When is a town "safe"?

You won't find the answer in a dictionary. Our Webster's New Collegiate Dictionary defines "safe" as "freed from harm or risk" or "secure from threat of danger, harm, or loss." That describes the condition of being safe, but it doesn't help you tell if a community is safe.

Moreover, common sense will tell you that no town can guarantee you complete safety by either of those definitions. All you can ask for—in this life, at any rate—is *relative* safety. And even there you have no guarantees. All you can go by is the town's past record and present situation.

There's a personal side to the problem, too. You can live in the safest of our Safe Places, but if that town has just one crime that year and it affects *you*, you're not likely to think of it as "safe" anymore.

We can't protect you from all danger. "That's life," as the saying goes. All we can do is show you the steps we used to select towns that are *relatively* safe. We think our steps are pretty thorough. We also think the odds will be much more in your favor if you live in one of our Safe Places. But if your number's up, it's up.

Essentially, there were three steps in our selection process for the *Safe Places for the 80s*.

STEP 1: DETERMINE THE OVERALL CRIME RATE

First, we calculated a town's overall crime rate. There are two elements that determine the rate: the town's population and the number of crimes committed in the town.

If a town has a population of 10,000 and 10 crimes are committed in it this year, we can say that it has a crime rate of 1 incident per 1,000 inhabitants.

But remember: Crime rates are all *relative*. Town X is safe only in comparison with Town Y and it's not as safe as Town Z. If they each have different populations, how can you compare their crime rates?

The easiest way—the only way, actually—is to take the statistics on the *number of offenses* in the town, determine the *population* of the town, and then project its *crime rate per 100,000 population.* That tells you what the odds are that you'll be hit by a crime in that community. The town's actual population may be way under 100,000 or way over it, but this is the only way to compare towns and cities of varying populations.

For example:

Pleasant Town has a population of 10,000 and it has 80 crimes this year. When you visit Pleasant Town, it *looks* safe. You *feel* safe there.

Kook City, on the other hand, has a much larger population: 2,500,000. And it has 10,000 crimes this year. "That's a lot of crimes," you say to your spouse. Besides, like most places that large, Kook City has a much more cosmopolitan population. There are cultures you don't understand, there are industrial areas and a port area that *look* forbidding, and—let's face it—there are a lot of kooks running around. You just don't *feel* safe there.

You decide that Pleasant Town and its 80 crimes *must* be safer than Kook City with its 10,000 crimes, so you move to Pleasant Town. And, in consideration of the two places' crime rates, you made a mistake. Your odds of being a victim of crime are much greater in Pleasant Town than they are in Kook City.

Let's go back to those statistics.

Pleasant Town's 80 crimes and 10,000 population project to a *rate* of *800 crimes per 100,000 population.* It's easy to see how this works, since we deliberately picked round figures: 10,000 is one tenth of 100,000, and 80 × 10 = 800.

Kook City's 10,000 crimes and 2,500,000 population project to a *rate* of *400 crimes per 100,000 population.* Again, we picked easily divisible figures: 2,500,000 is 25 × 100,000 and if we divide the 10,000 total number of crimes by 25, we get the figure of 400 crimes per 100,000.

Pleasant Town has a crime rate of 800 per 100,000, while Kook City has a crime rate of only 400 per 100,000. That means you are twice as likely to be the victim of a serious crime in Pleasant Town.

This is not an academic or irrelevant example. It happens all the time when people judge only by their emotions and off-the-cuff reactions—or get fooled by the larger *numbers* of crimes in a bigger city—and don't bother to check the statistics and compare *rates.*

In real life, of course, you don't get population figures and crime figures that divide and multiply so easily. So we used a calculator, following the same arithmetic process. And in real life, unfortunately, the crime rates aren't nearly that low.

When we started on our travels in 1982, the most recent statistics on U.S. crime rates were for the year 1980. And in that year these were the actual crime rates for the United States:

U.S. Total:	5,899.9 crimes per 100,000 population
U.S. Metropolitan Areas:	6,757.6 crimes per 100,000 population
U.S. Rural Areas:	2,290.4 crimes per 100,000 population

The first thing those figures tell us is: This is a horrendous amount of crime. The population of the United States in 1980 was roughly 225 million and the number of reported crimes was more than 13 million.

The second thing those figures tell us is: Big cities have the highest crime rates and rural areas are the safest. Most of us have figured that out instinctively, but if you have to be hit over the head with statistics before you believe something, there they are.

STEP 2: CHOOSE A TOP LIMIT ON THE OVERALL CRIME RATE

Having calculated the crime rates for all of the cities and towns of interest to us, we now face an arbitrary decision: We must decide what will be the top acceptable crime rate.

We say this is an "arbitrary" decision because, once again, all crime rates are relative. The U.S. rural crime rate—2,290.4 crimes per 100,000 population—is "safe" compared with metropolitan levels of crime. But even that is horrendously high compared with the crime rates of countries like Japan or England.

Also we have to add a number of factors other than crime to our equation. Most of us have to work for a living and in today's society that means most of us are going to have to live in a metropolitan area—that's where the jobs are. Well, we can say that we're not going to accept any crime rate above 1,000, but that dream world won't leave us with many choices of places in which to live. We're liable to get pretty hungry.

So we pick a figure that seems likely to satisfy both our need to find a reasonable number of places in metropolitan areas and our need to find places that offer some genuine sanctuary from rampant crime.

We began with an arbitrary crime-rate limit of 3,000. If a community's crime rate was higher than that, we wouldn't consider it for this book. It's almost inevitable, we reasoned, that even a safe town or suburb in a metropolitan area is going to have more crime than a place out in the boondocks. The figure 3,000 was reasonably higher than the 2,290.4 rate for rural areas and yet it was less than one-half the rate (6,757.6) for metropolitan areas. A nice compromise, we said, and we proceeded to look for communities with a crime rate of less than 3,000 per 100,000 population.

That worked fine for a while. Particularly in the Northeast, you are likely to find a number of suburbs that meet that standard, even if the central city has exceptionally high crime. But then we started looking for potential Safe Places in the South and West. We quickly discovered that crime rates are much higher in those areas of the country. In many metropolitan areas, sometimes entire states, we couldn't find any communities that would qualify as Safe Places.

We had to revise our standards. If necessary, we would accept an overall crime rate as high as 4,000. But, of course, we'd choose communities with lower crime if they were available and if they were desirable places in which to live in other ways as well.

STEP 3: COMPILE THE RATES FOR EACH CATEGORY OF CRIME

As we continued our research, we made another discovery. A town could have an overall rate of crime that was low enough to qualify it as a Safe Place (that is, under 4,000) and still be high in some individual categories of crimes that made us very nervous.

The seven categories of major crimes are murder, forcible rape, robbery, aggravated assault, burglary, larceny-theft, and motor vehicle theft. Our crime charts list the crime rates per 100,000 population in each of these seven categories.

To illustrate this problem, we picked up one of our crime charts at random while writing this chapter—it turned out to be the chart for Nassau County, New York, a suburbanized area of Long Island. We went down the list of towns until we found one that illustrated our problem very forcefully: Old Westbury Village. It happens that Old Westbury Village is a lovely community renowned for its lavish old estates.

The overall crime rate for Old Westbury Village was 3,759.6 per 100,000—low enough so far (under 4,000) to qualify as a Safe Place. But when we calculated its crime rate for each of the seven categories, it ranked above U.S. metropolitan levels for rape, robbery, and burglary. In larceny-theft and motor vehicle theft, it ranked between U.S. rural levels and U.S. metropolitan levels. Only in murder and aggravated assault did it rank below U.S. rural levels.

That was unacceptable—particularly the high rape, robbery, and burglary rates. As lovely as it is, we would not pick Old Westbury Village as a Safe Place.

We found it impossible to devise hard-and-fast rules about how many categories we'd allow to rise above a certain level. As bad as property crime is, we knew we'd be even more strict about the levels of crimes of violence. Beyond that, if we had too many questions about the community's crime rates, we just wouldn't pick it.

As it turned out, we are proud to say that we think we've discovered some real gems. Time and again, we've taken the statistics for a metropolitan area that has exceedingly high crime, dissected them, and discovered one or two communities with crime rates that are largely below U.S. rural crime levels. It wasn't easy—it involved more hours than we care to think about, doing nothing but poring over dry crime statistics. But we think the final products—our Safe Places—made all the tedium worthwhile, and we hope you do too.

Alabama

On February 18, 1861, on the steps of the state capitol in Montgomery, Jefferson Davis was inaugurated President of the Confederate States of America. Montgomery became the first capital of the Confederacy and the momentous telegram was sent, authorizing Beauregard to fire on Fort Sumter.

Nearly a century later, on July 1, 1960, NASA's George C. Marshall Space Flight Center began operations in Huntsville and the northern Alabama city became the first "space capital" of the reunited states.

In 1860 Daniel D. Emmett wrote "Dixie (I Wish I Was in Dixie's Land)," the battle song of the Confederacy, in Montgomery.

A century later, the Muscle Shoals Sound Studio was recording gold records by Paul Simon, the Rolling Stones, Rod Stewart, Leon Russell, and Boz Scaggs, and an even more recent group, aptly named "Alabama," was taking country music *and* pop music audiences by storm.

Alabama—the old and the new. Even the new Alabama is a study in contrasts within itself. It is steel mills and barbecued ribs in Birmingham, fields of soybeans and heaping platters of soul food in the rich agricultural Black Belt, and a bustling port and seafood *en papillote* in Mobile.

Thanks to the destructive boll weevil, the Cotton State's agriculture was forced to diversify and thus to survive; today you're as likely to come across fields of corn, peanuts, watermelons, or potatoes, as of cotton. Some people were even thankful enough to erect a monument to the insect in the town square of Enterprise, Alabama. Even more important than agriculture in present-day Alabama is a variety of manufacturing, iron and coal mining, forestry, stock raising, commercial fishing, and tourism.

Most of Alabama consists of flat coastal plains, but ridges of the Appalachian highlands lend variety to the physical terrain in the northern part of the state. Water sports lure residents and tourists alike to the Gulf Coast and the TVA lakes of the Tennessee River, while auto races are a leading spectator sport. The Alabama International Motor Speedway in Talladega is said to be one of the fastest tracks in the world, with 33-degree banks in the turns, and is host to several "500" stock and sports car races.

BIRMINGHAM AREA

The Indians painted their faces and weapons red from the iron-laden earth. The first farmers in the Jones Valley considered the pigment to be worthless. But if the South had exploited the area's iron resources in time, Montgomery might still be the capital of the Confederate States of America. As it turned out, lack of iron for weapons was one of the critical deficiencies of the Confederacy. In desperation they built a few small blast furnaces and ironworks, but even these were destroyed by Wilson's Raiders before the war's end.

Birmingham was incorporated in 1871 and named after the English industrial center. Somebody apparently could tell what was coming. In 1887 the area's first steel furnace was built and named after Sir Henry Bessemer, the British inventor of the converter steel process. By 1891 there were more than fifty blast furnaces and nine rolling mills in the area and Birmingham became known as the Pittsburgh of the South.

David remembers traveling through Birmingham in the late 1950s on trips between Texas and Washington; the fog of pollution was so heavy it shut out the sun. But today Birmingham—like Pittsburgh—has cleaned up its act. And not only is the sky clear. The city has gleaming glass skyscrapers downtown with attractively landscaped walkways. Moreover, Birmingham has become a cultural center as well as an industrial one. World-renowned opera, ballet, and concert stars perform in the spring Festival of Arts and the Birmingham Museum of Art contains many prized collections, including part of the world-famous Kress collection of Renaissance art.

At the same time, unfortunately, Birmingham has a crime rate that is twice as high as the already horrendous U.S. crime rate. Other communities in the area are almost as bad off, as our Birmingham Area Crime Chart (page 7) reveals. On the fortunate side, though, we found two suburbs that readily qualified as Safe Places and that turned out to be among the most beautiful suburbs we found anywhere in the nation.

MOUNTAIN BROOK

POPULATION: 18,221
NO. OF CRIMES: 545
CRIME RATE: 2,991.1 per 100,000

Mountain Brook was an eye-opener for us. Call us biased or blame it on too many years of seeing Alabama portrayed through the lenses of the television networks and the pages of the New York *Times.* Whatever the cause, we never expected to be making our Safe Places trip across America comparing the new communities we saw with one we had seen in . . . in cornpone Alabama! Yet, after our visit to Mountain Brook, that's what we repeatedly found ourselves doing. "Not nearly as nice as Mountain Brook," we'd find ourselves muttering.

BIRMINGHAM AREA Crime Chart

	Crime Rate	Murder	Rape	Robbery	Aggravated Assault	Burglary	Larceny —Theft	Motor Vehicle Theft
United States								
U.S. Total	5,899.9	10.2	36.4	243.5	290.6	1,668.2	3,156.3	494.6
U.S. Metropolitan Areas	6,757.6	11.5	43.4	319.0	328.3	1,911.8	3,534.9	608.8
U.S. Rural Areas	2,290.4	7.5	15.5	22.5	136.9	830.2	1,143.9	133.9
Regional Crime Centers								
Birmingham	12,551.7	31.2	97.5	602.7	505.9	3,567.1	6,549.2	1,198.2
Fairfield	10,856.8	15.4	46.2	300.5	408.4	2,126.7	6,811.5	1,148.1
Homewood	9,995.3	4.7	47.0	282.2	84.7	1,693.3	7,111.9	771.4
Safe Places								
Mountain Brook	2,991.1	0	5.5	27.4	43.9	631.1	2,140.4	142.7
Vestavia Hills	3,149.2	0	12.8	51.1	31.9	657.9	2,159.1	236.3

As its name implies, Mountain Brook is built on the mountains—Red Mountain and Shades Mountain—south of Birmingham. Some of the drives offer panoramic vistas of the city below. Roads follow the contour of the land, winding every which way, and the homes that line them are beautiful. You'll find all the traditional architectural styles here, from Tudors to Georgian colonials and even areas of Spanish influence. While the luxurious mansions and estates are what stick to the memory, there are more modest neighborhoods that are charming as well and business neighborhoods filled with a choice assortment of shops and services.

Socially, Mountain Brook tends to be "old money," traditional, more insular than the other suburbs, and definitely a society-conscious community. Birmingham Country Club and Mountain Brook Country Club, both private, are centers of social life. You won't find many blacks living in Mountain Brook, but there is a sizable Jewish population. Mountain Brook's schools have traditionally been the best in the state, but at the time of our visit (July 1982) that academic ranking had been seized by the schools of our other Safe Place in the area, Vestavia Hills.

When we talked with Sonya Henderson of American Realty, Inc., the Century 21 affiliate in Mountain Brook, she proved to be a font of information on both communities. Sonya has lived here for fifteen years in the "poor" part of town she laughingly refers to as the ghetto of Mountain Brook. She remembered reading somewhere that it was supposed to be the eighth-wealthiest community in the United States.

Sonya wasn't surprised to learn that Mountain Brook is safe according to the statistics. She couldn't recall a murder ever occurring here. "And you hear about rapes all the time in Birmingham," she said, "but not in this area." Sonya jogs at night and the only persons to stop are women who ask if she wants a ride.

"We're not going to have anything in Mountain Brook that's displeasing," Sonya told us with a chuckle that let you know *that* was *that.* "We have more burglar alarms and security systems per square foot here than anywhere else in the country."

The lowest listing you'll find in Mountain Brook, Sonya told us, would be around $85,000. The highs would be $450,000 to $650,000 and the moderate price range here would be $139,000 to $179,000, with probably a 1/2-acre lot that is heavily wooded. With a $450,000 house you'll get 4 to 6 acres—if the house is "incredible," though, you might get just 2 acres for that price. Unlike the clay-soil flatlands of the South, you'll find basements here. Almost all Mountain Brook houses have at least 1 fireplace and the larger ones have at least 2. Hardwood floors with Oriental carpets are very big here and you'll find lots of greenhouses and a dazzling array of flowering plants.

The Crestline area is where Mountain Brook children buy their starter homes after they get married. For a price in the 80s, you can get 2 or 3 small bedrooms, 1 bath, dining room, kitchen, living room, and basement. There would likely be no garage, carport, or patio. Some would still have air-conditioning units, but by now most owners have installed central air-conditioning.

For $150,000, you will usually get a living room, den or great room (family room), formal dining room, large kitchen with an eat-in area, 4 bedrooms, 2 1/2 baths, basement, and 2-car garage. She showed us an exceptionally good buy for $150,000 where the dining room was especially elegant, the fourth bedroom was instead a study with fireplace, and you also got a swimming pool. (There are a good number of pools in Mountain Brook at the higher prices.)

In our comparison year of 1980, Mountain Brook had no murders, 1 rape, 5 robberies, and 8 aggravated assaults. In property crime it had 115 burglaries, 390 larceny-thefts, and 26 motor vehicle thefts. This placed it below U.S. rural crime rates for murder, rape, aggravated assault, and burglary, slightly above U.S. rural levels in robbery and motor vehicle theft, and above U.S. rural levels, but still way below U.S. metropolitan levels, in larceny-theft. This record is even more commendable when you contrast it with the superhigh crime rates of Birmingham, right down the mountainside.

Mountain Brook's police department has an authorized strength of forty-seven sworn officers, ten civilian employees, and twelve reserve police officers. We asked Police Chief John F. Haley if he could suggest some reasons that may account for the city's low crime rate and he was kind enough to oblige.

"An active, aggressive police patrol is effective in preventing crime," he told us. In Mountain Brook, "The 12-square-mile area of the city is divided into six patrol beats, in order to give better patrol coverage to the community and keep response time to a call for service to a minimum.

"The police department offers a house watch service," he noted, "so that residents who are temporarily away from home can call in and have their home checked daily by the beat officer."

In addition, Chief Haley told us, "A Neighborhood Watch program is active in the community and the residents are encouraged to report any suspicious or unusual activity to the police department. Signs and decals are furnished for this program also. We also encourage the residents to participate in Operation Identification. Engraving tools and decals for doors and windows are furnished by the department at no additional cost to those who wish to mark their items of value for identification."

Chief Haley caught our attention with his discussion of still another matter—his insistence on investigating crimes even when there are few "solvability factors." When we seemed puzzled by the term, he showed us the following list, taken from an offense report:

	Yes	No	Unknown
Was arrest made? How many?			
Was there a witness to the crime?			
Can a suspect be named?			
Can a suspect be located?			
Can a suspect be described?			
Can a suspect be identified?			
Is the stolen property traceable?			
Is physical evidence present?			
Is a significant M.O. present?			
Has evidence technician been called?			

"If the response to most of those questions is negative," the chief explained, "no follow-up investigation is made by many departments. Burglary is one crime that fits in the above category. Yet our experience is that even in these cases, an active investigative effort will result in solving many burglaries.

"Many 'experts' in the criminal justice community disagree with my philosophy in response to calls for service, house watch service, and investigating burglaries with a low solvability factor," Chief Haley told us. "But I believe that the combined effort reduces the criminal's belief that he can successfully commit a crime."

We'd say the record proves Chief Haley's point. And when you add to Mountain Brook's low crime rate all those other advantages of living here—the beautiful homes and landscaping, the mountaintop vistas, the convenient proximity to Birmingham—you'll understand why we say this is the type of community any metropolitan area in the country would be lucky to have as one of its neighbors.

VESTAVIA HILLS

POPULATION: 15,655
NO. OF CRIMES: 493
CRIME RATE: 3,149.2 per 100,000

Vestavia Hills was described to us by a resident of the area as "a newer community in age, a more contemporary community in outlook, than Mountain

Brook. Vestavia's population is younger and it offers a more casual style of living. Whereas Mountain Brook is 'old money,' Vestavia Hills is 'new money' and the upper middle class."

A city fact sheet says that the median price range for a home in Vestavia Hills is about $73,000. There are homes in the $50,000 to $70,000 bracket, but also many that are valued at $200,000 and up to $1 million. Sonya Henderson, our realtor contact in Mountain Brook, told us that Vestavia Hills doesn't have too many listings over $200,000, however, and $119,000 might be an average listing in that city.

The newness of Vestavia Hills was also noted by a correspondent from the chamber of commerce. "Vestavia Hills was incorporated in 1950," we were told, "and considered a very remote community building out on the fringes of the moonshine stills. We've come a long way. We're making our history as we go along, but we believe we have the finest community—second to none—in Alabama."

Vestavia Hills is located south and west of Mountain Brook, just past Brookwood Medical Center as you head south from Birmingham on U.S. 31 (Montgomery Highway) and after you make the climb up Shades Mountain. We found it a bit disconcerting that the business district is bisected by U.S. 31, a high-traffic artery, but the neighborhoods—both the more modest ones and the more expensive ones—were lovely and reflected the same kind of community pride evident in Mountain Brook. Vestavia Country Club, a private membership club, is located here and some of the homes enjoy striking views of the Birmingham area down the mountainside.

We had mentioned before that Vestavia Hills' schools were ranked tops in the state in 1982. There are two elementary schools (grades 1–5), a middle school with fifty-five fifth-grade students and all of grades 6 through 8, and a high school (grades 9–12). The Vestavia Hills Library is also considered one of the best in the area, with 14,396 active members and over 40,000 volumes. Since it is a part of the Jefferson County (Birmingham) system, its patrons can use any of the libraries in the county system. The library also contains the elegant Vestavian Room, available to the residents of Vestavia Hills for receptions, parties, and other special occasions.

As you'd expect in a younger community, the parks and recreation program is a busy one. Special pride is taken in the city park, which contains a civic center, two baseball fields, two softball fields, a soccer-football field, eight tennis courts, a quarter-mile track, and a swimming pool. A picnic area has barbecue grills and tables and benches. There are organized sports programs, a variety of classes, and tennis and swimming lessons. With active men's and women's tennis leagues, tennis has become a year-round, day and night activity in Vestavia Hills.

Taxes are $82.10 per $1,000 of assessed evaluation, which is 10 percent of actual value. On a $100,000 house, for example, the assessed value would be $10,000 and at $82.10 per $1,000, taxes would be $821. If the house is owner-occupied, however, there is a $13 state homestead exemption and a $27 county homestead exemption, leaving annual taxes of $781. This tax is distributed as follows:

State of Alabama	$ 52.00
Jefferson County	108.00
School Tax	415.50
City of Vestavia Hills	205.50
	$781.00

The police department, with twenty-three personnel, maintains a twenty-four-hour patrol of the city. A special program coordinated through the Exchange Club is the Nosey Neighbor program. The police department also has a highly skilled tactical squad, which has been trained at schools conducted by the FBI, Birmingham Police Department, and Jefferson County Sheriff's Department. "Like fire insurance, we have it but hope we never need to use it," a city fact sheet says. "However, in the event of a crisis, this squad will spring into action immediately."

Vestavia Hills' crime rate is just slightly higher than Mountain Brook's. In our comparison year of 1980, there were no murders, 2 rapes, 8 robberies, and 5 aggravated assaults. Property crime consisted of 103 burglaries, 338 larceny-thefts, and 37 motor vehicle thefts. This placed Vestavia Hills below U.S. rural crime rates in all categories except robbery, larceny-theft, and motor vehicle theft and in those categories it was still way below U.S. metropolitan levels.

Vestavia Hills and Mountain Brook have different ways of meeting the needs of persons moving to the Birmingham metropolitan area, but they share the important things—good homes, good schools, low crime, and community pride. Between them, you can't go wrong in these beautiful mountain communities rising above the industrial and commercial center of this part of the South.

Where to get further information:

State

Bureau of Publicity of Information, 532 S. Perry Street, Montgomery, AL 36130, telephone: 800/633-5761 outside Alabama or 800/392-8096 within Alabama.

Regional

Greater Birmingham Convention and Visitors Bureau, 2027 First Avenue N., North Commerce Building, Third Floor, Birmingham, AL 35203.

Local

Mountain Brook: City of Mountain Brook, 100 Tibbett Street, Mountain Brook, AL 35213.

Vestavia Hills: Vestavia Hills Chamber of Commerce, P.O. Box 20793, Birmingham, AL 35216.

Arizona

Arizona, admitted to the Union in 1912 as the forty-eighth state, is a land of exciting contrasts and spectacular colors. The Grand Canyon and the Painted Desert of northern Arizona, the rock formations near Sedona and beautiful Oak Creek Canyon, Prescott's Granite Dells, and many other areas are noted for the range of colors that has made *Arizona Highways* the best-known state magazine in the country. It is said that there are more than a hundred shades of red, orange, magenta, cerise, and lavender in an Arizona sunset.

Elevations range from 137 feet near the lower Colorado River to the 12,670 feet of Humphreys Peak near Flagstaff. You have your choice of the sun-drenched desert areas, comprising 30 percent of the state, or the plateau grasslands that make up 53 percent of Arizona, or the forests (including the world's largest stand of ponderosa pine), mountain meadows, canyons, and streams of the 17 percent of the state that is highlands. Six of the seven life zones are found in Arizona, providing a vast variety of flora and fauna, from cactus to aspen trees and from lizards to mountain lions.

You have your choice, too, of metropolitan density or wide-open spaces. Arizona is one of the nation's fastest-growing states, with a population that jumped from 1,302,161 in 1960 to 1,772,482 in 1970 and 2,715,357 in 1980, but three fourths of that population is centered in Maricopa County (Phoenix) and Pima County (Tucson). The state's population also includes one seventh of the total Indian population of the United States and one out of every twenty Arizonans is an Indian. Their twenty reservations comprise one quarter of the state's area and you will be fascinated by their powwows, tribal dances, and ceremonies. If you love delving into history, there are plenty of old cow towns and mining towns, ghost towns, lost mines, old trail routes, and sites of battles with outlaws and with Indians. You can watch or join in the rodeos, cowboy barbecues, and Pioneer Days celebrations. You'll find Cochise's last stronghold in the Dragoon Mountains near Tombstone and the sights of Old Mexico are just across the border.

Arizona has more national parks and monuments than any other state. With two national parks (Grand Canyon and Petrified Forest), fifteen national monuments, six national forests with over 11 million acres, two national historic sites, two national recreation areas, two national wildlife refuges, and one national memorial, some 83 percent of the state's land is government- or Indian-owned, causing land prices in some areas to be higher than you would expect, given the wilderness setting. There are also seventeen state parks. So, between the federal, state, and Indian lands, Arizona is one vast desert-mountain natural museum waiting to be explored by you.

Above all, though, Arizona is the Grand Canyon State to us. We will never forget our mule trip down the canyon, on switchback trails barely wide enough for two mules to pass each other, on the first *Safe Places* trip in 1970—an experience that cannot be duplicated anywhere else on the face of the earth. This time we were able to introduce Melissa to the canyon and the awe on a child's face confirmed our continuing wonderment. Grand Canyon is almost too much for anyone to comprehend.

Unfortunately, the same Mesopotamian valley that is thought to be the site of the Garden of Eden later recorded the rise of the city of Babylon. So, too, on this continent with Arizona. The awesome beauty of its natural wonders has not inspired any noticeable saintliness on the part of its residents. Oh, they're the same sort of folks as the rest of us, only in wide-open Arizona too many of them seem to think they have a license to commit mayhem. The Wild West of the old frontier was largely a creation of the fantasies of pulp-fiction writers. We doubt it could come close to matching the amount of actual crime committed in Arizona today.

We've mentioned a number of times in this book how crime is much more prevalent in the South and West than in the Northeastern parts of the nation. We call, as our next witness, the state of Arizona. Our search for a Safe Place in this state was almost as fruitless as Coronado's search for the golden cities of Cibola. Instead of gold, he found adobe mud in the poor Indian villages of the Southwest. And instead of Safe Places, we kept finding cities and towns whose crime rates matched or surpassed those of faraway evil cities like New York or Washington.

Arizona's overall crime rate in our comparison year of 1980 was the third-highest in the nation. Only Nevada and Florida were worse off.

Phoenix, Tucson, Tempe, and Casa Grande all had more crime per capita than New York City or Washington, D.C. Scottsdale and Flagstaff came close.

Phoenix could claim a special honor. Of the twenty-three cities in the United States with a population of 500,000 or more, only Boston and Dallas had more crime.

Indeed, of the seventeen Arizona communities listed by the FBI, only one qualified for this book with a *rate* of less than 4,000 crimes per 100,000 population—our lonely Safe Place of Sierra Vista.

After several days of research and hours spent trying to obtain crime statistics for some smaller communities, we finally managed to give Sierra Vista a little

ARIZONA Crime Chart

	Crime Rate	Murder	Rape	Robbery	Aggravated Assault	Burglary	Larceny —Theft	Motor Vehicle Theft
United States								
U.S. Total	5,899.9	10.2	36.4	243.5	290.6	1,668.2	3,156.3	494.6
U.S. Metropolitan Areas	6,757.6	11.5	43.4	319.0	328.3	1,911.8	3,534.9	608.8
U.S. Rural Areas	2,290.4	7.5	15.5	22.5	136.9	830.2	1,143.9	133.9
Regional Crime Centers								
Casa Grande	12,426.0	33.8	33.8	219.9	1,218.1	2,165.5	8,306.5	448.3
Flagstaff	9,523.0	2.9	91.9	215.4	244.1	1,751.8	6,835.0	382.0
Phoenix	11,453.6	13.3	62.8	392.9	439.3	3,123.0	6,676.0	746.3
Scottsdale	9,132.3	4.6	19.4	176.7	196.1	2,238.3	6,022.8	474.3
Tempe	10,390.7	6.6	71.5	187.2	458.1	2,447.7	6,769.1	450.6
Tucson	10,843.5	11.5	52.5	197.6	517.9	2,833.1	6,629.1	601.8
Safe Places								
Oro Valley	3,828.1	0	0	0	0	738.8	2,887.8	201.5
Sierra Vista	3,180.6	4.0	4.0	28.1	76.3	650.6	2,329.2	88.3

company with a tiny suburb of Tucson. But that's it for now. We are continuing our research in an effort to find at least one safe enclave in the sprawling Phoenix area and another in the northern part of Arizona. Meanwhile, these are your best bets as a home base from which to enjoy the splendid natural wonders of this magnificently sculpted state.

TUCSON AREA

Arizona's second-largest city is situated in high desert country at an elevation of approximately 2,400 feet. To the north and east, the Santa Catalina and Rincon mountains rise 6,000 feet above the desert floor, providing a spectacular backdrop and a quick change of climate—relief from the hot desert temperatures during the summer and skiing rather than sunbathing by the swimming pool in the wintertime.

Tucson is a winter resort center and an increasingly popular retirement center. Fashionable shops, fine restaurants, and a wide array of cultural events take advantage of the winter influx of monied refugees from northern climes. Many people come here for health reasons, too. The University of Arizona, with more than 30,000 students, makes this an educational center as well. Copper, cotton, and cattle are still other important industries. With a metropolitan area population of about 500,000, Tucson is large enough to enjoy a variety of cosmopolitan activities while still retaining a small city atmosphere.

In seeking a Safe Place in the Tucson area, our major problem was that virtually all the suburban areas outside the city limits are unincorporated. Thus their crime statistics are all merged and published as one overall set of figures for Pima County.

The Sheriff's Department did try to help us by breaking down their statistics for several sections of the county near Tucson. As precisely and accurately as possible, we then tried to obtain census-tract figures for the identical areas. We still were unsuccessful in our quest.

As a general rule, for instance, the most popular suburban areas are to the north and east of Tucson—between the city and the mountains. So we did our best to get an accurate match of crime statistics and census figures for the Tanque Verde area to the northeast. As far as we could tell, the crime rate was much too high. We had also heard that Green Valley, to the south, was increasingly popular with commuters to Tucson, but its crime rate also was too high.

Then we discovered, on the map, a small community due north of Tucson that apparently was incorporated. If it has its own police force, we reasoned, it would also maintain separate crime statistics, so we quickly headed north on U.S. 89. The result was our Safe Place of Oro Valley.

ORO VALLEY

POPULATION: 1,489
NO. OF CRIMES: 57
CRIME RATE: 3,828.1 per 100,000

Oro Valley is a small, predominantly residential community 6 miles north of the Tucson city limits. U.S. 89 is the only major thoroughfare, but even it is virtually devoid of businesses here, except for the just-opened Sheraton-Tucson El Conquistador, a posh hotel and resort complex. To the east of Oro Valley, just beyond El Conquistador, rise the Santa Catalina Mountains and the lands protected as Coronado National Forest. In all other directions, desert.

A farming area thirty years ago, Oro Valley is now at the edge of the Tucson metropolitan area. It is located at an elevation of 2,450 feet, covers a 3½-square-mile area, and was incorporated in April 1974. The goal was to provide better local services (including police protection) and to keep the area from being overdeveloped, as it is farther south on U.S. 89. The incorporation has had its desired effects.

Incorporation has been so beneficial, in fact, that neighboring areas have repeatedly asked to be annexed by Oro Valley. For its part, Oro Valley has always taken the position that it doesn't want to annex anyone who doesn't want in. Most recently, a development known as Pusch Ridge Estates asked to be annexed and was. In welcoming them to the town, the Oro Valley *Voice/Call* stated its opinion that "The annexation will bring benefits to Oro Valley—but they will be minimal in the near future. As the population of Pusch Ridge builds up, it will add to the town's base figure for state gasoline tax rebates, sales tax sharing, and other refunds.

"The more immediate gain," the *Voice/Call* added, "is to the residents of

Pusch Ridge. They will receive the protection of Oro Valley's small but diligent police department and the guarantee that their building and zoning standards will be set on the local, town level—not by a more remote and sometimes hard-to-reach county government."

Residents of Oro Valley pay county taxes but no additional town property taxes. Instead of property taxes, the town gets its revenue from the sales tax sharing and gasoline tax rebates mentioned by the *Voice/Call*, from building and business permits, and from a hefty number of traffic citations on U.S. 89.

So successful is this approach that Oro Valley is probably one of the few towns in the state that is comfortably in the black. At the time of our visit (August 1982), Mayor Steve Engle had just announced that the town had taken in about $92,000 more than projected for fiscal year 1981–82. Combined with a hard-line attitude on holding down expenses, that meant that the town had a surplus of about $108,000 in the bank.

With El Conquistador open, the financial picture should be even more rosy. This one resort alone may add $100,000 a year in sales tax revenues.

Though it consists of just the chief and four officers, Oro Valley's police department maintains a twenty-four-hour patrol of the community. Special attention is given to homes vacated by residents during the summer months and this led to an amusing incident related by the mayor.

Personally checking the house of a neighbor, Mayor Engle inadvertently set off the alarm. Assisted by Police Chief Gary Robb and another officer, they entered the house to turn off the alarm, only to get themselves in deeper trouble.

"The security control system was a bit complicated," the mayor recalls with a chuckle. "I pushed the wrong button, I guess. Anyway, right away you had the Oro Valley mayor, the police chief, and one of his officers locked in the house!"

Most of the time, though, the systems work the way they're supposed to and in our comparison year of 1980 Oro Valley had just 11 burglaries, 43 larcenies, and 3 motor vehicle thefts. There were no crimes of violence that year—and there rarely are. This placed Oro Valley below U.S. rural crime levels in all categories except larceny-theft and motor vehicle theft and in those categories it was still way below U.S. metropolitan levels.

Tucson General Hospital maintains a Northwest Emergency Center in the Oro Valley area and the metropolitan area's extensive medical facilities—including some ten hospitals—are within generally easy reach. Local educational facilities include the ultramodern Canyon del Oro High School. Most houses are 1-story ranches, with a mixture of Western, Spanish, and contemporary styles.

For information on Oro Valley housing costs, we talked to Bernard Rubin of Tucson Realty and Trust. Mr. Rubin moved to Oro Valley from New York City and in his eight years here he can recall only one serious crime incident—and its perpetrator was caught. "Oro Valley is definitely the safest part of the Tucson area," he agreed.

Prices in Oro Valley, Mr. Rubin explained, generally fall into two categories—

one for the houses around the Oro Valley Golf and Country Club, another for the remaining neighborhoods.

Houses at Oro Valley Estates (on the golf course) and Oro Valley Heights (near the golf course) usually range in price from $150,000 to $300,000, though there was nothing available for less than $175,000 at the time of our inquiry (April 1983). Elsewhere the range for single-family homes is from around $75,000 to $150,000.

Some building lots are still available, at prices from the low 30s to the low 40s for 1 acre. "Expect to pay $75 per square foot to custom-build your own house," Mr. Rubin told us. There has been a spurt of new construction, since it costs no more—and sometimes less—than buying an existing house. With your own plan, you get exactly what you want and another consideration is that the older homes are not as well-insulated as the new ones. Electricity was too cheap when they were built for anyone to be very concerned about energy conservation.

It happened that a house on the fairway with a swimming pool was available and listed at $165,000. Normally it would sell for more, but this was a distress sale due to foreclosure. Previously the house had 3 bedrooms and about 2,400 to 2,500 square feet of living area. The foreclosed owner had added a bedroom-and-bath guest area, bringing the total living area to around 3,000 square feet. "The lot alone would be worth $50,000 to $60,000 today," Mr. Rubin told us. Most homes of this size and price range have a living room, family room, dining room, and 2 or 2½ baths.

The less expensive homes, away from the country club, have more of a tract look and are more modest in size—usually some 1,700 to 1,800 square feet of living area, with 3, sometimes 4, bedrooms.

We had noticed a sign advertising 42 LUXURY TOWN HOMES at Fairway Point near the golf course. Those come in four plans, some with 2 bedrooms and a den, some with 3 bedrooms. They sell in the $150,000 range.

El Conquistador, too, built town homes as part of its resort complex. At prices generally ranging from $120,000 to $150,000, they sold out within six months. A second phase of town home development is in the works.

Taxes are reasonable, especially in comparison with what we face in the Northeast. Even with a new $250,000 house, you would likely pay no more than $1,200 a year. Older homes of equal value might pay only half as much, though an effort is being made to equalize the tax burden without regard to age.

After our frustrating search for a Safe Place in the Tucson area, Oro Valley appeared as an oasis in the desert. But it's no mirage. With low crime and low taxes and the protection of local zoning and police surveillance, Oro Valley offers you an easily accessible home base for enjoying all the delights of southern Arizona.

SOUTHEASTERN ARIZONA

South and east of Tucson is a land of dazzling natural beauty that brings to life some of the most famous legends of the Old West.

In the immediate vicinity of Tucson, first of all, are such attractions as Saguaro National Monument, which preserves some of the finest forests of saguaro cactus (the tallest and largest species of cactus), Old Tucson, an authentic re-creation of a Western town that you've seen countless times before in Western movies and television shows, and Misión San Xavier del Bac, restored to its original splendor.

Tombstone, the Town Too Tough to Die, is perhaps the most famous landmark in the far southeast corner of the state. Here you will find the O.K. Corral, scene of the famous gunfight, as well as Boot Hill Graveyard, Bird Cage Theatre, the gallows and other frontier mementos of the old Tombstone Courthouse (now a state park museum), and the saloons once frequented by Wyatt Earp, Doc Holliday, and Bat Masterson.

Nearby are the strongholds of the legendary Apache warriors Cochise and Geronimo. A 1½-mile foot trail in the desert north of Chiricahua National Monument leads you past an old Butterfield stagecoach station, the post cemetery, and Apache Springs to the ruins of old Fort Bowie. The Old Fort and historical museum at Sierra Vista's Fort Huachuca re-creates the Army's cavalry days and south of Sierra Vista is the Nature Conservancy's Ramsey Canyon Preserve, recognized as the Hummingbird Capital of the United States.

On the Mexican border is Coronado National Memorial, commemorating the first European expedition into the American Southwest and offering spectacular mountain views into Mexico. Patagonia is famous for its quarterhorse and cattle ranches and is home to the Museum of the Horse. Bisbee is an old-time mining town, replete with an awesome open-pit copper mine, Brewery Gulch, and the Copper Queen Hotel.

And in all directions . . . ghost towns, semi-ghost towns, deserted mines, and lost mines . . . all the colorful and vivid reminders that the rip-roaring days of the Old West were not so long ago.

SIERRA VISTA

POPULATION: 24,901
NO. OF CRIMES: 792
CRIME RATE: 3,180.6 per 100,000

Of all the Arizona communities with a population of 10,000 or more, only Sierra Vista qualified as a Safe Place. It is no coincidence that Sierra Vista is also a military town. Throughout the United States, we noted that the strong presence of a military base usually indicates a low-crime community. A military career obviously requires a measure of self-discipline and that quality is reflected in the communities where the military personnel live.

In Sierra Vista the military presence is Fort Huachuca, last of the U.S. Army's cavalry posts. Established in 1887, it now houses the U.S. Army Communications Command, the U.S. Army Intelligence Center and School, the U.S. Army Electronics Proving Ground, and TRI-TAC—the tri-service (Army, Navy, and Air Force) Tactical Communications Test Organization. As you would expect, Sierra Vista's economy is closely tied to these activities. Employment at the fort in 1981 consisted of 5,511 military personnel and 5,556 civilians for a total of 11,067. The next-largest employer in town was the Sierra Vista school system with a staff of 629.

The city itself is neither particularly attractive nor rundown. It's just there, teeming with a ragtag assortment of service establishments, fast-food outlets, and the like. The homes are modest to middle-class in size and appearance, sufficiently maintained but without much evidence of any desire to take advantage of the desert setting with the type of landscaping you see in California. But let's face it. Where else but in a Southwestern military town could you find a Taco-Seoul restaurant, specializing in Mexican and Korean food? We say Sierra Vista is the center of Mexi-Korean cuisine in America and challenge any other community to prove us otherwise!

What *is* magnificent about the town is its setting. Sierra Vista means "mountain view," a most appropriate name considering the city's location in the midst of the Whetstone, Dragoon, Mule, and Huachuca mountains. The elevation in town is 4,623 feet and Huachuca Peak rises in the west to an elevation of 8,406 feet, Miller Peak to heights of 9,466 feet. The desert-mountain vistas in all directions are breathtaking.

Sierra Vista is located approximately 70 miles southeast of Tucson and 192 miles southeast of Phoenix, but even here, in the middle of the desert, you can keep in touch with the world through an array of daily newspapers (one of them local), several weeklies, two AM and one FM radio stations (twelve additional FM stations available via cable), a local television station, and twelve more TV stations available via cable from Nogales, Tucson, Phoenix, Atlanta, Chicago, New York, Los Angeles, Denver, and Bristol.

Sierra Vista's public school system consists of five elementary schools, a middle school, and a high school. The fort maintains two elementary schools and one middle school, and three small private elementary schools are also located in town. Cochise Community College has a campus here and offers nearly 300 day and evening classes in a wide variety of college transfer and occupational programs.

Medical facilities include twenty-three physicians, twenty-two dentists, five chiropractors, and the 55-bed Sierra Vista Community Hospital. For emergencies, an overflow agreement makes the 110 beds of Fort Huachuca's army hospital available to the public.

Sierra Vista has thirty-six Protestant churches, as well as two Catholic parishes, a Jewish congregation, two Mormon churches, and four Army chapels.

As for crime, Sierra Vista had 1 murder, 1 rape, 7 robberies, and 19 aggravated assaults during our comparison year of 1980. Property crime consisted of 162 burglaries, 580 larceny-thefts, and 22 motor vehicle thefts. This placed Sierra Vista below U.S. rural crime levels in all categories except robbery and larceny-theft and in those categories it still remained way below U.S. metropolitan levels.

For information on housing costs, we found Ken Wilson of Cochise Realty most helpful. He told us that while you can find some small twenty-five-year-old homes available in the low 40s and at the other extreme a few houses sell for as much as $250,000, most of the housing in town is in the $47,000 to $120,000 range.

For $50,000, you could get a 3-bedroom ranch with about 1,200 to 1,300 square feet of living area, on a city-sized (80 × 100) lot. It would likely have 1¾ baths, living room, and an eating area off the kitchen.

For $120,000, you would get up to 4 bedrooms and a ½-acre lot. A house at this price level would probably have a living room, family room, formal dining room, and 2-car carport. It might even have a swimming pool, though they are more common beginning at $130,000.

Spanish architecture and flat gravel roofs, with just a slight angle for drainage, predominate. There are very few basements—perhaps two, three, or four in the entire town. At any price level, carports are more popular than garages and formal dining rooms appear in houses beginning in the 80s. Taxes are very low. Some typical assessments were $563 for a $89,000 house, $570 for $112,000, $737 for $115,000, and $596 for $132,000.

There is one condominium development in Sierra Vista. Its units sell in the 40s. They have 2 bedrooms, sometimes 3, but are generally small.

There are four or five groups of town houses, however. These sell from the 60s to around $100,000, with the most expensive ones located on a golf course.

City lots cost $8,000 to $10,000. A 1-acre lot in Village Meadow Estates in town was on the market for $28,000. One-acre lots south of town sell for $17,000 to $20,000.

Several dozen mobile home parks also dot the desert floor around Sierra Vista and an average rent for a 2-bedroom apartment would be about $350 a month.

While Sierra Vista is primarily an Army-oriented community, that hardly exhausts its possibilities. Its high elevation, clean air, abundant sunshine, and plentiful water supply make it appealing to all who love high desert living. The generally low cost of living helps to make it attractive as a retirement community. And the warm, dry air is a tonic for persons suffering from various respiratory ailments. A modern metropolis is just 70 miles away when you need it, but here you can enjoy to the fullest the wide-open spaces and star-studded skies that give you a glimpse of infinity each day and every night.

Where to get further information:

State

Arizona Office of Tourism, 3507 N. Central Avenue, Phoenix, AZ 85012.

Regional

Tucson: Tucson Convention and Visitors Bureau, 120 W. Broadway, P.O. Box 27210, Tucson, AZ 85726.

Local

Oro Valley: Town of Oro Valley, 680 W. Calle Concordia, Oro Valley, AZ 85704. Bernard Rubin, Tucson Realty and Trust, 4717 East Sunrise Drive, Tucson, AZ 85718.

Sierra Vista: Sierra Vista Chamber of Commerce, 372 N. Garden Avenue, Sierra Vista, AZ 85635. City of Sierra Vista, 2400 E. Tacoma, Sierra Vista, AZ 85635.

California

More than one out of every ten Americans now lives in California, making it our most populous state. Since the 1980 census, Los Angeles has undoubtedly replaced Chicago as the nation's second-largest city. And while people have been complaining for decades that California is too crowded to be attractive anymore, lots of people aren't listening. They still pack up their bags and head west for a fresh start, sunshine, jobs, California men, California women, or whatever it is that motivates them.

California's economy is so huge that it dwarfs the output of most of the nations in the world. Manufacturing is the major source of income, with the aerospace industry, food products, and tourism all playing a vital part. But California is also the nation's top agricultural state. It leads the nation in the production of more than thirty-five fruits and vegetables and grows commercially every U.S. crop except tobacco. Oil and gas, fishing, wine, and lumber are all important contributors to the economy.

Geographically, California ranges from Southwestern desert country to the subarctic peaks of the high Sierra; the highest point (Mount Whitney) and the lowest (Death Valley) in the forty-eight contiguous states are less than 80 miles apart. The state's 1,200-mile coastline includes the famed beaches of the southland as well as the rugged Big Sur and Mendocino coasts. As for the climate and weather, when it's good it's great and when it's bad it's *real* bad. How soon we forget the forest fires, mud slides, earthquakes, and smog inversions when it's sunny at Malibu or the powder's just right at Tahoe!

One of the great growth areas in the Golden State, unfortunately, is crime. As we discover also in Florida, criminals like to pursue fun in the sun as much as anyone else. There's nothing new about this, of course. Half a century ago, H. L. Mencken sought to rank the states in terms of their extent of "civilization" and California finished poorly in terms of "public order." "It is surely not news that California sees more gunplay than is comfortable," Mencken groused.

In our comparison year of 1980, California had the fourth-highest rate of crime among the fifty states—outpaced only by Nevada, Florida, and Arizona. And as we discovered elsewhere in the West and South, it was often difficult to find a single Safe Place in a major metropolitan area. The situation was so bad, indeed, that we ended up with *no* Safe Place, of any size, in the vicinity of San Diego—California's second-largest city and the nation's eighth-largest.

We painstakingly compiled the crime rates for 244 California communities with a population of 10,000 or more. Only a paltry 17 qualified as Safe Places—and they were concentrated in the Los Angeles and San Francisco areas, with just one exception in the middle of the state and one near San Jose. On the other hand, 33 of these California cities had higher rates of crime than New York City or Washington, D.C. (see our California's Crime Centers section, below).

Still, there are the havens. As our Safe Places in California, we picked four communities around Los Angeles and three around San Francisco, with one outside San Jose and the ninth in the center of wine country. Two of them are smaller communities that we recycled from our original *Safe Places*—they remain as attractive and safe as before. As with the weather, we can say that when California towns are bad they're *real* bad, but when they're good—witness the Safe Places in this chapter—well, they're just great!

CALIFORNIA'S CRIME CENTERS

Throughout the nation, New York City and Washington, D.C., have a reputation as cities in a state of siege, stalked by murderers, rapists, and assorted thieves. This is all too true, but what most people don't realize is that the situation today is even worse in hundreds of other cities—large and small—across the United States. This becomes apparent when we take the cities' population figures and crime statistics and project their crime *rates*—what your odds are of being hit by a crime in that city.

In our comparison year of 1980, New York City's crime rate was 10,094 crimes per 100,000 population; Washington's was 10,022.8. California alone had thirty-three communities with higher crime rates. Here they are, with their crime *rates* projected per 100,000 population:

Bakersfield	12,812.4
Berkeley	12,605.0
Beverly Hills	10,656.4
Calexico	10,704.7
Campbell	10,739.7
Ceres	12,007.0
Commerce	19,120.6
Compton	11,158.1
Culver City	11,519.3
El Segundo	10,845.4
Fresno	11,516.5
Hawthorne	10,683.4

Indio	17,995.6
Inglewood	10,367.1
Merced	10,981.8
Montclair	13,152.8
National City	11,527.7
Oakland	13,035.0
Palm Springs	14,304.4
Pomona	11,325.0
Porterville	12,024.6
Richmond	11,237.1
Sacramento	12,638.7
San Bernardino	14,028.1
San Francisco	10,446.4
San Pablo	16,431.1
Santa Cruz	11,595.5
Santa Fe Springs	15,595.0
Santa Maria	10,568.6
Santa Monica	12,063.5
South Lake Tahoe	13,716.3
Stockton	11,030.6
Tustin	12,602.3

LOS ANGELES AREA

Readers of the November 1982 issue of *Los Angeles* magazine were asked: "How Safe Is Your Neighborhood?" The article then began: "Beverly Hills . . . *the* safest place to live in the Los Angeles metropolitan area. You probably would have guessed that."

The implication here is that exclusive, posh communities like Beverly Hills *of course* are safe because they can afford protections like electric gates (mentioned in the same paragraph) and as many policemen as they need, unlike poor big cities with lots of minorities, like Los Angeles.

This implication is made explicit as the article continues. Los Angeles' police force, we learn, is down to 6,900 officers "since Proposition 13"—the tax-limitation proposition. *(Not,* mind you, because the city government gives priority to welfare handouts over protection of your life and property.) "And when it comes to hiring new officers and preparing new budgets, Beverly Hills doesn't suffer from the same restrictions as LAPD [Los Angeles Police Department] divisions do."

Los Angeles, like New York, has plenty of limousine liberals who love to wallow in guilt. The only thing wrong with this rich man/poor man theme, however, is that it isn't true. It's not true as a general proposition around the country, but the really funny thing is that it's not true about the specific communities *Los Angeles* magazine is talking about. Far from being "*the* safest place to live in the Los Angeles metropolitan area," Beverly Hills actually had a 1980 crime rate higher than Los Angeles!

Frankly, we can't figure out what was going on in the mind of *LA*'s writer, but we hope nobody moved to Rodeo Drive as a result of this article just to escape from crime. We can think of plenty of nice things to say about Beverly Hills, but a low crime rate is not one of them.

The more we looked into the article's figures, the curiouser it got.

First, *LA* restricted its statistical proof to "major" crime, which it defined as "meaning murder, rape, and assault." Granted, being burglarized isn't as terrible as being murdered or raped, but who says that the invasion and desecration of your home is not a "major" crime? Even more curiously, since when is robbery not a major crime? Even if we delete all the categories that are purely property crime, robbery—by the FBI's definition—employs "force or threat of force or violence." It also often ends up in another category—murder.

Of course, if *LA* had included robbery, it would have had to junk the thesis of its article. Beverly Hills, you see, had 247 robberies in 1980—which translates into a *rate* for robberies that is more than twice as high as the overall robbery rate for U.S. metropolitan areas!

Second, even in the figures it did use, *LA* didn't jibe with the statistics published by the FBI. *LA* says Beverly Hills had 1 murder, 18 rapes, and 24 assaults in 1980. The FBI counted 1 murder, 21 rapes, and 43 assaults that year.

Third, *LA* (to be fair) bases its claim that Beverly Hills is "safest" on 1981 statistics. But . . . in 1981, by *LA*'s own statistics, the number of crimes that supposedly occurred in Beverly Hills were 18.6 percent higher than the number of crimes that supposedly occurred in 1980 in the categories that *LA* cares to count. So that's no excuse for this rhubarb. Beverly Hills was even worse off in 1981 than it was in *our* comparison year of 1980.

Fourth, *LA* claims to be talking about "the Los Angeles metropolitan area," yet it doesn't even mention the towns that are the *real* Safe Places in the area!

But for that you've got us.

Despite the fact that it is seriously flawed in its comparisons of different communities and neighborhoods, the *LA* article has some fascinating nuggets of information about crime control in the central city. The lesson, to us, seems to be: More police do not ensure that you will solve your crime problem (witness Beverly Hills), but lack of a police force—in a city with the social problems of a Los Angeles—ensures that the criminals will run the show. Witness:

• In the Hollenbeck section of Los Angeles, a Latino neighborhood, the police operate with a ratio of one officer for every 16,666 residents. Moreover, there are more neighborhood youth gangs there (twenty) than there are individual police officers (eighteen) patrolling the area!

• In Hollywood the senior lead police officer admits candidly: "Our response time is about thirty minutes."

That should make the criminals tremble! And that is why you need our Safe Places if you are planning on living in the Los Angeles area.

We mentioned above that robberies are a major crime that too often lead to murder. Even as we were writing this chapter, we came across a confirmation of that in an interesting article in the *Daily Breeze* of Torrance. The article was on the number of murders in the town of Inglewood and noted that traditionally it has been hard for police to prevent murders since they tend to be crimes of passion between family members or acquaintances.

"But that may be changing," wrote Jim Hart. He then quotes officer Sergio Diaz of the Los Angeles Police Department as saying: "We're getting a much higher number of random killings in the course of another crime. Unfortunately, now it's more likely a criminal will be armed and willing to kill you for no other reason—and we've had crooks tell us this—than to get rid of a witness."

This observation is supported by Inglewood Police Chief Joseph Rouzan, Jr. "There's a whole new group out there who could care less about the consequences," he says. "At one time we could say they don't hurt witnesses, but you can't say that anymore."

"The silver lining in this trend," says *Daily Breeze* writer Hart, "may be that if the police can reduce the number of robberies, they can reduce the number of homicides."

That's a mighty big "if," but in Inglewood, at least, the police have been having some success. They're not sure why, but mentioned three programs that *may* be factors. These were the formation of a special anti-gang police detail, regular patrol checks of neighborhood bars (where arguments often lead to violence), and a crackdown on prostitution.

"When you get the girls off the streets," Chief Rouzan explains, "I think you get narcotics off the streets, too, as well as the guns and the knives that the pimps are carrying."

Another police spokesman estimated that Inglewood has its prostitute problem 75 percent licked, thanks largely to a change of tactics that other communities may want to consider: They started booking suspected prostitutes more on public nuisance charges than for actual solicitation, which is difficult to prove in court.

In searching for some Safe Places in the Los Angeles area, we were relieved that we were able to find any at all—they are that rare. But we do like to get as wide a range of Safe Places as possible, of varying levels of affluence, and here we were unsuccessful—so far—at finding a lower-middle-income community that qualified. We plan to continue our search, but for now we must hope that you can afford one of the havens we describe. Two of them (the most affluent ones) are neighbors on the ocean, one is situated in the foothills east of Los Angeles, and the fourth is in Orange County. So they do provide at least a wide range of geographical diversity and a mix of community lifestyles.

LOS ANGELES AREA Crime Chart

	Crime Rate	Murder	Rape	Robbery	Aggravated Assault	Burglary	Larceny —Theft	Motor Vehicle Theft
United States								
U.S. Total	5,899.9	10.2	36.4	243.5	290.6	1,668.2	3,156.3	494.6
U.S. Metropolitan Areas	6,757.6	11.5	43.4	319.0	328.3	1,911.8	3,534.9	608.8
U.S. Rural Areas	2,290.4	7.5	15.5	22.5	136.9	830.2	1,143.9	133.9
Regional Crime Centers								
Beverly Hills	10,656.4	3.1	65.1	765.2	133.2	3,138.1	5,278.6	1,273.2
Commerce	19,120.6	28.6	57.1	723.3	1,294.4	4,368.5	10,212.2	2,436.5
Compton	11,158.1	70.7	147.6	1,327.3	1,222.5	3,506.1	2,742.8	2,141.0
Culver City	11,519.3	26.0	41.6	1,258.3	369.2	2,552.9	5,667.3	1,604.0
El Segundo	10,845.4	7.3	80.0	290.8	378.0	3,038.5	5,887.9	1,163.0
Hawthorne	10,683.4	21.3	101.2	1,066.6	759.6	2,764.9	4,692.2	1,277.8
Inglewood	10,367.1	57.4	140.3	1,585.3	489.8	3,264.1	3,092.0	1,735.1
Los Angeles	9,952.1	34.2	95.3	868.3	744.7	2,930.6	3,826.6	1,452.4
Montclair	13,152.8	26.6	66.5	469.9	549.7	3,205.1	7,828.7	1,006.3
Pomona	11,325.0	23.7	76.6	797.7	1,040.6	4,342.8	4,064.3	979.1
San Bernardino	14,028.1	30.0	86.4	783.0	724.0	3,935.7	7,121.8	1,347.0
Santa Fe Springs	15,595.0	13.7	96.2	666.4	1,394.6	4,815.9	6,670.8	1,937.3
Santa Monica	12,063.5	17.0	76.0	748.8	329.0	3,302.6	6,129.9	1,460.1
Tustin	12,602.3	3.7	70.3	303.5	266.5	3,852.8	7,154.2	951.2
Safe Places								
Palos Verdes Estates	2,802.2	7.0	27.9	27.9	83.6	982.9	1,526.6	146.4
Rancho Palos Verdes	2,675.1	0	31.0	19.7	126.8	1,237.5	1,102.2	157.9
Sierra Madre	2,391.6	9.3	18.5	27.8	64.9	1,038.2	1,066.0	166.9
Yorba Linda	2,471.9	0	7.1	32.1	85.5	1,100.6	1,079.2	167.4

PALOS VERDES ESTATES

POPULATION: 14,346
NO. OF CRIMES: 402
CRIME RATE: 2,802.2 per 100,000

RANCHO PALOS VERDES

POPULATION: 35,476
NO. OF CRIMES: 949
CRIME RATE: 2,675.1 per 100,000

"This is the most magnificent, serene, and idyllic place to live if you don't have to deal with the real world."

We were talking with Jay Abraham, a direct-response writer and entrepreneur who lives in Palos Verdes Estates. His "real world" was a reference to Los Angeles in particular, and Jay's point was that he didn't have to worry about commuting to an office downtown or on Wilshire Boulevard or anywhere else. His office is right next to his home and he can communicate with his clients by telephone and telecopier.

We don't know how many others in these two communities work at home or have offices nearby, but that certainly is the way we would want it if *we* lived here. The chamber of commerce says downtown Los Angeles is "just" 23 miles north, but that overlooks two major obstacles: First you have to *get* to a freeway (there aren't any that come directly to these two communities); then you have to survive your rush-hour trip *on* the freeway once you've reached it. Jay has the right idea.

Palos Verdes Estates and Rancho Palos Verdes are neighboring communities on the Palos Verdes Peninsula, which juts out into the Pacific due south of Los Angeles. This is a magnificent peninsula of plateaus, cliffs, canyons, and hills that reach a height of almost 1,500 feet above the Pacific. On a clear day you can see Santa Catalina Island, more than 20 miles at sea to the southwest. And around here almost every day is clear, thanks to the prevailing westerly winds of the Pacific. Smog is for Los Angeles and if you turn around on your hilltop and face north you can also see the reddish clouds that mark the spot.

Our two Safe Places share the peninsula with two smaller towns, Rolling Hills and Rolling Hills Estates, and two unincorporated areas, Westfield and Academy Hill. While we weren't able to get their crime statistics due to time limitations, we suspect that these four areas share the safe characteristics of their two larger neighbors. Rolling Hills, in particular, has private streets and gatehouses at all entrances and you have to be a resident or invited guest to get in. That should do the job, we'd think!

A quick economic profile will put these peninsula communities in perspective:

	AVERAGE HOME VALUE	PER CAPITA INCOME (1975)	% OF HOMES OWNER-OCCUPIED
Rolling Hills	$660,708	$19,886*	97.4%
Palos Verdes Estates	387,067	11,162	94.0
Rancho Palos Verdes	274,790	10,000**	81.7
Rolling Hills Estates	284,268	10,396	94.5
Westfield–Academy Hill	302,344	10,000**	92.0

* Highest in the state
** Estimates

Mediterranean architecture dominates Palos Verdes Estates, which was planned in the 1920s to reflect a "new Riviera." All homes are custom-built, with neighborhoods where all you'll see are red tile roofs, others where shingle roofs predominate. While there are setback requirements, billboards are prohibited, and an architectural review and approval is required before any new building is allowed, you'll find different-sized homes adjacent to each other, resulting in less of a tract look. Also, intense landscaping and the fact that a quarter of the town lies in parklands gives this area a garden-suburb atmosphere.

Rancho Palos Verdes is less compact and more recently developed. Rambling ranch styles and striking contemporaries are common and you'll find most of the peninsula's condominiums here. Here you'll find 7½ miles of unspoiled coastline with fishing access and a county beach and such promontories as Point Vicente, Long Point, Portuguese Point, and Inspiration Point. At one place along the coastal highway, signs warn CONTINUOUS EARTH MOVEMENT and the road gives evidence that the sign is not a hoax. The peninsula's two tourist attractions are here, too—Marineland and the Wayfarers' Chapel.

By almost any standard, these are top-quality communities.

The peninsula's unified school district is considered one of the best in the state; some say only Beverly Hills is better. Its students regularly rate among the top 5 percent statewide in achievement. There are ten elementary schools (grades K–5), four intermediate schools (6–8), and three high schools (9–12). Transportation to and from schools is available from a private bus company for a fee. Also on the peninsula are Marymount Palos Verdes College, a coeducational two-year liberal arts college with both lay and religious teachers, the Chadwick School (grades K–12), a coeducational, nondenominational school with 590 students, Rolling Hills Country Day School (K–8), coeducational and with 375 students, and St. John Fisher (1–8), a Catholic school with 309 students.

For an area with a total population of just about 63,000, library facilities are unsurpassed. The central library has 200,000 volumes, 600 periodical subscriptions, 30 newspapers, and a file of 20,000 government documents and pamphlets, plus special collections. Two branches have a total of another 70,000 volumes and members also have use of twenty-seven other libraries in Los Angeles County. This library district ranks third-largest in circulation and use in the state of California.

Retail shopping facilities are restricted to a few specific areas. The main complex is the modern, mile-long Peninsula Center development. The original section contains more than 300 shops, including major department stores. The new 13-acre Courtyard houses another 75 shops, including Bullock's Wilshire and the May Company, plus an Ice Capades ice rink, community theater, and community rooms. The Malaga Cove business center in Palos Verdes Estates, with its Mediterranean-style architecture and picturesque Plaza Fountain, has been the locale of many motion pictures, television dramas, and commercials.

Recreation facilities and programs are also superb. The peninsula has hundreds of organizations and committees, cultural activities are legion, and the summer recreation schedule distributed to all residents is breathtaking in its scope. Horseback riding is particularly popular on the peninsula and you will find more than 60 miles of equestrian trails plus stables and riding clubs. The peninsula also has three 18-hole golf courses, with a fourth projected for the near future. One of the clubs is private and the rest are open for public use. A special attraction is the South Coast Botanical Gardens, home to more than 200,000 plants, with approximately 140 families, 700 genera, and 2,000 different species represented. The garden was built over a landfill on a self-supporting basis, so that the project cost nothing to the taxpayers. Numerous gardening and horticulture classes are offered.

Palos Verdes Estates has its own police and fire departments. Its firemen receive special training to prepare them for the unusual hazards of brush-filled canyons and steep ocean cliffs. The U.S. Coast Guard, which has a facility at Point Vicente, cooperates on cliff, beach, and water rescues. Rancho Palos Verdes has county police and fire protection. An undercover Burglary Apprehension Team (BAT) has been assembled to reduce the number of burglaries.

In our comparison year of 1980, Palos Verdes Estates had 1 murder, 4 rapes, 4 robberies, and 12 aggravated assaults. Property crime consisted of 141 burglaries, 219 larceny-thefts, and 21 motor vehicle thefts. This placed the city below U.S. rural crime levels in murder and assaults and slightly above U.S. rural levels in all the other categories—not bad for an affluent community in a metropolitan region.

In Rancho Palos Verdes there were no murders, 11 rapes, 7 robberies, and 45 aggravated assaults. Property crime consisted of 439 burglaries, 391 larceny-thefts, and 56 motor vehicle thefts. This community placed below U.S. rural levels in four of the categories and above them in three.

At the Merrill Lynch Realty office in Palos Verdes Estates, Ellen Davidson gave us a wealth of information on housing costs. At the time of our visit (August 1982), properties on the market in Rancho Palos Verdes ranged from a low of $189,000 to a high of $1,150,000. In Palos Verdes Estates the low listing was for $219,000, the highest for $4,500,000.

Normally, the usual sales range in Rancho Palos Verdes is $250,000 to $300,000, in the Estates $300,000 to $500,000. A feature of the recessionary market, though, was that the bottom and top levels were selling better than the middle and $500,000 was the mean selling price for the Estates. Also, in good times there is a considerable amount of shifting from one home to another within the peninsula, but that had largely stopped under the impact of the recession.

In Rancho Palos Verdes you can expect to get a house with 1,400 to 1,800 square feet of living area in the $200,000 to $250,000 range; for $250,000 to $300,000, 1,800 to 2,400 square feet. In the Estates you'll find less house for your money—perhaps 2,400 to 3,000 square feet for $500,000—but smaller houses may also have a pool and view for the price.

Ellen had a good buy for $255,000 in Rancho Palos Verdes. With 2,300 square feet on 1/2 acre, this rambler had 4 bedrooms, 2 baths, family room, living room, formal dining room, kitchen, and a 2-car garage.

In the same area, for $259,000, you could get a 3-bedroom, 2-bath house, with 1,400 square feet of living area and "an absolutely smashing coastal view." It was on a large 70 × 136 lot. This was a fixer-upper, with work needed in the bathrooms and particularly in the kitchen. So you pay for the view and fix it up yourself.

With prices that start at these levels, the peninsula communities obviously are not for the faint of heart or for those of us with lean wallets. But if you can pay the dues, these communities are unsurpassed in the Los Angeles area for their views, community programs, and overall quality of life. The peninsula offers Southern California living at its best.

SIERRA MADRE

POPULATION: 10,788
NO. OF CRIMES: 258
CRIME RATE: 2,391.6 per 100,000

"This is it!" Russ Kudsk vividly recalls his reaction the first time he passed through Sierra Madre. He was fresh from Boston, transferred by his company and looking for a home. The small town flavor of Sierra Madre made an immediate impression on him and it's been his home ever since.

Sierra Madre's small town atmosphere is as inviting as ever today, perhaps more so because the explosive growth of Southern California has produced dozens of look-alike, interchangeable bedroom communities with no distinctive personality. There is an unhurried pace to life within the town, for which we can largely thank the absence of any freeways or even county roads. Yet when you need it, the Foothill Freeway is just a mile south of town and will speed you on your way to downtown Los Angeles, a quick 17 miles to the southwest. For that matter, an hour's drive in different directions from Sierra Madre will bring you to Pacific beaches, desert resorts, or alpine retreats—whichever you prefer.

Sierra Madre rests in the foothills and canyons of the San Gabriel Mountains in the Sierra Madre Range. The town's altitude is about 1,000 feet and pure mountain water, rich, loamy soil, and proud homeowners have made this a showplace of subtropical vegetation and flowering trees. In earlier days Sierra Madre was a resort community. Los Angelenos, particularly those with respiratory problems, would take the trolley from downtown in the summer. Present-day Kersting Court is where the trolleys completed their journey to Sierra Madre.

The town was also popular with early mountain hikers. They followed the scenic 7½-mile trail into the mountains—as you can today—that was first blazed by Benjamin (Don Benito) Wilson to bring down timber for his ranch. In 1889 a different kind of cargo was carried up the trail on burros. The burros were hauling telescopes and scientific equipment for the first Mount Wilson Observatory, established by Harvard College.

As you drive through Sierra Madre today, you get an impression of middle-class solidity but no particular display of wealth. The more modest homes are found south of Sierra Madre Boulevard and the homes get larger, more attractive, and more expensive the farther north and higher in elevation you go. You will find all architectural styles here—even a splendid Victorian on Lima Street—but mostly California-style Western and contemporary ranches.

If you take Canon Drive and Woodland Drive up the Little Santa Anita Canyon, you pass through Sierra Madre's artist colony. These houses are smaller and more ramshackle in appearance but in such a picturesque way that you realize that is the intended effect. The canyon road ends at Sierra Madre Dam. On either side of the canyon are areas of more expensive homes set alongside winding and twisting mountain roads. Their irregular shapes and locations are designed to fit the contour of the land and it isn't unusual to have a house perching high above you on one side of the street, with a street-level garage on the other side that serves a home below you.

Downtown Sierra Madre is in scale with the rest of this compact town—no shopping centers or malls, just a few blocks of attractive, pleasantly designed shops and businesses. Also downtown is the civic center and Sierra Madre Community Hospital, providing respiratory therapy, medical/surgical, maternity, and extended-care facilities, as well as a natural childbirth center.

Sierra Madre is part of the Pasadena Public School District, with an elementary school located in town. A community nursery school and Catholic and Episcopal parochial schools are also located here. Recreational facilities scattered throughout town include a large swimming pool, hiking trails, shuffleboard and tennis courts, Little League and Pony League ballparks, a Community Recreation Center, four town parks, and 900 city-owned acres of wilderness area in the mountains.

Criminal activity in Sierra Madre is minimal for a California community. In fact, this is the safest town with a population of 10,000 or more in all of the Los Angeles area and the second-safest in the state. In our comparison year of 1980, Sierra Madre had 1 murder, 2 rapes, 3 robberies, and 7 aggravated assaults. Property crime consisted of 112 burglaries, 115 larceny-thefts, and 18 motor vehicle thefts. This placed Sierra Madre below or just above U.S. rural crime levels in all categories.

Russ Kudsk, the man who said, "This is it!" when he first saw Sierra Madre, was our source of information on housing costs in Sierra Madre. He is associated with Max Fields Realtors, the Century 21 affiliate in town.

The cost of housing, Russ told us, ranges from $90,000 to $700,000, but the medium price would be around $150,000 and most houses sell in a range of $135,000 to $175,000. Within that range you would probably get 3 bedrooms, 1¾ baths, living room, family room or den, kitchen, and either a dining room or dining area. Many homes have a dining area adjacent to the living area. In many cases you could get a pool and generally you would have a 2-car garage and either central or wall air-conditioning.

The small homes in the canyon, Russ said, might sell for as low as $50,000—except that they never come on the market. The mountainside homes on either side of the canyon sell for $135,000 to $160,000, depending on their view and how recently they have been built or remodeled. In the older, more level part of town, the lots are usually only 45 feet wide, but some go up to 200 feet deep, particularly along Carter Avenue and adjacent streets.

We asked about natural disasters. Russ told us he's been here since 1964 and there have been some fires in the mountains but none that came into the town. The dam and its channel usually take care of any danger from flooding or mud slides, although about five or six years ago there was *some* mud damage to low-lying homes in the canyon.

Even more impressive than the town's physical attractiveness is the public-minded spirit of its residents. This is reflected in the number of activities that are maintained on a volunteer basis, without recourse to taxation.

Sierra Madre, for example, is the only town represented in Pasadena's annual Rose Parade that depends entirely upon voluntary community participation. The town has had a float in the parade for over forty years and the money, time, and labor are all donated to the project.

Sierra Madre's Volunteer Fire Department was founded in 1921 and is still active and highly regarded today, utilizing the latest in fire fighting equipment. More than twenty-six regular and thirteen reserve volunteers are on call twenty-four hours a day and their dedication saves residents thousands of dollars annually in city taxes that would otherwise have to pay for this service.

But the most impressive example of all is Sierra Madre's nationally respected Search and Rescue Team. In its thirty-some years of operation as an all-volunteer organization, its members have helped save over 1,700 lives. "We will go anywhere someone in the wilderness needs help!" is their motto, and their wilderness training encompasses both the mountains and the desert.

Team members come from all walks of life, but they share a love of mountaineering and a drive for excellence. Before a person is accepted as a full team member, he or she must spend a year training with the team on missions and pass tests on area familiarization, rope management, helitac, mountain first aid, victim evacuation, specialized map and compass work, search and tracking, radio communications, ice and snow work, and more. Adding to the team's capabilities are associate members who help as pilots, ham radio operators, photographers, and dog handlers. The team owns specially trained bloodhounds that have also been used by local police agencies to search for lost children in the city and it uses German shepherds to search for avalanche victims, a program patterned after successful ones in Europe and the Northwestern United States.

In its dedication, the Sierra Madre Search and Rescue Team represents the finest aspirations of this special community in the San Gabriel foothills. You can't go wrong if you make this your home base for enjoying life in Southern California.

YORBA LINDA

POPULATION: 28,076
NO. OF CRIMES: 694
CRIME RATE: 2,471.9 per 100,000

Yorba Linda is assured of a spot in the history books if only as a footnote: It's the birthplace of Richard M. Nixon, thirty-seventh President of the United States. Yorba Linda is also our fourth Safe Place for the Los Angeles area, having the lowest crime rate in Orange County during our comparison year of 1980.

Actually, there are two Yorba Lindas, existing side by side. The western half is the Yorba Linda that was developed in the early part of this century and grew gradually as the trading center for a region of citrus and avocado orchards. Here you'll find older homes—mostly modest ranches—that avoid a tract look and give a small town appearance to the area. Also here is an old-fashioned Main Street, delightfully landscaped and shaded to add to the small town atmosphere.

The other Yorba Linda is the eastern half, a series of expensive suburban developments carved out of the ranches that once existed here. Here are modern, attractively designed, and relatively small shopping centers lining Yorba Linda Boulevard. Most of the homes—Western-style ranches, contemporaries, some 2-level splits—are crowded together on typically small tract lots, until you reach a maze of undeveloped bare streets in the shadow of bare, brown hills, waiting for the next surge of real estate expansion.

Average annual household income (1978 dollars) in the two Yorba Lindas is $25,203 in the west, $38,750 in the east.

Residents of Yorba Linda commute in all directions, and the proximity of Riverside Freeway makes it an easy jaunt to downtown Los Angeles, 25 miles northwest, or west to Anaheim, or south to Santa Ana and Newport Beach. If you need more extensive shopping facilities, the regional Orange and Brea malls are nearby too.

Since its incorporation in 1968, the goal of local government has been to keep bureaucracy to a minimum—to provide a low-cost, minimum-service level of government. Toward that end, as many services as possible are provided by outside contracts. The city contracts with Orange County for fire protection, for example, and with the neighboring city of Brea for police protection. If the crime rate is any indication, the system seems to work for Yorba Linda. The Brea Police Department provides around-the-clock patrols, two detectives, one motorcycle unit, a liaison staff member, and three cadets to assist with Yorba Linda crime-prevention programs.

Another Yorba Linda tradition is citizen assistance to local police. Sometimes this takes the form of traffic control during disasters, searches, and special events —or regular citizen patrols through the community, reporting suspicious incidences or hazardous conditions to the police.

In our comparison year of 1980, Yorba Linda had no murders, 2 rapes, 9 robberies, and 24 aggravated assaults. Property crime consisted of 309 burglaries, 303 larceny-thefts, and 47 motor vehicle thefts. This placed Yorba Linda below U.S. rural crime levels in four categories and just above rural levels in the other three.

Public school students attend five elementary schools, a junior high, and a high school in nearby Fullerton. Library resources include more than 100,000 volumes of books. Medical facilities include two fully accredited, general acute-care hospitals within city limits and more just a short distance away. Placentia-Linda Community Hospital and Esperanza Intercommunity Hospital provide all major medical, diagnostic, and surgical needs, including twenty-four-hour emergency service.

Beverly Pool, manager of S&S Realtors in Yorba Linda, told us at the time of our visit (August 1982) that the least-expensive single-family home on the market was priced at $112,500 and the most expensive one was $798,000. The usual price range, she said, is $150,000 to $180,000 in the older part of town and $200,000 to $350,000 in the newer areas.

For $179,900, she had a listing for a 2-story house with probably 2,400 square feet of living area. It had 3 bedrooms and a large bonus room upstairs that could be made into 2 additional bedrooms. It also had a dining room, family room, living room, kitchen with eat-in area, a 2-car garage, and wall air-conditioning units. The lot was irregularly shaped but basically 60 × 195 in size.

Another house in the same price range had a swimming pool and spa, with 4 bedrooms and central air-conditioning.

For taxes, Beverly said, figure 1.25 percent of the value of your house if you're in the western part of town; this includes school bonds and other levies. The eastern part of town also has a water bond levy, so figure on paying 1.43 percent in taxes there.

The newer, more expensive homes have all the appliances and modern conveniences that you expect today in a new house, plus central air-conditioning. Two listings in the local newspaper caught our eye.

For $259,900: a 4-bedroom home in a prestige area, with pool, 2 fireplaces, formal dining room, family room, maid's quarters, and study.

And for $475,000: a 3-bedroom, 3-bath custom home with privacy on over 1 acre of land; included was a guest house and swimming pool.

Whether you choose the older or newer section of Yorba Linda, you are not far from reminders of the agricultural bounty that prevailed before Orange County plowshares were turned into suburban mailboxes. You can still enjoy the fragrance of orange blossoms in the northwest and southeast portions of the city and in the center of town are Richard Sakamoto's gardens, producing some of the finest strawberries and vegetables in the county. Yorba Linda also has a large hothouse nursery stocked with flowers and tropical plants. Country touches such as these, combined with the easy access to all parts of Orange County and Los Angeles, make Yorba Linda not only a Safe Place to call home but an otherwise desirable one as well.

SAN JOSE AND SILICON VALLEY

Mention San Jose to someone (like us) who is not a Californian and you're likely to get some vague response about a song that was popular quite a few years back. And that's about it. There are so many California cities whose names start with "San" or "Santa" . . . San Francisco or Santa Barbara, *that* we're familiar with.

So here comes the 1980 census and San Jose is right up there with San Francisco in population and has probably passed it by now to be the third-largest city in California. What's going on?

SAN JOSE/SILICON VALLEY Crime Chart

	Crime Rate	Murder	Rape	Robbery	Aggravated Assault	Burglary	Larceny —Theft	Motor Vehicle Theft
United States								
U.S. Total	5,899.9	10.2	36.4	243.5	290.6	1,668.2	3,156.3	494.6
U.S. Metropolitan Areas	6,757.6	11.5	43.4	319.0	328.3	1,911.8	3,534.9	608.8
U.S. Rural Areas	2,290.4	7.5	15.5	22.5	136.9	830.2	1,143.9	133.9
Regional Crime Centers								
Campbell	10,739.7	3.8	60.2	353.5	323.4	2,399.1	6,806.3	793.4
Cupertino	8,326.8	3.3	39.0	172.3	247.1	1,781.8	5,683.4	399.9
Los Gatos	7,416.0	3.8	24.6	174.7	129.1	2,327.7	4,203.5	550.6
Mountain View	7,731.4	5.1	35.9	138.4	94.0	1,293.4	5,657.1	507.4
Palo Alto	9,702.3	3.6	58.3	215.0	96.6	2,436.0	6,409.9	482.8
San Jose	8,252.0	9.9	76.3	272.9	244.1	2,221.8	4,713.9	713.3
Santa Clara	7,943.4	3.4	57.3	178.7	232.5	1,894.5	4,959.6	617.4
Sunnyvale	6,369.6	4.7	26.3	112.8	122.2	1,087.8	4,581.4	434.3
Safe Place								
Saratoga	3,585.3	3.5	17.3	38.0	110.5	1,471.4	1,720.1	224.5

What's going on—in large measure, at least—is the Silicon Valley. You won't find that name on the map because it's not a geographical designation but an industrial one. It refers to a 30-mile stretch of California that has become the nation's first and foremost center in the development of computers and other products based on microelectronic and semiconductor technology. Silicon is the major nonmetallic element used in computers, thus the name. This is high technology industry—high tech for short—that is clean (no smokestacks billowing pollutants into the air) and that employs highly educated and highly skilled technicians and laborers. It's what every city and state has now decided it wants and it's what San Jose and the Silicon Valley area of California has, more so than any other place in the United States.

Put in geographical terms, the Silicon Valley is roughly that area at the south end of San Francisco Bay that stretches from Palo Alto to San Jose or from Stanford University to San Jose State University. Sunnyvale, with some 300 high tech companies and cartographic accuracy, advertises itself as the Heart of Silicon Valley.

With a metropolitan population of roughly 1,300,000, San Jose now compares in size with such other metro areas around the United States as Milwaukee,

Cincinnati, Kansas City, Buffalo, Portland, or New Orleans. An area that large has more than computers, of course, and San Jose has major headquarters or branches of such well-known companies as Lockheed, General Electric, FMC Corporation, and Ford Motor Company. Its aggressive business-seeking attitudes, combined with the natural beauty and ideal climate of the area, have made San Jose one of the fastest-growing cities in the nation.

We are always stuck with being the bearers of bad news about these fantastic places around the country, given the nature of our assignment, and San Jose and the Silicon Valley are no exceptions. The bad news is evident in our San Jose/Silicon Valley Crime Chart (page 37) and in the statistics, not only for San Jose but for most of the major cities in the area. It becomes obvious that this is not only a high tech area, it's high crime too. The situation is not as bad as it is 40 miles up the highway in San Francisco, but it's not something you want to brag about either.

Still, when we bring you bad news, we always follow up with some good news too—and around here the good news is . . .

SARATOGA

POPULATION: 28,952
NO. OF CRIMES: 1,038
CRIME RATE: 3,585.3 per 100,000

When *Fortune* magazine sent a reporter to check out the restaurants and lodgings of Silicon Valley in 1983, his first observation was: San Francisco it's not. "Nonetheless," wrote Roy Rowan, "nestled among the computer and semiconductor plants in the roughly 30-mile-long, 3,000-company complex are some dandy places to eat and sleep."

One of the spots that satisfied his stomach was our Safe Place of Saratoga. It "claims no major electronics company," Rowan noted. "Continental cooking appears to be its primary industry, the main street being known as 'restaurant row.' " He was particularly impressed with the "scattering of *intime* bistros like Le Mouton Noir in Saratoga, whose delectable cream of sorrel soup with fresh mussels, and veal sweetbreads with brown butter and capers, prove convincingly that high-tech and haute cuisine can indeed coexist in this computer mecca."

Before it became noted for its mussels and sweetbreads, Saratoga was known for its wines, mineral waters, and fruits (the kind you find in orchards). Saratoga's Paul Masson Vineyards, dating from 1852, are the oldest continuous wine-producing facilities in California. The city got its name from mineral springs that closely resemble, in chemical content, that of Congress Spring at Saratoga Springs, New York. And from the 1870s through World War II, Saratoga was famous for its orchards, which produced mainly prunes and apricots but some peaches and cherries as well.

After the war, when the population of the area began to expand, the residents of Saratoga decided to incorporate rather than face annexation by San Jose. It has always been a slow-growth community and a few years back a no-growth city council was elected to office. It's the old story of locking the barnyard gates once you're safely in. So while there is still room for expansion in Saratoga, you are probably better off looking for an existing house on the market.

Nestled as the town is in the foothills of the Santa Cruz Mountains, Saratoga's neighborhoods range from nice to super. We naturally gravitated toward the rustic back roads that follow the contour of the hills and meander alongside mountain streams. Lovely Spanish-style homes or ranches or contemporaries are discreetly set back from the road and shaded by tall oaks, redwoods, and madronas. A number of these homes will have gardens, pools, privately situated lanais, horses on the property. This is Northern California living at its finest.

The climate makes it that, too. During the summer, your average maximum temperature will be in the low 80s, nights will be cool and refreshing, and the humidity will be comfortably low. And on those few occasions when the temperature rises past 90 degrees, the relative humidity is likely to drop to around 32 percent. As for winter, even during your coldest months the average minimum temperature will be around 40 degrees.

Shopping facilities are sufficiently varied in town to supply most of your needs. The Saratoga-Sunnyvale Road is a wide, busy thoroughfare of no particular charm, but there are picturesque and interesting small shopping clusters, including downtown. Nearby regional shopping centers with major department stores include Valley Fair (Joseph Magnin's, Macy's), Westgate (Hart's, Penney's), and the new Almadén Fashion Plaza (The Emporium, Joseph Magnin's).

Medical facilities in the area include the Community Hospital of Los Gatos–Saratoga (180 beds) and Good Samaritan Hospital (225 beds), with many more in the area. Educational facilities include the public systems as well as three private elementary schools—Sacred Heart, St. Andrews, and Pacific Academy. West Valley Community College has a campus in Saratoga and among the outstanding colleges and universities within easy driving distance are Stanford University, Santa Clara University, San Jose State University, and the University of California at Santa Cruz.

Saratoga contracts with the Sheriff's Department of Santa Clara County for police protection. In our comparison year of 1980, Saratoga had 1 murder, 5 rapes, 11 robberies, and 32 aggravated assaults. Property crime consisted of 426 burglaries, 498 larceny-thefts, and 65 motor vehicle thefts. This placed Saratoga below U.S. rural crime levels in two categories, above it in the others, and nowhere near metropolitan crime levels in any of them.

For housing information, we had an informative talk with Shelley S. Williams, president of Shelley Williams Associates, realtors and consultants. He explained that the cheapest listing at the time of our visit (August 1982) was for a 3-bedroom, 1½-bath ranch at $112,000. At the upper end of the scale was an estate priced at $2,150,000, with a 5-bedroom, 5½-bath house containing 3,700 square feet of living area. The average price, he said, would be around $285,000 and anything under $200,000 would be atypical.

Within a certain price range, you must often choose whether you want more land or more house. For $343,900, for example, he had a "more land" listing, where the house had 2,150 square feet of living area and was on a 1-acre lot. It had 3 bedrooms, 2 baths, living room, family room with cathedral ceiling and dining area, a breezeway, and a double garage, with a workshop in back. For the same price, but with a 1/4-acre lot, you could expect to get a house with 3,100 square feet and perhaps 4 bedrooms, 2 1/2 baths, separate family room, and formal dining room.

Condominiums were selling for $131,500 to $339,000. The lower price was for a 2-bedroom, 1-bath unit where you could walk to village stores and public transportation. The higher price was for a town house unit with 2,100 square feet, including 3 bedrooms and 2 1/2 baths. It was still in the village but on a hillside, with swimming pool and tennis facilities.

Taxes are 1 percent of your purchase price, so the amount of taxes on a particular property will depend in large part on when and how often it has been sold. Add another 1/4 of 1 percent to cover various bond issues, with 1 1/4 percent the most taxes you would be paying.

Living in Saratoga, you will be able to take advantage of all the cultural and recreational activities of the community, everything from hikes up the scenic trails of the mountains to summer concerts at Paul Masson's Mountain Winery, from the productions of the Los Gatos–Saratoga Symphony Orchestra and the Saratoga Community Theatre to browsing in the antique shops that abound in the area. But that is just the beginning. The Pacific surf is a mere 26 miles away and San Francisco is a short drive to the north. With Saratoga as your home base—your *safe* home base—all of Northern California is yours to explore and to enjoy.

SAN FRANCISCO BAY AREA

"Every man should be allowed to love two cities—his own and San Francisco," wrote Gene Fowler. "San Francisco has only one drawback—'tis hard to leave," Rudyard Kipling observed quite a bit earlier.

Many other writers have paid their compliments to this Paris of the West and tourists from all walks of life have "voted with their feet"—several million of them a year. What they find—and obviously like very much—is a sparkling city rising on seven major hills and mountains and on thirty-three smaller ones, dominated by the water that surrounds it on three sides, a bustling port metropolis that has encouraged its immigrants to retain their ethnic heritages rather than try to assimilate them, a financial and insurance capital, a justly famed shopping center, topless and bottomless entertainment coexisting with opera and the symphony, above all a *city*—a real, genuine city, not just a sprawling mass.

Air-conditioned by nature, San Francisco has a moderate year-round climate, with temperatures seldom above 75 degrees or below 45 degrees. Morning and

SAN FRANCISCO BAY AREA Crime Chart

	Crime Rate	Murder	Rape	Robbery	Aggravated Assault	Burglary	Larceny —Theft	Motor Vehicle Theft
United States								
U.S. Total	5,899.9	10.2	36.4	243.5	290.6	1,668.2	3,156.3	494.6
U.S. Metropolitan Areas	6,757.6	11.5	43.4	319.0	328.3	1,911.8	3,534.9	608.8
U.S. Rural Areas	2,290.4	7.5	15.5	22.5	136.9	830.2	1,143.9	133.9
Regional Crime Centers								
Berkeley	12,605.0	9.7	65.9	586.6	291.9	3,108.6	7,627.0	915.3
Oakland	13,035.0	39.0	128.1	1,254.1	803.6	3,874.6	5,932.0	1,003.5
Richmond	11,237.1	18.9	130.7	623.9	989.1	3,471.2	5,169.1	834.1
San Francisco	10,446.4	16.3	112.6	1,116.5	639.9	2,491.3	4,861.2	1,208.5
San Pablo	16,431.1	30.4	30.4	846.1	1,008.3	3,597.3	10,087.7	830.9
Sausalito	11,302.4	0	32.5	438.5	308.5	3,361.5	6,252.0	909.4
Safe Places								
Belvedere	3,539.8	0	0	0	77.0	1,154.3	2,193.2	115.4
Hillsborough	2,009.0	9.6	0	38.5	57.7	970.9	894.0	38.5
Moraga	2,655.7	0	7.3	21.8	43.7	720.3	1,797.1	65.5

evening fogs are common, but actually San Francisco is one of the sunniest major cities in the United States (after Los Angeles, Denver, and Phoenix). September and October are generally the warmest months of the year, when bathing and sunning are most popular. While many will find this to be a brisk and invigorating climate, we know of southlanders and desert lovers who simply cannot adjust to what they consider the constant "chill" of this marine climate.

The two best ways to see this fabulous city are on foot and by cable car—if you don't wander into the wrong neighborhoods and stick to the safer, densely populated ones, and if the cars are back in operation when you're there. Our trip for this book brought us to San Francisco in August 1982, just before the city bit the bullet and shut down the cable cars for a long-overdue renovation and mechanical upgrading. We made the most of the fact that they were still clanging down California Street at a 17 percent grade and even steeper grades elsewhere. With the sun beating down and salt in the air, the three of us worked the collection of shops, galleries, restaurants, and plazas known as Ghirardelli Square, located in a nineteenth-century chocolate-spice-coffee-woolen works overlooking Aquatic Park. After lunch at the Mandarin, there were Chinese kites and copper-penny souvenirs to buy from the street vendors, clowns to enjoy, a puppet show—complete with Elvis and Gladys Knight and the Pips—to marvel at. Who wants to waste time struggling through more street crowds? So we hop in the back of a bicycle ricksha and weave dizzily through traffic, on and off sidewalks, with our driver clanging the bell constantly as we speed toward Fisherman's Wharf. Once there, we forget that we stuffed ourselves just a few hours ago. The fresh crabmeat and shrimp cocktails are irresistible; there is sourdough bread to buy for a picnic we're planning overlooking the Pacific . . . it's San Francisco!

After several months on the road, San Francisco was a much-needed tonic and change of pace. If there is any place where we love to splurge, this is it—and the place where we love to do it is the Stanford Court on Nob Hill, a haven of understated, quiet elegance. If there is a finer, more considerate hostelry anywhere in the country, we have yet to find it. And somehow, with a seven-year-old ingenue like our Melissa along who loves to talk and to make new friends, you do get to brush elbows with more interesting people. Warming up over a cup of tea in the hotel's lobby café, after the tiring day of traipsing about the city, who sits down at the next table but Mr. Jonathan Hart himself, Robert Wagner. And who charms her way into not only an autograph, but a *kiss* no less, than our you-know-who. . . . That cheek wasn't washed for weeks—and what a story to tell the other girls in third grade (and to make Mommy jealous)!

BELVEDERE

POPULATION: 2,599
NO. OF CRIMES: 92
CRIME RATE: 3,539.8 per 100,000

As you drive north on the Golden Gate Bridge, you pass from San Francisco to Marin County, a collection of plush bedroom communities, historic towns and villages, spectacular mountain vistas of San Francisco Bay and the Pacific, outstanding beaches and seashores, yacht clubs, and redwood groves. Drive north on U.S. 101—the Redwood Highway—for 8 miles, past Sausalito to Route 131 or Tiburon Boulevard. Follow this for 4 miles as it winds past stylish shopping centers and residential areas and you will find yourself on the Tiburon peninsula, consisting of the tiny village of Belvedere and its somewhat larger neighbor, Tiburon. Here you have some of the most sought-after addresses in the San Francisco Bay Area—and some of the most magnificent vistas.

Belvedere is without a doubt one of the most affluent and prestigious of our Safe Places. It definitely is not for everyone—just for those who have money and want to spend it in this way. It is a retreat for stockbrokers, for doctors and other professionals, for all kinds of top executives. Some lead a semiretired life here, keeping in close touch with friends and activities across the bay in San Francisco—or if younger you'll find them heading for work there by ferry, in what must be one of the most pleasant commuter rides anywhere.

In Belvedere social life centers around the oldest and most prestigious yacht clubs on the West Coast, around the tennis and country clubs, and in charitable and conservation club activity. If that's the life for you, you'll find it offered in high fashion here—at the San Francisco Yacht Club (oldest on the West Coast), Corinthian Yacht Club (second-oldest), Belvedere Sailing Society, Belvedere Tennis Club, and Tiburon Peninsula Club.

Belvedere itself is almost entirely residential, but it does share with adjoining

Tiburon the Boardwalk Shopping Center, which, upon its construction, won the highest award in competition sponsored by the Northern California Chapter of the American Institute of Architects. And Tiburon's Main Street is a quaint array of shops and restaurants, about two blocks long and just over the line from Belvedere. Many of the restaurants are on the waterfront side of the street and offer superb views of the Bay and San Francisco.

Here, too, in contrast to San Francisco itself and most of the Bay Area, you are relatively safe from the harsher aspects of crime. (See our San Francisco Bay Area Crime Chart, page 41.) Indeed, during our comparison year of 1980, Belvedere was the only Marin County community of any size to qualify as a Safe Place. Perhaps it is the relative isolation—almost all of Belvedere is really an "island," with two roads connecting it to the remainder of the Tiburon peninsula—but whatever the reason, crimes of violence are practically nonexistent here and in 1980 they consisted of just 2 aggravated assaults.

As for property crime, that Belvedere has—but it's nowhere nearly as bad as elsewhere in the county and it is actually reassuringly low considering the affluence of the community. In 1980 it consisted of 30 burglaries, 57 larceny-thefts, and 3 motor vehicle thefts. That placed Belvedere below U.S. rural crime levels in the last category and somewhat above rural levels—but still way below metropolitan levels—in the other two.

We are pleased to learn, too, that the crime situation has improved since our comparison year of 1980. "There were more residential burglaries in 1980 than in 1981 or this year [1982]," Police Chief Frank W. Barner told us. "Shortly after my inauguration in October 1980, we developed a comprehensive crime and neighborhood alert program which included Operation Identification and meetings with the establishment of block captains in an effort to further reduce crime in the city of Belvedere. This program has paid off with a one-third reduction in residential burglaries from the 1980 level."

Homes here are expensive, to put it mildly, but they have gorgeous landscaping around their perches on the mountainsides and along the waterfront and views—of the Golden Gate Bridge, San Francisco, Angel Island, Sausalito, Alcatraz—that would be hard to match in any metropolitan community. The name Belvedere is Italian for "beautiful view" and it is justified with every twist and turn in the road.

For nostalgia's sake, we looked back at what housing prices were when we selected Belvedere for our original *Safe Places.* There was one "poor" part of town where you could find a few houses in the 30s, but we were shocked—back in 1970—that elsewhere, "Houses in Belvedere seem to be unheard of at any price below $55,000." And "the ultimate in Belvedere is Golden Gate Avenue, on top of the mountain and therefore with the most sweeping views. Homes there will cost you from $150,000 to $300,000."

That was just in 1970. Read it and weep!

By 1982, when we returned to Belvedere for this book, the *average* price of its houses was more than a half million! To be specific, eighteen houses were sold in

1980 and their average price was $317,561. In 1981 sixteen houses were sold and their average price had zoomed to $531,375.

At the time of our visit, the least-expensive home on the market was listed at $265,000, the highest at $2,600,000. There were twelve listings under $500,000, twenty-two between $500,000 and $1,000,000, and seven over $1,000,000.

In the classifieds of the local newspaper, we noticed these listings:

- For a paltry $265,000: 2 bedrooms, 1 bath, country kitchen, and family room. This one's "a steal" at that price, the ad says.
- For $399,500: 2 bedrooms, 2 baths, family room, 50-foot dock, decks, and patio.
- For $445,000: a turn-of-the-century shingled home within walking distance of the town and ferry, with 4 bedrooms (3 + den), 2 baths, solar pool, patio, and garden.
- And for $595,000: 5+ bedrooms and 5 baths, with the master suite on its own level. A lower level, we are told, could be a separate 1-bedroom apartment or office.

And for the views—well, today you'd better count on paying $700,000 and up. Heavenly mansions and heavenly views don't come cheap in this part of the world. But they *are* heavenly.

HILLSBOROUGH

POPULATION: 10,403
NO. OF CRIMES: 209
CRIME RATE: 2,009.0 per 100,000

"While not wishing to seem rude, I must respectfully decline comment. The less said or published about this town, the better we like it."

Well, if you were the police chief of a town that includes the Bing Crosby estate, a town whose list of present residents includes Patty Hearst, what would *you* do? At least Hillsborough's Police Chief William A. Key was open and honest about his attitude.

We have no desire to cause any problems for the publicity-shy residents of Hillsborough, but with building lots alone costing a minimum of $200,000, they really don't have to worry about any sudden influx of new residents with the publication of this book. The real concern, of course, is not new residents but publicity—*any* publicity—and its potential for bringing in gawkers and trouble-makers. Frankly, our inclusion of Hillsborough may call it to the attention of outsiders who have never heard of it before (we hadn't), but we doubt Hillsborough is any secret to residents of the San Francisco Bay Area. We were in a San Francisco taxicab, heading for dinner at La Pergola and talking about our next day's schedule, when the driver exclaimed, "You're goin' to Hillsborough? That's where Patty Hearst lives. Quite a place!"

So much for anonymity in our celebrity-conscious age.

In our comparison year of 1980, Hillsborough came in as the safest town in California with a population of 10,000 or more. Naturally, that piqued our interest. What we found was a truly lovely residential community but with prices that confirm everything we non-Californians suspect about the level of sanity on the West Coast.

Hillsborough, it became clear, is the premier residential address on the San Francisco peninsula, the region directly south of the city. The peninsula is a scenic area of rolling, oak-clad hills and redwood-sloped mountains, nestled between the Pacific and the southern arm of San Francisco Bay. Particularly along the bay, it has become a mecca for corporations and research institutes that appreciate its suburban ambience and metropolitan accessibility.

Hillsborough's particular corner of the peninsula is closely tied, historically and commercially, to the town of Burlingame. Since Hillsborough has no businesses within its limits, Burlingame is the nearest place to shop and dine. And while Burlingame is nowhere as exclusive as Hillsborough—it has not only shopping areas but also three industrial parks near San Francisco Airport—it, too, is a coveted address. *Time* magazine once listed it as one of twenty-four nice places to live in the United States.

The area that is now Burlingame and Hillsborough was first selected as a site for exclusive estates by William C. Ralston, a prominent San Francisco banker and a partner in the development of the Comstock Lode. Ralston moved here in the 1860s, but his vision of a "sacrosanct colony" wasn't realized until the founding of the Burlingame Country Club—California's first—in 1893. As more and more visitors and guests came to the area, the colony grew into a village. Burlingame became an incorporated city in 1908 and Hillsborough followed two years later.

We mentioned that Hillsborough was California's safest city in 1980. Its actual number of crimes of violence that year consisted of 1 murder, no rapes, 4 robberies, and 6 aggravated assaults. Property crime consisted of 101 burglaries, 93 larceny-thefts, and 4 motor vehicle thefts. This placed Hillsborough below U.S. rural crime levels in four of the categories, just above rural levels in the other three categories—and way below metropolitan crime levels in all of them.

The neighborhoods of Hillsborough are marked by winding roads, often bordered on both sides by rows of tall and stately trees. Trim hedges and massive wrought-iron gates mark the boundaries and entrances of the old estates, most of which have been subdivided at least in part. The foliage is as dense and varied as you would expect in verdant California and the newer housing comes in a wide variety of styles. Hillsborough is not mountainous, but it is scenically hilly, with houses placed on irregularly shaped lots that follow the contour of the land.

To get some idea about housing costs in Hillsborough, we talked with Norman McKellar, a broker associate with Town & Country Realtors in Burlingame. The lowest listing he could find in Hillsborough was for $299,000—and that was on the fringes of the town. It did have 1⅓ acres of hilly grounds, with a swimming pool and canyon view. The house was a 6-room stucco-and-brick ranch, twenty-eight years old, with 3 bedrooms and a living room with fireplace.

The highest listing, Norman told us, was for $2,900,000. The usual range, though, was for around $600,000 to $700,000, for which you could get 3 or 4 bedrooms, 2 or 3 baths, and usually a living room, family room, and formal dining room. Sometimes you would get a pool and minimum lot sizes in town range from 1/2 acre to 2 acres.

The older homes, Norman told us, are the remainders of the old estates and usually have more rooms, more overall space, and more acreage. The newer homes have less space, but more modern conveniences.

A "typical" Hillsborough listing, at $725,000, was for a nine-year-old, 11-room ranch with a shingled roof. On a level corner lot, it had 5 bedrooms (including a master bedroom suite), 4 baths, a 2-car garage, and a swimming pool. Taxes were just $2,200 a year.

A better buy at $695,000, Norman thought, was a twenty-seven-year-old 10-room wood ranch with a shingle roof. It had 4 bedrooms (including an 18 × 14 master bedroom with suite), 2 1/2 baths, formal dining room, 26 × 15 living room with fireplace, and 17 × 13 family room with fireplace. There was an attached 3-car garage and the 1.48 acres of property included stables, a barn, and an orchard. Taxes were just $1,548.

Between Belvedere and Hillsborough, it is clear, affluent San Franciscans have a choice of two idyllic but contrasting styles of suburban living. If you are water-sports-oriented, head north for Belvedere; if you lean more toward horses or golf, turn south toward Hillsborough. For bayside views, it's Belvedere; for rustic countryside and more land, it's Hillsborough. And, of a more practical consideration, if you are a businessman who travels frequently by air, there is no getting around the much greater convenience of a Hillsborough address. Either way, though, whether it's on the Tiburon peninsula or the San Francisco peninsula for you, you know you're going through life first-class.

MORAGA

POPULATION: 13,744
NO. OF CRIMES: 365
CRIME RATE: 2,655.7 per 100,000

Back to reality. After Belvedere and Hillsborough, you may wonder what we're going to do for the poor working stiffs who can't afford to put down $700,000 for a 4-bedroom ranch. Well, for you—for us—we've got Moraga.

We hasten to add that Moraga is not exactly the poor part of town. It's an attractive and delightful upper-middle-class community with a feeling of country never far away. It only *seems* poor if you've been spending the previous two days gazing at the estates of Belvedere and Hillsborough.

Moraga is located in the central part of Contra Costa County. The name Contra Costa is Spanish for "opposite coast" and the name makes sense when you realize that the county originally included most of the east coast of San Francisco Bay—the Oakland-Berkeley area—and that the earliest Spanish settlements in the Bay Area were in San Francisco. From their location, this was the opposite coast.

Today you get to Contra Costa County by taking the San Francisco–Oakland Bay Bridge east to Oakland, then continuing east on the Route 24 expressway. You know you're in Contra Costa when you pass through Caldecott Tunnel, which burrows through the coastal mountain range that rises east of Oakland and Berkeley. This low mountain range separates the San Francisco Bay Area from inland California and the climactic difference is often immediately and dramatically noticeable. The Bay Area has a brisk and cool marine climate; east of the mountains you step into a semiarid climate, warm and dry, more typical of points far south of San Francisco.

Contra Costa is off the main tourist paths, but we have become more familiar with it since we have friends who reside and work there. For them, as for so many others, Contra Costa County combines the best of two worlds—the semiarid climate that they love and easy accessibility to Berkeley (with all the activities generated by the university) and San Francisco.

Contra Costa was pretty sleepy countryside until the completion of Caldecott Tunnel in 1937 and the end of World War II opened it up for suburban development. Our Safe Place of Moraga, for example, had been established by James Irvine and his Moraga Company in 1916, but it didn't take off. In 1953, though, the Utah Construction and Mining Company purchased most of the Irvine lands in Moraga and growth then proceeded rather rapidly. Moraga incorporated in 1974.

Moraga's natural setting is a peaceful and beautiful corner of the Diablo Valley, with the town's residences extending into the foothills of the coastal mountains. Some areas are heavily wooded; others are open grasslands broken by clusters of oaks. You can see cattle grazing on the undeveloped hills and horseback riding is popular on the trails maintained throughout the area. The redwood trees around here are all second-growth, since lumbering depleted the area of its original redwoods by the late 1850s.

Moraga's most notable landmark is the campus of St. Mary's College, with its exquisitely styled Spanish architecture. St. Mary's was founded in 1863 in San Francisco, moved to Oakland in 1887, and moved again to its present location in 1928. Founded by the Christian Brothers, it began as a men's college but became coeducational in 1970. It currently enrolls approximately 1,500 undergraduates and 600 graduate students.

Another landmark is the former Rheem mansion, known as the Hacienda de las Flores ("House of Flowers"). It had been the western headquarters for the Christian Brothers and is now the town's recreational and cultural center, where more than 150 different classes and programs are presented. The 10-acre park surrounding the mansion contains picnic tables, a nature trail, and botanical displays.

While the community is mostly residential, two attractive business areas make it possible to fulfill most of your shopping needs locally. Bus lines take you from Moraga to the Lafayette and Orinda stations on the BART (Bay Area Rapid Transit) line. Taking BART, it is a quick twenty-minute trip to the financial district in downtown San Francisco and the line runs from 6 A.M. to midnight. Driving, it will take you approximately twenty minutes to get to Berkeley or Oakland and thirty-five minutes to San Francisco.

Brent Abel, a realtor associate with Wallace, Underwood, & Scofield Realtors in Moraga, told us that prices for single-family houses begin at around $140,000 to $150,000 and extend up to $975,000. The usual range, though, is more around $200,000 and the Manor area of town—bounded by the triangle formed by Moraga Road, St. Mary's Road, and Rheem Boulevard—is more expensive, with houses there priced at $250,000 and up.

For $200,000, Brent told us, you could usually get a 3- or 4-bedroom ranch with about 2,200 square feet of living area on a 1/3- or 1/4-acre lot. It would probably have, in addition to the kitchen and living room, a family room, formal dining room, and hot tub.

Condominiums, Brent added, range from around $100,000 for a 1- or 2-bedroom unit to about $250,000. Lots run $135,000 for 1/3 acre or 1/4 acre and you pay more for a view. Building costs range from $80 to $100 per square foot, depending on the quality and what you want.

Most homes here are single-story in design and they don't usually have basements. Since most of them have been built in the last twenty years, they usually have central air-conditioning and heating, though the temperatures are normally so moderate that you don't really need the air-conditioning. Fog helps to cool off the mornings and evenings.

In terms of crime, Moraga consistently ranks as one of the safest suburbs in the Bay Area. In our comparison year of 1980, it was second in the area only to Hillsborough. Crimes of violence consisted of no murders, 1 rape, 3 robberies, and 6 aggravated assaults. Property crime consisted of 99 burglaries, 247 larceny-thefts, and 9 motor vehicle thefts. This placed Moraga below U.S. rural crime levels in all categories except larceny-theft and even there its rate was just about half the U.S. metropolitan rate.

What makes Moraga safe? When *San Francisco* magazine ran a profile, "The Bay Area's Safest Suburbs," in its February 1981 issue, it mentioned Moraga's geographical advantages—off the beaten path, 5 miles from the nearest freeway, and with just a few roads connecting it to the rest of the county. In addition, said Police Chief Larry Olson, "We have been very aggressive at stopping and talking to people who don't appear to belong in the community. We have a very strong police presence in the town."

We asked our favorite resident of Moraga, Virginia Tracy, if she agreed that it was safe.

"I've lived here for ten years and, yes, I think it's safe," Ginny answered. "I've only been burglarized once during that time."

Gee thanks, we said, what a great recommendation.

"No," Ginny quickly added with a chuckle. "That was our own fault. My husband and I were both gone, there were no cars in the garage, and we didn't take any of the precautions we should have taken. So they cleared us out of our sterling. We learned from that—even in a Safe Place you take sensible precautions to guard against theft."

Then she added the clincher: "I feel safe enough to run at five o'clock in the morning or ten o'clock at night—alone and without any qualms."

As for all the other aspects of Moraga, there was no doubt where Ginny stood. "Moraga is a fantastic community," she exclaimed, "and I can't speak highly enough about it. There's a very strong community spirit here. This week was Clean Up Moraga week and we had several hundred people show up to clean up the parkways. The schools are excellent. The high school that Moraga students go to, Campolinda, was just named one of the top five in the state. And there's a fantastic ecumenical crossover in the churches, especially at Easter, with joint services and celebrations."

If you knew Ginny like we know Ginny, you'd realize she is not the sort to give such an enthusiastic recommendation if she didn't mean it. And having seen the town for ourselves, we can understand and appreciate the attachment that its residents have for Moraga. Fine homes and schools, a storybook setting of hills and valleys, a vibrant community spirit, and ready accessibility to one of the nation's most exciting metropolitan regions all help to make Moraga one of the finest places to call home in the San Francisco Bay Area.

NAPA VALLEY

An hour's drive north of San Francisco is the lovely Napa Valley, world-famous for the varieties of choice California wines produced there. About 35 miles long and with a width of up to 5 miles, the valley is also famous for its exquisite beauty. On all sides are hills and mountains carpeted with forests of oak, pine, redwood, and Douglas fir. Reaching up the hillsides to meet the forests are small orchards, farms, and—everywhere—the beautiful vineyards. This is a land of old stone wineries, of geysers, hot springs, and mineral baths, of cattle spreads and quaint Victorian estates, of the ruins of silver- and mercury-mining towns, and of lake and river resorts.

Once the home of the Wintun and Wappo Indians, the Napa Valley experienced its first real influx of white population during the Gold Rush of the 1850s. Disillusioned miners sought refuge and work here after the first harsh winter in the gold fields. Then came the great Silver Rush in Napa Valley itself, the opening of quicksilver and mercury mines in the hills, and characters such as stagecoach robber Black Bart. The first wineries began operating in the 1860s and the latter half of the nineteenth century was also a heyday for such spas as White Sulphur Springs, Calistoga Hot Springs, and Napa Soda Springs.

When we first visited the Napa Valley in 1970, wine was the predominant industry, but there was also a plentiful supply of open land and farmland. Since then, of course, a revolution in drinking habits has occurred and Americans are now consuming a much higher percentage of wine, compared with the hard liquors. The results were not hard to see in the valley. The vineyards were *everywhere* when we returned in 1982.

Official statistics supplied by the Wine Institute supported what our eyes told us. Between 1971 and 1981, Napa County almost doubled its acreage devoted to wine-grape cultivation—from 14,834 acres to 26,971 acres. That pattern is true across the state, where a similar doubling of acreage took place. White varieties showed the biggest increase, especially French Colombard and Chenin Blanc. Cabernet Sauvignon had the largest increase in acreage among the red varieties.

An important byproduct of this wine industry is a phenomenal growth in tourism. More than 100 wineries and vineyards make the Napa Valley their home and most of them offer tours or at least an opportunity to sample and buy their wares. "The tourist industry should be a lucrative field in the coming years," we wrote in our 1972 book, *Safe Places.* But even we were surprised to learn that the Napa Valley now ranks as the number-one tourist attraction in California, having surpassed even Disneyland. It is a tribute to the local communities that the exploitation of this lucrative trade has been done tastefully, with beautifully restored historical attractions but no neon alleys. Jim Gordon, writing in the St. Helena *Star,* caught the spirit of the place when he noted that you cannot legislate good taste, but "most of the wineries and other businesses value the architectural integrity of the area and build in good taste without official promptings."

The valley certainly does offer one an opportunity to get soused in style—with one operator even offering chauffeured limousine tours of the wineries. At the Beringer Brothers winery you can see tunnels hewn out of the limestone by Chinese laborers in the 1880s, when St. Helena had its own Chinatown, joss house and all. Beaulieu is noted for the beauty of its gardens and the Christian Brothers Wine and Champagne Cellar is said to be the largest stone winery building in the world. The Charles Krug Winery, established in 1861 and the oldest operating winery in the Napa Valley, is now a California Historical Landmark. The Heitz estate features a nineteenth-century stone winery; the Robert Mondavi winery follows the secular architecture of the Early California period; and Inglenook's Neo-Gothic winery, built in 1883, is set deep in the basalt of Cellar Hill. It features vaulted cellars, oval casks hewn from oak of Germany's Black Forest, and wine antiques in the Sample Room dating back as far as 1498. Many of the wineries feature concerts during the summer.

If you extend your shopping beyond the valley to encompass the entire county, you can fill your pantry as well as your wine cellar. The map and guide distributed by Napa County Farming Trails illustrates where you can get freshly picked and grown fruits and vegetables—or pick your own. The variety is enticing and includes apples, blackberries, corn, cucumbers, figs, green beans, kiwis,

NAPA VALLEY Crime Chart

	Crime Rate	Murder	Rape	Robbery	Aggravated Assault	Burglary	Larceny —Theft	Motor Vehicle Theft
United States								
U.S. Total	5,899.9	10.2	36.4	243.5	290.6	1,668.2	3,156.3	494.6
U.S. Metropolitan Areas	6,757.6	11.5	43.4	319.0	328.3	1,911.8	3,534.9	608.8
U.S. Rural Areas	2,290.4	7.5	15.5	22.5	136.9	830.2	1,143.9	133.9
Regional Crime Centers								
Calistoga	6,695.0	0	0	0	425.1	1,381.5	4,357.1	531.3
Napa	7,903.1	6.0	32.1	100.2	432.9	1,735.7	5,101.0	495.1
Safe Place								
St. Helena	2,281.1	0	0	20.4	81.5	366.6	1,670.1	142.6

lemons, mandarins, melons, nectarines, olives, oranges, peaches, pears, persimmons, plums, pumpkins, raspberries, squash, tamarillo, tomatoes, walnuts, and yarrow.

Napa County has much more, as well, to entice you to move here. Water sports are popular at Lake Berryessa, California's second-largest lake. Deer hunting is popular at private hunt clubs. And Calistoga offers massage baths and physiotherapy services at its hot mineral springs, the Napa County Fair, Old Faithful of California (a geyser which shoots 200 feet up in the air every forty minutes or so), a forest of petrified redwood trees, and Robert Louis Stevenson Memorial State Park, where the famous writer honeymooned in 1880 and wrote *The Silverado Squatters.* Mount St. Helena (not to be confused with decidedly *unsafe* Mount St. Helens in the state of Washington) also was reportedly used by Stevenson when he described Spyglass Hill in *Treasure Island.*

And in the center of this wine-lover's paradise is our final Safe Place for California—a fine home base for enjoying all this natural and cultivated beauty.

ST. HELENA

POPULATION: 4,910
NO. OF CRIMES: 112
CRIME RATE: 2,281.1 per 100,000

St. Helena is a pleasant community of wide and clean streets, of colorful gardens and its shady Avenue of Elms, and of Victorian homes and atmosphere. While the mushrooming tourist trade has led to an increase in traffic since our last visit, the town remains as unspoiled as you could reasonably expect, given its central location. Thanks to deliberate slow-growth policies, life here is still unrushed and the problems of rapid growth have been avoided. In St. Helena you are within easy traveling distance of San Francisco, yet you can live in close proximity to the beautiful natural surroundings of the Napa Valley.

And it's safe. A few months before our visit, the San Francisco *Chronicle* featured St. Helena as the safest town in the nine-county area surrounding San Francisco Bay. A photograph showed St. Helena's police chief sitting in a park with nothing to do.

"I don't believe there is any magic formula for a low crime index," Police Chief A. V. Angel told us. "Deployment of patrol officers in marked police units is probably still the best deterrent. Simply a matter of seeing and being seen. We do work a lot of traffic, which to me is a good deterrent to crime.

"Perhaps one of our best ongoing programs," Chief Angel added, "is getting officers into the schools for presentations and keeping a good rapport with the students."

We noted that in our comparison year of 1980 there were no murders or rapes, 1 robbery, and 4 aggravated assaults. Property crime consisted of 18 burglaries, 82 larceny-thefts, and 7 motor vehicle thefts. This placed St. Helena below U.S. rural crime levels in all categories except larceny-theft and motor vehicle theft and even there it was just above rural levels. St. Helena's burglary rate was particularly—and commendably—low. In fact, it was considerably lower than when we had visited the town in 1970.

St. Helena's school system consists of an elementary school (K–5), junior high, and high school. A parochial school also provides instruction in the first eight grades. Pacific Union College, a four-year college run by the Seventh-Day Adventist church, and Napa College, a two-year institution, also serve the area. Napa College has a campus in St. Helena, which offers courses for the community.

Medical facilities include St. Helena Hospital, which has 108 acute patient beds and 72 beds in its Health Center. An Adventist hospital, it also emphasizes preventive medicine and has a mental health unit, alcohol recovery unit, weight control unit, and heart unit. There are forty-five active physicians and surgeons and twenty-two courtesy physicians on its staff. Other medical facilities in town include ten dentists, two optometrists, five chiropractors, a medical clinic, a convalescent hospital, a retirement home, and several nursing homes.

St. Helena's new public library houses the extensive Napa Valley Wine Library and the Silverado Museum, with Robert Louis Stevenson memorabilia. A wide variety of churches and civic organizations is found in the community.

For information on housing costs, we had a very helpful talk with Don Buller of Glenn Buller Realty, the Century 21 affiliate in town. It turned out that Don's grandfather is Horace Jenkins, who had been our real estate contact on our previous visit. Mr. Jenkins has retired, but we were delighted to see him again and to reminisce about the changes that have taken place in the valley.

Don told us that Napa County has been tightening its restrictions on the subdividing of land, seeking to keep a lid on growth. As a result, it is difficult to create a new parcel of less than 40 acres. The city can still subdivide, but it also has a slow-growth attitude. Both St. Helena and Calistoga currently have moratoriums on building permits and the last new building lot sold in St. Helena—a 1/4-acre lot—went for $65,000.

At the time of our visit, no previously approved building lots were on the market in St. Helena. A few parcels were available within a 10-mile radius, but 1/2-acre lots were selling for $50,000 or more. In the hills, your price will depend on building site possibilities. A 10-acre parcel and a 24-acre parcel were each available for $155,000.

Planted vineyards, Don told us, run $20,000 to $30,000 an acre, with a usual minimum of 40 acres in a vineyard. Raw land in the hills, suitable for planting, costs $7,000 to $10,000 an acre.

Given the slow-growth policies of the city and county, your best bet is to look for an existing property. In town, Don told us, prices start at $85,000 for a 2-bedroom house with about 900 square feet or $125,000 for a 3-bedroom house with 1,300 square feet. The newer houses with 1,700 to 2,100 square feet of living area will cost $170,000 to $225,000. These will usually have 3 or 4 bedrooms, 2 baths, a living room, a family room, and a 2-car garage. Some will have a formal dining room, but most have a combination family room and dining area. The lot size is usually 1/4 acre.

It is not uncommon, Don told us, to find homes selling in the $300,000 to $500,000 range—and up. For $525,000, for example, there was a six-year-old house on the market that had 3,000 square feet of living area, nestled on 4 acres of land with an in-ground swimming pool and a tennis court. A 2-story country-style home, it had 4 bedrooms, 2 1/2 baths, and a living room, family room, formal dining room, and 2-car attached garage.

And a few miles out of town, with stucco walls and tile roofs, was a new 3-story house, with 5,300 square feet of living area, selling for $640,000. It had 4 bedrooms, 3 baths, a living room, a large family room, a formal dining room, and a 3-car attached garage. Among the many extra features were 4 fireplaces, wood/slab floors, double entry doors of carved oak, stained moldings and baseboards, skylights, a tiled entry, a breakfast room, and solar-augmented hot water heating. *And* the property, about 1 1/2 acres in size, provided incredible views of the Napa Valley below.

The valley's most famous resident, Robert Louis Stevenson, once described it as a land where "the earth's cream is skimmed and garnered . . . and the wine is bottled poetry." The valley remains as beautiful today as it was in Stevenson's time and offers you an opportunity to throw away the fears and tensions of the city and create your own days of wine and roses.

Where to get further information:

State

California Chamber of Commerce, Tourism Department, Box 1736, Sacramento, CA 95808. Office of Visitor Services, P.O. Box 1499, Sacramento, CA 95808. California Office of Tourism, 1030 13th Street, Suite 200, Sacramento, CA 95814. State Parks ($2.00 for its *Guide):* Department of Parks and Recreation, P.O. Box 2390, Sacramento, CA 95811. National Parks:

Information Office, National Park Service, Fort Mason—GGNRA, San Francisco, CA 94123. For a list of their maps for sale: Map Center, 631 N. Market Boulevard, Suite F, Sacramento, CA 95834.

Regional

Los Angeles Area: Los Angeles Visitors and Convention Bureau, Arco Plaza, 505 S. Flower Street, Los Angeles, CA 90071.

San Jose and Silicon Valley: San Jose/Santa Clara Valley Information Center, 1762 Technology Drive, San Jose, CA 95110. San Jose Visitors Bureau, 1 Paseo de San Antonio, San Jose, CA 95113.

San Francisco Bay Area: San Francisco Convention and Visitors Bureau, 1390 Market Street, San Francisco, CA 94102. Redwood Empire Association, 360 Post Street, Suite 401, San Francisco, CA 94108.

Napa Valley: For a listing of wine country maps and tour guides for sale: Sally Taylor & Friends, 756 Kansas Street, San Francisco, CA 94107.

Local

Palos Verdes: Palos Verdes Peninsula Chamber of Commerce, P.O. Box 2484, Palos Verdes Peninsula, CA 90274. *A Guide to the Palos Verdes Peninsula* is an excellent publication of the League of Women Voters, Palos Verdes Peninsula, 700 Silver Spur Road, Suite 702G, Rolling Hills Estates, CA 90274. Neighborhood Crime Watch, P.O. Box 963, Palos Verdes Estates, CA 90274. Palos Verdes Peninsula Unified School District, 38 Crest Road W., Rolling Hills, CA 90274. City of Palos Verdes Estates, 340 Palos Verdes Drive W., P.O. Box 1086, Palos Verdes Estates, CA 90274. City of Rancho Palos Verdes, 30940 Hawthorne Boulevard, Rancho Palos Verdes, CA 90274. *A Homeowner's Guide to Fire and Watershed Management at the Chaparral/Urban Interface* includes "What to Do When Caught in a Wildfire" and is available from Deana Dana, Supervisor, Fourth District, County of Los Angeles, 500 W. Temple, Room 822, Los Angeles, CA 90012.

Sierra Madre: Sierra Madre Chamber of Commerce, 49 S. Baldwin Avenue, Sierra Madre, CA 91024. Sierra Madre Search and Rescue Team, P.O. Box 24, Sierra Madre, CA 91024. Sierra Madre Historical Society, P.O. Box 202, Sierra Madre, CA 91024.

Yorba Linda: Yorba Linda Chamber of Commerce, 4854C Main Street, P.O. Box 238, Yorba Linda, CA 92686. Yorba Linda City Hall, 4845 Main Street, P.O. Box 487, Yorba Linda, CA 92686.

Saratoga: Saratoga Chamber of Commerce, 20460 Saratoga–Los Gatos Road, Saratoga, CA 95070 (map $1.00; other literature without charge).

Belvedere: Belvedere-Tiburon Chamber of Commerce, P.O. Box 563, Belvedere, CA 94920. Belvedere City Hall, 450 San Rafael Avenue, Belvedere, CA 94920.

Hillsborough: Town of Hillsborough, 1600 Floribunda Avenue, Hillsborough, CA 94010. Burlingame Chamber of Commerce, 306 Lorton Avenue, Burlingame, CA 94010. San Mateo County Convention and Visitors Bureau, 888 Airport Boulevard, Burlingame, CA 94010.

Moraga: Moraga Chamber of Commerce, P.O. Box 512, Moraga, CA 94556. Town of Moraga, 1550 Viader Drive, Suite D, P.O. Box 188, Moraga, CA 94556. *At the Foot of the Mountain* is an informative booklet on the communities of central and eastern Contra Costa County, including Moraga, available from the League of Women Voters of Diablo Valley, 3557 Mount Diablo Boulevard, Lafayette, CA 94549.

St. Helena: St. Helena Chamber of Commerce, 1508 Main Street, St. Helena, CA 94574. For a copy of their map, send a self-addressed, stamped legal-sized envelope to: Napa County Farming Trails, 4075 Solano Avenue, Napa, CA 94558. The best and most detailed road map is published by the Napa County Board of Realtors, 2045 Jefferson Street, P.O. Box 3600, Napa, CA 94558. For an excellent weekly tabloid on activities in Napa and Sonoma counties ($18 for one year): *Wine Country Review,* P.O. Box 92, El Verano, CA 95433. For information on their self-guided tours of Napa, Yountville, St. Helena, and Calistoga: Napa Landmarks, Inc., P.O. Box 702, Napa, CA 94558.

Colorado

"Mountains" and "Colorado": the words are interchangeable and go together like "Texas" and "oil" or "Kansas" and "plains." Actually, the eastern two fifths of the state are an extension of the plains of Kansas and Nebraska, while the western one fifth of the state is a high plateau scarred by canyons and valleys. No matter. The remaining two fifths of the state is enough to give Colorado more than six times the mountain area of Switzerland. Its average elevation of 6,800 feet makes Colorado the highest state in the nation, with 1,143 mountains that rise to an elevation of 10,000 feet or more, 53 of them higher than 14,000 feet.

It was the awesome panorama from the summit of one of these promontories, Pikes Peak, that inspired Katherine Lee Bates to write "America, the Beautiful" in 1895.

Skiing is the sport most often associated with Colorado—and well it might be, with more than thirty ski resorts in the state. But this is paradise too for hunters and fishermen, for hikers and campers, and for golfers (more than 140 courses statewide), as well as those who want to see Colorado from the gondola of a hot-air balloon. With a jeep or other four-wheel-drive vehicle, you can explore the more than 400 ghost towns and mining camps that haunt the mountainsides and valleys. And if you get your thrills from shooting the rapids, you'll find more than forty white water rafting companies operating in Colorado.

Tourism and the pursuit of these outdoor activities are a major contributor to the state's economy. So, too, is mining and quarrying. Colorado leads all other states in the production of molybdenum, tin, uranium, granite, sandstone, and basalt. It ranks high in the production of coal, zinc, silver, and gold.

Agriculture has also become important with the utilization of irrigation. Potatoes, sugar beets, wheat, corn, cauliflower, fruit, and flowers are all cultivated here. Much of the state's industry is based on these mining and agricultural activities—beet sugar refineries, meat packing plants, flour mills, and smelters, for example.

When it comes to crime, Colorado acts like a typical Western state—with slim pickings in the way of Safe Places. In our comparison year of 1980, Colorado had the sixth-highest crime rate among the fifty states. The FBI listed twenty-one communities in the state with a population of 10,000 or more and not one of them qualified as a Safe Place. Four of them had crime rates higher than New York City or Washington, D.C. Denver's 1980 population was slightly under 500,000, so it didn't make our chart of the nation's largest cities. But if it had, it would have shown a higher crime rate than any other big city in the nation with the single exception of Boston.

Luckily for us, we have a friend in Colorado who shares our interest in Americana and in the nation's diverse regions and communities. He has outtraveled us, too, particularly in his adopted state of Colorado, so it was just natural to give John Bernick a call and tell him our plight. He did some homework with state and local police agencies while waiting for us to arrive in the course of our Safe Places trip—and it was thanks to John's diligent research that we have five Safe Places to offer you in the Silver State. They may be small, but in an area as crime-ridden as Colorado they are a bonanza of riches. Eureka!

DENVER AREA

In case you don't watch television's "Dynasty" and otherwise don't keep up with the really important things going on around the country, Denver is a boom town.

This is certainly nothing new in the history of the Mile-High City. This latest boom is based on Denver's role as a hub for energy exploration in the region that stretches from Colorado to Alaska. Earlier fortunes were made in mining camps, starting with the Pikes Peak and Central City gold rushes in 1859.

Actually, Denver learned quickly that it is more profitable over the long run to be the *hub* of all the boom activities than the source. Fortunes went up and down in the mining camps, but Denver's lease on life was its role as a trading city and in the end it won out over the rival settlements in the mountains. In the 1880s and 1890s, the new attraction was silver. Denver continued to grow, basing its economy on cattle, sheep, commerce, and a proliferation of federal offices in the Nation's Second Capital.

Things really started popping after World War II and Denver became a major business, financial, and manufacturing center. The federal government and tourism continued to assure the diversity of the city's economic base. Still, when we visited Denver in 1970, we thought it was pleasant enough itself and was located in beautiful countryside but was nevertheless overrated. We wouldn't say the same today. The energy boom of the past decade has added so much wealth to Denver that it holds its own with any comparably sized area in terms of shopping facilities, cultural activities and entertainment, residential neighborhoods, and restaurants.

With a population of more than 1,500,000, the Denver metropolitan area today is the home of more than half of all the residents of Colorado. Natives are an endangered species around here and the latest influx of newcomers has insti-

DENVER AREA Crime Chart

	Crime Rate	Murder	Rape	Robbery	Aggravated Assault	Burglary	Larceny —Theft	Motor Vehicle Theft
United States								
U.S. Total	5,899.9	10.2	36.4	243.5	290.6	1,668.2	3,156.3	494.6
U.S. Metropolitan Areas	6,757.6	11.5	43.4	319.0	328.3	1,911.8	3,534.9	608.8
U.S. Rural Areas	2,290.4	7.5	15.5	22.5	136.9	830.2	1,143.9	133.9
Regional Crime Centers								
Commerce City	10,582.7	0	55.4	160.2	659.1	1,884.9	7,281.0	542.1
Denver	12,013.1	20.2	143.9	483.5	480.5	4,046.2	5,764.3	1,074.4
Englewood	13,727.1	3.3	56.6	333.1	389.7	3,021.2	8,843.8	1,079.2
Safe Places								
Cherry Hills Village	3,081.7	0	0	19.5	19.5	1,423.8	1,521.4	97.5
Columbine Valley	3,467.0	0	0	0	216.7	1,191.8	2,058.5	0

gated a bumper-sticker war identifying drivers as a NATIVE, SEMI-NATIVE, or—defiantly—ALIEN. So if you're an alien to the area or about to become one, let us point you in the direction of two of the finest places to consider as your new home.

CHERRY HILLS VILLAGE

POPULATION: 5,127
NO. OF CRIMES: 158
CRIME RATE: 3,081.7 per 100,000

The main direction of growth in the Denver area today is south toward Colorado Springs. With commuting developments found as far down the highway as Castle Rock, 30 miles from downtown, Cherry Hills Village appears to be more conveniently located with each passing year. It's not just the short 8-mile trip downtown by Interstate 25, either. It's also the fact that many businesses have relocated in the fashionable southeastern suburbs, many of them in office parks with stunning architecture in Greenwood Village, adjacent to Cherry Hills Village.

For all the hustle and bustle in all directions, the Village itself maintains a tranquil, even rustic air about it. This is one place where gravel roads are a matter of deliberate choice rather than a lack of funds. The message you get from the unpaved roads, bridle paths, and acre-plus lots is: "This is executive country"—with emphasis on both words.

We don't dispute the attractiveness of the community. The homes themselves range from comfortably upper-middle-class to gorgeous and many of them enjoy views of the Front Range of the Rockies off to the west. There are attractive churches, Village Hall is modern and inviting, and the police have a reputation for acting swiftly when help is needed. But when the starting price for homes is around $300,000—and there we're talking about a quite-ordinary ranch—well, you know that a large part of what you're paying for is the address. Obviously, the people who live here believe it's worth it.

Lee LaCasse, branch manager of Cherry Creek Properties, Ltd., told us that at the time of our visit (August 1982) the top house on the market was listed at $1,600,000, with the starting price around $300,000. A lot (1 acre to 1½ acres) will cost you $150,000, he said—if you can find one.

We pleaded poverty and he showed us a $290,000 listing for a 3-bedroom ranch with 2,500 square feet of living area, on a 1.3-acre lot. You would get a living room, family room, dining room, kitchen, and basement. Taxes would be in the vicinity of $2,600.

For $312,500, we could get a 1-story contemporary rambler, a stone-faced house with tinted modern windows. This one had no basement, but it was on a 1.9-acre property zoned for horses. With about 2,700 square feet of living area, it had 3 bedrooms, 2 baths and 1 toilet, living room, 14 × 13 kitchen, and dining room. Because this was a new house, he estimated that taxes might come to $6,000 a year.

Cherry Hills Village is entirely residential, except for a small commercial site separated from the remainder of the community by U.S. 285 (East Hampden Avenue). There is some ½-acre zoning and one small area zoned for 16,000 square feet; otherwise, zoning is for a minimum of 1, 1¼, or 2½ acres.

The village is part of a public school district that encompasses a wider area of Arapahoe County. Two of the district's elementary schools are located in the village, but they will be consolidated into one school in 1984. Cherry Hills Village also has two private schools—St. Mary's, a Catholic girls' school that is coeducational in the lower grades, and coed Kent Denver Country Day School.

Crime levels in this bucolic community are appropriately rural. During our comparison year of 1980, there were no murders or rapes, 1 robbery, and 1 aggravated assault. Property crime consisted of 73 burglaries, 78 larceny-thefts, and 5 motor vehicle thefts. This placed Cherry Hills Village below U.S. rural levels of crime in all categories except burglary and larceny-theft, and in those categories it remained well below U.S. metropolitan levels.

In addition to a weekly newspaper, *The Village Squire,* there's an unofficial and self-supporting bimonthly newsletter for residents, *The Village Crier.* Between them you can keep up with local news and gossip, including tips on which young men will mow your lawn, babysitting services, and why you've seen peacocks strutting around. (The resident owners got them at the zoo. The peacocks used to go to the next-door neighbors to admire themselves in front of the glass doors. To protect the neighbor's privacy, the owners of the peacocks put a mirror against their house so the peacocks could see themselves at home.)

At the time of our visit, the big topic of conversation was an upcoming special election on "what to do about the resort hotel"—nothing like a zoning fight to stir up a community like this—and understandably so.

It seems that in 1958 a 68.8-acre parcel of land was given a special zoning allowing a resort hotel to be built on it. Finally, in 1981, the owner decided to proceed. Some residents protested and through a petition drive sought an election to vote on changing the zoning for the area, allowing only single-family residences.

They argued:

"To allow a 600-room hotel with approximately 200 condominiums housing 500 people, a ballroom accommodating 1,200 persons and 1,000 employees, adding at least 5,000 car trips per day, is so foreign to our community and so detrimental to the neighborhood, it violates the very concept for which Cherry Hills Village was created.

"The influx of traffic, noise, and air pollution will result in extremely negative consequences. The increase in tourists, conventioneers, transients, vehicles, and without doubt an increase in crime and loss in property values aggravates an already unconscionable situation."

In response, the developer was able to point to its legal rights and to offer both a carrot and a stick.

The carrot was that "the project will strengthen the local tax base. By 1987 the project will be paying (net of cost to the city) almost $1 million a year to the city of Cherry Hills and over $800,000 a year to the Cherry Creek School District." This would represent "yearly income to Cherry Hills Village in excess of its current annual operating budget."

Moreover, said the developer, this would be a quality project worthy of the community.

"Designed by the Frank Lloyd Wright Foundation, the heart of the project will be a resort hotel deserving of a five-star rating. Its closest competitor in Colorado would be the Broadmoor in Colorado Springs.

"Recreational facilities will include nine tennis courts, two swimming pools, an outdoor ice skating rink, and an 18-hole, par 70 golf course.

"In addition to the resort hotel, there will be a number of luxury condominiums. Combining condominiums with the hotel will give a residential atmosphere to the entire project.

"The Cherry Hills Resort Hotel and Luxury Residences will be the kind of resort where people just like the people who live in Cherry Hills come to relax and live."

On the other hand, the threatened stick was that legal fees could cost the city $100,000 "and open the door to an even higher density development of the land." And if the courts ruled that the rezoning was permissible but that the owner had to be compensated, "A conservative estimate of the compensation the city of Cherry Hills would be required to pay is $50 million."

Cherry Hills' residents decided to accept the carrot and voted against any change in the zoning by 1,738 to 496. The project, however, is nevertheless in the courts since the city says its zoning ordinance doesn't allow condominiums and the developer wants the court to define what the ordinance says.

With or without a five-star resort, Cherry Hills remains a five-star suburb well worth your consideration whenever fortune brings you to the Denver area.

COLUMBINE VALLEY

POPULATION: 923
NO. OF CRIMES: 32
CRIME RATE: 3,467.0 per 100,000

Nurseries, farms, and stables line Platte Canyon Road, the main highway passing through Columbine (pronounced CŎL-um-bine) Valley. East of the highway is the South Platte River and its valley. This is the southwest tip of suburban Arapahoe County, with Douglas County to the south and Jefferson County to the west. The foothills of the Rampart Range of the Rockies are just a few miles farther south.

Columbine Valley is countryside rapidly turning into suburbs. To the north of town you will find the Columbine Country Club and its fairway residential neighborhoods. The homes in this country club area are comfortably sized ranches. The neighborhoods have had time to age just enough so you are impressed by the green lawns, profuse trees, and mature landscaping. Farther south are a mixture of 2-story architectural styles and ranches, built in new developments on the prairie. The lawns are green and this is definitely an upper-middle-class area, but trees are scarcer and the houses are close together in tract-development fashion.

"Columbine Valley is unique in the Denver area because it does have real community spirit," Brian Hansen told us. "We have Town Hall meetings here and they are well-attended."

A realtor, Brian has his office in nearby Englewood. But he has been a member of the Columbine Country Club for ten years and has lived in the country club neighborhood for three years. He wasn't at all surprised to learn that the town had qualified as a Safe Place.

"It's safe, all right," he affirmed. "Neighbors will watch your house when you are gone and my next-door neighbor is probably the best burglar alarm we've got."

Another factor may be the relative stability of the community—particularly in the country club area. Brian noted that the entrance fee has risen from $4,000 to $15,500. "You don't tend to move quickly when you've put that much money down," he suggested. And turnover in the past year had been slight—just nine properties.

In our comparison year of 1980, Columbine Valley had no murders, rapes, robberies, or motor vehicle thefts. There were just 2 aggravated assaults, 11 burglaries, and 19 larceny-thefts. Because of the extremely low population base—less than 1,000—this meant that the community's crime rates in those three categories were above U.S. rural levels, but they were still far below U.S. metropolitan levels.

We noted that Columbine Valley is not in the most convenient location for commuting to downtown Denver—there's no interstate nearby and you must rely on U.S. 85, South Santa Fe Drive. Brian Hansen said that he had done a survey of the country club residents a couple of years back and only about 25 percent commuted to downtown Denver. Perhaps 40 percent worked in the southeast—at places like the office parks of Greenwood Village. The rest worked closer to home, in the southwest.

This is an up-and-coming area, yet the population is not likely to take off without faster highway access. It is a good place to turn a profit on real estate, Brian noted. People come in and buy one of the older houses, built in the sixties, for a price ranging between $75 and $83 per square foot. They modernize it and expand it somewhat and then sell it for more than $100 a square foot. He was just about to close such a deal. The owner had bought the house for $190,000, put in $58,000 in improvements, and was going to sell it for considerably more than $248,000.

We asked Brian about real estate costs and he said that the lowest price range is around $180,000, the highest around $425,000. There had been two extremely good buys in early 1983 (when we talked to him). Usually you couldn't find anything under $200,000, but two nonbasement ranches, each with about 2,400 to 2,500 square feet of living area, had sold for around $180,000.

The average sale price in the country club neighborhood would be $92 per square foot, he thought, or about $250,000. That includes the house and the land. You would have a minimum of 3 bedrooms and 3 baths, a maximum of 5 bedrooms and 5 baths. You would have a living room, family room, formal dining room, kitchen, and 2-car garage. The lots are just under 1/2 acre in size, though the country club and its golf course give you the illusion of more land.

The house that sold for $425,000 had 4,250 square feet of living area on the main floor, plus a finished basement of 1,800 to 2,000 square feet.

Six buildable lots remain available in the country club area, Brian told us. Two had recently sold for $60,000 and $70,000, but that was because they backed up to maintenance barns. For a lot on the fairway, you would pay $90,000 to $100,000.

In the newer areas to the south of the country club, you can expect to pay $150,000 to $275,000. Here you will find a mixture of ranches and 2-story styles and the lots are smaller—1/3 to 1/2 acre. For $155,000, he had a ranch available. It had 3 bedrooms and a basement, with a total of 2,400 square feet of living area, but it backed up to a busy street. For a 2-story, 4-bedroom, 2 1/2-bath executive house, you could expect to pay $225,000.

A quick look at some tax assessments showed a levy of $2,000 for a house valued at $240,000 and $2,900 for a $339,000 house.

If you're looking for a quiet neighborhood with community spirit at the edge of the Denver metropolitan area, Columbine Valley offers that with quiet good taste in the shadow of the Rockies.

COLORADO SPRINGS AREA

Tourism and the military have long been cornerstones of this magnificently located city at the foot of Pikes Peak. The growth of the metropolitan area has been rapid—from about 75,000 in 1950 to more than 300,000 as of 1981.

One of the features of this growth during the seventies was the diversification into new economic areas. While the number of military personnel stationed locally declined, manufacturing employment increased from 6,680 to 14,980. The combined employment in finance, insurance, real estate, and service industries jumped from 15,350 to 30,170. And Colorado Springs became a center for high technology microelectronics manufacturing. Some of these firms locating new facilities here were Digital Equipment, Honeywell, Inmos, Litton Data Systems, NCR, Mostek, Texas Instruments, and Rolm.

The U.S. Air Force Academy is the most visible military operation in the area, with visitors welcome and tours available. The least visible military operation is the North American Air Defense Command, buried in Cheyenne Mountain. Fort Carson Army Base, Ent Air Force Base, and Peterson Air Force Base are also located in the area. The Air Force's Consolidated Space Operations Center, which is scheduled to become operational in 1985, will control all military space missions and space shuttle operations.

COLORADO SPRINGS AREA Crime Chart

	Crime Rate	Murder	Rape	Robbery	Aggravated Assault	Burglary	Larceny —Theft	Motor Vehicle Theft
United States								
U.S. Total	5,899.9	10.2	36.4	243.5	290.6	1,668.2	3,156.3	494.6
U.S. Metropolitan Areas	6,757.6	11.5	43.4	319.0	328.3	1,911.8	3,534.9	608.8
U.S. Rural Areas	2,290.4	7.5	15.5	22.5	136.9	830.2	1,143.9	133.9
Regional Crime Center								
Colorado Springs	8,170.0	6.8	73.0	195.7	295.7	2,448.1	4,692.7	458.0
Safe Place								
Palmer Lake	2,389.4	0	0	*88.5	88.5	1,415.9	796.5	0

*A statistical aberration caused by low population and crime numbers.

The Colorado Springs area has many attractions. The Broadmoor Hotel is the top convention and resort area in Colorado, as well as a major sports center. Many Olympic skating events are held there and its 18-hole golf course is considered one of the finest in the nation. Scenic highways include the Pikes Peak toll road to the summit, Cheyenne Mountain Highway, Gold Camp Road, and High Drive. The historic mining town of Cripple Creek and Royal Gorge, with its suspension bridge 1,053 feet above the Arkansas River, are nearby. And everywhere to the west are the Rockies.

PALMER LAKE

POPULATION: 1,130
NO. OF CRIMES: 27
CRIME RATE: 2,389.4 per 100,000

Palmer Lake is a suburb of Colorado Springs, sitting at the edge of the Rampart Range of the Rockies. Colorado Springs is about 20 miles to the south and Denver is about 45 miles in the opposite direction.

Military retirees constitute a good proportion of Palmer Lake's population. Of those residents who work, many commute to jobs in Colorado Springs. Outside of a couple of stores in Palmer Lake, local shopping takes place a couple of miles down the highway in the town of Monument. Schools, too, are shared with Monument. The elementary school (K–3) is in Palmer Lake; the middle school (4–8) is in the Woodmoor section of Monument; and the high school (9–12) is in Monument.

The big attraction, here as elsewhere in Colorado, is the great outdoors. Palmer Lake sits at an elevation of 7,225 feet and it enjoys more than 300 days of sunshine each year. Days are warm, the nights cool, and the shelter of the Front Range offers protection from extremely cold winters. A small tree-shaded pond and park is located right in town and Woodmoor Country Club offers a championship golf course, tennis, and swimming. Pike National Forest is at your elbow, with miles of hiking trails, wilderness camping areas, and vast areas of natural beauty waiting for the backpacker and hiker.

David had fond memories of two weeks spent in Palmer Lake in 1957, attending a libertarian school run by Bob LeFevre, then the editor of the Colorado Springs *Gazette-Telegraph.* He still remembers the splendidly bright days and bracing nights, the hikes and horseback trips up the canyons of the Ramparts, and the pleasures of going to sleep with a window open, listening to the rushing waters of a nearby mountain stream. Returning to the area now, some twenty-five years later, he found it surprisingly little changed. Yes, it has grown in population, but there's a lot of country around to absorb the new population.

Palmer Lake's crime rate is reassuringly low in a high-crime corridor that stretches from Colorado Springs north to Denver and beyond. In our comparison year of 1980, there were no murders, rapes, or motor vehicle thefts. There were 1 robbery, 1 aggravated assault, 16 burglaries, and 9 larceny-thefts. This placed Palmer Lake below U.S. rural levels of crime in all categories except robbery and burglary. In those two categories, the town remains below U.S. metropolitan levels.

When it came time to get information on real estate costs in Palmer Lake, we talked with Kris Bolewicz of Tri Lakes Realty in Monument. She had moved here in the past year precisely because of worries about crime where she previously lived, in Lakewood, a suburb of Denver. Having a twelve-year-old daughter, she could never breathe easy until she saw the girl home after school, Kris told us, but here there were no such fears.

Kris told us that anything selling for less than $60,000 in Palmer Lake would be an older home—even forty, fifty years old. Wood-burning or free-standing stoves are popular here, she said, and are used much more than heat-losing fireplaces. Most sales are in the 60s and 70s.

For $59,000, Kris showed us a listing for a house built in 1950, with 920 square feet of living area and a lot of 75 × 125. It had 2 bedrooms (12 × 10, 10 × 10), 1 bath, and a 25 × 12 living room, 12 × 10 kitchen, and 2-car detached garage. There was no formal dining room. Taxes were $392.

For $65,500, she had a bilevel house with 1,800 square feet of living area, with 3 small bedrooms, 2 full baths, living room, family room, kitchen, and a 1-car attached garage. Taxes were $710.

For $74,000, you could get a 4-bedroom, 2-bath house with 2,482 square feet of living area, including a living room, family room, and kitchen. It had no garage, but the lot was approximately 1/3 acre and taxes were $638.

And for $80,000, Kris had a listing for a 2-story house, with 1,898 square feet, a 2-car attached garage with a deck over it, and a lot that was about 110 × 150. Taxes were $834. This house had 4 bedrooms (2 up, 2 down), 1 1/2 baths, a living room, and a family room with a combination kitchen.

The nicest homes in Palmer Lake are found in the Red Rock Ranch subdivision. The homes here are nestled in pine groves and maintain their rustic setting through the use of large lots and acreage.

For $168,000 in Red Rock Ranch, Kris had a new house with 4 bedrooms and a 20 × 14 living room, 14 × 12 dining room, 26 × 20 family room, and 12 × 12 kitchen. This house had 3,128 square feet of living area plus a 2-car attached garage and sat on 2.68 acres. It had not been assessed yet for taxes.

Another house in Red Rock, a 5-bedroom house with 3,425 square feet of living area, was on the market for $179,500. Sitting on a 265 × 200 lot, its taxes were $1,890. It had 3 bathrooms and a 20 × 16 living room, 12 × 10 dining room, 28 × 11 family room, and 23 × 13 kitchen. It had 2 fireplaces, with taxes of $1,890 due the developer.

Set at the base of the mountains in a largely rural area, yet easily accessible to both Colorado Springs and Denver, Palmer Lake offers you the best of both of those exciting and fun-filled worlds.

SOUTHWESTERN COLORADO

Southwestern Colorado contains some of the state's most spectacular mountains and canyons. This was our first time in the area and our travels along the Navajo Trail (U.S. 160) took us through magnificent country, including Colorado's largest stand of aspen, near Mancos. The scenery ranges from Southwestern desert vistas to the ever-shifting Great Sand Dunes National Monument, where the dunes reach heights of 700 feet, and to the high Rockies. This is great country for hunting and fishing, for campouts and four-wheel-drive explorations, for visits to ghost towns and abandoned mines, for river rafting, hang gliding, horseback trips into the back country, golf, tennis, or skiing at Telluride, Wolf Creek, and Purgatory.

Southwestern Colorado has "the world's oldest apartment house"—the Indian ruins of Mesa Verde National Park. The Black Canyon of the Gunnison, part of which is a national monument, is awesome because of the depths (1,730 feet to 2,425 feet) combined with narrow widths (sometimes 40 feet wide at river level, 1,300 feet wide at the rims). The steam-operated, narrow-gauge railroad that tackles the high country between Durango and Silverton—a 90-mile round trip—may be the area's most popular tourist attraction, and another rail adventure is the trip between Antonito, Colorado, and Chama, New Mexico. The countryside north of Ouray provided the scenery and the community of Ridgway provided the frontier town scenes for such movies as *True Grit*, *How the West Was Won*, and *Molly Brown*.

This is unbeatable country, but some of the towns are as boisterous as they were in frontier days. Durango, in particular, is the tourist hub of the area and has a crime rate that is higher than you will find in New York City or Washington, D.C. (see our Southwestern Colorado Crime Chart, page 67). In our search for a Safe Place, we found two adjacent communities that qualified and they offer you some of the most breathtaking views you will find in any of our Safe Places across the nation.

PAGOSA SPRINGS

POPULATION: 1,331
NO. OF CRIMES: 23
CRIME RATE: 1,728.0 per 100,000

PAGOSA

POPULATION: 1,351
NO. OF CRIMES: 48
CRIME RATE: 3,555.6 per 100,000

According to Ute legend, a plague fell among them and none of their medicines worked to stem its rage. In desperation, they built a huge fire to send a message to the chief of the happy hunting ground. Overnight, a pool of boiling water appeared on the spot where the fire had been built. They called this hot spring Pagosah or "healing waters."

Another legend has Coronado and his Spanish soldiers as the first non-Indians to visit the springs. The first recorded visit by a white man, though, was in 1859. In 1866 the Utes defeated the Navajos with the help of Col. Albert H. Pfeiffer of the U.S. Army. In 1873 it was the whites who took control of the area with the establishment of Fort Lewis. The area remained under military control through 1883, but the town of Pagosa Springs became a permanent settlement

SOUTHWESTERN COLORADO Crime Chart

	Crime Rate	Murder	Rape	Robbery	Aggravated Assault	Burglary	Larceny —Theft	Motor Vehicle Theft
United States								
U.S. Total	5,899.9	10.2	36.4	243.5	290.6	1,668.2	3,156.3	494.6
U.S. Metropolitan Areas	6,757.6	11.5	43.4	319.0	328.3	1,911.8	3,534.9	608.8
U.S. Rural Areas	2,290.4	7.5	15.5	22.5	136.9	830.2	1,143.9	133.9
Regional Crime Center								
Durango	11,091.0	0	38.3	86.1	918.7	1,368.4	8,095.7	583.7
Safe Places								
Pagosa	3,555.6	0	0	0	296.1	370.1	2,886.8	0
Pagosa Springs	1,728.0	0	0	0	450.8	225.4	976.7	75.1

and the Southern Ute Indian Reservation was established in the southern part of Archuleta County.

Though the springs are reputed to be the largest and hottest mineral springs in the United States and they contain the highest mineral content of any mineral springs in the world, they have never been fully exploited. Hot mineral baths *are* available in town, though, and people come for hundreds of miles to gain relief from rheumatism and other ills. Today they are being put to a new use as a source of geothermal energy for businesses and residences in Pagosa Springs. The temperature of the springs is a constant 153 degrees and their bottom has never been located.

Archuleta County adjoins New Mexico on the south. The northern and eastern parts of the county are mountainous, while the southern portion consists of mesas cut by stream valleys. Elevations in the county range from 6,000 feet to 13,272 feet and the elevation at Pagosa Springs is 7,079 feet. Only about a third of the county is in private hands. The federal government owns about half of the land as national forests and the Indian reservation includes 128,000 acres in the county.

Pagosa Springs' climate is typical of high mountain valleys. Winters are cold, but lots of sunshine and little wind make it a pleasant season. In January the average maximum temperature is 37.8 degrees, the minimum 1.4 degrees. Snowfall ranges from an average of 77 inches in town to about 500 inches at Wolf Creek Pass. Because of the numerous hot springs in the area, dense fog is common along the river and in the center of town during these colder months. Summers are mild, but again with plenty of sun and low humidity. In July the average maximum temperature is 83.2 degrees, the minimum 45.2 degrees (even summer nights get refreshingly cool here).

With a short growing season (an average of 75 days), agriculture is limited mostly to hay, with some wheat and corn grown in the southern part of the county. Mining has been limited, though oil and gas exploration has excited some interest in recent years. Cattle ranching is important. Timber has declined as an industry in recent years, but tourism and real estate development have expanded rapidly. The major development has been the Eaton Corporation's Pagosa in Colorado, which we will discuss shortly. The town is actively seeking light industry and new tourist-oriented businesses.

With Denver 278 miles to the north and Albuquerque 224 miles to the south, people come to Pagosa Springs for the attractions of the rugged outdoors, not metropolitan delights. Still, you can keep in touch with the world through the weekly newspaper, the local radio station, and television—three network stations from Albuquerque, an educational channel from New Mexico, and another station from Durango–Grand Junction in Colorado. Local stores and shops will supply your basic shopping needs, and the schools consist of an elementary school (K–5), middle school (6–8), and high school (9–12). Medical facilities are somewhat limited at the present time, but a new hospital is being built. The medical community presently consists of two doctors, two optometrists, one chiropractor, and one veterinarian. Emergency service provides care and ambulance service to two hospitals in Durango, 61 miles west of Pagosa Springs.

At the busy offices of the Pagosa Springs Chamber of Commerce, we had a pleasant talk with its manager, Lyn DeLange. She also heads the welcoming group for newcomers to town.

"We've probably had 1,500 new residents in recent years," Lyn told us, "but 60 percent of them have left. It's very hard to make a living here—and harder for the women, since the men have their hunting and fishing to occupy their time. But that's changing, too, as we get more and more activities going in town."

At the offices of Wolf Creek Land & Cattle, the Century 21 affiliate in town, Roberta Shaver told us that you can expect to pay $35 to $47 per square foot for new construction, but many of the homes that are selling are not new but have been previously occupied.

Because of the heavy snowfall, you need a relatively steep metal roof so the snow will slide off. A surprising number of houses don't have garages, considering the snow. Central air-conditioning is very unusual, since you have only two or three hot weeks out of the year, at most. Basements and family rooms are not very common. Most houses would have an eat-in kitchen instead or a combination living room with dining area. Most people around here have gone to wood stoves, since fireplaces are not nearly as effective in heating a house.

An average sale, Roberta estimated, would be around $63,000 for a house with 1,300 square feet of living area and a 1/4-acre lot. It would probably have 3 bedrooms, 2 baths, a living room, and an eat-in kitchen. Prices would rise to about $110,000 for a house with 1,500 to 1,600 square feet and $250,000 for a house with 2,500 square feet—but there aren't very many of that size on the market.

As for building lots, Roberta told us that a community or neighborhood water system is a real plus. Any subdivision with lots that are 3 acres or smaller in size is required to have a central water system. If you buy 5 acres or more, you would probably put in your own well.

The average price for a 3-acre parcel of land with central water would be $16,000. Larger acreage is scarce and river frontage even scarcer since there aren't very many rivers or large streams. If you find a 10-acre tract close to a national forest, you would probably pay $2,500 to $3,000 an acre. Some big ranches are dividing into 35-acre tracts, thus avoiding the subdivision laws. Such a parcel would run you $3,000 an acre—or more if the developer puts in a road.

Almost everything is owner-financed, with a 30 percent down payment and a 10-year mortgage at 12 percent. (Our visit was in July 1982 and the rate had just recently gone to 12 percent—it had been 10 or 11.)

Taxes would probably come to around $600 on a $63,000 house and about $1,000 for a house valued at $110,000.

Unlike most resort communities in Colorado, Pagosa Springs has low levels of crime in almost all categories. In our comparison year of 1980, there were no murders, rapes, or robberies, but there were 6 aggravated assaults. Property crime consisted of 3 burglaries, 13 larceny-thefts, and 1 motor vehicle theft. This placed Pagosa Springs below U.S. rural crime levels in all categories except assault. There the 6 incidents translated into a high metropolitan-level rate, though it was still less than half of what you would find in Durango.

Four miles west of Pagosa Springs is the largest by far of the real estate developments to take advantage of the attractiveness of this alpine region. Pagosa, with a total of 18,000 acres, was started in 1970 by the Eaton International Corporation and already boasts a total population as large as the town. Incorporation as a separate community is seen as a likely step in the near future.

While Pagosa has a strong recreational orientation, it is designed to be a year-round community with shopping areas and light industry. Perhaps half of the residents are retirees and many others use it as a vacation home for part of the year. It seems to be a popular place for Texans to go to escape the summer heat.

While we personally are not the biggest fans of planned communities, we do have to admit that the setting for Pagosa is unsurpassed and that the developer is creating a quality atmosphere. Many of the homes and condominium units are located in cluster villages—Pagosa-in-the-Pines around an award-winning 18-hole golf course, for example, and Lake Pagosa Park for those interested in water activities. The ranch community features larger tracts for people who want horses. Most of the areas have underground utilities and all above-ground structures must have their plans approved before construction begins by an environmental control committee. High-country meadows, seven lakes, streams, and forests of ponderosa pine, oak, aspen, and cottonwood give you a tantalizing variety of settings and views.

Jim Smith, a sales representative, told us that the average price for a 1/4-acre building lot is $10,000 to $15,000. The larger tracts for horse lovers are south of

U.S. 160, with 5-acre parcels selling for $25,000 to $35,000 and 10-acre tracts going for $30,000 to $45,000.

On the average, Jim told us, you can expect to pay $40 to $55 per square foot in building costs. The condominium units range in price from $48,000 for a small efficiency to $120,000 for one with 1,200 to 1,500 square feet of living area. These larger units have 2 or 3 bedrooms, 2 baths, and a large living room with fireplace.

One of the unique aspects of Pagosa, for an area that is presently unincorporated, is its Public Safety Office. This consists of five men, led by Director Roy D. Vega, who are commissioned as deputy sheriffs by the county and who are also certified as fire fighters and emergency medical technicians.

Crimes of violence are virtually nonexistent at Pagosa, as at Pagosa Springs. In our comparison year of 1980, they consisted of 4 assaults, with no murders, rapes, or robberies. Property crime consisted of 3 burglaries and 2 attempted burglaries, 38 larceny-thefts and 1 attempt, and no motor vehicle thefts. This placed Pagosa below U.S. rural crime levels in all categories except assaults and larceny-thefts and in those categories it remained below U.S. metropolitan levels.

Indeed, Pagosa's record is better than the bare statistics indicate at first glance. First of all, access control is a virtual impossibility. As Vega notes, this "is a wide-open area encompassing over 22 square miles and crisscrossed with a couple of hundred miles of public access roadway, many miles of which have already been accepted into the county road system."

Second, there's the high percentage of homes left vacant during part of the year. Vega classifies the population as "permanent" when they are present for more than six months out of a year and "transient" if they use Pagosa for less than six months a year. In 1980 the total population of 1,351 consisted of 878 permanent and 473 transient residents. That there should be only 3 burglaries and 2 attempts with such a high percentage of sometimes-vacant property is an enviable record indeed.

But that's not all. How many communities clear two thirds of their burglaries? "Of the three residential burglaries," Vega told us, "two were immediately cleared and one is still an open investigation. Of the two cleared burglaries, one involved suspects who were passing through the area and the other involved suspects who were residents of the area. Arrests were made in both of those burglaries and property recovered."

As for the larceny-thefts, Vega said, "We have no particularly serious problem in that area, except that as a growing community the incidents of thefts from construction sites is relatively high. Again, however, these are of a relatively minor nature when compared against the losses experienced at construction sites elsewhere in the country."

Great. Still . . . we get nervous when we see a growing, high-income resort community. Was 1980 a fluke? To be sure of our choice, we called Vega just before press time and obtained population and crime statistics for 1981 and

1982. Pagosa still qualified as a Safe Place for both of those years and during the entire 1980–82 period there were no murders, rapes, robberies, or motor vehicle thefts.

From his standpoint, Vega said, the critical point was that they had kept the increase in crimes down to 3 percent a year at a time when Pagosa's population was increasing by 12 to 15 percent a year.

Whether you live in Pagosa Springs, Pagosa, or the surrounding countryside of Archuleta County, there is always plenty to do. Pagosa Springs has a full calendar of events, led by the annual 4th of July Red Ryder Roundup—a two-day affair with a rodeo, parade, dances, and other activities. In addition to scores of tennis and golf tournaments and clinics, Pagosa features a fine arts and crafts festival, an old-time fiddler's concert, and children's Halloween and Christmas celebrations. One backcountry outfitter has nine-day horse trips each September that take you from Wolf Creek Pass to Silverton—a distance of 100 miles—along the Continental Divide. And the Pagosa Springs Chamber of Commerce has information on enough trails, waterfalls, and backcountry tours to keep you busy for as long as you want. Here, in the stunning high country of Southwestern Colorado, there is no seasonal limit on the good life.

Where to get further information:

State

Colorado Office of Tourism, 1313 Sherman Street, Room 500, Denver, CO 80203. Colorado Dude and Guest Ranch Association, Box 6440 Cherry Creek Station, Denver, CO 80206.

Regional

Denver Area: Denver and Colorado Convention and Visitors Bureau, 225 W. Colfax Avenue, Denver, CO 80202.

Colorado Springs Area: Colorado Springs Convention and Visitors Bureau, 801 South Tejon, Colorado Springs, CO 80903.

Local

Cherry Hills: Village of Cherry Hills, The Village Center, 2450 E. Quincy, Englewood, CO 80110.

Palmer Lake: Town of Palmer Lake, Palmer Lake, CO 80133.

Pagosa Springs: Pagosa Springs Chamber of Commerce, P.O. Box 787, Pagosa Springs, CO 81147. Pagosa in Colorado, P.O. Box 609, Pagosa Springs, CO 81147.

Connecticut

Connecticut is a tiny state—just 60 miles from top to bottom and some 90 miles across—but it packs a lot into that compact area. Like much of southern New England, it is highly industrialized and urbanized. Yet there is also much unspoiled countryside, ranging from the coastal marshes and inlets of Long Island Sound to the hills and gentle mountains of Litchfield County in the northwest. Grim cities coexist with a hundred lovely villages and small towns.

The Nutmeg State serves as home to numerous refugees (and potential home to countless would-be refugees) from New York City. But the first thing we discover when we look at the statistics is that crime—major crime—is no stranger to Connecticut. High rates of property crime are common throughout the state and there are even areas where you are more likely to be murdered or mugged than around Times Square.

Consider, for example, the crime statistics for Connecticut's five cities with a population of more than 100,000. When we compare them with New York City's, we find to our surprise that . . .

Hartford, the state capital, is worse off than New York in ALL seven crime categories . . .

New Haven, home of Yale University, is more dangerous for rape and for all three categories of property crime . . .

Bridgeport, the state's largest city, has higher rates in the two main categories of property crime—burglary and larceny-theft . . .

Even *Waterbury*—the most stable and homogenous of the state's big cities—has more larceny-theft than New York . . .

And even *Stamford*, the most affluent and suburbanized of these cities, comes uncomfortably close to New York City rates in burglary and larceny-theft.

Fairfield County's posh suburbs are certainly safe compared with New York City for crimes of violence. But beware of the safety of your house, your possessions, your automobile! Westport, for example, is a favorite haunt for commuting New York City executives, yet it has more larceny-theft per capita than the Gotham these executives leave behind after work.

So you'll want to choose carefully where you live in Connecticut. Fortunately, there *are* enclaves of quiet and safety in the midst of all this mayhem. Of the seventy-three reporting communities in the state, we found five that score lower than the U.S. rural crime rates in six of the seven categories. For the commuting towns of Fairfield County, soaring property crime forced us to resort to a slightly less safe community, but it still scores below U.S. rural rates in five of the seven categories of crime and it's your best bet in this exclusive corner of the state.

Of these six safe towns in Connecticut, we discarded Naugatuck and Windsor Locks. They're visually unattractive to us and Naugatuck in particular is highly industrialized. If that doesn't bother you, look them up.

On paper, Waterford looked like a good bet. Just down the highway from New London, it lies in the midst of the state's top tourist and recreational attractions, among them Mystic Seaport, the Groton submarine base, the U.S. Coast Guard Academy, Connecticut's major beaches, and the historic river port of Essex. But when we visited Waterford, we were less than enthusiastic. There were nice areas, to be sure, but instead of a compact town center, there was a sprawling mass of congested shopping centers. Without a sign, you wouldn't know where New London ended and Waterford began. Also Waterford is home to the Millstone Nuclear Power Station. By coincidence, we happened to be in Harrisburg, Pennsylvania, the Friday that the Three Mile Island incident began. Having noted the panic evacuation of the area, we have personal reservations about living close to a nuclear power plant.

That left us with three remaining Safe Places in Connecticut, but they are real finds, rare gems in this congested and industrialized Northeast Corridor of the United States.

SIMSBURY

POPULATION: 19,810
NO. OF CRIMES: 421
CRIME RATE: 2,125.2 per 100,000

This lovely and historic New England town has accepted the twentieth century—but on its terms.

Barely 10 miles northwest of downtown Hartford, modern Simsbury is, in effect, a bedroom community, a suburb of the sprawling Hartford metropolitan area. Most breadwinners commute to jobs in the city. Yet Simsbury has avoided the too familiar look of interchangeable suburbs. For one thing, there are no interstates or superhighways to force development in this direction. For another, Talcott Mountain rises between Simsbury and Hartford, capped by the 165-foot tower of the former home of the Heublein family (now part of a state park). Hartford seems far away.

Moreover, development has been carefully controlled within the historic center of town. No neon alleys or lakes of asphalt here. In addition to individual stores, there are two small shopping centers, both very attractive. The shingle and clapboard decor of Simsburytown Shops is a pleasant contrast with the very modern assembly of shops and stores at Drake Hill Mall down the road. And for a *real* mall, with acres of parking lots, you have to travel 5 miles to the Farmington Valley Mall at the edge of town. Everything is convenient without being disruptive.

Straddling the Farmington River, early Simsbury was once burned by hostile Indians. Around 1700 the town witch, Debby Griffen, was observed entering and leaving the locked Meeting House via the keyhole. The town boasts many firsts, including the first mining and smelting of copper in America (1705), the minting of the first copper coins struck in America (1737), the introduction and manufacture of the first safety fuse (1836), and the first silver plating of spoons and forks in America (1845). You can learn more about this fascinating history at Massacoh Plantation, a complex of authentically furnished buildings and historical exhibits.

The safety fuse industry is still thriving in Simsbury. Ensign-Bickford Industries can boast that its fuses were used for the construction of the Panama Canal and its rows of neat and well-maintained red brick buildings actually add their own charm to the town. The tobacco industry is also important in Simsbury, with large plantings by the American Sumatra Company and Cullman Brothers. And the cattle of Holly and Folly Farms are well-known to breeders throughout the country.

As our Connecticut Crime Chart, page 78, shows, Simsbury's crime ranks below rural U.S. levels in all categories except larceny-theft and even there it's just above the rural level. In the most recent town report available at the time of our visit, Police Chief Thomas J. Hankard reported that the number of serious crimes had actually decreased locally. As he noted, this "is unusual during these unstable times."

In addition to the public schools, Simsbury is home to two private academies of note—the Ethel Walker School for girls and the Westminster School for boys.

The 1982 tax rate was 48.3 mills (it may be 3 points higher by the time you read this), plus 1.5 mills for the fire district, based on a 70 percent assessment. We were told that taxes for a $120,000 house typically would come to $2,100.

For information on housing costs, we talked to Harry Ryan, Simsbury manager for Heritage Group Real Estate. Of approximately 6,300 residential units in the town, 180 were on the market at the time of our visit (April 1982). Their average asking price was $142,000, but homes in a somewhat lower price range were selling better. For around $120,000, you can expect to get a 4-bedroom, 2½-bath 2-story colonial with 2,200 to 2,400 square feet of living area on a lot of about 1 acre. Most houses in this predominant style would include fireplaces in both the living room and the family room, a formal dining room, eating space in the kitchen, a full basement, and a 2-car attached garage.

Condominiums are also available at prices ranging from $76,000 to $112,000.

If you're historically minded, you may want to see if an older home is on the market. *Historic Simsbury Houses* is a booklet that includes photos, capsule histories, and the names of present owners for thirty-four eighteenth-century houses in Simsbury and an additional sixteen that were built between 1800 and 1850. Be forewarned, though. Simsbury may be relatively free of modern crimes, but we cannot guarantee that the spirit of witch Debby Griffen won't slip in through your keyhole to cause some mischief!

BETHEL

POPULATION: 15,730
NO. OF CRIMES: 371
CRIME RATE: 2,358.6 per 100,000

Most of New England's metropolitan areas lost population during the past decade. One striking exception was the Danbury, Connecticut, area. Its 26.8 percent growth rate was exceeded only by the 32.4 percent jump in Nashua, New Hampshire, a tax haven across the state line from Boston, Taxachusetts.

From the Revolutionary War until the 1950s, Danbury was known as Hat City—the hat-manufacturing center of the nation. And when hats went out of fashion, its economy pretty much collapsed. In time, though, a much more diversified industrial base was established and with the construction of Interstate 84, which provides easy access to all of New England and New York, the local economy took off.

Today signs of continued growth are everywhere. Union Carbide, one of the nation's largest corporations, has moved its world headquarters from Manhattan to a pastoral setting astride I-84 in Danbury. Hilton has put up a hotel, with competition from Sheraton and Marriott in the works. Construction has also started on what will be New England's largest shopping mall, featuring six major department stores and some 150 smaller shops.

In recessions such as the one we've been experiencing, that sort of expanding economy isn't sneered at by too many people. Growth equals jobs, a scarce commodity in a recession. Of course, growth can also bring congestion, rootlessness, and—too often—increased crime. The trick is to situate yourself where you can enjoy the benefits and minimize the risks.

Which brings us to Bethel.

Bordering Danbury on the southeast, Bethel benefits from the economic vitality of the region. At the same time, the big jumps in growth *(and* problems) are in other directions: to the north and west of Danbury.

Bethel has other compelling advantages besides location.

Its crime rate is the lowest in the area—indeed, the lowest in all of Fairfield County, that part of Connecticut nearest New York City. Bethel ranks below rural U.S. levels in all categories of crime except larceny-theft and even that isn't disturbingly high.

Bethel is also a visually attractive mixture of small town, suburban, and country elements, all in a compact 17 square miles. As recently as 1955, three quarters of its population lived within walking distance of downtown. Despite the growth during the sixties and seventies, Bethel retains that feel of an all-American small town.

But most surprisingly, for this part of the country, Bethel is affordable. We had a most pleasant talk about this at the chamber of commerce offices with realtor Mary Baillie of RealTech. A native of Scotland, she has lived in Bethel for twenty-three years and seen its population change from predominantly blue-collar to executive.

The nice thing about Bethel, Mary pointed out, is the variety of housing it offers newcomers. You can choose an old colonial on a city lot or a new house in a suburban development or something more isolated in the rolling countryside. Houses are available from $60,000 (a rarity elsewhere in Fairfield County) to $160,000 and up (that would be a new house in a subdivision with 2 acres). She mentioned a particularly nice 3-bedroom older house on a city lot where the asking price was $79,000.

Condominiums are also available, mostly in small developments of twenty to forty units and in a price range of $60,000 to $80,000.

Most of Bethel's shops are compactly and conveniently grouped along Greenwood Avenue (the main street), from the train station to P. T. Barnum Square—the master showman was born here in 1810. There's some local industry—electronics, chemicals, wire, and bicycle parts—but most people work in Danbury or commute south to jobs in Norwalk or Stamford. Others use Interstates 84 and 684 to commute to corporate headquarters in White Plains, New York, and a few hardy souls even commute to New York City. Manhattan is just 60 miles away as the crow flies, but if you're not a crow, you face a miserable two-hour journey via the dilapidated train system. Better to work closer to home and enjoy the many advantages Bethel has to offer.

NEW CANAAN

POPULATION: 17,845
NO. OF CRIMES: 427
CRIME RATE: 2,392.8 per 100,000

Money can't buy happiness, but if you want to see what it *can* buy, come here. Everything in New Canaan is elegant, stylish, meticulously maintained—the downtown shops, the homes and estates, the graceful churches and public buildings. The term for places like this used to be "top drawer," but being a little behind the times, we're not sure what the equivalent term would be today. But you get the picture when the real estate agent explains that anything under $200,000 buys just a starter home, with 2 bedrooms and 1 bath, or, if you're lucky, a small Cape or ranch with 3 bedrooms.

We mean no slight to Bethel, itself a lovely community, when we point out that New Canaan and Bethel are both in Fairfield County and that there the similarity ends. A new Jaguar and a new Pontiac are each nice tools to have and it just depends on which you can afford.

Take, for example, per capita income—always a deceptively low number, since this census figure represents total earnings divided by total population, including all children, retirees living on social security, and, we suspect, cats and dogs. Anyway, in New Canaan per capita income is $13,826, outranked in Fairfield County only by Darien's $14,632. In Bethel the figure is less than half that—$6,284. Not surprisingly, the median age in Bethel is the lowest in the county, 29.7, and New Canaan's is the second-highest at 38.4 years.

Downtown Elm Street is lined with high-fashion shops, jewelry stores, dealers in Oriental rugs, and other adornments appropriate to an affluent haven such as New Canaan. There are also plenty of real estate offices, befitting an executive community where one third of the population moves each year.

The Silvermine Guild of Artists offers instruction in art and dance for adults and children, maintains outstanding galleries, and is noted for its prestigious New England Exhibit and the biennial National Print Show. And this is bird-watching territory: note the space and prominent location given to natural history and field guides at the New Canaan Book Shop. A bird sanctuary and wildlife preserve offer trails, ponds, brooks, and bridges, and the town's nature center features excellent nature displays, greenhouse exhibits, plants for sale, special seasonal events, and trails to explore.

And the homes! At RealTech's offices, Sue Hallberg and office manager Sharon Daley showed us their book of listings—houses on the market. The biggest segment was in the $300,000 to $400,000 range. The average sale price was somewhat lower, at $285,000. For that you get a center-hall colonial on 2 acres, with 4 bedrooms and 2½ baths. Needless to say, prices for larger homes range into the millions.

New Canaan is also noted for its stylish clusters of town house condominiums. Indeed, in our travels around the country, we have found no community with town houses as architecturally pleasing as the ones we've found here. You *can* get a 1-bedroom, 1-bath condo for $94,000, but the average price is $275,000 and they stretch to $380,000. "But these are really nice homes," Sue reminded us, "and most have a pool."

Executive transferees from Southern California will take prices like this in stride and even regard them as a bargain, but the rest of us may be pardoned for deeming them rather astronomical. As usual with real estate, the reason *why* they're high is threefold: location, location, and location. In Fairfield County that means prices rise the farther south you go, in the direction of the New York-bound expressways and railroad. New Canaan is the terminal for a spur of the New Haven railroad line, with a busy schedule of commuter trains, and the scenic Merritt Parkway passes through the southern part of the town.

With all this affluence, it's surprising that property crime rates are as low as they are. Only the burglary and auto theft rates exceed those for U.S. rural areas and even those are below city levels. Serious crimes of violence are predictably rare. In a town like New Canaan, the only violence you're likely to encounter is in the sand trap at the country club.

CONNECTICUT Crime Chart

	Crime Rate	Murder	Rape	Robbery	Aggravated Assault	Burglary	Larceny —Theft	Motor Vehicle Theft
United States								
U.S. Total	5,899.9	10.2	36.4	243.5	290.6	1,668.2	3,156.3	494.6
U.S. Metropolitan Areas	6,757.6	11.5	43.4	319.0	328.3	1,911.8	3,534.9	608.8
U.S. Rural Areas	2,290.4	7.5	15.5	22.5	136.9	830.2	1,143.9	133.9
Regional Crime Centers								
Hartford	17,347.4	33.7	87.3	1,511.9	861.2	4,442.5	6,616.1	3,794.7
New York City	10,094.0	25.8	52.7	1,429.2	618.0	2,994.9	3,545.2	1,428.2
Safe Places								
Bethel	2,358.6	0	0	19.1	101.7	692.9	1,443.1	101.7
New Canaan	2,392.8	0	11.2	5.6	78.5	1,087.1	963.9	246.6
Simsbury	2,125.2	5.0	0	10.1	111.1	696.6	1,206.5	95.9

Where to get further information:

State

Connecticut Development Commission, P.O. Box 865, State Office Building, Hartford, CT 06115 (tourist information and materials for inquiring businessmen). State Park and Forest Commission, State Office Building, Hartford, CT 06115 (camping and state parks). Department of Agriculture and Natural Resources, State Office Building, Hartford, CT 06115 (hunting, trapping, and fishing regulations). Connecticut Commission on the Arts, 340 Capitol Avenue, Hartford, CT 06106 (for *The Arts in Connecticut,* bimonthly calendar, $2.50 per year).

Towns

Simsbury: Annual town report and guide/map from Town Clerk's Office, Town Hall, Simsbury, CT 06070. Free brochures on Massacoh Plantation, the Phelps House, and Tobacco Valley tourist attractions from Simsbury Historical Society, Massacoh Plantation, 800 Hopmeadow Street, Simsbury, CT 06070. Various historical booklets also for sale.

Bethel: Town map and brochure, *Why Bethel?,* from Violet Mattone, Executive Secretary, Bethel Chamber of Commerce, 14 P. T. Barnum Square, Bethel, CT 06801. Annual town report from Selectmen's Office, Town Hall, Bethel, CT 06801. *Bethel,* information booklet, available for $3.00 from Cyndy Price, Unit Leader, League of Women Voters, Codfish Hill Road, Bethel, CT 06801; or pick up at Bethel Linen Closet, 109 Greenwood Avenue.

New Canaan: George W. Griffin, Jr., Executive Director, New Canaan Chamber of Commerce, 24 Pine Street, P.O. Box 583, New Canaan, CT 06840. Annual town report from Board of Selectmen, Town Hall, New Canaan, CT

06840. *Know Your Town, New Canaan* from League of Women Voters of New Canaan, P.O. Box 383, New Canaan, CT 06840.

Ridgefield: Our home town is not formally listed as a Safe Place, but it certainly qualifies and we note its attractions in the Introduction. Interested readers can obtain literature from the following sources. Tom Carroll, President, Ridgefield Chamber of Commerce, 27 Governor Street, Ridgefield, CT 06877. *Annual Report* from the Town of Ridgefield, Town Hall, 400 Main Street, Ridgefield, CT 06877. Real estate information, as well as *Ridgefield: A Town for All Reasons* and *Education in Ridgefield,* from Harry H. Neumann, Sr., Harry H. Neumann Associates, Inc., 395 Main Street, Ridgefield, CT 06877. The League of Women Voters' *This is Ridgefield* ($1.00), the Ridgefield Conservation Commission's *Ridgefield Walk Book* ($3.00), George Rockwell's *History of Ridgefield* ($29.50), and Silvio Bedini's *Ridgefield in Review* ($7.95) are available from the Ridgefield News Store, 389 Main Street, Ridgefield, CT 06877, or Books Plus, 409 Main Street, Ridgefield, CT 06877. The *Centenary* edition (1975) is also available for $2.50 from the Ridgefield *Press,* 16 Bailey Avenue, Ridgefield, CT 06877.

Florida

With nearly 10 million residents, Florida now ranks eighth in the United States in total population. More people move here than to any other state when they retire, but that accounts for just part of its phenomenal growth. Industry and agriculture, too, are both expanding, ensuring a steady increase in population among all age groups.

Tourism is the major industry, with more than 30 million visitors a year. Agriculture is also vitally important to the state's economy; Florida grows more citrus fruit than any other state and is second only to California in winter vegetables. Florida waters provide more than sixty kinds of food fish, including nearly half of all the shrimp we eat. Cattle raising is also big in the Sunshine State and other important industries include food processing, chemical and electronic research, cigars, and resort apparel.

The Florida lifestyle is outdoors-oriented. When people move here, the first thing they do is shed their winter clothing. Florida's 8,462-mile coastline is the longest of any of the forty-eight contiguous states, providing unlimited opportunities for recreational boating, swimming, and saltwater fishing. Canoeing in the lakes and rivers, water skiing, and skin and scuba diving all have their enthusiasts. More than 500 courses await the golfer and who can count all the tennis and shuffleboard courts? Spectator sports are equally diversified. The list would have to include professional football, baseball, and soccer, as well as jai alai, pro golf tournaments, rodeos, auto races, polo matches, and dog and horse races.

All is not fun in the sun in the Sunshine State, however. Ever since Ponce de León failed to find his fountain of youth, Florida has disappointed as well as delighted its guests.

First, let us repeat a few caveats we included in our 1972 book, the original *Safe Places:*

Many people are moving *into* the state, but another sizable group is moving a second time *within* the state. We were told throughout our Florida sojourn of people who had packed their bags with all their possessions and headed south. Having moved to one of the glamour spots, they found that the climate also included a lot of rain and plenty of bugs, that they had escaped one giant traffic jam only to help develop another, and that not only decent people but far too many criminals also liked the easy life in the sun. And so they were searching again for a new home, hoping to regain their dreams.

You can avoid their mistake, if only you will take your time in deciding whether or not to move to Florida, and if so, where. By all means, spend some time in your prospective new home during the *bad* time of the year. See how you like the rain, the humidity, the bugs in the summer. You'll have to put up with these, unless you are prosperous enough to escape somewhere else during the summer.

When we wrote those words, crime was already a festering sore in Florida. Today the situation might better be described as an epidemic. Consider:

- Of all the fifty states, only Nevada has a higher crime rate than Florida.
- When most people think of crime, they think of a place like New York City. Yet, in our comparison year of 1980, *forty-two* Florida cities had a higher crime rate than the Big Apple (see our Florida Crime Centers table, pages 82–83).
- In just five years (1977 to 1981), the crime rate jumped 24 percent.
- Meanwhile, during those years, the percentage of crimes cleared *decreased* from 23.6 percent to 20.9 percent.

That five-year trend—an increasing crime rate and a decreasing percentage cleared—applies to each of the seven categories of major crime, as well as to the overall crime rate. Murder, for example, increased by 54 percent, while the percentage cleared fell sharply from 80 percent to 61.2 percent. Forcible rapes, too, increased by 48 percent, while the percentage cleared dropped from 55.4 percent to 48 percent.

That's a pretty dismal picture, a dark side of the state its boosters and promoters don't like to think about.

To help you surmount this crime problem, we spent more hours than *we* care to think about evaluating and comparing the crime statistics for some 335 Florida towns and cities. We were looking for places that had not only a low overall crime rate, but low rates as well in most of the seven individual categories of crime. And since 1981 statistics were available by the time we went to Florida, we chose only communities that qualified both years.

The result is the seven towns and cities we describe in this chapter. They're not the only Safe Places in Florida, by any means, but they do combine safety with prime locations and other attributes that make them the practical cream of the crop among Florida's sun-drenched communities.

FLORIDA CRIME CENTERS

New York City, the nation's largest city, is generally thought of as also being the nation's leading crime center. Actually, several hundred cities and towns across the United States* have higher crime rates. More of these communities —forty-two of them—are in Florida than in any other state.

* We compared only those towns and cities with a population of 10,000 or more.

In our comparison year of 1980, New York City had 10,094 crimes per 100,000 population. Now compare:

Altamonte Springs	10,389.5
Belle Glade	14,447.6
Cocoa Beach	11,754.0
Coral Gables	12,611.4
Dania	19,507.7
Daytona Beach	18,256.7
De Land	13,637.1
Fort Lauderdale	13,604.1
Fort Myers	13,928.1
Fort Pierce	13,138.7
Gainesville	11,562.2
Hallandale	11,005.7
Hollywood	10,964.5
Homestead	17,332.1
Jacksonville Beach	10,697.7
Key West	12,460.8
Kissimmee	15,589.4
Lake Worth	11,659.8
Leesburg	11,410.0
Miami	15,650.1
Miami Beach	11,160.8
Miami Springs	10,711.4
Naples	11,251.3
New Smyrna Beach	10,246.4
North Miami	11,257.5
North Miami Beach	12,255.7
Oakland Park	20,029.6
Ocala	12,313.8
Opa-Locka	21,468.3
Orlando	13,717.2
Plant City	10,758.4
Pompano Beach	12,733.1
Riviera Beach	14,098.1
Sanford	11,254.3
Sarasota	10,825.9
South Miami	17,833.5
Tallahassee	12,006.1
Tampa	14,477.8
Vero Beach	10,373.9
West Palm Beach	20,264.1

Winter Haven	10,173.7
Winter Park	10,685.5

MIAMI AREA

The year 1981 was a historic one for Dade County, the county dominated by Miami. For the first time in over thirty years, more people left the county than moved into it.

We were in Florida when the Metro-Dade Planning Department released its blockbuster. Department spokesmen and news commentators left no doubt why the tide had turned: fear of crime and the Latinization of Dade County. The flight that's taking place today is mostly an Anglo flight.

Only a record number of births prevented the county from showing an actual overall loss in population that year.

MIAMI AREA Crime Chart

	Crime Rate	Murder	Rape	Robbery	Aggravated Assault	Burglary	Larceny —Theft	Motor Vehicle Theft
United States								
U.S. Total	5,899.9	10.2	36.4	243.5	290.6	1,668.2	3,156.3	494.6
U.S. Metropolitan Areas	6,757.6	11.5	43.4	319.0	328.3	1,911.8	3,534.9	608.8
U.S. Rural Areas	2,290.4	7.5	15.5	22.5	136.9	830.2	1,143.9	133.9
Regional Crime Centers								
Coral Gables	12,611.4	7.1	23.6	532.5	372.3	2,530.8	8,483.0	662.1
Miami	15,650.1	65.5	96.8	2,052.3	1,203.1	4,089.4	6,725.0	1,417.9
Miami Beach	11,160.8	18.7	65.0	733.2	424.9	3,768.3	5,266.6	884.0
Miami Springs	10,711.4	8.2	8.2	606.5	663.8	2,499.6	6,007.2	917.9
North Miami	11,257.5	14.2	68.7	914.2	566.1	3,015.1	5,843.1	836.1
North Miami Beach	12,255.7	21.4	36.7	835.0	520.0	3,251.3	6,679.9	911.5
Opa-Locka	21,468.3	70.2	126.4	2,009.1	3,322.8	6,090.6	8,366.7	1,482.3
South Miami	17,833.5	19.0	37.9	1,726.4	1,660.0	6,791.9	6,867.8	730.4
Safe Places								
Bay Harbor Islands	1,670.4	0	0	103.1	20.6	433.1	1,010.5	103.1
Biscayne Park	2,730.8	0	0	162.5	0	1,560.5	877.8	130.0

"For the first time that we know of," said Charles Blowers, head of the research division of the Metro-Dade Planning Department, "our growth is due to a natural increase [that is, due to more births than deaths]. If we hadn't had the record high of births, we would have actually had a decline."

Sergio Pereira, assistant to the county manager, said in response: "The reports in the media about crime and refugees make some people want to leave because they don't want to deal with it."

That's "liberal" code language for: "Some people are leaving because they're so selfish they don't want to give up their lives and their possessions at the point of a gun."

Notice that Mr. Pereira didn't admit that actual *crime* was the reason for the flight. No, indeed, it was *reports* of crime. People aren't fleeing because they—or members of their family or their friends and neighbors—are being robbed, raped, burglarized, ripped off, and too often murdered. No, they're leaving because those damn newspaper and television and radio reporters are scaring them with ghost stories.

In reply to which, we gag ourselves from saying what we really want to say and answer instead: Balderdash! (How's that for self-control?)

If anyone wants to see the grim reality, let him look at our Miami Area Crime Chart (page 83). Miami Beach, Miami Springs, and North Miami are relative havens—their crime rates are just a little higher than New York City's. On the other hand, Coral Gables, Miami, and North Miami Beach have crime levels more than *double* the national crime rate. And Opa-Locka and South Miami have crime levels more than *triple* the national crime rate.

And that's just *reported* crime. We all know that in high-crime metropolitan areas much of the crime goes unreported. "What's the use?" the victims say. "Even if the criminals are caught—and few are—they'll get off in the courts and then they'll come after me again—with vengeance."

Let us make one thing perfectly clear at this point. *We* are not implying that Latinization per se is the problem. That's the way the problem is often perceived around here, but we'd suggest instead that the massive uprootedness of the Latin population is the key. We've walked at midnight along the back streets of Madrid and Seville and some cities in Mexico and felt safer than we do in broad daylight in New York City or Washington, D.C. And as we show in our chapter on Texas, that state's large cities actually get safer as the Latin proportion of their population increases.

The reason, we suspect, is that Latin society in Texas is relatively stable and traditional. Strong family, cultural, and religious ties bind the community together. There's a sizable middle-class element that has roots in the community. And though the illegals are an exception to this stability, they have to watch their step or face deportation. They are highly visible because their numbers don't overwhelm the population and indeed they're more often victims than offenders.

In South Florida, on the other hand, there's been a massive, sudden tidal wave of migration. An entire culture—hundreds of thousands of families—was uprooted almost overnight and fled here. But at least the initial waves of migration included enough professionals and middle-class businessmen and entrepreneurs to make Miami the vibrant crossroads of Latin commerce in the Americas. Then, to add insult to an already injured culture, Cuba's prisons and jails were emptied and dumped onto the streets of Miami in the spring and summer of 1980. It was all too much, too fast, for decent people—for the hardworking, decent refugees—to cope with.

All of which brings us to our search for the needle in the haystack. Would you believe we actually found *two* needles? Yes, in the midst of all this mayhem we were delightfully shocked to discover two Safe Places. They are tiny, but none of the larger communities around them qualified and they'll convince you of the saying "Good things come in small packages."

BISCAYNE PARK

POPULATION: 3,076
NO. OF CRIMES: 84
CRIME RATE: 2,730.8 per 100,000

"You know what I call this area? I say it's an oasis in a desert of crime."

That's how Police Chief Dan Marx once described Biscayne Park. He retired in 1982 and we met new Police Commissioner Peter Hinck. It is testimony to Biscayne Park, he told us, that many police officers from throughout northern Dade County have moved their families here. They *know* it's a good place to live.

The village employs six full-time police officers. They are assisted by two reserve officers. Biscayne Park is a tiny, compact area, just slightly more than 1/2 square mile in size. But in 1981 this force put in 57,894 patrol miles—an average of 158.6 miles a day. Even so, some residents were complaining that they wanted still more police visibility.

One of the most active groups in town is the Citizens Crime Watch. It assists the police by training fellow residents how to recognize a possible crime situation, how to report a crime coherently, and how to take a description of a suspect or vehicle.

In refreshing contrast to the rest of Dade County, Biscayne Park had no murders, rapes, or aggravated assaults in 1980. There were 5 robberies, 48 burglaries, 27 larceny-thefts, and 4 motor vehicle thefts. This placed Biscayne Park below U.S. rural crime rates in all categories except robbery and burglary and even in those categories it placed below U.S. metropolitan crime levels.

The next year was even better, with the total number of crimes dropping from 84 in 1980 to 55. Again there were no murders or rapes and there were just 1 robbery, 3 aggravated assaults, 35 burglaries, 14 larceny-thefts, and 2 motor vehicle thefts.

In past years there was pressure on local communities to abolish their separate forces and get their protection from the Dade County Metro Police Force. But Biscayne Park Mayor Ed Burke, who's held the post since 1964 and personifies the village, resisted those pressures. "The bigger government becomes, the less efficient it becomes," he says. "They [Biscayne Park's policemen] know their neighborhood like the back of their hand."

Biscayne Park is used to fighting for its rights. In 1969 the village defeated an attempt by the state highway department to build a major east–west highway, the Opa-Locka Expressway, which would have split the community in two. That fight earned Biscayne Park the description "the mouse that roars like a lion."

Tucked away between Miami Shores and North Miami, Biscayne Park is a haven of peace and quiet. It was a product of the real estate boom of the 1920s and strict zoning laws passed in 1944 have kept it a residential community. Duplexes are allowed, but buildings cannot exceed 2 stories. The town has one 5-acre park, one church, and one public building that houses the village hall and police. Built by the Works Progress Administration in 1933, the hall is made entirely of Dade County pine. County historians say it was made from a kit.

About 35 percent of Biscayne Park's residents are of Latin origin. From the homes, mostly modest in size, a visitor gathers that this is a comfortable community, financially, but not particularly affluent. What *is* apparent is community pride, reflected in the well-maintained homes and public areas. Many of the streets are actually residential boulevards. Their median strips and the yards that line the streets are landscaped with a colorful array of shrubs, flowers, and trees.

An annual art festival is one of the village's big events. Students go to Miami Shores public schools and then North Miami High School or to St. Rose School and then Madonna High School.

Paul Libovitz, a former Brooklynite who manages Heritage Realty in North Miami, told us that houses in Biscayne Park range in price from the 50s to over $100,000. The highest sale price ever recorded, he thought, was a doctor's house at $250,000.

Two-bedroom homes with 1,200 to 1,300 square feet of living space will usually be priced in the 50s and low 60s.

Three-bedroom homes with 1,600 to 1,800 square feet will be in the high 60s to high 80s.

Duplexes cost between $60,000 and $100,000, depending on the number of bedrooms and baths and overall size.

With Florida's homestead exemption, taxes for an owner-occupied 3-bedroom, 2-bath house would probably be around $800 to $850. Taxes for the larger houses might run anywhere between $1,500 and $3,000.

One listing that caught our eye was a 2-bedroom, 2-bath house built in 1945 and sitting on a 75 × 105 lot. At $79,900, its price was higher than usual for a 2-bedroom house because of its special features and larger size—1,948 square feet. This house had a living room, large Florida room, dining area, large country kitchen, enclosed front porch, and 2-car garage. Its roof was tile and Cuban tile was featured inside the house.

Despite the problems which beset South Florida, foremost among them crime, there's no denying the many charms and pleasures it also offers. The quiet, lushly landscaped streets of Biscayne Park have a way of making those problems seem distant and the pleasures more immediate. With its affordable homes, low crime rate, and community pride, Biscayne Park is indeed an urban oasis that cannot be matched—a unique treasure of Dade County.

BAY HARBOR ISLANDS

POPULATION: 4,849
NO. OF CRIMES: 81
CRIME RATE: 1,670.4 per 100,000

Biscayne Park and Bay Harbor Islands are just 3 miles apart, but they couldn't be more different.

Whereas Biscayne Park is landlocked, the very name of our second Safe Place reveals that it is surrounded by water. In fact, the town consists of two islands set in northern Biscayne Bay. Broad Causeway connects them with North Miami to the west and Bal Harbour to the east.

And whereas Biscayne Park is a middle-class community of modestly priced homes, Bay Harbor Islands is an expensive upper-middle-class retreat. Houses here *begin* at prices that are above the highest prices you'll find in Biscayne Park.

Moreover, whereas Biscayne Park is all residential, Bay Harbor Islands is a mixed-use community. The western island is reserved for single-family homes, while the eastern one is dominated by businesses and condominiums.

Bay Harbor Islands is part of an exclusive area that includes northern Miami Beach, Indian Creek Village, Surfside, and Bal Harbour. The islands' own shops are nice enough, but just a couple of blocks down the street in Bal Harbour is one of the poshest and most elegant shopping malls in America, featuring names like Saks, Neiman-Marcus, Gucci, and Tourneau.

This small island community is also distinguished by having two first-rate French restaurants. La Belle Époque rates four stars with *Mobil Travel Guides* ("outstanding—worth a special trip") and Café Chauveron, a refugee from Manhattan, is one of the few restaurants anywhere to rate five stars ("one of the best in the country"). (When it closes for the summer, maitre'd Jean Claude returns to our neck of the woods to serve as maitre'd of Le Chateau of South Salem, New York.)

With the generally older population that such affluence suggests and with housing dominated by condominium units that rarely accept children, it's no surprise that Bay Harbor Islands is not your Little League type of family town. However, more younger families with children have been moving here in recent years. These children go to the elementary school on one of the islands, then use school bus transportation to continue at Nautilus Junior High, in the nicest area of Miami Beach, and Miami Beach Senior High.

If you're going to live in an affluent enclave, with all its temptations for the criminal class, an island has obvious crime-control benefits: it limits access, as well as potential escape routes. The town's police department doesn't believe that's cause for complacency, however, and periodically holds Help Stop Crime seminars for town residents. The thrust of the seminars is how residents and police can work together to prevent crime.

They must be doing something right, for in our comparison year of 1980 Bay Harbor Islands ranked below U.S. rural crime rates in all categories except robbery. There were no murders or rapes, 5 robberies, 1 aggravated assault, 21 burglaries, 49 larceny-thefts, and 5 motor vehicle thefts.

The following year, unfortunately, there was a considerable rise in the number of crimes, from 81 in 1980 to 125, and a rise in the overall crime rate, from 1,670.4 per 100,000 to 2,563.6. That's still well within the parameters for qualifying as a Safe Place and especially in as criminally active an area as Miami. Nevertheless, it's a step in the wrong direction. We hope that's all it is—not a trend.

Our real estate contact in Bay Harbor Islands was a friendly and informative broker, Adele Fredel, in the realty offices of Stein McHugh Company.

Single-family houses, she told us, range from $150,000 to $700,000. The average price for an off-water house, though, would be around $250,000. Waterfront properties are rarely seen below $300,000 to $350,000.

At the time of our visit, there were seven listings in Bay Harbor Islands for single-family homes. The cheapest at $160,000 was a 3-bedroom, 2-bath Bahamian-style ranch with a tropical pool. It was on an 80 × 125 lot and had 1,900 square feet of living area. Taxes were $2,110. The most expensive was a $650,000 waterfront home with 4 bedrooms, 4 baths, marble floors, heated pool, and a 15.2 × 76 cabana dock for your yacht. Taxes were $7,072.

Twenty-six condominium units were also available in Bay Harbor Islands at the time of our visit. Eighteen were priced between $45,000 and $95,000 and five of these had 2 bedrooms. Then there was a jump to $149,500, with the highest-priced condominium listed at $225,000. That particular one had 2 bedrooms, each with private bath, a spacious living area, a powder room, views overlooking Indian Creek, a condo pool, and lobby security. Taxes were $2,712 and the maintenance fee was $427.40.

A few rental apartments were advertised in the classified section of a Miami Beach newspaper. You could get an efficiency for $300, a 1-bedroom apartment for $360, and 2-bedroom units for around $500.

High-priced addresses are no novelty in the Miami area, the playground of the rich. What *does* distinguish Bay Harbor Islands, though, is the sense of security and safety you also enjoy here while soaking up the sun. In this neck of the woods, that's a *lot* to be thankful for and well worth the stiff price of admission.

GOLD COAST

North from Miami stretches one of the fastest-growing and most glamorous areas of Florida, packed in a narrow strip between the Atlantic Ocean and the Everglades.

Fort Lauderdale has been called "the Venice of America" and "the country's largest yacht basin." With 165 miles of navigable waterways within city limits—

consisting of rivers, inlets, and man-made canals—and 30,000 boats that call it their home port, both titles are credible. Its 6-mile stretch of ocean beach is just as famous, playing host during winter and spring vacations to 40,000 to 50,000 college students.

GOLD COAST Crime Chart

	Crime Rate	Murder	Rape	Robbery	Aggravated Assault	Burglary	Larceny —Theft	Motor Vehicle Theft
United States								
U.S. Total	5,899.9	10.2	36.4	243.5	290.6	1,668.2	3,156.3	494.6
U.S. Metropolitan Areas	6,757.6	11.5	43.4	319.0	328.3	1,911.8	3,534.9	608.8
U.S. Rural Areas	2,290.4	7.5	15.5	22.5	136.9	830.2	1,143.9	133.9
Regional Crime Centers								
Dania	19,507.7	59.0	84.3	1,323.6	1,736.6	5,968.6	8,464.0	1,871.5
Fort Lauderdale	13,604.1	28.6	61.0	834.2	303.8	4,620.4	6,679.0	1,077.0
Hallandale	11,005.7	27.2	87.0	739.7	998.0	2,243.6	6,050.8	859.3
Hollywood	10,964.5	10.3	49.6	499.9	451.1	3,147.3	6,057.4	748.9
Lake Worth	11,659.8	7.7	53.6	264.3	643.5	3,769.1	6,067.3	854.2
Pompano Beach	12,733.1	25.2	71.7	440.0	754.0	3,564.6	7,022.7	854.8
Riviera Beach	14,098.1	19.6	136.9	434.1	1,482.1	4,286.1	7,109.6	629.6
West Palm Beach	20,264.1	10.3	128.3	1,149.2	1,414.3	6,213.1	10,119.2	1,229.6
Safe Places								
Atlantis	1,250.9	0	0	0	0	662.3	441.5	147.2
Highland Beach	2,837.2	0	0	49.8	0	647.1	2,040.8	99.6

Palm Beach, on the other hand, is much more sedate. Here you can rub elbows with high society at the Breakers, admire the Mediterranean mansions along Ocean Boulevard, and shop in the fashionable salons of Worth Avenue.

In between these two cities and all the way down to Miami is a continuous stretch of oceanfront communities, inland resorts, retirement havens, and commercial centers that have blossomed on the swampy coastal plain to service them.

Pervading virtually all of these communities is the same plague of rampant crime we noticed in the Miami area. A careful look at our Gold Coast Crime Chart (above) reveals that West Palm Beach and Dania have crime rates more than three times as high as the national rate. And eight of the major cities of this area have crime rates worse than New York City's.

Once again, though, a couple of small communities have managed somehow to insulate themselves from this epidemic of crime. One is on the ocean and the other's an inland country-club resort—and between them you have two safe ports in which to ride out the rough times.

HIGHLAND BEACH

POPULATION: 2,009
NO. OF CRIMES: 57
CRIME RATE: 2,837.2 per 100,000

Midway between Fort Lauderdale and Palm Beach is a narrow 3-mile-long spit of land, part of a longer island that is bounded by the Atlantic and the Intracoastal Waterway and filled with beautiful homes and sparkling high-rise towers.

Your eyes sense a difference between this 3-mile stretch and all the other towns you've passed through. It's more distinctive, somehow, and as you think about it you piece together the jigsaw puzzle that explains why.

Part of the answer is the mystery of the oceanfront houses that hide behind a slight bluff, a lush patchwork of flowers and vegetation buffering them from curious passing eyes on the coastal highway. Part of the answer is the lack of congestion, even with the high rises. Part of the answer is the purely residential nature of the community. And certainly another part of the answer is the obvious care and attention given the architecturally pleasing homes you've been passing.

That community is Highland Beach and the distinctive atmosphere you've been piecing together is no accident. If allowed to expand unhindered like so much of Florida, it could have supported a population of 27,000, complete with hot dog stands, car washes, mobile home parks, and similar delights. But that wasn't allowed to happen. Instead, Highland Beach became one of the first communities in the state to adopt a comprehensive land-use plan and a series of zoning ordinances established ever more stringent restrictions on such matters as density, preservation of the dunes along the ocean, setback requirements from property lines, height of buildings, and the open space required between buildings. As a result, the maximum population this town should ever have is approximately 8,000.

Highland Beach has come a long way since its incorporation in 1949.

The twenty-one original residents had two reasons for their decision to form a town—to provide a source of good water and to prevent the intrusion of trailer parks. They succeeded on both counts.

Water has always been a central concern, since wells drilled locally give water that is brackish and salty in taste. Early residents had to buy 5-gallon bottles of water for drinking and cooking. Today the town has a modern water plant and well field located in Boca Raton, with storage tanks and a repump station behind the Highland Beach municipal center. Current capacity is 2 million gallons a day, with consumption running about 1 million gallons a day.

Early police protection was provided by the sheriff in West Palm Beach. The only problem was that responses to calls often took forty-five minutes. Today there's an experienced seven-man force that has apprehended many criminals, including a gang of jewel thieves. At all times, there are two police officers patrolling Highland Beach's six tenths of a square mile.

Similar advances have marked other town services. Four fire fighters are on duty at all times in the Highland Beach Fire Station and at least one of them is a paramedic and another is an emergency medical technician. Town employees man the post office under contract with the U.S. Postal Service. A fee is received from the Postal Service, but half of the cost is met by town taxes.

Another focus of civic pride is the handsome new municipal center, opened in March 1982. It houses town administrative offices, Town Commission chambers, the library, and the post office.

The bottom line on crime in Highland Beach is that there were no murders, rapes, or aggravated assaults in our comparison year of 1980. The year's 57 crimes consisted of 1 robbery, 41 larceny-thefts, 13 burglaries, and 2 motor vehicle thefts. Highland Beach placed below U.S. rural crime rates in all categories except robbery and larceny-theft and even there it remained below metropolitan levels.

In 1981 the number of crimes was reduced to 51—1 aggravated assault, 13 burglaries, 35 larceny-thefts, and 2 motor vehicle thefts. Only in larceny-thefts did it rise above U.S. rural crime rates.

If you've been suspecting that a quality oceanfront community like this isn't cheap, you guessed correctly. The least expensive listing we saw in local newspapers was a 1-bedroom, 1½-bath condominium for $118,500. The tenth floor of its building does offer spectacular views.

On the Intracoastal side of the highway, away from the ocean, you could get 2-bedroom, 2-bath condominium units for $135,000 and up. One building, Seagate of Highland, had a 3-bedroom, 3-bath apartment on the first floor selling for $169,000 and a 2-bedroom, 2-bath furnished unit renting for $1,200 per month seasonally (with a four-month minimum) or $750 per month annually.

Just opened was the Clarendon, directly on the ocean. This 12-story, 42-unit building has 2-bedroom and 3-bedroom corner apartments ranging from 2,192 to 2,448 square feet and four posh 2-story penthouses, aptly described as "mansions in the sky," with approximately 4,000 square feet of living space. Prices here begin at $265,000.

Apartments in another oceanfront luxury condo began at $249,000 and went up in price to $695,000 for the penthouses. Your $249,000 would get you a 2-bedroom, 2½-bath unit on a lower floor. It would have 2,050 square feet, not counting the balcony.

And as we were dreaming of one of those single-family homes on the oceanfront, we saw an advertisement for just such a "very private hideaway, beautifully furnished"—no doubt the house of our dreams. Its owner was letting it go for a pittance—a mere $875,000. End of daydream.

Highland Beach, it's apparent, is not for everyone—you must be able to pay the dues. But if you can and the ocean is your passion, do yourself a favor and look into it today. Tomorrow you could be running in the surf, tasting the salty spray as it settles on your lips, digging your feet into the finely ground sand . . .

ATLANTIS

POPULATION: 1,359
NO. OF CRIMES: 17
CRIME RATE: 1,250.9 per 100,000

We confess we're not the country-club type. Neither of us plays golf, to begin with, and we prefer dining and socializing in our favorite commercial haunts or trying out a new one.

We also confess that we have no use, ourselves, for planned communities of any sort, including—or should we say, especially—retirement communities. We would find it terribly distressing to be surrounded only by people in our own age bracket and all of us cut from the same economic and social cloth. We like variety and we enjoy maintaining daily contact with people both younger and older than we are.

That's us.

Notwithstanding, we realize that many people feel otherwise. They thrive on a busy social life with people they find compatible, who share their own social values and outlook. There's nothing wrong with that. That's how they express their personality.

All of this has a direct bearing on a book such as this. Do we select only towns that we personally like? Or do we seek a mix that extends beyond our own preferences, as long as each community meets our standards as a Safe Place?

It's inevitable that this book will reflect our personal tastes. In any selection process, there's no such thing as pure objectivity.

At the same time, however, we do try to provide you with an appealing variety of communities that extends way beyond our own tastes. There are *many* towns in this book in which we wouldn't want to live ourselves. We seek only to ensure that they're quality communities, with a distinctive character, and—of course—safe.

Which brings us to Atlantis.

Atlantis describes itself as "one of Florida's finest country-club communities." We agree. It's not *our* cup of tea, but if a country-club community is what *you* are seeking, you couldn't do much better than this.

Incorporated as its own town, Atlantis is conveniently located in Palm Beach County, southwest of Lake Worth. The ocean, at South Palm Beach, is just 3 miles away. The distinctive shops of Palm Beach are a short drive away and no place on the entire Gold Coast, even as distant as Miami, is more than an hour away.

Atlantis offers you a choice of individual homes, apartments, or villas. The villas combine the privacy of a home with the convenience of apartment living.

Each villa cluster has its own pool and recreation area; some have their own tennis courts.

Strict architectural control is maintained by the community. Utility lines are underground and authentic gas lamps light the streets at night. The lawns are exquisitely manicured, with a profuse variety of Florida's tropical plants and trees. If anything, we found it all *too* perfect: no uncut lawn, no dented jalopy in anyone's driveway, no peeling paint anywhere. We kept expecting it to turn out to be a mirage or perhaps an exquisite movie backdrop painted on a gigantic billboard. Real-life neighborhoods just aren't this perfect, we kept telling ourselves.

The two country clubs are cast in the same mold. Atlantis Country Club and Inn is a semiprivate club with a championship 18-hole golf course, pro shop, restaurant, lounge, and snack bar. No bond or initiation fee is required. Annual membership charges are $1,365 (single) or $1,627.50 (family), with a $603.75 trail fee for those wanting to use their own golf cart.

Atlantis Golf Club is private, with a championship 27-hole golf course, pro shop, restaurant, and lounge. Membership requires a refundable bond of $5,000, an initiation fee of $10,000, and annual dues of $1,750. The trail fee is $550 for golf cart owners and there's an annual food and beverage minimum of $400. At the time of our visit, total membership was limited to 385 and there was a waiting list, but applications were being accepted.

Atlantis Enterprises Realty Company told us that new homes cost $295,000. These have 3 bedrooms, 3 baths, and a pool. Resale homes ranged in price from $179,000 to $555,000.

New villas began at $135,000 (2 bedrooms, 2 baths) or at $149,500 (2 bedrooms, den, 2 baths). Resale villas were on the market at prices ranging from $144,500 to $199,000.

New apartments (2 bedrooms, 2 baths, furnished) were $155,000 and up and all of them overlooked the lake and golf course. Resale apartments were priced from $94,900 to $165,000.

Residential lots were also available at prices from $88,000 to $198,000. So too were seasonal rentals: $2,100 per month for a town home, $2,300 for an apartment, and $2,700 for a villa.

Atlantis has its own police department and access to the community is limited. Despite its affluence, the crime rate is very low.

In our comparison year of 1980, there were no crimes of violence at all and just 9 burglaries, 6 larceny-thefts, and 2 motor vehicle thefts. That placed Atlantis below U.S. rural crime rates in all categories except motor vehicle theft.

The following year, there was one more crime but the population had increased to 1,454, so the crime rate actually inched downward. There were 1 aggravated assault, 6 burglaries, and 11 larceny-thefts. That year Atlantis placed below U.S. rural crime rates in all seven categories.

In medical facilities you are also well-served. John F. Kennedy Memorial Hospital, a major facility, is situated right outside the town on Congress Avenue.

The combination of safety and quality is Atlantis' unique advantage. If you're looking for a country-club community with characteristics like that, you need look no farther.

SOUTHWESTERN FLORIDA

The beaches of southwestern Florida are located as far south as those on the Gold Coast. Here, though, you're on the Gulf of Mexico, with a noticeably more gentle surf than you'll find along the Atlantic Coast.

That's a disappointment if your interest is in surfing or rollicking in powerful incoming waves. It's an advantage if you're looking for beaches that are suitable for young children and timid adults. Here the beaches slope so gradually into the Gulf that you can often walk out hundreds of yards during low tide and still find the warm waters barely lapping at your knees.

Gentle slopes and surf are a *distinct* advantage if you enjoy the sport of shell hunting. In particular, the beaches on Sanibel and Captiva islands are deemed one of the three best shelling sites in the Western Hemisphere. Each tide brings thousands of new shells within reach. The two islands also make up the Sanibel National Wildlife Refuge, a Safe Place for more than 200 varieties of birds. A causeway links the islands with the mainland.

SOUTHWESTERN FLORIDA Crime Chart

	Crime Rate	Murder	Rape	Robbery	Aggravated Assault	Burglary	Larceny —Theft	Motor Vehicle Theft
United States								
U.S. Total	5,899.9	10.2	36.4	243.5	290.6	1,668.2	3,156.3	494.6
U.S. Metropolitan Areas	6,757.6	11.5	43.4	319.0	328.3	1,911.8	3,534.9	608.8
U.S. Rural Areas	2,290.4	7.5	15.5	22.5	136.9	830.2	1,143.9	133.9
Regional Crime Centers								
Fort Myers	13,928.1	32.8	81.9	360.4	1,488.1	3,104.5	8,415.2	456.0
Naples	11,251.3	17.0	62.5	90.9	392.1	3,028.8	7,432.7	227.3
Sarasota	10,825.9	12.3	86.1	305.3	477.5	3,245.9	6,262.3	436.5
Safe Place								
Cape Coral	3,164.6	0	3.1	9.4	43.9	868.8	2,176.6	62.7

Inland, southwest Florida is aptly described as "a total family entertainment area." That means that while there are many golf, tennis, and boating activities for Mom and Dad, they'll also be busy carting the kids to places like the Everglades Jungle Cruise, or the Everglades Wonder Gardens, with its panthers, alligators, and crocodiles, or Jungle Larry's African Safari Park, where Jungle Larry is assisted in his rounds by Safari Jane. ("Me *Larry,* you Jane"?)

Crime is not nearly as much of a concern here as it is in the Miami area and along the Gold Coast. Still, you *do* have to exercise caution if you're thinking of moving here. As our Southwestern Florida Crime Chart reveals (page 94), Fort Myers, Naples, and Sarasota each have crime rates higher than you'll encounter in New York City.

Fortunately, though, there's another spot in southwestern Florida where the situation is dramatically different.

CAPE CORAL

POPULATION: 31,884
NO. OF CRIMES: 1,009
CRIME RATE: 3,164.6 per 100,000

In this fast-growing region of Florida, the fastest-growing city of all is Cape Coral. The chamber of commerce goes so far as to call Cape Coral the fastest-growing city in the nation.

Well, it didn't even exist at the beginning of 1957, so with a population base like that you can work wonders with the statistics. Our caustic remarks aside, this *is* our largest Safe Place in Florida, with its population of more than 30,000, and that's a pretty fair growth rate for just twenty-six years.

Cape Coral is located at the mouth of the mile-wide Caloosahatchee River, with Fort Myers opposite. It could be described (our description, not the chamber's) as the poor man's Fort Lauderdale. It was laid out with 10 miles of residentially developed riverfront and more than 400 miles of canals, compared to Fort Lauderdale's 165 miles of waterways. Yet housing prices here are way below anything on the Gold Coast.

Though it began as basically a retirement community, the average age in Cape Coral has steadily dropped. The latest figures show that 25 percent of the population is between the ages of five and twenty-five years, 48 percent between the ages of twenty-six and sixty-five, and 22 percent over sixty-five years of age.

What this reflects is a growing business base in town. More than two hundred businesses are already located in Cape Coral's industrial park and a new commercial park was opened in 1979. The authors of the *Places Rated Almanac*, which evaluates 277 U.S. metropolitan areas, rank the Cape Coral/Fort Myers metropolitan area as the second-best in the nation for economic opportunity, following Reno, Nevada. (On the other hand, they also ranked it as the third-hottest area in the nation.)

Cape Coral's commendable record explodes the idea that a fast-growing area necessarily pays for its growth in high crime rates. In our comparison year of 1980, the city had no murders, 1 rape, 3 robberies, 14 aggravated assaults, 277 burglaries, 694 larceny-thefts, and 20 motor vehicle thefts. The following year, there was a slight increase in the number of crimes from 1980's 1,009 to 1,024. But with a growth in population to 35,037, the crime *rate* decreased.

Both years, Cape Coral placed below U.S. rural levels of crime in all categories except burglary and larceny-theft and in those categories it was still way below U.S. metropolitan levels.

You should be aware that Cape Coral's public schools have students bused in from Fort Myers, which has a sizable minority population. This bureaucratically dictated program is as unpopular here as it is everywhere else in the nation and as a result a number of private schools have opened in the area.

Harmon A. Cole, whose H. A. Cole Realty is the Realty World affiliate in Cape Coral, told us that housing prices range everywhere from the 50s to $300,000. The average price of homes would be about $70,000, however, with very few selling for more than $200,000.

A major factor determining the price is whether you want river frontage, frontage on a canal with access to open water, or frontage on a landlocked canal.

Without access to open water, you will probably pay $70,000 for a 2- or 3-bedroom home on an 80 × 125 lot, with 2 baths, kitchen, dining-el off the living room, Florida room, 2-car garage, and screened porch. New construction will also have central air-conditioning. Taxes will be about $700.

The same house with access to open water can run you $100,000. Such a lot, alone, will cost you $35,000 and the price is going up fast because so few are left.

Almost all condominium units have 2 bedrooms. Prices range from $50,000 (off-water) to $80,000 (waterfront).

There are always many rentals available as well—apartments, private rooms in houses, condominiums, duplexes, and houses. A look at the classified ads showed apartment rentals ranging between $240 and $350 and condominiums renting for $400 to $500. Houses for rent were listed at prices ranging from $325 to $600.

Away from the water you can get building lots at much cheaper prices—say, $15,000. There are even areas where the price is as low as $3,000 to $4,000, but those are out on the prairie, in undeveloped areas without city water and sewage. The 1981–82 recession put a crimp on further development of this area, but local boosters have no doubt that the long-range prospects are for continuing growth. As proof of the confidence that business has in this area, they note that two large discount grocery chains and the Holiday Inns chain plan to build in Cape Coral.

When the next real estate boom takes off, today's prices are likely to look like bottom-of-the-recession bargains. That's all the more reason to consider Cape Coral *now,* if you see southwestern Florida in your future.

TAMPA–ST. PETERSBURG AREA

Tampa and St. Petersburg are Florida's third- and fourth-largest cities, respectively. Together with the beach communities of the Pinellas (County) Suncoast, they constitute one of the most popular vacation and resort areas of Florida.

Tampa is Florida's "different" city. It is the state's major industrial center, with thirty-three industrial parks. Its port, eighth-largest in the nation, is home to the world's largest shrimp fleet and unloads tons of bananas and other fruits from South America. More than 3 million cigars a day are manufactured at Ybor City, a colorful Spanish-Cuban-Italian enclave.

At the same time, tourism is a growing force in Tampa. It has some of the most popular restaurants in the state and a major theme park, Busch Gardens (The Dark Continent), where more than 1,000 animals can be viewed by monorail. A popular annual event is the Gasparilla Pirate Invasion, where buccaneers take over the city and command everyone to celebrate Florida's version of the Mardi Gras.

St. Petersburg has been a popular retirement community for some time, but in recent decades it has also attracted a younger population with its expanding industries (aerospace, appliances). Sunshine City is also the major winter resort of Florida's west coast. Popular attractions include Sunken Gardens, with more than 7,000 varieties of semitropical and tropical plants, including more than a thousand kinds of orchids, the full-sized replica of Captain Bligh's *Bounty*, anchored at the municipal pier and originally built for MGM's film *Mutiny on the Bounty*, and the historical figures and chamber of horrors (created by Tussaud's of London) at the London Wax Museum in St. Petersburg Beach.

The major direction of growth in recent years has been mostly north from St. Petersburg, in Pinellas County—the beach communities on the Gulf of Mexico and cities such as Largo, Clearwater, and Dunedin, where tourism, retirement, and light industry all contribute to the expanding economy. Tarpon Springs, the northern gateway to this metropolitan region, is famous for its sponge industry and colony of Greek fishermen.

TAMPA-ST. PETERSBURG AREA Crime Chart

	Crime Rate	Murder	Rape	Robbery	Aggravated Assault	Burglary	Larceny —Theft	Motor Vehicle Theft
United States								
U.S. Total	5,899.9	10.2	36.4	243.5	290.6	1,668.2	3,156.3	494.6
U.S. Metropolitan Areas	6,757.6	11.5	43.4	319.0	328.3	1,911.8	3,534.9	608.8
U.S. Rural Areas	2,290.4	7.5	15.5	22.5	136.9	830.2	1,143.9	133.9
Regional Crime Centers								
Clearwater	8,519.4	4.6	49.3	151.3	444.7	2,272.8	5,309.0	287.7
St. Petersburg	9,021.1	9.4	66.4	314.7	732.7	2,510.6	5,108.9	278.3
Tampa	14,477.8	16.4	129.5	698.5	1,049.5	4,447.2	7,455.6	681.0
Safe Place								
Belleair Bluffs	2,430.3	0	0	79.7	0	637.5	1,633.5	79.7

A less welcome growth industry in the region is crime (see our Tampa–St. Petersburg Area Crime Chart, above). Tampa's crime rate is nearly as high as Miami's. Elsewhere the situation isn't that bad, but it isn't good either. Both St. Petersburg and Clearwater come uncomfortably close to New York City levels of crime.

In our search for a Safe Place in this area, we were able to find only three small communities whose overall crime rate (less than 4,000 crimes per 100,000 population) qualified. When we visited the first one, Kenneth City, we found it to be a drab, uninspiring assortment of tract homes. The next community, Belleair, was the poshest of the three, but when we broke down its crime rate by categories, its burglary rate was way too high. Our last hope was Belleair Bluffs. Luckily for us—and for you—it turned out to be just what we were looking for: an attractive, friendly community that would be an asset to any metropolitan region in the country.

BELLEAIR BLUFFS

POPULATION: 2,510
NO. OF CRIMES: 61
CRIME RATE: 2,430.3 per 100,000

Belleair Bluffs is not a plush community, by any means, yet its middle-class neighborhoods are pleasant, quiet, and well-maintained. Everything is 1-story here, with stucco exteriors common to the older residences and brick also popular in the newer ones. We always gravitate toward water frontage, so our favorite homes were the ones on the west side of Bluff View Drive, facing onto Clearwater Bay.

West Bay Drive is the main east–west artery and Indian Rocks Road intersects it in a southwest–northeast direction. More than 150 businesses line those two streets, including an attractive array of specialty shops in the Belleair Bazaar Shopping Center. Belleair Bluffs is a residential community. With Clearwater to the north and Largo to the east, there's no shortage of additional shopping facilities in the area.

There are no schools within city limits. Students go to Mildred Helms Elementary, Largo Middle School, and Largo High School. A number of private schools are also available in the area.

Three major hospitals, all of them well-equipped, are within five minutes of the city. The nearest one is just a few blocks away.

The Gulf of Mexico beaches are also just five minutes away. Belleair Causeway takes you across Clearwater Bay to Belleair Beach, Belleair Shores, and the other oceanfront communities.

Belleair Bluffs has a six-man police department and a combination paid and volunteer fire department. Both have an average response time to emergency calls of less than two minutes and the promptness of the police is undoubtedly an important factor in the low crime rate. Fire department employees are trained in emergency care and advanced life-support techniques.

In our comparison year of 1980, Belleair Bluffs had no murders, rapes, or aggravated assaults. There were 2 robberies, 16 burglaries, 41 larceny-thefts, and 2 motor vehicle thefts. This placed Belleair Bluffs below U.S. rural crime rates in all categories except robbery and larceny-theft and in 1981 the community had *no* robberies.

Our real estate contact in Belleair Bluffs was Philip Mayfair of Rogers & Cummings, the Merrill Lynch Realty affiliate in town. He said that most houses in Belleair Bluffs are listed between $55,000 and $100,000. There are some more expensive homes, but not too many. People who can afford a higher price range usually try to get into Belleair, where most of the houses cost $100,000 to $300,000.

Philip explained that split-plan houses are popular here. That means that the master bedroom is on one side of the house and any other bedrooms are on the other side.

For a price of, say, $65,000, you could expect to get a 2-bedroom split-plan house with about 1,300 square feet of living area. Most likely, it would have a combination living room-dining area, which in turn would open up to a Florida room—the equivalent of a rec room in the north. It would have central air-conditioning, stucco exterior, a 1-car garage, and a 50 × 110 lot. Since it is an older house, taxes would probably be around $600.

For $97,900, he had a listing for a two-year-old house with many special features: cathedral ceilings, fireplace, lanai adjacent to the master bedroom, 13 × 17 screened porch, and sprinkler system. It had 3 bedrooms and 2 baths in a split-plan, with 1,750 square feet of heated living area and a 2-car garage. Being a newer home, it had an exterior with more brick than stucco and had been assessed more recently for taxes. As a result, taxes would probably amount to $1,200.

There are several small condominiums in town, where the units cost between $30,000 and $60,000. Port Belleair is a much larger condominium development, where prices are in the $100,000 range because it's on the bay.

At the time of our visit, Baywest Condo had a furnished 1-bedroom unit available for $43,900, with only $3,900 down. There were also several listings for houses which were larger and more expensive than usual.

For $169,900, you could get a 3-bedroom, 3-bath house on a large lot with a view of Clearwater Bay. This one had a family room, screened pool, office or maid's quarters with separate entrance, and a large kitchen and dining room.

And for $274,900, you could get an estate home on a large lot with lovely landscaping. It had 6 bedrooms, 3 baths, 2 kitchens, and a swimming pool.

In all, Belleair Bluffs offers you moderately priced housing in attractive neighborhoods, a location convenient to beaches and shopping, and low crime—a combination that makes it an unbeatable community in Pinellas County and the Sunshine Coast.

FLORIDA PANHANDLE

Florida's panhandle is that part of the state that stretches west of Tallahassee. Georgia and Alabama form its border to the north, the Gulf of Mexico to the south.

Paradoxically, this northernmost part of Florida is the most "Southern" part of the nation's southernmost state. Yankees and Midwesterners have pretty much taken over the rest of Florida, but the panhandle is where Southerners moved when they wanted to migrate to the ocean. In particular, the Fort Walton Beach–Destin area drew most of its early residents from the South and their descendants are now second- and third-generation Floridians.

There are two big attractions here—the beach and fishing. By comparison, everything else pales into insignificance.

The panhandle's beach is known as the Miracle Strip—approximately 100 miles of uninterrupted beauty, stretching from Pensacola to Panama City. Until you've sampled it, you won't believe how white and luxuriously soft this sand is. The swimming season around here is a long summer, so the best times to sample the waters—if you want to avoid the crowds—are right before Easter and just after Labor Day.

FLORIDA PANHANDLE Crime Chart

	Crime Rate	Murder	Rape	Robbery	Aggravated Assault	Burglary	Larceny —Theft	Motor Vehicle Theft
United States								
U.S. Total	5,899.9	10.2	36.4	243.5	290.6	1,668.2	3,156.3	494.6
U.S. Metropolitan Areas	6,757.6	11.5	43.4	319.0	328.3	1,911.8	3,534.9	608.8
U.S. Rural Areas	2,290.4	7.5	15.5	22.5	136.9	830.2	1,143.9	133.9
Regional Crime Centers								
Panama City	9,963.8	12.1	60.4	108.8	568.0	2,546.8	6,320.2	347.4
Pensacola	9,622.0	5.3	38.5	281.8	694.9	2,424.3	5,839.3	337.8
Tallahassee	12,006.1	9.9	121.3	268.7	752.9	3,323.5	7,049.4	480.4
Safe Place								
Valparaiso	652.6	0	0	32.6	32.6	326.3	179.5	81.6

The fishing is just as fantastic. Destin has the state's largest charter-boat fleet, and its big event each year is the Destin Rodeo—a "rodeo" held at sea, not in a corral. We arrived on the scene right after 1982's rodeo, just in time to see pictures in the papers of such trophies as a 34-pound, 2-ounce red snapper.

As our Florida Panhandle Crime Chart reveals (above), the state capital of Tallahassee has a crime rate more than double the U.S. average. Panama City and Pensacola are each approaching New York City levels of crime. Of the major population centers, only Fort Walton Beach came close to being a Safe

Place. Its overall crime rate in 1980 was 4,103.7—not quite low enough to qualify as a Safe Place, but amazingly low considering how crowded it is most of the year with hordes of tourists. There aren't many bustling resorts with a permanent population of 20,000 that can match that record.

Considering the relative safety of Fort Walton Beach, we weren't too surprised when it turned out that our Safe Place for the panhandle was going to be a small town and suburb just a few miles away.

VALPARAISO

POPULATION: 6,129
NO. OF CRIMES: 40
CRIME RATE: 652.6 per 100,000

The central fact of Valparaiso life is Eglin Air Force Base. The base is its next-door neighbor and its economic mainstay. The base also buffers Valparaiso from Fort Walton Beach and the other bustling communities along the miracle strip.

In area, Eglin Air Force Base is the world's largest. It includes more than 720 square miles of base and test ranges, ten auxiliary fields, and twenty-one runways. During World War II, this was where Gen. Jimmy Doolittle and his Raiders trained. A monument in Valparaiso commemorates their exploits.

Upon considering the close relationship between Valparaiso and the base, who would want to live in this town if they were *not* an air force family?

ANSWER: Anyone who enjoys quiet, small town living in a picturesque setting of bays and bayous.

ANSWER: Anyone who wants the above and at the same time wants to take advantage of some of the best real estate prices around.

ANSWER: Anyone who wants all of the above and wants to enjoy it, moreover, in an essentially crime-free environment.

Although there's no denying the presence of the Air Force in Valparaiso, it doesn't follow that only air force families are welcome here. The welcome mat is out for all.

We found Valparaiso's neighborhoods to be quietly seductive, luring us with views of Boggy Bayou, Tom's Bayou, and Choctawhatchee Bay. Homes are nestled among pine forests, moss-draped oaks, and other southern-style vegetation. They are mostly modest ranches, but some areas feature larger, custom-built residences. The south end of Grand View Avenue, for example, has especially lovely ranches fronting on Boggy Bayou, and they enjoy what truly is a "grand view" of the bay. Pleasant little parks are also scattered throughout the town, some offering picnic sites on the waterfront.

Valparaiso has local businesses and more extensive shopping facilities are just a short drive away in Niceville (on the other side of Boggy Bayou) and Fort Walton Beach. Okaloosa-Walton Junior College is conveniently located in Niceville and Twin Cities Hospital serves Valparaiso and Niceville with medical care and twenty-four-hour emergency service.

Valparaiso's crime rate is almost "out of sight"—on the low end, that is. In our comparison year of 1980, there were no murders, no rapes, 2 robberies, 2 aggravated assaults, 20 burglaries, 11 larceny-thefts, and 5 motor vehicle thefts. This placed Valparaiso below U.S. rural rates of crime in all categories except burglary and even there the local rate was still way below U.S. metropolitan levels. The result was an overall crime rate of just 652.6 per 100,000—a worthy accomplishment *anywhere* in this day and age, but especially so in Florida.

In 1981, moreover, the overall crime rate decreased slightly, and there were no murders, rapes, or robberies. That year Valparaiso ranked below U.S. rural rates in all categories of crime.

Donna Brzuska of Rupert Miller Realty ("the area's oldest") was very helpful and informative. She stressed the friendliness of the people—a natural trait in a community where everybody's from somewhere else.

"There are about eighty people in my Sunday school class," Donna told us. "Only one of them was born in this area. That's typical."

Donna also informed us of a welcome change in Florida's $25,000 homestead exemption. In the past, you had to be a resident of the state for five years before you could take advantage of this tax break. Now you get a $5,000 exemption when you first move to the state and the $25,000 exemption applies immediately after the following January 1.

That homestead exemption is one reason property taxes are so low here. If you are an owner-occupant and your dwelling is assessed at, say, $60,000, the first $25,000 is exempt and the local property tax rate applies only to the remainder—in this instance, $35,000. Donna told us that in Valparaiso taxes would be about $400 on a $60,000 house.

Prices in Valparaiso range from a bottom of $20,000 to $200,000-plus for waterfront properties. But the average is around $65,000 to $70,000.

Building lots range from $8,000 to about $50,000 for waterfront locations. Lots are usually 75 × 150.

A 2-bedroom town house condominium will cost you in the neighborhood of $50,000.

And if you want to build, *you* decide the price by what you put into the house. A builder will charge you 10 percent of whatever else you spend. If the cost of your custom design is $50,000, his fee for building it will be $5,000.

You can get a very nice house for relatively little money in this part of the world—or so it seemed to us, coming from a Northern metropolitan region where prices veer toward the other extreme. Donna had just sold a new 1,500-square-foot contemporary ranch in a nice neighborhood—for $54,000. It was designed with the master bedroom and bath on one end of the house and 2 other bedrooms and Hollywood bath on the opposite end. (A Hollywood bath, she informed us, is one that you can enter from both adjacent bedrooms.) This house had a formal dining room, eat-in kitchen, "great room," wet bar between the kitchen and great room, heat-recovery system, and 2-car garage.

While driving through town, we had noticed two architecturally striking new homes facing the water on Bay Shore Drive. One was a contemporary, the other Spanish, and they demonstrate what—besides ranches—can be built with a little imagination to take advantage of these lovely settings. Donna was familiar with the contemporary—a 3-level house with extra-large windows that take advantage of the water views, an unusual floor plan, cedar trimming, and an indoor heated swimming pool. She estimated that it would cost $200,000—we would say *just* $200,000—to build this house in this location in Valparaiso.

Florida's panhandle has many attractions. If you want to take advantage of them, the Fort Walton Beach area allows that with the least exposure to crime. And if you want to move to this area, there's no better choice than Valparaiso. All the shops and beaches, all the hustle and bustle of the miracle strip, are no more than a half hour away. Yet here, at home, you can enjoy the leisurely pace and tranquil beauty of a picturesque small town. Not a bad arrangement, we thought. Not bad at all.

Where to get further information:

State

Florida Division of Tourism, Visitor Inquiry, 126 Van Buren Street, Tallahassee, FL 32301.

Regional

Miami Area: Metro-Dade Department of Tourism, 234 West Flagler Street, Miami, FL 33130. Visitor and Convention Authority, 555 17th Street, Miami Beach, FL 33139.

Gold Coast: Fort Lauderdale–Broward County Chamber of Commerce, 208 S.E. Third Avenue, Fort Lauderdale, FL 33301. Palm Beach Chamber of Commerce, 45 Cocoanut Row, Palm Beach, FL 33480.

Southwestern Florida: Metropolitan Fort Myers Chamber of Commerce, P.O. Box CC, Fort Myers, FL 33902. Naples Area Chamber of Commerce, 1700 N. Tamiami Trail, Naples, FL 33940. Visitor Information Center, Tamiami Trail and 6th Street, Sarasota, FL 33579.

Tampa–St. Petersburg Area: Greater Tampa Chamber of Commerce, P.O. Box 420, Tampa, FL 33601. St. Petersburg Area Chamber of Commerce, 225 4th Street S., Box 1371, St. Petersburg, FL 33731. Chamber of Commerce, P.O. Box 2457, 128 N. Osceola Avenue, Clearwater, FL 33517.

Florida Panhandle: Greater Fort Walton Beach Chamber of Commerce, 34 Miracle Strip Parkway, S.E., Fort Walton Beach, FL 32548. Tourism Information Center, 803 N. Palafox Street, Pensacola, FL 32501. Bay County Resort Council, Box 9473, Panama City, FL 32401.

Towns

Biscayne Park: A monthly *Village Bulletin* is available to residents from the Village of Biscayne Park, 640 N.E. 114th Street, Biscayne Park, FL 33161.

Bay Harbor Islands: A monthly newsletter and a town map are available to residents from the Public Relations Department, Town of Bay Harbor Islands, 9665 Bay Harbor Terrace, Bay Harbor Islands, FL 33154.

Highland Beach: Several brochures are available from the Town of Highland Beach, 3614 S. Ocean Boulevard, Highland Beach, FL 33431.

Atlantis: The exclusive sales agent for all Atlantis properties is Atlantis Realty Co., 144 Clubhouse Boulevard, Atlantis, FL 33462.

Cape Coral: A wide variety of maps and literature, including an annual visitor's guide, is available from the Cape Coral Chamber of Commerce, 2051 Cape Coral Parkway, Cape Coral, FL 33904. A *Community Newsletter* is available to residents from the City of Cape Coral, P.O. Box 900, Cape Coral, FL 33910.

Belleair Bluffs: A brochure and map are available from the City of Belleair Bluffs, 115 Florence Drive, Belleair Bluffs, FL 33540. The city is also served by the Greater Largo Chamber of Commerce, 395 First Avenue, S.W., Largo, FL 33540.

Valparaiso: Niceville–Valparaiso Bay Area Chamber of Commerce, 170 John Sims Parkway, Valparaiso, FL 32580.

Georgia

Georgia began as a haven for debtors and dissenters and at one time its lands reached all the way to the Mississippi. It lost the parts that now constitute the states of Alabama and Mississippi, but what remains is still the largest state east of the Mississippi River.

The hub of modern-day Georgia is the state capital of Atlanta, the commercial, industrial, and financial center of the Southeast. Augusta and Savannah are other industrial centers. Textiles and lumber products are key industries, while tourism brings more than $2 billion to the state's economy each year. Agricultural products range from peaches and watermelons to peanuts and pecans, where Georgia leads the nation in production. It's also the country's second-largest producer of chickens and eggs.

Geographically, the Peach State is marked by a fall line that extends from Augusta on the South Carolina border, through Milledgeville and Macon to Columbus on the Alabama border. Below this line are the coastal plains, Okefenokee Swamp (home of Pogo and his friends), and the Atlantic coast with its luxury resorts at Jekyll and Sea islands and a chain of barrier islands, part of them now comprising Cumberland Island National Seashore. Above the fall line is the Piedmont country, which slowly rises until it reaches the Appalachian and Blue Ridge mountains in the far northern part of the state.

Winters in the mountain regions bring an average snowfall of 1½ inches and late October and early November are the peak foliage season. Atlanta itself enjoys a four-season climate unlike other Southern cities such as Houston, New Orleans, or Miami. With an elevation of 1,050 feet, it is the third highest large city in the United States, following Denver and Phoenix. In the coastal and plains areas, spring arrives in mid-March and state propaganda assures us that "summers are only slightly warmer than those in Chicago and New York areas." You believe it!

ATLANTA AREA

Culture, family entertainment, sports, and nightlife—Atlanta has plenty of each to offer you. Nearly all of the nation's 500 top corporations have offices or plants in Atlanta, and the city has become a mecca for the young—both singles and young families. Jobs and salaries are good, while the cost of living is low. One of the most impressive aspects of Atlanta is its housing—numerous city neighborhoods and surrounding suburbs filled with beautiful homes and luxuriously landscaped yards. They are especially attractive during the time of the Dogwood Festival in April and in the fall foliage season.

As you tour Atlanta, you're likely to notice that all areas of the city seem to be relatively new—and not just the gleaming downtown with its glass skyscrapers and ultramodern hotels. There are no old neighborhoods along the lines of what you'll find up and down the Eastern corridor of the United States and for good reason: General William Tecumseh Sherman. During the War Between the States, he gave Atlantans a preview of twentieth-century barbarism as he bombarded civilians and military alike during the forty-day siege of the city. Then, when Atlanta surrendered under terms that promised protection of life and property, he burned and destroyed 90 percent of the dwellings and buildings.

Atlantans built a new city on the ashes of the old. Its selection as the capital of Georgia, but mostly railroads, soon made it a larger city than had existed before the war.

Atlanta is fighting a different kind of war today, only the siege seems to be permanent and the enemy is homegrown. Crime—rampant and pervasive crime—is taking away much of the luster and glamour of Atlanta. Sensible people consider large areas of the city—including downtown—uninhabitable at night and we know of hardened New Yorkers who get apprehensive when business or a convention calls for them to visit Atlanta. And with good cause. Atlanta's crime rate is much worse than New York's—approximately 40 percent worse—and in categories of violent crime such as murder, rape, and aggravated assault, Atlanta is two or three times worse than New York.

In a metropolitan area with a population of roughly 2 million, Atlanta accounts for only one fourth of the total. So the crime problem is not confined to Atlanta. It spills over everywhere. Atlanta, with its population of 422,000, had an overall crime rate in our comparison year of 1980 of some 14,059 crimes per 100,000 population. In comparison, Morrow, with a population of 3,791, had a crime rate of 16,275. Chamblee, with a population of 7,137, had a rate of 12,498. Marietta, with a population of 30,805, had a rate of 12,384. So communities of all sizes are affected.

And, as the Metropolitan Atlanta Crime Commission reports in one of its studies, "The crime statistics contained herein are based on crimes that come to the attention of law enforcement—not total crime. For some offenses as much as 50 percent of the crimes go unreported."

ATLANTA AREA Crime Chart

	Crime Rate	Murder	Rape	Robbery	Aggravated Assault	Burglary	Larceny —Theft	Motor Vehicle Theft
United States								
U.S. Total	5,899.9	10.2	36.4	243.5	290.6	1,668.2	3,156.3	494.6
U.S. Metropolitan Areas	6,757.6	11.5	43.4	319.0	328.3	1,911.8	3,534.9	608.8
U.S. Rural Areas	2,290.4	7.5	15.5	22.5	136.9	830.2	1,143.9	133.9
Regional Crime Center								
Atlanta	14,058.6	47.6	158.8	1,120.3	1,294.8	3,979.4	6,509.7	948.0
Safe Place								
Avondale Estates	0	0	0	0	0	0	0	0

Outside Fulton County, which contains Atlanta, the largest metropolitan population is found in DeKalb County (pronounced De-CAB'). It has approximately 445,000 residents compared to Fulton's 630,000. And while DeKalb's overall crime rate (5,402 crimes per 100,000 population) is still too high for us, it *is* less than one half the rate in Fulton County (11,785). DeKalb also has the highest clearance rate (36.4 percent) of any of the counties in the metropolitan area.

DeKalb is the most affluent county in the Southeast, and while basically white-collar and commuting in its orientation, it also ranks third in the state in manufacturing. It was in DeKalb that we found our incredibly safe Safe Place.

AVONDALE ESTATES

POPULATION: 1,305
NO. OF CRIMES: 0
CRIME RATE: 0

We blinked and blinked again when we saw the crime statistics for Avondale Estates. Zero! Granted it's a small place, there still must be some mistake, we thought. But we checked its crime statistics for the last four years and the pattern seemed to hold. In 1977, there were 16 crimes—10 burglaries and 6 larceny-thefts. In 1978 no crimes. In 1979, 4 burglaries and 2 larceny-thefts. And in 1980 no crimes. Even in its "high-crime" year of 1977, the overall crime rate came to a mere 997 crimes per 100,000 population.

Avondale Estates has a police force consisting of a chief and six men, with three patrol cars and two motorcycles—not bad for a community this small in population and in area. They maintain a twenty-four-hour patrol, and are assisted by an auxiliary (civilian) force of about twenty. The members of this group also patrol Avondale streets, two at a time. Street signs say: WARNING: THIS IS A MUTUALLY PROTECTED NEIGHBORHOOD.

In addition to having a highly visible police force, Avondale has a reputation as a place you don't want to speed through—"They hand out tickets right and left," we were told. Also, trucks with three or more axles are prohibited from driving through the residential areas. We assume this ordinance was enacted to control traffic and noise, but it undoubtedly has another good effect of reducing the possibility of a truck pulling up to a house and making away with the contents while the owners are away.

From its name, you could be excused for assuming that this is an affluent enclave of exclusive estates. Actually, it's a very middle-class community where the homes and neighborhoods show evidence of pride and care but no particular display of affluence. A variety of architectural styles, both traditional and contemporary, are present, and while most lots are relatively narrow (80 feet), they can be as much as 300 feet deep in some areas. The town's original builder apparently used Stratford-upon-Avon, the home of William Shakespeare, as his inspiration for the development of Avondale Estates, which also explains the Old English architecture of some sections of the business district.

Avondale Estates is located in central DeKalb County, on U.S. 278 (Covington Highway) between Decatur to the west and Interstate 285 to the east. Executive Square Office Park is located east of the city; DeKalb General Hospital is about a mile and a half north and to the south are two shopping centers, Columbia Mall (with Rich's, Davison's, and a Sears) and Belvedere Mall.

This is a residential community, with the few businesses located in the vicinity of the main thoroughfare, Covington Highway. City limits are bordered, in part, by Forest Hills Golf Club to the south and the American Legion Country Club to the north. The Avondale Swim and Tennis Club has a pool, tennis courts, and playground, and there are other clubs active in town as well—the Avondale Garden Club, the Avondale Historical Society, and Avondale Community Action, which was bringing all the Georgia gubernatorial candidates to town for speeches at the time of our visit (July 1982).

The school system consists of an elementary school (K–8) and a high school (9–12).

City Manager Dewey Brown, Jr., told us the tax rate was $13.50 per $1,000, with evaluation at 40 percent of full value. This reflected the city's first increase in eleven years, he told us. In addition, residents pay a $75 annual sanitary tax.

At Ford Realty of Avondale, Sandra Ford told us that the cheapest houses would cost $50,000. For that, you'd get a 3-bedroom, 1-bath house that would need a lot of work. While prices on some houses listed as high as $200,000, none had actually sold for that much. Many of these are older homes with new interiors.

The median range at the time of our visit, Sandra told us, was $75,000 to $95,000. These would usually have 3 bedrooms, 2 baths, living room, dining room (usually a formal dining room), kitchen, and sometimes a breakfast area and a den. Usually there'd be a 1-car garage in the older homes, built in the twenties, thirties, and forties. Perhaps half the homes have basements, she said, since the rolling topography lends itself to them.

Avondale Estates is a remarkable community in a vast metropolitan region. Its exceptionally good record on crime would be reason enough to seek out a home here, but you also have plenty of other reasons that point to Avondale Estates as a good place to call home—its close-knit community spirit, the attractive parks and neighborhoods, and the determination to keep it this way. From your vantage point in Avondale Estates, you can enjoy to the fullest all the advantages of the Southeast's most exciting metropolis.

Where to get further information:

State

Tour Georgia, Georgia Department of Industry and Trade, P.O. Box 1776, Atlanta, GA 30301, telephone 800/241-8444. Office of Information, Department of Natural Resources, 270 Washington Street, S.W., Atlanta, GA 30334.

Regional

Atlanta Convention and Visitors Bureau, Suite 200, 233 Peachtree Street, N.E., Atlanta, GA 30303. DeKalb County Chamber of Commerce, 515 Decatur Federal Building, Decatur, GA 30030. Metropolitan Atlanta Crime Commission, 100 Edgewood Avenue, N.E., Atlanta, GA 30303.

Local

News from City Hall, from City of Avondale Estates, 10 N. Clarendon Road, Avondale Estates, GA 30002. *Newsletter* from Avondale Community Action, 31 Avondale Plaza, Avondale Estates, GA 30002. Avondale Historical Society, 10 N. Clarendon Avenue, Avondale Estates, GA 30002.

Idaho

Idaho is one of our least-known states and we suspect many of its residents would just as soon keep it that way. Too many foreigners from places like California might mess up their beautiful wilderness.

The Idaho baking potato is probably the best-known product associated with the state. Sun Valley, the internationally renowned ski resort, would undoubtedly be one of the most-recognized names from within the state. Beyond that, images tend to blur. Most Easterners probably think of it as part of the Wild West without being able to put it into focus—the way they associate Arizona with the desert and Grand Canyon, Texas with cowboys and oil, or Colorado with skiing.

Actually, the baking potato and Sun Valley do signify two important aspects of the state, agriculture and tourism.

IDAHO Crime Chart

	Crime Rate	Murder	Rape	Robbery	Aggravated Assault	Burglary	Larceny —Theft	Motor Vehicle Theft
United States								
U.S. Total	5,899.9	10.2	36.4	243.5	290.6	1,668.2	3,156.3	494.6
U.S. Metropolitan Areas	6,757.6	11.5	43.4	319.0	328.3	1,911.8	3,534.9	608.8
U.S. Rural Areas	2,290.4	7.5	15.5	22.5	136.9	830.2	1,143.9	133.9
Regional Crime Centers								
Caldwell	11,358.0	5.7	11.4	136.4	403.4	2,545.5	7,892.0	363.6
Coeur d'Alene	9,103.6	5.0	29.9	94.6	483.1	1,713.1	6,264.9	512.9
Safe Place								
Salmon	1,545.5	0	0	0	121.2	727.3	636.4	60.6

Agriculture is the single most important industry in the state and is concentrated in the southern areas—the wide valley of the Snake River and its tributaries. Here you'll find the largest contiguous irrigated area of the United States, with more than 4,600 separate irrigation projects. They have transformed a land of sagebrush and greasewood into farmlands with superlative yields. Another major agricultural area is the Palouse Hills area around Moscow, some of the most beautiful wheat country we've ever seen.

Idaho's sheep industry is centered in the southwest. Cattle raising and dairying are also important, as is the lumber industry, with 40 percent of the state covered by prime timberland. Mining is not as prominent as it used to be, but Idaho still is a major producer of silver, zinc, lead, phosphate, and gold. Tourism is based on the state's wilderness attractions. With three quarters of Idaho publicly owned (mostly as national forests), the wilderness is going to be around for some time.

And when you think of the wilderness in Idaho, you think of two of the West's great rivers, the Snake and the Salmon. The Snake has been tamed by dams in the agricultural region, but still runs very wild in the nation's deepest gorge, Hell's Canyon. The Salmon is as untamed as ever and that's where we will find our Safe Place for Idaho.

SALMON

POPULATION: 3,303
NO. OF CRIMES: 51
CRIME RATE: 1,545.5 per 100,000

Salmon, Idaho, is not for everyone. It's not for anyone who wants easy access to the amenities of a big city, for a "big city" in these parts is a place with 25,000 population and you have to drive 140 miles over winding mountain roads to find one that large. Salmon *is* a veritable Garden of Eden, though, for anyone who wants all the challenge of a rugged wilderness unspoiled by swanky neon-lit motels and congested freeways. Salmon is a haven for the true outdoorsman—whether he is a hunter, fisherman, backpacker, logger, or rapids runner. It is headquarters for those who get their sport—and those who earn their living—shooting down the mighty gorge of the Salmon River, the River of No Return.

Lewis and Clark were the first white men to arrive in the Lemhi Valley. Here in 1805 they made contact with the Shoshone Indians and obtained the horses they needed for the next lap of their expedition. Not much happened again until gold was discovered on Napias Creek in 1866. Within a year 7,000 people were living in Leesburg, the gold rush city. The town of Salmon grew up 14 miles east of Leesburg as a supply point for this $16-million mining boom, and when the gold ran out, Leesburg died. Salmon survived.

Salmon today is a logging, mining, agricultural, and outdoor sports center, with the businesses and services you would expect in a town of just over 3,000. It rests in a fertile (when irrigated) valley bordered on the east by the lofty Bitterroot Range and the Continental Divide, on its western side by the Salmon River Mountain Range and a vast untamed territory constituting the Salmon, Challis, Boise, Payette, Bitterroot, and Nezperce national forests, and the Idaho Wilderness Area, the nation's largest.

Flowing through this wilderness empire is the Salmon River and its main tributary, the Middle Fork of the Salmon. Rising at elevations of above 8,000 feet, the Salmon River cascades to an elevation of 905 feet at its mouth, where it joins the Snake River, which in turn empties into the mighty Columbia. The Salmon remains one of the few Western rivers unimpeded by power dams; there are no man-made barriers here to hamper the migratory run of steelhead trout and chinook salmon.

As it flows northward through Salmon, rapidly but calmly, the river gives little hint of the turbulence to come. Twenty-two miles north of Salmon, at the little town of North Fork, it departs from this south-to-north path and turns due west. For 49 miles, as the country gets rougher, you can follow it along the River Road, passing outfitters' camps and sportsmen's retreats. You continue through the town of Shoup, where many of the old houses you see are relics of the early mining days before there was a road. In those days everything was transported down the river in rough barges, which were then broken up and used for building material. You pass the discovery site of a prehistoric man who preceded you thousands of years ago and continue until you are near the end of the road, where the Middle Fork joins the parent Salmon River. Make your way up to Long Tom Lookout, and you'll behold one of the spectacular sights of North America—the Middle Fork Canyon, one of the deepest in the world. You are viewing it from an elevation of some 8,000 feet and the mountains on either side of the canyon rise to heights of 9,000 and 10,000 feet, but the river is a full mile below you.

The Salmon, now joined by its Middle Fork, rushes westward for 79 miles before it is breached by another road. That stretch of the river is what gave it the name River of No Return. For more than 150 years after the first white men came to this valley, only one-way trips down the river were possible. Today, with the advent of powerboats, it is possible for highly skilled river men to return up the river, but it remains a tricky business. In these 79 miles, the Salmon drops a total of 969 feet, about 12 feet per mile. There are more than forty stretches of rapids, one of them, Ruby Rapids, more than 3 miles in length. Stretches of calm water and deep, quiet pools alternate with these rapids and 4-, 6-, and 8-foot waterfalls. This is the second deepest gorge on the continent (only the Snake River's Hell's Canyon is deeper), one fifth of a mile deeper than Grand Canyon. Approximately 180 miles of the Salmon canyon is more than a mile deep.

The towns of Salmon and North Fork are the home base for those who choose to enjoy this primitive wilderness—whether by fishing, hunting, backpacking, riding the trails by jeep or horse, or shooting the rapids. If your interest is in running the rapids, you will have your choice of rubber rafts, kayaks, powerboats, and flatbottom barges.

For fishermen, the river's most popular offerings are chinook salmon and steelhead trout. The chinook migrate from the Pacific, leaping their way upstream through the rapids to spawn in the headwaters of the Salmon and other

Western rivers. After spawning, the adult salmon die and the young spend one to two years in the fresh water before heading for the ocean to grow and mature. Instinct leads the mature salmon back to the very stream of their birth and the cycle begins again. Steelhead trout also spawn in the headwaters of the Salmon and other rivers. The young migrate to the ocean for about a two-year stay, reaching a size of 10 to 20 pounds before returning to the stream of their birth. Unlike salmon, steelhead do not die naturally after spawning, but a second visit to the ocean is extremely unlikely, due to the rigors of the journey. Experienced steelhead fishermen find fishing for smaller trout tame sport by comparison.

For hunters, there are few areas featuring open seasons on as many big-game animal species. Here they apply to bighorn sheep, Rocky Mountain elk, cougar, black bear, Rocky Mountain goat, mule and white-tailed deer, and pronghorn antelope. One outfitter advertises mountain lion hunts. Moose frequent the area but are on the protected list. Rattlesnakes inhabit the area, so always carry snake bite kits and know how to use them.

Fascinating trips can be made around Salmon to ghost towns and other reminders of the past. One of the most interesting of these is the original gold rush town of the area, Leesburg. Or you can take the Middle Fork trip, through the mining town of Cobalt to the ghost town of Yellowjacket, where the 5-story hotel building—never completed—gives mute testimony to the earlier mining boom.

A trek north and east will take you to Gibbonsville, which once counted more than 3,000 in its population, and on to Big Hole Battlefield National Monument, site of one of the big battles in Chief Joseph's War. And from Salmon to Leadore on Route 28 you follow the route of the old Gilmore and Pittsburg Railroad, which served Salmon from its completion in 1909 until 1939—when it was abandoned and sold for scrap, the scrap going to Japan a year before Pearl Harbor. Railroad buildings still stand in Leadore and along the way is the ghost town of Gilmore, with many old buildings still standing. A side trip takes you to Lemhi Pass, where Lewis and Clark crossed the Continental Divide. Just over the top of the pass on the Montana side is a memorial named for Sacajawea, the Shoshone squaw who traveled with the expedition as its guide. On your way you can make still another side trip to the old mud wall which is all that remains of Fort Lemhi, the first white settlement in this area.

There are also archaeological sites and relics throughout the Salmon area, including pictographs that give evidence of Indian habitation 8,200 years ago. You will also have dozens of mountain lakes to discover, old caves and mining shafts, and hot springs to dip into. Only a few have ever been developed for commercial use, but men and wildlife have used them for ages. Hydrogen sulfide gas gives many of them a peculiar odor.

Livestock raising is the major industry of the Lemhi County area. Others are logging, sawmills, cheese production, mining, and tourist-related activities—including the outfitting and guide services for big-game hunting and fishing. Federal and state activities are also a major influence upon the local economy, with offices here of the U.S. Forest Service, the Bureau of Land Management, the State Fish and Game Department, the Agricultural Stabilization and Conservation Service, the Farmers Home Administration, and the Soil Conservation Service.

Salmon has the normal range of services necessary for most day-to-day needs —retail stores, garages, service stations, motels, restaurants, pharmacies, and banks. For more specialized shopping needs, the nearest cities of any size are Missoula (population about 33,000) and Butte (population about 37,000), both about 140 miles away over the Montana line. Idaho Falls, Idaho (population about 40,000), is 156 miles away. You'll find Steele Memorial Hospital, doctors, and dentists in town.

Salmon River Days, the town's old-fashioned 4th of July celebration, features a parade, rodeo, marathon, Lewis and Clark pageant, demolition derby, and raft races. The weekend before Labor Day brings the Lemhi County Fair, with 4-H livestock judging, agricultural demonstrations, illustrated talks, a parade, and a rodeo. Salmon's rodeos attract some of the most important names in the rodeo profession and some of those names have addresses in Salmon, as this is one of the relatively few rodeos in the nation to be staged in working ranch country. Other activities in town include a summer arts and crafts festival, the summer program of the Salmon River Playhouse, and a Winter Carnival in January.

The nearest skiing facilities are at the Lost Trail Ski Area, about 45 miles north on U.S. 93. A little over 100 miles away, over some back roads, are several ski areas in the Beaverhead National Forest in Montana. The most extensive ski facilities are available at the Missoula Snow Bowl, 140 miles to the north, and at Sun Valley, 176 miles south by U.S. 93, or about 140 miles south if you follow another route with some back roads.

In our comparison year of 1980, Salmon had no murders, rapes, or robberies, and just 4 aggravated assaults. Property crime consisted of 24 burglaries, 21 larceny-thefts, and 2 motor vehicle thefts. This placed Salmon below U.S. rural rates in all categories of crime. As our Idaho Crime Chart (page 110) shows, the same cannot be said for all Idaho communities. Caldwell and Coeur d'Alene have crime rates comparable to New York City or Washington, D.C.

We were told that the state of Idaho—Salmon included—has become increasingly popular as a retirement spot for Californians, who are escaping the crowds along the West Coast. Cary Cook, of Cook Real Estate, confirmed this but added that people have been moving in from other areas as well. Colorado ranchers sell out at a nice price to ski developers or the oil companies, then move here, buy a new ranch, and start all over—in much better financial condition, no doubt. Other people are coming from a wide area—Michigan, Pennsylvania, Texas. The common denominator seems to be that they first learned of the Salmon area by coming here to hunt or to run the river.

The lowest-price houses, Cary told us, would be $30,000 to $42,000 for an older 3-bedroom, 1-bath house with a 1-car garage. For 2 baths and a 2-car garage, you'd have to pay at least $42,000 to $48,000. Nicer homes with fireplaces and custom touches then go up to $55,000. And custom-built houses with more than 1,500 square feet of living area cost up to $90,000 or more.

For $47,500, he had a 3-bedroom, 2-bath house built about five years ago. Located on a 75 × 100 city lot, this house had a professionally landscaped yard and patio and a 2-car attached garage. Its 1,200 square feet of living area included a living room and combination kitchen-dining area. Taxes on this property were $412.

And for $107,500, Cary had an eight-year-old custom ranch-style house 3 miles north of Salmon. It had about 2,400 square feet of living area, including 4 bedrooms, 3 baths, formal living room and dining room, den with lava-rock fireplace, an eat-in kitchen, and built-ins like a microwave oven and trash compactor. It had a 2-car attached garage, shake siding, and patios. This house came with 8 acres of property. The two wells were used solely for domestic water use. Springs in the back of the property provided year-round running water; in addition, the property came with ditch rights (irrigation rights) from a nearby stream. Taxes were about $495. (Taxes run about 40 percent higher inside city limits because of city water and sewage.)

Cary told us that homes are available both north and south of Salmon that have year-round water supply. Most of these are priced between $57,000 and $100,000. For land alone, you will pay between $3,800 and $4,500 an acre—and usually over $4,000 an acre—for a 5-acre parcel of "irrigated" land. That means you have water surface rights from a nearby stream, usually obtained by an irrigation ditch. This water is not used for your domestic supply, which comes from a well. At the high end of this price range, you can also get actual water frontage on a stream or the Lemhi and Salmon rivers. And without frontage or irrigation water rights—relying solely on well water for all your needs—you would pay $3,000 to $3,500 an acre.

If you think the rugged outdoor life of Idaho would appeal to you, do as so many others have done before you. Try it out, first on a vacation trip to sample the hunting, fishing, or white water adventures. You too may decide that this is too good a life to live just a few weeks each year and pull up stakes and move here.

Where to get further information:

State

Idaho Travel Committee, Statehouse Room 108, Boise, ID 83720. Among their publications are very attractive ones on each of six regions in the state. Salmon is in the area designated Mountain River Country.

Local

Salmon Chamber of Commerce, 202 Main Street, Salmon, ID 83467.

Illinois

This Midwestern state is one of the nation's giants economically, ranking third in the value of its manufactured goods. From meat packing to steel mills, from oil refineries to farm equipment—you'll find it here in Illinois.

But Illinois is a leader not only in manufacturing but in agriculture and mining as well. With 85 percent of its land in cultivation, it ranks first in the production of soybeans, second in corn, sixth in oats, and eighth in wheat. It also ranks second in hog production and marketing. Just as it ranks third in value of manufactured goods, it ranks third in income derived from crops and livestock. And in mining, it is the nation's largest producer of coal.

There are aspects of Illinois that surprise even the most seasoned traveler. We all know about the level plains, but how many realize that a nine-county area in the south contains the Illinois Ozarks? We all know this is the Land of Lincoln, but how many realize that the southern tip of the state is as "Southern" as any Deep South state, complete with cottonfields and deltalands along the Mississippi and Ohio rivers? Here, too, are limestone bluffs along the upper Mississippi valley and historic towns like the Mormon center of Nauvoo and the old lead mining center of Galena, today a treasure trove of Victorian, Federal, Greek Revival, and Italian-Colonnade architecture. But when all is said and done, Illinois is best known to the world through its magnificent metropolis, the Windy City, "the city that works," Chicago.

CHICAGO AND CHICAGOLAND

Rudyard Kipling called Chicago "a real city" and his sentiments have been echoed by countless visitors over the years. There's a vigor, a solidity, to Chicago that somehow seems to capture the spirit of America more than any other city. Its colorful individuality and innovativeness have fired the imagination of poets and writers ranging from Carl Sandburg to Saul Bellow.

Chicago has always been a transportation hub—first the rail center of the nation, now home to the nation's busiest airport and an inland port connected by the St. Lawrence Seaway to the North Atlantic and by the Illinois Waterway to the Mississippi River and the Gulf of Mexico. While exporting its manufactured goods and agricultural products, Chicago also imports many things, the most important of which have been waves of immigrants—first Easterners in search of fortunes in the West, then Europeans speaking a dozen tongues, then Southern blacks and Appalachian whites, now the Chicanos and Asians. The result is an ethnic mosaic that rivals those of the nation's coastal cities, though by now many of the European immigrants have become suburbanized and the city population is predominantly black and Chicano. One result of these population shifts could be seen in the election of April 1983, when the nation's second largest city elected its first black mayor.

Chicago is a city of many superlatives. It is the world's largest convention and trade show center, with more than 1,200 of them each year. It has the nation's tallest building (Sears Tower), tallest apartment-office building (John Hancock Center), largest hotel (Conrad Hilton), largest commercial office building (Merchandise Mart), leading futures trading market (Chicago Board of Trade), leading commodity exchange (Chicago Mercantile Exchange), busiest street corner (State and Madison), largest printing firm (R. R. Donnelley & Sons), largest newspaper plant (Chicago *Tribune),* and largest exhibition center (McCormick Place).

Economically, Chicago is number one in candy manufacturing, commercial printing, construction machinery, envelopes, industrial machinery manufacturing, mail order business, metal products manufacturing, musical instruments and parts, office machines, sausages and prepared meats, service industry machines, soap and other detergents, steel production, surgical appliances and supplies, tool and die making, wire products, and much more.

To get to the specific point of our book, is it also number one in crime?

To begin with, Illinois ranked twenty-seventh among the fifty states in crime during our comparison year of 1980. Its overall record on crime, therefore, is so-so—about half the states are worse off with higher crime, the other half better off with less crime.

The surprise is with Chicago, portrayed in so many movies as the gangsters' town that the nation has come to believe it. Yet it has an overall crime rate of 6,583.4 crimes per 100,000 population. That means the nation's second largest city ranks twentieth in crime out of the nation's twenty-three largest cities—only Milwaukee, Philadelphia, and Indianapolis have lower crime rates. Chicago, it turns out, has 35 percent less crime than the nation's largest city, New York, and it has 34 percent less crime than the nation's third largest city, Los Angeles.

Chicago, then, does seem to get a bum rap from the movies—until we break down its overall crime rate into the seven separate categories (see our Chicagoland Crime Chart, page 119). Then we begin to understand the image of gangland violence, for it turns out that Chicago has very high rates in all four categories of violent crime—murder, rape, robbery, and aggravated assault. The reason its *overall* crime rate is relatively low is because it has exceptionally low rates of burglary and larceny-theft for a city of this size and in sheer numbers those usually constitute the largest number of crimes.

We compiled and compared the crime rates for 167 communities in Illinois with a population of 10,000 or more. We came up with a number of interesting facts.

High-crime spots, for example, seem to be divided equally between the Chicagoland area and the rest of the state. Of the twenty-three communities with an overall crime rate of 8,000 or more, eleven were in the Chicagoland area. Of the top ten, five were in Chicagoland. In addition to the four Chicagoland communities we've noted in our crime chart, Kankakee, Alton, and East St. Louis all have crime rates higher than those for New York City or Washington, D.C.

Low-crime spots, on the other hand, are overwhelmingly found among Chicago's suburbs. This follows the pattern we've found in other Northeastern states, of a surprising number of safe suburbs located on the rim of high-crime metropolitan areas.

Of the 167 communities in Illinois, 48—or 29 percent—actually qualified as Safe Places, with crime rates of less than 4,000 per 100,000 population. Compare that with our problems in Southern and Western states, where it was often difficult to find even one or two communities that qualified.

We had so many Safe Places in Illinois, in fact, that we narrowed the field of consideration to those with a rate of 3,000 or less. That still left us with twenty-one Safe Places in Illinois—seventeen of them Chicago suburbs!

Now let's see if we can arrive at any generalizations about the different suburban *areas* in Chicagoland.

Of the twenty-three highest-crime cities in Illinois, we noted that eleven were in Chicagoland. Of those eleven, five were suburbs to the south of Chicago, two in the southwest, none to the west, one in the northwest, and three along the north shore.

Of the seventeen safest suburbs, the west had nine, one was in the southwest, three in the south, one in the northwest, two in the north, and one along the north shore.

To make the pattern clearer, let's put those numbers in the form of a chart:

CHICAGOLAND SUBURBAN AREAS	SAFEST SUBURBS	HIGHEST-CRIME SUBURBS
North Shore	1	3
North	2	0
Northwest	1	1
West	9	0
Southwest	1	2
South	3	5

As a general pattern, then, we can say this: *Chicago's western suburbs are the safest. The highest crime will be found in the south and along the Gold Coast north shore of Lake Michigan, yet you will find individual communities in both areas that are quite safe.*

We picked four Safe Places that we think will give you a good variety of Chicagoland suburbs.

Hinsdale: The safest city in Illinois in 1980. And one of the most pleasant suburbs we found anywhere in the nation.

CHICAGOLAND Crime Chart

	Crime Rate	Murder	Rape	Robbery	Aggravated Assault	Burglary	Larceny —Theft	Motor Vehicle Theft
United States								
U.S. Total	5,899.9	10.2	36.4	243.5	290.6	1,668.2	3,156.3	494.6
U.S. Metropolitan Areas	6,757.6	11.5	43.4	319.0	328.3	1,911.8	3,534.9	608.8
U.S. Rural Areas	2,290.4	7.5	15.5	22.5	136.9	830.2	1,143.9	133.9
Regional Crime Centers								
Chicago	6,583.4	28.9	44.5	544.5	341.7	1,148.1	3,444.6	1,030.9
Harvey	13,145.2	22.6	118.8	885.2	376.1	3,911.3	5,468.8	2,364.3
Markham	10,604.7	0	60.6	451.1	619.4	4,470.8	4.255.3	747.4
Matteson	11,801.2	0	0	88.4	108.1	756.6	8,931.9	1,916.1
Zion	11,336.7	11.2	28.1	95.6	759.2	3,368.4	6,573.7	500.5
Safe Places								
Hinsdale	843.6	0	0	35.9	53.8	406.8	227.3	119.7
Lake Forest	2,494.1	0	0	6.6	46.3	416.8	1,997.9	26.5
Niles	2,474.5	0	0	26.4	13.2	455.9	1,575.9	403.1
Palos Heights	2,243.9	0	0	36.5	9.1	419.6	1,651.0	127.7

Lake Forest: Safest of the Gold Coast communities. And let's drop the reverse snobbism and admit it: If they could afford it, this would be the No. 1 choice of most people. Your authors included.

Niles: Let's face it, though, we can't all afford Lake Forest or even Hinsdale. If you have champagne taste but a beer or bourbon budget, you'll find this a stable, pleasant, and community-minded middle-class haven.

Palos Heights: Newest, most recently developed of our Chicagoland suburbs. Therefore most "typical" of the new middle-class to upper-middle-class suburbs that spread around the country in the sixties and seventies.

Geographically, these represent the west, north shore, northwest, and southwest, in that order. A locally published directory, *Chicagoland's Community Guide,* rates them on a scale of 1 (upper crust) to 9 (average) in "socioeconomic class," and it gives a rating of 1 to Lake Forest, 2 to Hinsdale, 3 to Palos Heights, and 6 to Niles. So you have a choice of directions as well as styles among our Chicagoland Safe Places. Happy hunting!

HINSDALE

POPULATION: 16,715
NO. OF CRIMES: 141
CRIME RATE: 843.6 per 100,000

Founded more than a hundred years ago, Hinsdale is one of the oldest commuting suburbs in Chicagoland. It has aged well and is also one of the loveliest suburbs you will find here.

The first settlers, seeking higher ground, headed west from the shores of Lake Michigan and followed the old Black Hawk Indian trail—now Ogden Avenue. One of the first tasks undertaken by William Robbins, the Father of Hinsdale, was to plant thousands of young shade trees. That tradition is maintained to this day and Hinsdale's quiet streets are lined by stately elms, oaks, and maples. There's a settled New England flavor to the town that distinguishes it from the newer suburbs that abound in all directions.

For one thing, there's no suburban sprawl here. Downtown Hinsdale is attractively maintained and offers a wide variety of shops and services housed in rows of brick and stone buildings. But it is compact and only 3 percent of the community's area is devoted to commercial enterprises. The rest is mostly single-family homes. There are attractive parks and the village's offices and library are located in an imposing and stately Georgian brick building.

Long before we ever visited Hinsdale, we were aware of its existence through our friendship with book publisher Henry Regnery. Before starting his Chicago-based Henry Regnery Company, he had published a series of thoughtful booklets under the imprint Human Events Pamphlets. This later evolved into the Washington newsletter, *Human Events,* where both of us worked at a later time.

Quality—the maintenance of high standards—has always been a trademark of Henry Regnery's work and we just assumed it would be reflected in his home town as well. We weren't disappointed. Hinsdale will hold its own in comparison with the finest suburbs you may pick in any of the nation's other metropolitan areas.

Hinsdale's image is one of "old money" and there is plenty of reality to back up the image, but that doesn't mean you have to be wealthy to afford a Hinsdale address. Houses are available at prices ranging from $65,000 on up. Still, the reputation derives from the prestigious homes in the southeastern part of town. Kettering (General Motors) and Legge (International Harvester) are two of the most prominent family names associated with Hinsdale. Others who have lived in Hinsdale at one time or another include Justin Dart (Dart Industries), George Robbins (Armoured Car Company), Henry's brother William H. Regnery (Joanna-Western Shade), the Butlers of Butler Aviation and other enterprises, and the families that manufactured the Cable piano and the Kimball piano and organ.

The arts have flourished here, too. Some of the active groups and programs you'll find in town include the Hinsdale Community Artists, the Village Associates of the Art Institute of Chicago, the Hinsdale Area Women's Committee of the Chicago Symphony Orchestra, the Celebrity Series sponsored by Grace Episcopal Church, the Hinsdale Community Concert Association, the Hinsdale Opera Theatre (which has received regional and national attention), the Hinsdale Village Players, and the Music Club.

For years, the Salt Creek Summer Theater brought stars such as Melvyn Douglas and Bert Lahr to the town. Today, the KLM Concert Series arranges performances by groups such as the Bourbon Street Jazz Band, Ferrante and Teicher, Dizzy Gillespie, and the Chicago Pops Orchestra. And counted among the town's residents have been poets Virginia Barnes Trask and Adaline Bjorkman, dancer Loie Fuller, and writers such as Frances Seith, Paul Teschner, and Ron Hilts. *The Doings,* Hinsdale's newspaper, has been named the best weekly newspaper in the state five times since 1970. Finally, we note that playwright Philo Higley's Broadway production, *Remember the Day,* had a Hinsdale setting.

We've already mentioned in our introduction that Hinsdale had the lowest crime rate in Illinois, among communities with a population of 10,000 or more, in our comparison year of 1980. When we break down its crime rate into the seven categories, we find that it places below U.S. rural crime levels in all categories except robbery, and in that category its six incidents during 1980 placed it slightly above U.S. rural levels. This is a commendable record for a community in a major metropolitan area.

In addition to its very low levels of crime, Hinsdale has other attractive qualities. Its schools are considered among the best in the area, with more than 80 percent of the graduates going on to college. In addition to the public schools, there are Catholic, Lutheran, and Seventh Day Adventist elementary schools. Medical facilities include the 440-bed Hinsdale Sanitarium and Hospital, a Seventh Day Adventist hospital, and Suburban Hospital and Sanitarium, which started as a Cook County tuberculosis facility and is now a private general hospital, still noted for its treatment of pulmonary diseases. More than a hundred doctors and twenty-five dentists are in private practice in Hinsdale and the Kettering family endowed the noted Robert Crown Center for Health Education. It offers exhibits and classes in four general areas—health, family living, environment, and drug abuse—and 275 Chicagoland school districts have participated in its programs. "We seek to teach the young that good health is determined largely by our own attitudes and behavior," says the Center's president, Arthur Wiscombe. "All of our programs are designed to motivate nonabusive patterns of thought and living."

Commuters will find Hinsdale an easy trip from the Loop on the Burlington Northern: twenty-two minutes by express train, thirty-nine minutes on the local. Shopping facilities are plentiful downtown and Oak Brook Center—one of the region's most modern shopping centers—is just a few minutes away. An interesting aspect of local shopping was noted by Sarah Mann in a perceptive article on Hinsdale for *Chicago's Suburbia.* She focused on Hinsdale's "entrepreneuses"—some thirty-seven women active in town as owners and managers of local businesses.

For real estate information, we found Carole Van Dahm very helpful, in the offices of Jeff Jensen Realtor, the Realty World affiliate in Hinsdale. At the time of our visit (September 1982), the prices of houses on the market ranged all the way from $65,000 to $975,000.

An average price, Carole told us, would be about $110,000 and for that you could get one of the older 2-story houses on a 60 × 150 size lot. It would probably have 3 bedrooms, 1½ baths, a full basement and 1-car garage, living room, formal dining room, and sometimes a first-floor family room.

Slightly higher was a classic example of a Hinsdale house—a 2-story brick Dutch colonial, with 3 bedrooms, old woodwork, basement, and downstairs rec room. Its price was $121,000.

As a starter home in Hinsdale, a 3-bedroom ranch with a fireplace in the living room was on the market for just $67,900.

With relatively little space in which to build, anything less than twenty years old is a new house in Hinsdale. To find them, you have to go south of Fifty-fifth Street and the prices usually start at $200,000. For $205,000 reduced to $175,000 in the market slump of 1982, Carole showed us a listing for an 11-room house at the edge of Hinsdale. Thirteen years old and with taxes at $3,071, it had 5 bedrooms, 2½ baths, living room, family room, dining room, and rec room, plus a 2½-car garage.

Straddling the line between Cook and DuPage counties, Hinsdale offers the charm and friendliness of a small town in a vast and sprawling suburban sea. Small wonder that it is the suburb of choice for those who know Chicagoland well.

LAKE FOREST

POPULATION: 15,116
NO. OF CRIMES: 377
CRIME RATE: 2,494.1 per 100,000

You know you're in the poor part of Lake Forest when you can see the homes from the highway.

Well, that's a bit of an exaggeration, we admit, but it serves to give you a feel for this prestigious North Shore community. There are a number of good addresses along Chicagoland's ritzy Gold Coast, but we suspect Lake Forest would hold its own against any challengers as *the* place to live. If it's good enough for the Armours and the Swifts . . . well, you get the point.

Along with Lake Bluff to its north, Lake Forest is situated on high bluffs overlooking Lake Michigan, with ravines stretching inland that add to the natural beauty of the setting. Roads follow the curves of the ravines and everywhere there is a bountiful array of handsome trees and dense foliage. It came as no surprise to us to learn that Lake Forest was designated a Tree City, U.S.A., in 1981 and 1982 by the National Arbor Day Foundation. The forested, carpeted look is one of its most attractive features as you drive through.

And the homes. There were plenty of beautiful neighborhoods and impressive estates all over town, but as a general rule the closer you get to Lake Michigan, the more exclusive the area. The residences tend to reflect the traditional architectural styles, as you'd expect, but every so often you turn a corner and are jolted by the contrast of an eye-catching contemporary.

After driving through a community like this, it always comes as a shock to learn that you *can* get something for as low as $65,000. You know it's going to be a tiny, older home that needs plenty of renovation, but your first reaction still is: "Somebody's kids are off to college and the parents must be selling their treehouse." Have no fear, though. Most likely you will have to pay at least $200,000 for a standard "executive" house in one of the newer, more suburbanized areas of town, so you will pay your dues for the Lake Forest address.

Lake Forest began as a university town, when a group of Presbyterian ministers and laymen selected the area as the site for Lind University. A town grew up to service the college community and in later stages the town became a popular locale for summer houses and then for executives who commuted to the Loop by rail. Even today, three private railroad cars are available for groups of Lake Forest commuters on the Chicago and North Western line.

Lind University became Lake Forest College and in 1876 became one of the first colleges in the nation to admit women. It is today an independent, coeducational, four-year liberal arts college with an enrollment of about 1,100. It is joined in Lake Forest by Barat College, an independent and exclusive liberal arts college for women run by the Society of the Sacred Heart. Barat has an enrollment of about 800.

From the beginning, Lake Forest was planned as a quality community. The New York firm that had designed Central Park was asked to design the new town and at their suggestion the work was done by a young St. Louis engineer and landscape architect, Jed Hotchkiss. He designed the town in parklike fashion, with Deerpath as the main street.

Then, after the turn of the century, Chicago's industrialists discovered the northern retreat. J. Ogden Armour built a 1,000-acre estate, Mellody Farms, and others followed. Something had to be done with the ragtag business district, so it was remodeled according to the suggestions of the Lake Forest Improvement League. The result, Market Square, is claimed to be the nation's first shopping center and remains impressive today as the core of the compact business area by the train station. Comprehensive, protective zoning plans were passed in 1923, 1955, and 1978. Also in 1978, most of the original part of the city was added to the National Register of Historic Places.

For present-day residents, shopping facilities downtown includes branches of fine Chicago stores. Commuters can reach the Loop by rail in an hour (forty-five minutes by express train) from both the Chicago and North Western and Milwaukee railroad lines. By automobile, you can take U.S. 41 to the newly rebuilt Edens Expressway. Medical facilities include 243-bed Lake Forest Hospital, an all-specialist health care center with twenty-four-hour emergency room service, stress testing, executive physicals, and a cardiology laboratory, a new audiology department, and the only oncology unit in Lake County.

The public school system consists of five elementary (K–4) and intermediate (5–6) schools, a junior high school (7–8), and a high school divided between a west campus for freshmen and sophomores and an east campus for juniors and seniors. In a scholastic test, Lake Forest's eighth-grade class ranked among the nation's top 5 percent and more than 80 percent of the high school graduates continue their education in college. Private and parochial schools in town, in addition to the two colleges, include Lake Forest Academy–Ferry Hall, a coeducational four-year prep school, Woodlands Academy, a four-year Catholic prep school for girls adjacent to Barat College, coeducational Lake Forest Country Day School (K–9), the School of St. Mary, a Catholic parochial school (K–8), and a number of preschools.

Recreational and cultural activities are as extensive and varied as you would expect in a wealthy suburb with several small colleges. Private clubs in the area include the Lake Forest Club, the Lake Forest Winter Club, the Knollwood Club, and the exclusive Onwentsia Club and Lake Bluff Bath and Tennis Club.

In terms of crime, Lake Forest was the only North Shore community to qualify as one of Chicagoland's safest suburbs. In our comparison year of 1980, it had no murders or rapes, 1 robbery, and 7 aggravated assaults. Property crime consisted of 63 burglaries, 302 larceny-thefts, and 4 motor vehicle thefts. This placed Lake Forest below U.S. rural crime levels in all categories except larceny-theft and even there it remained way below U.S. metropolitan levels.

For real estate information, we talked to Marilyn Curtis, of Koenig & Strey, Realtors. At the time of our visit (September 1982), there were houses on the market ranging in price from $64,900 to a $3,500,000 estate with annual taxes of $32,000. If you wanted a more reasonable tax bill—say, just $15,000 a year—there was a $3 million mansion on Lake Road with 17 rooms, 8 baths, more than 4 acres of land, and steps leading to your private beach on Lake Michigan.

If that still doesn't fit your pocketbook, here's an example of what you could get for just $195,000, with annual taxes of $3,200: an 8-room executive house with about 3,000 square feet of living area, 2-car attached garage, and an irregularly shaped lot basically 86 × 174 in size. It had 4 bedrooms, 2½ baths, living room, family room, formal dining room, kitchen with eat-in area, full basement, 1 fireplace and 2 patios.

And for $60,000 you could get a very small house that needs a lot of work—but it's in Lake Forest. For $86,000 and $1,500 in taxes, you could get a 6-room house that was probably forty to fifty years old, with a 1-car detached garage. It had 2 bedrooms (12 × 11, 12 × 12), 1 bath, 23 × 13 living room with fireplace, 15 × 13 dining room, 11 × 11 kitchen, a 9 × 7 room with a child's bed in it, and a 23 × 9 enclosed front porch.

We also looked at some classified ads and found a few listings for apartments and condominiums renting from $330 to $900 a month. Most enticing was a listing for a 3-room lakefront cottage with a 50-foot deck and woodburning fireplace, for $525 a month plus utilities. A 4-bedroom unfurnished house was also available for $600. Condominiums were selling for $74,500 (2 bedrooms) to $123,500 (3 bedrooms) and to build your own house there was one parcel of 1½ landscaped acres going for $195,000. A 5-bedroom New England colonial was listed for $375,000, and for $449,000 you could get a traditional country house with a master bedroom featuring a fireplace, 5½ baths, maid's quarters, heated garden room, paneled library with fireplace, a circle driveway, and 4+ acres.

With its distinctive Market Square, gas lighting along the streets, exclusive colleges and acclaimed educational facilities, and above all its beautiful residential areas, Lake Forest has pretty much accomplished the goal of the old Lake Forest Improvement League: to make it "the best, safest, healthiest, and the most beautiful suburb of Chicago." If you can afford it, why accept anything else?

NILES

POPULATION: 30,269
NO. OF CRIMES: 749
CRIME RATE: 2,474.5 per 100,000

Bordering Chicago, this northwest suburb is just 15 miles and a half hour from the Loop. But easy access to the city is just one of its many advantages. Niles also offers affordable housing, low crime, a family-oriented community, and a determination to give residents their money's worth in local services.

Perhaps it is precisely because Niles is *not* as wealthy as many of its neighboring suburbs that the need to stretch the dollar is felt more acutely here, but whatever the reason, less does seem to accomplish more here. Taxes are relatively low in Niles—the village claims to have the lowest property taxes of the northwest suburbs—yet fire and police protection is excellent, the schools encourage levels of academic achievement usually boasted about in more affluent districts, and the community can point to a number of unique local achievements.

Niles, for example, is the first community in the nation to establish a no-fare courtesy bus system within the town, linking all public facilities, parks, shopping centers, and neighborhoods. It is the first in the area to provide, at the local government level, a full-time youth commission, senior center, family counseling agency, and consumer fraud department. It operates the first playground in the state that is handicapped-accessible. And despite extensive shopping areas, it is unique in its total lack of any parking meters. The cost-conscious town was the first of thirty-one communities to join an insurance pool, thus reducing the cost of its insurance sharply and when a village hall was needed, it converted a vacant supermarket facility rather than build a new one.

A major reason why property taxes aren't higher is the income obtained from a thriving local business community. Niles is a regional shopping center, with some 600 retail and service businesses located within its boundaries and sales taxes levied on their customers account for more than half of the village's revenues.

Then, too, some 18 percent of Niles' land area is set aside for light industry and more than 180 national and international corporations take advantage of the village's convenient location and excellent services. Many of these companies are leaders in their fields, too. Niles is the home to such firms as American Hospital Supply's V. Mueller Division, the nation's largest producer of surgical instruments, Wells Lamont Corporation, the largest manufacturer of gloves in the world, Sound Video Unlimited, the country's leading wholesaler of video tapes, home movies, and electronic games, and Republic Molding Corporation, the largest manufacturer of plastic household items. The A. B. Dick Company has its headquarters here, with 13 acres of manufacturing and office space under one roof, and other familiar names in town include the Coca-Cola Company of Chicago, Harcourt Brace Jovanovich, and the Sony Corporation of America.

Particularly in view of the large number of retail establishments, the low crime rate is a major accomplishment for Niles. Many communities with extensive shopping facilities find that high rates of robbery, larceny, and motor vehicle theft come with the territory. (See, for example, Matteson—home of the Lincoln Mall—in our Chicagoland Crime Chart, page 119.) The numbers of crimes in those categories are undoubtedly higher than they would be if Niles were a strictly residential community, but the situation seems to be under control here.

In our comparison year of 1980, Niles had no murders or rapes, 8 robberies, and 4 aggravated assaults. Property crime consisted of 138 burglaries, 477 larceny-thefts, and 122 motor vehicle thefts. This placed Niles below U.S. rural crime levels in four categories and just slightly above it in robbery and larceny-theft (but still way below U.S. metropolitan levels in those categories). Only in motor vehicle theft did Niles approach the national level—but even here it still remained below it.

In seeking the reasons for Niles' relatively low crime rate, we were impressed with the answers we received from Martin J. Stankowicz, commander of the police department's administrative division.

"I know many agencies may boast that they do this or that," he began, "and that's why their crime rate may be low, but I can't be so sure. We do pretty much what the neighboring agencies do in the way of training, community programs, equipment, etc."

But then he came up with some differences.

"We may have an advantage by utilizing the village computer system," Commander Stankowicz told us. He explained that this allows the police to analyze patterns and types of crime and to utilize patrol officers most efficiently.

"Another factor," he added, "may be that the building of homes is now taking place farther away from the city of Chicago and Niles. This area is now stabilized and the residents have lived here some time. The growing is now taking place further out and it may be that crime is following the new growth. However, this is only an assumption on my part."

Then he made one more observation that seemed to us perhaps a critical one. "All our officers live in the community," Commander Stankowicz told us, "and they just might take a little more interest in the affairs of the community by living here. I know I do, so I'll speak for myself."

That brought us back to the strong family orientation of Niles. This family orientation is reflected in the more than 150 recreational programs offered annually by the community, as well as in the schools. Niles has nine elementary schools—four public, three Catholic, and two Lutheran. The three high schools consist of two in the public system, where 85 percent of the professional staff holds master's degrees or beyond and more than 80 percent of the students continue on to some form of higher education, and Notre Dame High School, a boys' school conducted by the Holy Cross Fathers (who also run Notre Dame University), where 92 percent of the students continue their education at major universities and colleges. Both public and parochial schools boast a wide range of academic and athletic accomplishments, including National Merit competition and multiple conference championships.

Niles College is a branch of Loyola University, with twenty-two undergraduate degree programs plus a seminary. Oakton Community College, in addition to its two-year undergraduate program, works with the high schools in the area to offer more than 700 adult education courses each year. Residents of Niles can use its 60,000-volume library as well as their own Niles Public Library, which has 140,000 volumes and access to more than 15 million volumes through an interlibrary loan system.

Medical facilities are also comprehensive. Lutheran General Hospital, a 777-bed facility in adjacent Park Ridge, is the fourth largest privately owned teaching hospital in the Chicago area. Its specialized units include psychiatric and cancer care, physical rehabilitation, and a perinatal center for high-risk infants and mothers. Other hospitals in the immediate area include Resurrection Hospital in Chicago (442 beds), Holy Family Hospital (247 beds) in Des Plaines, and Skokie Valley Hospital (271 beds).

In its housing availability, too, Niles is diversified. You will find more than 9,000 single-family homes here, but also over 2,000 apartment, town house, and condominium units. Bunker Hill Estates, facing the Edgebrook section of Chicago, has homes in the $175,000 range, but otherwise prices and the dwellings are more modest. Solid brick construction is a feature of local neighborhoods and the 1980 census placed the median home value at $79,700. Apartment rents range from $250 to $500 per month with perhaps $350 for a 2-bedroom unit in a "six-flat" building (a building with six apartments). Condominiums sell at prices ranging from $40,000 to $90,000.

We talked with Betty Cusinano of Johnson Real Estate about local housing costs. In the 70s, she said, you can find some older Cape Cods and ranches without basements, usually with 2 bedrooms.

For $90,000, Betty said, you could get a 3-bedroom ranch with a finished basement and a 2-car garage, on a 50 × 125 lot. It would probably have a powder room in the basement and a full bath on the main floor, a living room, and an eat-in kitchen. Taxes would be around $1,000 to $1,100 a year.

And for $130,000 you would find a newer bilevel or trilevel house, from six to ten years old. It would usually have a family room with fireplace and a half-bath downstairs, with a living room, dining room, kitchen, 3 bedrooms, and 1½ baths on the main floor. Taxes would be about $1,300.

No discussion of Niles would be complete without reference to two local landmarks.

The Bradford Museum of Collector's Plates is the world's leading gallery of limited-edition ceramic plates. The collection includes all of the major plates currently traded—the works of more than sixty makers from twelve countries—and is valued at more than a quarter of a million dollars. A sunken garden, complete with a stream and stone walkways, serves as the backdrop for the exhibits.

And then there's the Leaning Tower of Pisa—oops, Niles. A half-size reproduction of its Italian inspiration, it was constructed in 1933 by Chicago industrialist-inventor Robert Ilg. It originally stored water for park swimming pools and in recent years was used by NASA for some experiments in rocket reentry systems. A gift shop is open on the first level. So don't waste time trying to figure out what it's doing in a Chicago suburb. Just take your snapshots and tell your friends you took an Italian vacation!

PALOS HEIGHTS

POPULATION: 10,963
NO. OF CRIMES: 246
CRIME RATE: 2,243.9 per 100,000

Palos Heights gets its name from the heavily forested hills in the area. Along with numerous ponds, sloughs, and ravines, they are the remaining scars of ice-age glaciers. The hills are probably the steepest in the Chicagoland area and are a popular weekend destination for Chicagoans as well as local residents.

Some 11,000 acres are set aside as the Palos Preserves of the Cook County Forest Preserve District. In the preserve, the broad Sag Valley is rimmed by hills on the north and south. Hidden in the preserves, along with the ponds, creeks, and springs, are a narrow rock-lined canyon and two old limestone quarries. Pheasants and wild turkeys, mink, raccoon, foxes, and deer all make it their home. The mostly oak forests provide a spectacular autumn setting and at any time of the year it is hard to remember that you are just about 20 miles from Chicago's Loop and on the rim of a metropolitan area of 8 million people.

Palos Heights itself is a relatively new community, barely forty years old since it was laid out as half-acre "farmettes." South and slightly west of Chicago, it is bounded on the north by the Sag Channel connecting the Calumet River with the Des Plaines River, an outgrowth of the Illinois-Michigan Canal. The school district and other shared facilities and activities tie Palos Heights to the adjoining outer suburbs of Palos Park and Orland Park.

The Palos communities are suburbs comprised of subdivisions and developments with names like Ishnala, Navajo Hills, Palos Pines, Westgate, and Palos Gardens. Ranches and bilevels are the predominant styles and the price range extends from the 60s to $250,000. In the 1980 census, the median home value was $92,400. Condominiums range in price from $70,000 to $125,000. Oak Hills Country Club Village is a distinctive condominium and town house complex, with housing clustered around a 9-hole golf course. Prices there start in the low 70s for the condos and from $130,000 and up for fairway homes.

Gretta Otte of Arquilla DeHaan & Triezenberg Realtors told us that a popular price level is just under $100,000. For $95,800, for example, she had a 3-bedroom brick ranch with a 1½-car attached garage on a 70 × 145 lot. It had draperies and air-conditioning units, a living room, formal dining room, kitchen, 3 bedrooms, and 1 bath. There was no basement—just crawl space. Taxes were $1,084.

For $120,000 you could get a larger brick ranch on a larger lot—with 4 bedrooms, 2 baths, and a full basement.

The most expensive homes in town, Gretta told us, were in the Ishnala development. Most of these are less than fifteen years old. We asked about colonials and for $150,000 she found one in Ishnala that was ten years old, on an 85 × 130 lot, and with a 2½-car attached garage. It had an entry hall, living room, dining room, family room, kitchen, 4 bedrooms, and 3 baths. Taxes were $1,900. Another 4-bedroom, 2½-bath colonial was five years old, sitting on a 180 × 130 lot, and selling for $190,000.

Palos Heights has a police force of thirty-three persons, including almost twenty officers. It is a highly trained and educated force, with seven squad cars maintaining twenty-four-hour patrol. Recently, the force was honored by having not one but three of its members selected to train at the FBI Academy. All of its officers have associate or bachelor degrees in criminal justice and at least four are pursuing a master's.

In our comparison year of 1980, Palos Heights had no murders or rapes, 4 robberies, and 1 aggravated assault. Property crime consisted of 46 burglaries, 181 larceny-thefts, and 14 motor vehicle thefts. This placed Palos Heights below U.S. rural levels of crime in all categories except robbery and larceny-theft. In those two categories, it was slightly above U.S. rural levels but still way below U.S. metropolitan levels.

The public school district consists of seven elementary, two junior high, and two high schools. Private schools include Lutheran and Catholic elementary schools and the Chicago Christian High School, affiliated with the Christian Reformed and the Reformed Church. In Palos Park, the Joseph P. Kennedy, Jr., School for Exceptional Children has educational and workshop programs for children of ages six through twenty. There are also two local colleges—Moraine Valley Community College and Trinity Christian College, a four-year liberal arts college with 400 students. In the nearby area is Lewis University in Lockport, a coeducational Catholic institution with more than 4,000 students.

Palos Community Hospital is an interfaith, not-for-profit general medical facility. It is expanding to 497 beds and is located in the midst of 42 parklike acres. Also in Palos Heights is the Southwest Industrial Clinic, specializing in emergency medical care for people injured while on the job. More than sixty doctors and twenty-five dentists practice in the Palos area.

Commuters have a choice of transportation. The Regional Transit Authority has rush-hour bus trips between Palos Heights and downtown Chicago. The Norfolk & Western Railroad stops in adjacent Palos Park. Additional rail service is available 9 miles east in Blue Island, at the ICG 127th Street station.

Shoppers will find plenty of local stores and services along the city's main thoroughfares and in its three shopping plazas. Major department stores—Marshall Field's, J. C. Penney's, Carson's, and Sears—are just minutes away at the Orland Square Shopping Center.

A wide variety of recreational and cultural activities are found in the Palos area. The Palos Village Players may be the oldest amateur theater group in Chicagoland and it has more than 100 major productions to its credit. The sixty-five-member Southwest Symphony Orchestra presents three concerts each season and the Town and Country Art League of Palos maintains a gallery and sponsors the annual Festival of Art held in the Lincoln Mall in Matteson.

As for recreation, there is a wide offering of activities and facilities by the Palos Heights Recreation Department. The Wimbledon Tennis and Racquetball Club has extensive facilities for those two sports. Target shooting is the activity at the Palos Gun Club, which has four national and five world skeet champions among its members. It holds five registered shoots each year. The Great American Balloon Company offers rides and instruction and has a hot air balloon port in Palos Park. And surrounding the Palos communities are a half-dozen golf clubs and some fourteen stables. High-toboggan rides are a winter favorite in the forest preserves.

The forest preserves. As you take a break from the workday routine and spend some time in the forests, perhaps looking for old Indian trails and burial grounds, you can understand why this area has been a popular homesite from the time of the Potawatomi tribe. With its serene setting, the Palos area offers you a pleasant base from which to enjoy all the attractions and take advantage of all the opportunities that abound in Chicagoland.

Where to get further information:

State

Illinois Adventure Center, 160 N. LaSalle Street, Room 100, Chicago, IL 60601. Office of Tourism, Illinois Department of Business and Economic Development, 222 S. College Street, Springfield, IL 62706, or 205 W. Wacker Drive, Chicago, IL 60606. Illinois Travel Information Center, 208 N. Michigan Avenue, Chicago, IL 60601.

Regional

Chicago Convention and Tourism Bureau, McCormick Place-on-the-Lake, Chicago, IL 60616. Chicago Association of Commerce and Industry, 130 S. Michigan Avenue, Chicago, IL 60603.

Chicagoland's Community Guide is available for $5.95 from the Law Bulletin Publishing Co., 415 N. State Street, Chicago, IL 60610, Attention: Lorene Nystrom, Circulation Manager.

Community Profiles is one of the relocation booklets available from Koenig & Strey, Inc., Realtors, 819 Waukegan Road, Northbrook, IL 60062, Attention: Connie Rosene, or from the firm's Relocation Department, 999 Waukegan Road, Glenview, IL 60025.

Local

Hinsdale: Hinsdale Chamber of Commerce, 22 E. 1st Street, Hinsdale, IL 60521. *Your Village Board Reports* (a newsletter for residents), recreational brochures, and *A Statement of Objectives and Policies* are available from the Village of Hinsdale, 19 E. Chicago Avenue, Hinsdale, IL 60521.

Lake Forest: Lake Forest Chamber of Commerce, P.O. Box 242, Lake Forest, IL 60045. The *Lake Forest Annual Report* is available from the City of Lake Forest, 220 E. Deerpath, Lake Forest, IL 60045. An informative and beautifully produced booklet is *Lake Forest Portrait,* published by the League of Women Voters, Gorton Community Center, 400 E. Illinois Road, Lake Forest, IL 60045.

Niles: Niles Chamber of Commerce and Industry, 8101 Milwaukee Avenue, Niles, IL 60648. Village of Niles, 7601 N. Milwaukee Avenue, Niles, IL 60648. The Bradford Museum, 9333 Milwaukee Avenue, Niles, IL 60648.

Palos Heights: Palos Heights Chamber of Commerce, 6410 W. 127th Street, Palos Heights, IL 60463. City of Palos Heights, 7607 W. College Drive, Palos Heights, IL 60463.

Indiana

Indiana has often been called the typically American state. We doubt that any such creature as the "typical American" actually exists, but perhaps what's really meant is that Indiana has a little in it of *many* American characteristics while not bound too closely to any one of them, so that we all can see a bit of ourselves reflected in it. Mississippi is too Southern, New York too ethnic, and California too kooky for the rest of us to look at it and say, "*That's* America." But Indiana? Why, it's as American as . . . as apple pie and Johnny Carson and all those "typically American" television anchormen with no definable accents or peculiarities.

Indiana is one of our most industrialized states, for example, and ranks ninth in the total value of its manufactured goods. Yet there's a down-home flavor that permeates even its largest cities and the visitor is more likely to remember a state of cornfields and natives who speak with a distinct country twang, rather than steel mills and city slickers.

In politics, too, there's a diversity as wide as the broader American landscape, despite the popular image of a conservative Republican state. This "Republican" state has a congressional delegation that is predominantly Democratic and in its postwar years Indiana has elected everyone from superconservative William Jenner to superliberal Birch Bayh. Indianapolis was the major headquarters for America's labor unions before they all headed for Washington, D.C., and in 1958 it also served as the birthplace of the John Birch Society.

Even in its sectional sympathies, this is a hodgepodge of a state. From Indianapolis north, attitudes tend to be more Northern and to reflect the early settlement of this part of the state by pioneers from the Northeastern and New England states. From Indianapolis south, in turn, attitudes are more Southern and reflect the area's early settlement by pioneers coming from Kentucky and Virginia. Indiana fought on the Union side in the Civil War, but there were plenty of Southern sympathizers around and most people forget that after the war the Ku Klux Klan achieved more power here than in virtually any other state.

In literature too Indiana has made major contributions that reflect the nation's creative diversity. James Whitcomb Riley was the epitome of Hoosier letters with his homespun verse and stories like "The Old Swimmin' Hole" and "Little Orphant Annie." Any compendium of Indiana authors would also have to include Edward Eggleston, Jessamyn West, A. B. Guthrie, Jr., Lew Wallace, George Ade, Booth Tarkington, Theodore Dreiser, Elmer Davis, Ernie Pyle, Gene Stratton Porter, and Kurt Vonnegut, Jr. A literary kaleidoscope indeed.

In its economy, Indiana is both the second largest producer of raw steel in the nation and the state that ranks third in hogs and tomatoes, fourth in corn, and fifth in soybeans. The Calumet region outside Chicago is one of the major industrial concentrations in the world and central Indiana is one of the richest agricultural regions in the world. That's the economic diversity that is Indiana.

INDIANAPOLIS AREA

We lived for four years in Indianapolis—more accurately, in our Safe Place of Carmel—so we're not exactly objective observers and can write about it from a broader experience than a quick visit. We arrived knowing that we would never want to live the remainder of our lives in a place this far from the ocean and any mountains. We left, four years later, with our prejudices intact and even strengthened. Yet that doesn't mean we think there was anything really wrong with Indianapolis; indeed, we found a number of qualities about it we admired. It merely underscores the truism that no place can be all things to all people. (That's also why we have tried to get such a wide variety of Safe Places; this book's not for us but for you, and we're all looking for different things.)

On the positive side: Indianapolis has few of the critical problems that plague most cities today. Of the twenty-three cities in the United States with a population of a half million or more, Indianapolis has the lowest crime rate. Any residents who complain about traffic congestion, air pollution, and things like that are people who have never lived anywhere else. Its slums and poverty are minimal for a city of this size.

At the same time, Indianapolis' economy is diversified and one of the strongest in the country. During the years we lived there, a number of studies placed Indy right behind energy-rich Houston in terms of its economy. Since then, we suspect that the collapse of oil prices has given the residents of Indianapolis new cause to appreciate the value of their diversification.

And Indianapolis is a city of fine neighborhoods. Nothing flashy or opulent, mind you, but clean, well maintained, peaceful, and good places to raise kids. Even the mansions along North Meridian tend toward understatement.

On a more personal level, too, we'd have to say that service in Indianapolis was uncommonly good. Whether in the department stores or your neighborhood supermarket or with the gasoline station owner who came to start your car in an icy winter storm, service was uniformly courteous and helpful.

With all that going for it, what was wrong with Indianapolis? In five words or less, *it was a bore.* Indianapolis was as bland as a slice of processed American cheese and if your idea of a good native cheese is a chunk of tangy, aged Vermont cheddar, well, you're going to be disappointed.

When we decided to make a list of the things about Indianapolis that were memorable—not just nice, mind you, but memorable—we ended up with the Indy 500 (a truly spectacular event), the Indianapolis Museum of Art (lovely inside and out), the Children's Museum (largest in the nation and a treat), and the homes of Benjamin Harrison and James Whitcomb Riley (pleasant Americana). And that's it. Pretty slim pickings for one of the nation's largest cities.

CENTRAL INDIANA Crime Chart

	Crime Rate	Murder	Rape	Robbery	Aggravated Assault	Burglary	Larceny —Theft	Motor Vehicle Theft
United States								
U.S. Total	5,899.9	10.2	36.4	243.5	290.6	1,668.2	3,156.3	494.6
U.S. Metropolitan Areas	6,757.6	11.5	43.4	319.0	328.3	1,911.8	3,534.9	608.8
U.S. Rural Areas	2,290.4	7.5	15.5	22.5	136.9	830.2	1,143.9	133.9
Regional Crime Center								
Indianapolis	5,326.6	15.3	58.7	313.8	249.4	1,441.7	2,705.7	542.0
Safe Place								
Carmel	3,823.6	0	0	16.6	27.7	398.4	3,148.5	232.4

To talk about Indianapolis nightlife is an oxymoron. It's not even that we whoop it up all that much; it's just that we like to know there's something around besides singles bars when the urge hits us. We *do* insist that fine restaurants are the mark of any civilized metropolis and we'd hate to tell you what mark we'd give Indianapolis in that regard. (Besides, we suspect it's probably improved a bit in the years since we left.) We decided that the root cause of Indy's blandness, culinary and otherwise, was its lack of any ethnic identification and pride. America is nothing if not an immigrant nation and the Midwestern cities with character—above all, Chicago—flaunt their ethnicity. Here they hide it, as quickly as possible.

Long before we ever thought we'd be spending a few years in Indianapolis, a native Hoosier visiting us in New York said, after ordering roast beef in a French restaurant, "We don't have any French restaurants in Indianapolis. Why should we? We don't have any Frenchmen living there." It was a joke and yet not a joke. By the evidence of our years there, they also don't have any Italians, Germans, Spaniards, Jews, Chinese, Japanese, Scandinavians, Hungarians, Russians, or Indians living there—at least not enough to open a decent restaurant worth the name. Perhaps that's also one reason they often call it India-no-place.

Enough already. Now that we've got that off our chests, we can go on to tell you about the Safe Place outside Indianapolis that really *does* have a lot going for it.

CARMEL

POPULATION: 18,072
NO. OF CRIMES: 691
CRIME RATE: 3,823.6 per 100,000

Some years back, Indianapolis expanded and instituted a "metro" form of government, absorbing all of Marion County except for a few previously incorporated areas. That's one reason why Indianapolis has so few suburban communities around it. Those suburban neighborhoods, almost all of them, are part of the city.

Carmel is one of the exceptions. It's an Indianapolis suburb *and* its own independent community. Because it is located in Hamilton County, just north of Marion County, Indianapolis couldn't touch it.

Until fairly recently it was more of a rural trade center than a bedroom community. Then countywide (Marion County) school busing hit Indianapolis and Carmel grew like hotcakes. In the process, the residents built a community of excellent schools and beautiful homes. Today Carmel is generally considered to be one of the finest communities in the entire Indianapolis region, so the reasons for moving here now are quite positive ones. And for transferred business executives there's an additional reason as well. The resale market is likely to be stronger here than elsewhere, when it comes time to pull up stakes and make the next company transfer.

Carmel is just five minutes north of Interstate 465, the belt parkway that circles Indianapolis. That means all of the metropolitan area is easily accessible. Downtown Indianapolis is just 13 miles south and the airport is about thirty minutes away. Major department stores are just minutes away, too, at Castleton Square (exit 35 off I-465) and down Keystone Avenue. But for your day-to-day shopping needs, as well as scores of interesting little stores and shops, you'll find them right next to you within Carmel itself. Indeed, you'll want to explore the antique and gift shops not only in Carmel, but also in the nearby communities of Zionsville, Westfield, and Atlanta.

Churches: There are twenty-five in Carmel itself, more just minutes away. Hospitals: Depending on where you live in town, you'd be closest to 172-bed Riverview Hospital in Noblesville or 555-bed St. Vincent Hospital in Indianapolis. Indy has other hospitals too and a medical center of national reputation. Two nursing homes are located within Carmel. Schools: The public system now consists of five elementary schools, two junior highs, and one high school. In addition, Carmel has several nursery schools, the Tabernacle Christian Academy Elementary School, and Our Lady of Mt. Carmel Catholic School (through grade 8).

As for crime, we've already noted that Indianapolis has a relatively low crime rate for a city of its size. That still allows for plenty of crime, though, and the difference between Indianapolis and Carmel is most marked when it comes to crimes of violence (see our Central Indiana Crime Chart, page 134). Carmel's below-rural burglary rate is also remarkable for an affluent community in a metropolitan area.

In our comparison year of 1980, Carmel had no murders or rapes, 3 robberies, 5 aggravated assaults, 72 burglaries, 569 larceny-thefts, and 42 motor vehicle thefts. This placed it below U.S. rural crime rates in all categories except larceny-theft and motor vehicle theft.

Jerry Lowe, chief of police in Carmel, has lived there since 1963, when the population of the town was 2,000 or less. "The unique thing about Carmel residents," he told us, "is their involvement in the community. A lot of them have moved to Carmel in search of high quality education for their children and security for their families."

Chief Lowe told us that the Carmel police department consists of twenty-seven full-time officers, eight full-time civilians (dispatchers), and six reserve officers. All records are computerized and the department is linked by computer to state and national agencies. In general, Carmel's department is regarded as very professional by other police agencies in the area.

"All officers," Chief Lowe told us, "are selected by rigid and thorough background investigation, psychological tests, polygraph tests, and department interviews. When an officer comes on the department, he is required to complete the Indiana Law Enforcement Academy and to attend all in-department training sessions.

"We have specially trained officers," the chief continued, "in several categories such as accident investigations, burglary investigations, hostage negotiations, breathalyzer operations, interview techniques, hypnosis, and several others. About half of our officers have criminal justice degrees beside the required training in the department."

What's the most important factor, we asked, that contributes to a low crime rate? "The willingness of citizens to get involved," he responded. "Not as vigilantes, but as good citizens cooperating with their police department, such as reporting criminal or suspicious activity. And they should demand from their political leaders a professionally well-trained police department."

The first thing one notices when visiting Carmel is the fine selection of homes. They come in varying sizes, from modest ranches to large 2-story homes in "estate" developments and the variety of architectural styles is equally pleasing. You can probably find what you're looking for here, whether it be a colonial, contemporary, Tudor, Spanish, Western ranch, or whatever. Some areas, it's true, have a tract development look to them—because that's what they *are.* But just as many neighborhoods have winding, tree-shaded streets that are pleasing to the eye. One enterprising developer even managed to turn an eyesore of a swamp into a "lake" that now shores up the values of the houses fronting on it.

When it came time to get an update on Carmel housing prices for this book, we turned to the person who had proved so knowledgeable and helpful when we first moved there—Myra Rooze Medley, a leading realtor/broker with A. H. M.

Graves Realtors in Carmel. As we expected, prices had continued to rise in Carmel—no reason for it to be different from the rest of the nation in that regard. Carmel has never been cheap, but when you consider that this is one of the premier locations in the metropolitan area, prices aren't bad either. Also, our observation has been that you get better construction and more features for your money here than in some areas of the East or the West.

The lowest-priced house, Myra told us, was $25,900, but the listings quickly jumped to $60,000 and above. There were only two houses priced above $400,000. Two big blocs of houses will be found in the $90,000 to $115,000 range and in the $120,000 to $160,000 range. And for $175,000 you can get a very fine 4-bedroom, 2-story home.

For $114,500, Myra showed us a listing for a traditional 2-story home in Brookshire North. It had 4 bedrooms, 2½ baths, a full basement, and a living room, formal dining room, family room with fireplace, and kitchen with a separate breakfast area—in all, probably 2,100 to 2,300 square feet of living area. It sat on a "typical" 110 × 150 lot and taxes were $459 per half year.

(That's another advantage of Carmel, Myra noted. A comparable house in Indianapolis would have taxes of $560 to $570 per half year—roughly 20 percent more.)

We had always considered the Eden Park subdivision to be one of the nicest in Carmel, since it is heavily wooded, with streams and large traditional homes that are a visual delight. Myra told us there were only two listings on Eden Glen Drive for under $200,000. One house had actually sold for under $150,000 in 1982, but that was very unusual, a reflection of the soft recessionary market. Another concentration of executive-style homes will be found in Crooked Stick Estates, where most are priced between $200,000 and $350,000.

Building lots in a subdivision will cost you $18,000 to $30,000 and there's one new area in Carmel where the lots cost $60,000. If you're not in a subdivision, you must have acreage—3 to 5 acres is the usual.

Condominium units generally begin in the 60s. Wilson Village is the only apartment complex that has been converted to condominiums; the others, such as Carmeltown, were built from the start as condominium developments.

As for rentals, about the nicest development in town is Woodland Trace. At the time of our visit (October 1982), their apartments rented for $315 (1 bedroom), $365 (2 bedrooms), and $450 (3 bedrooms). The rental price includes water and residents pay individually for gas heat and electricity. Carports are $15 a month extra.

Woodland Trace also has 2-story town houses for rent that are spacious and attractively designed, with brick colonial exteriors. A 2-bedroom town house with 1,616 square feet rents for $450, while a 3-bedroom town house with 1,800 square feet rents for $525. With the 3-bedroom unit you get 2½ baths, 14.4 × 12 master bedroom with walk-in closet and dressing area, 18.6 × 13 living room, 11.6 × 10 dining room, 14 × 12 family room with free-standing gas fireplace, kitchen with built-ins, and washer-dryer hookup. A few ranches ($525) and cottages ($565) are also available.

Whatever is most important to you—beautiful homes, good schools, excellent shopping facilities, metropolitan access, good resale values—we think you'll find it in Carmel. It was our personal choice when we moved to Indianapolis and, we think, the best choice we could have made.

Before we leave Carmel, though, we must put in a final recommendation that you visit Conner Prairie Pioneer Settlement in adjacent Noblesville. It's an entire pioneer village with activities and exhibits for each season of the year. If you're like us, your entire family enjoys "Little House on the Prairie" and this is an unparalleled opportunity to see just how a frontier settlement on the prairie really operated all year long. One visit and you'll be hooked for many more.

SOUTHERN INDIANA

In many ways, Southern Indiana is the most interesting area of the state.

Brown County is a pleasant respite from the flat prairies farther north. Its wooded hills are full of log cabins and the views are especially popular during the Spring Blossom Festival and the fall foliage season. Nashville, the county seat, is an arts and crafts center and has several restaurants that specialize in country cooking and wild game. You'll also find the John Dillinger museum here.

Limestone country stretches from Bloomington south to the Ohio River. The campus of Indiana University in Bloomington includes a number of stately ivy-covered buildings and the notable Lilly Library of Rare Books. In West Baden, don't miss the grandiose turn-of-the-century resort that once was the 750-room West Baden Springs Hotel and now houses the Northwood Institute. (Rooms are once again available, with meals served by the students.) The surrounding countryside is interesting, too, filled as it is with mineral springs, caves, sink-holes, and streams that disappear underground.

Finally, there's the lovely Ohio River Valley, which—between Louisville and Cincinnati—is lined by hills with commanding views of vineyards, tobacco farms, and always the river and its ever-fascinating barge traffic. Vevay, in Switzerland County, has more than 300 structures built before 1883. But the most remarkable gem in this Rhineland of America is our Safe Place of Madison.

MADISON

POPULATION: 12,467
NO. OF CRIMES: 76
CRIME RATE: 609.6 per 100,000

Madison became the gateway to the Northwest Territory with the building of the famous Michigan Road and later the first railroad west of the Allegheny Mountains (from Madison to Indianapolis). As it prospered, its citizens sought to recapture the flavor of their former homes in the South or New England. The result was an architectural heritage that cannot be matched anywhere else in the Midwest.

A walking tour of Madison explains that "within a few blocks can be found houses showing direct descent from Bulfinch and Latrobe, splendid examples of the Federal style, the classic revival as sponsored by Jefferson, and the Americanized Italian villa style which became popular in the reign of Victoria. For much of its fine architecture Madison is indebted to Francis Costigan, who came to the bustling, growing town in 1837 from Baltimore. He had trained under the influence of Benjamin Henry Latrobe, who, up to that time, was American's most highly educated architect and the man who established the Greek Revival in this country."

For a brief period, Madison was the largest city in Indiana. Eventually rail transportation supplanted river transport, however, and Madison waned in influence. That may have been an unfortunate situation for the residents of Madison at that time, but it proved to be most propitious for everyone today who loves beautiful classic architecture. The town sat sleepily on the banks of the Ohio River until postwar affluence led to a new renaissance starting in the 1960s. Everywhere else, so much had been lost as communities grew and tore down their old buildings to make way for the new; here, virtually everything was intact —a present from the previous century.

During World War II, the Office of War Information selected Madison as the "typical American town" and featured it in a widely distributed movie. In 1958, Madison was the setting for the movie *Some Came Running*. *Life* was preparing a photo essay on the riverfront town when the magazine went under. And more recently, the National Geographic Society has paid its respects to the town. Madison is not without its admirers.

It is impossible in our limited space to give any comprehensive survey of Madison's treasures—fully 133 of its blocks are included in the National Register of Historic Places. But we must mention a few of the highlights, to give you the flavor of the place . . .

The James F. D. Lanier mansion (1840–44), now a state memorial, is one of the finest examples of classic revival architecture in the Midwest. It is preserved with original furnishings, and features a 3-story free-standing spiral staircase.

Shrewsbury house (1846–49) is an equally splendid example of Regency architecture, with large, high-ceilinged rooms, intricate plaster cornices, and majestic columns. The long windows, iron balconies, and widow's walk enjoy a panoramic view of the Ohio River.

The *Jeremiah Sullivan house* (1818) is an excellent example of Federal architecture, a style indigenous to early America. Poplar and ash woodworking predominate throughout the home and it contains the only restored Federal serving kitchen on record in the country.

The *Holstein-Whitsitt house* (1840) shows the Greek Revival influence of the houses in Salem, Portsmouth, and Kennebunk designed by Bulfinch and McIntyre.

Mrs. John Paul's house (1837) is a good example of Baltimore style. Edward Eggleston, celebrated author of *The Hoosier Schoolmaster,* lived here around the turn of the century.

Trinity Methodist Church (1873) shows Norman-Gothic style as influenced by English taste.

The *old jail* has been kept intact with its thick iron doors, heavy chains, and very large locks on dungeonlike cells.

Dr. William Hutchings' office and hospital (1845) is furnished with most of his original equipment.

The *Madison Volunteer "Fair Play" Fire House* was erected in the 1880s in the style of the Italian towers of the Renaissance.

Priest's house is a fine adaptation of the garden houses designed by Vignola for the Popes at Villa Lante north of Rome in the sixteenth century.

The *auditorium* (1835), now the headquarters of Historic Madison, Inc., is one of the most notable examples of Greek Revival style in the Midwest.

Christ Episcopal Church (1847–48) is one of the earliest relatively pure examples of English Gothic style in the Northwest Territory.

And *Mulberry Street,* between the river and Main, has survived almost without change, making this block one of the most perfect period pieces to be found anywhere today. This was the street used by passenger traffic from the wharf on the river to the center of town and examples of Federal style dominate.

This historic district hugs the river, but present-day Madison has grown beyond it, with suburban-style neighborhoods on the hills overlooking the old town. The city's school system is considered to rank among the top 10 percent in the state, and consists of eight elementary schools, one junior high, and one high school. Madison also has a parochial elementary school, a parochial high school, and Indiana Vocational Technical College. Medical facilities consist of two clinics, four nursing homes, twenty-four-hour ambulance service with licensed technicians, and 140-bed King's Daughters' Hospital, a private, nonprofit facility. Madison State Hospital for mental care is also located here. For shopping, Madison has an extensive business district, and two-hour drives will take you to Indianapolis, Cincinnati, or Louisville.

Present-day Madison is also an active community, with some festival or event always going on or being planned. The annual Madison Regatta is a week full of activities, highlighted by races on the river of big hydroplanes—"the world's fastest boats"—that reach speeds of almost 200 miles per hour. The Chautauqua of the Arts is a prestigious arts and crafts festival, with limited, juried shows. Then there are historic home tours, a wine festival, rodeos and square dances, cruises on the *Delta Queen* and the *Belle of Louisville* and much more. In the summer there's the farmer's open air market and tobacco auctions in the autumn and winter.

Just outside town is Clifty Falls State Park, popular for its waterfalls, canyons, views, wildflowers, wildlife, and hiking trails. And 4 miles southwest of town is one of the most beautiful college campuses we have seen anywhere in the United States. Hanover College was founded in 1827, making it the oldest private four-year liberal arts college in Indiana. Its 550-acre campus is set on rugged bluffs overlooking the Ohio River and contains more than thirty handsome buildings of Georgian architectural design constructed since World War II.

Serious crime in Madison is extremely low. Indeed, in our comparison year of 1980, Madison had the lowest crime rate in Indiana for any community with a population of 10,000 or more. Its 76 crimes that year included no murders, rapes, or aggravated assaults, and consisted of 4 robberies, 24 burglaries, 27 larceny-thefts, and 21 motor vehicle thefts. That placed it below U.S. rural crime rates in all categories except robbery and motor vehicle theft and even in those categories it remained way below metropolitan levels.

Our Southern Indiana Crime Chart (page 142) contrasts Madison's low rate with those of the Louisville-area towns of Clarksville and New Albany, Indiana.

In determining whether a community is "safe" our primary concern, of course, is with crime. You should be aware, however, that 17 miles downriver from Madison the Marble Hill nuclear plant has been under construction. As we went to press with this book, however, a halt in construction—seemingly for good—was announced.

Our contact for Madison real estate was the knowledgeable and friendly Phil Vayhinger of Wooden & Vayhinger Real Estate. Phil was born and raised in Madison and went to Hanover College. He became an accountant and moved around, but when his company wanted to transfer him to Chicago, Phil and his wife decided instead that they wanted to raise their family in Madison—a decision they haven't regretted.

Phil told us that Madison is attracting a number of retirees and semiretired professionals. Some learn a craft or a trade in order to earn a living here and others commute from Madison to a number of surrounding towns.

We were incredulous when he told us that houses were available for as low as $7,000. That wouldn't be much, most likely a 2- or 3-bedroom recreational cabin upriver, with electricity but no indoor plumbing. But for $12,000 to $16,000 you *could* get a year-round residence. He told us of one, a 4-room cottage with about 500 square feet of living area. It had a living room, 1 bath, 2 bedrooms, and an eat-in kitchen. The present owner was a carpenter who had put in new wiring and plumbing and the cottage had a river view from the front porch, hills in back.

Another small house, at $13,950, was recently remodeled and would be great for an elderly couple because it was just a couple of blocks from a store, a pharmacy, and a laundromat.

Hilltop houses, Phil told us, were constructed starting in the 50s. About a

SOUTHERN INDIANA Crime Chart

	Crime Rate	Murder	Rape	Robbery	Aggravated Assault	Burglary	Larceny —Theft	Motor Vehicle Theft
United States								
U.S. Total	5,899.9	10.2	36.4	243.5	290.6	1,668.2	3,156.3	494.6
U.S. Metropolitan Areas	6,757.6	11.5	43.4	319.0	328.3	1,911.8	3,534.9	608.8
U.S. Rural Areas	2,290.4	7.5	15.5	22.5	136.9	830.2	1,143.9	133.9
Regional Crime Centers								
Clarksville	10,753.5	13.2	86.1	119.2	470.1	1,397.2	7,714.2	953.5
New Albany	9,402.2	10.8	8.1	121.3	285.8	1,736.5	6,716.6	523.1
Safe Place								
Madison	609.6	0	0	32.1	0	192.5	216.6	168.4

third of these are in the smaller sizes, about 1,000 to 1,200 square feet, and sell for $25,000 to $45,000 depending on the size of their living area, how well they've been maintained, and the amount of modernization they've had.

Another third are about 1,200 to 1,600 square feet in area and sell for $40,000 to $85,000. The top-priced ones in this range have super locations. These are the biggest sellers in town and are where he makes his living, Phil told us.

The balance of the hilltop houses are larger. One with 3,000 to 5,000 square feet will sell in the $100,000 to $140,000 range, and a very few—with 5,000 to 6,000 square feet and several acres—sell for $200,000 or more.

Downtown houses are predominantly of Federal design and of brick 2-story construction. These will have 2,400 to 3,500 square feet and a 2-car garage, but no central air-conditioning and no yard to speak of. Their prices range from $40,000 to $100,000, depending on location, appearance, and the quality of the house.

Several of the historic homes were on the market for $239,900 and $250,000, but most cost much less. There was a beautiful, large historic property on the market for $175,000 that had recently been remodeled. Built in the 1850s, it was one of the few houses in town with a widow's walk. It featured a large, beautiful staircase and a full basement where all doors were stone archways made of limestone.

Rentals are very scarce and if you're lucky you can snatch one for a minimum of $150 (an apartment) or for $265 to $425 (a town house). Some of the bigger homes that sell for $40,000 to $90,000 are being remodeled and converted to rentals. You can often get your money back in five years with a rental property.

With its fantastic array of historic homes and buildings, Madison is the historic architectural jewel of the Midwest. But it's also much more than a period piece. Good schools and recreational opportunities are just some of its modern advantages. Put them all together, as they are in Madison, and you'll see why we call this one of our favorite places anywhere in the Midwest.

Where to get further information:

State

Indiana Department of Commerce, Tourism Development Division, 440 N. Meridian, Indianapolis, IN 46204. Ask in particular for their booklet *SceniCircle Drives,* and the annual Indiana Festival Map.

Regional

Indianapolis Area: Convention and Visitors Bureau, 100 S. Capitol Avenue, Indianapolis, IN 46225.

Southern Indiana: Brown County Chamber of Commerce, P.O. Box 164, Nashville, IN 47448. Conventions and Visitors Bureau of Monroe County, 441 Gourley Pike, Bloomington, IN 47401. Springs Valley Area Chamber of Commerce, P.O. Box 347, French Lick, IN 47432. Clark-Floyd County Convention and Tourism Bureau, 540 Marriott Drive, P.O. Box 608, Jeffersonville, IN 47130.

Local

Carmel: Carmel-Clay Chamber of Commerce, 30 W. Main Street, P.O. Box 1, Carmel, IN 46032, has a map and brochures on the city. For their fact sheet on Carmel: Mrs. Myra Rooze Medley, A. H. M. Graves Co., Inc., Realtors, 1119 Keystone Way, Carmel, IN 46032. For a descriptive brochure: Conner Prairie Pioneer Settlement, 13400 Allisonville Road, Noblesville, IN 46060.

Madison: Madison Area Chamber of Commerce, 301 E. Main Street, Madison, IN 47250. Historic Madison, Inc., 500 West Street, Madison, IN 47250. Jefferson County Board of Tourism, Room 103, Jefferson County Court House, Madison, IN 47250. Madison Regatta, Inc., P.O. Box 341, Madison, IN 47250. Hanover College, Hanover, IN 47243.

Iowa

This incredibly productive land is responsible for one fifth of all the corn grown in the United States, even though in size it measures just 300 miles east to west and 200 miles north to south. Iowa also ranks second in soybean production and first in hogs. One fifth of all the hogs and one fourth of all the cattle grown in the United States are processed for the market in this state. More of its land (about 95 percent) is cultivated than of any other state.

At the same time, Iowa has more than 4,000 manufacturing firms. Agricultural and livestock products, insurance, publishing, appliances, and tractors and farm equipment are just some of the products helping to diversify the state's economy.

One of the more fascinating areas of Iowa is the group of seven communities known as the Amana Colonies. The Amanas were the New World home for members of the Society of the True Inspirationists. Adopting a communal way of life, each of the colonies' members—of German, Swiss, and Alsatian ancestry—handed down his skills from father to son, from mother to daughter, in the Old World tradition.

Then, in 1932, came the Great Change, as it is called in the Amanas—the communal way was dropped, private enterprise was adopted in large measure, and church and state were separated. The irony has been noted by Bertha Shambaugh, who writes that "while much of the unrest of the world is seeking relief in trends that are communistic and socialistic, long-time communistic Amana seems to have found salvation in a modified, cooperative capitalism, with wages, profits, and private ownership, in which communism functions as an overtone. Here is a community that, having functioned for seven generations as a benevolent and self-perpetuating church autocracy, is now operating as a one-man-one-vote industrial democracy . . ."

The Great Change has brought prosperity to the Amanas, with an ever-growing market of outsiders pleased by the excellence and fine craftsmanship of the products they've bought there: solid walnut and cherry furniture . . . hickory smoked hams . . . bacons and sausages . . . fine woolen goods . . . bakery products . . . food freezers, refrigerators, and air conditioners . . .

rhubarb and grape wines . . . and handicraft and gift items. The restaurants of the Amana Colonies are yet another reason to stop here. They have a deserved reputation for excellent German cooking, served family-style.

With their dedication to craftsmanship and quality, and the Great Change to profits and private ownership, you might say the Amanas have blended together the best of the Old World with the best of the New.

GRINNELL

POPULATION: 8,864
NO. OF CRIMES: 245
CRIME RATE: 2,764.0 per 100,000

"Go West, young man . . ."

Most of us will remember that it was Horace Greeley who gave this well-known bit of advice in his New York *Tribune.* But not many, outside of history buffs and the Grinnell Chamber of Commerce, will recall that he gave this advice personally to J. B. Grinnell, a young Congregational minister. Grinnell heeded Greeley's words and came to Iowa to form a colony whose members would share his views on education, religion, slavery, and temperance.

IOWA Crime Chart

	Crime Rate	Murder	Rape	Robbery	Aggravated Assault	Burglary	Larceny —Theft	Motor Vehicle Theft
United States								
U.S. Total	5,899.9	10.2	36.4	243.5	290.6	1,668.2	3,156.3	494.6
U.S. Metropolitan Areas	6,757.6	11.5	43.4	319.0	328.3	1,911.8	3,534.9	608.8
U.S. Rural Areas	2,290.4	7.5	15.5	22.5	136.9	830.2	1,143.9	133.9
Regional Crime Centers								
Cedar Rapids	8,727.4	0.9	17.3	103.5	176.2	1,837.0	6,173.0	419.5
Council Bluffs	9,207.9	8.9	39.0	165.1	294.6	2,365.9	5,736.3	598.1
Des Moines	10,145.7	6.8	52.9	259.3	253.0	2,003.0	6,981.3	589.3
Safe Place								
Grinnell	2,764.0	0	0	22.6	33.8	755.9	1,793.8	157.9

Founded in 1854, Grinnell a few years later was a center of abolitionist sentiment and a stop on the Underground Railroad, which assisted the escape of fugitive slaves. John Brown, with his party of runaway slaves and his arsenal of weapons used in the Kansas guerrilla wars, was cordially welcomed by the town and helped on his way to Canada. Today Grinnell retains many of the characteristics and much of the heritage of its early settlers from Ohio and New England. The Protestant ethic still rules here.

Grinnell serves as the trading and processing center for a chunk of the rich Iowa farmlands we mentioned previously. What Grinnell also has, however, are the cultural, social, athletic, and recreational advantages of having in its midst one of the nation's most respected small liberal arts colleges.

The first four-year college west of the Mississippi River, Grinnell College is now coeducational, nonsectarian, and privately endowed and supported. It purposely remains a small college, with its 1,200 students coming from nearly all of the fifty states and from fifteen other countries. More than 70 percent of its faculty hold the doctorate or its equivalent, and Grinnell is consistently rated as one of the top ten institutions of its kind in the United States.

Al Pinder of the Grinnell *Herald-Register* served as a memorable host to us during our first trip to Grinnell, when we selected the town for our 1972 book *Safe Places*, and has kept in touch since then. We were quite pleased—but not that surprised—to find that Grinnell still rates as a Safe Place a decade later. With the town's determination to maintain a quality community in all aspects we expected its crime rate to be kept under control.

You might think that a corn-and-hogs state wouldn't know anything about big city-type crime. If so, take a look at our Iowa Crime Chart (page 145). Des Moines' crime rate is as high as New York City's. Council Bluffs and Cedar Rapids both have overall crime rates far above U.S. metropolitan rates of crime.

Grinnell, on the other hand, had no murders or rapes in our comparison year of 1980. It had 2 robberies, 3 aggravated assaults, 67 burglaries, 159 larcenies, and 14 motor vehicle thefts. This placed it below U.S. rural crime rates in all categories except robbery, larceny-theft, and motor vehicle theft. And in those categories, it was still way below U.S. metropolitan area levels of crime.

Grinnell's medical resources include the 84-bed Grinnell General Hospital, which offers twenty-four-hour emergency room service and radiological, laboratory, physical therapy, and other facilities for its patients. There are four private family clinics in town, ambulance service is available, and facilities for the aged include the Mayflower Home, Friendship Manor, and St. Francis Manor. Grinnell also provides low-cost apartments for the elderly.

Grinnell has four elementary schools, a junior high, and a senior high school. Other facilities for the education of children include the Grinnell Community Day Care Center, the Head Start program, and the Grinnell College Pre-School. Adult evening classes are provided through a program of Marshalltown Community College.

Recreation facilities include a private 9-hole golf course, a public 18-hole course, one public and one private swimming pool, the indoor pool at Grinnell College (open to the public), a dozen city tennis courts, an indoor track, plus the tennis and handball courts at the college. Fishing, camping, and swimming facilities are available at Rock Creek State Park, 6 miles west of Grinnell and the largest man-made lake in the country created solely for recreational purposes. The Grinnell Area Arts Council, Grinnell Community Theater, and City Parks and Recreation Department all have year-round programs.

More than 250 businesses serve the Grinnell community. Among the major employers and their products or services are the Cargill Seed Corn Company (research, production, and sales of hybrid seed corn), DeKalb Agricultural Research, Inc. (production and distribution of hybrid seed corn), DeLong Sportswear (men's and boys' jackets and headquarters for branch plants), Farmhand, Inc. (farm machinery), General Telephone Company (Midwest headquarters for Iowa, Missouri, Nebraska, and Minnesota, computer center, training center), Grinnell College, Grinnell Mutual Reinsurance Company (farm reinsurance and direct insurance headquarters), Heneke Hybrid Corn Company, and Golden Sun Feeds (livestock feed). The Grinnell Industrial Park has 83 of its 182 acres still available for new industry.

Housing costs in Grinnell remain low in comparison with many other areas of the country. According to the chamber of commerce, the average purchase price of homes is $45,000 (2 bedrooms), $55,000 (3 bedrooms), or $58,000 (4 bedrooms). A typical lot size would be 80 × 135 and would sell for $18,000.

Rentals range from $150 to $250 for a 1-bedroom apartment, from $200 to $330 for a 2-bedroom unit, and from $200 to $300 for a 3-bedroom apartment. Mobile home parks are also available in Grinnell and a lot in one of them will run you about $70 per month.

Here, in the middle of America you can live the good life free of the pressures and crises faced by big city residents. Yet a top liberal arts college keeps you in touch with the nation's best cultural and entertainment offerings. It's an ideal combination, as the 9,000 residents of Grinnell already know.

Where to get further information:

State

Tourism and Travel Division, Iowa Development Commission, 250 Jewett Building, Des Moines, IA 50309.

Regional

Amana Colonies Travel Council, Amana, IA 52203.

Local

Grinnell Area Chamber of Commerce, 834 Broad Street, Grinnell, IA 50112.

Kentucky

Kentucky is a gently beautiful land stretching all the way from Virginia to Missouri, linking our Eastern states with the Midwest. Daniel Boone opened it up with his Wilderness Road, beginning in 1769, and settlement proceeded so rapidly that by 1792 Kentucky was admitted as a state. It was very much a border state of divided sympathies and in the War Between the States it provided both sides with their president: Abraham Lincoln was born in Hodgenville, Jefferson Davis at Fairview.

Kentucky is dominated by the Appalachian Mountains in the east, with the highest and most rugged country found in the southeast near Virginia. The land becomes more and more gentle as you head west, until one reaches the delta country of the Mississippi. Its winding northern border is formed by the Ohio River.

Kentucky's major crop is burley tobacco; it produces two thirds of the nation's supply. It is also the nation's leading producer of bituminous coal. Its two most famous products, however, are Kentucky bourbon and the thoroughbred horses of the Bluegrass region.

We picked two Safe Places in Kentucky. The first, Fort Thomas, is a suburb of Cincinnati. The other, Georgetown, is a college town in the Bluegrass country near Lexington and was one of our choices in our 1972 book *Safe Places*. We were delighted to learn that the passage of a decade had not changed the town as we remembered it. It's still safe and it's still unspoiled.

NORTHERN KENTUCKY

With a population of about 250,000, the towns of northern Kentucky constitute the second largest metropolitan area in the state. Only Louisville is larger. This is an area that takes pride in its German heritage and calls itself the Rhineland of America. Cincinnati provides a picturesque backdrop across the Ohio River and seven bridges link the Queen City with its northern Kentucky suburbs. The earliest of these bridges, the Suspension Bridge, was the longest single bridge span when it was completed in 1867. Designed by John Roebling, it served as his prototype for the Brooklyn Bridge.

Throughout this area, you'll find steep cobblestoned streets, Germanic architecture, and stately churches. Restorations are taking place along Newport's Monmouth Street, at Covington's Old Town Plaza, and most notably at the thirty-block area of West Covington known as Main Strasse Village. The water tower there contains one of the two American-made animated clocks in the world, with twenty-one figures that perform the story of the Pied Piper of Hamelin. In Newport, the George Wiedemann Brewing Company is the only operating brewery in Kentucky. The Cathedral Basilica of the Assumption in Covington was built in 1901 of French Gothic design, patterned after Notre Dame, and has one of the largest stained glass windows in the world and four large paintings by Frank Duveneck. And one of the most unusual museums you'll find anywhere is the Vent Haven Museum in Fort Mitchell. Its subject is ventriloquy, with more than 500 ventriloquist dummies and other memorabilia of the art.

In the center of this mixture of urban, suburban, and rural settings, we found one of the safest communities in Kentucky. To be specific, in our comparison year of 1980 Fort Thomas was the second safest community in Kentucky with a population of 10,000 or more. Only Glasgow was safer and Glasgow sits in the middle of countryside, not a major metropolitan area. That piqued our interest and we decided to see what Fort Thomas was like.

FORT THOMAS

POPULATION: 15,924
NO. OF CRIMES: 241
CRIME RATE: 1,513.4 per 100,000

What we found when we looked into Fort Thomas was a peaceful residential community with a small-town atmosphere, hugging the hills and bluffs on the southern side of the Ohio River.

With the completion of Interstate 471 and its bridge into Ohio, Fort Thomas is just five minutes away from downtown Cincinnati. That makes it a more convenient downtown commute than nearly any of the Ohio suburbs. Interstate 275 also provides direct access westward to the Greater Cincinnati International Airport in Boone County, Kentucky.

The community of Fort Thomas was incorporated in 1867 as the District of Highlands. It took its present name in 1914. The military fort in town was established in 1887 and named for a prominent Union general. It is now a Veterans Administration nursing home and parts of the former military reservation have been turned into city parklands and recreational areas.

Fort Thomas has a few local businesses to meet your day-to-day shopping needs, but you will probably also want to patronize the Newport Shopping Center located right down Grand Avenue, the Newport Mall in downtown

CINCINNATI AREA Crime Chart

	Crime Rate	Murder	Rape	Robbery	Aggravated Assault	Burglary	Larceny —Theft	Motor Vehicle Theft
United States								
U.S. Total	5,899.9	10.2	36.4	243.5	290.6	1,668.2	3,156.3	494.6
U.S. Metropolitan Areas	6,757.6	11.5	43.4	319.0	328.3	1,911.8	3,534.9	608.8
U.S. Rural Areas	2,290.4	7.5	15.5	22.5	136.9	830.2	1,143.9	133.9
Regional Crime Center								
Cincinnati	8,609.7	12.5	92.1	440.1	481.1	2,311.8	4,822.1	450.0
Safe Places								
Fort Thomas, Ky.	1,513.4	0	6.3	6.3	69.1	458.4	935.7	37.7
Montgomery, Ohio	2,372.4	0	13.3	26.5	26.5	490.4	1,756.1	59.6

Newport, and the department stores of downtown Cincinnati. The nearest major medical facilities are right in Fort Thomas, with 300-bed St. Luke Hospital of Campbell County.

At the time of our visit (October 1982), residents were preparing to enjoy cable TV, with a 55-channel capacity and five premium services being offered. The school system was introducing children in grades 4, 5, and 6 to the joys and mysteries of Apple computers. The planning commission had rezoned most of the undeveloped lands overlooking the Ohio River, with new limits of one housing unit per acre rather than the 4½ units per acre previously allowed. We learned belatedly that the Snappy Tomato had opened in town, offering New York pizza and hoagies right here in River City. And the recreation department announced the completion of a new picnic shelter in Tower Park ("The demand for shelters is tremendous," the director noted). We were impressed with one of the department's summer playground programs—a program of day camp activities for sixty mentally or physically handicapped children from throughout the county.

From the town's public works department came a tip that we immediately noted and which we trust will be equally useful to others who live in countrified areas: "The best way to handle the problem of dogs and raccoons in your garbage cans is to saturate a rag in household ammonia and attach it to your lid."

Fort Thomas' sixteen fire fighters include four who are state-trained paramedics, with two others in training. A new, modern 1,250-gallons-per-minute pumper may have arrived by the time you read this, replacing an old 1959 pumper.

The police department, at the time of our visit, had established intelligence networks with other police agencies in northern Kentucky and southern Ohio and was setting up several citizen programs—Neighborhood Watch and a program to coordinate all residential and business alarm systems. Chief Norman H. Hughes announced "a significant reduction in residential burglaries" in 1982, which is pretty impressive considering that the town's burglary rate was already below U.S. rural levels.

In our comparison year of 1980, there were no murders in Fort Thomas and the 241 crimes consisted of 1 rape, 1 robbery, 11 aggravated assaults, 73 burglaries, 149 larceny-thefts, and 6 motor vehicle thefts. This placed Fort Thomas below U.S. rural crime rates in all categories.

In 1981, there was a slight increase to 278 crimes. There were no murders or rapes that year, but the number of larceny-thefts increased to slightly above U.S. rural levels.

For real estate information, we talked with Chet Mason of Schoepf-Mason, Inc. He told us that a few houses can be found in the $25,000 to $40,000 range, but most will be found between $45,000 and $80,000. A few more houses, again, will be found selling at prices up to $200,000. Fort Thomas doesn't have very many two-family homes, but those that do exist sell between $60,000 and $100,000.

For $60,000, he could offer us a 2-story brick house with approximately 1,000 square feet of living area. It sat on a 50 × 136 lot with woods in back. It had a living room, dining room, kitchen, 3 bedrooms, 1 bath upstairs, and a full basement with a commode and shower.

For $89,000, you could get a nice-looking 2-story brick and shingle house on a large wooded lot, with natural woodwork, large porches, and 4 or 5 bedrooms but only 1 bath.

The most expensive listing in town was a brick English Tudor at $190,000. It had 3 to 5 bedrooms, depending on how you used the rooms, and 3 full baths. The many attractions of this house included a charming foyer, beautiful family room, living room with fireplace and built-in bookshelves, custom drapes, and solid oak floors. It had a 2-car built-in garage and a full basement.

A secluded and peaceful location on the banks of the Ohio, small-town friendliness, and yet a mere five minutes away from downtown Cincinnati—we think you'll find that as enticing a combination as we did. It's a combination only Fort Thomas can offer and it's well worth your consideration if you are planning a move to this metropolitan area.

BLUEGRASS REGION

Man O' War . . . Citation . . . Native Dancer . . . The list could go on and on, illustrating why this central portion of Kentucky has come to be known as the Kingdom of the Horse. They are the famous sons of this century, just as Daniel Boone, Abraham Lincoln, Jefferson Davis, and Henry Clay were the region's claim to fame in previous centuries.

Kentucky's Bluegrass region. Technically, Bluegrass country is an extensive area that covers as much of Tennessee as of Kentucky and it is almost as famous for its Tennessee walking horses as it is for its Kentucky thoroughbreds. But in the public mind, Bluegrass country is the rolling land surrounding Lexington, Kentucky, the horse breeding capital of America.

Lexington has had its share of Kentucky history. Abraham Lincoln used to come calling on a Miss Mary Todd of Lexington and that old brick home where she grew up and was courted still stands on Main Street. Among the students at Transylvania College, the oldest institution of high learning west of the Appalachians, was Jefferson Davis, the Confederate president during the War Between the States. Other students who made their mark on history included Stephen F. Austin, the Father of Texas, Vice President John C. Breckenridge, and Gen. Albert Sidney Johnston. The public is invited to Ashland, home of Henry Clay, where he entertained Lafayette, Daniel Webster, and President Martin Van Buren, and to Hopemont, home of Gen. John Hunt Morgan, the Thunderbolt of the Confederacy.

But Lexington is very much a modern city, too, the home today of such nationally recognized firms as IBM and General Electric and Dixie Cup—in all, more than fifty major industries and concerns. It is an educational center, too, with the University of Kentucky and Transylvania College among its institutions. And it is the world's tobacco and horse capital.

Surrounding Lexington are the famous, beautiful horse farms with their miles of fences and their big houses with stately columns. There are more than 300 of these horse farms surrounding Lexington, some of them open to the public at no charge. You can visit their barns, watch the young colts at play, view the horse cemeteries where their champions are buried. The most famous product of these farms is remembered with a statue by the noted sculptor Herbert Haseltine. It honors Man O' War, the "greatest race horse and leading money winner of his day." Winner of twenty of twenty-one starts, "Big Red" in retirement sired sixty-two stakes winners.

Adjoining Fayette County (Lexington) is the northernmost county of the Bluegrass region of Kentucky, Scott County. Gently rolling in the south, the county becomes hilly and broken in the north. A section of Interstate 75 passing through the county was selected as one of the most beautiful such stretches in America for two consecutive years. Names of hamlets such as Great Crossing and Stamping Ground recall the herds of buffalo that once passed through this land; Stamping Ground got its name from the fact that herds of crowded buffalo would tread or stamp the earth, as those on the outside attempted to get inside and thus secure protection from the Indians.

There, in Scott County, is where we found our Safe Place for the Bluegrass region of Kentucky.

GEORGETOWN

POPULATION: 10,954
NO. OF CRIMES: 368
CRIME RATE: 3,359.5 per 100,000

Bourbon whiskey, which rivals race horses as Kentucky's most famous product, got its start here in 1789, at the still of a (would you believe it?) Baptist preacher. It is said that while he was seasoning white-oak staves to make barrels to hold sour mash, the staves caught on fire and burned to a deep char. It was discovered that the charred part of the stave, placed inside the barrel to reinforce its holding ability, removed foreign particles from the sour mash, changed its color, and mellowed the sharp taste. Thus was born the first bourbon whiskey and it remains an industry in Scott County today with the Schenley Distillery located at Stamping Ground.

Georgetown, the county seat, was named in honor of George Washington and grew up around Royal Spring, one of the greatest springs in Kentucky and at one time a mile long. It is a city of gracious antebellum and Greek revival homes and mansions, and a business district that has thirty-nine buildings (mostly Italianate and Renaissance revival in design) listed in the National Register of Historic Places. Their centerpiece is the Scott County Courthouse, a striking example of Second Empire style.

Georgetown is also a college town. Georgetown College is the second oldest college west of the Alleghenies (after Transylvania College in Lexington). The oldest permanent building on its campus is Giddings Hall, with its unusual columns of brick. It was built in 1840 by faculty and students with handmade bricks burned on the premises and is one of the finest examples of Greek revival architecture in the United States.

Local medical facilities include 45-bed John Graves Ford Memorial Hospital, two physicians' complexes, twenty-four-hour ambulance and emergency services, and four nursing homes. The county public school system consists of four elementary schools, a middle school, and a high school, with a Montessori school also located in Georgetown. Shopping facilities are ample for day-to-day needs in Georgetown, with Lexington's malls just 10 miles to the south. A special local attraction is the Georgetown Antique Mall, which, with more than seventy-five dealers, is the largest in the state.

In our comparison year of 1980, Georgetown had no murders or rapes and its crimes consisted of 1 robbery, 7 aggravated assaults, 78 burglaries, 267 larceny-thefts, and 15 motor vehicle thefts. This placed Georgetown below U.S. rural crime rates in all categories except larceny-theft.

In the following year, the overall crime rate decreased to 1,442.4 per 100,000 population—a drop of more than 50 percent.

For information on housing costs, we talked with Ron Hastings, of Smith Realty Group in Georgetown. He told us that the overall price range is all the way from $15,000 to $200,000.

Homes selling for $15,000 or $16,000 are older homes in older neighborhoods —"something that is repairable but needs it."

The best-selling range, he told us, is from $40,000 to $60,000. For $50,000 to $60,000, you can get a modern ranch with 3 bedrooms, 1½ baths, living room, and kitchen, with a 1-car garage, sitting on ¼ to ½ acre.

KENTUCKY BLUEGRASS REGION Crime Chart

	Crime Rate	Murder	Rape	Robbery	Aggravated Assault	Burglary	Larceny —Theft	Motor Vehicle Theft
United States								
U.S. Total	5,899.9	10.2	36.4	243.5	290.6	1,668.2	3,156.3	494.6
U.S. Metropolitan Areas	6,757.6	11.5	43.4	319.0	328.3	1,911.8	3,534.9	608.8
U.S. Rural Areas	2,290.4	7.5	15.5	22.5	136.9	830.2	1,143.9	133.9
Regional Crime Center								
Lexington	7,664.9	5.4	35.0	172.8	269.8	1,977.0	4,798.1	406.7
Safe Place								
Georgetown	3,359.5	0	0	9.1	63.9	712.1	2,437.5	136.9

Executive homes are in the top range of $180,000 to $200,000. These are usually either colonials or very contemporary houses with solar heat. They would have 4 or 5 bedrooms, 2½ baths, and a family room, living room, dining room, eat-in kitchen, and (sometimes) a full basement. These houses would have a 2-car garage and sit on 1 to 5 acres of land.

Building lots in town range from $10,000 to $12,000 in price for 1 acre. Areas out of town are now zoned for a minimum of 5 acres, to keep the farmlands from being overdeveloped. Such a 5-acre tract will cost you $15,000 to $20,000.

Georgetown has no condominiums or town houses, though a town house complex is in the planning stage. Ron told us that of the new residents in town, perhaps 40 percent work in Georgetown or Scott County (there are two small industrial parks in town, as well as local businesses) and 60 percent work in Lexington.

The beautiful campus of Georgetown College, the antebellum farmhouses, the stately old homes lining Main Street, and the lush, rolling pastures of the horse farms with their miles of painted fences—this is the magnificent setting that can be your Safe Place in the Bluegrass region of Kentucky.

Where to get further information:

State

Department of Tourism, Capitol Plaza Tower, Frankfort, KY 40601. Telephone 800/626-8000 from outside the state or 800/372-2961 from within Kentucky.

Regional

Northern Kentucky: Northern Kentucky Convention and Visitors Bureau, 605 Philadelphia Street, Main Strasse Village, Covington, KY 41011.

Bluegrass Region: Lexington Convention and Tourist Bureau, 421 N. Broadway, Lexington, KY 40508.

Local

Fort Thomas: Municipal News is a booklet prepared for residents by the City of Fort Thomas, 130 N. Fort Thomas Avenue, Fort Thomas, KY 41075. *Fort Thomas Living* is published monthly ($10 per year) by Community Publications, Inc., 3666 Paxton, Cincinnati, OH 45208.

Georgetown: The Georgetown-Scott County Chamber of Commerce, 114 N. Broadway, Georgetown, KY 40324, has a brochure on the town, another on the town's big spring, and a map. An informative booklet is also available for $3.00.

Maine

Should we be surprised that the residents of Maine have a reputation as sturdy individualists? How else could they survive in this far-northern land of long and harsh winters? Those with tenacity accept the limitations imposed by geography and climate and, indeed, learn to look upon them as blessings; the less tenacious head south or return there.

It's not all that bad, of course, but our point is that there's a vast difference between living in Maine year round and popping in during the short but glorious summer. We've warned elsewhere: Before you pull up stakes and move to a new part of the country, spend some time there during whatever season offers the most extreme living conditions. And in Maine, that's the winter.

You may very well find the weather and the relative isolation of the state to be invigorating, not forbidding. Not everyone thrives in eternal summer. One of the most interesting trends of recent years has been the return to the countryside, among all age groups. Maine is one of the places they've been coming to, giving rise to a mini-industry of homesteading books and magazines.

You'd be forgiven if you assumed that Maine's nickname was the Lobster State, but it isn't. This is the Pine Tree State and a drive anywhere within its borders will demonstrate the appropriateness of that designation. Forests cover 85 percent of the state and lumber, pulp, and paper operations are its main industries. Machine tools and other metal products are also manufactured here, as well as woolens and woven cotton goods, boots and shoes, and other leather goods. Agriculturally, Maine is one of the three major potato-growing states and it's also well known for its blueberries. And naturally there's the fishing industry. Lobsters are the most valuable catch among the fish and shellfish and only California brings in more herring.

Tourism is yet another important industry. The state's 2,500 lakes are a popular destination and wilderness lovers head for the northern woods and rivers, including Baxter State Park with its 5,267-foot Mount Katahdin. But two thirds of the tourist dollars are spent along the fabled coast. As the crow flies, that Maine coast stretches 230 miles. The actual shoreline is more like 3,500 miles long, which gives you some indication of the wild profusion of inlets, bays, and capes. One of the most popular resorts is Acadia National Park, where granite mountains and deep-blue seas produce a thunderous symphony as frothy waves pound against jagged cliffs.

MAINE Crime Chart

	Crime Rate	Murder	Rape	Robbery	Aggravated Assault	Burglary	Larceny —Theft	Motor Vehicle Theft
United States								
U.S. Total	5,899.9	10.2	36.4	243.5	290.6	1,668.2	3,156.3	494.6
U.S. Metropolitan Areas	6,757.6	11.5	43.4	319.0	328.3	1,911.8	3,534.9	608.8
U.S. Rural Areas	2,290.4	7.5	15.5	22.5	136.9	830.2	1,143.9	133.9
Regional Crime Center								
Portland	11,533.9	4.9	37.4	191.6	609.0	3,205.8	6,803.1	682.1
Safe Places								
Kennebunk	3,183.3	0	0	16.1	64.3	948.6	1,961.4	192.9
Rockport	2,891.6	0	0	0	120.5	441.8	2,168.7	160.6

Water sports dominate the summer scene—swimming at the beach resorts, windjammer cruises, deep-sea and surf fishing along the coast, canoeing and freshwater fishing inland. The autumn brings foliage tours and agricultural fairs. Skiing is king of the winter sports, but there's also plenty of snowshoeing, ice fishing, skating, downhill sledding, snowmobiling, and snow camping. Ice boats are becoming increasingly visible on the lakes and dog sledding is enjoying a revival of popularity.

Unfortunately, crime is no stranger to this outdoors-oriented outpost. Portland, the major city, has an overall crime rate that is higher than New York City's, though it is weighted more toward property crime. Even the small towns and cities surprised us; most of them, including some of the prettiest and most popular ones, had too much crime to qualify as Safe Places. Nevertheless, we did find some tantalizing havens throughout the state.

Someday, we hope to have more time to explore Maine's inland regions and their low-crime communities. For now we must concentrate on two of the most popular areas: the state's lower coast and its midcoast. Our havens in those two areas are visual delights and prime examples of Down East living at its best.

KENNEBUNK

POPULATION: 6,220
NO. OF CRIMES: 198
CRIME RATE: 3,183.3 per 100,000

After the Civil War, Kennebunk and Kennebunkport became popular summer resorts for well-to-do residents of Boston and other congested cities. Here they could enjoy the leisurely pleasures of "surf-bathing," canoeing and boating on the Kennebunk and Mousam rivers, sailing on the ocean, clambakes on moonlit beaches, and picnics in the piny woods. There were special celebrations too, such as the 4th of July, the launching of ships at the shipyards, and the Lobster Boat and Canoe Club's annual river parade of decorated and illuminated boats.

Vacationers of that era would most likely take one of the seven trains leaving daily from Boston. Others would travel overnight by steamship to Portland, then catch a train in the opposite direction. Once at the Kennebunk station, stagecoaches would take them to their hotel or boarding house or to their own "cottage" by the sea. During these years, nearly forty hotels were built in the two towns.

Much of the architectural wealth of that era has been preserved for your enjoyment today. Kennebunk and its sister port town contain some of Maine's choicest examples of eighteenth- and nineteenth-century residential architecture —magnificent colonial, Federal, Greek Revival, and Victorian homes, many of them preserved in two national historic districts.

Among these architectural treasures in Kennebunk is the Storer House, built in 1758 and the home of Revolutionary General Joseph Storer. The Taylor-Barry House typifies the Federal period with its low-hipped roof, large double chimneys, and fan-shaped window over the front and side doorways. The Bourne Mansion is a square 3-story home with chimneys at each of its four corners. And the photographers' favorite is the Wedding Cake House, which gets its name from its icinglike carved lace-wood trim.

Today's tourists are most likely to arrive by automobile or first by air—the new Portland International Airport is thirty minutes away, Boston and its Logan International Airport just an hour and a half. They come not only from the entire northeastern United States, but from Canada as well. Residents of Montreal, Quebec, and Toronto find this a convenient and relaxing summer retreat.

It would be wrong, however, to think of Kennebunk as merely a resort. This is a year-round residential home to more than 6,000 people, with local manufacturing of plastics, engineering supplies, and electric components. Others commute to Sanford, Biddeford, even Portland. Still others retire in these beautiful surroundings.

As to crime, we were able to accept Kennebunk as a Safe Place but had to reject Kennebunkport. The port town's crime rate was double that of Kennebunk; its pattern of high property crime and low rates of crimes of violence is a familiar one for resort towns, where the tourist hordes bring not only dollars for the local economy but also an increase in burglaries, larceny-thefts, and auto vehicle thefts.

The reassuring fact is that Kennebunk has been able to buck the tide. It's not as heavily inundated with tourists as Kennebunkport but is still on the tourist trail. Property crime rates are above those for U.S. rural areas, but not by much. Violent crime is quite low. Also, we were able to get 1981 statistics before putting this book to press and they show that Kennebunk's 1981 crime rate actually went down from 1980 levels.

The low crime rate came as no surprise to Thomas J. Reagan III, of R. E. Marier Real Estate. Tom is a native of the area; after graduating from Kennebunk High School he went off to college but returned to live here.

Tom told us that real estate in the Kennebunks ranges from the high 40s (you'll get nothing more than a small cottage at this price) to $300,000–$400,000 for the choicest waterfront properties. He also had a very special Queen Anne Victorian, with 100 acres, selling for $350,000.

In the more modest 60s and 70s, however, you can expect to find a good 2-, 3-, or 4-bedroom home in a quiet Kennebunk neighborhood. At the time of our visit (November 1982), for example, $74,500 would get you a conveniently located town home, with a new roof and vinyl siding on the exterior, and fine interior design, woodwork, and moldings from a bygone era. The first floor has an entrance foyer, double parlors with sliding pocket doors, a dining room with butler's pantry, a modern kitchen with pantry, a utility room, a half bath, and front and rear stairways. Upstairs you will find 3 bedrooms and 1 bath, plus a large finished third-floor master bedroom with bath. Taxes on this property are $600 to $700.

There's a continuing demand for ranches in this price range, Tom told us, but not many are available. He was expecting a 2-bedroom ranch to go on the market soon, priced in the 70s.

New 4-bedroom, 2½-bath colonials start in the 80s and the better the location the higher the price.

At higher prices, we saw two listings that were particularly interesting:

• For $135,000: an attractive custom-built Garrison colonial located off historic Summer Street, with a 2-car garage and beautifully landscaped grounds. It has 5 bedrooms, 2½ baths, a den, a formal living room with fireplace, and a dining room. The family room features a fireplace, a patio entrance, and a rear stairway. Off the custom kitchen is a laundry-hobby room with ample built-in shelves and closets. Taxes are $1,400.

• And for $162,500: the Lyman-Kingsburg house in Kennebunk's historic district. This exquisite 14-room colonial has been tastefully restored, preserving many of the antique features. It has 8 bedrooms, 2½ baths, 7 fireplaces, and lots of unique features. And it's located on 2½ acres in Kennebunk's shipbuilding area, with frontage on the Kennebunk River!

Tom Reagan told us that some undeveloped land is still available. A decent lot that passes all local environmental requirements costs $10,000–$12,000 for 20,000 square feet; $15,000 to $17,000 will get you the same sized lot but with a better location. Two or 3 acres with river frontage or a river view will set you back $20,000 to $30,000.

Kennebunk also has a few condominium units—residential condos, not resort-type condos, Tom hastened to add. Most 2- and 3-bedroom units sell in the mid-to-upper 60s or the low 70s. A luxury development also has 2 bedroom units selling for $129,000. These are not town houses, but single-story ranches with a Cape design. They feature 2 bedrooms, 2 baths, a living room, a dining room, a den or family room, a kitchen, a concrete patio, and a 2-car garage.

Ironically, Kennebunk also has some condominiums priced in the 80s, but they are not selling as well as these luxury units or the lower-priced units.

Even though you are located near the ocean, winters bring plenty of snow this far north. Maine's Yankees have plenty of experience with snow, however, and it rarely causes a prolonged problem here—the snowplows work, they know how to use them, and there's no panic of the sort you'll encounter in border or more southern areas of the country. If you're like us and you dream of a white Christmas of the kind so beautifully depicted by Currier and Ives, then Kennebunk may be just the place for you to enjoy it.

ROCKPORT

POPULATION: 2,490
NO. OF CRIMES: 72
CRIME RATE: 2,891.6 per 100,000

One of our major disappointments in the Northeast was the discovery that crime in Camden, Maine, has risen too high for us to include it in this book. Otherwise the town remains the same as when we featured it in 1972's *Safe Places:* one of the most beautiful coastal villages to be found anywhere in the United States.

Our cutoff point, for overall crime rates in this volume, was 4,000 crimes per 100,000 population. In 1980 Camden had a crime rate, adjusted for its population, of 3,970.3—it squeaked by, barely, but the rate was uncomfortably high. When we got 1981 figures just before going to press, the crime rate had risen to 4,995.6. Clearly the trend is in the wrong direction.

Even so, we must point out that these figures represent mostly property crime. Not that property crime isn't serious; it's just not as serious as a crime against your body. Anyway, in 1980 Camden had 1 robbery and 6 aggravated assaults. In 1981 it had *no* crimes of violence. So if you can't tear yourself away from Camden—and we can't say that we'd blame you—just take all the necessary steps to protect your home, your automobile, and other property.

We have an even better suggestion: Live right next door in Rockport. Its residential areas and views are as lovely as Camden's and all it lacks is the varied businesses of its larger neighbor. But how lazy can you get? Those are just down the road, no more than a mile or two, and by moving into quieter Rockport you also move into a much safer neighborhood. Rockport's 1981 crime rate (2,146.2) actually represents a major drop from the 2,891.6 figure for 1980. And, like Camden, even that small amount of crime is almost entirely property crime. In 1980 there were 3 aggravated assaults, in 1981 no crimes of violence whatsoever.

"We are pleased," says Police Chief Forest Doucette, "that many more residents are placing their property on the property checklist when they are leaving for vacation or a few days. I do want to encourage this because of so many break-ins in the neighboring communities."

Like adjoining Camden, Rockport is situated in an area of Maine's midcoast where the mountains meet the sea. Like Camden, it has become a favorite haunt of artists and craftspersons and boasts a beautiful harbor. Its harbor is not as busy as Camden's, but it is increasing in popularity as both a home port and a place to drop anchor while touring the Maine coast. Here you'll find Rockport's most famous resident, André—an orphaned seal, now honorary harbormaster, who performs with his adopted trainer each afternoon during the summer.

Rising above the harbor are the white frames of handsome New England houses, situated on winding, hilly roads. A few businesses are clustered around the harbor, in the village, along with the centers of cultural life. The Rockport Opera House offers a year-round series of classical concerts, as well as summer presentations of Maine folk music and folklore. The Russell Avenue gallery of Maine Coast Artists has exhibits of paintings and sculpture, lectures, and classes. Another gallery is maintained by the Maine Photographic Workshop. Nearby is Vesper Hill Chapel, with its garden landscaped according to biblical text, and if you look closely you may see a herd of Belted Galloways—unusual beef cattle from Scotland—as you drive along Russell Avenue toward Camden.

In Camden, we had a talk with Joe Jaret of Jaret Real Estate. He moved to Camden about ten years ago and recalls having seen an article in which we listed Camden as one of our ten favorite Safe Places around the country. At that time, Joe told us, Camden-Rockport was a seasonal community. Now it has grown into a year-round community and the real estate market lasts throughout the year too.

Rockport offers a wide variety of housing in a wide price range, he added. Prices get higher the closer you get to the harbor and the village center.

Our favorite location in town was Mechanic Street, offering beautiful views as it winds above the north shore of the harbor. Naturally, that's one of the most expensive locations in town too. He happened to have a listing there: a house on the harbor side of the street, set amidst 2 acres of extensively landscaped grounds. It has 4 bedrooms, a living room and a family room each with fireplace, a large kitchen, a den and a sitting room with fireplace, as well as an efficiency apartment over the 2-car garage. You could have this distinctive property for between $500,000 and $600,000.

Not too many properties come onto the market in the village center area, Joe told us. There were three such listings this year, all with some view of the harbor, and each of them was priced between $110,000 and $145,000.

At the time of our visit (November 1982), a beautiful 3-story New England farmhouse was on the market. Of white frame construction with black shutters, it was located in the village on 1.3 acres, with 345 feet of frontage on Goose River and a view of the harbor. It is presently divided and used as three apartments—the owner's unit alone had 3 bedrooms, a living room, a dining room, a kitchen, and a sunporch—but could easily be converted to single-family use. With an attached shed and barn, the asking price was $134,500.

Outside the village was a much lower-priced ($46,000) farmhouse. Built around the turn of the century, it had been renovated in the 1940s and was in good condition. The house had 3 bedrooms, 1 bath, a living room, dining room, and kitchen. A 3-level barn was attached and it was situated on an acre of land.

Six condominium units are located right on the harbor. They offer 2 bedrooms, 2 baths, a living room, a dining room, a kitchen, a deck overlooking the harbor, and a single-car garage. Built in 1974, they didn't sell for years, and when they did, the highest price paid was $74,500. In 1982 one of these was resold for $145,000—a nice jump for 2½ years.

For a luxury development of condominium homes overlooking Penobscot Bay, look into Eastward on the Ocean. Built on a 62-acre estate with half a mile of shoreline, these will be individual homes built in clusters, protected by a gatehouse and full-time security. Their prices are in the $200,000–$400,000 range. Construction has just started and already there is considerable interest, Joe Jaret told us, from professionals, affluent retirees, even European buyers.

The mountains or the ocean? That's a hard decision for many of us to make. Here, in the shadow of Mount Battie and Mount Megunticook and on the shores of Penobscot Bay, you can enjoy both all year long. And then you can exclaim, with the poet Edna St. Vincent Millay, "More sea than land am I."

Where to get further information:

State

For a state highway map and a wide variety of tourist literature: Maine Publicity Bureau, Gateway Circle, Portland, ME 04102. Maine Vacation Center, 1268 Avenue of the Americas, New York, NY 10020. Maine State Development Office, 193 State Street, Augusta, ME 04333. Department of Conservation, Bureau of Forestry and/or Parks and Recreation, Augusta, ME 04333. InfoRoad USA, Centre Capitol Suite 2030, 1200 Avenue McGill College, Montreal, Quebec H3B4G7. For fishing regulations and license information: Department of Inland Fisheries and Wildlife, Information and Education Division, 284 State Street, Augusta, ME 04333. For a free private guide: *The Traveler,* P.O. Box 29, Bridgton, ME 04009. The monthly *Maine Real Estate Guide* is available ($2.00 single copy, $20 annual subscription) from Box 999, Andover, MA 01810.

Towns

Kennebunk: A wide variety of materials—including a fact sheet on the town, an area map, and the vacation guides *Discover Maine in the Kennebunks* and *Kennebunk-Kennebunkport-Wells Summer Guide*—is available from the Kennebunk-Kennebunkport Chamber of Commerce, 41 Main Street, Kennebunk, ME 04043.

Rockport: Many materials on the area are available from the Rockport-Camden-Lincolnville Chamber of Commerce, P.O. Box 246, Camden, ME 04843. When in Rockport, drop by the town offices at the corner of Main and Camden streets to get a street map (25¢) and the most recent annual town report. For a truly handsome sales prospectus, with breathtaking photographs of the Rockport-Camden area, write to Eastward on the Ocean, Box 445, Rockport, ME 04856.

Maryland

For a small state, Maryland has a surprisingly diverse terrain. Most of it is coastal plain, bounded by the Atlantic Ocean and the waters of Chesapeake Bay. As you travel west from Baltimore, the coastal plain rises to rolling Piedmont countryside and then quickly to the Blue Ridge Mountains and the Alleghenies west of them.

Everywhere throughout this short distance Maryland seems to be squeezed between other states. The geographically distinct area east of Chesapeake Bay is known as the Eastern Shore, but that peninsula is shared with Delaware and Virginia—thus its designation as Delmarva (Delaware-Maryland-Virginia). The state's western panhandle is so squeezed between West Virginia and Pennsylvania that at one point the Cumberland Narrows (Maryland's portion of land) is only 2 miles wide. Even the less-narrow band of mainland between Chesapeake Bay and the northward-headed stretch of the Potomac River was diluted when Maryland donated land for the District of Columbia to the young nation it had helped create.

The economy is as diverse as the terrain. Baltimore, with a population of more than 2 million in the metropolitan area, is the center of industry and commerce. It tends to be overshadowed, nevertheless, by the nearby presence of Washington. The federal government—along with science- and government-related research—is the economic mainstay of Prince Georges and Montgomery counties. Tobacco retains its colonial importance in the area south of Washington and Annapolis; tourism, agriculture, and seafood dominate the Eastern Shore and the west has livestock, orchards, and mining.

For our Safe Places in Maryland, we picked one of the most historic and aristocratic towns of the Eastern Shore and three suburbs of crime-ridden Washington, D.C.—actually, two suburbs and one exurb farther out in Montgomery County.

Baltimore's crime rate is almost as high as Washington's and we wanted to get at least one suburb there as well. In the limited time at our disposal, however, we were unsuccessful in this quest. In part, this was because Maryland crime statistics are not broken down very effectively by municipalities. And, in part, it was the result of Baltimore's crime problem overflowing to the surrounding suburbs.

The crime rate for Baltimore County, at 7,160.8 crimes per 100,000 population, was not that far below the city's crime rate of 9,964.8—and way above the 4,000 limit we set as the definition of a Safe Place. Corresponding rates were 5,900.3 for Howard County, 5,489.3 for Anne Arundel County, and even 4,240.5 for more rural Harford County.

This wouldn't have been fatal if we could have found small towns or suburbs within those counties that were safe. We had been able to do that in the Washington suburbs, but here, unfortunately, separate statistics were available for only a few individual communities and all of them had far too much crime.

Another time, perhaps. For now we do have four communities that will provide you with an excellent introduction to the bounteous pleasures of tiny Maryland.

EASTERN SHORE

In colonial times, Chesapeake Bay served to unify Maryland, since most of the larger settlements were along the Atlantic seaboard and most commerce was moved by boat. That changed, however, as population expanded westward and the railroad became the main engine of commerce and transportation. Now the bay served to isolate the Eastern Shore from the more populous part of the state to the west.

By the middle of the twentieth century, the difference between the two shores was pronounced. The Western Shore, dominated by Baltimore, was ethnically diverse and sustained economically by a wide range of industries. The Eastern Shore, in contrast, was still agriculturally based in its economy, provincial in its social outlook. H. L. Mencken, the Sage of Baltimore, bemoaned the Eastern Shore's "frankly peasant culture." More important to the business interests in the west was the fact that they had lost almost all of the Eastern Shore market to Wilmington and Philadelphia. Their solution was the majestic, 4.35-mile Chesapeake Bay Bridge, which opened as a link between the two shores on July 30, 1952.

In its three decades of operation, the bridge has certainly changed the Eastern Shore, yet not beyond recognition. By making it more accessible to the Baltimore and Washington metropolitan regions, the bridge served to broaden the Eastern Shore's economy beyond agriculture and seafood, into manufacturing, services, real estate, and tourism. That, in turn, helped to reverse the population decline of the Eastern Shore. Yet the bridge had surprisingly little impact in one of the areas where it was supposed to matter most. Today, as before, most of the seafood and nearly 90 percent of the Eastern Shore's poultry products still head north to markets in Wilmington, Philadelphia, and New York City. What the bridge *has* done, agriculturally, is to help revive vegetable farming on the

Eastern Shore, since fresh produce can now be moved quickly to Washington and Baltimore.

MARYLAND Crime Chart

	Crime Rate	Murder	Rape	Robbery	Aggravated Assault	Burglary	Larceny —Theft	Motor Vehicle Theft
United States								
U.S. Total	5,899.9	10.2	36.4	243.5	290.6	1,668.2	3,156.3	494.6
U.S. Metropolitan Areas	6,757.6	11.5	43.4	319.0	328.3	1,911.8	3,534.9	608.8
U.S. Rural Areas	2,290.4	7.5	15.5	22.5	136.9	830.2	1,143.9	133.9
Regional Crime Centers								
Baltimore	9,776.8	27.5	71.4	1,277.2	736.1	2,250.8	4,697.4	716.3
Salisbury	11,782.0	36.7	18.4	226.3	48.9	2,746.7	8,129.9	575.0
Washington, D.C.	10,022.8	31.5	69.1	1,400.6	509.4	2,560.0	4,890.8	561.7
Safe Places								
Glenarden	1,061.5	0	0	60.1	40.1	600.8	340.5	20.0
Oxford	400.0	0	0	0	0	133.3	266.7	0
Poolesville	2,382.3	0	0	0	29.4	941.2	1,323.5	88.2
Somerset	2,363.6	0	0	90.9	0	818.2	1,363.6	90.9

The changes since the bridge was built are most noticeable on the Atlantic coast. When cumbersome ferries moved traffic across the bay, Ocean City might have a population of 20,000 on a hot summer weekend. Today, post-bridge, it regularly attracts 250,000. Yet even here it wasn't just the bridge that was responsible. The broadening of U.S. 50 (the Ocean Gateway) and several decades of postwar affluence were also necessary to make regular weekend jaunts and second homes an integral part of the Washington–Baltimore–Eastern Shore scene.

As the Eastern Shore has changed, the desirability of "unspoiled" locations has increased accordingly. Which brings us to our magnificently unspoiled Safe Place on the Eastern Shore, historic Oxford.

OXFORD

POPULATION: 750
NO. OF CRIMES: 3
CRIME RATE: 400.0 per 100,000

In 1983, Oxford celebrated its 300th anniversary. In 1683 the colony's general assembly had designated it a port and appointed the first commissioners to govern it, making Oxford the oldest community on the Eastern Shore. Indeed, it existed as a town long before Baltimore and for a while was as important as Annapolis.

Except for the presence of automobiles, hardtop, and utility lines connecting

Oxford to the outside world, the twentieth century hardly protrudes. The predominant architectural styles reflect the eighteenth and nineteenth centuries and the entire town maintains that atmosphere to a splendid degree.

Oxford is almost entirely surrounded by water—Town Creek and the broad Tred Avon River near its junction with the even broader Choptank River. Present-day Oxford remains both a yachting and a boatbuilding center and its marine orientation is visible in such establishments as the Tred Avon Yacht Club, Mears Yacht Haven, Oxford Boatyard, Town Creek Marina, Cutts & Case Boatyard, Applegarth's Boatyard, Bates Marine Basin, and Pier Street Marina. Other than these, there are a couple of small grocery stores, a bank, some antique shops and gift shops, a few real estate offices—and the lovely homes. The fairest of the fair, in our estimation, were found facing the water on the Strand and along Jefferson and Truax streets.

We haven't forgotten the Robert Morris Inn. How could we! This magnificent structure was built prior to 1710 by ship's carpenters with wooden pegged paneling, ship's nails, and hand-hewn beams. In 1730 it was bought by an English trading company for use as the residence of Robert Morris, who represented their shipping interests in Oxford. This was the father of Robert Morris, Jr., who later moved to Philadelphia, became Washington's good friend, and went down in the history books as the financier of the Revolution.

Among the notable features inside the inn are the staircase leading to the guest rooms, an example of the enclosed type of the Elizabethan period, and the massive fireplace in the taproom. Four impressive murals in the dining room portray the plains of West Point, a Winnepeg Indian village, Natural Bridge of Virginia, and Boston Harbor. These were painted by an unknown French artist, and printed on a screw-type press using 1,600 woodcut blocks carved from orangewood.

The inn is not only an architectural delight, but a gastronomical tour de force as well. We were there for lunch—a luncheon more memorable than most dinners we've had in the pseudo-Continental restaurants springing up in every alley across America.

The fare was Eastern Shore at its best. A rich and flavorful crab cake was served hamburger-style on a bun with lettuce and tomato, accompanied by fresh tartar and cocktail sauces, French fries, and crisp, cold cole slaw. After washing that down with ale, we decided to sin all the way by devouring a generous slice of strawberry pie—large, luscious Eastern Shore strawberries resting in a bed of creamy but firm custard. We justified our indulgence by noting that this was, after all, lunch. We could work it all off by taking a walking tour of Oxford, and by fasting at dinnertime. (Ah, but that's so hard to do on the Eastern Shore. Wouldn't you know, dinnertime found us right in the vicinity of this great seafood house . . .)

The walking tour of old Oxford was a necessity after that lunch, at any rate, and among the old homes we passed was the Academy House on Morris Street, built in 1848 to serve as officers' quarters for the Maryland Military Academy—

the nation's first military academy. Other interesting houses in town include the Barnaby House, with its corner fireplace and an unusually lovely handmade staircase, the Grapevine House, whose vines were brought from the Isle of Jersey in 1810 by a sea captain, and Byberry, which was built sometime before 1695. There's also a replica of the first customs house in the United States, and the Tred Avon Ferry that connects Oxford and Bellevue. Started in 1760, it is believed to be the oldest continually operated ferry in the United States that runs "free"—that is, not attached to a cable.

Annual events in Oxford include a three-day regatta each August, sponsored jointly by the Tred Avon Yacht Club and the Chesapeake Bay Yacht Club of Easton. The third annual International Oxford Triathlon, held in June of 1983, consisted of a 2.4–statute mile swim course, a 20-mile running course, and a 50-mile bike course.

Crime is hardly any problem in this peaceful hamlet. In our comparison year of 1980, there were just 3 crimes—1 burglary and 2 larceny-thefts. Oxford's crime rate was below U.S. rural crime rates in all categories.

Because of its desirability, you'll find that real estate costs are higher in Oxford than in most of the Eastern Shore. The least expensive homes in the town proper are off the water. Even there you'll be set back a minimum of $80,000 or $90,000 and can expect to invest another tidy sum in renovation. An attractive home in good shape will cost at least $150,000 to $200,000 and one of those lovely homes we saw with water frontage will cost $295,000 or more.

"Everyone tells me, 'I want a little shack on the water.' I always tell them the shacks are gone."

Our conversation was with Mary Hanks, the resident manager in Oxford for Freeman & Kagen, Inc. She wasn't surprised by our interest in her town. *Newsweek* once listed it as one of the ten nicest places to live, she recalled, and *Town & Country* has had several articles on Talbot County. "It's sort of a Shangri-la. I've lived here thirty years and I'm very much in love with Oxford."

Noting the interesting and friendly people who live here, Mary mentioned her friends John and Lucille Wallop. Both are noted authors, but you may be most familiar with his *The Year the Yankees Lost the Pennant,* which became the Broadway hit *Damn Yankees.*

One of the best buys in recent months, Mary told us, was a 3-story Victorian that sold for $90,000. It had 7 bedrooms and 3 baths, one on each floor—rather unusual since Victorians don't often have that many baths. Of course, the new owners will have to spend a bundle on renovation, which is why they got it at that price.

On the market in the same price range was a double house. More accurately, each *side* of this double house was in the same price range—$95,000 recently reduced to $85,000. Like the Victorian, this was also on the land side of Morris Street, and each unit had a living room, dining room, kitchen, and powder room downstairs, with 3 bedrooms and 1 bath upstairs. These were fine for weekend use, Mary thought, but probably would be too small for most people as full-time residences.

Waterfront properties with names like "The Lighthouse" and "Tred Haven" have been selling for $425,000. A recent sale on the river side of Morris Street was for just $295,000, however—"a good price." That's because of its smaller town-sized lot, but the house itself had some interesting features. One was a huge keeping room (family room, in today's parlance) that could house a party for one hundred guests. Another was its fine master bedroom with a porch overlooking the river.

We did notice too, in the Easton newspaper, an advertisement for town house condominiums in Oxford. For $95,000 you could get 4 bedrooms, fireplaces, a screened porch, and a patio.

If your interests are water-oriented, and your aesthetic preferences are traditional, Oxford may be just what you've been looking for. Washington and Baltimore are each just 75 miles to the west, the Atlantic surf is the exact same distance to the east, and Chesapeake Bay is—at most—a couple of city blocks away. That makes it an ideal site for a second home or a retirement home or just plain *home* if you can bring your work with you.

Now embarking on its fourth century, Oxford has plenty of experience at making you feel at home. Enjoy the best of its first three centuries—and all the conveniences of today.

WASHINGTON, D.C., AREA

Persons contemplating a move to the Washington, D.C., area have a choice of fine suburbs in both Maryland and Virginia. Within Maryland, the two suburban counties are Montgomery and Prince Georges. Montgomery is the more upscale of the two, with such established prestige suburbs as Bethesda and Chevy Chase, while Prince Georges, in general, has newer and less expensive suburbs.

Many of our remarks in our section on northern Virginia (pages 402–405) apply to these Maryland suburbs as well. Here, too, there was a rush to the suburbs in the fifties and sixties. And here, too, the growth of the federal government in the sixties and afterward led to the establishment of numerous government agencies throughout the Maryland countryside.

Prince Georges County has its share of federal offices, among them the U.S. Census Bureau, Federal Records Center, Defense Mapping Agency (Oceanographic Office), Federal Communications Center, National Agricultural Research Center, Goddard Space Flight Center, and the Air Research and Development Command at Andrews Air Force Base.

The close-in portion of Montgomery County is home to such agencies as the National Institutes of Health, National Library of Medicine, National Naval Medical Center, Walter Reed Army Medical Center, and Defense Mapping Agency (Topographic Center and Reproduction Plant). And as the interstate system made the outer reaches of Montgomery County more accessible, other government departments moved farther out, among them the U.S. Department of Energy, National Bureau of Standards, and U.S. Treasury Department Laboratory.

Crime is a matter of great concern anywhere in the Washington area. Its center, of course, is Washington itself, with a rate of 10,022.8 crimes per 100,000 population. On a countrywide basis, Prince Georges has a higher crime rate (7,870.2) than Montgomery (5,482.3). Yet we were able to find individual communities with lower crime rates in Prince Georges County than in Montgomery County.

Within Prince Georges County, there was a great variation in crime rates between the numerous municipalities. High-crime centers included Laurel (9,700.1), Bladensburg (10,102.7), and Cottage City (12,834.2). When broken down by individual categories as well as the overall crime rate, our Safe Place of Glenarden was the safest community in the county—and the safest of all the Washington suburbs for which separate crime statistics are reported. Only Capitol Heights had a lower overall crime rate, but the robbery rate was twice as high there as in Glenarden.

In Montgomery County, a complicating factor was the lack of separate statistics for most of the communities. Most rely on protection from the county police, so that their statistics are all lumped together. There were exceptions, however, communities that are incorporated and maintain their own crime statistics. In some of these, the overall crime rate was higher than in Washington itself—Kensington, for example, with a rate of 14,444.4 compared to Washington's 10,022.8. Our two Safe Places in Montgomery County, close-in Somerset and farther-out Poolesville, were the two safest communities in the county reporting separate statistics.

All three of these communities are quite different from each other. Between them, there should be an excellent place for you within commuting distance of the nation's capital.

GLENARDEN

POPULATION: 4,993
NO. OF CRIMES: 53
CRIME RATE: 1,061.5 per 100,000

Around the turn of the century, a white plantation owner in Prince Georges County divided his land among several black people who lived and worked in the area. That was the beginning of the Glenarden neighborhood, but for decades it remained an impoverished rural community lacking town water, gas, electricity, or sewage facilities, not to mention such luxuries as sidewalks, paved streets, and public transportation.

By 1939 the Glenarden Civic Association had its fill of unanswered pleas for assistance and decided what the solution was: "Let's do it ourselves!" And they did. Under the leadership of W. H. Swann, they successfully petitioned the state legislature for incorporation and became the third all-black community chartered in Maryland.

For twenty-eight years, beginning in 1941, Mayor James R. Cousins, Jr., was "Mr. Glenarden." Under his leadership, Glenarden was transformed from a rural slum to a relatively affluent Negro suburb. Water and sewage systems were installed, a town hall was built through public donations and a bank loan, and Glenarden became the first city in Prince Georges County to receive an urban renewal grant from the federal government. It was used to renovate and modernize the community's Old Town area.

With his long period of service, Cousins became the dean of Maryland mayors and was the first black to be elected president of the Prince Georges County Municipal Association.

"We are people who are proud," Cousins once told the delegates to the county's constitutional convention. "If we need something done, we do it ourselves.

"We got hard surface roads through our own efforts . . .

"We sold bonds and built our municipal center, and the people of Glenarden are enjoying it now. It was built as our own achievement.

"We feel as a town we are a credit to Prince Georges County."

After World War II, the town began to grow when returning black GIs settled there. A series of annexations provided room for expansion and the income and educational levels of the residents continued to rise. More and more college-educated technicians and professionals moved to Glenarden and they wanted to modernize town government. In 1969, after twenty-eight years as mayor, Cousins was finally ousted by Decatur W. Trotter. Two thirds of the town's voters turned out despite rain and snow and the vote was narrow. The hard-fought campaign was typical of the community involvement and vigorous politics for which Glenarden has become noted in the Washington area.

"Municipalities are the answer to our problems," the new mayor told his constituents.

"Cleveland, Philadelphia, and New York are plagued with money problems," Trotter noted. "They are approaching bankruptcy because there are no more areas to tax to carry on the functions of government. If these areas were divided into smaller municipalities, responsible for recreation, police protection, water and sewage services, etc., the cost of government would not be as high as it is today."

Mayor Trotter added that he wouldn't mind seeing some white people moving into Glenarden.

"We want to open up," he said. "We don't care what color they are. We think we've got a good thing going."

Glenarden has continued to grow and prosper and when we visited the town in October 1982 we found a suburban community of attractive middle-class neighborhoods, with modern facilities at the Glenarden Municipal Center and the Martin Luther King Recreation Center. We met Glenarden's current mayor, Herbert Jackson, Sr., who told us of the town's history and gave us copies of *The Glenarden Guardian,* a bimonthly town publication full of news about town services and community activities.

The municipal center is used for much more than governmental activities. Its Gold Room is rented out for meetings, receptions, banquets, cocktail parties, cabarets, and proms. Community affairs include Halloween and Christmas parties, a Mardi Gras ball in February, and an annual talent show. Glenarden's library is another busy center of community life, with an especially active schedule of programs in February centered on black history month.

In addition to town-sponsored activities, the county's parks and recreation department also sponsors programs in Glenarden. Be sure to pick up their current program guide at the library. In the fall 1982 guide, for example, we found listings for children's classes in arts and crafts, preschool play, Civil Air Patrol, and ballet, tap, and modern dance. Teen and adult activities included a beauty and poise club, bowling night, drill team, beginning karate, men's fitness, slimnastics, tennis, woodcrafts, volleyball, and modern, jazz, and African dance. There were also recreational game programs in backgammon, pool, bid whist, and checkers.

As we mentioned in our introduction to the Washington area, Glenarden is about the safest community in the region. In our comparison year of 1980, there were just 53 crimes—no murders or rapes, 3 robberies, 2 aggravated assaults, 30 burglaries, 17 larceny-thefts, and 1 motor vehicle theft. That placed Glenarden below U.S. rural crime rates in all categories except robbery. Even in that category—the category in which Washington, D.C., exports its crime most pervasively—Glenarden was below U.S. metropolitan levels.

Obviously, a good part of the reason for this low crime rate in the midst of a sea of crime is the nature of the community itself—the heavy involvement of Glenarden's residents in what goes on within their town. Another reason can be found in the dedication of police officers like Sgt. Clyde Walker, who had been named police officer of the year before our visit. Since 1977 Sergeant Walker has given the youth of Glenarden his special attention.

"I have the opportunity to help people and to be of service to people," Walker said in accepting his award. "I enjoy it [being a policeman] especially when I can prevent a kid from going to jail, or when someone says 'thanks,' or when I ride down the street and the kids mob my car because they are glad to see me. This is why I joined the force."

We got information on the cost of Glenarden real estate from Betty Garvey, of Sterling Properties, Inc., in Camp Springs. She told us that homes are available in Glenarden in a wide price range, from the low 50s up to $100,000.

In the 50s, 60s, and 70s, the homes are usually smaller and twenty-five to thirty years old. Very nice newer homes will be found in the 80s and 90s. Betty mentioned a new all-brick rambler that had recently sold for $92,000. It had 5 bedrooms, 3 full baths, a rec room downstairs, fireplace, dining area, and eat-in kitchen.

Almost all lots in Glenarden are 6,000 to 7,000 square feet in size, although some of the larger homes built in recent years may have lots up to 10,000 square feet in area. Betty told us that a 6,000- to 7,000-square-foot "finished lot"—meaning it is on a surfaced street, with water and sewage connections, ready for building—will cost $10,000 to $12,000.

If you move to Glenarden, you'll also find the location an asset. The George Palmer Highway (Route 704) speeds traffic toward downtown Washington, and you are right inside Interstate 495, the Capital Beltway, which provides access to the entire metropolitan area. Landover Mall, a major shopping center, is at the southeast edge of town.

With its low crime, strong civic pride, and accessible location, Glenarden offers you suburban living that matches convenience with a friendly hometown flavor. It's unique and knows it and is well worth your consideration.

SOMERSET

POPULATION: 1,100
NO. OF CRIMES: 26
CRIME RATE: 2,363.6 per 100,000

Montgomery County used to call itself the bedroom of Washington. The phrase sounds rather quaint today, with bedroom communities surrounding Washington in all directions, but in the thirties and forties it made sense. Two of the larger Montgomery County suburbs in particular—Chevy Chase and Bethesda—became *the* prestige addresses during those decades for Washington's top-level bureaucrats, association executives, and politicians.

Working in Montgomery County's favor during the suburban era was the fact that it had remained virtually undeveloped and unspoiled in previous decades. This was just pleasant farmland, reaching westward to the Blue Ridge foothills. The Chesapeake and Ohio Canal that was going to open up the West never got farther than Cumberland; there was no railroad until 1873. The War Between the States and the Industrial Revolution both seemed to pass by Montgomery County without having any noticeable impact.

Bethesda and Chevy Chase remain two of the most pleasant suburbs of Washington today. Age has given them a refinement and grace that you just don't find in a new tract development. Many of these areas *were* new developments at one time, of course, but today that is obscured by the lush vegetation and foliage that has grown up everywhere, by the varying architectural styles (most of them traditional) that have won favor over the years and that now offer a diversity lacking in the newer suburbs, and by the permanence suggested by old brick, stone, and ivy.

Somerset is one of those gracefully aging neighborhoods. It's a tiny neighborhood by today's standards, tucked in between River Road, Little Falls Parkway, the Chevy Chase Country Club, and the Friendship Heights section of Chevy Chase. It's entirely residential, though you are within walking distance of Saks Fifth Avenue, Brooks Brothers, and other fine stores on Wisconsin Avenue. Somerset enjoys a village atmosphere, though a nearby Metrobus terminal places downtown Washington within quick and convenient reach.

While Montgomery County has a countywide system of public schools rather than separate systems for each community, Somerset is fortunate in having an elementary school within its town boundaries. After completing sixth grade at Somerset Elementary School, students attend Westland Intermediate School and Bethesda-Chevy Chase High School.

A stimulating aspect of the Somerset school is its international composition. Parents of many of the students are staff members of foreign embassies and international organizations. In one recent year alone, some of the languages spoken by Somerset students included Chinese, French, German, Hebrew, Hungarian, Italian, Korean, Persian, Portuguese, Russian, Spanish, Swahili, and Swedish. The customs, music, art, food, and traditions of these students are used to enhance the curriculum and learning experiences of all the students.

Montgomery County parents, themselves highly educated, place great emphasis on achievement in their schools. In 1980 Montgomery County had almost three times more Merit Scholarship semifinalists than the national average—and more, in actual numbers, than in all the other Maryland public school systems combined.

Another test, this time of the lower grades, resulted in Montgomery students again having the best performance of any county in Maryland. The State Accountability Program tabulated 216 scores in grades 3, 5, and 7. Montgomery County's average was highest in 209, or 97 percent, of these scores.

As we've previously noted, Montgomery County's record on crime is more mixed. On a county-by-county basis, it has a higher crime rate than Fairfax County, Virginia, but is lower than Virginia's Arlington County or Prince Georges County in Maryland.

Separate statistics are not available for most of the communities and neighborhoods, since they are served by a county police force and their statistics are all lumped together. Somerset, however, was incorporated as a town in 1906 and *does* maintain its own statistics. They show that in our comparison year of 1980, there were only 26 crimes—no murders, rapes, or aggravated assaults, 1 robbery, 9 burglaries, 15 larceny-thefts, and 1 motor vehicle theft. This placed Somerset below U.S. rural crime rates in all categories except robbery and larceny-theft and the one incidence of robbery created a statistical aberration because of the town's small population. More remarkable is the fact that this affluent suburb, located less than a mile outside the District of Columbia boundary, could have a lower-than-rural rate of residential burglaries.

At Chris Coile, Inc., the Merrill Lynch Realty affiliate in Bethesda, Marjorie Rosner told us of two listings in Somerset. Both were in the same price range.

For $187,500, you could get a twenty-seven-year-old rambler with a brick and aluminum exterior. It had a living room, kitchen, formal dining room, entrance foyer, 3 bedrooms, and 2 baths on the main floor, with another bedroom and bath on the basement level. Taxes were $2,767 and the lot backs up to town parkland.

For $184,500, a New England-style stone and clapboard colonial was also available. It was forty-seven years old but was remodeled just two years ago. The first floor had a living room, dining room, kitchen, and bath, with 2 bedrooms and 1 bath upstairs. Taxes were $2,158.

While those were the only two houses on the market at the time of our visit, a number of houses had been sold in recent months. Jeanne Dorsett, relocation director of Allied Realty in Chevy Chase, was kind enough to review them with us. The twenty-two houses ranged in price from $95,000 to $349,950. The two houses at the bottom of the list ($95,000 and $122,500) were way below the norm. There were eight houses in the $154,000–$175,000 range, five priced from $185,000 to $198,000, three that sold for $213,500 to $255,000, and four that sold for $300,000 to $349,950.

Among the more expensive homes was a classic 4-bedroom, 3-bath center hall colonial for $329,500, a 4-bedroom, 5-bath Victorian for $349,950, with brick walks and front porch, a marble entrance foyer, and 3 fireplaces, and, for $300,000, a 4-bedroom, 3½-bath contemporary in a magnificent woodland setting that had been featured in the *AIA Guide to Washington Architecture.*

Somerset's homes, in short, are everything you'd expect in a prestige suburb of a leading metropolis. That, plus its close-in location, fine schools, and low crime, makes us confident that you could not do better than to consider Somerset when making your move to the nation's capital.

POOLESVILLE

POPULATION: 3,428
NO. OF CRIMES: 81
CRIME RATE: 2,382.3 per 100,000

The magic words in Poolesville are "controlled growth." The town's slogan could very well be: "Don't let Poolesville become another Gaithersburg!"

Gaithersburg, as you probably surmise, is the nearest town to explode with seemingly uncontrolled growth in recent years. Government agencies like the U.S. Department of Energy and the National Bureau of Standards have fed that growth. Poolesville, 12 miles due west of Gaithersburg, is determined not to let the process be repeated within its borders.

Actually, Poolesville has a number of things working in its favor in this battle to retain its semirural flavor. First, it's off any major thoroughfare, such as Interstate 270 which slices up Gaithersburg. Second, the town is virtually surrounded by an agricultural zone. Known more specifically as the Agricultural Reserve or Rural Density Transfer Zone, it's a zoning ordinance that is intended to help keep operating farms in operation. With few exceptions, only one house is allowed per 25 acres. Third, even without the Agricultural Reserve it would be hard to get permission to build a house on 5 acres or less. This is because of the high concentration of clay in the soil. Once outside town, you're on individual wells and septics and the county is responsible for checking percolation.

Located in the northwest corner of Montgomery County, Poolesville is the second oldest town (after Rockville) in the county. It's been an agricultural trade center for most of its existence and probably was most prominent during the War Between the States. That was because the Union army used it as a communications center, stationing 15,000 troops here and sending dispatches about Federal troop maneuvers across the country with a Poolesville dateline. The Confederates, in turn, stationed 8,000 troops across the Potomac near Leesburg, Virginia, our other Safe Place in this neck of the woods.

Downtown Poolesville has a number of homes and business structures that date back to the eighteenth and nineteenth centuries. They are now entered in the National Register of Historic Places as the Poolesville Historic District. Chief among these buildings is the John Poole House (c. 1793), the town founder's combination residence and log store. Another historic attraction is the Seneca Schoolhouse Museum (1866), a one-room school built of Seneca sandstone and restored with period furnishings and a shop. Also near town is White's Ferry, the only one remaining on the Potomac River. There's been some sort of ferry there since the 1700s and it connects Poolesville with Leesburg at the point where Generals Jeb Stuart and Robert E. Lee crossed with their armies in the Confederate invasion of Maryland.

We had interesting talks in town with Richard Buckingham, Jr. of Woodbyrne Realty and then with Mayor Charles W. Elgin, Sr. Mr. Elgin described himself as "retired but working almost full-time" as mayor. He and his father were born here and he has children and grandchildren living in Poolesville.

Both men told us that many Montgomery County police live in Poolesville ("over seventy," according to the mayor). Since many of them now have take-home cars and they work various shifts, there are always plenty of police cars visible in the town's neighborhoods. That alone would seem to be a deterrent factor with any visiting criminals.

Whatever the reasons, crime is relatively low here. In our comparison year of 1980, there were just 81 crimes—no murders, rapes, or robberies, and 1 aggravated assault, 32 burglaries, 45 larceny-thefts, and 3 motor vehicle thefts. That placed Poolesville below U.S. rural crime rates in all categories except burglary and larceny-theft and in those categories it remained well below metropolitan levels.

Poolesville has complete school facilities in town—elementary, junior high, and high school. There's also a branch of the Montgomery County library system. Mr. Buckingham told us there's an extremely active sports program for the young people and it's a great town in which to raise children. As with so many semirural communities, though, boredom and restlessness can be a problem when youngsters reach the teenage years. If they're not into athletics, they complain of having very little to do.

That goes for some of the adults as well, Mr. Buckingham noted. "People either love or hate semirural living."

Commuters are fairly well split between those who work in the outlying areas of the county and those who work in the District of Columbia and nearby areas of northern Virginia. If you're headed for D.C., you can catch the Amtrak commuter train at Barnesville. Most people commute by car to their work, either individually or in car pools.

Since the seventies, there's been a sewage moratorium in town. Hence, no new subdivisions during that time. Mayor Elgin told us, however, that he expects construction to begin on a new sewage treatment plant in the spring of 1983, with completion in 1984. Next, he said, the town will need a second water-storage facility to match the increased sewage-treatment capacity and the demands of the controlled growth.

Richard Buckingham told us that single-family subdivision housing ranges in price from $74,000 to $95,000. In all subdivisions, lots average 1/3 acre and range from 11,000 to 21,000 square feet in size (the larger ones being cul-de-sac lots). The older houses downtown come on the market only occasionally. Larger country houses with acreage will bring $150,000 to $200,000. There are also three town house communities in the area, with units ranging in price from $58,000 (3 bedrooms) to $67,000.

At the $74,000 low end of the range for single-family residences, Mr. Buckingham said, you're likely to get a smaller 3-bedroom split level, with 1 bath upstairs. When new, most of these were sold with an unfinished basement, but many of their subsequent owners have put in a bath and rec room in the basement area.

At the $95,000 high end of the range, he said, you would probably be in Westerly subdivision. Your home would be well maintained and perhaps upgraded, about five years old, and would include a 2-car garage, screened porch in back, and perhaps a backyard pool.

As the man said, you'll either love semirural living or hate it. If the exurbs *are* for you, Poolesville offers that style of living with just the right dash of southern charm.

Where to get further information:

State

For the *Maryland Guidebook,* state highway map, outdoor recreation and campgrounds guide, annual calendar of events, and directory of product/factory outlets: Maryland Office of Tourist Development, 1748 Forest Drive, Annapolis, MD 21401, or call 800/638-5252 from outside Maryland, 800/492-7126 within Maryland. For information on Maryland State Forests: Maryland Forest and Park Services, Tawes State Office Building, Annapolis, MD 21401.

For the quarterly publication *Maryland* ($7.50 a year): Department of Economic and Community Development, *Maryland* Magazine, 2525 Riva Road, Annapolis, MD 21401.

Regional

Chesapeake Bay Area: Tourism Council of the Upper Chesapeake, P.O. Box 66, Centreville, MD 21617. *Chesapeake country life,* Port Republic, MD 20676, is a monthly publication available for $14.95 a year.

Washington, D.C., Area: Information Officer, Montgomery County Office of Economic Development, Executive Office Building, 101 Monroe Street, Suite 1500, Rockville, MD 20850. Prince Georges Travel Promotion Council, Inc., 6600 Kenilworth Avenue, Riverdale, MD 20737.

Towns

Oxford: Talbot County, Maryland—A Tourist's Guide, from the Talbot County Chamber of Commerce, P.O. Box 1366, Easton, MD 21601. *A Guide to Oxford, Maryland,* from Commissioners of Oxford, Oxford, MD 21654. *History and Tariff Schedule,* from Robert Morris Inn, P.O. Box 70, on the Tred Avon, Oxford, MD 21654. For information on the Oxford Triathlon: Fletcher Hanks, P.O. Box 268, Oxford, MD 21654.

Glenarden: For a history of the town and a copy of the town publication, *The Glenarden Guardian,* write Mayor Herbert Jackson, Sr., Town Hall, 8600 Glenarden Parkway, Glenarden, MD 20706.

Somerset: Address inquiries to Mrs. Marty Cline, Clerk-Treasurer, Town of Somerset, 4510 Cumberland Avenue, Chevy Chase, MD 20815. Information on the area may be obtained from the Bethesda–Chevy Chase Chamber of Commerce, 7401 Wisconsin Avenue, Bethesda, MD 20014. For a brochure on their program: Somerset Elementary School, Warwick Place and Cumberland Avenue, Chevy Chase, MD 20015. And for a brochure, *About the Schools in Montgomery County, Maryland,* write: Department of Information, Montgomery County Public Schools, 850 Hungerford Drive, Rockville, MD 20850.

Poolesville: Town street map available from Town Hall, Poolesville, MD 20837. *Poolesville Area Business and Services Directory* available from the Poolsville Chamber of Commerce, P.O. Box 256, Poolesville, MD 20837. *Poolesville Town Walking Trail,* a historical booklet, is available from either Sugarloaf Regional Trails, Box 87, Stronghold, Dickerson, MD 20753, or Historic Medley District, Box 232, Poolesville, MD 20837.

Massachusetts

As anyone with even a cursory acquaintance with American history knows, the Bay State has had an influence on the United States far beyond anything its small size might indicate. Rebels, writers, philosophers, artists, noted teachers and religious leaders, politicians—Massachusetts has provided them in abundance, beginning with the first permanent settlement at Plimoth Plantation. The American Revolution began here; so too the Civil War, if we count the militant abolitionist movement as its genesis.

Fishing and small-scale agriculture have played their role in the state's economy from the beginning; even today, most of the world's cranberries come from Massachusetts bogs and two thirds of the nation's sea scallops are brought to port here. But with the advent of modern manufacturing processes, the state's economy turned primarily industrial—and Massachusetts became famous for its shoes, textiles, and paper goods. Mill towns were soon as much a part of the landscape as the fishing villages and coastal resorts. Since World War II, higher education and technological research have again transformed the economy.

Geographically, Massachusetts is marked by the Berkshire Hills in the west (highest elevation: 3,491 feet), separated by the Connecticut River Valley—known here as the Pioneer Valley—from the forested plains that dominate the eastern part of the state. But the most popular feature is the shoreline—the rocky, craggy coast of Cape Ann north of Boston, the sandy beaches and dunes of Cape Cod, Nantucket, and Martha's Vineyard to the south. The climate is definitely four-season, though the amount of snow and the harshness of the winter decline the closer you are to the ocean. Recreation in the Bay State is as varied as the geography: skiing and winter sports in the Berkshires; swimming, boating, and fishing along the coast. In addition, Boston has professional football, baseball, basketball, and hockey; horse racing and dog racing are popular everywhere and history itself is one of the state's biggest recreational pursuits, with such attractions as Bunker Hill, the Freedom Trail, Lexington, Concord, Plymouth, Old Sturbridge Village . . . the list goes on.

Massachusetts does have disadvantages, one of them denoted by its recent nickname, "Taxachusetts." Politically it is probably the most liberal and Democratic state in the union, which doesn't endear it to you if you're from the other party, and the corruption that inevitably follows one-party rule is as expensive to the inhabitants as it is amusing to us outsiders.

Crime is no stranger, either. Both Boston and neighboring Lynn have crime rates that are higher than New York City's. Even more surprising, so too do the beach communities of Yarmouth and Barnstable on Cape Cod. True, it's mostly property crime in those resorts, but this does demonstrate why we have chosen no Safe Places from Cape Ann or Cape Cod or Nantucket or Martha's Vineyard —there were no Safe Places to be found in all those lovely settings.

What Massachusetts *does* have, when you get away from the resort areas— and this is in marked contrast to most of the Southern and Western states of the United States—is a good supply of attractive, even beautiful, small towns and suburbs that are quite safe from the scourge of crime. We chose five of them for this book. Three are near Boston—Wellesley and Dover from the fashionable western suburbs, Winthrop to the near north. Holden is a suburb of Worcester, the second largest city in all of New England. And Stockbridge, the hometown of Norman Rockwell, is the embodiment of Norman Rockwell's America and a true gem of the Berkshires.

GREATER BOSTON AREA

With its population of 2,763,000, this collection of eighty-three towns and cities ranks as the tenth largest metropolitan area in the nation. At its core, with a population of a half million, is one of America's most charming and delightful cities—the Boston of Beacon Hill and Back Bay, of the Common and the Charles River, of Faneuil Hall and Old North Church, of Filene's and antiquarian book shops, of great universities and outstanding medical centers, of the Boston Museum of Art and the summer outdoor concerts of the Boston Pops Orchestra.

It is an area of stark contrasts. The city that seems to have invented ethnic politics is also a center of the "new elite" of intellectuals, scientists, engineers, and technicians. For although manufacturing remains vital to the area's economy, it is now eclipsed by the research-and-development and higher-education industries. Route 128, the main highway encircling the region, is lined by industrial research laboratories; signs along the expressway now dub it America's Technological Highway. More than sixty colleges and universities are located here, among them Harvard University, Massachusetts Institute of Technology (MIT), Radcliffe and Wellesley colleges, Boston College and Boston University, Brandeis, and the Boston and New England conservatories of music. Metropolitan Boston is also one of the foremost medical and medical research centers of the world, with the Harvard, Tufts, and Boston University medical schools, such famous hospital centers as Massachusetts General and the Lahey Clinic, and numerous additional hospitals that specialize in particular kinds of diseases.

As you would expect, the crime rates for these dozens of communities are as

BOSTON AREA Crime Chart

	Crime Rate	Murder	Rape	Robbery	Aggravated Assault	Burglary	Larceny —Theft	Motor Vehicle Theft
United States								
U.S. Total	5,899.9	10.2	36.4	243.5	290.6	1,668.2	3,156.3	494.6
U.S. Metropolitan Areas	6,757.6	11.5	43.4	319.0	328.3	1,911.8	3,534.9	608.8
U.S. Rural Areas	2,290.4	7.5	15.5	22.5	136.9	830.2	1,143.9	133.9
Regional Crime Center								
Boston	13,465.6	16.4	86.0	1,337.8	777.8	3,027.5	4,483.8	3,736.3
Safe Places								
Dover	1,722.3	0	0	0	63.8	574.1	893.0	191.4
Wellesley	2,552.8	0	0	22.2	121.9	639.1	1,518.4	251.2
Winthrop	1,496.9	0	0	20.7	0	331.5	543.8	600.8

varied as all other aspects of the region. Boston, Lynn, Brookline, Chelsea, and Cambridge are the worst offenders, in that order. As for the more suburban-type communities, you'd probably guess that the further away they are from Boston, the safer they are—but then you would often be wrong. Fashionable Concord, west of Route 128, has a crime rate three times as high as close-in Winthrop's.

In the Boston area, the suburbs are generally divided into three regions: the north shore, the south shore, and the western suburbs. We could find no Safe Places—no towns that met our strict standards—on the south shore. On the north shore, however, we had a rich choice that included coastal Marblehead, hunt-country Hamilton, and peaceful Lynnfield, but we passed them up in favor of a delightfully different and rather old-fashioned town, Winthrop, which gives the appearance more of a city neighborhood than of a suburb. And in the prestigious west, we found three adjoining towns that met our standards: Weston, Wellesley, and Dover. We picked the last two, one a built-up college town and the other a pastoral mélange of exurban dwellings and conserved open spaces.

Wellesley, Dover, Winthrop—three very different home bases from which to explore the delights of Greater Boston.

WELLESLEY

POPULATION: 27,068
NO. OF CRIMES: 691
CRIME RATE: 2,552.8 per 100,000

Wellesley is a special place for us. It is, first of all, Holly's hometown. Here she was born and raised and here her parents still live in the stylish colonial her father built when she was a young girl. More likely than not, you'll find her mother, Mary Lambro, checking out the latest acquisitions on British royal history—her passion—at the town's beautiful and substantial library. Pat, her father, will be styling a customer's hair in his shop on Crest Road, drawing on his many years in Wellesley and his active participation in the town's service clubs to answer any questions that may arise about what's going on in town.

But more than childhood memories make it special to us. David, too, came under Wellesley's spell during his first visit here and has ever since been impressed by the attractiveness of the town. Few communities can match the beauty of Wellesley's neighborhoods, which are laid out along the irregular and winding paths of its tree-shaded streets, thus avoiding the development look of later suburbs.

Wellesley was being transformed from an isolated town into a suburban community in the days before World War II, when quality and good taste were more highly regarded among developers than they are now and that stylishness is reflected today in the beautiful homes, with the colonial style predominating, to be found throughout Wellesley, in the larger Tudor and French provincial homes of the Cliff Estates section of town, and culminating in the luxurious Honeywell mansion along Washington Street. Add to those neighborhoods a number of business sections that are in themselves attractive and stylish, a downtown that avoids the neon-alley look predominating in America today, and stately, well-proportioned churches. Also several lakes, streams with hiking trails alongside, ponds on the parklike grounds surrounding the old Town Hall (originally the library) where you can watch the geese and ducks at play. And the beauty added by the campuses of the town's three colleges—the more than 500 acres of woodlands, hills, and meadows bordering on Lake Waban, where Wellesley College has its dozens of buildings with architectural styles ranging from Gothic to contemporary and, in other parts of town, the heavily wooded campuses of Babson College and Massachusetts Bay Community College.

Add all these together and you begin to understand the charm of Wellesley.

There is still another advantage of Wellesley living that should be noted: location. No interstates or turnpikes have chopped up Wellesley, but just east of town passes Route 128, the famed expressway that circles Boston and just north of Wellesley is the Massachusetts Turnpike. Route 128 offers Wellesley residents unhampered access to the computer-age industries and shopping centers that have been built along its path, while the Mass Pike can speed you 15 miles east to downtown Boston itself. Wellesley allows you to enjoy both the charm of life in a small-town community of 27,000 and the excitement and variety of one of the nation's largest metropolitan areas.

Wellesley has a reputation as a doctors' and dentists' town. It does have more than its share of these, being one of the more affluent suburbs of New England, along with a mix of other professionals, executives, managers, and white-collar workers. A number of active and retired college professors also make it their home.

Wellesley was one of our Safe Places in the original book and we were delighted to find that it still qualified. Indeed, the crime rate here is less than one fifth the reported rate in Boston. Despite its convenient location, crime here is below the U.S. rural rate in all categories except larceny-theft and motor vehicle theft. Your chances of being robbed are sixty times greater in Boston. Even your car is fifteen times safer here than in Boston.

Most homes in Wellesley are of frame construction, with brick and stone also popular. Nearly all have basements, attics, and working fireplaces. Wellesley developed as a town—gradually—before the big suburban boom of the 1950s and 1960s and so very few of its neighborhoods have the tract appearance of new developments. A variety of traditional styles is found in the town, with colonial probably the most popular. There is a profusion of trees and greenery and almost all homes have lots of at least 10,000 to 15,000 square feet.

We talked with Robert W. Buntin, of the DeWolfe Company, about real estate costs in Wellesley at the time of our visit for this book (November 1982). He told us that homes then on the market ranged from the high 70s to $500,000, with most of them selling in the 130s and 140s or in the $149,000–$210,000 range. Property taxes are rather high—you'd probably pay around $2,100 a year on a house costing $125,000 or $130,000. This is a built-up suburb, with virtually no land remaining for building a new home. If you do find a lot, expect to pay at least $55,000 for a half acre.

The weekly *Wellesley Townsman* carried a good number of real estate ads, with photographs. The cheapest listing was for a "snug" 5-room Cape selling at $99,750. It had a living room with fireplace, a large adjoining porch overlooking the private backyard, a dining room with bay windows, and a modern kitchen and lavatory on the first floor. Upstairs were two bedrooms, one with a fireplace and full bath.

Slightly more expensive ($103,900) was a 4-bedroom English colonial on a quiet side street, with an eat-in kitchen, large living room with fireplace, heated Florida room, extra large dining room, and 1½ baths. An 8-room village Victorian was selling for $129,900, and for $159,500 you could get an older 9-room colonial with 5 bedrooms, 2½ baths, beamed-ceiling living room, and a detached 2-car garage, all on ⅓ acre.

Perhaps the most prestigious area of town is that section known as the Cliff Estates. We saw several listings there for under $200,000, but more common were listings at $250,000 and up. For $375,000 you could get a twin-chimney, 4-bedroom brick colonial with a fireplace in the library. And $425,000 would bring you a 12-room colonial on ¾ acre, sporting a living room with fireplace, 15 × 16 dining room, stunning family room with fireplace, vaulted ceiling, and sliders to the patio.

Wellesley has reached its optimum size, but as in all executive-class communities, there are always enough residents being transferred by their companies to provide a considerable amount of real-estate turnover. If you are moving to the Boston area, Wellesley offers you a pleasant and cultured style of life that few other communities can match. If you can afford it, grab it!

DOVER

POPULATION: 4,703
NO. OF CRIMES: 81
CRIME RATE: 1,722.3 per 100,000

When Wellesley people speculate about "moving to the country," more often than not they're thinking of Dover.

Located just south of Wellesley and west of Needham and Route 128, Dover has managed to retain its rural atmosphere and charm through a happy combination of natural conditions and purposeful action.

The natural attributes have to do with the terrain. The Charles River forms one border of the town, and flood-control laws restrict development along its shores and those of its tributaries. Soil and water-table considerations make other areas of the town just as unsuitable for any sizable number of septic tanks. As a result, few areas are even thinkable for tract or commercial development.

And just to make sure, the town's zoning and development laws ensure the orderly and slow growth of the area. There are places in the center of town—areas that were already established when the zoning laws went into effect—with smaller lot minimums, but nearly all of Dover is zoned 1-acre or 2-acre. Some areas have up to 5-acre zoning.

Dover already has a considerable amount of deeded conservation land. Many of the larger estates are in the hands of "old money" families who are determined that their land will never be developed. If economic necessity does require the selling of an estate, Dover has a very active conservation commission and a private conservation group that is ready to buy up properties and keep them intact.

The Dover you see today, therefore, is the Dover you're likely to see tomorrow.

And that's a very pretty sight, indeed. The countryside, with its unpredictable patterns of woodland, open space, and wetlands, is reminiscent of the English countryside the town name evokes. The town hall and a few businesses are concentrated in the center of town; there is no sprawl whatsoever to confuse the delineation between village and countryside.

Crime? Only auto theft rises above U.S. rural crime rates and that barely. Crimes of violence rarely disturb this peaceful haven.

We had a most pleasant chat with Peg Crowley and Judy Birch of Brown Realty Company, the Realty World associate in Dover. They told us the lowest-priced property in town was $70,000. The highest-priced—apart from the mammoth Saltonstall estate that had recently been sold—was tagged at $750,000. But those were the exceptions and most homes had been selling in the $150,000 to $200,000 range.

The lower prices usually go with the older and smaller homes in the center of town. For $119,500, for example, you could get an attractive dark-stained Cape on a lot of 14,000 square feet, in the center of the village. It has a living room with fireplace, a dining room, 2 baths, no garage. It has 2 bedrooms upstairs and 2 down—or those downstairs could be utilized as a bedroom and a den. Taxes were $1,366 on this property.

For $195,000, Peg and Judy could offer a 9-room executive colonial on a lot of more than 1 acre and on a private cul-de-sac. This house has 4 spacious bedrooms, a living room with fireplace, a family room with wood stove, a separate library, a finished walk-out basement, and a large screened porch. Taxes here are $2,346.

Of course, a little more money will bring you the older-type properties you dream about . . .

For $249,000, for example, a tastefully restored old colonial on 3.84 acres of lovely grounds accented by a patio, terrace, and gazebo, not to mention the 2-stall barn with paddock area. This one has fireplaces in the living room, dining room, and library. The eat-in kitchen has been updated. There are 4 bedrooms on the second floor and yet another bedroom and studio on the third floor. But drool on . . .

Up the ante to $425,000 and you can enjoy an antique colonial on over 5 acres of beautiful land with Charles River frontage. Here the reception room, living room, dining room, and library all have working fireplaces. So does the master bedroom suite, with its 2 dressing rooms, and the guest suite. Front and back stairs, barn, studio—all help to make this a lovely country estate barely a half hour from downtown Boston.

You don't have to be a Saltonstall to enjoy the Dover lifestyle. But let's face it, a little money doesn't hurt!

WINTHROP

POPULATION: 19,294
NO. OF CRIMES: 290
CRIME RATE: 1,503.1 per 100,000

After determining the crime rates for several hundred Massachusetts communities and comparing them, we were ready and able to let the secret out: The safest suburb of Boston is—Winthrop!

Winthrop? The proper name itself was familiar, of course, since John Winthrop was the first governor of the colony and father of two other colonial governors. Holly had a vague recollection of the town being on the water, but it evidently wasn't the sort of place you head for in the summer like the Cape.

Out came the map. We checked the index, ran down the coordinates, and found it on a neck of land that sticks out into the ocean, separating Boston Harbor from the larger Massachusetts Bay. There it was, right past Logan International Airport, buffered from the mainland by the grounds of the Suffolk Downs Race Track, and with a prison—a "house of correction," pardon us—at the very tip of the peninsula. Hardly an auspicious location, we mused, that close to Boston and with those surroundings. It must be an industrial low-rent area, we speculated, with nothing in it to interest the crooks. We've seen *that* kind of Safe Place elsewhere; thanks but no thanks.

Still, duty required us to check it out. Leaving downtown Boston, we drove a mere 5 miles in ten minutes to get past Logan, past Suffolk Downs, and over the bridge for Belle Isle Inlet that links Winthrop to the mainland. What we found wasn't exactly President Reagan's "shining city on a hill," but it was a very pleasant surprise nonetheless.

Winthrop, we discovered, is not your "typical" suburb, with wave after wave of lookalike housing developments clustered around shopping malls with their asphalt lakes. No, this had more of the feel of a self-contained small town (thanks to its geographical isolation) or at least a sizable city neighborhood. Most of the housing is single-family, but the lawns are compact and cutting them poses no threat to your hernia. Business areas are scattered throughout the town and there are no massive asphalt lakes here—just the real thing, the ocean, all about you.

The views are what especially set Winthrop apart from otherwise similar areas—views of the downtown Boston skyline beyond Logan Airport, of the islands in Boston Harbor and the Quincy hills beyond to the south, of the open ocean to the east. Low hills and the streets that wind up them add just a hint of San Francisco to the salty atmosphere. As for Logan, its runways run in directions away from most of Winthrop; we didn't notice jet noise anywhere except on a narrow neck of land that connects Cottage Hill with Point Shirley. Even there we found it fascinating to park at the public landing and watch the jumbo jets set down and take off—a form of relaxation, of technological reverie, no king was ever able to enjoy before our day.

With its views and close-to-downtown convenience, Winthrop started to be "discovered" during the seventies. Housing values jumped 340 percent during the decade—a greater advance than in many more prestigious suburbs. Even so, prices are still average to low for the Boston area and frequently you see homes being renovated. (Winthrop used to be a summer beach colony for Bostonians; many of those cottages make affordable "starter" homes today, but need to be renovated and winterized.) With the trend toward in-city living accelerating, we suspect that Winthrop is a good bargain—and a prudent investment—for the wise home buyer. In short, it's a real find, the sort we wish we could have found in each of the metropolitan areas we visited.

Auto theft is the only category in which Winthrop's crime rate rises above U.S. rural levels. And let's face it, all of metropolitan Boston has stratospheric rates for auto theft; everyone around Beantown, it seems, has a love affair with someone else's automobile. Winthrop Police Chief David C. Rice has a few succinct reasons to offer why the overall crime rate is so low:

"Our response time is about three minutes anywhere in town.

"We have a crime-watch program.

"We stop all suspicious persons and vehicles.

"Most of our department performs quite well.

"That," says the chief in explaining Winthrop's safety, "is about all I can say." And he does seem to have covered the bases quite well with a few words.

When we were in town, the weekly *Sun Transcript* had a story about a resident who became suspicious when a strange man entered a neighbor's house; she quickly called the police and the police just as promptly arrived to nab a would-be thief. Watchful neighbors and quick police response can work wonders.

George Rio, a salesman with John T. Conway Real Estate, took out a Winthrop street map and marked off the different neighborhoods for us. It's an example of what makes Winthrop fascinating that there *are* a number of neighborhoods, each with its distinctive style, in this compact area.

Picture Winthrop, if you will, as a roughly round-shaped mass of land separated from the mainland by Belle Isle Inlet and Broad Sound, and linked to the mainland by two highways. In the center of this area is the part known, appropriately enough, as Center-town. Court Park, to the northwest, and Cottage Park, to the southwest, face Logan Airport and the downtown Boston skyline. Facing east is the low-lying beach neighborhood and a promontory known as the Highlands. Protruding into the ocean to the south is a narrow neck of land with three "bumps" or enlargements. The first is Cottage Hill, otherwise known as Water Tower Hill, and the second is Point Shirley. The third, at the southernmost tip, is Deer Island, and it contains the Suffolk County House of Correction. It's part of Boston, not Winthrop.

Center-town contains the major business district, most of the public buildings such as the town hall, library, and schools, the expanding facilities of Winthrop Community Hospital, a municipal golf course, several apartment complexes, and a residential mix of single-family and multifamily homes. Mr. Rio told us that the single-family homes sell mostly in the 70s. Two-family or multifamily houses are more expensive, in the 80s and 90s, because they are larger and you can expect a rental income. Conway Real Estate was offering a single-family home, for example, with 7 rooms—living room with fireplace, dining room, kitchen, enclosed sun porch, and 3 bedrooms with a very large bath. The asking price was $67,500.

Court Park and Cottage Park feature homes with natural hardwood floors, high ceilings, the details that constitute older charm. Some of the homes on Court Road had, in our opinion, the finest views of Logan and the Boston skyline. In these neighborhoods, you can expect to pay in the 80s and 90s even without a view, but a charming 7-room home in the Cottage Park area was going for $59,000 because it needed work. Its slate roof, however, was in excellent condition.

Homes in the Highlands area are of a more modern vintage and can sell for as much as $125,000 to $150,000. For $135,000, Conway Real Estate was offering a single-family house on the water, with an outstanding view. It had 4 bedrooms, a modern kitchen and baths, a wraparound porch, and many other extras.

The Highlands area also has the only genuine high-rise in Winthrop—the 10-story Seal Harbor Condominiums. Its prices range from $85,900 for a small 1-bedroom apartment to $229,000 for a penthouse. A 2-bedroom apartment will cost you $125,000.

The beach area has a couple of drawbacks: It took a beating in the 1978 storm that battered New England and it gets a little crowded and noisy in the summer. We saw a listing here for a 6-room house with an additional 3-room "in-law area," offered at $59,900. There were also 2-family houses listed in the 60s and 70s and a 3-family house listed at $85,000.

Cottage Hill (Water Tower Hill) was one of our favorite areas, along with Court Park and Cottage Park. The homes on Harbor View Avenue and Faun Bar Avenue enjoy especially striking views of the ocean below. Apparently, others are as impressed as we were, for we found no listings on the market in this neighborhood.

Point Shirley, finally, has many of the summer cottages we mentioned earlier. If they're on the water or have a particularly good view of the Boston skyline, they can go for $125,000 or $130,000. There was a 5-room colonial, however, with a garage, selling for $73,500. A number of the smaller homes appear to be in a somewhat run-down condition, but with the continuing built-in value of a harbor view, we suspect they also offer some of the best prospects for renovation and value appreciation.

With Boston just a skip (or a short swim) away, with views that are hard to match elsewhere in the metropolitan area, with relatively low prices and excellent living conditions—Winthrop may prove as pleasant a surprise for you as it was for us.

WORCESTER AREA

Worcester (pronounced Wuś-ter) is the second-largest city in New England. Few people outside Massachusetts, however, seem even to have heard of the city, much less know anything about it. It has a low profile for a city with a respectable list of economic and cultural contributions to the nation.

Even among those who know something about Worcester, it retains an image of a somewhat dismal industrial city. Industry is still important, with more than 750 factories in the area, but new construction has transformed the appearance of downtown Worcester.

Historically, Worcester County was the home of Eli Whitney's cotton gin, Elias Howe's sewing machine, the carpet loom, the steam calliope, and streetcars, and more recently, liquid-fuel rocketry (Dr. Robert Goddard launched his first rockets from Pakachoag Hill in nearby Auburn) and the birth-control pill (developed and tested at the Foundation for Experimental Biology in Shrewsbury).

For Worcester contributions on other fronts, consider Isaiah Thomas' Revolutionary-era newspaper *Massachusetts Spy* and Dorothea Dix's humane innovations in the treatment of the mentally ill. And we must not forget the ice cream sundae, first dished out at Easton's on Harrington Corner.

Worcester's twelve colleges include Holy Cross, the oldest Catholic college in New England, and Clark University, with its Goddard Library and Exhibit dedicated to the rocketry pioneer.

WORCESTER AREA Crime Chart

	Crime Rate	Murder	Rape	Robbery	Aggravated Assault	Burglary	Larceny —Theft	Motor Vehicle Theft
United States								
U.S. Total	5,899.9	10.2	36.4	243.5	290.6	1,668.2	3,156.3	494.6
U.S. Metropolitan Areas	6,757.6	11.5	43.4	319.0	328.3	1,911.8	3,534.9	608.8
U.S. Rural Areas	2,290.4	7.5	15.5	22.5	136.9	830.2	1,143.9	133.9
Regional Crime Center								
Worcester	8,041.7	3.7	36.6	374.9	309.2	2,660.7	3,374.6	1,282.0
Safe Place								
Holden	1,454.2	0	0	7.5	7.5	610.3	806.2	22.6

Culturally, the Worcester Art Museum is highly regarded nationally. The Worcester Music Festival is the country's oldest (124 years old this year). Charles Dickens once read *A Christmas Carol* at Mechanics Hall, where the Hook organ—first installed in 1864—has just had its 3,500 pipes cleaned and tuned, a fact which, along with other modernizations, marks it as one of the best-preserved, largest, and oldest recital-hall organs in the United States. The elegant reading room of the American Antiquarian Society is a favorite haunt for scholars and genealogists. And for all you romantics, the Higgens Armory Museum offers the nation's largest display of medieval and Renaissance armor, arms, and art, including paintings, tapestries, stained glass, and metalwork.

HOLDEN

POPULATION: 13,272
NO. OF CRIMES: 193
CRIME RATE: 1,454.2 per 100,000

Holden is located just ten miles northwest of Worcester's city hall via Route 122A. As befits a town established in 1742, a handsome Congregational church with a tall white steeple marks the center of town.

In 1809, the textile industry discovered Holden, with its abundant waterways. Within twenty-five years, eleven cotton and woolen mills were built here. And two boot and shoe manufacturers produced 15,800 pairs of footwear annually.

That era ended with the Great Depression. The remaining mills closed during those years and the numerous small mill villages have disappeared except for a few homes which have been renovated into apartments.

Holden today is basically a bedroom community; its breadwinners commute to Worcester and sometimes even Boston, 40 to 50 miles to the east. A recent newspaper article listed Southborough, Paxton, and Holden as the area's most affluent communities, in that order. Holden does have an easygoing, pleasant look about it, but it is not particularly stylish. Route 122A is the main street, with no centralized business area. The terrain is slightly rolling and heavily wooded.

An interesting supplement to the *Holden Landmark* carried the observations of area realtors as to why Holden is one of the favorite suburbs in central Massachusetts. The school system, regarded as one of the best in the area, was the most frequently cited reason. "There are good homes, recreation, an excellent police department, good access roads, and a board of selectmen who are doing a fine job," said Robert K. Daw. "What more could people want: You're fifteen minutes from Worcester center and we have a community that is lively but conservative, in the best sense of those words."

This comment was echoed by Larry O'Connell. "I think, by nature, the population in Holden and in this general area is conservative," he said. "They don't particularly want swimming pools and wet bars—they want a spacious, energy-efficient home where they can be comfortable."

Worcester is not a major crime center on the level of Boston or New York City, but like that of any other major or middle-sized city, its crime rate is still too high. Holden, on the other hand, ranks below the crime rates for U.S. rural areas in all categories. Crimes of violence are especially rare. If you move to Holden, ask the police department for a formal security survey inspection. Using a detailed checklist, an officer will come to your home, note the security precautions that exist, and make recommendations for improvements.

We had a most informative chat with Ginny Hynes, a realtor with Robert B. Love & Company. She told us that the eastern suburbs of Worcester were traditionally the preferred area for commuters to Boston—a logical decision, since Boston is to the east. But with the building of Interstate 190, a Holden commute to the east takes just a few minutes longer and offers better schools and more house for the money.

Ginny told us that you can find homes in Holden ranging from the 50s to around $285,000, but most houses up for resale are in the 60s and 70s. These are usually ranches, built about fifteen years ago, and they don't need much updating because they were well built originally. Most of these would have 3 bedrooms, 1 or 1½ baths, a living room with fireplace, a family room finished off in the basement, and a 1-car garage. Some will have formal dining rooms.

You could also get, at the time of our visit, a 7-room split-level house on a quiet dead-end street, with 3 bedrooms, 2½ baths, and a double garage, for $76,900.

The new homes that "everyone" looks for—with 4 bedrooms, 2½ baths, a 2-car garage, and all the conveniences found in new construction—will usually cost $150,000 and up in Holden. At this price level, you'll find Georgian colonials and contemporaries but not too many ranches, on a lot of at least 1/2 acre. (The land alone will cost you $28,000–$30,000.)

"Nice, clean, and well organized." Those are the qualities noted by one realtor. And those qualities make Holden a good place to call home.

BERKSHIRES

Gentle mountains . . . . serene vistas . . . . idyllic villages. It's hardly surprising that the Berkshire Hills of western Massachusetts have long been a haunt of writers, artists, musicians, sculptors, dancers, actors . . . . and plenty of ordinary folk who get as much inspiration from their surroundings as do the creative celebrities they pass in the corner grocery or pharmacy.

Nathaniel Hawthorne's *Tanglewood Tales* made the Berkshires famous. Matthew Arnold found the views "beautiful and soul satisfying." In the latter part of the nineteenth century, fine mansions began to adorn the region as it became a popular summer retreat for the rich. In our own day it's the sound of music and the sounds of the other creative arts that perpetuate the fame of the region.

BERKSHIRES Crime Chart

	Crime Rate	Murder	Rape	Robbery	Aggravated Assault	Burglary	Larceny —Theft	Motor Vehicle Theft
United States								
U.S. Total	5,899.9	10.2	36.4	243.5	290.6	1,668.2	3,156.3	494.6
U.S. Metropolitan Areas	6,757.6	11.5	43.4	319.0	328.3	1,911.8	3,534.9	608.8
U.S. Rural Areas	2,290.4	7.5	15.5	22.5	136.9	830.2	1,143.9	133.9
Regional Crime Center								
Pittsfield	6,268.5	0	42.4	86.6	300.3	2,137.0	3,309.5	392.8
Safe Place								
Stockbridge	1,546.4	0	0	0	0	945.0	472.5	128.9

Tanglewood, the summer home of the Boston Symphony Orchestra, is the most widely known of these attractions. In Lee, the Jacob's Pillow Dance Festival is perhaps the foremost summer dance festival in the country. Pittsfield has Arrowhead, Herman Melville's home where he completed *Moby Dick,* and the Hancock Shaker Village west of town, with twenty restored buildings in the religious community founded in 1790. The beautiful campus of Williams College in Williamstown is home to the Clark Art Institute, with its major Renoir and French impressionist collections.

And then there are the villages that look like Norman Rockwell paintings—that *were* Norman Rockwell paintings—like Stockbridge.

STOCKBRIDGE

POPULATION: 2,328
NO. OF CRIMES: 36
CRIME RATE: 1,546.4 per 100,000

What do Nathaniel Hawthorne, Daniel Chester French, Norman Rockwell, Cyrus Field, and Reinhold Niebuhr have in common?

What, for that matter, do Katharine Hepburn, James Cagney, Robert E. Sherwood, and Thornton Wilder have in common?

The answer, as you've undoubtedly guessed, is Stockbridge. This picture-postcard New England town has touched all their lives and has contributed to the creative accomplishments of each of them. There's nothing in Stockbridge to spoil the charm and beauty of the past two centuries, nothing to intrude—except, of course, that horseless carriage you dared to ride into town.

If we had to name just one person most often associated with Stockbridge in the public mind, he would have to be Norman Rockwell. This was his home and it was memorialized in one of his famous paintings, *Main Street, Stockbridge.* Today the Old Corner House displays over 200 of his paintings, drawings, and sketches and his studio is being prepared for public viewing.

Another Stockbridge landmark is the Berkshire Playhouse, designed by the eminent architect Stanford White in 1886. Now the oldest and most famous of the original strawhat summer theaters, it is also the only institution in the country dedicated to preserving the nation's theatrical heritage by producing works exclusively of the American repertoire. Katharine Hepburn, James Cagney, Montgomery Clift, Dustin Hoffman, and Al Pacino all credit the Playhouse's Berkshire Theatre Festival with launching their careers. Other noted artists played here repeatedly—Ethel Barrymore, Tallulah Bankhead, Jessica Tandy, Julie Harris, Eli Wallach, Maureen Stapleton, Anne Bancroft, and Joanne Woodward among them. Playwrights Robert E. Sherwood, William Inge, Thornton Wilder, and William Gibson have directed here and sometimes acted in their own works on its stage.

Tanglewood, though located near the village of Lenox, is actually within the township of Stockbridge. Hawthorne's original Little Red House, located near Tanglewood, burned in 1891 but was rebuilt on the original foundations in 1947.

And that merely begins the list of attractions you'll find in this small but amazing town.

The Red Lion Inn opened in 1773 as a tavern stop on the Albany-to-Boston stagecoach route. It is one of the few remaining New England inns to be in continuous use since before 1800.

The present building of St. Paul's Episcopal Church was designed by the noted architect Charles F. McKim. Its chancel window is by John LaFarge, the baptistry by Augustus Saint-Gaudens, and a window in the nave by Louis Comfort Tiffany.

Jonathan Edwards wrote his *Freedom of the Will* while he was minister of the First Congregational Church, on Main Street.

Cyrus Field was one of the town's most famous residents. In the summer of 1858, the first message from his transatlantic cable was relayed to his office near the present Soldier's Monument.

And then there are the homes and estates open to the public. Like Naumkeag, another Stanford White creation and home of Joseph Hodges Choate, President Wilson's ambassador to the Court of St. James. And Chesterwood, the summer home and studio of the famous sculptor Daniel Chester French. French created the Minute Man statue in Concord and the seated Lincoln in the Lincoln Memorial in Washington, D.C. His home and studio were designed by Henry Bacon, the architect of the Lincoln Memorial.

It seems almost sacrilegious to turn to prosaic present-day concerns like crime and housing, but this *is*, believe it or not, a community very much alive today, not just a period piece. And an interesting mix of people it is you'll find here today—traditional New Englanders, theatrical and musical celebrities, and cultural transplants and visitors from Boston and New York.

Indeed, there's not only the artistic emphasis but also a cultural trendiness evident here that you won't find in a more "typical" New England village. It was evident in the posters, announcements, and ads we found on the community bulletin boards when we visited in November 1982. For example: a fall series of yoga classes. A myotherapy pain-erasure clinic. A Middle Eastern deli. Clay pottery designs. Antiques, art galleries, restaurants, summer theaters. Autumn-painting weekend workshops. Guitar lessons. Canoes on the Housatonic River. Concerts of all sorts. A game farm selling fresh pheasant, partridges, quail, duckling, and wild turkey.

Crime is not a major public concern anywhere in the Berkshires, we suspect, but that surface tranquillity can be deceptive and misleading. Pittsfield, the largest city in the area, exceeds the crime rates for U.S. metropolitan areas in rape and burglary. There are some safe hamlets, where the populations are counted in the hundreds, but most of the towns of any consequence have surprisingly high property crime rates when you adjust the figures for population. Only Stockbridge among them is truly safe. Crime here is below the U.S. rural rate in all categories except burglary and even there it's way below metropolitan levels.

As you might already suspect, most houses in this fashionable village are on the expensive side. But we did find a few moderately priced properties. The cheapest listing we saw was for $60,000—an old clapboard colonial with lovely trees and river frontage, within walking distance of the theater and the village. For $75,000 you could get a 6-room stucco Cape Codder on 4 acres. It had 3 bedrooms, new plumbing and wiring, a wood-stove hookup. A newer wood-shingled saltbox on an acre was selling for $80,000 and an attractive colonial with two fireplaces and a servant's wing had an $85,000 price tag.

If you're looking for a newer colonial with modern conveniences, we saw two listings. For $145,000: a ten-year-old house on 2½ acres, with 4 bedrooms, 3½ baths, a fireplace in the family room, a finished basement, a pool, and a 2-car garage. For $168,000: an eight-year-old 9-room colonial on 3.2 acres, with a large living room, family room with fireplace, 5 bedrooms, and 2½ baths.

Other interesting properties were available:

• A converted carriage house on 3.5 acres with beautiful views. For $127,000 you get 3 bedrooms, a living room with fireplace, a dining room, a large deck, a full basement that includes a darkroom, a laundry room, and a 4-car attached garage with studio.

• An unusual 9-room colonial of fieldstone and stucco, nestled on 20 acres, with a 4-car garage and a workshop. For your $225,000 you also get woods and meadows, a brook with a beautiful pond site, and long frontage on two town-maintained roads.

• And for $200,000 elsewhere in town you can take care of all your relatives or open up your own New England inn. The mountainside property advertised at this price was designed at Yale around 1900 and has 7 main bedrooms, 3½ baths, and 6 working fireplaces, plus the 7-room guest/servant floor. Built of stone and cedar with a great room, it is located on 10½ acres with a spring-fed fountain and faces south with views of fenced pasture and woods. Of course, they didn't say how much it would cost to heat this fascinating "cottage."

So, if you're looking for an unspoiled New England village for retirement or have a career that can be pursued in a small town . . . if you have a special love for the theater, for top-quality music and dance . . . if you want to stay in touch with New York or Boston, yet be far enough away . . . then consider Stockbridge. There aren't too many places left, after all, where you can simultaneously live in the past *and* enjoy today's life to the fullest.

Where to get further information:

State

For a state highway map and a wide variety of tourist literature: Massachusetts Department of Commerce and Development, Box 1775, Boston, MA 02195, and New England Vacation Center, 1268 Avenue of the Americas, New York, NY 10020.

Regions

Greater Boston Area: Greater Boston Convention and Tourist Bureau, P.O. Box 490, Boston, MA 02199.

Worcester Area: Central Massachusetts Tourist Council, Mechanics Tower, Suite 350, 100 Front Street, Worcester, MA 01600.

Berkshires: Berkshire Hills Conference, 20 Elm Street, Pittsfield, MA 01201.

Towns

Wellesley: A map-brochure from the Wellesley Chamber of Commerce, 287 Linden Street, P.O. Box 715, Wellesley, MA 02181.

Dover: Maps from Brown Realty Co., Inc., 10 Springdale Avenue, Dover, MA 02030, and from the South Middlesex Area Chamber of Commerce, 615 Concord Street, Framingham, MA 01701.

Winthrop: Map from John T. Conway Real Estate, 207 Hagman Road, Winthrop, MA 02152.

Holden: Map of Holden and Paxton and brochure *Holden, Massachusetts—Planning to Buy,* from Robert B. Love, Realtor, 1133 Main Street, Holden, MA. *Here's Holden,* a booklet published by the League of Women Voters, from the Worcester Area League of Women Voters, P.O. Box 881, Worcester, MA 01613.

Stockbridge: Booklet *Welcome to Stockbridge,* from the Stockbridge Chamber of Commerce, Stockbridge, MA 01262. *The Berkshires' Homebuyers Guide,* a monthly publication, from Box 76, Trumbull, CT 06611, or Box 136, Richmond, MA 01254.

Michigan

Michigan came of age at the beginning of the twentieth century with the genius of Henry Ford. His invention of the Model T and his revolutionary concepts—mass markets, the assembly line, and the use of higher wages as a competitive lure for industrial workers—changed the economies of Detroit and Michigan beyond recognition and helped to propel the United States to its role as the world's leading economic superpower. Today, despite the grinding recession of the 1980s, automobiles, auto parts, and recreational vehicles remain Michigan's major industry.

While the automobile comes first, Michigan is intensely industrialized and produces countless other products as well. Pharmaceuticals, rubber goods, chemicals, and food processing (breakfast cereals at Battle Creek) are major components of the state's economy. They barely begin to dent the list of Michigan products and services.

Tourism is a $4.7 billion-a-year industry in its own right. Michigan has some 11,000 lakes, including frontage on four of the five Great Lakes. That gives it more freshwater shoreline than any other state and makes it a center for water sports of all kinds. Skiing (some fifty developed ski areas), fishing, and hunting are also popular.

In mining, Michigan ranks second behind Minnesota in the production of iron ore and fifth in the mining of copper. Agriculturally, it is a major producer of cherries, blueberries, and other fruits.

In looking for some Safe Places, we concentrated our limited time on the suburbs of Detroit, one of the nation's major cities and metropolitan regions.

DETROIT–ANN ARBOR AREA

The place the French called *d'étroit* (city of the strait) is now referred to as Motown, a derivation of Motor City. And at the time of our visit (October 1982), Motown was singing the blues in more ways than one. The recession of the early 1980s had hit it as hard as any place in the nation and we passed untold numbers of businesses that had closed and boarded up their windows. With the city's dominant industry in depression, everyone suffered.

We hope that by the time you read this, the crunch is over and Detroit—and the nation—are bouncing back. Detroit is not, after all, a fun-in-the-sun kind of tourist mecca. It's a monument to work—productive work—and everyone here just wants to hear those factories humming again.

As Detroit became the nation's auto capital, it expanded in a number of directions, including westward to Dearborn. That's where the Ford Motor Company established its massive Rouge Assembly Plant and that's where Henry Ford built his tribute to American ingenuity, Greenfield Village, and dedicated it to Thomas Edison. More than eighty historic buildings were moved here from all over the country, among them Edison's laboratory, a courthouse where Abraham Lincoln practiced law, the Wright brothers' cycle shop, and the birthplaces of Henry Ford, Noah Webster, and many others. You won't find anything like this anywhere else in the country.

South and west of Dearborn is the Detroit Metropolitan Wayne County Airport—Metro Airport for short—and beyond that a stretch of countryside until you come to Ypsilanti and Ann Arbor. Ypsilanti has varied industries and is the home of Eastern Michigan University (18,000 students). Ann Arbor is the home of the huge University of Michigan (35,000 students) and of more than a hundred research and high technology firms.

We stress this westward flow of population from Detroit since that's where our Safe Place is located—halfway between Detroit and Ann Arbor. And it wasn't easy to find a Safe Place anywhere in the entire metropolitan region.

Detroit itself has one of the worst crime rates of any big city in the United States. Some would like to blame this on unemployment, but Detroit was notoriously crime-ridden even when the factories were busy. In our comparison year of 1980, Detroit had the fourth-highest crime rate of any big city in the United States. Only Boston, Dallas, and Phoenix were worse off.

In most northeastern metropolises, moreover, there are at least *some* very safe suburbs close in to the core city. Here, Detroit's crime spills over to nearly all its suburbs. In most instances they were not as high-crime as Detroit, but they did have far too much to qualify as Safe Places. Detroit's most prestigious suburbs are the Grosse Pointe communities; we had crime statistics for three of them and all were too high. The same was true of the fashionable newer northwestern suburbs like Farmington, Farmington Hills, Birmingham, and Royal Oak.

We did find some other suburbs that qualified *technically* as Safe Places—their overall crime rates were below 4,000 crimes per 100,000 population. But when we broke down their statistics by categories, we were unhappy about the level of certain kinds of crimes in most of them. In the end, we were comfortable only with Van Buren and Sumpter townships, which adjoin each other. Van Buren, we thought, was not only the safer of the two but also better located and so it became our Safe Place for the Detroit–Ann Arbor region.

DETROIT AREA Crime Chart

	Crime Rate	Murder	Rape	Robbery	Aggravated Assault	Burglary	Larceny —Theft	Motor Vehicle Theft
United States								
U.S. Total	5,899.9	10.2	36.4	243.5	290.6	1,668.2	3,156.3	494.6
U.S. Metropolitan Areas	6,757.6	11.5	43.4	319.0	328.3	1,911.8	3,534.9	608.8
U.S. Rural Areas	2,290.4	7.5	15.5	22.5	136.9	830.2	1,143.9	133.9
Regional Crime Centers								
Ann Arbor	8,574.6	4.0	29.0	111.8	332.5	1,879.3	5,899.4	318.5
Dearborn	8,926.0	3.3	15.5	202.0	192.1	867.7	6,138.7	1,506.8
Detroit	10,642.1	45.7	109.7	1,121.6	668.1	3,411.6	3,429.8	1,855.6
Ypsilanti	10,361.8	16.7	83.3	370.5	1,136.5	2,730.9	5,470.2	553.7
Safe Place								
Van Buren Township	555.0	0	0	15.9	37.0	132.1	338.3	31.7

VAN BUREN TOWNSHIP

POPULATION: 18,918
NO. OF CRIMES: 105
CRIME RATE: 555.0 per 100,000

As our Detroit Area Crime Chart (above) demonstrates, the entire Detroit-to-Ann Arbor area suffers from a burden of crime. We've already mentioned how Detroit has one of the highest crime rates of any big city in the U.S. Ypsilanti, our figures show, is virtually tied with Detroit. Dearborn and Ann Arbor look good only by comparison with them; in actuality, they still have much higher crime than vastly larger cities in other areas of the United States, like Chicago and Philadelphia.

Yes, you read that right. If you thought all that went on in Ann Arbor was collegiate hanky-panky and high tech computer thievery, think again. Its crime rate is a full 30 percent higher than Chicago's.

All of which makes the crime figures for Van Buren Township that much more remarkable. Granted, it is still basically rural and exurban in character, but it *is* right in the midst of these high-crime centers. And Van Buren's crime rate is not only below U.S. rural crime rates in all categories, but *substantially* below rural levels in all categories. That's quite an accomplishment.

In addition to its super-low crime rate, Van Buren has location going for it. The township is bisected by two interstates that make it accessible to the entire metropolitan region. Interstate 94 speeds you east to Detroit or west to Ann Arbor and beyond. Interstate 275 provides access southward to Toledo and the Ohio Turnpike or northward to Detroit's northwestern suburbs and the vacationlands of northern Michigan.

That makes Van Buren Township a good location for white-collar and blue-collar workers alike. Downtown Detroit is just half an hour away during off hours, forty-five minutes during rush periods. The research and development industries of Ann Arbor are even closer. Metro Airport is just ten minutes away (though we heard no airplane noise during the entire period we spent in the area). And if you need accessibility to the automotive industry, you've got it. The Ford Motor Company Wayne Plant and the Detroit Diesel Allison Division are just beyond the township's borders to the northeast; to the west in Ypsilanti you'll find Ford's Rawsonville Plant, the GM Hydramatic Division, and the Chevrolet Division Truck Plant. De Vilbiss, Kelsey-Hayes, and Huron Valley Steel Corporation are other major employers in the area and Ford owns large tracts of land that it's holding for future development.

Van Buren Township, in sum, enjoys a pretty strategic location. We're betting that along with economic recovery, real estate values here will jump higher than they will elsewhere in the Detroit area.

Van Buren Township is one of the westernmost townships of Wayne County. Mott and Van Born roads form its northern boundary with Canton Township. Hannan Road forms its eastern boundary with Romulus Township. Bemis Road constitutes its southern boundary with Sumpter Township. And the Wayne-Washtenaw county line forms its western boundary with Ypsilanti Township.

Belleville, a small town in the center of Van Buren, has its own police force and maintains separate crime statistics. The surrounding countryside is flat prairie land, partly wooded and mostly still undeveloped. The subdivisions that do exist are concentrated near Interstate 94 and Belleville Lake, a long and relatively narrow lake formed by the Huron River and flowing west to east. The southeast corner of the township is part of the Lower Huron Metro Park, a lovely area of nature trails, picnic grounds, and play areas.

Van Buren Township is the home of Willow Run Airport, which in turn was the home of the B-24 bomber of World War II fame. Old-timers among the residents still like to talk about their contributions to that particular war effort. Today Willow Run is the commercial airport of the Detroit region and the laboratory of the University of Michigan's aeronautical research department. Just east of the airport, the university also maintains an Environmental Research Institute.

The Wayne County Fair Grounds and 4-H Fair Grounds are located within the township. Pine Creek Country Club and Lemontree Golf Course are in the vicinity of Belleville Lake, while Lower Huron Golf Course is on the grounds of that Metro Park.

The Van Buren School District serves both the township and the city of Belleville with eight elementary schools, two junior highs, and one high school. A parochial grade school is also located here and Wayne County Community College has its western regional campus here.

Depending on your location within the township, you would use the facilities of Beyer Memorial Hospital or St. Joseph's Hospital in Ypsilanti, Annapolis

Hospital in Wayne, or Oakwood Hospital and Sumpter Family Medical Center in Sumpter Township.

Day-to-day shopping needs can be met in Belleville and the stores located near Interstate 94. Major malls are just twenty minutes away—either Ann Arbor's Briarwood or Dearborn's Fairlane Center.

We had an enjoyable talk about Van Buren real estate with Judy Sullivan, of Community, Inc., the local affiliate of Century 21. Judy told us that the price range for houses in the township is $20,000 to over $300,000, a wide span that reflects everything from the small frame homes in the countryside to the choice waterfront properties on Belleville Lake.

Most properties, Judy thought, would probably range between the high 20s and about $125,000. With a deep recession at the time of our visit, houses were selling substantially below their asking price and a rental market had developed. People would rent their houses for $300 to $400 a month, just enough to cover their mortgage payments.

Judy told us about a small brick ranch that had recently sold for $31,000—$5,000 under its real market value, she thought. It had a living room, kitchen, utility room, 1 bath, and 3 bedrooms. There was no basement, but it had a 2½-car attached garage and sat on a 60 × 120 lot. Taxes were $1,071.11 a year.

South of Belleville, a colonial listed at $107,000 had sold for $95,000. Built in 1967, it sat on 1¾ wooded acres with a stream and above-ground pool on the property, as well as a custom-built underground sprinkling system. It had 4 bedrooms, 2½ baths, living room, family room with fireplace, formal dining room, and a "dream kitchen" with work and eat-in areas. It also featured ceramic baths, a redwood deck patio, and central air conditioning and was sold with its appliances. Taxes were $3,000.

We asked about lake properties and Judy told us about a ranch listed at $170,000 that had sold for $140,000. It was custom built and had fireplaces in both the living and family rooms, a formal dining room, a kitchen with dinette area, 4 bedrooms, 3 full baths, and a full basement. There was no central air conditioning (most homes on the lake don't have that). It sat on 2½ acres and included a boat dock with a deck above it. Taxes were $3,581 a year.

With prices like that, an exceptionally low crime rate, and its accessibility to the entire metropolitan area, Van Buren Township should be the first place you investigate if you're planning a move to the Detroit area.

Where to get further information:

State

Travel Bureau, Michigan Department of Commerce, Box 30226, Lansing, MI 48909, telephone 800/292-2520 within Michigan or 800/248-5700 from out-of-state.

Regional

City of Detroit, Department of Public Information, 608 City-County Building, Detroit, MI 48219. Metropolitan Detroit Convention and Visitors Bureau, Renaissance Center, Suite 1950, Detroit, MI 48243. Dearborn Chamber of Commerce, 15544 Michigan Avenue, Dearborn, MI 48126. Ypsilanti Area Chamber of Commerce, Visitors and Convention Bureau, 11 N. Adams Street, Ypsilanti, MI 48197. Conference and Visitors Bureau, 207 E. Washington Street, Ann Arbor, MI 48104. Visitor Relations Office, University of Michigan, Ann Arbor, MI 48109.

Local

Belleville Area Chamber of Commerce, 116 4th Street, Belleville, MI 48111. Van Buren Township Hall, Tyler Street, Belleville, MI 48111.

Minnesota

The nation's twelfth-largest state is about 400 miles long, north to south, with an average width of 225 miles. That area is divided between rolling western plains and prairies, northern coniferous forests, and eastern hardwood forests. Much of it is wilderness and parts of that wilderness are preserved as Boundary Waters Canoe Area, the nation's only wilderness canoelands, and Voyageurs National Park, where French-Canadian voyageurs transported furs for a century and a half.

Indeed, for a state that is 1,000 miles from either ocean, Minnesota is defined to a surprising degree by its water resources. Three major river systems begin here: the Mississippi eventually empties into the Gulf of Mexico, the St. Lawrence into the Atlantic, and the Red River of the North into Hudson Bay. The Land of Ten Thousand Lakes actually has about 15,000 of them—more natural lakes than any other state. Three of the state's most scenic tours are along the bluffs of Lake Superior, the Hiawatha Valley of the Mississippi, and the valley of the Jolly Green Giant along the Minnesota River. At Duluth, Minnesota actually has a major freshwater inland port.

The North Star State is a sportsman's paradise. Its lakes and streams are filled with walleye, northern pike, trout, bass, and sunfish. Its woods abound with moose, white-tailed deer, black bear, timber wolves, fox, opossums, otters, and squirrels. In a state where the average first fall freeze is October 13 and the average last spring freeze is April 30, with more than 46 inches of snowfall in between, you shouldn't be surprised to find 225 downhill and cross country ski facilities, plus over 9,000 miles of snowmobile trails.

This is also a land of legends, myths, and speculation about ancient explorations. Foremost among the legendary figures are Paul Bunyon and Babe the Blue Ox, and if you don't believe Bunyon existed, you can have your photograph taken by his gigantic cradle in his birthplace of Akeley. In Minnesota, you can also find Casey Jones' Old 201 locomotive. And you'll be shown a mooring stone, a sword believed to be over 700 years old, and a rune stone inscription, all of which is said to indicate that Vikings explored this part of America 130 years before Columbus discovered us.

Of more recent vintage are the pioneers—in Minnesota, overwhelmingly Swedish, German, Norwegian, Irish, Danish, Finnish, and Bohemian. In the eastern part of the state, you can see an actual Little Red School House, built in 1905, and in the west you can visit the village of Walnut Grove, made famous by the books of Laura Ingalls Wilder and the "Little House on the Prairie" television series. Not all of the characters from frontier days were good guys, of course, and you can visit a town where Jesse James and his gang tried to rob the bank, as well as the town where his gang was finally broken up.

Minnesota's byways and shunpikes will lead you to still more delights. You can watch modern-day Indians fashion peace pipes from pipestones, just as their ancestors did, or visit the Halloween Capital of the World or the Bullhead Capital of the World. You can view the world's largest open-pit iron mine, or go on the only tour of an underground iron mine, visit the facilities of Le Sueur or Land O Lakes, or make an Americana pilgrimage to Redwood Falls, birthplace of Sears, Roebuck & Co. You can tour the Mayo Clinic, the boyhood home of Charles Lindbergh, Sauk Centre, the town made famous by Sinclair Lewis in *Main Street*, or the state's only two-story outhouse, in Belle Plaines. (Which makes us wonder, how many two-story outhouses does *our* state have?)

As you tour Minnesota, you'll find more live theaters (122 at last count) than in any place between Los Angeles and New York. You'll also find festivals and special events of every description—ethnic festivals such as Svenskarnes Dag, Kaffe Fest, and the Finnish Festival, the lobster-crayfish races and turtle races of Pequot Lakes, or King Turkey Days in Worthington, with its Gobbler Gallop matching Minnesota and Texas turkeys, everything from Jesse James Days to the month-long Minnesota Renaissance Festival.

And you thought they just sat around like frozen icicles all year long!

TWIN CITIES AREA

Minnesota has some of the richest farmland in the world, and ranks first in the United States in production of oats and second in spring wheat. Minneapolis is the processing and distributing capital for this agricultural bounty. It has four of the five largest milling companies in the world, including Nabisco, Pillsbury, and General Mills. Other major corporations include Honeywell and Control Data Corporation.

St. Paul, Minneapolis' neighbor to the east, is a governmental center as state capital of Minnesota. It is also a distribution center and South St. Paul has stockyards and is one of the nation's top markets in dairy cows and veal calves.

Minneapolis and St. Paul are also educational centers for the northern Midwest. The University of Minnesota, with 50,000 students, is located in Minneapolis, along with private institutions such as Augsburg College and Seminary and the Minneapolis School of Arts. St. Paul is home to a number of educational institutions, including Macalester College, Concordia College, and others.

TWIN CITIES AREA Crime Chart

	Crime Rate	Murder	Rape	Robbery	Aggravated Assault	Burglary	Larceny —Theft	Motor Vehicle Theft
United States								
U.S. Total	5,899.9	10.2	36.4	243.5	290.6	1,668.2	3,156.3	494.6
U.S. Metropolitan Areas	6,757.6	11.5	43.4	319.0	328.3	1,911.8	3,534.9	608.8
U.S. Rural Areas	2,290.4	7.5	15.5	22.5	136.9	830.2	1,143.9	133.9
Regional Crime Centers								
Minneapolis	9,676.8	9.7	100.8	612.4	335.3	3,136.2	4,728.7	753.7
St. Paul	8,245.3	6.0	52.2	326.3	372.5	2,718.3	4,262.7	507.4
Safe Place								
Apple Valley	2,591.0	0	9.2	13.8	27.5	632.9	1,820.6	87.1

The Twin Cities both have park systems that are considered among the finest in the country. Minneapolis has 153 parks and 22 lakes; St. Paul has almost 100 parks itself. Both cities have modern downtown shopping complexes—Nicollet Mall in Minneapolis and St. Paul's Town Square. Both cities are cultural and sports centers as well.

The overall metropolitan area has a population of about 2 million. Both of the central cities have high crime rates, but especially surprising to us was the high level of crimes of violence in Minneapolis. Its robbery and rape levels are roughly *double* the already horrendous rates for U.S. metropolitan areas. The suburbs of these cities are a mixed bag in regard to crime, but we found one with an excellent record on crime and made it our Safe Place for the Twin Cities area.

APPLE VALLEY

POPULATION: 21,806
NO. OF CRIMES: 565
CRIME RATE: 2,591.0 per 100,000

South of Minneapolis–St. Paul is a community with the charming name of Apple Valley, which conjures up images of orchards in a gently rolling river valley. You'll find plenty of woods around, but we were unsuccessful in our quest for orchards. As it turns out, there *may* have been some apple trees around at one time, but nobody's sure even about that. "Apple Valley," it seems, was a developer's name for a subdivision, later expanded to cover the entire area.

Before the 1960s, this was a farming area known as Lebanon Township. Then, in 1963, developer Orrin Thompson built his Apple Valley subdivision and the housing boom was on. A few years later residents decided to incorporate as a village and thought Apple Valley sounded better than Lebanon. By 1974 there were enough people for the municipality to change status from village to city.

Despite its rather unromantic, unhistorical roots, Apple Valley is a pleasant and attractive suburban community. Its location is convenient to both Minneapolis and St. Paul, about 15 to 20 miles north, and to the Minneapolis–St. Paul International Airport, located on the way north to the cities. The commute north includes a scenic crossing of the Minnesota River and its valley.

As with most larger suburban communities, you can find a diversity of subdivisions. All are well maintained, though they differ greatly in the size of the homes and terrain of their lots. The older subdivisions, with the smaller homes, tend to be close to Route 42. The homes are mostly one story in height and there is a tract-development look to them. Also along Route 42 are most of the businesses you'll find in Apple Valley, scattered along the highway but also concentrated in two adjacent shopping centers, Apple Valley Square and Apple Valley Center.

North of Route 42 (toward Minneapolis–St. Paul), the homes get larger along with their lots. Apple Valley Senior High School has an exceptionally modern plant, with large duplex condominiums across the street. Attractive ranches line the shores of Alimagnet Lake. And the largest homes are found north of 140th Street and the Apple Valley Golf Course (par 32, "open to the public"). You'll find ample numbers in both traditional and contemporary architectural styles, mostly 2-story and 3-story in height, with larger, wooded lots and winding streets. To the very north, forming a boundary between Apple Valley and Eagan, is Minnesota Zoological Garden, noted for its natural habitats housing 250 species of animals and 2,000 varieties of plants.

For real estate costs in Apple Valley, we talked to Sheila Myhervold, of Eberhardt Fox–Herfurth Real Estate, the local affiliate of Better Homes and Gardens. She told us that condominiums and town houses start in the mid-50s and go up into the 90s—the "twin homes" we saw by the high school. Single family homes start in the mid-60s and go up to $395,000. Between January and July 1982, 388 homes had been on the market. The median sale price for this suburban area was $76,000; for Apple Valley by itself the price undoubtedly would have been higher.

For $100,000, Sheila told us, you could get an Orrin Thompson tract home—a split-level house with perhaps 2,000 square feet of living area. As a tract builder, Sheila said, Thompson was very good, so that these older homes from the sixties would be comparable in many ways to today's custom-built houses. At this price, you'd get 3 bedrooms in a rambler, 4 in a split (2 up, 2 down), 1¾ baths, and either a family room on the first floor or an amusement room in the lower level of a split. There aren't too many formal dining rooms here, but you could expect to get a formal living room and a country kitchen with eating area. A rambler would have a basement; you'd be using that area in a split-level house. There would be a 2-car attached garage and a good sized lot, 100 × 150 on the average.

A medium-priced house—say, $149,900—would have 4 bedrooms, 3 baths (including a master bath), kitchen, dining room, living room, family room, and amusement room. With 2,400 square feet, it would have a 3-car garage and a 110 × 160 lot.

Building lots start at $21,000. That's both the 1 acre lots and standard-sized lots, since the price depends on location and the land. There are many lots available in the $24,000–$25,000 range, Sheila told us.

A table distributed by the Northwest Metropolitan Chamber of Commerce compared 1982 estimated taxes on a $75,000 homestead in some ninety-six communities in the Minneapolis–St. Paul area. It was estimated that the tax load in Apple Valley would be $483. In the ranking from 1 (high) to 96 (low), Apple Valley was 64—moderate to low in its tax rate.

Sheila Myhervold, our real estate contact, had also given us some tax estimates and they were somewhat higher. She thought taxes on a $100,000 house in Apple Valley would probably be around $800 and around $1,500 for a $150,000 house.

As you would expect in a growing suburban community, where everyone is from somewhere else, there's a strong emphasis on community activities and "getting involved." In addition to the good work that gets done, it's a great way to make new friends. The list of civic groups distributed by the chamber of commerce includes some sixty-eight organizations and activities. The parks and recreation department lists eight parks available for the activities and enjoyment of residents, plus the facilities of the Apple Valley Pool and Racquet Club, the Apple Valley Sports Facility, the Lebanon Hills Golf Course, and the Westview Community Building.

With all these activities going on in the community, there's certain to be something of interest to you. Add in the countless activities and attractions of Minneapolis and St. Paul, so conveniently near, and you'll see why the Twin Cities area is regarded as one of the finest places to live in the northern half of the United States.

Where to get further information:

State

Minnesota Tourist Information Center, 480 Cedar Street, St. Paul, MN 55101; telephone 800/328-1461 from out-of-state or 800/652-9747 from within the state.

Regional

Minneapolis Convention and Tourism Commission, 15 S. 5th Street, Minneapolis, MN 55402. Greater Minneapolis Chamber of Commerce, same address. St. Paul Convention, Exhibition and Tourism Commission, Landmark Center, 75 W. 5th Street, St. Paul, MN 55102. St. Paul Chamber of Commerce, 701 N. Central Tower, 445 Minnesota Street, St. Paul, MN 55102.

Bloomington Convention and Visitors Bureau, 8200 Humboldt Avenue, S., Suite 213, Bloomington, MN 55431.

Local

Apple Valley Chamber of Commerce, 7373 W. 147th Street, Apple Valley, MN 55124.

Mississippi

Even in Mississippi, cotton is no longer king. The Magnolia State still produces more long-staple cotton than any other state and ranks second in total cotton production, but soybeans are now its leading cash crop. Rice, corn, wheat, fruits, and sugarcane are also important crops today and the state's overall economy has diversified to the point where oil and gas production, the chemical industry, food-processing, forestry products, livestock, and seafood are all significant contributors. Mississippi's Gulf Coast for example, produces nearly one half of the oysters and one fourth of all shrimp canned in the United States.

The antebellum charm of Natchez and the Confederate shrines at Vicksburg remain major tourist attractions, but the subtropical Gulf Coast is by far the most popular resort and vacation area. It is also a leading center for jobs and retirement, making this 85-mile coastline a natural place in which to seek a Safe Place.

MISSISSIPPI'S GULF COAST

Strung along the Mississippi Gulf Coast is a chain of pleasant towns and cities that are dependent upon industry, commercial fishing, and tourism as the keystones of their economy. Chief among them are Biloxi, Gulfport, and Pascagoula.

Biloxi, with a population of about 50,000, is the major resort and the cultural and historical center of the coast. Keesler Air Force Base, the major electronics training center of the U.S. Air Force, is a key part of the economy. As a resort, Biloxi offers 25 miles of coastline, motels and resort hotels catering to the tourists who flock to the white sand beaches along the seawall and Beach Boulevard, and deep-sea fishing expeditions. Beauvoir, the last home of Confederate President Jefferson Davis, leads the list of historical attractions and cultural activities include art festivals, symphony concerts, and ballet, opera, and theatrical productions.

Gulfport, population 40,000, is the commercial and business center of the coast. Its industries include the manufacturing of paper products and you will find Central and South American ships unloading at the banana terminal in its deep-sea harbor.

Pascagoula, population 30,000, has one of the South's great shipyards and an oil refinery. It also is the site of the oldest building still standing in the Missis-

MISSISSIPPI GULF COAST Crime Chart

	Crime Rate	Murder	Rape	Robbery	Aggravated Assault	Burglary	Larceny —Theft	Motor Vehicle Theft
United States								
U.S. Total	5,899.9	10.2	36.4	243.5	290.6	1,668.2	3,156.3	494.6
U.S. Metropolitan Areas	6,757.6	11.5	43.4	319.0	328.3	1,911.8	3,534.9	608.8
U.S. Rural Areas	2,290.4	7.5	15.5	22.5	136.9	830.2	1,143.9	133.9
Regional Crime Centers								
Gulfport, Miss.	11,203.7	20.2	75.8	275.2	1,426.7	2,999.8	5,825.3	580.8
Mobile, Ala.	10,575.1	27.1	72.2	479.4	762.7	3,575.5	5,109.5	548.6
New Orleans, La.	9,605.4	39.1	105.4	833.2	487.5	2,537.6	4,602.0	1,000.6
Safe Place								
Ocean Springs, Miss.	2,275.2	6.9	20.7	41.4	372.3*	1,592.7	**	241.3

* Includes simple assault as well as aggravated assault. ** Not available.

sippi Valley—the Old Spanish Fort. Built in 1718 by the French, it became a Spanish possession fifty years later. The Pascagoula River, near here, is known locally as the Singing River, for the low humming noise that crescendos, dies, then starts again. There is an Indian legend to explain the mystery, something scientists have not resolved.

And just short distances away are two of the South's most interesting cities, New Orleans and Mobile.

No survey of the Gulf Coast would be complete, either, without mention of the seven islands lying off the coast of Mississippi, accessible only by boat and now preserved as the Gulf Islands National Seashore Park. Petit Bois and Horn islands are bird and wildlife sanctuaries, respectively. Sailing vessels used to stop at Round Island, and Deer Island, adjacent to Biloxi, has legends galore of buried pirate treasure and is a favorite for moonlight picnics. The Isle of Caprice disappeared below the surface in the 1930s, but its artesian well still serves as a drinking fountain at sea. Cat Island was the scene of the first mutiny on American soil, in 1757, and in 1814 Jean Couevas, called the Hero of Cat Island, refused to lead the British fleet through the tricky passages of the coastal area, thus giving Andy Jackson time to prepare for the Battle of New Orleans. Its fort, called Fort Twiggs by the Confederates and Fort Massachusetts by the Union forces, changed hands three times during the War Between the States. Excursion boats will take you there from Biloxi and Gulfport.

The entire Mississippi Gulf Coast is popular today with retirees, as well as young families seeking jobs that will also allow them to take advantage of the area's superb recreational opportunities. Unfortunately, these new residents often discover that crime—something they probably thought they were leaving behind—is worse here than in their previous home. As our Mississippi Gulf Coast Crime Chart shows (page 209), the entire area from New Orleans to Mobile is marked by exceptionally high rates of crime—and most notably crimes of violence.

There is a community, however, that allows you to enjoy the coast without having to fear constantly for your life or your property. It was one of our original Safe Places in 1972 and we're pleased that it is still a Safe Place today.

OCEAN SPRINGS

POPULATION: 14,504
NO. OF CRIMES: 330
CRIME RATE: 2,275.2 per 100,000

Across from Biloxi, on the eastern side of the Bay of Biloxi, we discovered a community not quite like the others along the Mississippi Gulf Coast. This one is almost entirely residential and it occupies the highest point on the Mississippi coast, an area of densely wooded and slightly rolling terrain.

Ocean Springs is willing to let Biloxi, Gulfport, and Pascagoula be the commercial and industrial centers of the coast. It seems content to be a pleasant and charming place to live and among its residents are many of the executives, technicians, and white-collar workers from those busier communities. We found charming lanes in Ocean Springs, shaded by huge oak and pecan trees. We found older homes that fed one's nostalgia for an earlier period, as well as modern but tasteful houses set in the forest or along a bayou or lagoon. We also found delightful shops—pottery stores, antique and gift shops, and galleries that have given Ocean Springs a reputation as an artists' and craftsmen's colony.

The original French establishment of Biloxi, founded by Pierre Lemoyne d'Iberville in 1699, was on the grounds now occupied by Ocean Springs. Iberville's men didn't seem to respect the law prohibiting fraternization with Indian maidens, so a few years later several frigates brought in some young French ladies—accompanied by four nuns who stayed until the ladies were all safely married. When Biloxi was moved across the bay to its present location, the original settlement became known as Old Biloxi and survived as an Indian trading post. Years later it was the site of a Spanish garrison and with the Louisiana Purchase in 1803, it became part of the United States.

In the nineteenth century the name of Ocean Springs was coined, for a number of springs thought to have healing power were located here (they have since mostly disappeared) and the area had become popular as a health resort. Steamboats between New Orleans and Mobile made it a regular stop and the Ocean Springs Hotel was the oldest on the coast. As late as the turn of the century, the Louisville & Nashville Railroad offered $1.00 round-trip excursions from Mobile and New Orleans. Later, Ocean Springs became a shipping center for pecans and citrus (mostly satsumas), but with a series of cold winters the groves died off and were not replanted once the Great Depression set in.

Today, the major tourist attraction in Ocean Springs is the headquarters for Gulf Islands National Seashore Park. In addition to a campground on the mainland, there are daily boat tours of the shore area, seasonal boat excursions to one of the wilderness islands, and charter fishing boat services. The park draws more than a half million visitors a year.

A number of small firms are located in Ocean Springs. Among them are three that deal with optical systems and components, a boatbuilder, an apparel manufacturer, a lumber-products company, and a pottery. The Gulf Coast Research Laboratory is also here; although it deals primarily with marine resources research, it also offers courses in marine biology and geology.

Ocean Springs' residents are busy throughout the year with a full calendar of cultural and recreational activities. Annual events include the d'Iberville Landing Celebration, the Fall Arts Festival, the Christmas Tour of Homes, and an annual judged art exhibit of the Ocean Springs Art Association. Shearwater Pottery is located in the home of Walter Anderson, a renowned artist who died in 1965 and whose life story was recently made into a television documentary. The Ocean Springs Community Center, with its murals by the artist, actually serves as an Anderson museum and plans for a true museum are in preparation.

In addition to the national park, Ocean Springs' recreational facilities include nine town parks (with a full schedule of activities), the only YMCA facility located on the Mississippi Gulf Coast, and a small-craft harbor. The Ocean Springs Yacht Club and the Treasure Oak Country Club are located in town, with three 18-hole golf courses also located just minutes away.

We ran into some difficulties when we tried to determine Ocean Springs' crime rate. We had a few questions about the statistics we had received for our comparison year of 1980, from the chief of police at that time. When we called early in 1983, we talked with the town's new chief, Capt. Kevin Alves.

In short, the statistics for previous years are in somewhat of a mess. It's not that they are incomplete or deceptive. They just aren't categorized properly for reporting purposes. As the new chief, Captain Alves is looking forward to the installation of a computer which will help in storing statistical information and he promises that we will have detailed, accurate figures for our next edition of *Safe Places*.

Meanwhile, the figures for 1980 (see our Mississippi Gulf Coast Crime Chart, page 209) reflect 1 murder, 3 rapes, 6 robberies, 231 burglaries, and 35 auto thefts. We had received no figures for larceny from the previous chief and the 54 assaults includes simple as well as aggravated assault. As a general pattern, most of these would be simple assaults and therefore not counted in our crime totals. We went ahead and included them anyway, since we *didn't* have figures for larceny-theft.

So, our total crime rate for 1980 is an estimate and not as accurate as in our other chapters. We are convinced, however, that even with the most accurate statistics Ocean Springs would still qualify as a Safe Place. Our overall crime rate of 2,275.2 is way below our cutoff point of 4,000 crimes per 100,000 population, so we feel secure in retaining Ocean Springs as a Safe Place.

This feeling was augmented by going over 1981 and 1982 statistics with Captain Alves. We did our best to make sense of the statistics and records that he had inherited and even when we threw in "everything but the kitchen sink," we ended up with crime rates still low enough to qualify the town as a Safe Place.

One further point about those 1980 statistics. You will note that in most crime categories, Ocean Springs is above the U.S. rural levels of crime. In this regard, it's not as safe a community as many of the others in this book. The important comparison, however, is with the other communities in this Gulf Coast area. Ocean Springs' crime rates were not only below U.S. averages in the different categories; they were *way* below the rates for this region. This is a high-crime region, so you will never have cause for complacency, but by comparison with surrounding communities you're in a Safe Place.

On to real estate. At Harbor Realty, we talked with Sherry Vollmuth, an agent, and Connie Smith, the broker. We were told that while properties range in price from the low 20s to $300,000, the average price was probably in the $68,000 to $70,000 range because of the large number of military personnel who buy homes in Ocean Springs.

In the $72,000 to $80,000 range, you would find the best-selling types of houses in the two best subdivisions for that price range. These could be contemporaries or ranches, with all amenities and 1,500 to 1,700 square feet of living area, on a 100 × 175 lot. You would likely get 3 bedrooms, 2 baths, an eat-in kitchen, and a 2-car garage. Since 1980 most houses have a formal dining room and a "great room," which serves as a combination living room and family room.

Executive homes start at $85,000 and go up in price, occasionally, to $400,000. You will find these on heavily wooded, irregularly shaped lots, in areas that do not have a subdivision look. For $125,000, you could get a Williamsburg or Southern colonial executive house with 4 bedrooms, 2½ baths, and a total of 1,800 to 2,200 square feet of living area.

Town houses and condominiums are beginning to make their appearance. In Ocean Springs, you can get a 2-bedroom condominium for $80,000 to $100,000.

Sherry told us that a nice building lot, with trees, will cost $20,000 and up in Ocean Springs. She had two lots available in the Fort Bayou area of town. One lot, 90 × 152, was selling for $22,000. The other, at $24,500, was slightly smaller (86 × 140) but had a water view. Actual water frontage is more expensive, as you'd expect. Sherry had a lot in town that had 221 feet of frontage on Fort Bayou and it was listed for $50,000.

We have traveled through virtually all of the U.S. coastline along the Gulf of Mexico. There are certainly other areas that are equally charming—the Florida panhandle, the eastern shore of Mobile Bay, the Galveston and Padre Island areas of Texas come to mind. But for an interesting and convenient location,

Ocean Springs is hard to beat. Being halfway between New Orleans and Mobile, you are close enough to enjoy them when you want yet far enough removed to enjoy peace and quiet the rest of the time. The relaxing, informal atmosphere you will find in Ocean Springs is contagious, so consider yourself forewarned before you set foot in this enchanting spot on the Gulf of Mexico!

Where to get further information:

State

Division of Tourism, Mississippi Department of Economic Development, P.O. Box 849, Jackson, MS 39205; telephone 800/647-2290.

Regional

Mississippi Gulf Coast Convention and Visitors Bureau, P.O. Box 4554, Biloxi, MS 39531. Biloxi Chamber of Commerce, P.O. Drawer CC, Biloxi, MS 39531. Gulfport Chamber of Commerce, P.O. Drawer FF, Gulfport, MS 39501. Pascagoula–Moss Point Area Chamber of Commerce, 825 Denny Avenue, P.O. Drawer P, Pascagoula, MS 39567. Long Beach Area Chamber of Commerce, P.O. Box 396, Long Beach, MS 39560. Pass Christian Chamber of Commerce, P.O. Box 307, Pass Christian, MS 39571.

Local

Ocean Springs Chamber of Commerce, P.O. Box 187, Ocean Springs, MS 39564. W. P. Crawford, Superintendent, Gulf Islands National Seashore Park, U.S. Department of the Interior, National Park Service, Ocean Springs, MS 39564.

Montana

Montana, the nation's fourth-largest state, averages 550 miles in length, east to west, and 275 miles in width, north to south. The eastern third is plains country, the central third, plains and isolated mountain ranges, the western third, high mountains and mountain valleys. This western section contains both the highest and the lowest points in the state and is bisected in a north to south direction by the Continental Divide. And it is this western portion that offers the dramatic vistas most people associate with Montana, from the northern reaches of Glacier National Park to the thermal wonders of Yellowstone.

Montana is basically an agricultural state. Livestock is the most important single product, with hard winter wheat, barley, hay, and sugar beets also important to the economy. So are lumber and lumber products and mining—for copper, silver, gold, lead, zinc, oil, natural gas, and much more.

This is the Old West, memorialized by the great Western painter Charlie Russell and by A. B. Guthrie, Jr., in *The Big Sky.* The title of his classic has become the state's nickname and nobody who has ever been to Montana needs any explanation why this is called the Big Sky Country.

RED LODGE

POPULATION: 1,896
NO. OF CRIMES: 54
CRIME RATE: 2,848.1 per 100,000

Take a very Western-looking town with a wide Main Street and shops displaying Stetsons and Levis in their windows, give it 1,896 friendly and neighborly residents (well, there may be a couple of bad hombres among them, though we didn't meet any), then place that community at the base of some of the most spectacular terrain in the United States—and you have Red Lodge, Montana.

North of Red Lodge is countryside sloping gradually downward toward Billings, the commercial and cultural center of southern Montana. Just a convenient 60 miles away, Billings is a shopping center, a regional medical center, and an all-around pleasant small city of some 67,000 people.

South of Red Lodge is the majestic Beartooth Range of the Rocky Mountains, containing the highest point in Montana (Granite Peak, 12,799 feet high), Grasshopper Glacier (which takes its name from millions of grasshoppers embedded in its glacial ice), and vast expanses of forests, primitive areas, lush meadows, and gushing mountain streams. In all, Beartooth country has more than twenty-five mountain peaks that rise higher than 12,000 feet, ten rock-strewn plateaus that lie above 11,000 feet, numerous glaciers, more than 300 lakes, over 5,000 waterfalls, and everywhere in the spring and summer a profusion of alpine wildflowers.

Traversing that range, between Red Lodge and Yellowstone National Park, is an engineering wonder—the Beartooth Highway. Starting outside Red Lodge at an elevation of 5,650 feet, a series of five switchbacks provides a gradual climb to 10,942 feet. You then traverse arctic tundra and skirt glacial lakes, following the most spectacular route into Yellowstone. Small wonder that CBS News correspondent Charles Kuralt, who's been around, calls this the most beautiful drive in America.

Then there's Yellowstone itself, the world's first national park and the nation's largest: over 10,000 geysers, fumaroles, hot springs, boiling terraces, and bubbling mud volcanoes known as paintpots, home to some of the most abundant wildlife in the country.

All of this, you might say, is in Red Lodge's backyard. They make backyards rather big in this part of the country.

We were interested in the origins of the town's name and just a short way south on U.S. 212 we found an explanation on a roadside sign, courtesy of the Montana Highway Department. "According to tradition," it said,

> a band of Crow Indians left the main tribe and moved west into the foothills of the Beartooth Range many years ago. They smeared their council teepee with red clay and this primitive artistry resulted in the name Red Lodge.
>
> This region is a bonanza for scientists. It is highly fossilized and Nature has opened a book on Beartooth Butte covering about a quarter of a billion years of geological history. It makes pretty snappy reading for parties interested in some of the ologies—palaeontology for example. Dinosaur eggs have been found that grade just as high in omelet value as the Gobi Desert products.
>
> Some students opine that prehistoric men existed here several million years earlier than heretofore believed. Personally we don't know, but if there *were* people prowling around that long ago of course they would pick Montana as the best place to live.

Now, when was the last time you've seen a highway department sign that was as much fun to read as that?

Red Lodge is hardly a place where one would expect to find a tamburitza band or a native group of Tyrolean dancers, but such Yugoslavian and German influences are joined by others from Scotland, Italy, Scandinavia, England, Finland, and Ireland. In its early days, it seems, Red Lodge was a mining town and attracted persons from throughout the European continent. The Italians and

Finns came to work the coal mines, the Germans and Scandinavians to till the surrounding farmlands. In 1951 the citizens of Red Lodge decided to celebrate this ethnic diversity with an eight-day Festival of Nations each year and that observance has done much to put this small community on the map. Each day the heritage of one of the nationalities is highlighted with entertainment programs, arts and crafts, and cooking events; there are art exhibits, a flower show, bagpipes, and parades. Yet, impressive as the Festival of Nations is for a town this size, it is only one of a number of observances put on annually by this high-spirited town.

In winter, for example, there are dog sled races in January and the Red Lodge Winter Festival and tracks competition in March. April brings the Peak-to-Prairie Triathlon. Summer events include the Run-to-the-Sun Old Car Rally, the Beartooth Run, the annual 4th of July Home of Champions Rodeo (with a parade, fireworks, and evening street dances), the Carbon County Fair, and the Top-of-the-World Bar. (That's when the Red Lodge Chamber of Commerce buys motorists a drink from a snowbank on top of Beartooth Pass, one day every year in July—the exact date always kept a secret.) The town is also home to the Red Lodge International Ski Race Camp and the Red Lodge Music Festival, a private music camp that draws students from all over the country, with faculty and student concerts open to the public.

Red Lodge has a historic district of buildings and houses on and off Main Street that were built between 1893 and 1910, during the height of Red Lodge's coal mining boom. Reminders of the ethnic groups that settled Red Lodge are preserved in Hibug Town, Finn Town, and Little Italy. Other attractions include the Carbon County Arts Guild Gallery, the Carbon County Museum, the summer theater offerings of *The Great Pretenders,* and the Red Lodge Zoo, the state's largest, with more than 200 native and exotic animals and birds.

The year-round backbone of the local economy is farming (hay, wheat, and barley) and ranching. Tourism is also important—Yellowstone traffic in the summer and skiing in the winter at the Red Lodge Mountain Ski Area, where the longest run is 2 miles with a vertical drop of 2,016 feet. The more than 100 businesses in town include two banks, five grocery stores, two drugstores, four clothing stores, five service stations, real estate offices, law offices, and many other services.

The Red Lodge school system has 450 students enrolled from kindergarten through high school. A large percentage of the graduates have been recipients of national scholarships. The nearest colleges are Eastern Montana College and Rocky Mountain College in Billings and Northwest Community College in Powell, Wyoming—all within a radius of 60 miles. Eastern Montana College has a summer session in Red Lodge.

Medical facilities consist of the Carbon County Memorial Hospital (28 hospital beds and 24 nursing-home beds), the Carbon County Health Care Center (an 80-bed skilled nursing facility), four medical doctors in residence, two dentists, and an optometrist.

Churches in town are St. Agnes Catholic Church, Red Lodge Community

Church, United Church of Christ, Church of Latter Day Saints, Messiah Lutheran Church, Red Lodge Alliance Chapel, Calvary Episcopal Church, and the Southern Baptist Church.

Red Lodge has an alpine climate at an elevation of 5,555 feet. In a sample thirty-year period, there were only three days per year with a maximum of 90 degrees or warmer and twenty-six days a year of temperatures of zero or colder. Red Lodge averages a 52-inch snowfall per year and has an average of 104 freeze-free days between June and September.

In our comparison year of 1980, Red Lodge had no murders, rapes, or robberies, but 7 aggravated assaults. Property crime consisted of 21 burglaries, 17 larceny-thefts, and 9 motor vehicle thefts. This placed Red Lodge below U.S. rural crime rates in all categories except aggravated assault, burglary, and motor vehicle theft. Carbon County had an even lower crime rate.

As our Montana Crime Chart (below) shows, other communities in the state do not fare as well. Great Falls, Helena, and Missoula all have crime rates that are higher than those of New York City and Washington, D.C.

MONTANA Crime Chart

	Crime Rate	Murder	Rape	Robbery	Aggravated Assault	Burglary	Larceny —Theft	Motor Vehicle Theft
United States								
U.S. Total	5,899.9	10.2	36.4	243.5	290.6	1,668.2	3,156.3	494.6
U.S. Metropolitan Areas	6,757.6	11.5	43.4	319.0	328.3	1,911.8	3,534.9	608.8
U.S. Rural Areas	2,290.4	7.5	15.5	22.5	136.9	830.2	1,143.9	133.9
Regional Crime Centers								
Great Falls	10,884.2	0	17.7	99.0	166.2	2,586.3	7,384.0	631.1
Helena	11,969.9	8.4	25.2	67.2	130.2	2,258.8	8,976.4	503.8
Missoula	13,239.0	9.8	55.3	87.8	260.3	1,229.9	10,935.4	660.5
Safe Place								
Red Lodge	2,848.1	0	0	0	369.2	1,107.6	896.6	474.7

At the chamber of commerce, we had a pleasant talk with its director, Jim Coates. We discovered that he and his wife came originally from Houston—in fact, his wife was from the Memorial Drive area that is represented as one of our Safe Places for the Houston area. They moved first to Idaho, then here to Red Lodge, and much prefer the small-town and Big Sky setting.

And at Beartooth Realty, Leighton Herigstad brought us up to date on real estate costs.

At the low end of the price range, Leighton said, you can get a small 1-bedroom house in town for as little as $17,000, but it would need considerable plumbing work and other renovation. In the $30,000 to $40,000 range, you'd still have an older home but it would be more updated. For $49,500, he had a house on an average-sized (40 × 140) lot, with city water and sewage. It had a bedroom and a bath on the first floor, and 2 bedrooms and a 3/4 bath upstairs.

For $79,500, he had a newer home (built in the past ten years) with a double garage in back and situated on a 50 × 150 lot. The main floor of this house had a living room with dining area, kitchen, 2 bedrooms, and a bath. Then in the finished basement was a 2-bedroom apartment that rented for $350 a month. Taxes on this property were $744 a year.

Leighton told us there were four or five homes available in the deluxe category, priced between $79,500 and $117,000. These are homes built in the past few years, in top condition, with all the newer appliances and built-ins. They usually are located in choice spots with views and the lots range in size from 1/3 acre to over 1 acre. For $117,500, he had such a 3-bedroom, 2-bath house on an acre of land.

We asked about land outside town. "We get calls every day for 5-acre and 10-acre tracts," Leighton replied, "but there's hardly any for sale." He explained that Montana has a lot of regulations that are meant to keep the state from being developed too rapidly and with anything under 20 acres the seller has to go through a lot of red tape. But he did have *some* land available.

First, outside town, next to a nice subdivision, one 2-acre tract and one 3-acre tract were available. These were being offered for $7,000 per acre, and you would have to put in your own septic and well.

Another lot, just over an acre in size, was located less than 2 miles north of Red Lodge on the main road to Billings, and had frontage on the trout creek next to the highway. This is a choice location and sanitation restrictions have been lifted on the property, which means you are allowed to put in a septic system. It was being offered for $17,500.

And about 5 miles north of town, there was a ranch of 175 acres of irrigated hay ground. Leighton said the owner would consider selling a 40-acre parcel for $1,200 an acre.

There you have it—one of the nation's most majestic mountain ranges, one of its most scenic alpine highways, one of the world's few thermal playgrounds, and a vast wilderness and wildlife empire, all easily accessible from the rustic Western town of Red Lodge. Big-city conveniences are an easy drive away at Billings, while Red Lodge combines small-town friendliness and a rural pace with a healthy and varied community life. With that sort of combination it's like sitting on top of the world.

Where to get further information:

State

Travel Promotion Bureau, State of Montana, Helena, MT 59620; telephone 800/548-3390.

Local

Red Lodge Area Chamber of Commerce, P.O. Box 998, Red Lodge, MT 59068.

Nevada

Nevada is one of our largest states in area and one of the smallest in population. Even though it's our fastest-growing state, there still are fewer than eight residents per square mile. It has two industries of consequence—gambling and mining—although its low taxes have now made it a warehousing center as well and livestock are raised on a major scale. In 1980, about 48 percent of the state's revenues were raised by gambling—called gaming here.

Gold was first discovered in 1850, but it wasn't until the discovery of the fabulous Comstock Lode of silver and gold in 1859 that the territory was really on the map. For another seventy years, mining booms were followed by mining busts and residents decided they wanted a sounder base for the state's economy. So, in 1931, gambling was legalized and the marriage and divorce laws were liberalized. The Reno area boomed with the arrival of casinos in the city and divorce ranches in the surrounding countryside.

At this time, Las Vegas was a sleepy little desert town in southern Nevada. But in 1931, construction of Hoover Dam started on the Colorado River, at a point where it forms the border between Nevada and Arizona. This was then the largest hydroelectric construction project in the world and soon the influx of workers boosted the area's population 50 percent to nearly 6,000. With the combination of legalized gambling and cheap water and electricity from the dam project, the desert bloomed—but with neon signs rather than agriculture.

After World War II came the growth of the resort hotels and with them big entertainment to lure customers to the gaming tables. Downtown's Fremont Street—"the world's most brightly lit street"—has some of the earlier casinos, such as the Mint and the Nugget, with its traditionally Western decor. But the most famous concentration is along the Strip, Las Vegas Boulevard south of downtown. This is where you'll find Caesar's Palace, the Dunes, the Flamingo, the Sahara, the Tropicana, and so many other dazzling casinos and hotels.

Today, Las Vegas has a population of 165,000, with a total of about 460,000 in all of Clark County. It also attracts over 12 million visitors a year. Las Vegas can justly be called the gambling capital of the world and the entertainment

LAS VEGAS AREA Crime Chart

	Crime Rate	Murder	Rape	Robbery	Aggravated Assault	Burglary	Larceny —Theft	Motor Vehicle Theft
United States								
U.S. Total	5,899.9	10.2	36.4	243.5	290.6	1,668.2	3,156.3	494.6
U.S. Metropolitan Areas	6,757.6	11.5	43.4	319.0	328.3	1,911.8	3,534.9	608.8
U.S. Rural Areas	2,290.4	7.5	15.5	22.5	136.9	830.2	1,143.9	133.9
Regional Crime Centers								
Henderson	5,896.6	8.2	61.4	118.7	110.5	1,816.8	3,384.1	396.9
Las Vegas	10,743.5	23.9	75.5	684.0	363.8	3,769.1	4,934.9	892.3
North Las Vegas	10,276.7	32.7	107.6	575.3	1,174.1	3,786.5	4,006.4	594.1
Safe Place								
Boulder City	3,469.4	0	0	41.5	20.8	955.6	2,306.0	145.4

capital of the world. It is also one of the major sports centers and convention centers of the nation.

When gambling was legalized, faro and poker were the most popular games. Today blackjack is king of the gaming tables, with craps, roulette, and baccarat among the other leading attractions and poker regaining some of its former popularity. One-armed bandits—the slot machines—are everywhere. You'll find them in restaurants, grocery stores, drugstores, even launderettes and gas stations. If you're a compulsive gambler, you had better never even visit here, much less consider moving to the area. But if you can take it or leave it, as the pocketbook decrees, then living near Las Vegas or Reno opens up one of the greatest entertainment bargains anywhere.

BOULDER CITY

POPULATION: 9,627
NO. OF CRIMES: 334
CRIME RATE: 3,469.4 per 100,000

Boulder City, Nevada, started out as a company town. The "company," in this case, happened to be the United States government, which started building massive Hoover Dam in 1931 and needed a place to house the engineers, superintendents, and workers on the project. The result was Boulder City, a planned community of pleasant homes, open spaces and parklands, schools and churches, recreation areas, and a new innovation—off-street parking. Here, on a plateau 2,500 feet above sea level, air currents made the summers cooler and the winters warmer than in other desert locales and the soil was favorable for the growth of grass, shrubs, and trees. With water, which was plentiful once the Hoover Dam was completed, the town became an oasis in the Southwestern desert—or, as it likes to put it, "the best little city by a dam site."

Congress established Boulder City as an independent municipality in 1958,

and in front of the railroad depot." Boulder City, on the other hand, "was such a green oasis, had such a small-town atmosphere, and an unhurried tranquil air."

That desert oasis is still there. With all the recreational opportunities of Lake Mead at your doorstep, and with Las Vegas just 23 miles down the highway, Boulder City combines the best of small-town living with outdoor and indoor activities that can't be topped anywhere in the United States.

Where to get further information:

State

Nevada Department of Economic Development, Capitol Complex, Carson City, NV 89710.

Regional

Las Vegas Chamber of Commerce, 2301 E. Sahara Avenue, Las Vegas, NV 89104. Latin Chamber of Commerce, 829 S. 6th Street, Suite 3, Las Vegas, NV 89101. Las Vegas Convention and Visitors Bureau, 3150 S. Paradise Road, Las Vegas, NV 89105. Allied Arts Council, 300 Las Vegas Boulevard N., Las Vegas, NV 89101.

Local

Boulder City Chamber of Commerce, 1497 Nevada Highway, Boulder City, NV 89005. Superintendent, Lake Mead National Recreation Area, Boulder City, NV 89005.

New Hampshire

"Live Free or Die" is its motto, emblazoned on New Hampshire license plates. The Granite State was the first of the thirteen colonies to establish an independent government, with the adoption of a written constitution by the Provincial Congress meeting at Exeter, on January 5, 1776. And it cast the ninth vote that was necessary for the acceptance or rejection of the U.S. Constitution.

That spirit of independence lives on today. Modern-day New Hampshire is most visible every presidential election year, when its primary, the earliest in the nation, kicks off the race for the White House. In between, the state is a symbol of hope for beleaguered taxpayers everywhere, being the only one remaining without either a state income tax or a sales tax—and it's determined to stay that way.

Skeptics are quick to point out that the lack of a state income tax or sales tax places the burden of supporting state and local government almost entirely on property taxes—allowing renters to enjoy a free ride. Nevertheless, plenty of property owners in Massachusetts have been happy to accept that burden. The flight from "Taxachusetts" has made the Nashua area the fastest-growing metropolitan area in New England and New Hampshire the fastest-growing state in the region.

Although there are still many attractive small towns to maintain the New England image (we've picked three), New Hampshire's economy changed from an agricultural base to an industrial one in the nineteenth century. It is now the second most industrialized state in the union, on the basis of percentage of population so employed. Shoes and leather goods, textiles, lumber, wood and paper products, electronic equipment, and machinery are manufactured here. Tourism is the second largest contributor to the economy. In agriculture, dairy products, poultry, and vegetables are most important, but McIntosh apples and maple syrup and its products are perhaps most symbolic. More than 200 minerals are also found here—granite, mica, and feldspar being of chief commercial interest, along with sand and gravel.

Geographically, New Hampshire resembles a right triangle, about 180 miles north to south, with a width that ranges from some 20 miles in the far north to

100 miles in the far south. This compact area is dominated by the White Mountains, the highest in the Northeast—in fact, one third of the state has an elevation of 2,000 feet or more. Mount Washington is the highest peak at 6,288 feet. There are also some 1,300 lakes in New Hampshire, the largest being Lake Winnipesaukee, about 20 miles long and 12 miles wide. The state's Atlantic shoreline is just 18 miles long, but it includes the interesting maritime city of Portsmouth. That city was first called Strawbery Banke, but the name now dominates an area in which thirty-five homes and other structures, built from 1695 to the 1800s, have been restored.

As for the climate—well, the natives like to call it "invigorating." Summers are cool and refreshing and winters get colder the higher in elevation and the farther north you go, with a mean annual winter temperature of 17 degrees along the Canadian border. Snowfall ranges from 150 inches in the mountains to 50 inches annually along the coast. This climate is, in fact, a major attraction of the state: thirty-four major ski areas dominate winter sports, fall is foliage time, and spring is the time to visit maple-syrup sap houses and to enjoy the blossoms—the shadbush in early May, followed in turn by the cherry, apple, lilac, and laurel.

NEW HAMPSHIRE Crime Chart

	Crime Rate	Murder	Rape	Robbery	Aggravated Assault	Burglary	Larceny —Theft	Motor Vehicle Theft
United States								
U.S. Total	5,899.9	10.2	36.4	243.5	290.6	1,668.2	3,156.3	494.6
U.S. Metropolitan Areas	6,757.6	11.5	43.4	319.0	328.3	1,911.8	3,534.9	608.8
U.S. Rural Areas	2,290.4	7.5	15.5	22.5	136.9	830.2	1,143.9	133.9
Regional Crime Centers								
Boston, Mass.	13,465.6	16.4	86.0	1,337.8	777.8	3,027.5	4,483.8	3,736.3
Hampton, N.H.	9,892.3	0	38.1	104.8	142.9	3,078.2	5,708.6	819.6
Safe Places								
Hampstead	1,558.8	0	0	0	52.8	1,030.4	264.2	211.4
Kingston	2,091.9	0	0	0	24.3	973.0	827.0	267.6
Peterborough	1,879.5	0	0	0	81.7	326.9	1,287.0	183.9

Although crime in New Hampshire is not the problem it is in some other states, there still is no cause for apathy. Nearly all of the larger towns and cities and even most of the smaller towns had crime rates too high to be regarded as Safe Places. Capturing the dubious honor of being New Hampshire's crime center—among communities with a population of 10,000 or more—is coastal Hampton. Its overall crime rate is nearly as high as New York City's, though, as our crime chart shows, it consists almost entirely of property crime.

For our Safe Places, we picked two hamlets within commuting distance of Boston—Kingston and Hampstead—that are still unspoiled by the developers.

And in the Monadnock region we picked Thornton Wilder's *Our Town,* Peterborough, an eye-pleasing community nestled in eye-pleasing countryside. Enjoy!

KINGSTON

POPULATION: 4,111
NO. OF CRIMES: 86
CRIME RATE: 2,091.9 per 100,000

The most distinctive feature of this Rockingham County town is its elongated common—three or four blocks long, in fact, and a single block wide, lined by attractive homes, the town hall, and a small business center containing a neighborhood food store, pharmacy, cleaners, and restaurant. A plaque on the common honors one of Kingston's most distinguished citizens, Dr. Josiah Bartlett. A signer of the Declaration of Independence and the Articles of Confederation, he served New Hampshire as chief justice and as its first governor. He was also an innovator in medicine and practiced in Kingston for forty-five years.

This pleasant village-turned-suburb is almost entirely residential. A small shopping plaza is under construction; it will contain a food market, a hardware store, a bank, and some other shops to meet local needs. For more extensive shopping facilities, it is just a short drive to Exeter, Portsmouth, or Manchester.

Kingston's crime rate is low and the crime that does take place is almost entirely property crime. In 1980, there was just 1 aggravated assault; property crime consisted of 40 burglaries, 34 larceny-thefts, and 11 motor vehicle thefts. Adjusted for population, Kingston's crime rate was below U.S. rural levels in all categories except burglary (where it was just above rural levels) and auto theft (where it was high, like most of the Boston area).

In 1981, Kingston's crime rate actually decreased by one third. There were 4 aggravated assaults, but only 21 burglaries, 21 larceny-thefts, and 11 motor vehicle thefts. That year the town placed below U.S. rural rates of crime in all categories except motor vehicle theft.

Kingston's residents work throughout southern New Hampshire and northeastern Massachusetts. The town is located just 10 miles and fifteen minutes west of exit 1 of the New Hampshire Turnpike (Interstate 95). It is an equally short 10-mile drive south, on Route 125, to the Massachusetts border and I-495.

Gloria Stone, of the Kingston Real Estate Company, was most helpful in providing information on local properties. She explained that Kingston has a number of summer cottages on Kingston Lake and Pow-Wow Pond, as well as the larger homes built for year-round living. Some of the summer cottages are being converted to year-round homes, but that often poses a septic problem because of their small lots. Before buying such a property, be sure you check with town authorities and are certain that a full septic system will be allowed.

At the time of our visit (November 1982), there were five lake cottages on the market, priced from $31,900 to $45,000. For $38,900, for example, you could get a white shingle cottage that is at least twenty-five years old, with 5 rooms—2 bedrooms, 3/4 bath, living room, dining area, and kitchen. It has no garage or fireplace and was described as a "good starter home on good-sized lot. View of Pow-Wow Pond across street. If you are handy—this could be a dandy." Taxes in 1981 came to $477.30.

Seventeen year-round single-family homes were on the market, too, with prices as low as $49,000 and as high as $165,000. We picked three that seemed to be good examples of what you can find here:

- For $76,500: a tan clapboard colonial, about two hundred years old but well-preserved, with wide pine floors, wood stove, and stencil reproductions on several walls and hallways. It is near the center of town on a lot that measures 160 × 150 × 197 feet of street frontage. The second floor has 1 1/2 baths and 5 bedrooms, the largest measuring 12 × 16. The first floor consists of the living room, family room with dining area, eat-in kitchen, den, laundry, and 1/2 bath. Taxes in 1981 were $1,272.80.
- For $120,000: a white clapboard farmhouse that was renovated around 1970 and which is located on the town common. The 10 rooms consist of 6 bedrooms, including one that's 16 × 32, a full bath upstairs and 1/2 bath downstairs, and the living room, kitchen with dining area (16 × 32), den, office, and laundry. There is no fireplace and the garage is in a large attached barn. Taxes were $2,134.90 in 1981.
- And in the same price range, at $124,900: a new redwood contemporary on 2.1 acres, with a view of the beach and beach rights at Country Pond. This custom-built home has a living room, dining area and kitchen, family room, and full bath on the first floor, 3 bedrooms and a 3/4 bath on the second. Designed for wood heat, it contains two wood-stove heating units.

With prices like these, which would be hard to beat in Massachusetts, Kingston offers easy access to interstates and jobs throughout the area—a combination worth your consideration.

HAMPSTEAD

POPULATION: 3,785
NO. OF CRIMES: 59
CRIME RATE: 1,558.8 per 100,000

Hampstead is another idyllic village in southern Rockingham County, about 10 miles southwest of Kingston. If anything, it is less suburbanized and more countrified than our other Safe Place in the county.

Route 121 serves as Hampstead's main street and the village center is anchored by a handsome Congregational church and town hall. You'll find a bank, restaurant, pharmacy, and gas station here and that's about all. There are several small or medium-sized shopping areas elsewhere in the township, but otherwise it's rolling countryside—an exurb, as these rural-flavored commuter towns are sometimes called.

You're wondering why we picked two small towns so similar and so near to each other? The answer is that southeastern New Hampshire is the state's fastest-growing area, because of its proximity to Boston. And within a reasonable commuting distance, Kingston and Hampstead were the safest places around. Let us show you how our processes of elimination led us to these two peaceful communities.

We've mentioned that to qualify as a Safe Place, a town's overall crime rate had to be less than 4,000 per 100,000 population. And by the time we visited New Hampshire (in November 1982), we had its 1981 crime statistics as well as the ones for 1980, so we checked both years.

In Rockingham County, the only towns that qualified both years were Epping, Hampstead, Kingston, Newmarket, and Newtown. But then we determined the towns' rates in each of the seven index categories. Thus broken down, Newtown was too high in five categories one year and in two the other year; we felt uncomfortable with it. Epping and Newmarket were rather far north to begin with and when the figures were broken down, Epping was high in four categories each year, Newmarket in three. We discarded both of them and looked into Hampstead and Kingston, finding them satisfactory in the other amenities of life as well.

In Hillsborough County, another five towns had crime rates of under 4,000 both years. But when we broke down those rates into separate categories, we discarded Hollis, Hudson, and Merrimack as being too high in too many categories—including too many rapes in Hudson and Merrimack, too many robberies as well in Hudson. Amherst was very safe, but we thought the 9-mile congested trek to Nashua, much less to any place in Massachusetts, was too arduous to consider it a good commuting town. That left us with Peterborough, which we were delighted to accept, but it is still farther west and certainly is not a Boston commute.

So, on to Hampstead. In 1980, it had 2 aggravated assaults, 39 burglaries, 10 larceny-thefts, and 8 motor vehicle thefts. This meant it placed below U.S. rural rates in all categories except burglary and auto theft and those were still way below metropolitan rates.

In 1981, Hampstead's crime actually decreased by one third. There was 1 murder and 1 aggravated assault, as well as 25 burglaries, 8 larceny-thefts, and 5 motor vehicle thefts. It ranked below U.S. rural rates across the board except for murder, where the one incident and the small population created a statistical aberration.

About that murder: Police Chief William J. Letoile, Jr., reports that both victim and perpetrator were from out of state. After an investigation that took six weeks and led them into four states, both were identified and the culprit arrested.

"Despite the fact that we are a part-time department," Chief Letoile adds, "we are available twenty-four hours a day with an officer able to respond to any emergency. The phone is also manned twenty-four hours a day by either officers or volunteers, not an answering service. Two cruisers, radar units, mobile and portable radios, a snowmobile, a camera, and numerous other pieces of equipment are at our immediate disposal to aid in our continuing effort to serve residents more efficiently."

The town's low crime rate was no surprise to Joseph J. McGillicuddy, president of Hampstead Associates, a realty firm. He also had praise for the town's highly trained rescue squad. Twelve years ago he knew he wanted to get into real estate; he looked all over this region of New England and settled on Hampstead. One positive aspect about the town, he said, especially after moving from the Boston area, was the honesty and accessibility of local government.

Joe told us that you can't find anything in Hampstead today under $65,000 and a new 4-bedroom colonial will cost you $125,000. You could get a 3-bedroom, 2-story Garrison colonial for $90,000, paying taxes on it of $1,200 to $1,400. That Garrison would likely have a living room, a family room with a dining area (sometimes a formal dining room), 1½ baths, and a 2-car garage.

There is some rollover of homes on the town's attractive main street but not much. Depending on the one that becomes available, these houses fall into the same price range.

One attractive property was a centrally located 1800 brick Federal house, offering an excellent site for a home professional practice. With 4 large bedrooms, a great room with separate formal living room, a formal dining room, 2 full baths, a large barn, and an in-ground pool, it was on the market for $119,000.

Hampstead does have a mobile-home park for its elderly citizens, so they won't have to move out of town when the family homestead becomes too much of a burden to keep up. There are a few apartments for them too. House rentals are scarce here—sales are too brisk, even during the recession, to create a rental market.

The cost of the land itself is a major factor in the overall price of your house, Joe told us. The cheapest lot today will probably cost $18,000. Add $8,000 for a well and septic system (there's no town water or sewage) and you've spent $26,000 for an approved lot before you even begin to build.

Not that much land remains available for development, with a 1-acre minimum and other zoning restrictions. You should be able to find a parcel within the foreseeable future, but it's not likely that Hampstead will ever become a metropolis. For all who appreciate it as a quiet and handsome village, that is good news indeed.

PETERBOROUGH

POPULATION: 4,895
NO. OF CRIMES: 92
CRIME RATE: 1,879.5 per 100,000

New Hampshire hamlets seem to hold a strong attraction for novelists. One of the towns in the state's lakes region is reputed to be the real-life *Peyton Place.* Peterborough is Thornton Wilder's *Our Town.*

Wilder was ensconced at the MacDowell Colony, a retreat for established writers, composers, painters, sculptors, printmakers, photographers, and filmmakers. The colony was founded in 1907 at the home of Edward MacDowell, America's first internationally known composer, and has hosted such talents as Wilder, Edward Arlington Robinson, Stephen Vincent Benét, and Willa Cather. Colonists have won more than thirty-seven Pulitzer Prizes and numerous other awards over the years.

What these artists found in Peterborough was the quintessential New England village, with handsome red-brick public buildings and the type of natural setting you see depicted in Currier and Ives prints. This is the Monadnock region of New Hampshire, named for the mountain peak that dominates the area. Mount Monadnock rises 3,165 feet above sea level and 2,000 feet above the surrounding countryside. Emerson, Thoreau, Mark Twain, Kipling, James Russell Lowell, and Oliver Wendell Holmes have all added to its fame and only Mount Fuji has more hikers reach its summit each year.

Dublin, a few miles west of Peterborough on Route 101, is the highest town in New England (at 1,493 feet above sea level) and home to *Yankee* magazine and the *Old Farmer's Almanac.* Peterborough itself has two weekly newspapers and a number of periodicals that are published here, including the children's history magazine *Cobblestone* and *Byte,* a computer publication. The town also has some manufacturing enterprises, including a ball-bearing plant. If you've ever needed some esoteric gadget that nobody at your local hardware store ever heard of, you probably obtained it finally through Peterborough's Brookstone Company, which specializes in "hard-to-find tools and other fine things."

With Monadnock Community Hospital located here, Peterborough has a wide variety of medical specialists practicing in town. In addition to the downtown stores, there's an attractive business plaza on the edge of the village. New Hampshire's major metropolitan areas are less than an hour away and Boston is an hour and a half to the southeast.

Cultural resources here are superb. Monadnock Music has Saturday concerts during the summer at the Peterborough Town House and other concerts are presented in churches and town halls throughout the area. The Apple Hill Chamber Players also win critical acclaim. At the Sharon Arts Center you'll find not only a wide range of art and photography courses, but also instruction in jewelry crafts, quilting, smocking, basketmaking, glassblowing, dye-painting, stenciling, bookbinding, printmaking, weaving, ballet, pottery, calligraphy, you name it—even T'ai Chi Ch'uan, a sequence of Chinese body exercises. The Peterborough Lyceum, founded in 1829, brings to the community well-known names in government, science, and literature and the other arts. There are summer theater with the Peterborough Players, crafts classes given by shops in town, folk music entertainment at the Folkway, and art galleries to sample. You may view the collections of the largest local historical society in the state and for a really offbeat museum visit the Game Preserve, which houses over 800 early American board and card games, going back to 1820.

Outdoor activities are also profuse. In addition to the many trails of Mount Monadnock, Miller State Park—New Hampshire's oldest state park—is right in town, with spectacular views from the auto road leading to the top of Pack Monadnock Mountain. There are picnicking, boating, and fishing at the MacDowell Recreation Area and all the sports activities sponsored by the town recreation department and civic organizations. Not to mention three nearby ski areas, golf and tennis at the Monadnock Country Club, spring visits to maple-sugar houses, autumn foliage tours, and annual events such as the Winter Festival and the Monadnock Antique Show and Sale.

Crime is blissfully low in Peterborough. Police officers check eighty-eight buildings on the foot beat and eighty-seven buildings from their cruiser at least twice daily. If you leave your doors or windows insecure, you're likely to get a call from the police in the late evening or early morning hours to come to town and lock them.

In 1980, Peterborough had 4 aggravated assaults (no other crimes of violence) and 88 property crimes; this placed it below the crime rates for U.S. rural areas in all categories except larceny-theft and motor vehicle theft. In 1981, the number of crimes was reduced to 58 (with just 1 aggravated assault); that year *all* crime categories were below U.S. rural rates.

Most properties that we saw listed at the time of our visit were selling for under $100,000. Barbara Willis Real Estate advertised a 4-bedroom frame house for $49,000, a dormered Cape on 2 acres for $51,900, and a country house with plenty of brick and fireplaces, diamond-paned windows, and cozy nooks and crannies, for $69,900.

For $89,900, you could get a stone and stucco home overlooking Nubanusit Falls; French doors lead to a screened porch. A 2-bedroom, 2-bath contemporary with a ceiling-to-floor brick fireplace was on the market for $92,500. And an attractive colonial on a quiet cul-de-sac, with 2 fireplaces and a country kitchen, was selling for $98,500.

And look what you could get for $265,000: a 3- or 4-bedroom polished red-cedar log home, surrounded by towering pines; a living room with a fieldstone fireplace facing a magnificent view of Mount Monadnock; a fully cabineted kitchen with another view from the breakfast area; an underground passage to an office area with a fieldstone fireplace; and 26 acres of woods, fields, trails, streams, and bridges.

Barbara Willis also had 139 acres of gently sloping land, with river frontage and a year-round brook, selling for $69,500. Cornerstone Real Estate had a 7-room (3-bedroom, 2-bath) brick ranch going for $99,500. And Burwick & Walsh Real Estate was selling a 2-bedroom, 2½-bath colonial town house in a condominium community for $82,900.

With all this going for Peterborough—the full calendar of cultural and outdoor activities, plus the low crime and housing variety—you, too, may decide to make *Our Town* your town.

Where to get further information:

State

For a state highway map and a wide variety of vacation information: Office of Vacation Travel, P.O. Box 856, Concord, NH 03301. New England Vacation Center, Shop No. 2, International Concourse, 630 Fifth Avenue, New York, NY 10020.

Regional

Seacoast Region, Box 476, Exeter, NH 03833. Merrimack Valley Region, Box 29, Manchester, NH 03105. Monadnock Region, Box 269, Peterborough, NH 03458.

Towns

Kingston: For the town's annual report, stop at the town hall and ask for a copy.
Hampstead: For the town's annual report, stop at the town hall and ask for a copy.
Peterborough: Peterborough Chamber of Commerce, Box 401, Peterborough, NH 03458.

New Jersey

If you visited New Jersey for the first time and traversed it solely on the Jersey Turnpike, you would have good cause to wonder what irony led to the state's nickname, the Garden State, after seeing countless miles of industrial plants.

Actually, agriculture is an important part of the state's economy. But that is just one of the distortions you get by limiting your acquaintance with the state to the turnpikes. New Jersey has much more than suburban congestion and industrial sprawl.

Small as it is, the state has a wide variety of scenery and living conditions. The northwest part of the state is dominated by the Appalachian Mountains, with the valley of the rippling Delaware River forming a peaceful boundary with Pennsylvania. East of the mountains, prosperous dairy farms, glacial lakes, and handsome small towns greet your eye until you hit the urban and suburban mass of the northeastern part of the state.

Another suburban mass gathers around Philadelphia in the southwestern part of the state, but most of southern and central New Jersey is dominated by farmlands, the extensive pine barrens of the coastal plain, and the coast itself—with 127 miles of beaches extending from Sandy Hook to that mecca of gingerbread Victorian architecture, Cape May. This southern part of the state is below the Mason-Dixon line, and there's even an area that gives the illusion of being in Texas, with cattle ranches, red clay gullies, and Saturday night rodeos.

In a future edition, we hope to acquaint you with some of the Safe Places in these less congested parts of the state. But for now, we must limit our attention to the northeastern suburbs. That's where help is most needed. If you must commute to a job in New York City or in that area of New Jersey, you face a bewildering array of hundreds of towns and suburbs. Which one to pick as your home?

Crime is a major consideration, since it runs rampant throughout much of the state. In our New York chapter, we mentioned that in our comparison year of 1980, there were seventeen towns and cities in New Jersey with worse crime rates than New York City. Some are places you'd suspect (Newark, Trenton, Camden), but others you may never have heard of—like Egg Harbor Township.

NEW JERSEY Crime Chart

	Crime Rate	Murder	Rape	Robbery	Aggravated Assault	Burglary	Larceny —Theft	Motor Vehicle Theft
United States								
U.S. Total	5,899.9	10.2	36.4	243.5	290.6	1,668.2	3,156.3	494.6
U.S. Metropolitan Areas	6,757.6	11.5	43.4	319.0	328.3	1,911.8	3,534.9	608.8
U.S. Rural Areas	2,290.4	7.5	15.5	22.5	136.9	830.2	1,143.9	133.9
Regional Crime Centers								
Newark, N.J.	12,902.9	49.4	165.4	2,073.6	1,125.7	3,444.7	3,342.0	2,702.2
New York, N.Y.	10,094.0	25.8	52.7	1,429.2	618.0	2,994.9	3,545.3	1,429.1
Paramus, N.J.	16,601.2	0	7.6	238.0	79.3	2,364.6	10,852.2	3,059.6
Safe Places								
Berkeley Heights	1,657.5	0	0	8.0	31.9	533.9	1,043.9	39.8
Cliffside Park	2,581.1	4.7	0	32.6	23.3	1,057.6	1,048.3	414.6
Dumont	3,114.4	0	0	5.5	38.2	872.7	2,018.1	180.0
New Providence	2,406.2	0	0	24.1	80.5	619.7	1,601.5	80.5
River Vale	1,538.6	0	0	0	10.5	695.5	737.7	94.8
Summit	2,159.4	0	9.5	19.0	28.5	768.8	1,134.3	199.3

Atlantic City, with 30,981.5 crimes per 100,000 population, actually had the highest crime rate of any city in the nation.

You don't have to accept that sort of social climate, however. There are excellent places to live in the Jersey suburbs—and the towns that have put a lid on crime are first-rate communities in many other ways too. In the pages that follow, we describe six of these for you.

BERGEN COUNTY

Bergen County lies in the northeastern corner of the state, right across the Hudson River from New York. The main traffic artery connecting the two states is the George Washington Bridge, built in 1932 and described by LeCorbusier as the most beautiful bridge in the world.

That proximity has its negative aspects as well as its positive ones. Many Bergenites suspect that one of the negative aspects is crime: that much of their crime is imported from New York City. That view found support from former New York Police Commissioner Patrick V. Murphy, in a New York *Times* round table "Crime in the Suburbs."

"I think there might be a distinction," Mr. Murphy said, "between counties like Bergen, which sit right alongside New York City [and suburbs farther out]. When you're that close, a lot of criminals probably come over from the city to commit daytime burglaries. It's a little different in a suburb that's 25 miles away. The further from the city, the better the information the police seem to be able to get from one another, and information is the lifeblood of police work. If there's a burglar in town, the police are going to pick that up a lot faster than a chief who is overwhelmed by many burglars coming in every day."

That's a common-sense observation that probably holds true *as a general rule.* Yet, as we studied the crime statistics for Bergen County, we were pleasantly surprised to find a number of Safe Places. We actually could pick and choose for this book. So while proximity to a crime center doesn't help a suburb, it doesn't mean you have to give up and open the gates to the criminals. Here are three Bergen County communities that still manage to remain peaceful and pleasant places in which to live.

CLIFFSIDE PARK

POPULATION: 21,464
NO. OF CRIMES: 554
CRIME RATE: 2,581.1 per 100,000

Cliffside Park is right across the Hudson River from Manhattan, but its crime rate is just one fourth that of New York City's.

Look directly across the river from Cliffside Park and you'll see the tower of Riverside Church and the buildings of Columbia University's campus. Look north and you'll see the George Washington Bridge, a little south and there's the Midtown Manhattan skyline.

Cliffside Park sits atop the cliffs known as the Palisades, which provide such a commanding view of Manhattan. Drive down winding Edgewater Road to the foot of the cliffs and you're in Edgewater. The two towns may be next to each other, but they're worlds apart in character. Edgewater occupies a narrow band of land along the Hudson, below the cliffs, and consists predominantly of the docks and industries along the river.

Cliffside Park is compact; its entire population is squeezed into less than 1 square mile of land. Perhaps that helps explain the low crime rate. Even more important, we suspect, is the permanence of the population. When the children of a family grow up, they tend to stay in the community—at least more so here than elsewhere. This is not a transient community. One indication is that when we visited Cliffside Park, there were only nine single-family homes on the market, with a population of over 20,000.

Cliffside Park is not for everyone. If your goal is land and a rambling house with a 2-car garage, forget it. It reminds us more of a busy Brooklyn or Queens neighborhood than of a sedate suburb and that vitality is part of its charm. Anderson Avenue, the main business center, is lined with stores and filled with shoppers. No decaying downtown here.

There's a mix, too, of apartment houses, condominiums, multifamily houses, and single-family homes, of row houses and detached residences. As a general rule, the larger and nicer detached homes will be found between Palisade Avenue and the cliffs. Real estate costs for most of these types of housing tend to be lower than what you'd find in the prestigious suburbs farther away from the city.

The exception is a house with a view of the river and Manhattan. You pay for that.

We talked about real estate with Dr. Oscar Muscariello, Ph.D., a sales representative with Anderson Group Associates. The single-family homes on the market, he told us, ranged in price from $59,900 to $235,000. Two-family and multifamily homes ranged from $65,000 to $335,000. Condominiums in the Cliff House cost from $158,000 to $259,000 and when we looked at the classified ads in local newspapers, the available apartments rented for $250 to $785.

For $250, you could get a large studio or a 2½-room apartment, singles preferred. The $785 listing was described as a beautiful 5½-room apartment in a 2-family house, with 2 baths, basement, patio, and off-street parking. In between, most apartments were 3½ to 5 rooms, renting for $400 to $600.

In 2-family homes, for $139,900 you could get a forty-five-year-old house with stone and shingle exterior, on a 50 × 101 lot, and with no garage or fireplace. Taxes were $1,162. The main apartment consisted of a living room, kitchen, formal dining room, and large bedroom on the first floor, and a full, finished basement that included a bedroom, bath, living room, laundry room, and storage area. Another 2-bedroom apartment with a large eat-in kitchen was on the second floor.

The cheapest single-family house on the market, at $59,900, was a twenty-eight-year-old 1-story brick house on a 24 × 104 lot. It consisted of a 14 × 24.2 living room, kitchen, 2 bedrooms (9 × 12, 12 × 16), and 1½ baths. Taxes were $1,176.

Seemingly a good buy at $95,400 was a 9-room brick house, with a 2-car garage, on a 50 × 106 lot. On the first floor were a living room, dining room, den, kitchen, and porch, on the second, 2 bedrooms and a bath. The finished basement contained a ½ bath and the large attic had a closet and finished oak floors. Taxes were $1,395.

And then, for a beautiful view of the Manhattan skyline, you could get a 9-room house for $235,000. Thirty years old, it had 4 bedrooms, 3 baths, and 2 fireplaces. The house sat on a 63 × 100 lot, but your part of the cliff gave you more than an acre of land. Taxes were $3,319.

As for crime, in our comparison year of 1980, Cliffside Park had an overall crime rate just above the rate for U.S. rural areas. Violent crimes were especially low, with just 1 murder, 7 robberies, and 5 aggravated assaults. Property crime consisted of 227 burglaries, 225 larceny-thefts, and 89 motor vehicle thefts. Only that last category represented a rate common to metropolitan regions.

Whatever your finances allow, Cliffside Park offers you a vibrant—and safe—community just minutes from Manhattan.

DUMONT

POPULATION: 18,334
NO. OF CRIMES: 571
CRIME RATE: 3,114.4 per 100,000

In the center of Bergen County, 9 miles northwest of the George Washington Bridge, is the town of Dumont. In the center of town, at the intersection of Washington and Madison avenues, is the town's showpiece—historic Old North Reformed Church. Its sanctuary is deemed one of the finest examples of early American church architecture and its churchyard is the resting place of many Revolutionary War soldiers.

In our comparison year of 1980, Dumont had no murders or rapes and just 1 robbery and 7 aggravated assaults. Property crimes consisted of 160 burglaries, 370 larceny-thefts, and 33 motor vehicle thefts. In terms of the crime rate, Dumont placed lower than U.S. rural crime rates in all categories except larceny-thefts and motor vehicle thefts. In both those categories, it was still way below U.S. metropolitan crime levels.

In 1981, the crime rate dropped slightly.

During our visit in October 1982, Ronald G. Mansoldo, sales director of the Mansoldo Agency, told us that housing costs in Dumont ranged from $65,000 to $130,000. The average sale, he said, was probably in the $90,000 to $95,000 range.

At the lower price level—say, $75,000 to $90,000—you will find a number of older frame houses. Most often these will need some renovation.

For $90,000 to $95,000, you might get a split-level house on a 70 × 100 lot, approximately twenty-five years old. Most of the homes in this price range have a living room, dining room, family room, kitchen, 3 bedrooms, 1½ baths, and a 1-car garage. There would probably be no fireplace.

At the higher price range, you'll find the newer homes, under ten years old, perhaps in the area around the Prospect Avenue golf course. Such a home might be a 2-story colonial on a 75 × 100 or 125 lot, and with 4 bedrooms and 2½ baths.

At the time of our visit, a Bergen County newspaper had an advertisement for a Dumont house for sale. For $99,000 you could get a spacious brick colonial with a living room, dining room, den, family room, 4 bedrooms, and 1½ baths.

In appearance, Dumont is neat and attractive, but without any particularly stylish elaboration. Most of the homes are smaller and older than in new suburbs, but nevertheless well maintained. As the prices indicate, this is a relatively inexpensive town.

Perhaps the compact nature of the town—1.79 square miles—helps the police keep the crime situation under control. The middle-class and lower-middle-class nature of the population is probably another help, since thieves today seem to head for the more affluent communities, where the pickings are the best. And although Dumont is just 9 miles from Manhattan, it is also off any beaten path such as an interstate or parkway. That too helps to keep criminals out of the area.

Whatever the causes of its safety, we found Dumont to be an excellent choice either for a family's starter home or for elderly persons considering a retirement move to a smaller home. Both the young family and the retiree need a safe environment and relatively low housing costs. Dumont has both.

RIVER VALE

POPULATION: 9,489
NO. OF CRIMES: 146
CRIME RATE: 1,538.6 per 100,000

Of our three Bergen County communities, River Vale is the farthest removed from New York City. Sandwiched between the Hackensack River and Lake Tappan on the east and Pascack Brook to the west, it shares its northern border with New York State.

Of our three Bergen County communities, River Vale is also the one that looks most like a traditional suburb. It is not a city neighborhood like Cliffside Park or a self-contained town like Dumont. It is almost entirely residential, with winding, rural roads and dense foliage that preserve privacy while allowing neighbors to be close enough to watch out for each other.

Rivervale Country Club, Edgewood Country Club, and Parkvale Golf Club are all located here. Yet this is not an exclusive, upper-class town. It appears to be solidly middle class, but old enough to avoid the tract-development look of newer suburbs. Colonials are the predominant residential style.

The town's only business district (Four Corners) is a small one at the intersection of Westwood Avenue and Rivervale Road. It contains some specialty shops, a grocery market, and a Chinese restaurant. More extensive shopping facilities are located in neighboring towns, and the huge Bergen Mall Shopping Center in Paramus is just a short drive away.

The Jewish Hospital and Rehabilitation Center of New Jersey, a small facility, is also in the Four Corners area. Pascack Valley Hospital, a general facility, is a couple of miles away.

Commuters to New York can avail themselves of New Jersey's excellent bus transportation network and catch a bus in town. Those who take a train catch it in Westwood, Hillsdale, or Park Ridge, all west of River Vale. And car commuters take the Palisades Interstate Parkway to the George Washington Bridge.

River Vale has two elementary schools (K–5) and a middle school (grades 6–8). Students then go to the Pascack Valley High School in neighboring Hillsdale.

We talked about real estate with Dianne Mitchell, of Leslie Noonan Associates, Inc. She told us that it's hard to find a single-family house in River Vale for less than $100,000—not impossible but hard. There were six such starter homes on the market, but they go fast and three already had deposits on them. Almost always, a house in this price range will be a Cape or a ranch, with 3 or 4 bedrooms.

In the moderate $98,000 to $129,000 range, you'll find ranches, bilevels, and split levels. A newspaper ad at the time of our visit listed two homes in this price range. A Dutch-style hi-ranch, 2 years old, with 4 bedrooms and 2 baths, was listed at $109,900. And a secluded ranch priced at $112,000 had a huge living room, formal dining room, modern kitchen, 3 bedrooms, 2 baths, and a large rec room.

An executive-type home—say, a 4-bedroom, 2½-bath colonial, with a 2-car garage and all the modern amenities—will cost you at least $159,900 here.

Dianne told us that she had seven homes on the market priced over $200,000. Nine more were in the $160,000 to $200,000 range. The most expensive house on the market was a new 4-bedroom, 2½-bath Tudor, with lots of special features, such as a large family room with a cathedral ceiling and a brick hearth fireplace, and sliding glass doors that open to a wraparound deck with a barbecue. Its price was $229,000.

Taxes on most of the previously mentioned houses would probably run between $2,000 and $2,500, but here the bill might come to $4,000.

An average building lot in this area, Dianne told us, will cost around $65,000. And a few condominiums and town houses are located in town. A 1-bedroom, 1-bath condo will run in the mid- or upper-80s, and larger ones will cost over $100,000. "These will give you country-club-style living for a single person or a couple," she said.

As for crime, River Vale has the lowest rate of any of our New Jersey Safe Places—below U.S. rural crime rates in all seven categories. In 1980, for example, there were no murders, rapes, or robberies, and just 1 aggravated assault, 66 burglaries, 70 larceny-thefts, and 9 motor vehicle thefts.

Secluded, serene, and secure, River Vale fulfills the image its name suggests and offers you one of the most pleasant places to call home in suburban New Jersey.

UNION COUNTY

Union is the state's second smallest county in area, yet it ranks third in industry. Located southwest of Manhattan, it includes part of Newark International Airport, the industrial centers of Elizabeth and Linden, and swatches of the New Jersey Turnpike and Garden State Parkway.

The part that interested us, however, was the western corner of the county, where we found three communities, all in a row, with remarkably low crime rates. That's a rare occurrence in a major metropolitan area and we knew they must be something special.

They are. Summit, New Providence, and Berkeley Heights qualify individually as Safe Places, but we're placing them together in the same section since they are joined to each other not only geographically but also in their economic and cultural life.

SUMMIT

POPULATION: 21,071
NO. OF CRIMES: 455
CRIME RATE: 2,159.4 per 100,000

NEW PROVIDENCE

POPULATION: 12,426
NO. OF CRIMES: 299
CRIME RATE: 2,406.2 per 100,000

BERKELEY HEIGHTS

POPULATION: 12,549
NO. OF CRIMES: 208
CRIME RATE: 1,657.5 per 100,000

Our three towns in Union County occupy the rolling, wooded hills on the northwestern slope of the Watchung Mountains, extending to the Passaic River. Beyond them to the west is one of the unique natural habitats of the state, the Great Swamp National Wildlife Refuge.

It's a delightful setting, with New York, Newark, and the industrial concentrations of northeastern New Jersey just minutes away—and yet far, far away. They are as accessible, or remote, as you want them to be.

Summit is the largest and oldest of the three communities, as well as their business and cultural center. Back in the late 1800s, it was a fashionable resort community with many fine hotels. Today it has an extensive business area, a traditional downtown that has not been allowed to decay—except for the train station and there are renovation plans for that. The neighborhoods are tree-shaded and maintained with loving care. Throughout Summit, you have the feeling of being in an attractive small town of an earlier era rather than in a spanking new suburb. It's a pleasant ambience and a refreshing change from the lookalike mold.

New Providence and Berkeley Heights are newer and predominantly residential. Here the homes are farther apart, following a suburban rather than small town pattern of development, but still the special qualities remain. Berkeley Heights in particular has rolling terrain that enhances the homes' setting. New Providence's Murray Hill Square is a distinctive brick square with fountains, surrounded by colonial shops offering modern-day wares.

All three towns share a reputation for excellent schools. New York *Times* editor Gene I. Maeroff, in his book *Guide to Suburban Public Schools,* described Summit's high school as "an academic powerhouse." New Providence High School enjoys one of the highest academic and extracurricular ratings in the state and is known for its special education programs. Governor Livingston

High School in Berkeley Heights has more National Merit Scholars than any school in New Jersey except Princeton High.

The same can be said for medical facilities. Summit's Overlook Hospital is regarded as one of the top medical centers in New Jersey and is affiliated with Columbia Presbyterian Medical Center and St. Vincent's Hospital in New York. Other local medical facilities include Fair Oaks Hospital, a private psychiatric institution, and the John E. Runnells Hospital for Chest Diseases in Berkeley Heights.

A roster of some of the groups active in Summit gives an indication of the emphasis on cultural affairs. Among them are the Summit Community Concerts, Chamber Music Guild, Summit Chorale, Summit Folk Dancers, Summit Symphony Orchestra, and Summit Art Center. Theatrical groups include the Playhouse, Encore Players, Metropolitan Musical Theater, and Penny Lane Players.

For commuters to New York, the Summit station of the PATH (Port Authority Trans Hudson) line is an express stop and has late-night service. The World Trade Center and Thirty-third Street in Manhattan are forty-five to fifty-five minutes away. New Providence and Berkeley Heights are stops on a branch line. Bus lines speed you to Newark or Morristown, while neighboring Springfield has service to the Port Authority Bus Terminal in New York. And Newark International Airport is just 15 miles and a half hour from Summit.

With all these assets, it is no surprise that many top corporations have opened major plants or operations in the three towns. Summit has CIBA Pharmaceuticals, Celanese Research, and Kemper Insurance. Berkeley Heights is home to Dun & Bradstreet's National Business Center and to the famed Bell Laboratories, where so many of the major communications discoveries that have changed our world have originated.

What originally brought these towns to our attention, of course, was their low crime rates. In our comparison year of 1980, Summit was below the crime rates for U.S. rural areas in all categories except motor vehicle theft and even there it was way below U.S. metropolitan levels. New Providence ranked below U.S. rural levels in all categories except robbery (its 1 robbery that year raised it slightly above U.S. rural rates in that category) and larceny-thefts. Berkeley Heights was the safest of all and ranked below the crime rates for U.S. rural areas in all seven categories.

In 1981 the number of crimes in New Providence and Berkeley Heights actually decreased from their already low levels. The number of crimes increased slightly in Summit—but nothing to indicate a problem or a trend.

Frank J. Formichella, Summit's chief of police, noted that "because of incompleted major highways, few major roadways, and the traffic conditions in general, rapid criminal escape routes are held to a minimum."

Another possible factor in the town's low crime rate, he indicated, was population stability. "Our community is basically a 'zero population growth' community," he told us. "Although a certain amount of our residents change periodically, most are long-time residents who are aware and concerned for community betterment. Their awareness of and closeness to their neighbors eliminate, to some degree, the ability of strangers to roam freely without being reported to authorities."

Among the programs instituted by the Summit Police Department are Neighborhood Watch and Project ID. Also, "Members of the crime prevention unit check homes and business houses to alert owners of deficiencies in securing and maintaining their property."

In Berkeley Heights, Police Chief Ralph M. Del Duca attributed their especially low crime rate to four major factors:

"*Community involvement, citizen participation.* Our residents are quick to report suspicious activity, and are cooperative as witnesses when called upon. Our Neighborhood Watch program has been instrumental in this.

"*Response time.* Our police response time is approximately two minutes, which is well below the national average.

"*Selective enforcement.* We know what areas have a tendency to promote criminal activity and concentrate on these areas . . ."

And:

"*Morale.* The morale among the rank and file is extremely high, which tends to promote dedication and efficient law enforcement."

If, by now, you're ready to move to one of these homes, you'll find a refreshing variety of residential architectural styles. Your choice is likely to include Tudor, Normandy, English country, contemporary, Queen Anne, Spanish, French provincial, Regency, Williamsburg, Cotswold, Elizabethan, Garrison colonial, Pennsylvania Dutch, saltbox, Dutch colonial, and Swiss chalet.

The towns' newspapers were filled with display and classified real estate ads. Here's a sampling of what we found.

In Summit there were four listings for houses under $100,000. There were concentrations of houses in the $108,000–$115,000 and $160,000–$185,000 ranges, with the upper crust represented by homes selling for $325,000 and $475,000.

For $79,000, you could get a brick front Cape Codder with aluminum awnings and a side screened porch. It had 2 bedrooms, a full bath, a full basement with workshop and laundry room, wall-to-wall carpeting, and all-hardwood floors.

For a classic look, there was a $185,000 brick front Williamsburg colonial with wood-shingle roof. This one had 4 bedrooms, 3 full baths, a large country kitchen with extra cabinets, a bay window in the dining room, 2 fireplaces, and a 2-car garage.

The $425,000 listing was one of Summit's finest historic residences, built in 1907 on the site where General Washington set up Signal Station No. 10 during the Revolutionary War. We don't have space to tell you about all its special features, but it's just the place for you if you've always wanted a master bedroom suite with not 1 but 2 fireplaces! The price also includes 2 acres, a separate carriage house with apartment, and a 3-car garage.

Also in Summit were a 3-bedroom house renting for $875 a month and apartments ranging from $300 (an efficiency) to $1,400. That one was a 3-bedroom luxury garden apartment with 2,200 square feet. A wooded 100 × 150 lot was selling for $85,000, others from $69,900. Town house condominiums were priced from $96,500 (1 bedroom) to $179,900 (2 bedrooms).

New Providence houses were selling in a range from the 70s to $140,000. The nine listings under $100,000 included a number of ranches. For $124,500 you could get a custom Tudor featuring a sunken living room with beamed ceilings and fireplace, a cedar-paneled den, and 3 bedrooms. And for $138,900, there was a large 5-bedroom, 2½-bath home with a family room, full basement, and 3-car garage.

A 4-bedroom Cape in New Providence was renting for $750 and the only apartment listings were for a studio ($275) and a 4-room apartment ($380).

The main section of Berkeley Heights had homes listed between $88,900 and $219,000 with the bulk of them under $130,000. The seven listings under $100,000 included both ranches and colonials.

A prestige area of Berkeley Heights is Murray Hill, near the Bell Laboratories. There you could get a spacious center-hall colonial with 5 bedrooms for $229,500. Murray Hill Square is a stylishly designed and landscaped condominium development. Its fifty residences, no two of them alike, are priced from $120,000 to $320,000.

In sum, one word describes our three neighboring communities in Union County: quality. In their schools, their community facilities, their cultural life, and their houses, that's the message that kept coming through. And that, we suspect, is just what you're looking for.

Where to get further information:

State

New Jersey Division of Travel and Tourism, CN384, Trenton, NJ 08625.

Regional

Bergen County: Bergen County Office of Cultural and Historic Affairs, 355 Main Street, Room 1-1, Hackensack, NJ 07601.

Union County: Union County Cultural and Heritage Programs Advisory Board, 300 North Avenue E., Westfield, NJ 07090.

Local

Dumont: A *Guide to Dumont* is published by the Dumont Jaycees, P.O. Box 212, Dumont, NJ 07628.

River Vale: A letter to new residents from the mayor is available from the Township of River Vale, 406 Rivervale Road, River Vale, NJ 07675.

Summit, New Providence, and Berkeley Heights: The Chamber of Commerce of Summit, New Providence, and Berkeley Heights, 16 Maple Street, P.O. Box 824, Summit, NJ 07901, has these materials available: *Map and Shopping Guide; The Best of New Jersey* (booklet); *Summit, New Jersey* (brochure); *Summit, New Jersey: A Management Perspective* (brochure); *Berkeley Heights Merchants Guide;* and *Annual Report and Buyers Guide.*

New Mexico

Europeans explored this country almost a full century before the founding of Jamestown and Plymouth settlements. Missions were established here a century before the padres trekked to California. History here is no recent affair; it has richness, pride, romance.

The famous and the infamous have preceded you: Cabeza de Vaca, Don Juan de Oñate, Geronimo, General Douglas MacArthur, Billy the Kid, Kit Carson, Pancho Villa—even a famous cub given the name of Smokey the Bear. Ghosts inhabit the desert sweeps, the mesas and valleys, the tall mountains . . . the ghost of Sheriff Pat Garrett, ambushed . . . the anonymous ghosts of countless anonymous miners, prospectors, gamblers, Indians, pioneers, missionaries, cowboys, soldiers, outlaws . . . and they left behind intriguing traces of their sojourn here: wind-strewn pueblo walls, petroglyphs and arrowheads, abandoned tunnels into the earth, solitary fragments of railroad trestles, the crumbling ruins of towns, trading posts, and stagecoach stops.

In startling contrast, this is also the land where the modern world was ushered in with a ball of blinding light, heat, and destructive power on a scale never before imagined—on July 16, 1945, as the first atomic bomb was exploded in the desert. And where other alchemists devised ways of launching our first missiles, improving and expanding their work over the years until one day we would be able to send a man to the moon.

No visit to New Mexico is complete without a tour of Carlsbad Caverns, with its spectacular limestone formations, or a visit to one of the pueblos in the northern part of the state (we took Melissa to Taos, one of the largest and most interesting of the dwellings).

Having become, by necessity, experts on the motels of America, we don't usually write about Holiday Inns except in angry letters to their managers, but in southwestern New Mexico we found one that really is different and that provided one of our most enjoyable stopovers during the Safe Places trip. Holiday Inn de Las Cruces in a step back in history, a re-creation of the area's Spanish and territorial days. "The basic concept for the whole building was to be a hacienda," says owner C. W. "Buddy" Ritter, "but we went a step farther and created a Mexican town with a plaza."

We had a room with a balcony opening to that huge plaza, filled with the Pancho Villa Cantina and restaurant, several swimming pools (one with a Spanish tile waterfall), trees and lush foliage, and interesting shops. An alameda (tree-lined passageway) takes you to a restaurant and lounge decorated with authentic antiques from New Mexico's territorial days. The bar at the Billy the Kid Saloon is a particularly fascinating link with history, since at least twenty-seven men were killed at it before it was moved here from Cimarron. More about this bar, later.

NORTHERN NEW MEXICO

Northern New Mexico is dominated by high mountain country (the Sangre de Cristo range) where some peaks are snow-capped the year around. The culture is a colorful mixture of Indian, Spanish, Mexican, and Anglo influences.

Albuquerque's population of 332,000 makes it the largest city in the state. It sits on the west side of Sandia Peak (10,678 feet high), which is scaled by the longest aerial tram in the world, and is itself at an elevation of nearly 5,000 feet. Albuquerque has a reputation as a health center and the astronauts were given their qualifying examinations at the Bataan-Lovelace Medical Center, which is patterned after the Mayo Clinic. Major industries include electronics manufacturing and research, communications, the military (Kirtland Air Force Base), tourism, and livestock. The largest employer (of 6,000 people) is Sandia Laboratories, which is engaged in nuclear and solar research as well as the development and testing of nuclear weapons.

Santa Fe, the state capital, has a population of just 50,000 but is one of the nation's most popular cultural and artistic centers. The dominant architecture, protected by zoning, is in the Indian pueblo style. The elevation is a bracing 7,000 feet. Santa Fe has been a capital under four flags—Spain, Mexico, the Confederacy, and the United States—and here you will find the oldest church in the nation (beautiful San Miguel Mission) and the oldest public building in the United States which has been in continuous use (the Palace of the Governors, constructed in 1610). Canyon Road, once an Indian trail, is the center of the art colony and the Santa Fe Opera enjoys an international reputation.

Santa Fe's biggest problem, right now, is that it's the trendy place to be. It has long been a haven for artists and writers, but now it's been "discovered" by the new-rich and by the crowd that used to be known as the "beautiful people." There are fears that Santa Fe will become another Aspen, fears described in a poignant column in *The New Republic* by "R.S." (Ronald Steel?). "Half a century ago," R.S. wrote, "pale-faced strangers like Mabel Dodge and D. H. Lawrence came to northern New Mexico in search of ancient gods and noble savages. Today their followers are looking for a real estate deal and a mellow lifestyle. All of a sudden, Santa Fe, for years the haven of ne'er-do-well sons, second-string painters, and restless divorcees, is *le dernier cri.* Just check with *People* magazine and *Esquire.* Hollywood literati and Oklahoma oil barons have descended upon this pokey town a thousand miles from nowhere, snatching up mud adobe houses and embellishing them with the fantasies of Scottsdale decorators."

Taos (population 2,475, elevation 6,952) is a much smaller version of Santa Fe, popular not only with artists and writers but also with skiers. One of its fans, Donal Henahan, chief music critic of the New York *Times,* described it as a mixture of "art-colony sophistication, powder-hog machismo, and Tex-Mex culture."

NORTHERN NEW MEXICO Crime Chart

	Crime Rate	Murder	Rape	Robbery	Aggravated Assault	Burglary	Larceny —Theft	Motor Vehicle Theft
United States								
U.S. Total	5,899.9	10.2	36.4	243.5	290.6	1,668.2	3,156.3	494.6
U.S. Metropolitan Areas	6,757.6	11.5	43.4	319.0	328.3	1,911.8	3,534.9	608.8
U.S. Rural Areas	2,290.4	7.5	15.5	22.5	136.9	830.2	1,143.9	133.9
Regional Crime Centers								
Albuquerque	8,918.1	15.2	68.4	302.0	529.1	2,457.4	5,111.3	434.6
Las Vegas	7,108.8	0	28.0	98.1	1,351.7	2,038.1	3,298.8	294.2
Santa Fe	9,619.5	4.1	32.7	116.4	937.4	2,407.9	5,512.3	608.6
Taos	11,843.3	0	0	29.7	2,523.0	3,087.0	5,372.5	831.1
Safe Places								
Cimarron	1,013.5	0	0	0	450.5	225.2	337.8	0
Los Alamos	2,945.5	0	22.7	0	28.4	540.2	2,257.5	96.7

"Even first-time visitors become possessive about Taos," Henahan wrote, describing his appreciation of Taos Ski Valley. "They like its refusal to act like the average Rockies ski resort. There are at least as many pickup trucks in the parking lots as sports cars. The dialect most frequently heard in the lift lines seems to be West Texan, which is close enough to English so that an Easterner can understand a few necessary phrases in a short time."

For our purposes, it must be noted that the spectacular scenery and picturesque adobe villages are matched by high levels of crime (see our Northern New Mexico Crime Chart, above). Albuquerque and Santa Fe are each way above U.S. metropolitan levels of crime, while tiny Taos outdoes even New York City or Washington, D.C.—in fact, it outdoes *all* of our major cities other than Boston. True, here it consists mostly of property crime, but look at Taos' astronomical rate of aggravated assault. Those machismo powder-hogs having a little fun off the slopes?

We don't know, but we *do* have a couple of Safe Places for you in this fantastic country. Appropriately, one is as modern and science-oriented as the other is historic and cowboy-oriented. That's New Mexico.

LOS ALAMOS

POPULATION: 17,586
NO. OF CRIMES: 518
CRIME RATE: 2,945.5 per 100,000

Los Alamos enjoys one of the most dramatic and breathtaking locations in America. It sits atop the Pajarito Plateau at an elevation of 7,300 feet, 1,700 feet above the Rio Grande Valley. In all directions are piñon- and juniper-covered red rock mesas. Beyond them to the west are the forested and meadow-strewn Jemez Mountains, and to the east, the towering peaks of the Sangre de Cristo Mountains.

As you drive the steep winding highway to the top of the mesa, you begin to understand why the federal government picked this location for its top-secret city, the city where the secrets of the atom would be unraveled. This is not the most accessible spot in the country! Before Uncle Sam took it over, this was (from 1917 to 1943) the site of an exclusive boys' school, the Los Alamos Ranch School. Long before, between A.D. 1150 and the sixteenth century, it was home to the Anasazi, the Ancient Ones.

During World War II, the federal government displaced the school and turned Los Alamos into a closed-to-the-public laboratory and support community devoted to the research and development of atomic energy, which led to the production of the first three atomic bombs. After the war, the work of the laboratories was expanded and placed on a permanent basis. Twelve square miles were carved out of Sandoval County to form a new combined city-county, but it was still a closed town. All real estate, both residential and commercial, was owned by the federal government in the form of the Atomic Energy Commission.

During the fifties, the first steps were taken to open the town to the public and to sell residential land to private owners. In 1962, Congress passed the Disposal Act and over the next six years commercial and residential properties were sold to residents, municipal services became a county responsibility, and the Los Alamos School District assumed the ownership of school property. The building boom of this period led to the creation of the White Rock bedroom community at an elevation 800 feet below Los Alamos.

As before, the main employer in town is the Los Alamos National Laboratory. Only today the scope of its research has broadened considerably. One of the two major national research facilities in New Mexico, it now has programs in medicine, solar and geothermal energy, lasers, and industrial uses of atomic energy. The laboratory is managed by the University of California for the U.S. Department of Energy and laboratory employees are employees of the university.

We are well aware that picking Los Alamos—the atomic city!—as a *Safe*

Place will be met with derision in some quarters. This is not a political book, but we feel we should explain our position.

As we see it, there are two lines of protest—ideological and practical. (You can bet which one makes the most noise.) We don't have any use for the ideologues, but we do admit to a few qualms on the practical side.

The ideological line is that atomic energy is somehow "bad" or "evil." If that's so, Los Alamos is obviously an evil community, populated by the very people who let the genie out of the bottle. In part this is an emotional reaction, since the first use of atomic energy was with weapons of destruction, but we think most Americans are mature enough to realize that the same arguments could be used against any technological development since the stone ax. It's just the scale of potential destruction that has progressively increased, and at any rate everyone gets a little fuzzy when he tries to explain how he's going to get the genie back in the bottle and keep him there.

In large part, we think the emotional arguments are just a smokescreen to hide political motives and goals. And to *that* we don't hesitate to say that we're immeasurably thankful that it was the United States, not Germany, that got the genie out *first;* we're just as thankful that it was the United States, not the Soviet Union, that dominated the field for so long, and we're equally fearful that this is no longer the case.

On the other hand, there are two practical considerations that do merit attention. The first is the possibility, any place where atomic energy is employed, of a radiation accident. We have no inside information, so it's just our guess that this would be a minimal problem here in Los Alamos. The scientists and technicians here are the cream of the crop. They know what they are doing. And *their* lives are more at stake than the lives of any bystanders.

The other practical consideration would be that, in the event of war, Los Alamos would undoubtedly be a prime Soviet target. That certainly seems logical. But we don't know what to "do" about it other than perhaps move to our Safe Place on the coast of Oregon; the maps we've seen indicate that virtually the entire rest of the country, including most of our Safe Places in this book, will be prone to nuclear targeting or radioactive fallout. So, for the purposes of this volume, we will assume the absence of nuclear war and continue to pick our Safe Places on the basis of their crime rates.

In conclusion, nobody's forcing you to move to Los Alamos. If you have a fear of atomic energy research, stay away. There are plenty of other places in this book.

Now, who would *want* to move here, other than those who are employed by the Los Alamos National Laboratory and their families?

For one thing, if you're both outdoors-oriented and of a scientific bent, you might find the atmosphere here quite congenial. Los Alamos is not your typical Southwestern town. Because of its scientific base, it has the highest percentage of Ph.D.s and the highest per capita income in New Mexico. Just to say that sounds snobbish, though, when in reality this is a very informal and friendly Western town. It's just a very *educated,* informal, and friendly Western town.

That has other advantages, too. The Los Alamos schools have been rated in some studies as one of the ten top systems in the country. That's an important consideration if you have children—and, again, in stark contrast to what you'll find in most remote communities in the Southwest. Library facilities here—with more than 80,000 books—are comparable to what you'd usually find in much larger cities.

Cultural life, shared with Santa Fe, is also uncommonly and tantalizingly diverse. Opera and the fine arts coexist very nicely with rodeos and pueblo corn dances.

If you have a small business that requires an educated and intelligent work force, Los Alamos has a secret weapon: a large pool of highly educated—and largely underutilized—lab spouses, mostly women.

And finally, for all of us but *especially* if you're a retiree, there's the low taxes. This is largely a legacy of Uncle Sam (i.e., the rest of us taxpayers), since most of the public facilities were built by the federal government and given to the county; the major cost today is maintenance. Taxes on a house assessed at $100,000 would be around $600 and most homeowners pay only $200 to $300 a year. That's one reason a number of retirees are moving here. They can sell their house in an expensive, high-tax metropolitan area, get a less expensive but just as nice house here, and have virtually no taxes to worry about.

A word of caution. If you have heart or blood-pressure problems, the 7,300-foot elevation might aggravate them. Otherwise, it's just something to get used to. You may find that you are more easily winded or have a tendency to be sleepy. It takes longer to bring liquids to a boil or to bake potatoes and conversely foods cool quickly. Not least, the altitude will affect your ability to consume alcoholic beverages!

Housing costs, we were told by Mary Deal of Mary Deal Realty, range from $45,000 to $225,000. That low figure represents the cost of one fourth of a quadraplex—four housing units to a building. The medium price for a home here would probably be $85,000.

For $85,000, you could get a house with 1,600 to 1,700 square feet of living area, on a 1/4- to 1/2-acre lot. It would probably have 3 bedrooms, 1 3/4 baths, living room, family room with fireplace, and a dining area more often than a formal dining room. (Homes reflect the informal lifestyle around here.)

Most of the homes selling at the time of our visit (July 1982) ranged from $75,000 to $100,000, Mary told us. The more expensive ones have up to 4,000 square feet. It's a trade-off between Los Alamos proper and White Rock; in town you pay for the location, there you pay for the newer home.

What originally brought Los Alamos to our attention, of course, was its crime rate. The FBI's *Crime in the United States* listed fourteen cities in New Mexico with a population of 10,000 or more and of them only Los Alamos qualified as a

Safe Place. In our comparison year of 1980, it had no murders or robberies, 4 rapes, and 5 aggravated assaults. In property crime it had 95 burglaries, 397 larceny-thefts, and 17 motor vehicle thefts. This placed it below U.S. rural rates in all categories except rape and larceny-theft and in those categories it was way below U.S. metropolitan levels. Also, by the way, there were no rapes in either 1979 or 1981, so that the 4 occurrences in 1980 were not a normal pattern.

Using this mesa-top retreat as your home base, you can enjoy all the cultural and recreational attractions of northern New Mexico—from horseback riding and archaeological explorations to skiing or white water river rafting on the Rio Grande, from Indian festivals and crafts to symphony concerts and gallery exhibits. It's an exciting and fascinating world, different from any other area of the United States, and from your home on Pajarito Plateau you're sitting on top of that world!

CIMARRON

POPULATION: 888
NO. OF CRIMES: 9
CRIME RATE: 1,013.5 per 100,000

To keep peace in the family, let's say it right up front: This is *David's* extra Safe Place for New Mexico! Holly says, "No way." Or to paraphrase Willie Nelson, her mama didn't raise her to be a cowgirl—not unless you're talking about something like Southfork ranch, of course.

"I will always love John Wayne," says Holly, "but I like to live in a place that is alive with more than just history and lizards!"

Cimarron is every bit as dusty and remote a cow town as you'd think it was from its name and from Holly's reaction. It's located on the eastern side of the Sangre de Cristo Mountains, in cattle country and cowboy country as distinguished from the Indian country and artiste country on the other side of the mountains. This is wide-open sagebrush country until you take U.S. 64 west toward the mountains. Then you're quickly in a scenic canyon cut by the Cimarron River. On our 1972 Safe Places trip, we were there in November and the canyon was ablaze with colors—every bit as vivid and dramatic as Oak Creek Canyon in Arizona and without the bumper-to-bumper traffic.

Founded in 1841, Cimarron was a stop on the Santa Fe Trail. At one time it was the capital of the famous Maxwell Land Grant. The home of Lucien B. Maxwell, built in 1858, was a popular stopping place for stagecoach travelers. Later, as the historical marker along the highway puts it, "Cowboys, trappers, and outlaws congregated in Cimarron's saloons and gambling halls. Ranchers made and lost fortunes overnight in games of poker, faro, roulette, and monte. Fighting broke out frequently, and the *Las Vegas* [New Mexico] *Gazette* once reported: 'Everything is quiet in Cimarron. Nobody has been killed for three days.' "

Things are a lot quieter now, as you can guess from David's selection of Cimarron as a Safe Place. But it wasn't always that way. If you'll recall our introduction for this state, we mentioned our stay at the Holiday Inn de Las Cruces and the famous bar in their saloon, where twenty-seven men had been killed. Well, that bar was taken from the old St. James Hotel here in Cimarron. The hotel is still here and its museum documents the shootings. The hotel's guest register includes such names as Bat Masterson, Billy the Kid, Pat Garrett, Buffalo Bill Cody, Butch Cassidy, the Sundance Kid, Doc Holliday, and Governor Lew Wallace.

A gristmill, the old jail, and several other historic buildings still stand in Cimarron. You'll also find Rosebud's Country Store, a Ben Franklin's, the Southwest Shop, Pacific Studs Lumber Manufacturers, and a motel—the Kit Carson Inn and Restaurant. There's not much else, except for a few streets of weathered houses that look like they've been around as long as the St. James.

Of course, if you were a Boy Scout as a kid, you may remember Cimarron from something besides the old Westerns. Four miles south of town is the Philmont Boy Scout Ranch and Explorer Base, host each summer to 15,000 scouts from around the world. Seven miles south of the headquarters is the Kit Carson Museum and another museum displays the artwork and library of the first chief scout of the Boy Scouts of America, Ernest Thompson Seton. The surrounding camp also has herds of buffalo, deer, elk, and antelope.

Bill Littrell, of Cimarron Realty Company, told us that he deals primarily in ranch real estate and he was talking about *real* ranches of 2,000 acres and up—not 5-, 10-, or 40-acre parcels bought by dudes like us. You won't find those sorts of parcels available around here.

Bill told us that a few houses, perhaps a half dozen of them, are usually on the market in Cimarron. These are mostly older houses, since there's very little that is new in town. The low end of the price scale ranges from $17,000 to $60,000, while relatively newer homes—often with better views—cost from $75,000 to $125,000.

For $40,000, Bill had a small 3-bedroom house that was about twenty-five years old. It had a living room, kitchen, dining room, and detached 1-car garage and was on a lot of slightly less than 1/4 acre.

For $100,000, he had a 2-story house that was just about twelve years old, with a 2-car attached garage and 1/2 acre of land. It had 3 bedrooms, 2 baths, living room, den, and combination kitchen-dining area. Taxes on this property were around $275 to $300 a year.

In our comparison year of 1980, Cimarron had no murders, rapes, or robberies. There were 4 aggravated assaults, 2 burglaries, 3 larceny-thefts, and no motor vehicle thefts. That placed it below U.S. rural crime levels for all categories except aggravated assault. There the 4 incidents resulted in a *rate* higher than for U.S. metropolitan areas. Well, a cowtown's got to keep up its image somehow.

Where to get further information:

State

Tourism and Travel Division, New Mexico Commerce and Industry Department, Bataan Memorial Building, Santa Fe, NM 87503; telephone outside the state 800/545-2040. U.S. Bureau of Indian Affairs, P.O. Box 8327, Albuquerque, NM 87108.

Regional

Greater Albuquerque Chamber of Commerce, 401 2nd Street, N.W., P.O. Box 25100, Albuquerque, NM 87102. Hispano Chamber of Commerce, 407 Rio Grande Boulevard, N.W., Suite 2, Albuquerque, NM 87104.

Santa Fe Chamber of Commerce, 200 W. Marcy Street, P.O. Box 1928, Santa Fe, NM 87501. Hispano Chamber of Commerce de Santa Fe, P.O. Box 4206, Santa Fe, NM 87502. Santa Fe Opera, P.O. Box 2408, Santa Fe, NM 87501. Orchestra of Santa Fe, P.O. Box 2091, Santa Fe, NM 87501. *The Santa Fean Magazine* ($14.25 for one year, 12 issues), P.O. Box 1424, Santa Fe, NM 87501.

Taos Chamber of Commerce, Drawer I, Taos, NM 87571.

Local

Los Alamos: Los Alamos Chamber of Commerce, P.O. Box 888, Los Alamos, NM 87544. *Welcome to Los Alamos* is a splendid introduction to the laboratory and the community, available from the Public Affairs Office, Los Alamos National Laboratory, Los Alamos, NM 87545.

Cimarron: Cimarron Chamber of Commerce, P.O. Box 604, Cimarron, NM 87714.

New York

New York City gets a bum rap. Merely mention the word "crime" and what place do you think of? Yep.

Heaven knows, there's more than enough crime to go around in Gotham. We're not denying that. It's just that plenty of other places are even worse off.

New York got its reputation as the nation's crime capital because it is the nation's communications capital. The television networks and most of the newspaper wire services are headquartered here. Thus it's only natural that the nation's most influential communicators would be most familiar with this area's crime problems and unwittingly spread the idea that New York City is somehow unique when it comes to crime. When you think about it, perhaps the single most important reason was Johnny Carson and his jokes about New York, all those years he was broadcasting from Rockefeller Center.

It also doesn't help that New York City is by far the nation's largest city. From here, any other (smaller) place *looks* safe by comparison.

But as we emphasize continually, appearances and off-the-cuff reactions can be awfully deceiving. To put New York City in accurate perspective, we checked the crime rates for all U.S. cities and towns with a population of 10,000 or more. New York City's crime rate in 1980, our comparison year, was 10,094 crimes per 100,000 population. *There were 229 other cities and towns with a higher crime rate!* Florida alone had forty-two cities worse off than New York and there were thirty-three in California, seventeen each in Michigan and New Jersey, and eleven in the state of Washington. By far the worst place was New Jersey's Atlantic City, with a rate of 30,981 crimes per 100,000 population—three times higher than New York City's rate.

What makes this all the more remarkable is the disparity between New York's size and the size of the other cities, since as a general rule, crime increases as the cities grow. Even if we narrow the field to the nation's largest cities—those with a population of a half million or more—you are more likely to be the victim of a major crime in Boston (the *real* big city crime capital of the United States in 1980), Dallas, Phoenix, Detroit, or San Francisco.

We mention this not to justify or belittle New York's crime problem. We just want to put it in proper perspective and set the record straight. And we don't want to let others become overconfident. You can't exorcise your own area's crime problems by pointing the finger at big bad New York.

Now, this is the chapter for New York State, so let us explicitly acknowledge that, yes, we are fully aware that there is much more to the state than New York City. We have had the pleasure of seeing most areas of the Empire State and unless you've done that, you have no idea how varied, how beautiful—how rugged, even—New York State can be. With powerful resources and a population of more than 17 million, it could constitute a formidable nation by itself.

There are several reasons, nevertheless, why we are concentrating on the area around the *city* in this volume.

First, we just didn't have time to cover all of the state. After nearly four months on the road across the United States, we had to limit further explorations and meet our publishing deadline.

Second, although crime is a problem anywhere in the state, it's not nearly as much of a problem upstate as it is around the city. So we concentrated our limited time on the area where the problem is the worst.

Third, metropolitan New York City overwhelms the rest of the state in population and job opportunities. So if you are being transferred or for some other reason are moving to New York State, the odds are that you are planning a move to the vicinity of the city.

For these reasons, we have concentrated our efforts on finding you some Safe Places within commuting distance of Manhattan. In this chapter, that means Long Island and Westchester County. You'll also want to look at our chapters for Connecticut and New Jersey. As you will see, you can live but minutes away from the Big Apple and enjoy near-rural crime rates. You just have to know where to look in this maze of hundreds of communities and that's the job we have done for you.

LONG ISLAND

The Indian name for Long Island is Paumonak ("Isle of Shells"). With more than 250 miles of coastline, this is where New York State meets the Atlantic Ocean. Indeed, if you look at its shape on a map, you can envision a giant 125-mile-long beached whale, with a forked tail, nibbling at Manhattan. (As if the city doesn't have enough problems!)

The island's total population of more than 7 million includes two New York City boroughs, Brooklyn and Queens. But when most people talk about Long Island, they're thinking of the suburbs and resorts beyond the city and that's the area of concern to us now.

More than 2.5 million people live in that area's two counties. Nassau County, adjoining the city, is the more densely populated and suburbanized of the two. You see more and more patches of surviving countryside the farther east you go in Suffolk County, until you hit the fields of potatoes, corn, and strawberries.

Then you remember that this was the original home of the cauliflower and still lends its name to the famous Long Island duckling.

Caught in a seemingly endless traffic jam as you head for the beach on a summer weekend, you might easily pick up the impression that Long Island is one vast sea of Levittowns. There's more than enough of that, to be sure, but much more as well.

The south shore, facing the ocean, has popular Jones Beach State Park, the famous barrier island and national seashore Fire Island, and the socially chic summer resorts known collectively as the Hamptons. Beyond them lies the salty fishing village of Montauk (remember *Jaws?)* and at the very tip Montauk Point Lighthouse, perched majestically atop a bluff and facing Portugal.

The north shore faces Long Island Sound, with Connecticut visible on the other side of the water. Here you'll find old whaling towns, some of America's greatest mansions and estates, and countless bays and harbors brimming with white sails in the summertime.

More than 450 marinas and yacht basins line these two shores. The waters, warmed by the Gulf Stream, are filled with more than 470 species of fish and are noted for bluefish, striped bass, swordfish, giant tuna, and marlin. This is an angler's paradise, with thirty-five world records for sport fish caught off Long Island. This is also the home of Blue Point oysters, Little Neck clams, and bay scallops.

It's clear that if you are marine- and water-oriented, Long Island is one of the first places you'd want to consider when moving to metropolitan New York City. The problem is in finding a community that hasn't exported the city's crime industry. Ideally, such a community would also retain some personality and character and not be inundated with the tract housing that spread through Long Island in the fifties and sixties like wild weeds.

We are pleased to report that we have found *four* such communities—each not only safe, but also a beautiful place to call home. It wasn't easy. And while four is not a large number when you're talking about an area as heavily populated as Long Island, that's also part of what makes a special place special.

Bear in mind that between 1970 and 1980, the number of burglaries and robberies rose more than 100 percent in thirty Nassau communities. And in our comparison year of 1980, less urbanized Suffolk County actually had a higher overall crime rate than Nassau County.

Late in 1982 the New York *Times* printed a round table discussion, "Crime in the Suburbs." Included were these interesting comments from Nassau County District Attorney Denis E. Dillon:

> Our perception in Nassau County . . . is that the violent criminals, for the most part, are coming out from the city. The city has probably been picked fairly clean and so these people have just found out that there are areas where they can practice their criminal endeavors very lucratively, such as the north shore—big estates where they can get in and get out very quickly by car with very little chance of detection.
>
> We also find when we arrest these people from the city that they have been convicted

many times before and yet have been punished very lightly. They haven't been deterred yet, they haven't even been quarantined and kept away from the communities.

Despite this influx of city-based crime, the Nassau DA reports some progress:

We have about 5,000 felony arrests a year (it was about 3,000 when I was first elected). Still, we eliminated plea-bargaining after indictment. Once we go to indictment, it's all over. From that point, the defendant, if he wants to plead to anything, has to plead to the count in the indictment that covers the heaviest maximum punishment. Serious violent crime we don't plea-bargain at all where we have the evidence. For other crimes that affect the quality of life, such as residence burglaries, we will not take any plea less than a felony, which gives the judge the flexibility to give four years in state prison.

We've managed to reduce the number of felony cases awaiting trial in Nassau County by 80 percent, although the felony arrest rate has almost doubled in that period. And we've done all this without adding any judges or any assistant district attorneys. More than that we can't do. One thing we have to remember is that the criminal justice system can only do so much.

The rest *you* have to do, first by selecting a safe community to begin with and then by taking sensible precautions to protect yourself and your property.

When we started our search for Safe Places on Long Island, we began—as elsewhere—by dismissing all communities with a rate of more than 4,000 crimes per 100,000 population. First we looked at the FBI's statistics for all communities with a population of 10,000 or more.

That was an eye-opener. Instead of Safe Places, what we found were decidedly *unsafe* places like Hempstead in Nassau County and even East Hampton in Suffolk County, the "Home Sweet Home" of John Howard Payne's immortal song, where the crime rates are almost as high as New York City's (see our Long Island Crime Chart, p. 259). Only two places qualified with under-4,000 crime rates: Floral Park and Lynbrook. And when we broke down their crime rates into the seven categories, we were unhappy with both of them. They were safe only by comparison with their neighboring communities and had too many robberies and too much property crime for us to feel comfortable about them.

That meant we had to look for some smaller havens, with populations under 10,000.

Even here we were shocked, particularly by high levels of property crime. The situation was especially ludicrous in some of the small summer beach resorts that are hard hit by thefts and off-season residential burglaries. When we projected their crime rates per 100,000 population, in order to be able to compare them with larger communities, we found one that set new records—with a *rate* of over 50,000 crimes per 100,000 population in 1980 and over 73,000 the following year! That means that three out of four residents of this village were victims of a major crime in 1981!

But you don't have to head back to the city. We found a delightful middle-class suburb on the south shore, with the most reasonable housing prices of our four Long Island havens. Our two north shore villages are expensive, but what a way to live if you can afford it! And to round them out, we present an elegant whaling village at the end of the island. It's not within commuting distance of the city, but it makes a nice retreat for anyone who wants to combine metropolitan accessibility with the enticements of the ocean.

MALVERNE

POPULATION: 9,269
NO. OF CRIMES: 203
CRIME RATE: 2,190.1 per 100,000

Malverne is the largest in size, the lowest in crime, and the least expensive of our four Safe Places on Long Island.

We found it tucked away—almost hidden—on the south shore of Long Island between Valley Stream, Lynbrook, and Rockville Centre. You can get there from the city by taking exit 17 south off Southern State Parkway or by riding the Long Island Railroad to the Malverne or Westwood stations. Manhattan's Penn Station is about forty-five minutes away when the train runs on schedule.

Malverne has a small town flavor that is enhanced by the age of the homes: Most were built thirty-five to forty-five years ago or, at the latest, twenty-five years ago. The older architectural styles give the town a look distinctively different from newer developments, a difference we appreciate. The homes are comfortably sized but not enormous and business areas are similarly kept in scale. Nothing is run-down in this town; the residents obviously take great pride in their community and their homes.

Malverne is a quiet town of predominantly single-family homes and we suspect most of the residents would just as soon keep their secret to themselves. It got more publicity than it cared for in the sixties, when Malverne became the test site for busing on Long Island. "A decade later," says the Malverne School District brochure, "integration is working. There is peace in the Malverne schools. Children are being educated."

Malverne's public schools consist of two elementary schools (grades K–4), a middle school (5–8), and a high school (9–12). The school brochure caught our approving eye when it stated forthrightly that in Malverne, "Children are not exposed to reading-readiness. Here, kindergarten pupils actually *read*, using a program developed with the Bank Street College of Education. It is small-group instruction, heavily based on the phonetic approach to reading and decoding skills. The program has significantly improved the reading achievement of the children. The results have been so dramatic, it may be a method of turning out a generation of super-readers."

We were also pleased to read that "Malverne schools are organized on a tracking system in which students are placed in classes according to their levels of performance. The district calls this modified homogeneous grouping; there are three levels for each grade with placement determined by test scores."

LONG ISLAND Crime Chart

	Crime Rate	Murder	Rape	Robbery	Aggravated Assault	Burglary	Larceny —Theft	Motor Vehicle Theft
United States								
U.S. Total	5,899.9	10.2	36.4	243.5	290.6	1,668.2	3,156.3	494.6
U.S. Metropolitan Areas	6,757.6	11.5	43.4	319.0	328.3	1,911.8	3,534.9	608.8
U.S. Rural Areas	2,290.4	7.5	15.5	22.5	136.9	830.2	1,143.9	133.9
Regional Crime Centers								
East Hampton Town	9,956.7	0	79.4	26.5	935.7	3,062.9	5,446.2	406.0
Hempstead Village	9,345.6	9.9	27.2	549.5	522.2	2,566.6	4,836.2	834.1
New York City	10,094.0	25.8	52.7	1,429.2	618.0	2,994.9	3,545.3	1,429.1
Safe Places								
Kensington	2,460.5	0	0	0	0	1,230.2	966.6	263.6
Lloyd Harbor	2,389.9	0	0	0	86.4	835.0	1,382.1	86.4
Malverne	2,190.1	0	0	0	43.2	679.7	1,327.0	140.3
Sag Harbor	3,220.6	0	0	0	0	845.4	2,093.4	281.8

Our Lady of Lourdes School has also played an important role in the community for thirty years. It enrolls children in grades 1–8.

Crimes of violence in 1980 consisted of 4 aggravated assaults; there were no murders, rapes, or robberies. Malverne placed below the crime rates for U.S. rural areas in all categories except larceny-theft and motor vehicle theft and in those categories it was just above rural rates. There was actually a small decrease in crime in 1981.

Tina McNally of the Malverne Realty Company told us that houses sell from the low 80s to around $185,000, but the usual range is from the mid-80s to $150,000.

Least expensive are the Capes; they're the ones selling in the mid-80s. An expandable Cape is one with room and space upstairs that remain to be finished. In this price range, you will usually get a living room, dining room, kitchen, 2 bedrooms, a finished basement, and a 1-car garage, on a 50 × 100 lot.

(Malverne is basically a 1-car garage town, since the homes were built before the advent of multicar families.)

In the neighborhood of $100,000, you can expect to get 3 bedrooms, 2 baths, and a finished basement, den, or Florida room. An expanded ranch is a 3-bedroom home that has been expanded on the upper level with 2 or more bedrooms and a bath; these go for $135,000 to $145,000. Tudors and colonials are among the most expensive homes in town. Larger homes are likely to be on a 100 × 100 lot.

We noted, finally, that under the impact of the recession a number of houses seemed to be listed at lower than usual prices. For $69,990, for example, you could get a Cape with a family room, dining room, living room with fireplace, 4 bedrooms, a small eat-in kitchen, and a basement garage. For just $85,000 there was a listing for a 5-bedroom Tudor; it had a living room with fireplace, family room, dining room, eat-in kitchen, basement, and 2-car garage. Other listings around town included a 3-bedroom, 2-bath split-level house for $90,900, a 3-bedroom, 2-bath colonial for $92,000, and a larger 3-bedroom, 2-bath split-level house for $105,000.

There are no condominiums, very few 2-family houses, and just one small apartment complex across from the railroad station. Malverne is basically a town of single-family homes.

An easy New York City commute, low crime, affordable and attractive housing, schools that take education seriously, and quick access to some of the finest beaches in the Northeast make this a gem of a find on congested, crime-ridden Long Island. Don't pass this one by!

KENSINGTON

POPULATION: 1,138
NO. OF CRIMES: 28
CRIME RATE: 2,460.5 per 100,000

From *A Week-End at Kensington,* a 1915 sales brochure published by the Rickert-Finlay Realty Company of New York City, developers of Kensington:

To us it seems that Kensington would suit almost any refined man of moderate tastes—especially if he be an out-of-doors man, with a family—for here he can play golf, or tennis, and here he knows his family are in the midst of a healthy, beautiful and convenient neighborhood, made up of socially delightful folks . . .

You enter Kensington through an imposing gateway, like that of a private estate, and immediately find yourself in a veritable fairyland of natural beauty. The main drive through the property, known as Beverly Road, is lined on either side with lindens and elms thirty years old, forming a continuous archway of green for nearly three-quarters of a mile . . .

You make a quick survey of the houses as you pass and see that almost without exception they are of an unusually high standard of architecture, in a pleasing variety of styles—Colonial, English and Italian, and all evidencing that combination of simplicity, restraint, and careful handling of proportions so requisite in successful architecture . . .

Among the larger country homes within a few minutes' drive of Kensington, are those of William K. Vanderbilt, Jr., W. R. Grace, Harry Payne Whitney, Clarence Mackay, E. D. Morgan, Charles Steele, William C. Whitney and H. M. Earle. The famous Piping Rock Club and the Westbury Polo Field—the latter the scene of the International Polo Matches—are also in this wonderful section of Long Island . . .

The cost of houses and land in Kensington ranges from $15,000 upwards . . .

Under no circumstances will the Company rent houses which have been erected for sale. Kensington is a community of homeowners and not a colony of renters . . .

The land-values in Kensington are remarkably low. Large, well-situated plots cost from $4,000 to $6,000 and are priced on a basis of 30 cents to 60 cents per square foot.

Eat your heart out. Those $15,000 homes now sell for a minimum of $250,000 and usually in a range of $250,000 to $350,000.

When we talked with Pearl Diskin, the broker-owner of Pearl Diskin Ltd., she had a listing for a Kensington home—an all-brick, very pretty colonial—for $299,500. There are 4 bedrooms in the main house, with servants' quarters located over the 2-car garage. Taxes are under $5,000.

Prices aside, today's Kensington looks very much the same as when it was being built early in the century. Entirely residential, the village consists of four main roads running parallel, forming a long, narrow neck. Taxes are high because the village has its own police force and highway department; fire protection and garbage collection are provided under contract.

Kensington is located in the center of the Great Neck peninsula of Long Island's north shore, just 22 miles from midtown Manhattan and bordering on Queens, the largest borough of New York City. Composed of nine incorporated villages (among them Kensington) and an unincorporated area, Great Neck is known for its general affluence, its quality schools, its first-rate library system (with the largest book collection on Long Island), and its extensive cultural and recreational facilities. Great Neck is also the home of the U.S. Merchant Marine Academy, set on the beautiful Chrysler estate in the village of Kings Point.

Great Neck has extensive shopping facilities just outside the Kensington boundaries and on Northern Boulevard in adjacent Port Washington you'll find branches of major stores, including Bloomingdale's, Lord & Taylor, B. Altman, Abraham & Straus, and W. & J. Sloane.

We picked Kensington specifically as our Safe Place because it has the lowest crime rate of the Great Neck communities. There were no crimes of violence in either 1980 or 1981. The main crime problem, as you might suspect, is with residential burglaries—14 in 1980, 18 the following year. This is above the U.S. rural rate for burglaries but still way below metropolitan rates in this category.

Outside of the industrial giants, Great Neck's most famous resident may have been F. Scott Fitzgerald. He wrote *The Great Gatsby* in 1922, while living here at 6 Gateway Drive. By that time, Great Neck was already noted for its concentration of famous people—the Chryslers and the Sloanes, Eddie Cantor, Will and Ariel Durant, Maurice Chevalier, the Marx brothers, and Lillian Russell among them.

To Fitzgerald, Great Neck was West Egg, an abode of the newly rich and "one of the strangest communities in North America." To another resident, Gene Buck, producer of eleven Ziegfeld Follies, it was "a magnificent peninsula of undulating hills, jutting into the sound, embraced by beautiful bays, and almost completely surrounded by real estate dealers."

Even today, Great Neck continues in that tradition. Move here and you may find that your next-door neighbor is a writer like Bruce Jay Friedman or an artist like Harry Lieberman, America's oldest living primitive painter, or a musician-composer like Peter Nero or Morton Gould, or Broadway producer, actor, and comedian Alan King.

Lucky you. And lucky them, to have you as a neighbor in this luxurious corner of Long Island.

LLOYD HARBOR

POPULATION: 3,473
NO. OF CRIMES: 83
CRIME RATE: 2,389.9 per 100,000

"It is a place of quiet and rural charm. Its wooded hills, bluffs, meadowland, marsh, and beach—all outlined by the variegated waters of harbor, inlet, and sound—combine to create an area of great natural beauty. The rolling terrain is enhanced by extensive stands of native shrubs and trees. Freshwater streams and ponds, salt marsh and tidal wetland, each support distinctive plants and wildlife. And on all sides there are the sweeping water views. Not unexpectedly, effort has been made here to protect nature's handiwork. Lloyd Harbor today, at a commuting distance of some thirty-five miles from New York City, affords a quiet haven for a resident population daily involved with urban concerns."

We cannot improve on this capsule description of present-day Lloyd Harbor by Irene K. Alexander, in her official history of the village. This is truly a rural retreat from the metropolitan and suburban congestion that abounds in all directions.

Lloyd Harbor maintains its rural flavor with 2-acre zoning and its restriction to single-family residences. Geography helps a great deal too. The village is perched on the northwestern corner of Suffolk County and Huntington Township. A causeway and a narrow spit of land connect its two sections—Lloyd Neck and, on the mainland, West Neck. There is limited road access to the rest of Huntington Township and all major traffic arteries are much farther south. Nobody goes through Lloyd Harbor to get somewhere else.

When the village was incorporated in 1926, it was dominated by the estates of business giants such as Albert G. Milbank, Walter Jennings, the Standard Oil magnate, and Marshall Field III, whose 1,500 acres were regarded by many as the finest country estate in America. Over the years, these have disappeared or been converted to tax-exempt uses. That puts the tax burden squarely on the smaller property owners, of course, but when they consider the alternatives—such as business or industrial intrusions—it's a burden they willingly accept as the lesser evil.

One such intrusion was a plan by the Long Island Lighting Company to build a nuclear power plant, which would have drastically changed the character of Lloyd Neck. Faced by vehement local opposition, the company abandoned that plan. Local residents had no choice when Uncle Sam decided in 1955 to build a Nike guided-missile site here, but that program was phased out in 1963 and private residences have replaced the silos. Still more controversy was generated when Friends World College, a project of the Religious Society of Friends (Quakers), planned to convert the estate it bought into a campus for 400 to 500 students. The college abandoned those plans and instead joined the University Without Walls consortium, in which students are scattered around the world instead of on one campus. Friends World College is now deemed a "good neighbor."

Over 40 percent of the village's land area is presently used for tax-exempt purposes. The Field estate was sold to the state and turned into Caumsett State Park; it remains primarily a conservation and wildlife refuge, however, and public uses are limited to cross-country skiing, hiking and nature trails, saltwater fishing, bridle trails, and bicycle paths. Also within the village boundaries are Target Rock National Wildlife Refuge, properties owned by the Nature Conservancy and the Society for the Preservation of Long Island Antiquities, the Seminary of the Immaculate Conception, and the United Nations Mission of the Republic of the Ivory Coast.

Lloyd Harbor has several sites of historic interest. Lloyd Manor was built by Henry Lloyd in 1711 and that year was the birthplace of Jupiter Hammon, America's first black poet. A black oak tree visible from Lloyd Harbor Road was designated the largest black oak in the United States by a 1950 survey of the American Forestry Association. And during the Revolutionary War, Lloyd Harbor was dominated by the British. British officers were stationed at Lloyd Manor; Target Rock, a 14-foot-high boulder in Long Island Sound, was used by them for gunnery practice; and Fort Franklin was built by the British with American labor and served as a refuge for Tories fleeing Connecticut. De Lancey's loyalist brigade was stationed here and repulsed Rochambeau's French fleet in 1781.

Enough history. What does it cost to get into Lloyd Harbor today? At least $200,000, we were told by Edward W. Vossen, manager of Carll Burr, Inc., the Merrill Lynch Realty affiliate in neighboring Cold Spring Harbor. If you find something "cheap"—for $189,000, say—you can bet it needs work and you'll likely end up pumping $50,000 more into renovations.

A vacant building lot (a minimum of 2 acres, remember) will cost you at least $110,000. At the time of our visit, the average sale price for houses was in the $270,000–$280,000 range.

At the low end of the scale, Ed did have a house available on Gerry Lane that had dropped in price to $199,000 from $250,000. This was a 7-room ranch with 3 bedrooms.

For $450,000, you could get an 11-room (4-bedroom) contemporary with a winter water view (no leaves on the trees). And $510,000 would land you a carriage house with skylights, a floating staircase, and vaulted ceilings. It sits on 2 acres with award-winning landscaping and an in-ground pool.

The crime rate, as we promised, is low. Crimes of violence are especially rare: just 3 aggravated assaults in 1980, and no murders, rapes, or robberies that year or the following year.

In our comparison year of 1980, Lloyd Harbor was below U.S. rural crime rates in all categories except burglary and larceny-theft and in those it was just above rural levels. In 1981, the overall crime rate, including burglaries, decreased; Lloyd Harbor was above rural crime rates in just the larceny-theft and motor vehicle theft categories.

Ralph A. Hummel, the village's chief of police, told us that "one factor contributing toward Lloyd Harbor's low crime rate is geographical. More than 80 percent of its 9.2 square miles is serviced by a single roadway, which reduces the chance of a successful getaway."

Of greater importance, in his view, is the careful choosing of members of the force. "A police officer in a small department," he explained, "soon develops what has been called 'territorial imperative,' which is taking criminal activity as a personal affront rather than an expected occurrence. This feeling of personal pride has been most responsible for Lloyd Harbor's long-standing low crime rate."

As we've noted, Lloyd Harbor is an incorporated village in the town of Huntington. That township has a population of more than 200,000, with local blue-chip industries and businesses such as Estee Lauder, *Newsday,* Gould, Mergenthaler Linotype, and Poly Pak Industries. There's no immediate change once you leave Lloyd Harbor, however. The adjoining areas of Huntington are also quietly residential, and directly south is Cold Spring Harbor, a nineteenth-century whaling center that is now one of the most attractive village restorations in the country.

Students go to elementary school in Lloyd Harbor and then to nearby Cold Spring Harbor High School. Huntington has extensive shopping facilities, including Lord & Taylor and other fine stores. Commuters to Manhattan make it in an hour from Huntington station—*when* the trains run on time. Huntington is the last stop on the Long Island Railroad's electric line; if you live farther east, you must first catch a diesel train and then switch.

That's an additional pain you don't need, especially when the serene haven of Lloyd Harbor offers you such an attractive respite from the city, right here on the Gold Coast of Long Island.

SAG HARBOR

POPULATION: 2,484
NO. OF CRIMES: 80
CRIME RATE: 3,220.6 per 100,000

At its eastern end, Long Island splits into a south fork and a north fork. Between them lies Shelter Island and the waters of several bays and sounds.

Sag Harbor is located on the northern shore of Long Island's south fork; that is, it faces north toward Shelter Island and the protected waters of Shelter Island Sound and Gardiners Bay. This location made it an ideal home port for whaling ships and for nearly 100 years—from 1775 to 1871—whaling was the town's major industry. At its peak, in 1845, there were sixty-three vessels in the fleet and twelve large shipping firms in the business. You would see more masted ships in Sag Harbor's bay than in New York City's harbor and only New Bedford, Massachusetts, had a larger whaling industry. James Fenimore Cooper based many of the characters in his sea stories on real-life Sag Harbor salts.

As an interesting historical sidelight, it was *not* Commodore Matthew Perry but Southampton's Captain Mercator Cooper, commanding the Sag Harbor whaleship *Manhattan,* who was the first American to sail into a Japanese port and be allowed to anchor and fly the Stars and Stripes. That was in 1844 and was historically appropriate, since Sag Harbor residents can also lay claim to having the first American flag with stars and stripes used in battle—the famous Hulburt flag, commemorated by a bronze plaque on the grounds of the Hulburt house on Main Street.

The whales and their hunters are gone now, but you can relive those days at Sag Harbor's Whaling Museum, a Greek Revival edifice with Corinthian columns and roof ornamentation of carved wooden blubber spades and harpoons. You enter this museum by passing through the jawbones of a right (Greenland) whale. The Whaler's Presbyterian Church on Union Street has one of the most beautiful church interiors in America, hand-carved by ship's carpenters. Indeed, the flavor of those whaling days can be savored throughout the historic district of Sag Harbor.

The Gold Rush of 1849 was the turning point for the whaling industry—too many ships and men were lost to the lures of California. Sag Harbor's economy floundered for a while, then was buoyed by a variety of small industries after the arrival of the railroad in 1870. The railroad also brought summer travelers, who have continued to "discover" Sag Harbor to this day.

In recent years, the town has become popular with people who must commute into New York City just once or twice a week: with retirees, and with writers and artists, artisans and craftsmen. This is a year-round town, though, in contrast to resorts like the Hamptons. If you enjoy *Travels with Charley* as much as we do, you may remember that John Steinbeck began his journey from his Sag Harbor home.

In our comparison year of 1980, Sag Harbor had no crimes of violence. Its 80 property crimes placed it slightly above the U.S. rural rate for burglary, and somewhat higher in larceny-theft and motor vehicle theft—but still way below U.S. metropolitan crime rates in those categories. In 1981 the overall crime rate fell by 25 percent.

Ann Greaves, of the Sagg Harbour Agency, was delightfully informative about local real estate. She told us that prices have risen drastically in recent years, making it hard to find a building lot for less than $25,000 or a house for less than $100,000.

At that low end of the scale, you may get a 3-bedroom ranch. But if it's in a nice area with a little property, you are more likely to pay $150,000.

Old houses are much sought after here, even though they almost always need more work done on them. The cheapest one Ann had available at the time of our visit was $135,000 and that was a 2-family residence.

For $185,000 she did have a Federal house in the village with 3 bedrooms, 2 baths, and a sunporch, on little more than 1/4 acre. It also had a new roof and central heating system.

Two Victorians were also available, at $160,000 and $189,500. Each had 3 bedrooms and 2 baths.

Another home in the village, about 200 years old, was selling for $235,000. This 10-room house happened to be on a large lot and had a swimming pool, but the absence of landscaping kept the price down. It had 4 bedrooms, living room, dining room, family room, and 1 1/2 baths. Oak floors had been built over some original wide-board flooring.

Very little waterfront property is left. A couple of lots were available, but on Upper Sag Harbor Cove not Shelter Island Sound. A 1/2-acre lot with 118 feet of water frontage was going for $105,000, with another lot selling for $95,000.

Sag Harbor, unlike most oceanside resorts, has limited summer rentals available. The summer people here tend to be families and professional people in their thirties, whereas younger crowds inhabit the resorts. You can expect to pay between $4,000 and somewhere above $20,000 for a three-month summer rental, though most of them range between $5,500 and $8,000.

If the sea calls you and you want a town that's off the most-beaten paths but still accessible to the city, look into this haunt of James Fenimore Cooper and John Steinbeck. You may find it to be as hospitable a home port as they did, and the captains and seamen who shaped its salty character.

WESTCHESTER COUNTY

Westchester County is the most affluent of the suburban counties surrounding New York City. In the 1980 census, it had a population of 866,599, and with a per capita income of $10,744, ranked nineteenth among the 3,137 counties in the United States.

Persons familiar with the Westchester image may be surprised that it's that far down on the list. That image is conjured up by suburbs like fashionable Scarsdale or Bedford in the horse country farther north. What the image doesn't take into account is the fact that the southern portion of the county is heavily built up, with good-sized cities that share all of the problems of other metropolitan areas.

Yonkers (population 195,351) is the largest of these cities and the fourth largest in New York State. With more than 100 industries, including major ones like the Otis Elevator Company, it is an employment center in its own right and more than a suburb of New York City. White Plains (population 46,999) is the county seat and headquarters for a large number of Fortune 500 corporations, as well as a regional shopping center. New Rochelle (population 70,794) still benefits from its portrayal as a fashionable suburb in so many movies of the forties and fifties and television shows of the fifties. Today, it still has its nice areas . . . but there are just as many that we wouldn't want to traverse at night. The truly significant fact is that even with cities like these, Westchester County pulls through as the most affluent of the region's suburban counties.

WESTCHESTER COUNTY Crime Chart

	Crime Rate	Murder	Rape	Robbery	Aggravated Assault	Burglary	Larceny —Theft	Motor Vehicle Theft
United States								
U.S. Total	5,899.9	10.2	36.4	243.5	290.6	1,668.2	3,156.3	494.6
U.S. Metropolitan Areas	6,757.6	11.5	43.4	319.0	328.3	1,911.8	3,534.9	608.8
U.S. Rural Areas	2,290.4	7.5	15.5	22.5	136.9	830.2	1,143.9	133.9
Regional Crime Centers								
Elmsford	10,026.8	0	0	357.0	29.8	2,915.8	6,158.9	565.3
Larchmont	7,783.8	0	0	79.3	111.0	2,251.1	5,057.1	285.4
Mount Vernon	7,627.6	6.1	33.3	525.6	272.6	2,282.5	3,736.6	770.9
Safe Places								
Briarcliff Manor	1,200.1	0	0	0	14.1	833.0	211.8	141.2
Eastchester	2,010.0	0	5.0	15.0	40.0	730.0	1,050.0	170.0
Irvington	2,350.1	0	0	34.6	34.6	846.7	1,365.1	69.1

This variety of communities within the county is reflected in their crime statistics. Overall, crime levels here are not as pervasively high as on Long Island. You have more communities that are safe or fairly safe and even the crime centers are not as bad off as New York City—or some places on Long Island. As indicated by our Westchester County Crime Chart (above), the worst offenders in the county are Elmsford, Larchmont, and Mount Vernon. Here again, we see how appearances can be deceptive. Who would guess that tranquil-looking Larchmont has a higher crime rate than Mount Vernon or New Rochelle or White Plains?

EASTCHESTER

POPULATION: 20,000
NO. OF CRIMES: 402
CRIME RATE: 2,010.0 per 100,000

Most people just pass by Eastchester. That's easy to do, since the Hutchinson River Parkway skirts the town's eastern border, the Bronx River Parkway follows its western border, and the Cross County Parkway cuts an east–west path just south of town.

Perhaps this explains the town's relative anonymity. We are fairly familiar with Westchester County, yet we had to look on a map to see where Eastchester was located. We found it tucked away right in the middle of that built-up southern portion of Westchester County we talked about. Its neighbors are all better known: New Rochelle to the east, Mount Vernon to the south, Yonkers to the west, and Scarsdale to the north.

The entire town actually includes two incorporated villages, Bronxville and Tuckahoe, that maintain their own police departments and school systems. When *we* speak of Eastchester, we're referring to the rest of the town, since all three areas maintain separate crime statistics.

Eastchester is quite low in crime, especially for such a densely populated area. Tuckahoe would still qualify, barely, as a Safe Place (it has a crime rate of slightly less than 4,000 per 100,000), but there are many safer communities in the area. Exclusive Bronxville doesn't release its crime statistics even to the state's crime-reporting agency.

In our comparison year of 1980, Eastchester had no murders, 1 rape, 3 robberies, and 8 aggravated assaults. Property crime included 146 burglaries, 210 larceny-thefts, and 34 motor vehicle thefts. That placed the town below U.S. rural crime rates in all categories except motor vehicle theft and there the town was still way below metropolitan levels.

The following year, the number of crimes dropped still further—from 402 to 341. With an estimated population that year of 20,298, this constituted a rate of 1,680 crimes per 100,000. The only disturbing note was an increase to 10 robberies, bringing that category above rural crime levels.

In 1928, Eastchester was acclaimed the Cradle of American Golf. Among the Eastchester residents of this era who won titles were Will MacFarlane (the U.S. Open, 1925, defeating Bobby Jones), Jess Sweetser (the British Amateur Championship, 1926), Johnny Farrell (the U.S. Open, 1928, again with Bobby Jones as the victim), and Tom Creavy (the PGA title, 1931).

Today, the town is still home to the Siwanoy Country Club, the Leewood Golf Club, and Lake Isles Country Club. The last was bought by the town in 1980 and is one of the prize attractions of the community. Among its facilities are four swimming pools, a diving tank, eight tennis courts, and an 18-hole golf course. The club also has a restaurant and caters to parties, weddings, and other special events.

From all this you might get the impression that Eastchester is one of those exclusive Westchester enclaves of the rich. Actually, it's a hodge-podge collection of middle-class neighborhoods sandwiched between some genuinely affluent neighbors and a problem of the town is the loss of a strong identity, of community cohesiveness. The northern portion of Eastchester is all too ready to accept a much more fashionable Scarsdale mailing address. And the southern part of town gravitates more toward Bronxville, which was established early in the century as a planned community of affluence.

The main business area is neither run-down nor distinguished in appearance. The most attractive building is Town Hall, a large Pennsylvania-style building with stonework and a slate roof. Further north is the Vernon Hills Shopping

Center, with such distinguished tenants as Bonwit Teller, Lord & Taylor, Brooks Brothers, and Bloomingdale's.

We talked with Edna Haber, president of E. Haber Real Estate, and she told us that average sales in Eastchester are in the $120,000–$130,000 range. For that you'll get a small house of about 1,800 square feet, with a living room (perhaps with a fireplace), dining room, 3 bedrooms, and 1 or 1½ baths. Most likely such a house would have just a carport or a 1-car garage.

Not much is available under $100,000, she told us, or above $300,000. Lake Isle houses, with lake rights, are $200,000 and up, as are some new condominiums on Mill Road.

We noted two recent sales, one at the bottom of the price scale, the other in that $200,000 range.

For $98,000, someone had bought a 1940 white frame colonial, with 1,600 square feet of living area, situated on a 51 × 109 lot. The first floor has a living room with fireplace, dining room, eat-in kitchen, and porch. Three bedrooms and 1 bath constitute the second floor. There's also a semifinished attic and a basement with laundry area, toilet, and utilities. The house has a 1-car garage. Taxes are $1,500.

For $210,000, another buyer got a 1962 redwood-frame, brick, raised ranch. With 2,600 square feet of living area and a 2-car garage, it is on a 100 × 150 lot. This house has a living room, family room with fireplace, dining room, eat-in kitchen, 5 bedrooms, 3 baths, a maid's room with bath, and a laundry room. Taxes are $4,653.

Eastchester offers a convenient location near New York City and in the center of Westchester County. With its low crime rate and impressive recreational facilities, it offers pleasant homesites for families of varying economic levels—perhaps for you, too.

IRVINGTON

POPULATION: 5,787
NO. OF CRIMES: 136
CRIME RATE: 2,350.1 per 100,000

Scenic grandeur and colorful history combine to make the Hudson one of America's great rivers. The Statue of Liberty and Ellis Island at its mouth . . . the unmatched Manhattan skyline . . . majestic George Washington Bridge . . . the Palisades . . . Bear Mountain and West Point—with all that these names evoke, we've still covered just a small portion of the river's total length.

On the east bank of the lower Hudson, where the river widens to form the Tappan Zee, you'll find three communities known around the world as Sleepy Hollow country. The man who made the area famous was, of course, Washington Irving, America's first internationally successful author. His two most famous stories, "Rip Van Winkle" and "The Legend of Sleepy Hollow," celebrated the legends and history of this Dutch-settled area.

The three communities that constitute Sleepy Hollow country are Irvington, Tarrytown, and North Tarrytown. The derivation of Irvington's name is obvious. As for Tarrytown, Irving said it was so named by housewives "from the inveterate propensity of their husbands to linger about the village tavern on market days."

On the border between Irvington and Tarrytown is Washington Irving's home, Sunnyside. One of the most intriguing homes in America, it was originally a tenant farmer's house, to which Irving added Dutch-stepped gables, ancient weathervanes, various Gothic and Romanesque features, and a 3-story tower with slanting roof known as the Pagoda. In this home, Irving entertained such eminent visitors as Oliver Wendell Holmes, Thackeray, and Louis Napoleon.

Today's Irvington, for all its changes since Washington Irving's day, is still a charming and picturesque Hudson River town. In our previous visits, we knew Irvington only from Broadway (U.S. 9), the north–south thoroughfare that parallels the Hudson through Westchester County and into New York City. Stately homes, mansions, and estates survive up and down Broadway, many of them now occupied by corporations, foundations, or educational institutions. In Irvington, one of these splendid edifices is now the home of Leonard Read's Foundation for Economic Education, one of the leading centers of free-market economics in the United States. We've enjoyed some delightful and instructive visits there.

After choosing Irvington as a Safe Place, however, we discovered the rest of the town. East of Broadway we found most of the newer, suburban-style residences. And west of Broadway the chief concentration of population is along Main Street, which leads uphill from the Hudson to Broadway. Along Main Street are the usual stores and shops—a drugstore, bank, stationery store, several small grocers and delis. And at right angles off Main Street are a series of short streets, lined by small stucco and frame row houses with tiny yards, giving an appearance of a city neighborhood here in the suburbs.

It's quite a variety of homes, then, that you'll find in Irvington—old mansions and estates, traditional New England and Dutch colonials, gingerbread Victorians, ranches, and even row houses.

At the foot of Main Street, on the Hudson, you'll find the train station (about forty-five minutes to Grand Central), several businesses (including Lord & Burnham, manufacturers of greenhouses), the Irvington Boat Club, and Matthiessen Park, with its children's play areas, riverfront beaches, paddle tennis courts, and picnic tables and grills set under spreading trees. It's a lovely setting for concerts, movies, and the traditional Independence Day fireworks celebration.

Though a small village, Irvington is noted for its excellent recreational facilities. In addition to Matthiessen Park, these include the complete sports facilities at Memorial Park and indoor recreation at Benjamin Community Center. A list of activities sponsored by the village's Recreation and Parks Commission is available at Village Hall and is quite impressive.

Another center of activities is Irving's Sunnyside. All year long there are exhibits, displays, and special events such as shadow puppet performances. Thanksgiving is celebrated with the preparation of traditional family foods, according to nineteenth-century recipes, in Irving's own kitchen. And at Christmas, the house is festooned with evergreens and holly and special candlelight tours re-create many of the English traditions Irving popularized in "Old Christmas."

Crimes of violence here are rare. In our comparison year of 1980, there were no murders or rapes, and just 2 robberies and 2 aggravated assaults. For property crime, there were 49 burglaries, 79 larceny-thefts, and 4 motor vehicle thefts. This gave the village a low rate of 2,350.1 crimes per 100,000 population.

The following year saw a drastic reduction in the number of crimes. With just 1 robbery, 1 aggravated assault, 21 burglaries, 58 larceny-thefts, and 3 motor vehicle thefts, the total rate dropped to just 1,450.0 per 100,000.

We had an instructive talk about Irvington real estate with Stephen H. Hart, an insurance broker on Main Street. Although not a real estate broker, he's thoroughly familiar with housing prices in town.

Irvington real estate is expensive, he told us. Because it is unique and retains a small-village atmosphere, people are willing to pay handsomely to live here. Many houses are sold by word of mouth and apartments rarely get into a newspaper when they become available.

The small row houses we saw off Main Street sell for $60,000 and up, Mr. Hart told us. A few are 2-family homes, but most are single-family residences. A single usually has 6 to 8 rooms, of which 2 or 3 are bedrooms. Only a few of these houses have garages.

Elsewhere in Irvington, residential properties range from $125,000 to the million-dollar estates. East of Broadway, prices usually begin at $150,000. We saw a Treefrog Realty listing for that area at $162,000—a 3-bedroom, 2½-bath split-level house on ½ acre. Its features included a bay window in the living room, a dining-el, and an eat-in kitchen with deck.

The newest houses east of Broadway, Mr. Hart said, are priced at $250,000 to $300,000. These are spacious luxury homes on ½-acre to 1-acre lots. Built in the past year, they are selling briskly despite the recession.

Irvington also has one co-op, Half Moon Apartments, where a 2-bedroom apartment will run $70,000 and up. Half Moon is quite popular because it's adjacent to the train station and the river and is well maintained.

With its river-town charm and small-village ambience, Irvington is a special place even within Westchester County, where you have a larger than usual choice of desirable communities. For this reason, it may take a while to find just the home for you—a simple matter of supply and demand. We think you'll find Irvington well worth the effort, though. Sleepy Hollow country has charmed its visitors for centuries and is waiting to cast its spell on you.

BRIARCLIFF MANOR

POPULATION: 7,083
NO. OF CRIMES: 85
CRIME RATE: 1,200.1 per 100,000

Briarcliff Manor was founded in 1890 by British merchant Walter B. Law. Buying local farmlands, he amassed 5,000 acres of land and established Briarcliff Farms. With nearly 500 employees, the "Lord of Briarcliff" operated one of the finest farms in the country, noted for its dairy, agricultural, and poultry products. The farm delivered 4,000 quarts of fresh milk nightly to New York City and in 1900 won first place at the Paris Exposition for the best cream and butter in the world.

At the pinnacle of his estate, 500 feet above sea level, Law constructed a Tudor mansion known as Briarcliff Lodge. Here he could entertain his wealthy friends, such as Andrew Carnegie, and by the 1920s it was the foremost resort hotel in America. Its famous guests included Tallulah Bankhead, Alfred E. Smith, and Franklin Roosevelt. Gene Sarazen was the golf pro, John Weissmuller tried out for the 1924 U.S. Olympics in the pool, and in 1926 the lodge was the site of the U.S. Olympic winter trials.

Another part of present-day Briarcliff Manor has always retained a somewhat separate identity. Scarborough is that part of the village on the Hudson River and has been described as one of the most beautiful residential areas in the country. Wealthy city residents first began building their estates here in the 1890s. In the early 1900s, a president of New York's National City Bank, Frank Vanderlip, encouraged his vice presidents to build their homes here. One of our favorite spots is Scarborough Park, a tiny, grassy knoll with a splendid view of the wide Hudson.

Rustic and uncongested in character, today's Briarcliff Manor retains many pre-Revolutionary homes, century-old churches, mansions, monuments, and parks and trails. Situated between the Taconic State Parkway and the Hudson, Briarcliff Manor lies mostly in Ossining Township. The business area is small and compact; specialized shopping needs can be met in nearby Ossining, Pleasantville, Tarrytown, and White Plains.

Two colleges are located within the village boundaries—Pace University and King's College, an evangelical liberal arts college occupying the old Briarcliff Lodge. Also here are the Briar Hall Golf & Country Club and the Sleepy Hollow Country Club, built on what Washington Irving, in "The Legend of Sleepy Hollow," called "the quietest spot in the world."

Driving through the Briarcliff Manor countryside, we came across the corporate headquarters of Burns International Security Systems. They certainly picked a quiet hamlet as their home. In our comparison year of 1980, Briarcliff Manor had no murders, rapes, or robberies. There were 1 aggravated assault, 59 burglaries, 15 larceny-thefts, and 10 motor vehicle thefts. This placed Briarcliff Manor below U.S. rural crime rates in all categories except burglaries and there it was just barely above the rural rate.

Real estate, as you would expect from this background, is more expensive here than in our other Westchester County Safe Places. Irene Tracy, of Weber Tufts, Inc., Briarcliff Manor realtors, told us there was nothing available in the village under $106,000 and most sales are in the $150,000-and-up range. Land alone will cost you $60,000 an acre.

In the way of rentals, for $1,800 a month you could get a one- or two-year lease on a stone and stucco Tudor house, sitting on 1.75 acres that are fully landscaped with flowering trees and shrubs. The living room has a beamed ceiling and a fireplace and there are 4 bedrooms and 3 baths.

About the only condominiums available were some 2-bedroom units near the Scarborough train station, selling for $100,000 and up.

We noted listings that indicate what's available in two price ranges, for commuters who want to be within walking distance of the Scarborough train station.

For $168,000, you could get a gray frame split, built in 1956, situated on 1.24 acres. With a total of 2,230 square feet of living area, it has town water and sewage and lies in the Briarcliff Manor school district (some parts of Scarborough are in the Ossining school district). The "sub" floor has a family room with fireplace, bedroom, 1/2 bath, and brick terrace. The first floor contains a living room with fireplace, dining room, and eat-in kitchen. And the second floor has the master bedroom and bath plus 2 more bedrooms and a bath. A 2-car attached garage and storage shed are also included. Taxes are $5,116.

For $338,000, you could get a historic house on River Road, built in 1928, on 2.96 acres. The beautiful setting has views of the Hudson River and a 1-acre lake, and the home—a white frame and stone colonial—features quality construction, a new kitchen, new carpeting, a partial new roof, 4 air conditioners, a burglar system, and a sprinkling system. You're on town water and sewage here too. Taxes are $5,364.

On the first floor of this fine home, you'll find a center hall, living room with fireplace, dining room, family room, kitchen, pantry, powder room, and terrace. On the second floor, the master bedroom with fireplace, 4 more bedrooms and 2 baths, and 2 maid's rooms with a bath. There's also a full basement with laundry and storage facilities, cedar closet, toilet, and 4 rooms.

On the less expensive side, we noted one advertisement in a Westchester newspaper for a $118,000 4-bedroom ranch, featuring a master suite with skylit bath and private patio, a new deck, and a living room with fireplace.

While the days of the Lord of Briarcliff are behind us, it is obvious you can still lead a pretty good life in Briarcliff Manor. Whether you choose the rustic countryside further inland or the river views and commuter-train accessibility of the Scarborough area, you will be partaking of Westchester-style living at its finest.

Where to get further information:

State

For a state highway map and a variety of tourist information, including the *I Love New York Travel Guide:* State Department of Commerce, Division of Tourism, 99 Washington Avenue, Albany, NY 12245.

For information on state parks and recreation areas: Office of Parks and Recreation, Albany, NY 12238.

For information on recreation areas within the Adirondack and Catskill forest preserves: Department of Environmental Conservation, Albany, NY 12233.

Regional

Long Island: Long Island Tourism and Convention Commission, Administrative Headquarters, Long Island MacArthur Airport, Ronkonkoma, NY 11779; or Nassau Veterans Memorial Coliseum, Hempstead Turnpike, Uniondale, NY 11553. Long Island Association of Commerce and Industry, 425 Broad Hollow Road, Melville, NY 11747. New York Department of Commerce, Long Island District Tourism Office, 55 Jericho Turnpike, Jericho, NY 11753. Long Island State Park and Recreation Commission, Babylon, NY 11702. *Long Island Heritage,* 29 Continental Place, Glen Cove, NY 11542, is a monthly ($8.00 for 12 issues) guide to the island's history, antiques, arts, and architecture.

Local

Malverne: Information on town services is given in a mayor's letter available at the Town Hall, 99 Church Street. A directory of community organizations is available at the Malverne Public Library. Brochures on the Malverne School District and Our Lady of Lourdes School are available from their respective offices.

Kensington: Chamber of Commerce of Great Neck, 1 Great Neck Road, Great Neck, NY 11023. Copies of *A Week-End at Kensington* are available at the Kensington village hall. Descriptive brochures are also available from the U.S. Merchant Marine Academy, Kings Point, NY 11024.

Lloyd Harbor: At village government offices on Middle Hollow Road, you can obtain the village newsletter and, for a small charge, a copy of Irene K. Alexander's *A History of the Incorporated Village of Lloyd Harbor, 1926–1976.* Also, a wide variety of Long Island materials are available from the Huntington Township Chamber of Commerce, 151 W. Carver Street, Huntington, NY 11743. Particularly useful are the *Annual Town Guide: People, Places, Facts & Figures* and *The Arts Spectrum,* which describes the offerings of members of the Huntington Arts Council.

Sag Harbor: Sag Harbor Chamber of Commerce and Merchants' Association, P.O. Box 116J, Sag Harbor, NY 11963.

Eastchester: Town of Eastchester, 40 Mill Road, Eastchester, NY 10709, has a booklet on the town, plus a periodic newsletter for residents.

Irvington: Sleepy Hollow Chamber of Commerce, 80 S. Broadway, Tarrytown, NY 10591, covers Irvington and the Tarrytowns. Recreational brochures and a newsletter for residents are available from the Village of Irvington, 71 Main Street, Irvington, NY 10533. Brochures on Sleepy Hollow country, Sunnyside, and a calendar of events are available from Sleepy Hollow Restorations, Inc., Tarrytown, NY 10591.

Briarcliff Manor: Greater Ossining Chamber of Commerce, 13 Croton Avenue, Ossining, NY 10562, has an attractively illustrated map and history of the area. Briarcliff Manor–Scarborough Historical Society, Box 11, Briarcliff Manor, NY 10510, has a historical brochure. Weber-Tufts, Inc., 1123 Pleasantville Road, Briarcliff Manor, NY 10510, publishes a homebuyer's guide for the area. And various brochures on town services may be picked up at the Briarcliff Manor Village Hall, 1111 Pleasantville Road, Briarcliff Manor, NY 10510.

North Carolina

North Carolina stretches more than 500 miles from east to west, offering a vacationer's dream—something for everyone—along the way.

The eastern border contains the famous Atlantic surf and sand dunes of Cape Hatteras National Seashore (70 miles of coastline accessible by automobile) and Cape Lookout National Seashore (another 58 miles of unspoiled barrier islands accessible only by boat). Here, too, is Fort Raleigh National Historic Site (site of the first English attempt at colonization in 1585, and of the Lost Colony of 1587) and the Wright Brothers National Memorial, where mankind first learned to fly.

The western border is a land of densely forested peaks, mountain villages, and mountain arts, crafts, and festivals. Half of Great Smoky Mountains National Park is in North Carolina, the other half in Tennessee. It is America's most popular national park and contains 1,300 flowering plants, 52 species of fur-bearing animals, and 130 species of trees. The Blue Ridge Parkway, America's most popular scenic parkway, has about 250 miles in North Carolina, built at an average elevation of over 3,000 feet. In all, the state has forty-three mountains where the summits are higher than 6,000 feet in elevation and Mount Mitchell (6,684 feet in elevation) is the highest point in the eastern United States.

The land between the ocean and the mountains is divided between coastal plains and Piedmont country. Here you'll find the state's manufacturing and agricultural centers and its attractive major cities. Here, too, are some of the most popular year-round golf resorts in the country, at Pinehurst and Southern Pines.

Agriculturally, North Carolina grows two thirds of the nation's bright-leaf, flue-cured tobacco. Corn, cotton, peanuts, and fruits are also important crops. The vast forests have led to an important furniture-making industry. Other major manufacturing areas include textiles, with one half of the nation's hosiery coming from North Carolina, and tobacco products. Tourism is a major industry.

Diverse geographically and diversified in its economy, North Carolina is also noted for a progressive business attitude and a fine university system. Our Safe

Place in North Carolina is located in one of its most famous centers of learning and high-technology industry.

RESEARCH TRIANGLE

The triangle formed by the cities of Raleigh, Durham, and Chapel Hill is known generally as the Research Triangle of North Carolina. In the center of this triangle is a 5,500-acre development known formally as Research Triangle Park. The corporations and institutes located in the park have made this one of the premier research and high tech centers of the nation, but the unique character of the area is shaped as well by the three major universities—the University of North Carolina at Chapel Hill, Duke University in Durham, and North Carolina State University in Raleigh. Between the universities and the firms, this area is reported to have the highest ratio of Ph.D.s to total population of any comparably sized area in the world.

Research Triangle Park was formed in 1958 and began with an emphasis on textiles research. A number of federal government facilities then attracted toxicology research, IBM brought more microelectronics firms to the park, and in 1981 the North Carolina Biotechnology Center was formed here. Today, more than forty research centers employ over 20,000 people with an annual payroll of nearly one-half billion dollars. About 2,000 acres in the park are still available for development.

It is thought that the next step for the tri-city area might be to go beyond microelectronics research to the actual manufacture of the micro chips. There is concern, however, that the area not become a Silicon Valley East, with connotations of overcrowding and urban sprawl. There's already a rush-hour traffic problem that has everyone upset. The research park itself, however, doesn't seem to be in any danger of overdevelopment, since its covenants and restrictions require each tenant to buy at least 6 acres of land and to build on no more than 15 percent of the land that they buy. In fact, manufacturing is not allowed inside the park—just research and development.

What about the communities around the park?

Chapel Hill, with a population of 31,000, is a university town. The University of North Carolina is the oldest state university in the United States, and its beautiful campus includes Old East dormitory, the oldest state university building in the country. Attractions in Chapel Hill include Morehead Planetarium, Ackland Art Museum, the North Carolina Botanical Garden, and the Morehead-Patterson Bell Tower, whose twelve bells duplicate those at West Point. The Blue Cross–Blue Shield building in town has attracted international architectural attention with its unique rhomboid shape.

Durham (population 100,000) is a cigarette manufacturing center and its tobacco auctions are a popular attraction from September through December. It is also a major medical center, with five hospitals and clinics, more than 2,000

RESEARCH TRIANGLE Crime Chart

	Crime Rate	Murder	Rape	Robbery	Aggravated Assault	Burglary	Larceny —Theft	Motor Vehicle Theft
United States								
U.S. Total	5,899.9	10.2	36.4	243.5	290.6	1,668.2	3,156.3	494.6
U.S. Metropolitan Areas	6,757.6	11.5	43.4	319.0	328.3	1,911.8	3,534.9	608.8
U.S. Rural Areas	2,290.4	7.5	15.5	22.5	136.9	830.2	1,143.9	133.9
Regional Crime Centers								
Chapel Hill	6,899.4	6.5	26.1	78.2	319.4	1,610.0	4,650.6	208.6
Durham	10,561.0	12.0	66.2	270.7	292.8	2,864.9	6,572.1	482.3
Raleigh	7,196.0	8.1	43.1	175.2	301.8	1,602.1	4,761.9	303.8
Safe Place								
Cary	2,903.2	0	22.7	18.2	86.3	536.1	2,158.1	81.8

patient beds, more than $400 million spent annually on health-related research, and 22 percent of the work force employed in health-related jobs.

The major tourist attraction in Durham is Duke University, with Georgian architecture prevailing on its East Campus and Gothic architecture on its West Campus. Duke Chapel, on the West Campus, is reminiscent of Canterbury Cathedral and has a fifty-bell carillon and a new 5,000-pipe Flentrop organ.

With a population of 150,000, Raleigh is the largest city in the area. It is also the state capital, and its attractions include the Greek revival-style state capitol, the governor's mansion, North Carolina Museum of Art, North Carolina Museum of History, and North Carolina Museum of Natural History. Andrew Johnson's birthplace and other eighteenth-century buildings are preserved in Mordecai Historic Park, while Victorian architecture prevails in the historic Oakwood neighborhood.

As our Research Triangle Crime Chart (above) indicates, all three of these cities—attractive as they are in other ways—have crime rates that are higher than those for U.S. metropolitan areas nationwide. Fortunately, however, you *can* enjoy all the advantages of this metropolitan area and still reside in a Safe Place with neighborhoods as desirable as you'll find in its three larger neighbors.

CARY

POPULATION: 22,010
NO. OF CRIMES: 639
CRIME RATE: 2,903.2 per 100,000

Cary was a sleepy railroad town in the nineteenth century. Perhaps its most enduring legacy from that century was the expression, "It's a long time between drinks." Legend credits that remark to the governor of North Carolina, whose equally thirsty companion was the governor of South Carolina, on a trip from

Chapel Hill to Raleigh. It's an ironic legacy for a town named for a prominent Ohio temperance leader.

After the turn of the century, Cary began to get a reputation as a "sophisticated little town." Its most distinguished son, Walter Hines Page, became editor of the *Atlantic Monthly*—then regarded as "the premier editorial chair in the United States"—and Woodrow Wilson's ambassador to Great Britain during World War I. One of the state's first paved roads provided automobile access between Cary and Raleigh and when the General Assembly created a system of state high schools in 1907, Cary Academy became the first public high school in the state.

It took the creation of Triangle Research Park, though, to get the town really growing. And that's what it did. Between 1970 and 1980 Cary grew from 7,300 to 22,000, making it the fastest-growing town in the state. In 1980 it was also the state's safest town with a population of 10,000 or more, demonstrating that fast growth doesn't necessarily have to result in equally fast-growing crime.

A few years back, one of the first questions asked new residents was "Are you with IBM?" It was just assumed that you worked in Research Triangle Park. Cary never became a company town, however, and now it's a popular suburb for people who work in Raleigh too. Cary has its executive transferees, but it is also popular with people in the middle salary ranges, say $30,000 or $35,000. In recent years it has also shared in a nationwide trend of two-career couples, where both husband and wife are college educated and have well-paying jobs. Like most of the upscale communities in this area, the average educational level of the residents is very high.

The local population is not only well educated, it's young and family-oriented. The chamber of commerce estimates that only 3.7 percent of the population is over sixty-five years of age, while nearly half the population is under eighteen. As you'd expect, then, there's a strong emphasis on schools and recreational programs. About the only thing lacking is a public swimming pool, but that will probably come pretty soon; meanwhile, some residents join the Scottish Hills Recreational Club for its pool and other facilities.

In several aspects of its youth programs, Cary has won national recognition. It recently ranked second in the nation, on a per capita basis, on participation in scouting. And the Cary Band can count on the whole town rallying behind it as it marches in the Rose Bowl or Orange Bowl parades, or an inaugural parade in Washington or joins a festival as far away as Romania.

Cary's schools are part of the Wake County public school system, which merged with the Raleigh schools in 1976. We were told by residents that there is a minimum of busing and no forced busing, that there is, in fact, no race problem but instead some concern about drugs—as you'll find everywhere in the country. There are seven elementary schools, two junior highs, and one high school in Cary itself, and some students attend the neighboring town of Apex's middle school or high school. All elementary schools have kindergartens and there are also a good number of church and private kindergartens and nurseries.

We happened to be in Cary the week that *U.S. News & World Report* hit the stands with an article listing it as one of ten "great places to live" in the United States. "Livable Boom Town" was its heading for Cary. Each regional bureau of the magazine had been given the task of selecting one town for this admittedly unscientific listing. In an interview with the *Raleigh News & Observer,* the magazine's Atlanta-based reporter, Douglas C. Lyons, explained how he came to pick Cary. "One guidepost was economic conditions," he said, and the triangle area was holding up much better in the recession than most areas of the South.

"It could have been a community turned into a suburban sprawl," Lyons explained, but as he looked into Cary he realized that "developers were selling amenities as part of the package. I found it kind of fantastic. I saw households overlooking lakes, shopping areas that could be reached without going through traffic jams. I was impressed."

Because of its strict development regulations, it costs more to build a house in Cary than in Raleigh. Since the midsixties, for example, all subdivisions have had underground utility lines. Another area that impressed us very much was downtown. The Cary Historical Society has an attractive brochure, *A Walking Tour of Historic Sites,* that provides background on many of the homes and buildings in the central part of town. And when we were there, the town had started on the final phase of its downtown renovation project. Already, downtown merchants had renovated their buildings and the town had placed all utility lines underground and had installed antique-style street lamps and brick sidewalks. Now the major intersection was closed while the asphalt was being stripped away. In its place will be an attractive design of brick and concrete mixed with rocks, similar to a design found in Washington, D.C., and Tarboro, N.C.

One problem in Cary is the tax rate. When you combine the city tax with separate garbage, water, and sewage fees, Cary's taxes are the highest in the county. That has led to what the Raleigh *Times* calls "a fever of industry-hunting" (there seems to be no love lost between affluent-suburb Cary and central-city Raleigh). Marilyn Ryan, the town clerk, told us with satisfaction that "a number of industries have called in just the last few days as a result of the article in *U.S. News & World Report.*" The right kind of light industry, it is felt, would help lighten the tax burden while not detracting from the town's livability.

A knowledgeable source of information was Ben Gentry, president of Gentry & Associates, the Realty World affiliate in Cary. Ben gave us a good perspective on the town and told us that not many houses are available under $50,000. The few you'll find will usually be older, smaller houses near downtown but well maintained—there's no inner-city decay. And from there the prices go up, up, up, and up. Ben's computer printout of available properties showed eight listings under $50,000, twenty-four in the 50s, seventy-one in the 60s, fifty-four in the 70s, twenty-two in the 80s, and four in the 90s. Then there were twenty-four houses priced between $100,000 and $125,000, seventeen between $125,000 and $150,000, thirteen between $150,000 and $200,000, five with prices between $219,000 and $268,000, and one house for $425,000.

For $70,000 or so, Ben told us, you could get a 4-bedroom, 3-bath split level with approximately 2,000 square feet of living area. There would probably be a carport and a fireplace in the family room. You won't find basements, since the North Carolina clay makes them inadvisable. Your lot would be "residential size but private."

At the $150,000 price level, you could expect to get 3,100 to 3,300 square feet of living area. This would be a 2-story house with 4 bedrooms, 3 baths, formal areas, family room with fireplace, and a 2-car garage with a rec room above it. Your lot would probably be 3/4 acre and heavily wooded—if you don't have the trees, you can't sell the house.

In addition to the attractively restored downtown, Cary has five shopping areas, including a large mall with a Hudson & Belk department store. More shopping areas are being planned. We found the residential neighborhoods attractive; their trees and spacing help to avoid the harsh tract-development look found in so many fast-growing areas. When you add to these local features all the attractions of the Raleigh–Durham–Chapel Hill area, you can begin to understand the town's rapid growth. There are plenty of good reasons to move here!

Where to get further information:

State

North Carolina Travel and Tourism Division, Department of Commerce, 430 N. Salisbury Street, Raleigh, NC 27611.

Regional

Chapel Hill Chamber of Commerce, P.O. Box 127, Chapel Hill, NC 27514. Durham Chamber of Commerce, 201 N. Roxboro Street, Durham, NC 27701. Raleigh Chamber of Commerce, 411 S. Salisbury Street, P.O. Box 2978, Raleigh, NC 27602.

For an excellent free map of the Raleigh-Cary area, including a detailed map of Research Triangle Park, call 800/438-7406. *The Leader/Research Triangle Newsweekly* is published weekly ($12.50 a year) by Capitol Publications, Inc., Box 12054, Research Triangle Park, NC 27709. *The Triangle Pointer* is a weekly guide to activities ($16 a year) published by Triangle Pointer, P.O. Box 2777, Chapel Hill, NC 27514. *Business Properties* has a North Carolina Triangle edition that is published quarterly ($7.00 a year) by AAMCON, Inc., 3717 National Drive, Suite 101, Raleigh, NC 27612.

Local

Cary Chamber of Commerce, 119 W. Chatham Street, P.O. Box 51, Cary, NC 27511, has brochures and a city map. For questions regarding city government: Marilyn Ryan, Town Clerk, 316 N. Academy Street, P.O. Box 128, Cary, NC 27511. When in town, also pick up the current folder, *Community Education and Recreation in Wake County*, at the chamber offices, since it gives information on many activities throughout the county. The *Cary News* is a weekly ($10.40 a year inside Wake County, $13.52 a year outside the county) available from 212 E. Chatham Street, P.O. Box 519, Cary, NC 27511.

Ohio

Ever since John D. Rockefeller, Sr., founded the Standard Oil Company in 1870, Ohio has been synonymous with industry.

A roster of Ohio's industrial giants and their companies would have to include the Packard brothers, Fisher Body Company, and Champion Spark Plug Company in the automotive area, in rubber B. F. Goodrich, Harvey S. Firestone, and Frank Seiberling's Goodyear Tire & Rubber, in household products Procter & Gamble and Quaker Oats, and myriad others such as National Cash Register and Charles F. Kettering's Delco Labs. In the field of aviation, Ohio's contributions have ranged all the way from the Wright brothers to astronauts John Glenn and Neil Armstrong.

While Ohio has more large industrial cities than any other state, it also has (like its neighbor Pennsylvania) hundreds of thriving small towns and cities and an important agricultural economy. Corn, hay, soybeans, and wheat are leading crops, and dairying is also widespread. Ohio has a surprising number of vineyards and Liederkranz is an Ohio cheese. Coal leads the natural resources in importance.

Ohio is generally a flat state, except for the southeastern portion which is part of the Appalachian Mountains region. Surprisingly for a landlocked state, Ohio's most important physical features are two bodies of water—Lake Erie to the north and the Ohio River that forms its southern border.

In crime, Ohio's cities with a population of 10,000 or more run the gamut from safest Seven Hills (with a crime rate of 991.6 crimes per 100,000 population) to Lima (11,747.7). Ohio shares a characteristic with other states of the Northeast—high-crime metropolitan centers ringed by a number of very safe suburbs. This is most pronounced in the Cleveland area.

For our Safe Places in Ohio, we picked two of Cleveland's safest suburbs, plus a suburb of the Queen City, Cincinnati. We think they illustrate very nicely the opportunities for fine suburban living in the Buckeye State.

CLEVELAND AREA

Ohio's largest city is the center of a metropolitan area of nearly 2 million people. The Cuyahoga River Valley is one of the nation's most spectacular and impressive assemblages of industrial might, with its steel mills, oil refineries, and storage tanks. Cleveland is also a major Great Lakes shipping port and one of the centers of the U.S. automobile industry.

In its racial and ethnic composition, Cleveland is the epitome of a melting pot. You'll find communities of Poles, Germans, Czechs, Slovaks, Yugoslavians, Lithuanians, Italians, Romanians, Russians, Greeks—name them and you're likely to find them here. Cleveland was also the first large city in the United States to elect a black mayor.

In recent years, Cleveland has had a bad press as a result of its high crime and very real fiscal and political problems. Nevertheless, this also remains one of the cultural centers of the nation, with a noted symphony orchestra, art museum, and playhouse. It is a city also noted for its gracious affluent suburbs, of which the most famous—since World War I—is Shaker Heights. Pepper Pike, Gates Mills, and Chagrin Falls have become more recent favorites with the executive class.

For our Safe Places in the Cleveland area, however, we picked two middle-class communities that combine attractiveness with affordability and crime rates that are so low they're hardly believable in a metropolitan area such as this.

SEVEN HILLS

POPULATION: 13,614
NO. OF CRIMES: 135
CRIME RATE: 991.6 per 100,000

CLEVELAND AREA Crime Chart

	Crime Rate	Murder	Rape	Robbery	Aggravated Assault	Burglary	Larceny —Theft	Motor Vehicle Theft
United States								
U.S. Total	5,899.9	10.2	36.4	243.5	290.6	1,668.2	3,156.3	494.6
U.S. Metropolitan Areas	6,757.6	11.5	43.4	319.0	328.3	1,911.8	3,534.9	608.8
U.S. Rural Areas	2,290.4	7.5	15.5	22.5	136.9	830.2	1,143.9	133.9
Regional Crime Center								
Cleveland	10,058.7	46.3	122.8	1,187.8	645.4	3,117.0	2,462.2	2,477.2
Safe Places								
Bay Village	1,435.1	0	5.6	16.8	56.1	549.4	773.6	33.6
Seven Hills	991.6	0	0	7.3	36.7	279.1	624.4	44.1

Downtown Cleveland is just 10 miles north of Seven Hills, but when it comes to crime, those 10 miles constitute a world of difference.

Cleveland's crime rate is one of the highest in the nation for a big city. With 10,058.7 crimes per 100,000 population, it ranks between New York City and Washington, D.C.

Seven Hills' crime rate is less than one tenth as high—just 991.6 crimes per 100,000 population.

Cleveland has enormously high rates of murder and rape. Seven Hills had none in our comparison year of 1980.

The same pattern holds true in all the other categories of crime. Even adjusted for population, Cleveland has 11 times as many burglaries, 17 times more aggravated assault, more than 56 times as much motor vehicle theft and more than 162 times as many robberies.

In our comparision year of 1980, Seven Hills had just 1 robbery, 5 aggravated assaults, 38 burglaries, 85 larceny-thefts, and 6 motor vehicle thefts. This placed it below U.S. rural rates of crime in all categories.

Seven Hills has other things going for it as well. Its neighborhoods are clean and attractive—nothing flashy, just solidly middle class with modest and medium-sized suburban homes. Interstate 77 offers quick access to downtown Cleveland to the north, the Ohio Turnpike to the south. A major shopping center, Pleasant Valley, is located right across the city line in Parma. And what remains of the original seven hills (several have been leveled or filled in) sometimes offer vistas of the Cleveland skyline to the north or open pastures on the hills to the east of town.

Seven Hills is part of the Parma City School District, but three schools are located within its boundaries—Seven Hills Elementary, Col. John Glenn Elementary, and Hillside Junior High.

At Assad-Crea & Associates, the Century 21 affiliate in Parma, Bonnie Hurst was very helpful in giving us information on real estate costs in Seven Hills. At the time of our visit (September 1982), there were just around fifty houses on the market—not much turnover for a city of more than 4,000 homes. They ranged in price from $69,900 to $189,900, with the largest concentration in the 80s and 90s.

For $89,900, for example, you could get a twenty-five-year-old split level house with 3 bedrooms and 2 baths. This house had a 15 × 15 sunken living room, 14 × 22 family room, 14 × 10 dining room, and 25 × 12 eat-in kitchen. The 113 × 578 lot was wooded and had an above-ground pool. Taxes were $463 per half year.

For $139,000, you could get a 2-story colonial with a living room, family room, dining room, eat-in kitchen, 4 bedrooms, and 3 baths. The 78 × 159 lot included an in-ground pool. Taxes were $568 per half year.

The $189,900 listing was unusually high-priced for Seven Hills. This was a professionally decorated home of Spanish style, on a 100 × 200 lot with a circular drive. It had 3 bedrooms and 3 baths, plus special features like central air-conditioning, wood-burning fireplace, hardwood floors, all-electric utilities, and double-glass windows. Taxes were $695 per half year for this five-year-old house.

Just a couple of miles east of Seven Hills is the Cuyahoga Valley National Recreation Area, where some 32,000 acres of rural land and open space are preserved for recreation. This is a unique metropolitan-area park that blends National Park Service facilities with privately owned recreational and cultural facilities such as golf courses, youth camps, a music center, and a theater. You'll find plenty to explore, including historic buildings, remnants of the Ohio & Erie Canal, and 22 miles of the Cuyahoga River.

This blend of countryside adjacent to urban conveniences is just part of what makes Seven Hills special. Its very low crime rate, affordable and attractive homes, and accessibility to jobs in the area also make this a splendid location to consider whether you're already living in the Cleveland area or planning a move there.

BAY VILLAGE

POPULATION: 17,839
NO. OF CRIMES: 256
CRIME RATE: 1,435.1 per 100,000

Bay Village is about 12 miles due west of downtown Cleveland and fronts on Lake Erie. The waterfront is especially lovely, with both parkland and beautiful houses facing the bay. Another characteristic that made Bay Village appealing to us was its New England flavor. The profusion of trees and the colonial character of the homes, along with the water views, made us homesick for Connecticut and reminded us that this area of Ohio is known as the Western Reserve because it was held for settlement by Connecticut Yankees heading west.

Not only do you have a variety of traditional architectural styles in town, the houses also range in size and cost from modest cottages to frankly expensive mansions. As a general rule, the smallest and least expensive homes are to the east, nearest Cleveland, and then get larger and more expensive as you continue west, all the way to the Cuyahoga-Lorain county line.

Lake Erie does have its effect on the climate. Spring comes later here and is 5 to 10 degrees cooler than in one of the southern suburbs such as our other Safe Place of Seven Hills. That's because the winds whip into town after passing over still-icy waters. The reverse is true in the autumn, however. Then the water is still warm and raises the temperatures along the bayfront.

Bay Village started out as a summer resort for wealthy east-siders, the people who lived in places like Shaker Heights. Many of their summer cottages are still around, now converted to year-round use, and sell for $30,000 to $35,000. You do have a good number of corporate transferees in present-day Bay Village, but you also have many people who like it so much that they live here most of their lives. They begin with one of the smaller starter homes and whenever they can afford a larger, more expensive house they just head farther west within Bay Village. Many residents work in downtown Cleveland, but probably just as many work elsewhere in the metropolitan area. Office parks can be found everywhere now, not just downtown.

Bay Village is a nonindustrial community, but it does have a sufficient number of small- and medium-sized shopping areas. The city's public school system consists of four elementary schools, a middle school, and a high school, with a total enrollment of about 3,200 students. Another 950 Bay students attend private schools, including St. Raphael's Catholic School. The city also has four nursery schools and a school for retarded children.

We were especially impressed by the scope and facilities of the city's recreation department, considering that this is a community of just about 18,000 people. There are three city owned parks plus a county facility, Huntington Metropark, with picnic and sports areas, a playground, and a sand beach on the shore of Lake Erie. City-owned Community House is used for recreation programs and senior activities, while Bayway Youth Cabin serves as a similar center for young people. Seniors also have the Cahoon Memorial Senior Center and the West Shore Senior Activities Center in the Knickerbocker Apartment, the meeting place for the Bay Golden Age Club. The Bay Village Branch Library has numerous programs, while the Historical Society holds a number of annual events and operates Rose Hill Museum. Lake Erie Nature and Science Center has live animal collections, exhibits, nature trails, the Schuele Planetarium, and classes in the natural and physical sciences. Last, but certainly not least, the Baycrafters nonprofit organization promotes local arts and crafts. Their facilities include the Gallery House for classes and displays, the Station Shop retail outlet for handcrafted goods and supplies (it's located in the old railroad station, hence the name), and the Red Caboose play center for children.

Bay Village, you can see, is no ordinary, humdrum community.

Mayor James Cowles touches on another aspect of Bay Village when he describes it to newcomers as "the desirable and safe place in which we live." That it certainly is. In our comparison year of 1980, Bay Village had no murders, 1 rape, 3 robberies, 10 aggravated assaults, 98 burglaries, 138 larceny-thefts, and 6 motor vehicle thefts. That placed it below U.S. rural rates of crime in all categories.

Police Chief Peter J. Gray sees several reasons for the low crime rate.

"The first," he told us, "is that we have a highly trained police division that has a clearance rate on crime usually 30 percent above the national average. During the last year our conviction rate amounted to 99.97 percent. Our officers are trained through in-service and at universities.

"We also promote many successful crime prevention programs," he added, "one of which is called Bay Watch. Bay Watch enables the citizens of the community to help the police by patrolling in their own neighborhoods and reporting back suspicious activities via CB radio. Citizens are also invited to participate by being on our volunteer auxiliary police department."

We would also add, before leaving this subject, that the Bay Village police had more crime-prevention literature available for their residents than the police in any of our other Safe Places.

At HGM Hilltop Realtors, Jean Wilbert was most helpful and informative in discussing local real estate. The usual range of housing, she said, is from $40,000 to $500,000, with very little above $400,000. There are virtually no apartments and very little vacant land is available for building. Condominiums that will cost $200,000 to $500,000 are being built on the lake.

For a starter home at $56,900, she had a Cape Cod bungalow with a basement and 1-car detached garage, on a 45 × 135 lot. It had an 11 × 20 living room, 10 × 12 dining room, 10 × 10 kitchen, 1 bath, and 3 bedrooms (2 on the first floor, 1 on the second). Taxes were $434 per half year.

Above $85,000 nearly all your homes have 4 bedrooms, 2½ baths, a full basement, and a family room with wood-burning fireplace. The predominant style is the center hall colonial. The price differences are a result of location, house size, lot size, and the builder. Jean stressed that there is *no* tract housing in Bay Village. Each house was built separately, according to its own individual design.

Taxes on a $99,000 house will come to $750 per half year, on a $179,000 house $1,243 per half year.

With its lakefront location and New England atmosphere, its busy recreational and social programs and citizen involvement in fighting crime, we think you will find Bay Village to be something special in the Cleveland area. Others have discovered that once they move here, they don't want to leave. Perhaps you, too.

CINCINNATI AREA

Henry Wadsworth Longfellow called Cincinnati "a queen among cities," and to this day many would agree with his assessment. It is probably the most popular city in Ohio, among residents and visitors alike. Cincinnati has strong German and Southern overtones and topography alone—the hills straddling the Ohio River, with their narrow, winding streets—sets it apart from all other Midwestern cities.

Central to its existence is the Ohio River. More than a century ago, it was the basis for prosperity as Cincinnati supplied an agricultural South with manufactured goods and products. Today the river's towboats move twice as much tonnage each year as passes through the Panama Canal. Steamboat tours on the *Delta Queen* and *Mississippi Queen* are a popular way to discover the river's charms.

This is a truly cosmopolitan city, in the sense that it has something to offer almost any taste or to satisfy any psychic need. For the thrill of putting your life on the line, you can take the visiting team's side and face the fanatical Cincinnati Reds fans at Riverfront Stadium. If you're chicken and just want to pretend you're in danger, there's the Beast, the aptly named roller coaster at Kings Island, the Midwest's largest family entertainment center. Or if you want to reach for the sublime, you can visit the Taft Museum, one of the nation's finest small art museums, and view its Chinese porcelains, Limoges enamels, and paintings by Rembrandt, Turner, Goya, Gainsborough, and Corot.

There's an equivalent span on the gastronomical side as well. Cincinnati has four restaurants that rate four stars with Mobil, and one of only thirteen restaurants in the United States to rate five stars. On the other hand, Cincinnatians actually take *pride* in a local concoction they spread over spaghetti, no less, and have the audacity to call the result chili. (Mind you, this is the Texan half of your author team grumbling here . . .)

Tolerant souls that we are, we'll forgive Cincinnati its "chili" and keep it in the book. In this chapter, we'll introduce you to a Safe Place among its suburbs on the Ohio side of the river and in our Kentucky chapter we do the same for the southern Cincinnati suburb of Fort Thomas.

MONTGOMERY

POPULATION: 15,090
NO. OF CRIMES: 358
CRIME RATE: 2,372.4 per 100,000

The most prestigious suburb of Cincinnati is Indian Hill. That's where the Procters and the Gambles live, you see. But if you can't afford to live there, you move instead to Montgomery.

Our same informant on the social mores of the Queen City told us that Greater Cincinnati divides into the East Side and the West Side. The West Side gang is more traditional; it consists mostly of the German-Dutch who have lived there all their lives and who keep pretty much to themselves. The east-siders are more transient, more friendly, more open to new people.

We pass along this social chitchat not because we necessarily believe it's true or even verifiable, but because that's how at least one of the natives sees it; besides, merely repeating the gossip is bound to get us a dozen interesting letters datemarked Cincinnati and telling us more than we could possibly have learned in our brief visit. At this point, all we can verify from our research and our visit is that Montgomery is indeed both safe and a most desirable place to live in the Cincinnati metropolitan area.

You'll find Montgomery at exit 14 off Interstate 71, about a fifteen-minute drive northeast of downtown Cincinnati when there are no traffic jams. A little farther north on I-71 is Kings Island.

Most of Montgomery is a pleasant enough upscale suburb, with well manicured and maintained homes. What really sets it apart from the others, however, is the assemblage of beautifully restored shops along the main street,

CINCINNATI AREA Crime Chart

	Crime Rate	Murder	Rape	Robbery	Aggravated Assault	Burglary	Larceny —Theft	Motor Vehicle Theft
United States								
U.S. Total	5,899.9	10.2	36.4	243.5	290.6	1,668.2	3,156.3	494.6
U.S. Metropolitan Areas	6,757.6	11.5	43.4	319.0	328.3	1,911.8	3,534.9	608.8
U.S. Rural Areas	2,290.4	7.5	15.5	22.5	136.9	830.2	1,143.9	133.9
Regional Crime Center								
Cincinnati	8,609.7	12.5	92.1	440.1	481.1	2,311.8	4,822.1	450.0
Safe Places								
Fort Thomas, Ky.	1,513.4	0	6.3	6.3	69.1	458.4	935.7	37.7
Montgomery, Ohio	2,372.4	0	13.3	26.5	26.5	490.4	1,756.1	59.6

Montgomery Avenue. They're not alone, moreover, for the walking tour of historic Montgomery takes you to at least twenty structures, including three which comprise the Universalist Church Historic District, entered in the National Register of Historic Places. Most of them are nineteenth-century homes and churches, but there's also a "cottage" design gasoline station created in the 1930s by C. A. Peterson for the Pure Oil Company.

As late as 1950, Montgomery's population was just about 500. Then the suburban boom began, engulfed it, and by now has gone on even beyond Montgomery. Because Montgomery's zoning requires lots to be a minimum of 20,000 square feet, however, it has avoided a crowded tract look. And because traditional styles prevail among the newer homes, the early American character of historical old-town Montgomery does not clash with the rest of the community.

Montgomery is proud of its Sycamore Township school system. It's a major reason why people move here and is considered one of the best public school systems in the entire Cincinnati area—academically, in parental support, and in terms of the money spent on the system.

Shopping tends to be concentrated more at the suburban malls than downtown. A couple of exits south on Interstate 71 is one of those major centers, Kenwood Mall and Kenwood Plaza. Montgomery itself has a large shopping area, Montgomery Square, which unfortunately contributes to a distracting traffic jam along Montgomery Avenue, the town's main street.

Montgomery's recreational facilities include three parks, one of them a rugged, undeveloped nature preserve with a small, meandering creek. The athletic facilities of the high school, junior high, and three elementary schools are also open to the public when not used by students. The programs of the Montgomery Recreation Commission are complemented and supplemented by the programs of community groups such as the historical society, women's club, senior citizens center, garden club, and civic and business groups.

In our comparison year of 1980, Montgomery had no murders, 2 rapes, 4 robberies, 4 aggravated assaults, 74 burglaries, 265 larceny-thefts, and 9 motor vehicle thefts. This placed it below U.S. rural crime rates in all categories except robbery and larceny-theft and in those categories it was just above rural rates and way below metropolitan levels.

For a look at housing costs in Montgomery, we talked with Marlene Polisini, of Parchman & Oyler, Realtors, the Coldwell Banker affiliate in Montgomery. She told us that the range is from the 80s to about $300,000, though most houses that were selling at the time of our visit (October 1982) were in the $120,000 to $125,000 range.

For $125,000, you can get a 2-story home with 4 bedrooms, 2½ baths, living room, family room with fireplace, eat-in kitchen, and full basement. It would be on a ½-acre lot and be no more than ten years old.

In a lower price range would be a 3-bedroom, 1½-bath ranch for $89,900. It, too, would be on a ½-acre lot but would probably be twenty years old.

A well-rounded suburban community in its schools, shopping facilities, community activities, and homes, Montgomery enhances all of those qualities with the historical distinctiveness of its old-town area. Add them all together and you have one of the finest addresses in the Cincinnati area.

Where to get further information:

State

Ohio Office of Travel and Tourism, P.O. Box 1001, Columbus, OH 43216, telephone 800/BUCKEYE inside the state. For information on outdoor recreation: Department of Natural Resources, Publications Center, Fountain Square, Columbus, OH 43224. For historical information: Ohio Historical Society, 1982 Velma Avenue, Columbus, OH 43211.

Regional

Cleveland Area: Cleveland Convention and Visitors Bureau, Inc., 1301 E. 6th Street, Cleveland, OH 44114.

Cincinnati Area: Greater Cincinnati Convention and Visitors Bureau, 200 W. 5th Street, Cincinnati, OH 45202.

Towns

Seven Hills: Seven Hills Chamber of Commerce, 5733 Skyline Drive, Seven Hills, OH 44131. For the booklet *Seven Hills Past & Present:* City of Seven Hills, 7247 Broadview Road, Seven Hills, OH 44131, or Parma City School District, 6726 Ridge Road, Parma, OH 44129. For information on Cuyahoga Valley National Recreation Area and its programs: Canal Visitor Center, 6699 Canal Road, Valley View, OH.

Bay Village: Welcome to Bay Village and *Bay Village News Letter* from City of Bay Village, 350 Dover Center Road, Bay Village, OH 44140. *A Look Inside Bay Village* (map and brochure) from Bay Village Chamber of Commerce, P.O. Box 9783, Bay Village, OH 44140. For a booklet on educational and recreational activities: Bay Village Recreation Department, 300 Bryson Lane, Bay Village, OH 44140.

Montgomery: City of Montgomery Newsletter from City of Montgomery, 10101 Montgomery Road, Montgomery, OH 45242. *Parks and Recreation in Montgomery* (brochure) from City of Montgomery, Park and Recreation Commission, 10101 Montgomery Road, Montgomery, OH 45242. *Landmarks of Historic Montgomery—A Walking Tour,* from Montgomery Landmarks Commission, 10101 Montgomery Road, Montgomery, OH 45242. *Park District News* from Hamilton County Park District, 10245 Winton Road, Cincinnati, OH 45231.

Oklahoma

The name Oklahoma was derived from two Choctaw Indian words, *Okla* ("people") and *humma* or *homma* ("red"), thus literally meaning Red People. With more Indians here than in any other state, the name is appropriate. Thirty-five tribes and descendents of thirty-two more tribes are found in Oklahoma.

Oklahoma is also a cowboy state, the home of Hoot Gibson, Tom Mix, Gene Autry, and, of course, Will Rogers. Four major cattle trails traversed the state, the most famous being the Chisholm Trail.

This is a prairie state but a prairie state that has the Ouachita Mountains in the southeast, the Ozark Plateau in the northeast, and low ranges in the south and west such as the Wichitas, the Arbuckles, and the Antelope Hills. Livestock, tourism, and oil are the major industries. Oklahoma ranks fourth among the states in petroleum production, third in natural gas.

OKLAHOMA Crime Chart

	Crime Rate	Murder	Rape	Robbery	Aggravated Assault	Burglary	Larceny —Theft	Motor Vehicle Theft
United States								
U.S. Total	5,899.9	10.2	36.4	243.5	290.6	1,668.2	3,156.3	494.6
U.S. Metropolitan Areas	6,757.6	11.5	43.4	319.0	328.3	1,911.8	3,534.9	608.8
U.S. Rural Areas	2,290.4	7.5	15.5	22.5	136.9	830.2	1,143.9	133.9
Regional Crime Centers								
Oklahoma City	9,012.2	18.2	83.9	311.5	516.5	3,355.8	3,826.2	900.2
Tulsa	8,999.5	10.1	70.6	224.3	458.2	3,111.9	4,213.4	911.0
Safe Places								
Stillwater	2,437.2	0	21.0	26.2	68.1	699.7	1,512.1	110.1
Yukon	3,302.2	5.9	5.9	17.6	29.4	1,034.1	1,897.9	311.4

Oklahoma City, the state's capital and largest city, has a population of 400,000, with an equal number of people living outside city boundaries in the metropolitan region. Oil wells on the state capitol grounds are its most famous landmark. Stockyards and meat-packing plants make this the eighth largest livestock market in the country. With Tinker Air Force Base (largest supply and repair depot in the world) and the FAA Aeronautical Center at the airport, this is an important aviation center as well.

Tulsa is the state's second-largest city, with 360,000 residents. With more than 800 oil- and gas-associated companies, Tulsa bills itself as the Oil Capital of the World. Aviation and aerospace are the second most important industry.

Our two Safe Places in Oklahoma are Yukon, a suburb of Oklahoma City, and Stillwater, a university town halfway between the two largest cities.

YUKON

POPULATION: 17,019
NO. OF CRIMES: 562
CRIME RATE: 3,302.2 per 100,000

Yukon is a one-time farming community turned into a fast-growing suburb of Oklahoma City. When it was founded in 1891, Oklahoma City was a day's traveling distance away. Now the two city boundaries meet. Downtown Oklahoma City is just 18 miles to the east and you can get there in minutes via Interstate 40 or U.S. 66/270.

About the only place left where you can get the flavor of the old farming community is in the downtown area of Main Street. The grain elevator, railroad, and plains highway with its wide right-of-way are a familiar sight throughout the central states of the United States.

Once you leave Main, however, you are greeted by another just-as-familiar sight: suburban housing developments and shopping centers. Yukon's neighborhoods are comprised of well-maintained, middle-class homes and the town is just now getting its first subdivision of more expensive homes in the \$200,000 to \$300,000 range.

Yukon is located in Canadian County and the surrounding countryside consists of gently rolling prairies with moderate slopes and small creeks. The North Canadian River is about 1½ miles north of town. Yukon's elevation is 1,280 feet.

This area of Oklahoma is agriculturally diversified, with beef cattle, quarter horses, thoroughbred horses, small grain, alfalfa, hay, and wheat. Wheat is the major grain marketed at Yukon's Mid-Continent Co-op. Oats, milo, barley, soybeans, and corn are also processed there but in much smaller quantities.

The town actually has a famous landmark running through it and we were somewhat surprised that it hasn't been exploited more by the town boosters. We're referring to the Chisholm Trail. Jesse Chisholm and the other cattle drivers used this area as a campsite because of an overflowing spring that was located just south of the present junction of Main and Ninth streets. A small, easy-to-miss plaque is the only commemoration we saw.

Yukon bills itself as the Czech Capital of Oklahoma and a major event each year is the Oklahoma Czech Festival on the first Saturday in October. This full day of festivities includes a parade, art show, dances, special speakers, and crowning of the Czech Festival Queen. You can stuff yourself with kolaches and klobasy while you're enjoying all of this and the evening ends with a dinner and family dance at the Czech Hall.

Yukon's Czech Hall has been in the same location for eighty-three years, making it a historical part of the community. With its 3,200-square-foot wood dance floor, it is a popular social center. Country and western dances are held each Friday night and Czech and ballroom dances on other nights. Polkas, waltzes, circles, schottisches, the cotton-eyed Joe, flying Dutchman, Mexican hat dance, big-band ballroom dances—you can learn and dance them all here.

Another busy place is the Yukon Community Center, which includes a full-sized gym, game rooms, arts and crafts rooms, meeting rooms, weight room, teen center, lounge area, men's and women's locker rooms, and kitchen facilities. All the activities here are available free to city residents. Yukon also has six parks, including wooded City Park with its swimming pool and nature trail. An 18-hole golf course is located at Surrey Hills Country Club.

Additional recreational facilities include a motorcycle raceway, skating rink, five-screen theater center, and the facilities of the city's schools. Yukon has six elementary schools (K–6), a middle school (7–8), a mid-high school (9–10), and a senior high school (11–12). This is an independent school district and there is no busing. St. John's Parochial School (K–6) is also located in Yukon and a Protestant church school may have opened by the time this book is published.

As for other activities, the 1982 *Yukon Almanac* listed seventy-five clubs and organizations active in town and the town's Community Education Program conducts some eighty different classes. You won't lack for things to do here.

The cheapest homes in Yukon would be in the upper 40s, we were told by Pat Emerson, of Esquire Realty, the Century 21 affiliate in town. In that price range you would be likely to get 3 bedrooms, 1¾ baths, living room, kitchen with dining area, and a 2-car garage. You would have central heat and air, but no fireplace for this price.

A medium-priced house would be in the 70s. You would get the same rooms as for $49,000, except they would be larger and you'd have a fireplace. You would notice the size difference especially in the living room and master bedroom. You would probably have a U-shaped bar in the kitchen.

Basements are not common in this area. Nor are formal dining rooms. You also won't find too many houses with both a formal living room and a formal family room.

In the higher price ranges, you would have to pay $120,000 to $130,000 for a house with 2,400 square feet of living area. It would have 4 bedrooms, living room, and formal dining room as well as the dining area adjacent to the kitchen. The bath facilities would likely consist of a full bath, ½ bath, and ¾ bath (shower). Such a house would probably be on a 75 × 120 lot; there aren't too many with a full acre.

Opening in 1983 was the exclusive Spring Creek area, with houses in the $200,000 to $300,000 price range. At the time of our visit (July 1982) there were only a handful of houses in that range in Yukon.

Pat told us that homes are assessed at 12 percent of their last resale price, with a $1,000 homestead exemption applying to owner-occupied homes. The millage rate was .09723. The tax equation for a $100,000 house, therefore, would be: $100,000 × 12 percent − $1,000 × .09723 = an annual tax of $1,069.53.

In our comparison year of 1980, Yukon had 1 murder, 1 rape, 3 robberies, and 5 aggravated assaults. Property crime consisted of 176 burglaries, 323 larceny-thefts, and 53 motor vehicle thefts. This placed Yukon below U.S. rural rates in all categories of violent crime. Property crime was above U.S. rural levels but still way below U.S. metropolitan levels. (See our Oklahoma Crime Chart, page 293.)

J. D. "Sam" Ervin, Yukon's chief of police, told us that the number of auto thefts had increased in recent years "due to so many major auto dealers being located in our city limits." Other crimes, he thought, had not increased as fast as the town's population or as in neighboring Oklahoma City.

"Our biggest asset," he told us, "is a department of police officers willing to work hard and diligently—officers who are not concerned with what time of the day or night it is or how many hours they have put in, but just want to complete the job at hand in a proper and expedient manner."

Chief Ervin told us about some of the programs established beginning in 1980. In Operation ID, the police assist citizens in marking their property and valuables for identification purposes. A comprehensive Neighborhood Watch program was developed by the Kiwanis Club, with police assistance provided by Captain of Detectives James McDaniel. Yukon's police also distribute a number of pieces of effective literature. We saw two of them—the *Residential Security Manual,* full of detailed, practical suggestions for inexpensive ways to secure your home, and *Betsy & Bill & the Nice Bad Man,* written in picture-book format to warn children against accepting rides from strangers.

Chief Ervin was particularly pleased by "a decline in crimes committed by juveniles, which is quite astounding." He attributed this to a "very well-staffed Canadian County Youth Services Center," to his Detective Division, which has a full-time juvenile officer, and to combined efforts to rehabilitate youthful offenders.

Yukon's anticrime programs are typical of the community spirit you'll find here on the prairies west of Oklahoma City. And *that's* what makes this one of your best bets for a place to call home in central Oklahoma.

STILLWATER

POPULATION: 38,159
NO. OF CRIMES: 930
CRIME RATE: 2,437.2 per 100,000

One way to enjoy small town living with recreational and cultural advantages you'd usually find only in larger communities is by picking a town with a good college. In this case, we've picked a university town. And while Stillwater, with more than 38,000 residents (including the students), can't be considered a small town, it does still retain that flavor. Nothing seems rushed here and as large as the university is, it doesn't intimidate you with its size.

The university in question is Oklahoma State University, Oklahoma's largest institution of higher learning. There are 23,000 students enrolled at its main campus here. Having a university in town provides a number of advantages to residents, even if you're not enrolled or teaching at it . . .

Sports: Competing in the Big Eight Conference, OSU ranks third in the nation in the number of NCAA championships held in all sports.

Library facilities: If you are involved in writing or research, OSU's Edmond Low Library has more than 1.3 million volumes. Serving a university community, the city library also has exceptionally fine facilities.

Cultural activities: You can enjoy the programs at the University Theater, the Town and Gown Theater, Gardiner Art Gallery, and the Seretean Center—OSU's performing arts center. Available from the chamber of commerce is the *Stillwater Art Directory*, listing galleries, museums, and supply sources as well as artists specializing in paintings, drawing, graphics, jewelry, stained glass, fiber, wood, pottery, and ceramics.

Stillwater has a number of small museums, too: the Sheerar Cultural and Heritage Center Museum; OSU's Museum of Natural and Cultural History; the Museum of Higher Education in Oklahoma, operated by the Oklahoma Historical Society; the Fred Pfeiffer Museum, with its displays of early-day agricultural implements; and the National Wrestling Hall of Fame, the nation's only wrestling museum, which is located in the national offices of the U.S. Wrestling Federation.

Entertainment: You'll find more programs, performers, restaurants, theaters, and other forms of entertainment when you have a student body of 23,000 in town.

You notice the difference a university makes in other ways as well. The local newspaper, for instance, is of a higher quality and carries more interesting features than you'd likely find otherwise. Day-care facilities are going to be much more extensive than usual in a university town. If you want to rent rather than buy, that's always easier in a university town.

For your shopping needs, Stillwater has a downtown business district plus four major shopping centers and a number of smaller ones. In addition, downtown Oklahoma City is 65 miles to the southwest, Tulsa 75 miles east. Medical facilities include a 145-bed hospital (a regional medical center), four nursing homes with 379 beds, five clinics, and a large number of physicians and dentists.

Outdoor recreation is spread over a system of twenty-four parks, of which Boomer Lake is an especially popular spot for fishing, sailing, and picnicking. Oklahoma State University maintains Lake Carl Blackwell, a 19,364-acre recreational area, 7 miles west of the city. Stillwater's Parks and Recreation Department has a brochure outlining its extensive array of programs.

In our comparison year of 1980, Stillwater had no murders, 8 rapes, 10 robberies, and 26 aggravated assaults. In property crime, there were 267 burglaries, 577 larceny-thefts, and 42 motor vehicle thefts. This placed Stillwater below or just above U.S. rural rates of crime in all categories.

When we talked to David Goodrich of Global Real Estate, the Century 21 affiliate in Stillwater, there were 184 houses on the market. With an average price of $79,732 and an average size of 1,710 square feet, that comes to $46.62 per square foot as the average cost. Of these houses, thirty-one were 1- or 2-bedroom homes, 111 had 3 bedrooms, thirty-five had 4 bedrooms, and seven had 5 or more bedrooms.

David told us that most houses being built were in the $45,000 to $55,000 range. Such a house would have 3 bedrooms, 1½ or 2 baths, living room, and dining area (a formal dining room about half of the time). There could be either a 1-car or 2-car garage, and the lot would be sized 50 × 100 or larger.

In the fashionable area to the north, a house with 1,600 to 2,000 square feet of living area would cost $90,000 to $125,000. Generally it would have 3 or 4 bedrooms, living room, family room, and dining room. Mainly its rooms would be larger, and it would be on a larger lot—perhaps 100 × 200.

Building lots, David told us, run from $8,000 to $25,000 in this area. For a basic 80 × 125 lot, the usual price range would be $10,000 to $12,000.

Condominiums are starting to come to Stillwater, too. The overall range is $45,000 to $150,000 for 2 or 3 bedrooms, but most are in the $45,000 to $90,000 range.

Taxes for a house assessed at $40,000 to $50,000 would be $285 to $325 a year. David told us that most homeowners have a monthly tax bill ranging from $20 to $50.

With the countryside right at your doorstep, Oklahoma's two largest cities no farther than 75 miles away, and all the attractions of a major university right here, the state's eighth largest city welcomes you and offers you the best of both small town and university-city living.

Where to get further information:

State

Oklahoma Tourism and Recreation Department, 505 Will Rogers Memorial Building, Oklahoma City, OK 73105; telephone 800/522-8565 from within the state.

Regional

Oklahoma City Convention and Tourism Center, 4 Santa Fe Plaza, Oklahoma City, OK 73102. Oklahoma City Chamber of Commerce, 1 Santa Fe Plaza,

Oklahoma City, OK 73102. Metropolitan Tulsa Chamber of Commerce, 6156 Boston, Tulsa, OK 74119.

Local

Yukon: Yukon Chamber of Commerce, 1215-C S. 11th Street, Yukon, OK 73099.

Stillwater: Stillwater Chamber of Commerce, P.O. Box 1687, Stillwater, OK 74076.

Oregon

When you see Oregon, you have to say it was worth the effort of the pioneers to get there.

This is where Lewis and Clark ended their expedition in 1805, some 7,689 meandering miles after they left St. Louis to see what President Jefferson had bought in the Louisiana Purchase. Wood-hewn monuments mark the Oregon portion of their trail along the Columbia River, and at Fort Clatsop National Memorial near Astoria, you can see how they camped during the winter of 1805–6.

Lewis and Clark were followed by John Jacob Astor, other trappers, and missionaries. But it wasn't until 1843 that one small wagon train headed more directly west from Independence, Missouri, journeying 2,000 miles in covered wagons to Oregon, braving Indians, the weather, and the Rockies along the way. In the peak year of the Oregon Trail, 50,000 settlers made the perilous trek west. Today, you can follow the general path of their trail within Oregon by traveling Interstate 84 and visiting the Oregon Trail interpretive displays in the rest areas and state parks along the way.

Despite that migration and despite the 1859 gold rush to the Cascades, Oregon remained isolated from the rest of the nation until the railroads provided the missing link in 1883. Then, by 1890, Oregon's population quickly doubled.

Present-day Oregon is the nation's leading producer of lumber and lumber products. This is sometimes a mixed blessing, as in the recession of the early 1980s, when the nation's drastic slump in housing construction made Oregon the country's third most depressed state. Seafood, cattle and sheep, wheat, fruit and vegetable cultivation, and tourism are other important industries, and help to provide some diversification of the economy.

Oregon's Pacific shore is rimmed by the Coast Range of mountains. From the southwest corner of the state, the Cascade Range extends in a north-northeast direction into Washington. This is the dominant geographical feature of the state, with Mount Hood reaching an elevation of 11,235 feet, and it divides

Oregon into the mild coastal climactic zone to the west and a harsher inland climactic zone to the east.

Inside the *V* formed by the two mountain ranges is the Willamette Valley, containing bounteous fruit and vegetable farms as well as the manufacturing and commercial center of the state, Portland. East of the Cascades is cattle, sheep, and wheat country. The northeastern part of the state has 10,000-foot-high mountains and the awesome 6,000-foot gorge of the Snake River known as Hell's Canyon. The southeastern portion of the state, on the other hand, is a semiarid plateau.

Vying with the Pacific coast and the Cascades for the attention of the traveler is the majestic Columbia River Gorge, marking the Washington-Oregon boundary. Not only are the views of the broad river spectacular; so, too, are the dozen waterfalls that tumble down to the river valley from the Oregon side of the gorge.

Yes, indeed, the pioneers' trek—and yours—were both worth it.

PORTLAND AREA

The state's largest city has a population of 366,000 and is located at the junction of the Willamette and Columbia rivers. Portland is the nation's leading wheat port and a leading lumber port as well; overall, it ranks third in ocean-shipped cargo on the Pacific coast.

PORTLAND AREA Crime Chart

	Crime Rate	Murder	Rape	Robbery	Aggravated Assault	Burglary	Larceny —Theft	Motor Vehicle Theft
United States								
U.S. Total	5,899.9	10.2	36.4	243.5	290.6	1,668.2	3,156.3	494.6
U.S. Metropolitan Areas	6,757.6	11.5	43.4	319.0	328.3	1,911.8	3,534.9	608.8
U.S. Rural Areas	2,290.4	7.5	15.5	22.5	136.9	830.2	1,143.9	133.9
Regional Crime Centers								
Beaverton	7,349.8	6.2	49.5	123.8	204.3	1,783.3	4,792.6	390.1
Oregon City	7,343.5	0	54.1	74.5	575.3	1,401.0	4,812.2	426.4
Portland	11,168.8	12.6	99.6	615.2	628.6	3,003.0	6,195.0	614.9
Safe Place								
West Linn	3,203.1	0	23.0	15.3	306.5	781.6	1,946.4	130.3

One of the most enjoyable aspects of Portland is the topography. Here, as in few other U.S. cities, you can enjoy spectacular views of the skyline and the Cascade peaks to the east and north from the city's own hills and mountains. Viewing areas include Mount Tabor Park to the east of downtown, Rocky Butte in Joseph Wood Hill Park to the northeast, Washington Park to the west, and (highest of them all at 1,073 feet) Council Crest Park to the southwest. Many of the city's neighborhoods offer lovely homes in luxurious settings on the mountainsides.

Unfortunately, Oregon and Washington and their major cities of Portland and Seattle have a common problem in the midst of this Pacific Northwest paradise: crime. Perhaps a part of the reason is the transitory nature of the population; a census study after the 1980 count showed Oregon to have the lowest percentage of its population born within the state. At any rate, Oregon has the tenth highest crime rate among the fifty states, and when we consulted our FBI statistics we found that none of its twenty-five cities listed in the report qualified as a Safe Place. As a result, we knew we'd have to find smaller communities or unlisted communities as our Safe Places in Oregon.

That was easier said than done. We checked all cities and towns that report crime statistics in the metropolitan area of Multnomah, Clackamas, and Washington counties—twenty communities in all. None of these qualified as a Safe Place except for a tiny hamlet of 715 souls and the suburb that became our Safe Place in the Portland area. Portland itself (see our Portland Area Crime Chart, page 301) has a crime rate higher than you'll encounter in New York City and Washington, D.C. All the more reason to look just a few miles south when planning a move to this area.

WEST LINN

POPULATION: 13,050
NO. OF CRIMES: 418
CRIME RATE: 3,203.1 per 100,000

To get to this pleasant suburb from downtown Portland, you take Interstate 5 south toward Salem, then turn east on Interstate 205 (the bypass route around Portland). By the time you're on 205, you have left the built-up suburbs for the verdant Oregon countryside.

In a couple of miles, you see a scenic turnoff. Take it. When you get out of your car, you will behold one of the most important historical sites in the state—Willamette Falls on the Willamette River, with Oregon City on the opposite (southern) side of the river.

Oregon City was the end of the Oregon Trail and when Oregon was admitted as a territory in 1849, it became the capital. Dr. John McLoughlin, the chief factor of the Hudson's Bay Company, dominated the area's fur trading activities from 1824 to 1846 and his house in Oregon City has been restored and is open to the public as a national historic site. Before McLoughlin, this area and much of the Northwest was explored by a British fur trader named Peter Ogden; his grave is located in Mountain View Cemetery in Oregon City.

The falls, which are immediately below the scenic turnoff, were the site of an Indian salmon fishing village. As settlers moved in, the falls furnished power for a lumber mill, which began operation in 1842, a flour mill in 1844, a woolen mill in 1864, and the first paper mill in the Pacific Northwest in 1867. The first long-distance commercial electric power transmission in the United States was from this area to the city of Portland in 1889.

The Willamette Falls Locks, still in use below you, were opened on New Year's Day in 1873 and finally provided a solution to this age-old bar to navigation 26 miles above the mouth of the river. There are five locks in all, including a canal basin and guard lock at the upper end, and they provide a total lift of 50.2 feet.

The locks and the countryside about you are part of West Linn. Crown Zellerbach's paper mill on the river is the only local industry. Except for a few moderately sized business areas, West Linn is a residential community. Most of its breadwinners commute to jobs in Portland.

We've already noted one of West Linn's most distinctive features: It is the only Oregon community of any substantial size in the Portland metropolitan area to qualify as a Safe Place. In our comparison year of 1980, there were no murders, 3 rapes, 2 robberies, and 40 aggravated assaults. This was more violent crime than we like in a Safe Place, but as our Portland Area Crime Chart (page 301) indicates, West Linn still ranks way below the rest of the area in violent crime. Rape and aggravated assault rates are extremely high in the Portland area.

In property crime, West Linn had 102 burglaries and 17 motor vehicle thefts, which placed it below U.S. rural levels in those categories, and 254 incidents of larceny-theft, which placed it above U.S. rural levels but still way below U.S. metropolitan levels in that category.

Doris Ellis, of Tarbell Realtors in West Linn, told us that the climate on this side of the Cascades is moderate; there's not much snow locally and some years there is none. The last flood of the Willamette River occurred in 1964 and a repeat performance is not expected since dams have been built upriver which would control the flow of floodwaters.

Doris told us that West Linn offers a wide range of home prices, from $50,000 up to $300,000 and even $400,000. In 1981 the average sale price was probably in the $112,000 to $115,000 range, but by the time we visited the town in August 1982 that figure was down, due to the real estate and economic slump. The town has plenty of nice homes in the $60,000 to $80,000 range, too, she noted.

For $100,000 to $125,000, you could expect to get a new or fairly new home with 2,000 to 3,000 square feet of living area, on a lot ranging in size from 8,000 to 12,000 square feet. It would probably be a 1-story ranch or contemporary house, with 4 bedrooms and 2 or 3 baths. It would have either a formal dining room and family room, or a country kitchen that opens to an eating area and family area. There would be a 2-car garage, but there aren't many basements other than "daylight basements"—where the house is on sloping grounds, and your basement has a sliding glass door that opens to the outside.

As you approach the $200,000 price range, you can get as much as 5 acres of land with a view, either pastoral or of the mountains. Three listings in this range really caught our attention.

For $195,000, you could get a riverfront contemporary with 2,160 square feet of living area. This one was built in Northwest contemporary style, featuring beamed ceilings, skylights, and cedar walls. There were 3 bedrooms, 2 baths, a 16 × 31 family room with fireplace, living room with fireplace, and a country kitchen. The .41-acre lot includes a boat dock and slip on the river and the neighborhood has a recreational facility that includes tennis courts. Taxes were $2,000.

Also for $195,000, you could get a house in the center of town with 3,000 square feet of living area. The 1-acre lot offers views of the river and the mountains and contains an 18 × 30 heated greenhouse. You would have 4 bedrooms, 3 baths, a huge 15 × 31 living room, a country kitchen with an 11 × 9 eating area, a 15 × 25 master bedroom, 2 fireplaces, and a 2-car garage.

If you wanted acreage and a country feeling, there was an older, beautiful English Tudor available for $232,000. It had 3,135 square feet of living area and was located on 5 acres that had a barn, storage building, machine shed, and orchard. The house had 4 bedrooms, 2 baths, 20 × 33 family room, 15 × 21 living room, 14 × 31 formal dining room, 13 × 7 kitchen with eating nook, and a 2-car garage. Taxes were just $1,470, perhaps because this was zoned as farmland.

Perhaps the most expensive area in West Linn is a development called Ashdown Woods, off Johnson Road. The homes here are large, traditional mansions, on 1- or 2-acre sites, and prices range from $400,000 to $600,000. (At the time of our visit, a French Provincial with 3,100 square feet of living area was on the market for $415,000.) These homes are also surrounded by 160 acres of common land to preserve their privacy.

As you can see, there is no lack of fine homes in West Linn. We found this to be a pleasant, laid-back suburban community. The older areas downtown are not particularly pretentious, but neither have they been allowed to deteriorate. We were disappointed not to find much evidence of detailed landscaping by homeowners, the way you do in California, since the physical terrain certainly lends itself to some imaginative touches. But the natural foliage of the Pacific Northwest adds its beauty to the neighborhoods and the irregular paths and angles of the streets add to the country feeling of the community. Above all, there are the plentiful views of Mount Hood. That is always spectacular and helps to make West Linn a most pleasant as well as safe community to call home.

OREGON COAST

What can we say about Oregon's Pacific coast that hasn't been said already? A writer for the old *Holiday* magazine found: "Nothing in our experience compared to it, even the shores of the Mediterranean, Brittany, the Caribbean, the British Isles and Ireland, and the Pacific side of Central America." We cannot speak from such a worldwide geographical experience, but we *have* seen almost the entire coastline of the forty-eight contiguous states and we know that none of the rest of it can compare with what we've seen in Oregon.

This is a dreamland, a fairyland world, of densely wooded mountains sloping down to a narrow ribbon of tillable, habitable flatlands and valleys. Precipitous cliffs then complete the plunge down to the sometimes furious, sometimes calm Pacific below. And then the added touch that separates the Oregon coast from all others—the jagged, craggy rocks, not just along the beach where the cliffs meet the water, but out away from the shore as well. They are everywhere, it seems, some of them throwing waves hundreds of feet into the air, others teeming with sea lions. Beyond them is the blue-green eternity of the Pacific and at dusk the indescribable beauty of the setting sun. Once seen, this view will stay in your memory forever.

That narrow ribbon of habitable land we referred to is traversed by U.S. 101, one of America's magnificent scenic highways. As impressed as we are by the coastline, we are somewhat disappointed by the towns and villages that hug the Oregon coast along this highway. By and large, they have neither the stylish neighborhoods or architecture to be found in the Puget Sound area or on Portland's mountainsides or along parts of the California coast, nor the unique charm of New England's fishing villages—though many New Englanders settled here. The architecture, alas, is mostly twentieth-century blah.

More of a problem, though, is the matter of crime. Yes, incredible as it seems, you do have to worry about such a depressing subject even out here in the midst of all this beauty. Our Oregon Coast Crime Chart (page 306) lists only those communities with an overall crime rate of 7,000 or more per 100,000 population —that is, above U.S. metropolitan levels of crime—and still we found ten such communities. The other reporting communities along the coast were not as bad off but still too high in crime to qualify as Safe Places—except for two villages. In Clatsop County in the far north of Oregon's coast, Gearhart qualified (barely) as a Safe Place. However, it sits adjacent to Seaside, which has one of the highest crime rates among the coastal communities, and that is not a good situation. For our Safe Place on the Oregon coast we chose, instead, a quaint village along the even-more-beautiful southern portion of the coastline.

BANDON

POPULATION: 2,320
NO. OF CRIMES: 89
CRIME RATE: 3,836.2 per 100,000

This pleasant community at the mouth of the Coquille River has been a resort and commercial center for some time. As far back as the 1850s Gold Rush, an observer wrote: "The site of the town of Bandon was taken up, not for the gold that glittered in the front of it . . . but because of a convenient place for a ferry and from its admirable position for commercial purposes."

OREGON COAST Crime Chart

	Crime Rate	Murder	Rape	Robbery	Aggravated Assault	Burglary	Larceny —Theft	Motor Vehicle Theft
United States								
U.S. Total	5,899.9	10.2	36.4	243.5	290.6	1,668.2	3,156.3	494.6
U.S. Metropolitan Areas	6,757.6	11.5	43.4	319.0	328.3	1,911.8	3,534.9	608.8
U.S. Rural Areas	2,290.4	7.5	15.5	22.5	136.9	830.2	1,143.9	133.9
Regional Crime Centers								
Brookings	7,352.9	0	0	58.8	264.7	1,617.6	5,147.1	264.7
Cannon Beach	9,250.0	0	0	0	500.0	2,750.0	5,583.3	416.7
Coos Bay	9,547.5	6.9	82.9	117.4	103.6	2,756.5	5,796.2	683.9
Gold Beach	8,224.9	0	0	0	355.0	946.7	6,568.4	355.0
Lakeside	7,422.7	0	0	0	756.0	1,786.9	4,467.4	412.4
Newport	11,261.7	0	50.0	80.5	1,342.3	2,751.7	6,295.3	738.3
North Bend	8,682.3	10.2	40.9	30.6	449.4	1,634.3	6,138.9	377.9
Seaside	9,423.1	0	0	76.9	346.2	2,000.0	6,500.0	500.0
Tillamook	7,543.9	0	0	25.1	927.3	1,127.8	5,037.6	426.1
Warrenton	7,410.4	0	0	0	637.5	1,673.3	4,701.2	398.4
Safe Place								
Bandon	3,836.2	0	0	0	172.4	991.4	2,327.6	344.8

Sawmills and shipyards led to growth in the early part of the twentieth century and in 1908 the first direct steamer line was established between Bandon and Portland. Tourism grew and three years later Bandon had three good hotels.

Fires have been the bane of the town, however. In 1914 a fire destroyed almost all of the business district. In 1936 a forest fire all but destroyed the city. Only sixteen buildings, out of nearly 500, remained standing after the fire. Small wonder, then, that Bandon places great emphasis today on the training of its volunteer fire department.

When we talked with Virg Pearson, a real estate broker in town, he told us that Bandon is very popular with retirees, especially military retirees, and they may constitute half of the population today. He warned, however, that many people move here from Southern California after a visit during the glorious, sunny summer. They buy a place quickly and then find out, in a few months, that the winters are rainy. They also get homesick for relatives and for the busy cultural calendar and nightlife they left behind. As a result, half of them return to Southern California, while the other half adjust to Bandon's relative isolation and glory in it.

If you're not retired, one possibility is to commute 23 miles north to a job in Coos Bay or North Bend. Another possibility is to open or buy a business that caters to tourists. Other local industries are small. There's a cheese factory in town and the extensive cranberry bogs in the area have given Bandon the title of

Cranberry Capital of the State. Myrtlewood factories also abound in the area; the wood is noted for its deep grains and hardness, making it a favorite for bowls and wood gift items. Fishermen unload their catch at Bandon Harbor and a new commercial boat basin will provide docking facilities for another seventy-eight vessels from 30 to 80 feet in length.

The most extensive project going on in Bandon is the renovation and expansion of Old Town. This commercial area, a victim of the two fires, was the site at various times of a woolen factory, ship yards, banks, and brothels. Today it houses art galleries, crafts shops, cafés, a candy factory, fresh fish stores, the historical society, and an exhibit hall.

Medical facilities in Bandon include a 20-bed municipal hospital, a nursing home, and twenty-four-hour ambulance service. Four doctors, two dentists, one chiropractor, and one veterinarian serve the area.

Community activities include theatrical productions at the Bandon Playhouse, movies on weekends, and plenty of organizations—Lions, Rotary, Masons, Pythian Sisters and granges, mineral and rock groups, garden clubs, and more. Annual celebrations include fireworks on the 4th of July and a cranberry festival each fall.

In our comparison year of 1980, Bandon had virtually no crimes of violence—no murders, no rapes, no robberies, and just 4 aggravated assaults. Property crime consisted of twenty-three burglaries, fifty-four larceny-thefts, and eight motor vehicle thefts. While Bandon was well below U.S. metropolitan levels of crime in all these categories, the low burglary rate is especially impressive for a resort community where many homes are presumably vacant part of the year.

When we talked with Virg Pearson, he told us of two particularly nice listings then (August 1982) on the market. For $140,000, you could get a home with a wide, unobstructed view of the ocean—probably a 200-degree view—on an irregularly shaped, 1/3-acre lot. It had 3 bedrooms, 2 baths, a combination country kitchen–family room with cathedral ceiling, a separate living room, and a 2-car attached garage.

For just $95,000, he could offer us an oceanfront house where the beach would be just steps away. It was six or seven years old, had a new heavy shingle roof, and had been completely remodeled, featuring tile and teakwood floors, a fireplace with cedar mantel, and a greenhouse and sundeck outside surrounded by grape-stake fencing. It had only 2 large bedrooms and 1 bath, but there was room for expansion—and the views!

We also saw the printed listings of Portside Realty and Bandon Realty.

Bandon Realty listed oceanfront and ocean view homes ranging in price from $87,500 to $350,000. "Ocean-oriented" lots and acreage ranged from $12,500 to $210,000 in price; one listing was for 4+ and 7+ acres of oceanfront and ocean view parcels with deeded beach access, at $75,000 and $85,000. Bandon Realty also had businesses and commercial properties available at prices ranging from $15,000 for a corner lot to $350,000 for a myrtlewood sales and gift shop on 3 wooded acres, with a home and duplex included.

Portside Realty had extensive listings for town and country homes ($25,000 to $486,000), mobile homes ($28,000 to $79,000), vacant and unimproved land ($8,000 to $660,000), and commercial property ($95,000 to $650,000). The highest-priced listing for land was a 332-acre subdivision with forty lots, natural springs, a creek, and ocean and valley views. The highest-priced listing for commercial property was a stone-age museum and gift shop on 82 acres.

Remember Virgil Pearson's warning—year-round living in a relatively isolated small town is not for everyone. But if you really *do* want to get away from metropolitan life and the ocean is in your blood, you can't find a more spectacular setting than Bandon and the ever-charming Oregon coast.

Where to get further information:

State

Travel Information Section, Oregon Department of Transportation, 101 Transportation Building, Salem, OR 97310.

Regional

Portland Area: Greater Portland Convention and Visitors Association, Inc., 26 S.W. Salmon, Portland, OR 97204. Portland Chamber of Commerce, 824 S.W. Fifth Avenue, Portland, OR 97204.

Oregon Coast: Oregon Coast Association, P.O. Box 670, Newport, OR 97365. *Oregon Coast* magazine (one year, 6 issues, for $6.95), P.O. Box 18000, Florence, OR 97439. *Coastal Homes of Oregon* ($3.00 for six months, $6.00 for one year), P.O. Box 363, Coos Bay, OR 97420. *Fabulous Fifty Miles Recreation Guide* is a full-of-information annual publication available for $2.00 from *Western World* newspaper, P.O. Box 248, Bandon, OR 97411, or from the chamber of commerce (see below).

Local

West Linn: Oregon Tri-City Chamber of Commerce (includes West Linn), 719 Center Street, Oregon City, OR 97045. Corps of Engineers, Willamette Falls Locks, West Linn, OR 97068.

Bandon: Bandon Area Chamber of Commerce, P.O. Box 398, Bandon, OR 97411, has both a brochure and an illustrated guide and map available. For listings by the realtors mentioned in this chapter: Virg Pearson Real Estate, 890 2nd Street E., Bandon, OR 97411. Bandon Realty, 1160 Oregon Avenue (U.S. 101), P.O. Box 444, Bandon, OR 97411. Portside Realty, U.S. 101 and 11th Street, Bandon, OR 97411, telephone 800/525-8910, Extension F68.

Pennsylvania

The nation's fourth-most-populous state forms a rectangle on the map, 300 miles from east to west. Three hallowed names—Independence Hall, Valley Forge, and Gettysburg—symbolize the central role it has played in American history.

Geographically, Pennsylvania is dominated by long Appalachian ridges and highlands and the Allegheny Plateau north and west of the mountains. Coal and steel are the backbone of the economy in these areas, though the state has an amazing variety of industry and commerce. Productive farmlands dominate the southeastern lowlands and coastal plain.

Philadelphia in the east and Pittsburgh in the west serve as the state's population anchors. Outside those two areas, however, the state is a treasure trove of fascinating small towns. In our research for this book, we found more towns and small cities in Pennsylvania that qualified as Safe Places than in any other state. We see a direct relationship to a statistic unearthed by the Census Bureau in 1980: that Pennsylvania has the nation's most stable population. No other state has a higher percentage of its residents who were born within the state.

Our emphasis in this volume, as we've noted elsewhere, is on Safe Places within commuting distance of the major metropolitan areas. Thus we have picked three Safe Places in the Philadelphia area and two around Pittsburgh. One mostly rural region of the state holds such an attraction, however, that we couldn't ignore it. Therefore, we also have a Safe Place for you in the enchanting Pennsylvania Dutch country. Even so, we have barely tapped the treasures you can discover in the diverse and charming Keystone State.

PHILADELPHIA AREA

Soon after the 1980 census, William Penn's City of Brotherly Love lost its ranking as the nation's fourth largest city to Houston. As consolation, the city's newspapers trotted out statistics showing how total population figures didn't matter all that much, since Philadelphia was still by far the more cultured city. We remember in particular one set of statistics that showed that Philadelphia had vastly more books in its libraries. It was a quintessential Philadelphian response.

There is one area where Philadelphians should be glad to let Houston rank higher and that's in the number of crimes. As it turns out, Philadelphia *is* measurably safer. Houston has an overall crime rate of 8,886.3 per 100,000. Philadelphia's is 6,016.3. That's still an enormous amount of crime, but it goes down as one of the best big city crime rates in the country. Of the twenty-three U.S. cities with populations over a half million, only Indianapolis has lower crime.

Despite this relatively low crime rate for a big city, it's interesting to compare Philadelphia with Houston in the separate categories for crimes of violence. In murder, Houston easily outpaces Philadelphia, 39.1 to 25.9. Houston also has more rapes per 100,000 population: 88.8 compared with Philadelphia's 55.7. But Philadelphia has almost as many robberies (647.3 per 100,000) as Houston (670.8 per 100,000). And its rate of aggravated assaults actually surpasses Houston's by 300.0 to 176.0. Whoever thought there would be that many more brawls in the City of Brotherly Love than in the wild Texas frontier town?

PHILADELPHIA AREA Crime Chart

	Crime Rate	Murder	Rape	Robbery	Aggravated Assault	Burglary	Larceny —Theft	Motor Vehicle Theft
United States								
U.S. Total	5,899.9	10.2	36.4	243.5	290.6	1,668.2	3,156.3	494.6
U.S. Metropolitan Areas	6,757.6	11.5	43.4	319.0	328.3	1,911.8	3,534.9	608.8
U.S. Rural Areas	2,290.4	7.5	15.5	22.5	136.9	830.2	1,143.9	133.9
Regional Crime Center								
Philadelphia	6,016.3	25.9	55.7	647.3	300.0	1,483.5	2,433.4	1,070.4
Safe Places								
Haverford Township	2,518.4	0	7.6	19.1	101.3	915.3	1,310.8	164.3
Lower Moreland Township	3,045.4	0	8.0	8.0	32.1	1,122.0	1,578.8	296.5
Newtown Township	3,347.8	0	0	17.0	42.5	832.7	2,056.2	399.4

It is fascinating to us how different areas of the country have their crime peculiarities. We've noted elsewhere how everyone in Boston seems to have a love affair with someone else's automobile, since its rate of motor vehicle thefts is out of sight and is exported to Boston's suburbs. Well, here in Philadelphia robberies seem the favorite sport and one also exported to the suburbs. We broke down the crime statistics for fifteen Philadelphia suburbs whose *overall* crime rate was acceptable. Eleven had surprisingly high robbery rates. Among the four exceptions were our three Safe Places for the Philadelphia area.

Philadelphia is noted for its luxurious suburbs and exquisite exurban areas with their old stone houses and rolling fields. The most prestigious towns are found along the Main Line (the principal track of east/west bound trains of the former Pennsylvania Railroad), but unfortunately the Main Line also has unacceptably high levels of property crime. We didn't come up empty-handed, though. In Delaware County, west of the city, we found Newtown Township and Haverford Township. And in Montgomery County, north of Philadelphia, we chose Lower Moreland Township. Each has its unique characteristics that make it an attractive place to settle down in this corner of the world.

NEWTOWN TOWNSHIP

POPULATION: 11,769
NO. OF CRIMES: 394
CRIME RATE: 3,347.8 per 100,000

If you take the West Chester Pike (Route 3) out of Philadelphia, a brief jaunt will bring you to Newtown Square. This is the edge of the built-up suburbs, where fields are turning into developments to accommodate the continual surge out of the city. The recession may have slowed down the process, but the number of home listings in the newspaper classified columns give proof that it hasn't stopped.

Newtown Square is the compact center-town for this township. The pike—a wide, high-speed artery—breaks it up more than we like, but the beauty of the surrounding countryside makes amends for this blemish through the center of town.

Location is one asset touted by residents of the township. They have easy access both to the city (downtown Philadelphia is just 15 miles east) and to the fast-growing Valley Forge area to the north, with its employment opportunities and vast shopping arcades. At the same time, Newtown is much more convenient to the Philadelphia airport than is the Valley Forge area.

Buses will take you directly down the pike to downtown Philadelphia if that's where you are working; the trip takes about forty-five minutes. If you want to commute by train, the Bryn Mawr station is just twelve minutes away.

Some executives in town even commute to jobs in New Jersey. The Commodore Barry Bridge in Chester has very little traffic and speeds them over the Delaware River to industries on the other side. They much prefer the refined Pennsylvania countryside to the ticky-tacky overdeveloped suburbs in New Jersey.

Another asset of Newtown Township is the low tax burden. Taxes on an older home may come to no more than $800 a year; for a new $125,000 house they might be $1,200. And that's everything—township, county, and schools.

Roslyn Dowling, of the Newbold realty firm in town, told us that good-sized lots of at least 1/2 acre were common in Newtown. Also, more homes here were custom-built by people who moved out of the city in years past. That's why you'll often find pine paneling and other nice touches not usually found in a development house.

Another peculiarity of the local market is the number of ranches and their popularity. "We can't meet the demand," Roslyn told us.

The lowest price for a decent house, she said, would be in the $75,000 to $95,000 range. This would likely be a 3-bedroom, 2-bath house and past $80,000 you could also expect a 2-car garage. For a relatively new 4-bedroom, 2½-bath house, the minimum price would be $120,000 to $125,000. Prices go up to $200,000, with just a few estates above that.

We surveyed the newspaper ads and found two Newtown houses for rent: a country farmhouse for $300 and a 3-bedroom, 2½-bath ranch available for $650 a month. A third house—a larger 4-bedroom colonial—was selling for $126,900, but could also be rented for $950.

Among the houses for sale, we also noted the following:

- For $75,900: a 3-bedroom bilevel with a den or fourth bedroom, large family room, garage, patio, and grounds near a park.
- For $115,000: a 3-bedroom, 3½-bath brick ranch with 2 fireplaces, family room, and 2-car garage, plus a complete 4-room-and-bath apartment on the second floor with a private entrance, plus 2 acres with a stream.
- For $125,000: a center-hall colonial on a 1-acre lot, with 4 large bedrooms, 2½ baths, a sunny kitchen, a paneled den with fireplace, a covered barbecue patio, and a 2-car garage.

In crime, the township placed below U.S. rural rates in all categories of crimes of violence during our comparison year of 1980. Property crime was above U.S. rural rates, but still far below U.S. metropolitan levels. With no murders or rapes, 2 robberies, 5 aggravated assaults, 98 burglaries, 242 larceny-thefts, and 47 motor vehicle thefts, the overall crime rate was 3,347.8 per 100,000. In 1981, this fell to a rate of 3,295.1.

With its convenient location, low taxes, and reasonably priced range of housing, Newtown Township makes its bid for consideration as your home in the Philadelphia area.

HAVERFORD TOWNSHIP

POPULATION: 52,335
NO. OF CRIMES: 1,318
CRIME RATE: 2,518.4 per 100,000

Local governmental jurisdictions get awfully confusing at times, so we might as well begin by setting you straight on place names you'll encounter in this area.

The basic unit of local government around Philadelphia is the *township.* In a rural or semirural area, this can consist of a *town* and its surrounding countryside or several towns and their surrounding countryside. In metropolitan regions, however, it often happens that the town covers the entire township. They may or may not have the same name.

The town in Haverford Township is *Havertown.* To make things more confusing, one of the towns in adjoining Lower Merion Township is the *town* of *Haverford.* But we're not finished yet. Haverford *College*—which is probably what you've heard of—is mostly in Haverford Township and only slightly in Haverford the town. And (yes, there's more!), while most Haverford Township residents have Havertown, Pennsylvania, mailing addresses, those around the college have the more prestigious Haverford, Ardmore, or Bryn Mawr mailing addresses.

Now that we've got that clear, let's just say that in this section we're talking about Haverford Township, not the town, and since Havertown occupies most of the township, we won't duplicate and confuse by mentioning it again. Henceforth, all references to "Haverford" are to Haverford Township.

Next, we want to voice a reservation about the crime rate. In our comparison year of 1980, Haverford Township's crime rate was 2,518.4—low enough to be considered "good" for a metropolitan area. Moreover, when we broke the statistics down into their seven categories, it still looked good. The township was below U.S. rural crime rates in all categories of violent crime. It was somewhat above them in the three categories of property crime, but still way below U.S. metropolitan levels.

The problem was in 1981. The overall crime rate actually fell, from 2,518.4 to 2,405.0. Yet the number of crimes in each category of violent crime increased in 1981, often dramatically so. The number of murders rose from 0 in 1980 to 4 in 1981; the number of rapes increased from 4 to 8. Robberies jumped from 10 to 18, and aggravated assaults rose from 53 to 64. It was the drops in burglaries and larceny-thefts that accounted for the lower overall crime rate.

So, we're in a quandary.

On the one hand, Haverford Township is still quite safe, compared with its neighbors. And even with these increases in violent crime, it still ranks way below U.S. metropolitan levels of violent crime.

On the other hand, the trend is all in the wrong direction. We don't know if 1981 was an exceptionally violent year and things have since quieted down. But before you make a move to Haverford Township, ask the police department for the crime statistics for all years after 1981. See if the crimes of violence are still increasing or decreasing.

Be specific in what you ask for, however. Ask for the *actual number* of murders, rapes, robberies, and aggravated assaults each year. Why? Because police chiefs often are no different from other bureaucrats when it comes to boasting about the good news and trying to hide the bad news.

In the 1981 annual report of Haverford Township, for example, Police Chief James A. Myers compares the 1981 and 1980 crime rates. But look how he puts it: "There was actually a 5.5 percent decrease in Part One offenses, which include crimes of homicide, rape, robbery, burglary, assaults."

Now, from that, wouldn't you gather that each of those types of crime had decreased? Of course you would. But as we've already seen, each of the four categories of violent crime actually *increased*, while the *overall* crime rate did decrease by 5 percent.

Shame on Chief Myers, and you be forewarned.

Now to other matters. Haverford Township is a built-up community of more than 50,000. Economically, the neighborhoods range from lower middle class to Main Line upper crust.

As a general rule, the houses get larger and more expensive the farther north you go in the township. North of Merion Golf Club (Ardmore Road) you'll find mansions, set back from narrow roads where the trees and foliage shut out the sunlight. And as you'll notice throughout eastern Pennsylvania, there's heavy use of stone—stone curbs and walls covered with ivy and stone pillars marking the entrances to majestic stone houses with slate roofs. It's a pleasant world, indeed, in such a setting.

You don't have to come in at the top, however, to find this a good community. We drove extensively through the township and found no "problem" areas. Whatever their economic level, Haverford residents take pride in their homes and neighborhoods.

William R. Marnie, a realtor with Sloan Real Estate, told us that row houses sell in the $30,000 to $52,000 price range. Twins (two houses attached) range from $46,000 to $55,000. And single-family homes, he said, are from $52,000 to $130,000 and up, before you get into the Main Line neighborhoods.

For $61,000, Mr. Marnie told us, you could get a single-family 3-bedroom house on a 50 × 125 or 150 lot. These usually need some updating. For a house in prime shape, prices start in the mid-70s.

Rentals are also available in Haverford Township. A look at the classified ads showed that most efficiencies and 1-bedroom apartments rent for $300 to $350. Two-bedroom apartments range from $350 to $450. A 3-bedroom twin home was available for $525 and a 3-bedroom single-family house was renting for $600. Heat and water were sometimes included for an apartment, but not with the rental houses.

If you live in the northern part of the township, you're conveniently close to one of several Main Line train stations. If you live in the southern part of the township, the most convenient way to downtown Philadelphia is to take a bus to the Sixty-ninth Street Terminal in Upper Darby and transfer there to the subway.

Whatever your economic level, Haverford Township has much to offer. So keep tabs on those crime rates. If they do go down—as we hope and expect—you'll know you can consider a move to this fine community without any further hesitation.

LOWER MORELAND TOWNSHIP

POPULATION: 12,478
NO. OF CRIMES: 380
CRIME RATE: 3,045.4 per 100,000

Bryn Athyn Cathedral has to be one of the most impressive, yet least known, religious edifices in the United States. You come across it in the middle of the rustic Pennsylvania countryside, a majestic, awe-inspiring blend of fourteenth-century Gothic and twelfth-century Romanesque architectural styles. And it was built as the medieval cathedrals were built, by cooperative craft guilds.

Bryn Athyn Church of the New Jerusalem—its formal name—is the center of Swedenborgian worship in the United States. This religious sect is based on the teachings of Swedish religious philosopher Emanuel Swedenborg and has been active for several centuries. Their Academy of the New Church is adjacent to the cathedral.

Actually, the Swedenborgian properties are not in Lower Moreland Township, our Safe Place, but in Bryn Athyn Township. Their influence is felt in Lower Moreland, however, since their wealthy patron, John Pitcairn, is said to own much of the vacant land in Lower Moreland, keeping it out of development. Since Lower Moreland Township almost entirely surrounds Bryn Athyn, the social and economic ties are considerable.

Lower Moreland is largely rural in areas but mostly suburbanized with a countrified flavor. It was originally known as Goose Town because geese were raised here and floated down the Pennypack River to the eastern seaboard and even to Europe.

The township sits northeast of downtown Philadelphia and the Pennsylvania Turnpike skims its northern tip. The postal address for Lower Moreland and parts of three other townships is Huntingdon Valley, but there's no town or neighborhood by that name—the name was a post office contrivance.

Most people commute to jobs in Philadelphia. The Reading Railroad gets you downtown in twenty to thirty-five minutes, depending on whether you're on an express or local train.

We had a delightful talk with Manfred H. Speer, owner of the Century 21 real estate affiliate in Lower Moreland. He told us the township has very low mobility compared to other communities—professionals, businessmen, and executives move here and stay here. It's a particularly desired location because of the school system. Neighboring Bucks County has centralized school districts, but here in Montgomery County the schools are organized on a township basis.

In general, Mr. Speer told us, older homes can be bought for $70,000 to $80,000. Newer homes, however, will run $100,000 and up, with one estate on the market tagged at $1+ million. At the time of our visit, there were perhaps forty or fifty properties on the market in Lower Moreland, the bulk of them between $80,000 and $120,000 in price. This was a small amount of turnover compared with adjacent areas, reflecting the low mobility.

In real estate ads, we found a 2-bedroom, 2-bath custom ranch on 3/4 acre, with a basement and a 2-car garage, selling for $135,000.

For $220,000, you could get a 4-bedroom, 3 1/2-bath 2-story home with separate office or in-law quarters. An additional $5,000 would get you a nineteenth-century farmhouse on 4.3 acres, or a stone and brick 4-bedroom home with a pool and cabana.

In our comparison year of 1980, Lower Moreland Township had no murders, 1 rape, 1 robbery, 4 aggravated assaults, 140 burglaries, 197 larceny-thefts, and 37 motor vehicle thefts. This placed it below U.S. rural crime rates for all categories of violent crime. Its rates for property crime were above U.S. rural rates, but still way below U.S. metropolitan rates. And in 1981 the overall crime rate dropped by 15 percent.

With its northeastern setting, Lower Moreland Township is the most conveniently located of our three Safe Places if business or weekend jaunts take you to Bucks County, the Poconos, northern New Jersey, or New York. Add to that its countrified charm, reputable schools, and low crime, and you have more than enough reasons to pay a personal visit and consider it as your Philadelphia-area home.

PITTSBURGH AREA

America's largest inland port built its industrial empire on foundations of iron and steel. The valley of the Monongahela River, before its junction with the Allegheny River to form the Ohio, was known as Steel Valley. During the late nineteenth century and through World War II, this was the center of the American steel industry. At night the river's banks were bright red with the glow from steel-mill furnaces. Pittsburgh was the Smoky City.

During the past twenty-five years, a $3 billion civic renewal campaign has transformed the city. Modern skyscrapers have replaced slums in the Golden Triangle business district. The air is no longer smoky. Indeed, only one good-sized steel mill remains within the city limits.

This isn't all a success story. On the dark side of the picture, the U.S. steel industry has been decimated. Today it operates at 40 percent of capacity, its lowest level since before World War II, and naturally this is reflected in the Steel Valley. On the bright side, Pittsburgh's industrial economy became widely diversified in the past two decades. And today it extends beyond manufacturing, with more than 150 research and testing laboratories in the area. Still, massive unemployment is a fact of life here.

Although Pittsburgh itself has a population of less than half a million, the metropolitan area has expanded to more than 2,250,000. The picturesque physical setting of mountains and river valleys is matched by a vibrant cultural mosaic of immigrant population—Britons, Germans, Poles, Czechs, Slovaks, Hungarians, Russians.

Pittsburgh's first great wave of suburbs pushed south of the city. Of these, Mount Lebanon is the fashionable community for corporate transferees. Still farther south off Washington Road (U.S. 19), monied Upper St. Clair Township is the south side's upper crust. When it came time to choose a suburb here, however, we picked solidly middle-class Whitehall. It has affordable housing for those on moderate incomes and its crime rate is one of the lowest in the area, when broken down and measured by each of the seven categories of major crimes. Mount Lebanon's *overall* crime rate is reasonably low, but it has too many robberies, aggravated assaults, and larceny-thefts to make us feel comfortable.

Elsewhere, the newer eastern suburbs—such as Plum and Penn Hills—have generally a more affluent population than most suburbs in the region. You'll find many of the technocrats for the new research labs living here. In average income, they would probably be outranked only by Upper St. Clair Township and by the two towns we'll mention next. Those two towns are north of Pittsburgh.

To the northwest, above the Ohio River, is Sewickley Heights. A tiny enclave with a population of 899, it is believed by many to be *the* place to live. It helps to belong to one of the "fifty families" of steel magnate lineage, but even the younger generation of those families finds it hard to keep up the old ways.

Northeast of Pittsburgh and across the Allegheny River is Fox Chapel. Whereas much of Sewickley Heights is "old money," Fox Chapel is newly earned money. A recent newspaper article listed it as having the highest average income of any town in the metropolitan area.

In general, an identical house would cost $10,000 more in Fox Chapel than in Upper St. Clair. If your business requires you to use the airport frequently, Upper St. Clair is much more convenient. But for commuting every day to the Golden Triangle, pick Fox Chapel.

For a contrast of two different economic levels and lifestyles, we picked middle-class Whitehall and upper-middle-class Fox Chapel as our Safe Places in the Pittsburgh area.

WHITEHALL

POPULATION: 14,969
NO. OF CRIMES: 251
CRIME RATE: 1,676.8 per 100,000

Whitehall is one of the communities known collectively as the South Hills area. It is relatively new, formed in 1947. Castle Shannon is its older, more compact neighbor, with more modest homes. And Bethel Park is the southernmost major suburb in Allegheny County. Spread out, it mixes suburban developments with a hilly, rustic countryside setting.

If you live in Whitehall and work in downtown Pittsburgh, you'll find excellent commuter bus service. At rush hour the ride will probably take you forty minutes, during the off hours about fifteen minutes. A light-rail rapid transit system, partly underground, will service the area when it's completed. But that's still in the future.

Crime is under control here. Pittsburgh has a phenomenally large number of robberies—a condition common to the area's suburbs as well. We checked twenty-one towns and suburbs with a population of 10,000 or more and White-

PITTSBURGH AREA Crime Chart

	Crime Rate	Murder	Rape	Robbery	Aggravated Assault	Burglary	Larceny —Theft	Motor Vehicle Theft
United States								
U.S. Total	5,899.9	10.2	36.4	243.5	290.6	1,668.2	3,156.3	494.6
U.S. Metropolitan Areas	6,757.6	11.5	43.4	319.0	328.3	1,911.8	3,534.9	608.8
U.S. Rural Areas	2,290.4	7.5	15.5	22.5	136.9	830.2	1,143.9	133.9
Regional Crime Center								
Pittsburgh	7,166.1	11.8	70.5	766.6	358.1	2,120.9	2,527.3	1,310.9
Safe Places								
Fox Chapel	178.2	0	0	0	0	59.4	118.8	0
Whitehall	1,676.8	0	6.7	13.4	20.0	628.0	821.7	187.1

hall was the *only* one among them whose robbery rate was below the rate for U.S. rural areas.

In our comparison year of 1980, Whitehall had no murders, 1 rape, 2 robberies, and 3 aggravated assaults. In property crime, it had 94 burglaries, 123 larceny-thefts, and 28 motor vehicle thefts. This projects to below-rural crime rates in all categories except motor-vehicle theft, and there it still ranks way below U.S. metropolitan levels.

In 1981, moreover, the overall crime rate dropped by 15 percent.

While some municipalities try to hide the facts about the number of home burglaries in their jurisdiction, Whitehall officials take the opposite tact and publicize them. Their goal is to get all areas of the town active in the Neighborhood Watch program.

"While we wish there were no burglaries to report," says Mayor Edwin F. Brennan, "it is a fact that they do exist. We would far rather have our residents be alert than to be lulled into complacency."

Whitehall is also proud of its emergency medical service. Manned completely by volunteers (thirty-eight at last count), it provides twenty-four-hour help for the residents of Whitehall at no charge. The service responds to about forty-five calls a month, mostly from elderly residents.

One of the service's projects is called envelopes of life. A kit consists of a simple form for medical information, plus a plastic sleeve and sticker for placement on your home door or window. This makes it possible for the emergency workers to learn about your medical background in the event you are unable to supply it yourself.

We talked with Kermit Lindeberg, of the Bob Gooden Agency, about real estate costs in Whitehall. He said the overall range is from $32,000 to $140,000, though most houses probably fall into the $60,000 to $70,000 area.

The $32,000 price tag refers to one half of a double house. You would have 2 bedrooms, 1 bath, living room, dining room, kitchen, and a 1-car garage. Single-family houses start in the 40s.

For $60,000 to $70,000, you can get a 3-bedroom ranch with a double garage and a game room in the basement. Or you might prefer a 3-bedroom, 1-bath conventional 2-story house. For 2 baths and a family room (you'll find them only in the newer homes), expect to pay at least $75,000.

The top $140,000 price tag is for a newer 4-bedroom house with living room, family room, dining room, kitchen, entrance way, 2 fireplaces, finished basement (probably a game room there), and 2-car garage. This would be on a 65 × 150 lot, but there aren't too many houses this large and this expensive in Whitehall. You will find some houses in the $115,000 range that are basically the same, except with smaller rooms.

In short, Whitehall offers you a safe and secure community with reasonable access to the city and the airport. In this price range, you'll find few places to match it in the Pittsburgh region.

FOX CHAPEL

POPULATION: 5,050
NO. OF CRIMES: 9
CRIME RATE: 178.2 per 100,000

If we were going to move to Pittsburgh, this is where we'd want to live. Whether we could afford it is another matter, but there would be no doubting the desire.

Every major metropolitan area has at least one community that stands out from the crowd. Fox Chapel is Pittsburgh's entry and it can stand comparison with the best of most other regions. Its homes are handsome and distinctive, mostly in traditional styles, and the setting of gentle hills, rippling brooks, lush foliage, and sculptured parklands only enhances their charm.

There's no doubt that this is a community that knew what it wanted from the very beginning and that has never wavered in its determination to maintain its goals.

"Fox Chapel constantly strives to defend and maintain its rustic, rural character," the town's *Citizen's Handbook* tells us. "One of our most important tasks is to preserve this position. Not only is it desirable for Fox Chapel, it is desirable for the entire Pittsburgh area. Our wooded hills and uncrowded residential developments are a valuable regional asset. Fox Chapel is a classic example of what can be done to preserve openness and spaciousness in the very midst of urbanization and industrialization. This example must not be destroyed."

To maintain its ambience, 55 percent of the borough is zoned for 3-acre lots, 12 percent for 2 acres, and 26 percent for 1 acre. Private stables are permitted on the 3-acre lots. No commercial or industrial uses are allowed.

More than 200 acres of the borough are preserved as parklands available for passive recreation, such as walking trails and bird-watching. The most famous park area is the Trillium Trail. Each spring, hundreds of thousands of trilliums cover its grounds, drawing a crowd of admirers.

More land is in the hands of the three private clubs—Fox Chapel Golf Club, the Pittsburgh Field Club, and the Fox Chapel Racquet Club.

Fox Chapel's public school system is rated one of the best in Allegheny County. The district serves an area beyond Fox Chapel's own borders and extends into three other boroughs and two townships. There are also three private schools—a high school (9–12), a middle school (6–8), and a country day school (nursery through 5).

For their immediate shopping needs, Fox Chapel residents have extensive facilities available in adjoining O'Hara Township. For quality fashion and department stores, downtown Pittsburgh is a quick 12 miles away. (There's not enough population density for the stores to come out here.) It takes just twenty minutes to get to the Golden Triangle via the Allegheny Valley Expressway. A bus will take you thirty-five minutes because of frequent stops along the way.

Similarly, commuting to work in Pittsburgh is no problem. But many people work, as well as live, out in the suburbs and exurbs. Gulf Oil and Westinghouse are only two of the major corporations that have research laboratories in this area.

For such an affluent community, crime is amazingly low. In our comparison year of 1980, Fox Chapel had just 9 crimes—3 burglaries and 6 larceny-thefts. And in 1981, there were just 12 crimes—6 burglaries, 5 larceny-thefts, and 1 motor vehicle theft. That's not only below U.S. rural crime rates in all categories both years; it's so low it barely registers on the crime seismograph!

As is often the case with a top-bracket community, you'll find some cultural antagonism between Fox Chapel and the old manufacturing towns in the area. Two of them, Blawnox and Sharpsburg, are sometimes caustically referred to as Upnox and Downburg. (They are, respectively, up and down the Allegheny River from Fox Chapel.) We're sure the residents of those towns have an equivalent appellation for ritzy Fox Chapel.

We had a delightful visit with Mary Anne Barnes, an associate broker in the Fox Chapel office of Northwood Realty Company. She has lived in adjoining O'Hara Township for twenty-three years and was a gold mine of information about life in the Pittsburgh area.

The price range of Fox Chapel homes, she told us, runs all the way from $52,000 to $525,000 (and one estate was on the market at $1.4 million). But the largest bloc of available properties is in the $100,000 to $150,000 range and the ones that sell the fastest are the ones priced around $280,000. Corporate relocations explain the briskness of that higher-priced segment of the market.

While you can't build a new house on less than 1 acre, 7 percent of the existing homes are on 1/2-acre lots and naturally these dominate the lower price range. They really are the most practical and the easiest to heat, Mary Anne ventured, and on a 1/2-acre in Fox Chapel you can have all the privacy you want. The broken terrain and the fullness of the shrubbery ensure your privacy.

"I always ask, do you want privacy or seclusion?" she chuckled. Many people want privacy but also like the idea of having neighbors close at hand, and Fox Chapel allows you that combination.

For $125,000, on 1/2 acre or 1 acre, you can get a 4-bedroom, 2 1/2-bath colonial with a living room, family room, eat-in kitchen, basement finished off as a game room, and 2-car garage. Taxes will be around $2,000, give or take a little.

At $160,000, Northwood Realty had an aesthetically appealing large frame house with second-floor dormers. Its unique features included two screened-in porches, a 15 × 13 brick patio, a lily pond, and extensive flower gardens.

Really representative of "the Fox Chapel look" was a listing for a large, handsome white-brick colonial, which had just sold for $259,000, down 6 percent from the asking price of $275,000. Upstairs were 2 1/2 baths and the largest of the 5 bedrooms was 22.4 × 13.7. On the first floor were a 28 × 14.8 living room, 18.6 × 13.4 family room, 12.6 × 13.2 dining room, 19.7 × 13.4 kitchen, laundry room, and powder room. The 24 × 10 finished area of the basement could be used as a game room, bedroom, or office.

Special features of this mint-condition home included a beautiful screened porch, a concealed china closet in the dining room, a storage area and wine cellar adjacent to the 2-car garage, cable TV connections, and a wet bar in the family room. It's on a 1-acre lot and taxes are approximately $3,910.

With lovely homes like this, it's clear why Fox Chapel is such a special place. The homes and their setting work a special magic and we're certain you will be as easily seduced by Fox Chapel's charms as we were.

PENNSYLVANIA DUTCH COUNTRY

Beginning late in the seventeenth century, large numbers of dissenters fled the Rhineland and the Palatinate of Germany and found the religious freedom they sought in William Penn's "holy experiment," Pennsylvania. They settled first in the Philadelphia area, then moved west.

Today, the descendants of those immigrants reside in twenty-two states. One of their largest concentrations is in Lancaster County, Pennsylvania, where as the main attraction they draw over 3 million curious tourists a year. In the age of manned spacecraft and computer wizardry, many of them continue to use horse-drawn buggies rather than cars for transportation; the men still wear beards and black coats and hats and the women don bonnets and long, simple dresses.

These are the Plain People, so called because of their unadorned way of life. They follow the Old Order of their religious heritage—Amish, Mennonite, German Baptist, or River Brethren. Apparently they and other German immigrants became known as Pennsylvania Dutch as a result of linguistic corruption of the word *deutsch*.

In a modern city such as Lancaster (population 55,000), the Plain People are a minority and fade into the background. Tourism and other industries prosper here. So does crime. Lancaster has almost as high a crime rate as does Philadelphia (see our Pennsylvania Dutch Country Crime Chart, p. 322).

PENNSYLVANIA DUTCH COUNTRY Crime Chart

	Crime Rate	Murder	Rape	Robbery	Aggravated Assault	Burglary	Larceny —Theft	Motor Vehicle Theft
United States								
U.S. Total	5,899.9	10.2	36.4	243.5	290.6	1,668.2	3,156.3	494.6
U.S. Metropolitan Areas	6,757.6	11.5	43.4	319.0	328.3	1,911.8	3,534.9	608.8
U.S. Rural Areas	2,290.4	7.5	15.5	22.5	136.9	830.2	1,143.9	133.9
Regional Crime Centers								
Lancaster	5,855.5	7.3	18.3	119.0	120.8	1,618.1	3,494.3	477.7
Philadelphia	6,016.3	25.9	55.7	647.3	300.0	1,483.5	2,433.4	1,070.4
Safe Place								
Terre Hill (1981)	739.5	0	0	0	82.2	164.3	493.0	0

For the real flavor of Amish life, you must drive the country lanes, where the pace of traffic is set by the Amish buggies. And what splendid countryside it is! In our travels throughout America, we've seen no areas that can compare with this for well-maintained, prosperous-looking farms.

The scene is especially memorable from a high vantage point. In all directions you see gently undulating land, a patchwork pattern of fields under cultivation, and countless silos everywhere, reflecting the sun's rays, marking the location of each homestead. Absorbing that vista, it's easy to believe that the harvests from these fields are among the best in the country.

That's where we found our Safe Place for the Pennsylvania Dutch country—out there, amid all that agricultural bounty.

TERRE HILL

POPULATION: 1,217
NO. OF CRIMES: 9 (1981)
CRIME RATE: 739.5 per 100,000

Unspoiled and unrushed, the town of Terre Hill actually does sit atop a hill or plateau. Houses at the edge of town command sweeping vistas of the Pennsylvania Dutch countryside below.

As you approach town, families in carriages and young women on bicycles share the highway with you; chicken, sheep, cattle, and horses roam their pens and fields by the roadside. Once in town, your eyes focus on a historic-looking 2-story red-brick building, the Terre Hill Hotel, with its bar tucked into a corner on the ground floor.

Terre Hill is roughly 8 miles east of Ephrata and 17 or 18 miles northeast of Lancaster. They seem much farther. Not many tourists penetrate this far off the beaten path.

There's no business district in Terre Hill—just a few local stores here, a couple of shops there. A bank. The post office. A laundromat. A beauty shop and a barbershop in someone's house. An auto repair shop, a funeral home, an oil and solar heating service. A gas station, several antique shops, and a friendly-looking little restaurant offering homemade fare. The only sizable retail establishment among them is a food market, open 9 A.M. to 9 P.M. Down the hill are two local industries, a silo company and a manufacturer of concrete products. And that's about it.

Like the farms that surround it, Terre Hill is an immaculately neat and well-preserved town. Only it's not a restoration (like Colonial Williamsburg in Virginia) or a reproduction (like Massachusetts' Old Sturbridge Village), or even the unblemished re-creation of a genius' fantasy (as is Florida's Disney World). No, this is the authentic article—a real farm town and way of life set in the Pennsylvania Dutch countryside, where you only *feel* that you're stepping back in time.

Most of the residences are town homes—that is, 2-story frame or shingle houses on narrow lots. Around the edges, however, a few modern ranches can be seen. There is only one small suburban-type development in the entire town, where the street is lined by modest Capes, splits, ranches, and colonials.

We were visiting Terre Hill in the autumn and seasonal door decorations were visible everywhere—harvest wreaths, broomsticks, flower patterns, decorative ears of corn. Every so often we'd see a handwritten sign offering POTATOES FOR SALE, QUILTS FOR SALE, SWEET POTATOES.

In a small town like this, there's always some central location that becomes the people's bulletin board and here it was the entrance to the food market. Posters and handmade signs announced a garage sale, church bazaar, church women's bake sale, youth fellowship car wash and bake sale, adult education classes sponsored by the Eastern Lancaster County School District, babysitting services, an invitation to join the Ladies Friendship Circle at the nearby Mennonite church.

The preponderance of church-related activities reflects the traditional rural social environment, so strongly upheld here in Lancaster County. The churches in town reflect the special composition of the region, too—Berean Bible Fellowship Church, St. Paul's Church (Evangelical United Brethren), Trinity Evangelical Congregational Church, and the Weaverland Mennonite Church several miles out in the country. (Some Amish church services are held in the homes of members.)

Serious crime would be totally out of character in a setting like this and Terre Hill doesn't disappoint. Figures for 1980 were not available because Terre Hill's one-man police force didn't begin to report crimes to the state police until September. But in all of 1981 there were just 9 criminal offenses in town—1 aggravated assault, 2 burglaries, and 6 larceny-thefts. The result was a barely visible crime rate of 739.5 per 100,000.

Town Clock Hall, a handsome 2-story stone structure built in 1882, serves today as the Terre Hill Borough Office. Its name derives from the town clock in the steeple. It was used as a public school until 1900, then alternated as a meeting hall for the borough council and a fire hall. It was then privately owned until Terre Hill repurchased it in 1977 and renovated it. Today it is a Lancaster County Historic Preservation Trust Site.

We noticed a charming little house with a FOR SALE sign on it, next to the town hall. This was a 2-story white frame house with brown shutters and a vine-covered front porch. We talked with the agent, Elton Alvin Horning of the Horning Farm Agency in nearby Morgantown. He told us it had 6 rooms—3 bedrooms on the second floor, a living room, dining room, and kitchen on the first. It has since been sold for $41,000.

That's one of the cheaper houses in town, Mr. Horning told us. Older houses—usually 2½-story frame houses—sell for $45,000 to $50,000. Newer houses—say, one of the relatively few ranches—will go for $55,000 to $65,000.

We asked about the surrounding farmland. The price of a farm will vary, of course, depending on soil conditions and the state of its buildings. But in this area, Mr. Horning said, you can expect to pay $4,000 to $5,500 an acre for a 50-acre farm. He was in the process of selling one, 4 or 5 miles outside Terre Hill, for $7,000 an acre. They're not cheap.

Mr. Horning added that housing costs in Terre Hill are approximately 10 percent less than you'd pay for similar properties in, say, Ephrata or Morgantown. The reasons are the remoteness of the town and the scarcity of local businesses that might employ newcomers. The ones that are here, he said, hire mostly local people who have lived here all their lives, such as the farm girls we saw riding their bicycles out of town.

So, if you want to move to Terre Hill, plan on commuting to one of the larger towns in the area—unless, of course, you're retired or can bring your business with you. Above all, confine your relationship to a visit if you can't do without suburban amenities or the trappings of city life. Terre Hill is a genuine Pennsylvania Dutch country town, a delightful haven—but only for someone who truly enjoys country life. We wouldn't want it any other way.

Where to get further information:

State

The Pennsylvania Travel Bureau of Development, Department of Commerce, 416 Forum Building, Harrisburg, PA 17120, has a wide variety of tourist materials. Dial 800/323-1717 for a free vacation guide.

Regional

Philadelphia Area: Philadelphia Convention and Visitors Bureau, 1525 John F. Kennedy Boulevard, Philadelphia, PA 19102. Readable and accurate maps of metropolitan areas are difficult to find. For the Philadelphia area, we heartily recommend the Franklin's Map series. Newtown Township and Haverford Township are found on the Northern Delaware County map, and Lower Moreland Township is found on the Eastern Montgomery County map. For information, write: Franklin Survey Co., 1201 Race Street, Philadelphia, PA 19107.

Pittsburgh Area: Pittsburgh Convention and Visitors Bureau, 200 Roosevelt Building, Pittsburgh, PA 15222. Historical Society of Western Pennsylvania, 4338 Bigelow Boulevard, Pittsburgh, PA 15213.

Pennsylvania Dutch Country: Pennsylvania Dutch Visitors Bureau, 1799 Hempstead Road, Lancaster, PA 17601. Mennonite Information Center, 2209 Millstream Road, Lancaster, PA 17602. Lancaster Chamber of Commerce and Industry, P.O. Box 1558, Lancaster, PA 17603.

Towns

Newtown Township: Township Manager, Township of Newtown, P.O. Box 393, Newtown Square, PA 19073.

Haverford Township: Board of Commissioners, Haverford Township, 2325 Darby Road, Havertown, PA 19083.

Lower Moreland Township: President, Board of Commissioners, Township of Lower Moreland, 640 Red Lion Road, Huntingdon Valley, PA 19006.

Whitehall: Office of the Mayor, Whitehall Borough Office, 100 Borough Park Drive, Pittsburgh, PA 15236.

Fox Chapel: Office of the Borough Manager, 401 Fox Chapel Road, Pittsburgh, PA 15238.

Terre Hill: Terre Hill Borough Office, Terre Hill, PA 17581.

South Dakota

South Dakota is both an agricultural bastion of the Great Plains and an integral part of the Old West. Agriculture and tourism, accordingly, are the two anchors of the state's economy.

Geographically, the state is split by the Missouri River. Flat plains spread to the east and the rolling grasslands to the west are interrupted by buttes and in the southwest corner of the state by the Black Hills. The state's pioneer heritage has some foreign accents to it, mostly German, Czech, and Scandinavian.

For recreation, South Dakotans turn to water sports on the lakes created by the dams on the Missouri River, to hiking, mountain climbing, and winter sports in the Black Hills, to fishing for trout in the streams and for walleye and northern pike in the lakes, and to pheasant hunting east of the Missouri. Rodeos, auto races, horseracing, and dog races are popular spectator sports.

A greater percentage of South Dakota's population earns its living through agriculture than in any other state. The principal crops are hay, sunflowers, flaxseed, and alfalfa. Other industries found here include lumbering (in the Black Hills area), stock raising, meat packing, and mining (principally for gold, again in the Black Hills).

South Dakota's tourism industry is based on the attractions of the Black Hills —Mount Rushmore National Memorial, Badlands National Park to the east, Wind Cave National Park, Jewel Cave National Monument, tours of the Homestake Gold Mine, old western towns, scenic canyons and mountain roads, the buffalo herds of Custer State Park, Crazy Horse memorial, horseback riding, and much, much more. This is one of the most popular tourist destinations in the United States and deservedly so.

BLACK HILLS

Because of the popularity of the Black Hills area, we wanted to find a Safe Place in this region of South Dakota. In our 1972 book, we had chosen the mineral springs resort of Hot Springs. Unfortunately, crime has risen dramatically throughout the region—Hot Springs included—in the decade since that book appeared. Our task was further complicated by the fact that South Dakota's state government no longer compiles crime statistics from its individual communities; you have to get that information from each town and in these small towns record keeping is often notoriously incomplete.

BLACK HILLS Crime Chart

	Crime Rate	Murder	Rape	Robbery	Aggravated Assault	Burglary	Larceny —Theft	Motor Vehicle Theft
United States								
U.S. Total	5,899.9	10.2	36.4	243.5	290.6	1,668.2	3,156.3	494.6
U.S. Metropolitan Areas	6,757.6	11.5	43.4	319.0	328.3	1,911.8	3,534.9	608.8
U.S. Rural Areas	2,290.4	7.5	15.5	22.5	136.9	830.2	1,143.9	133.9
Regional Crime Centers								
Custer County	4,430.8	0	17.0	34.1	34.1	920.2	3,306.1	119.3
Hot Springs	6,150.9	0	0	84.5	528.4	1,373.9	3,699.0	465.0
Rapid City	8,027.6	8.6	51.8	148.9	198.5	1,965.9	5,202.8	451.0
Spearfish	5,369.4	0	0	0	0	990.1	4,112.7	266.6
Safe Place								
Fall River County	621.6	0	0	27.0	27.0	81.1	432.4	54.0

We made the rounds of local police departments, the Division of Law Enforcement Assistance of the state's Department of Public Safety, and the Division of Criminal Investigation of the state attorney general's office. Then we were fortunate to make contact with Jim Rowenhorst, a criminal justice planner for the Sixth District Crime Commission, headquartered in Rapid City. He sympathized with our plight in trying to obtain reliable crime statistics and he seemed to have a better handle on the situation than anyone else. Through him, we were able to obtain statistics on a number of the places of greatest interest to us.

That's when we discovered that Hot Springs, our former Safe Place, no longer qualified. In our comparison year of 1980, it had no murders or rapes, but it had 4 robberies, 25 aggravated assaults, 65 burglaries, 175 larceny-thefts, and 22 motor vehicle thefts. As our Black Hills Crime Chart shows (above), this placed it above U.S. rural crime levels in all those categories and above the U.S. national averages in aggravated assault and larceny-theft. The overall crime rate—6,150.9 crimes per 100,000 population—was well above our cutoff point of 4,000.

Rapid City, the big city of this area with its population of 47,000, was above U.S. metropolitan levels in its overall crime rate. We expected that; its crime rate has been high for some years.

We hoped that Custer County, including the town of Custer, might turn out to be a Safe Place. It was safer than most areas, but with an overall crime rate of 4,430.8 it still did not qualify.

"Hot Springs is still a nice place to live," Jim Rowenhorst told us, "but Spearfish would probably be the first choice of people living in South Dakota if they could live anywhere they wanted in the state. It's a college town in a scenic area, with beautiful old homes in town."

When we looked at Spearfish's overall crime rate, it was 5,369.4—too high to qualify as a Safe Place. But when we broke that down into separate categories, we discovered that Spearfish had *no* crimes of violence—no murder, no rape, no robbery, and no aggravated assault. It had 52 burglaries, which placed it just above U.S. rural levels in that category, and 7 motor vehicle thefts. What was really responsible for its overall high crime rate was its 194 incidents of larceny-theft. Since this category includes such crimes as shoplifting, purse snatching, and thefts from motor vehicles, we suspect that much of Spearfish's crime in this category is tourist-related.

Jim Rowenhorst suggested, too, that Spearfish's relatively high crime rate may be due to the fact that it has an excellent police force that turns in accurate, complete reports. The implication, of course, was that not all police departments are that circumspect about reporting everything.

This left one other political subdivision that we checked out: Fall River County, which contains our former Safe Place of Hot Springs. Outside of the town itself, Fall River County had no murders or rapes and just 1 robbery, 1 aggravated assault, 3 burglaries, 16 larceny-thefts, and 2 motor vehicle thefts. This gave it a very low crime rate of 621.6 crimes per 100,000 population. While we want to call this fact to your attention, we are not listing Fall River County as a Safe Place since its only community of any size—Hot Springs—has too much crime. You can find sparsely populated rural areas that are safe almost anywhere in the United States. What we're looking for are *communities* that are safe as well.

Where does that leave us in the Black Hills? Without a Safe Place, for one thing. We will continue to look into other communities in the area and perhaps in the future we'll be able to make a positive recommendation. For now, we would say that your relative best bets seem to be the town of Spearfish or Fall River County outside Hot Springs.

Meanwhile, we found a university town at the opposite end of the state where we had no such problems with the crime rate.

SOUTHEASTERN FARMLANDS

America the beautiful, and amber fields of grain. It was a bright, sunny day in late summer, the perfect time to be taking in the magnificent agricultural vistas of America's Great Plains. The fields were planted in corn, hay, wheat, alfalfa, oats, and soybeans. The farther north we went from the Missouri River, the more rolling the countryside became. Every so often we'd spot the spire of a white country church in the distance or a line of early-morning fog that indicated a river's path. Taking in the view from the top of a rise, you could always

SOUTH DAKOTA Crime Chart

	Crime Rate	Murder	Rape	Robbery	Aggravated Assault	Burglary	Larceny —Theft	Motor Vehicle Theft
United States								
U.S. Total	5,899.9	10.2	36.4	243.5	290.6	1,668.2	3,156.3	494.6
U.S. Metropolitan Areas	6,757.6	11.5	43.4	319.0	328.3	1,911.8	3,534.9	608.8
U.S. Rural Areas	2,290.4	7.5	15.5	22.5	136.9	830.2	1,143.9	133.9
Regional Crime Centers								
Rapid City	8,027.6	8.6	51.8	148.9	198.5	1,965.9	5,202.8	451.0
Sioux Falls	5,711.0	0	25.9	44.4	90.0	1,101.5	4,179.1	270.1
Safe Place								
Vermillion	2,919.1	0	29.6	9.9	187.4	463.5	2,120.3	108.5

tell the location of the farms by the clusters of trees dotting the fields. All farmhouses seemed to be protected by trees on at least three sides.

Sioux Falls, with a population of 81,000, is the largest city in this part of the state and serves as a regional meat-packing and agricultural center. Yankton was the first capital of Dakota Territory and this is where Jack McCall was hanged for the murder of Wild Bill Hickok. Mitchell has one of the most unusual and fascinating tourist sights in the country—its Corn Palace, a fairy-tale structure of Byzantine towers, spiraling minarets of Dakota grain, and huge outdoor mosaics decorated anew each year with colored corn and grasses. DeSmet is "Little House on the Prairie" country, where you can tour both the Ingalls family home and the surveyor's house of Laura Ingalls Wilder's *By the Shores of Silver Lake.* And across the state line is Sioux City, Iowa, a regional shopping and cultural center and a major U.S. livestock and grain center.

It was in this corner of the state, between Sioux Falls and Sioux City, that we found our Safe Place for South Dakota.

VERMILLION

POPULATION: 10,140
NO. OF CRIMES: 296
CRIME RATE: 2,919.1 per 100,000

Agriculture and education combine to make this a quietly prosperous small town, on the banks of the Vermillion River near its junction with the Missouri.

Clay County, of which Vermillion is the county seat, is a large producer of cattle and hogs. Its rich soil is planted in corn, oats, and soybeans, and four alfalfa mills in the area make the raising of alfalfa a large industry.

Education, however, is the major local industry. This is the home of the University of South Dakota, founded in 1862 and now the academic center of the state, with nearly 6,000 students. In addition to its contributions to the local economy, the university provides cultural, sports, and recreational opportunities enjoyed by few small towns of this size.

Vermillion is located on the route followed by the Lewis and Clark expedition, a trail later traversed by naturalist John J. Audubon and by fur traders, who established two trading posts in what is now Clay County. The town was originally located below its scenic bluffs, but disastrous floods in 1881 forced a move to its present site above the bluffs. The town's elevation is 1,225 feet above sea level.

Three small museums add to the city's cultural base. Austin-Whittemore Museum occupies a house built in 1882 and is maintained by the Clay County Historical Society. On the USD campus, the W. H. Over Museum features displays of native American and pioneer cultures and the Shrine to Music Museum is one of the major museums in the world devoted to the history of music and of musical instruments. It contains more than 2,500 musical instruments from around the world, along with an extensive supporting library. Also at USD is the Oscar Howe Gallery, highlighting the works of the native American artist and campus artist-in-residence.

Vermillion's medical facilities include the 47-bed Dakota Hospital and a 66-bed nursing home, with six major hospitals within 60 miles. The public schools consist of two elementary schools (K–4), a middle school (5–8), and a high school (9–12). St Agnes Catholic School also teaches kindergarten through grade 6.

In our comparison year of 1980, Vermillion had no murders, 3 rapes, 1 robbery, and 19 aggravated assaults. Property crime consisted of 47 burglaries, 215 larceny-thefts, and 11 motor vehicle thefts. This placed it below U.S. rural crime rates in all categories except rape, aggravated assault, and larceny-theft and in those categories it remained below U.S. metropolitan levels.

For information on local housing costs we talked with Ardyce C. Meisenholder, of Meisenholder Real Estate. She told us that area farmers move here to retire, though quite a few also go south in the winter. University professors and personnel also tend to stay here when they retire.

The overall range of housing, we were told, is from $12,000 to $167,000, but the usual range would be $50,000 to $60,000. The town qualifies for Farm Home Administration loans.

In that $50,000 to $60,000 range, you would be likely to get 3 or 4 bedrooms (usually 3 up and 1 down), 2 baths, a family room in the basement, living room, kitchen-dining area combination (older homes have a formal dining room), and a 1- or 2-car garage. This would be on a town lot.

On her board, we saw a 2-bedroom ranch that had recently sold for $52,000 and new ranches listed at $69,900. A 2-story traditional all-brick house was listed for $88,500. And for $105,000 you could get a new ranch with a 1-acre treed lot on the Missouri River, with a split-rail fence in front. It had a living room, family room, dining room, large kitchen, 3 bedrooms, and an unfinished but complete basement, along with a 1-car attached garage.

Some lots on the bluffs, with views overlooking the Missouri River Valley, had been selling for $20,000; only one was left at the time of our visit (August 1982). There were also bluff lots available in the Westgate area for $13,000, but these were not considered as desirable.

The southeast part of town has the highest real-estate values, Ardyce told us. This area has custom built homes that sell for $60,000 and up. Another prestige development is located on Route 50 west of town, but the southeast has the best resale values.

The University of South Dakota campus is one of the most unobtrusive ones we've seen anywhere for a state university. The campus seems to be well integrated into the community and merchants everywhere had put up signs: WELCOME BACK, STUDENTS. If you're looking for a small Midwestern town with the cultural leavening provided by a college or university, Vermillion is an attractive one that also places you in the midst of some of America's richest and most attractive North Plains farmlands.

Where to get further information:

State

South Dakota Division of Tourism, 221 S. Central, Pierre, SD 57501; telephone 800/843-1930 from out of state. Among its attractive brochures are ones on the Old West, history and heritage, parks and wildlife, lakes and streams, and Mount Rushmore and Crazy Horse.

Regional

Black Hills: Black Hills, Badlands and Lakes Association, P.O. Box 910, Sturgis, SD 57785. Rapid City Chamber of Commerce, Convention–Visitors Bureau, P.O. Box 747, Rapid City, SD 57709. Hot Springs Chamber of Commerce, 630 N. River Street, Hot Springs, SD 57747. Spearfish Chamber of Commerce, 722 Main Street, P.O. Box 550, Spearfish, SD 57783.

Southeastern Farmlands: Sioux Falls Chamber of Commerce, 127 E. 10th Street, P.O. Box 1425, Sioux Falls, SD 57101. Mitchell Chamber of Commerce, 604 N. Main, P.O. Box 206, Mitchell, SD 57301. Yankton Chamber of Commerce, 4th and Cedar, P.O. Box 588, Yankton, SD 57078. Sioux City Chamber of Commerce, 101 Pierce, Sioux City, Iowa 51101.

Local

Vermillion Chamber of Commerce, 5 Court Street, Vermillion, SD 57069. Public Information Office, University of South Dakota, Slagle 205, Vermillion, SD 57069. W. H. Over Museum, Vermillion, SD 57069. Shrine to Music Museum, USD Box 194, Vermillion, SD 57069.

Tennessee

If you have sampled the beauty of Tennessee's rolling hills and valleys, its wooded mountains and dozens of lakes, you need no sales pitch from us regarding the desirability and attractiveness of the Volunteer State. One visit is sufficient to convince most people that they want to return—either as tourists again, to explore new vistas or to come back to a favorite haunt, or as new residents.

Tennessee has three distinct regions: the lowlands area of West Tennessee, which reaches from the Mississippi to the Tennessee River; Middle Tennessee, an area of rolling hills and bluegrass which rises to the Cumberland Plateau; and East Tennessee, where the mountains keep getting taller, the valleys deeper, until you reach the highest mountain range in the eastern part of the United States.

The Great Smoky Mountains National Park, straddling the Tennessee–North Carolina border, is in fact the most popular national park in the nation. Northeast Tennessee, the area surrounding Cherokee National Forest, has just as spectacular views, among them the world's largest purple rhododendron gardens at Roan Mountain. The Cumberland Mountains along the Tennessee–Kentucky–Virginia border retain the rugged appearance of pioneer country that once greeted trailblazers such as Daniel Boone.

Tennessee's twenty-five largest lakes, with 600,000 acres of water and 10,000 miles of shoreline, are a water sportsman's paradise. They never freeze in the winter and there is no closed season on fishing. You can take a cruise starting near Nashville and, by the system of lakes, rivers, canals, and locks, work your way through Lake Barkley and Kentucky Lake and Pickwick Lake, swing down through Alabama and back up again to Knoxville—a trip of more than 800 miles.

Manufacturing has now replaced agriculture as the major contributor to the state's economy. Memphis, Chattanooga, Knoxville, and Nashville are the main centers, but smaller cities have prospered too. Kingsport, for example, has eleven major industries in town, including book printing and chemicals. Livestock and forestry are important; in crops, soybeans now outpace cotton and tobacco in value and limestone is the foremost mineral product. But the two most famous (and admired) products of the state, no doubt, are sour mash whiskey and Tennessee walking horses.

For our Safe Places in Tennessee this time around, we picked suburbs of the two major cities, Memphis and Nashville.

MEMPHIS AREA

This bustling Mississippi River port is best known for cotton, the blues, and rock 'n' roll, but in fact there are more than 800 industrial plants in the area and even the agriculture of the Delta country has diversified. Still, one third of the nation's cotton crop is bought or sold here and Beale Street is where W. C. Handy wrote "Memphis Blues," "St. Louis Blues," and other classics. In the fifties, "Elvis the Pelvis" Presley put the city on the musical map once more. His mansion, Graceland, must be the most popular tourist spot in the city today. You can also tour the Sun Recording Studio where Elvis and other rockabilly stars like Jerry Lee Lewis rocked and rolled their way to fame.

Memphis also has the South's largest medical center, a dozen colleges and universities, and some fine cultural attractions. There are excursions on the Mississippi River and annual events such as the Cotton Carnival, Mid-South Fair and Exposition, and Liberty Bowl football classic. De Soto Park is supposed to mark the spot where the explorer discovered the Mississippi. Confederate Park contains the ramparts that the Confederates unsuccessfully used to defend the city from the Union fleet. And Forrest Park has the grave of the Confederate hero and Memphis resident, Gen. Nathan Bedford Forrest.

There are plenty of places where crime is even worse, but it's bad enough in Memphis. In our comparison year of 1980, serious crimes increased by 14.4 percent over the previous year's levels—and murders jumped 40.6 percent. Which may help to explain the explosive growth of our Safe Place just southeast of the Memphis city limits.

GERMANTOWN

POPULATION: 20,190
NO. OF CRIMES: 493
CRIME RATE: 2,441.8 per 100,000

In contrast with Memphis, Germantown's crime rate dropped in 1980. There were 37 percent fewer burglaries, 23 percent less vandalism, and 9 percent fewer traffic accidents.

"I attribute it to police visibility and people calling in," said Germantown Police Chief Bob Cochran. "We have an awful lot of crime prevention [campaigning] where we go out and ask people to call in on any suspicious cars or any suspicious persons. And we go around to different groups and ask them to look out for their neighbor."

The Shelby County Sheriff's Department is responsible for covering 440

MEMPHIS AREA Crime Chart

	Crime Rate	Murder	Rape	Robbery	Aggravated Assault	Burglary	Larceny —Theft	Motor Vehicle Theft
United States								
U.S. Total	5,899.9	10.2	36.4	243.5	290.6	1,668.2	3,156.3	494.6
U.S. Metropolitan Areas	6,757.6	11.5	43.4	319.0	328.3	1,911.8	3,534.9	608.8
U.S. Rural Areas	2,290.4	7.5	15.5	22.5	136.9	830.2	1,143.9	133.9
Regional Crime Center								
Memphis	7,895.3	23.6	122.2	596.3	327.5	2,911.5	3,173.1	741.1
Safe Place								
Germantown	2,441.8	0	0	9.9	208.0	534.9	1,550.3	138.7

square miles of territory. To do its job, it has only six patrol cars—one for each of six districts.

In contrast, Germantown's police have to cover somewhere around 12 square miles. To do their job, they have three marked patrol cars and four unmarked ones. They maintain twenty-four hour, seven-days-a-week patrolling of the city. Their response time to calls for help is 4 minutes.

In 1980, Germantown had no murders or rapes, 2 robberies, 42 aggravated assaults, 108 burglaries, 313 larceny-thefts, and 28 motor vehicle thefts. This placed it below U.S. rural crime rates in all categories except aggravated assault, larceny-theft, and motor vehicle theft, and even in those categories it was well below U.S. metropolitan levels.

Germantown began as a utopian settlement, Neshoba, started by sisters Frances and Camilia Wright in 1825. Their goal was to show that slavery was not necessary for the Southern economy or social system and to train blacks with skills to prepare them for emancipation. Those noble goals weren't matched by practical details of organization or administration and the project folded after four years.

Germantown became an important station on the Memphis & Charleston Railroad and a center for sulfur springs resorts located north of the village, but it didn't grow much until the 1970s. Then it exploded in growth—from 3,474 in 1970 to more than 20,000 a decade later.

Census statistics show that 86.6 percent of Germantown's residents have lived there five years or less. It's a young and affluent crowd, too. Some 61.6 percent of the households have children under eighteen years of age, 40.1 percent of the heads of household fall in the twenty-five-to-forty-four age bracket, and the mean income is $26,025 a year.

In fact, Germantown is just about the most affluent suburb of Memphis and is considered to be where you strive to be able to afford to live. This used to be the place where people with horses and money had their summer homes. The equestrian heritage is kept up with two annual events, the Hunter Jumper Classic in early May and the Germantown Charity Horse Show in early June.

Another annual affair, the Germantown Festival, features exhibits and programs by artisans, craftsmen, and musicians. Recreational and educational classes are offered at the Community Center and numerous clubs and organizations are active in town. Germantown's chapter of Welcome Wagon has 800 members, making it one of the largest chapters in the United States. And the city's Arts Association has ten member groups—the Art League, Symphony Guild, Literary Society, Germantown Theater, Germantown Symphony Orchestra, Germantown Chorale, Germantown High School Fine Arts Department, the Memphis Guild of Handloom Weavers, the River City Sweet Adelines, and Friends of the Germantown Library.

We found Germantown to be an attractive and modern suburb, with a happy blend of both traditional and contemporary homes, all tastefully done. Germantown Village Square was an especially pleasing center of shops and restaurants.

For housing information, we talked with Paul Turner, whose firm is the Century 21 affiliate in Germantown. He told us that the overall price range is from $70,000 to $650,000 or more, but 80 percent of the listings are between $90,000 and $190,000.

Census statistics for 1980 showed the median value of all houses to be $92,900 and median rental for the 863 rental units coming to $320 a month. Both figures were about the highest in the county. Multiple Listing Service figures showed the average sales price for 293 Germantown homes to be $106,316—again, about the highest average price in the county for the first six months of 1982.

At the time of our visit (July 1982), Shelby County taxes came to $3.30 per $100, with assessment at 25 percent of true value. In addition, Germantown's tax was another $2.16. There are no additional assessments other than a 6 percent sales tax on everything. There are no income taxes on a state, county, or municipal level in Shelby County. On a $100,000 house, therefore, annual taxes would amount to something like $1,365.

The lesson is clear. Live in crime-ridden Memphis and you're likely to end up singing the blues. Live in nearby Germantown and your benefits include not only low and decreasing crime but attractive houses and neighborhoods, fine shops and department stores, and all the other advantages of a suburb that can afford to do things right.

NASHVILLE AREA

Nashville is, first and foremost, the country music capital of the world. That's what makes it famous around the world. But Nashville is much more as well.

It is also known, for example, as the Athens of the South, a reference to its fifteen colleges and universities (including Vanderbilt University), five religious publishing firms, and more than 700 churches. As further claim to that title, Nashville has a full-size replica of the Parthenon, housing an art museum.

Nashville is also the capital of Tennessee, with an impressive Ionic Greek capitol, and one of the state's major commercial centers. It is the largest investment banking center in the South.

Finally, Nashville is a city of lovely homes, attractive neighborhoods, wooded hills, a dramatic, modern downtown, and fine restaurants.

All of which make it one of the most interesting medium-sized cities in the United States.

NASHVILLE AREA Crime Chart

	Crime Rate	Murder	Rape	Robbery	Aggravated Assault	Burglary	Larceny —Theft	Motor Vehicle Theft
United States								
U.S. Total	5,899.9	10.2	36.4	243.5	290.6	1,668.2	3,156.3	494.6
U.S. Metropolitan Areas	6,757.6	11.5	43.4	319.0	328.3	1,911.8	3,534.9	608.8
U.S. Rural Areas	2,290.4	7.5	15.5	22.5	136.9	830.2	1,143.9	133.9
Regional Crime Centers								
Gallatin	5,394.8	5.9	11.9	83.2	457.5	1,485.4	3,095.5	255.5
Nashville	7,717.7	19.2	65.3	448.4	271.0	2,540.1	3,802.7	571.0
Safe Place								
Hendersonville	3,021.5	7.5	7.5	15.1	139.4	746.0	1,974.2	131.9

Back to country music. No visit to Nashville is complete without taking in a Saturday night radio concert at the Grand Ole Opry. The new auditorium, with seats for 4,400, is the world's largest broadcast studio. Ryman Auditorium (1891) hosted the Opry from 1943 to 1974; tours are available here, too. Nashville Music Row (Sixteenth and Seventeenth avenues South) houses the recording studios that make this the nation's second-largest music recording center. The Country Music Hall of Fame and Museum and the Country Music Wax Museum are full of memorabilia. And Opryland USA is one of the finest entertainment parks in the country, with twenty-one adventure rides, a petting zoo, gardens, mountain crafts demonstrations and displays, and fifteen live musical shows in five theme areas—not only country music but also jazz and blues, folk, Western, and rock.

HENDERSONVILLE

POPULATION: 26,543
NO. OF CRIMES: 802
CRIME RATE: 3,021.5 per 100,000

Johnny and June Cash are the most famous residents of Hendersonville. Their million-dollar home on Old Hickory Lake is a favorite spot for tourists, even though you can only see it from the road or by gawking through the gate. (Some persevering fans get a closer look by *cruising* to the house on the lake.) The Johnny Cash Museum on Main Street (U.S. 31E) has enough memorabilia to keep the most devoted fan busy for a while, including the one-piece-at-a-time Cadillac, built (as the song relates) entirely from Cadillac parts dating from 1949 through 1973.

Conway Twitty would have to rank next in prominence, we suppose. Certainly in visibility. Who else would build a museum and gift shop next door to his house and call the whole place Twitty City!

But look at who else is likely to be your neighbor if you move here. There's Roy Orbison, the Oak Ridge Boys, Barbara Mandrell, the Osborne Brothers, the Kendalls, Bobby Bare, Tammy Wynette, Jeannie Seely, Ferlin Husky, and dozens more.

Hendersonville is just a half-hour drive northeast of Nashville and less than that from the Grand Ole Opry. It was Tennessee's fastest-growing city during the decade of the seventies and now ranks eleventh in the state. Yet when you get away from its congested main street, it hasn't lost its small town, even rural, charm. The lake is always nearby and the houses and neighborhoods are attractive and sometimes even elegant.

Because Hendersonville is in Sumner County, not Nashville's Davidson County, you'll find taxes to be lower here. The residents say they get better schools for less money, too, and there's no busing. Hendersonville is a very sports-minded city and tends to be very friendly toward strangers since almost everyone here was a stranger not long ago. In contrast, it is said that the neighboring Sumner city of Gallatin has more of an old-crowd atmosphere, that it's hard to be accepted if you haven't grown up there.

Houses in Hendersonville start at around $80,000 and go up in price to $600,000. There are very few homes in the upper brackets, however, and most will be priced between $150,000 and $200,000.

There's still plenty of room for building here, too. Lots run $20,000 to $60,000 and that top price will get you an acre with lake frontage at Indian Lake, an exclusive area. There are also two condominium developments and eight or nine small apartment houses in town. Two-bedroom condominium units start at $30,000 and a 2-bedroom apartment would rent for about $345 a month.

For $80,000, you would get an older home that probably would be on an acre or more of land, with 3 bedrooms, a great room (no living room), possibly a dining room, 2 baths, and a 2-car garage.

Almost everything in this area is built with brick, though some houses are constructed of natural hardwood or hand-cut stone. Most houses have wall-to-wall carpeting, lots of wallpaper and built-ins, and a fireplace (usually in the family room). The trend in recent years has been back toward formal living rooms and dining rooms. Depending on the lot and what it will carry, some houses have full basements and others have half basements. They always have a 2-car garage.

For $150,000 to $200,000, you would probably get at least 4 bedrooms, 3 baths, a family room, an eat-in kitchen, a utility room, and a patio or deck, on little over an acre. In the $200,000 to $250,000 range you'll find lake frontage and houses with about 2,300 square feet or more in living area.

Taxes are low—not over $1,000 for most of these houses.

Most houses have central heating and air-conditioning, individual septic tanks, and city water.

Despite its rapid growth, Hendersonville has been able to keep its crime in check—and even to reduce its crime rate. In our comparison year of 1980, there were 2 murders, 2 rapes, 4 robberies, and 37 aggravated assaults. Property crime consisted of 198 burglaries, 524 larceny-thefts, and 35 motor vehicle thefts. This placed Hendersonville below U.S. rural crime rates in all categories except aggravated assault and larceny-theft, and even in these categories it was way below U.S. metropolitan levels.

In 1981, moreover, the amount of crime in Hendersonville was reduced by 41 percent.

Police Chief David Key sees a number of contributing factors behind this reduction in crime—Neighborhood Watch programs, programs for the elderly, vacation watch programs, and heavy emphasis on training of police officers.

Hendersonville has five officers with B.S. degrees and eight more seeking them. The three detectives each attend specialized schools dealing with criminal investigation. The lake patrol takes U.S. Coast Guard Auxiliary courses. HEAT (Hendersonville's Essential Action Team) is trained in special weapons and tactics that help them to cope with unusual situations; their equipment includes a fully equipped forward command post van.

Hendersonville is patrolled in four zones. The average response time for an emergency call is three minutes, for nonemergency calls about five minutes.

In addition to Neighborhood Watch and vacation watch, these programs were noted by Chief Key:

- An assurance program for the elderly who live alone. They provide police with their telephone number and a list of relatives to be contacted in case of emergency. Police make daily telephone calls to these elderly residents and if they can't be contacted, an officer is sent to the house to investigate the reason why.
- A security home survey for the elderly is provided upon request. Locks are suggested where appropriate and police try to furnish them free to underprivileged residents.
- Women are enrolled in rape seminars and firearms-safety classes.
- Businesses are also patrolled and in a recent year police discovered doors left open after business hours some 553 times. The officer who discovers an open door will not leave until someone has been contacted to secure the premises.
- The lake patrol uses its police boat to spot and prevent crime along Hendersonville's 25 miles of shoreline on Old Hickory Lake.

With programs such as these, it is easier to understand why crime has actually decreased in Hendersonville. At the same time, Hendersonville's exceptional housing and location make it easy to understand why the city is growing so fast.

Where to get further information:

State

Department of Tourist Development, 601 Broadway, P.O. Box 23170, Nashville, TN 37202.

Regional

Memphis Area: Memphis Convention and Visitors Bureau, 12 S. Main, Suite 107, Memphis, TN 38103.

Nashville Area: Nashville Area Chamber of Commerce, 161 Fourth Avenue N., Nashville, TN 37219. Ticket Office, Grand Ole Opry, 2808 Opryland Drive, Nashville, TN 37214. Mid-Cumberland Tourism Committee, 501 Union Street, Suite 600, Nashville, TN 37219.

Local

Germantown: Germantown Chamber of Commerce, P.O. Box 38441, Germantown, TN 38138.

Hendersonville: Hendersonville Chamber of Commerce, P.O. Box 377, Hendersonville, TN 37075.

Texas

Mention Texas and someone who has never been there is likely to conjure up images of cowboys, vast plains, and oil wells. As any Texan will tell you, there are plenty of cowboys, hundreds of miles of plains, and a staggering amount of oil to be found in the state. But Texas is much more, too, and it is the variety of this expansive land that makes it so attractive for visitors and residents alike.

Texas is especially attractive for retirees: The cost of living, outside of a few major cities such as Houston, is exceptionally low. The climate in West Texas will match that of Southern California and Arizona, the state's coastal climate is similar to Florida's, and the climate of the central Hill Country is considered the healthiest in the nation. But while the popular areas of California and Florida have been crowded for some time and most of Arizona's remaining land is owned by Uncle Sam, Texas still has plenty—*plenty*—of land in which to grow. There are, after all, some 267,338 square miles in the state, measuring 801 miles from north to south and 773 miles from east to west—one thirteenth of the total U.S. land area.

You can take your pick: moss-draped bayou country in the east; or the 23.4 million acres of woodland, including the Piney Woods and the dense Big Thicket in East Texas; or the coastal plains; or the subtropical vegetation and citrus groves of the Lower Rio Grande Valley; or the mesquite-covered brushlands of South Texas; or the rolling landscape and rushing streams of the Texas Hill Country; or the plains of the Panhandle and north central areas of the state; or the rugged mountain and canyon country "west of the Pecos." Texas elevations range from sea level to 8,751 feet in the Guadalupe Mountains, with ninety peaks more than a mile high. The rainfall varies from 56 inches a year along the Sabine River—nearly as much as in Miami—to less than 8 inches a year in the far west—or as little as in Phoenix. (In West Texas you'll get used to rivers without water.) Snowfall will vary from 24 inches each winter in the Panhandle to subtropical areas that have never seen a trace of snow. You can live in the nation's fourth largest city, bustling Houston, or in the fourteen other cities with a population of over 100,000 or in hamlets as tiny as Waylon Jennings and Willie Nelson's Luckenbach, Texas. Connecting them all together are more than 70,000 miles of highways—more than the total highway mileage of Russia.

Available for outdoorsmen of all types are ninety state parks, and over 1,100 roadside parks that provide welcome rest stops for the traveler (Texas pioneered this concept). Federal areas include two national parks, the country's largest national seashore, four national forests, three national grasslands, two national historic sites, a national historical park, two national recreation areas, a national memorial, and a national monument.

If it's the ocean you desire, Texas has 624 miles of coastline along the Gulf of Mexico. As for inland water, Texas has 6,300 square miles of it—a greater expanse than in any other state but Alaska. You will find more than 5,000 species of Texas wildflowers as you explore the state, more than 250 species of fin fish in the coastal waters, and another 200 species of freshwater fish inland. Texas winters 65 percent of the waterfowl in the Central Flyway of the United States; altogether, three fourths of all known American birds can be found in Texas. Its deer herd—estimated at 2,600,000 head—makes up 20 percent of the nation's total; other game animals include pronghorns, javelinas, and wild boars and Texas leads all states in wild turkey population, with some 250,000 birds.

Everyone agrees that oil is the single most important product in the Texas economy, but nobody agrees as to just how important it is. Roughly speaking, Texas has a third of the nation's oil production, it has a third of the nation's known reserves, and it refines more than half of the crude oil that it pumps out of the ground. Estimates of the overall role of the oil industry in the state's economy vary from 15 percent to 50 percent and the University of Texas Bureau of Business Research estimates that 25 percent of the Texas economy is directly related to oil and gas. This prominence of the oil industry led to the state's booming prosperity in the 1970s and similarly resulted in growing unemployment and a faltering economy when an oil glut developed in the 1980s. A consensus seems to be growing in the state that Texas must diversify and not remain hostage to the fortunes of a single industry—even if it's as important an industry as oil.

More diversification already exists than many people realize. Chemical manufacturing, agriculture, livestock, food processing, and tourism are all major industries. Military production, insurance, electronics, and other high tech industries are also important. Texas has more cattle, sheep, and goats than any other state and it is a leading producer of cotton, rice, wheat, citrus fruits, and truck crops.

Two demographic trends have transformed Texas in the past two decades. The first was the massive migration to the cities, which, in little more than a generation, changed a largely rural state into one that is predominantly urban in character. The second was the great influx of immigrants from the North and East. As a result, four out of five Texans now live in the state's twenty-six metropolitan areas and the state's population increased by more than 3 million between 1970 and 1980—a 27.1 percent jump. Texas is now the third most populous state in the nation and it is the only state to have three of the nation's ten largest cities. Nor is the end anywhere in sight. Texas may very well surpass New York in population before the decade of the eighties has passed.

To help you find a Safe Place to call home in the Lone Star State, we determined the crime rates for 152 Texas communities with a population of 10,000 or more. To our surprise, forty-one of these cities and towns qualified as Safe Places —a much better record than you will find anywhere else in the Sunbelt, with the single exception of Mormon Utah. Unlike the Northeast, however, relatively few of these Safe Places are suburbs of the big cities; only in Houston was there any selection to speak of. As a result, we have four Safe Places for you in Houston, but only one each in Dallas, Fort Worth, and San Antonio. And for those of you who still prefer the wide open spaces, we have brought back two towns that appeared in the first *Safe Places*—a small town in the popular Texas Hill Country and a real cow town in the fabulous Big Bend country of West Texas.

TEXAS POPULATION MIX—AND CRIME

In the Miami area, a considerable portion of the crime problem exists because Jimmy Carter let Fidel Castro empty his jails and ship his criminals to Florida. In Los Angeles, for whatever reasons, Latino youth gangs seem to be a serious problem. Here in Texas, though, the Mexican or Spanish-language population is a bulwark of law and order.

At this point, you'll hear a lot of Anglo Texans choking and guffawing at our statement. But we'll let the figures speak for themselves. When you look at the crime figures for the seven largest cities in Texas, the correlation is direct and almost 100 percent consistent—the larger the Spanish percentage of the population, the lower the crime rate.

The opposite direction appears when we look at the percentage of the population that is black. Here, the correlation is not quite as exact, but the trend is nevertheless clear: the higher the black population, the more crime in the city.

Before you get out your old George Wallace campaign buttons, however, bear this in mind: In Texas, as in the country in general, most crime committed by blacks is directed toward other blacks. We saw an analysis of murders published by the Dallas Police Department, for example, and in 86.4 percent of the cases, the suspect and the victim belonged to the same race or the same ethnic group (Anglo/Spanish). As for the remainder of the cases, there was no statistically significant difference between the number of cases in which whites had been victimized by blacks, compared with blacks victimized by whites.

In short, law-abiding blacks (the overwhelming bulk of the black population) should be the strongest advocates of a strong anticrime program. They are the principal victims of crime and they have the most to gain from firm enforcement of the law.

TEXAS CITIES RANKED BY

CRIME RATE
PER 100,000
(LISTED LOW TO HIGH)

1. El Paso (6,366.4)
2. San Antonio (7,343.8)
3. Corpus Christi (8,402,1)
4. Austin (8,754.8)
5. Houston (8,886.3)
6. Dallas (11,777.5)
7. Fort Worth (12,671.7)

% OF POPULATION
THAT IS SPANISH
(LISTED HIGH TO LOW)

1. El Paso (62.5%)
2. San Antonio (53.7%)
3. Corpus Christi (46.6%)
4. Austin (18.7%)
5. Houston (17.6%)
6. Fort Worth (12.6%)
7. Dallas (12.3%)

% OF POPULATION
THAT IS BLACK
(LISTED LOW TO HIGH)

1. El Paso (3.2%)
2. Corpus Christi (5.1%)
3. San Antonio (7.3%)
4. Austin (12.2%)
5. Fort Worth (22.8%)
6. Houston (27.6%)
7. Dallas (29.4%)

HOUSTON AREA

People don't come to Houston for the climate or the scenery. They come to make money.

Some of them may still dream of becoming legendary Texas millionaires, but for most people the goal is more down-to-earth: to get a better job, in a progressive city that is unashamedly capitalistic, and to enjoy life with less hassle than they've had to put up with in their previous home. That dream has made

Houston the nation's fastest-growing big city—and now the fourth largest city—in the United States.

And it's all happened so fast! The cold statistics are impressive in their own way, but they can't convey the sense of wonderment and even bewilderment that comes with being a native of the city, as one of your authors is. When David was graduated from Spring Branch High School in 1955, Houston's population was under 400,000. Today there are more than 1,600,000 people within city limits and more than 3 million in the metropolitan area. With all the change that implies, a visit to his family is like taking a trip to a strange land. In terms of steel and concrete, at least, the city is not recognizable as the same one in which he was raised.

The one thing that hasn't changed, however, is also the underlying explanation for Houston's success at a time when countless other cities are stagnant or in decline. That not-so-secret weapon is Houston's boundless human energy and optimism, its "can do" attitude in overcoming any obstacles, its confidence in the future. And as we go to press in the middle of 1983, Houston needs to summon forth as much of that attitude as it can. Always able to ride out previous national recessions, this time Houston faces unprecedented (for it) double-digit unemployment. The reason, of course, is oil. As the world's oil capital, Houston is reeling under the impact of the industry's current "bust" phase. But despite the almost-gleeful comments from a number of Frostbelt politicians and editors, we have no doubt that Houston will survive the recession and surge on to new records of growth and prosperity.

It may even be a sounder growth in the future. As Houston Mayor Kathy Whitmire puts it, "I think you'll see Houston out actively competing with other cities to attract new business and industry and specifically to attract a more diversified business base. There hasn't been a need [in the past] to focus on attracting anyone. They've come on their own."

Even in bad times, mind you, Houston looks pretty good when compared with the rest of the nation. It has the highest median family income in Texas and its per capita income is way above the national average. The city has managed to maintain its enviable AAA bond rating and in 1983 it again promises to lead the nation in housing starts—as it has for the past nine years. In fact, to put the matter in perspective, we must realize that in 1982 Houston built more new houses than the sixteen major metropolitan areas of the Northeast *combined.* Ditto with the twenty-one North Central markets *combined!*

Not that the city doesn't have problems from that kind of growth—traffic, for example. Houston is big in population but it's absolutely huge in land area—larger than New York City and Chicago combined—and the only way to get around is on the freeways (unless you're rich enough to commute by helicopter). During our last visit, we were amazed at the amount of traffic at two-thirty in the afternoon—and were told that this is pretty much a day-long phenomenon. Still, there's nothing like the long memory of a "reformed Yankee" from New York (his description) to maintain perspective.

"Traffic isn't a major problem," says Barry Kaplan, a former University of Houston faculty member who is now a consultant. "Not when you can endure the traffic jams in the privacy of your family car equipped with stereo and air conditioning. Try riding the New York subway, where a jostling 13-mile trip can take 90 minutes."

Or, we could add (getting into the spirit of the thing), try taking *any* of the commuter trains from *any* of the suburbs into Manhattan. You'll freeze in the winter and be dehydrated in the summer and you'll count yourself lucky if a wheel doesn't fall off the train or a strike isn't called before you are due to return home. Yes, Kaplan has a point.

"I'm not trying to sound like a Pollyanna," he says. "We have problems. But I'd rather take our problems than Cleveland's or Newark's. No place is a utopia."

Despite the familiar stereotypes, Houston constantly surprises. This "conservative" city, for example, has a woman mayor, a black police chief, and the nation's largest Oriental community outside California. Actually, Houston *is* a pretty conservative city by most standards, but in making such a statement you have to take into account the ambiguity inherent in such political labels.

The most detailed look at the attitudes of Houstonians comes from the Houston Area Survey, headed by Rice University associate professor Stephen L. Klineberg. The *Houston Post* reported the results of its polls in 1982 and again in 1983.

"It's a very simplistic thing to say we're liberal or conservative," says Klineberg. "While the city is much more conservative than is the nation as a whole on matters affecting the pocketbook, it is more liberal on lifestyle issues.

"It appears to be a fairly limited kind of conservatism," Klineberg explains, "one that is expressed primarily in the deeply held belief that individuals can succeed through their own efforts."

Houstonians are more "conservative" than the nation on such matters as the work ethic, welfare, and foreign aid. At the same time, Houstonians are apparently more "liberal" than the nation when it comes to matters such as sex-education courses in the public schools, protection of the environment, the role of women in the work force or as homemakers, abortion, and the legal right of adults to go to a theater to see sexually explicit films. And, above all, Houstonians are technology-oriented. They overwhelmingly welcome the computer revolution and 74 percent agreed that "science will find a way of solving the problem of shortages of natural resources."

Interestingly, Houstonians in the survey became less Republican but more conservative under the impact of the recession. Asked their party preference, the answers in 1982 were 30 percent Republican, 30 percent Democratic, and 35 percent independent. In 1983 this had changed to 23 percent Republican, 34 percent Democratic, and 36 percent independent. Asked to describe themselves in terms of ideology, though, the number of liberals declined from 20 percent to 17 percent, the number of moderates stayed constant at 35 percent, and the number of conservatives increased from 38 percent to 42 percent.

"Houston really is representative of the nation," Klineberg concludes, "more so than New York, San Francisco, Los Angeles, or Chicago."

There remains the matter of crime. Houstonians are alarmed at the amount of crime in their city and rightfully so. Like the city's population and area, the crime rate is growing faster in Houston than almost anywhere else in the country. It may not be as bad yet as in a number of other cities (see Appendix I, Crime Rates—U.S. Cities with a Population Over 500,000, page 435), but Houstonians fear that they're rapidly catching up.

Part of the reason for the residents' concern is the city's past. "There is not a tradition of burglaries" in Houston, for example, explains Police Chief Lee P. Brown. "It's been a part of New York's existence for years, but people who live in Houston talk about the old days, this generation, when you could leave your doors open at night. Well, those days are gone. Houston's a big city and all the problems that go along with being a big city are here."

One consoling and refreshing fact for law-abiding citizens is that your right to defend yourself and your property are respected in Texas—and in Houston in particular. We've all heard the horror stories of citizens in other parts of the country who have shot an intruder, only to find themselves treated as criminals by "their" government. Not here.

On November 21, 1982, the New York *Times* reported that "last year, residents of this city [Houston] shot and killed 25 criminal suspects. So far this year they have fatally shot 17 other suspects. All the cases were termed justifiable homicides."

To put that in perspective, the number of defensive killings in Houston is as large as the number in New York and Los Angeles combined. Yet the population of New York and Los Angeles combined is more than six times the population of Houston. Texans obviously are a lot more determined to protect themselves and to keep the criminals from taking over—but they also know that down here a distinction is still made between assault with criminal intent and self-defense.

Under Texas law, people are allowed to use force or deadly force to protect both life and property if there is no other reasonable way to do so. And in Texas, your right to bear arms (Amendment II of the U.S. Constitution) is actually respected. If you move to Houston, call the office of District Attorney John B. Holmes and ask for a free copy of the handbook they distribute on Texas weapons and self-defense laws. Mr. Holmes says that to his knowledge, no Houston resident who shot a suspect in self-defense or in defense of property has been indicted in years.

The direction of growth for the most fashionable sections of Houston is to the west. Our Safe Place for that part of town is known as the Memorial Villages—in actuality, three small incorporated Safe Places with a joint police force.

If you want to avoid the traffic jams on the freeways, try West University Place. You'll find it amazingly convenient to downtown, Rice University, the museums and parks of the South Main area, the Texas Medical Center, and the Astrodome.

If you are employed by the NASA Space Center or work somewhere else on the south end of Houston or just want to have a head start in getting to the Gulf of Mexico, look into Friendswood.

And if you are employed in the industrial belt that follows the course of the Houston Ship Channel, your best bet is not Mickey Gilley's Pasadena but its neighbor to the east, Deer Park.

Between these four Safe Places, you should be able to find a gracious and hospitable community to call home in this fourth largest city in the United States.

MEMORIAL VILLAGES

POPULATION: 17,050
NO. OF CRIMES: 368
CRIME RATE: 2,158.4 per 100,000

One of the ironies of modern Texas living is that for all of that land in all directions, most suburban residents are confined to standard tract lots and most housing developments look like rows of middle-class sardines.

The reason why can be found in the boom phenomenon that has prevailed for decades. With thousands of new residents arriving each week, builders strain just to meet the demand. There is no need to supply extra land around the houses and thus cut back your income from a tract of land when anything with a single blade of grass will sell before the last brick is in place.

That's what makes the Memorial Villages so special. Throughout most of their area, the houses are custom built and sit on good-sized lots or even acreage. Extensive landscaping and a dense covering of tall pines, moss-draped oaks and willows, crape myrtle, and honeysuckle give the area a subtropical garden atmosphere that lends a touch of gracious Southern living to this corner of busy Houston.

Of course, it's going to cost you to enjoy this pastoral setting. Houses begin at about $200,000 and you have a much better chance of finding something if you have $400,000 to $600,000 to spend. Most of that represents the land that you're buying.

The three Memorial Villages are Hunters Creek, Piney Point, and Bunker Hill. While each is a separately incorporated village, they share a police force among them. They are known as the Memorial Villages because all three are

HOUSTON AREA Crime Chart

	Crime Rate	Murder	Rape	Robbery	Aggravated Assault	Burglary	Larceny —Theft	Motor Vehicle Theft
United States								
U.S. Total	5,899.9	10.2	36.4	243.5	290.6	1,668.2	3,156.3	494.6
U.S. Metropolitan Areas	6,757.6	11.5	43.4	319.0	328.3	1,911.8	3,534.9	608.8
U.S. Rural Areas	2,290.4	7.5	15.5	22.5	136.9	830.2	1,143.9	133.9
Regional Crime Centers								
Houston	8,886.3	39.1	88.8	670.8	176.0	3,042.6	3,131.5	1,737.4
Pasadena	6,987.6	8.0	82.2	181.4	405.8	1,980.6	3,463.4	866.1
South Houston	6,539.2	7.6	75.9	311.0	311.0	1,395.8	2,844.8	1,593.1
Safe Places								
Deer Park	1,436.8	4.4	4.4	48.8	31.0	674.1	416.9	257.2
Friendswood	2,710.5	0	0	18.7	112.2	1,093.6	1,271.1	215.0
The Memorial Villages*	2,158.4	11.7	5.9	29.3	35.2	1,143.7	868.0	64.5
West University Place	3,499.3	16.7	16.7	116.9	108.6	1,286.2	1,745.6	208.8

*Consists of the Villages of Bunker Hill, Hunters Creek, and Piney Point.

bisected by an east–west residential traffic artery, Memorial Drive. While it carries a good amount of traffic, Memorial Drive remains a countrified two-lane drive through miles of choice residential neighborhoods. With their money and their political clout, the residents of the Memorial Villages have been successful in keeping major highways out of their area.

The southern border of the villages is Buffalo Bayou, which flows lazily eastward to bisect Houston and eventually become the Houston Ship Channel. North of the villages is Interstate 10 (Katy Freeway), which runs in a straight east–west direction. A fourth enclave, Hedwig Village, is on the south side of the freeway, but it has a commercial district and maintains its own police force. Two other communities, Spring Valley Village and Hilshire Village, are north of the freeway and complete the collection of incorporated villages. They are pleasant neighborhoods, too, but clearly not as affluent as the villages south of Katy Freeway. A railroad runs alongside the freeway and this is one place where there truly is a "right" and a "wrong" side of the tracks in terms of prestige.

With their joint police force and their lack of commercial districts or major traffic routes, the Memorial Villages are able to maintain one of the best records for low crime in Harris County, which is mainly Houston. If you appear to be sizing up the area after dark and don't have a resident's sticker on your car, expect to have a patrolman stop you and ask to see your license.

In our comparison year of 1980, the Memorial Villages had 2 murders, 1 rape, 5 robberies, and 6 aggravated assaults. Property crime consisted of 195 burglaries, 148 larceny-thefts, and 11 motor vehicle thefts. This placed the villages below U.S. rural crime levels in four categories and slightly above rural levels in two—robbery and burglary. Because of the small population base, the 2 murders translated into a rate equal to the U.S. metropolitan rate for murder—but still less than one third of the murder rate in Houston that year.

The two murders were an unusual occurrence and there were none the following year and just 1 in 1982. In fact, the overall crime rate for the Memorial Villages decreased to 1,988.3 per 100,000 in 1981 and decreased again to 1,841.6 in '82. So the trend here is in the right direction—down.

The traditional enclave of wealth in Houston has been River Oaks, with its columned mansions of the city's cotton and oil barons—"old money" by Houston standards. As the city moved out in all directions, the fashionable area of growth continued to the west. A second "downtown" developed in the area around the intersection of Westheimer Road and the West Loop (Interstate 610). Here you'll find plush hotels like the Houston Oaks and the Galleria Plaza and the Galleria itself—the nation's first temperature-controlled, enclosed shopping mall, which was quickly copied around the country. The Tanglewood residential neighborhood in this area is a second prestigious address.

Still further west, yet just 8 miles from downtown Houston, are the Memorial Villages. They incorporated in the midfifties to escape annexation by Houston and since then Houston has spread like a prairie fire west as far as Katy, surrounding the villages completely. That makes the villages pretty centrally located today and in terms of median household income they rank as the poshest neighborhood in Harris County—even higher than River Oaks or Tanglewood. In all of Texas, in fact, the only community with a higher median household income was our Safe Place of Westover Hills in the Fort Worth area. Its figure was $75,000+ in 1980, while Piney Point was second with $67,120, followed by Hunters Creek ($63,678) and Bunker Hill ($62,495). Highland Park, the supposedly posh neighborhood of Dallas, lags way behind with a median household income of "just" $36,910.

Small wonder, then, that the Memorial Villages have their share of well-known residents, people like Vic Damone in Hunters Creek, basketball star Elvin Hayes in Piney Point, and Nancy Ames in Bunker Hill. Others who live in the villages include Gerald Hines, Houston's leading developer, Don Jordan, president of Houston Lighting and Power, and Bernard Weingarten, the Bayou City's grocery king.

In a 1983 profile of the Memorial Villages in *Texas,* the Sunday magazine of the Houston *Chronicle,* Ken Hammond wrote that "golfers tend to belong to the Houston Country Club or Lakeside Country Club, while tennis buffs try to get into the Houston Racquet Club on Memorial Drive. It's not easy. Membership is limited to 1,000 for the 41-court club. Despite initiation fees of $12,000, the waiting list is so lengthy, it sometimes takes two years to get in."

And then there's the houses. The Memorial Villages are three of the five communities in Texas where the median value of owner-occupied homes is over $200,000. (River Oaks and Tanglewood are part of Houston, and thus are not listed separately.) All types of architecture are available here, from French château-styled estates to striking contemporaries and renovated farmhouses. The differences among the three villages are subtle and based mostly on lot sizes. One subdivision of Bunker Hill has 10,000- and 11,500-square-foot lots, but most are village 1/2 acres of 20,000 square feet. Hunters Creek has a 1/2-acre minimum lot size and a 1-acre minimum is the rule in Piney Point, where residents seek to maintain a semirural, rather than suburban, ambience.

At the time of our visit (July 1982), we talked with Klaus Zimmern, president of A.-Klaus & Associates, a Century 21 affiliate on Memorial Drive. He told us that the starting price for a home in the Memorial Villages would be around $200,000. A lot alone, in fact, would cost that much now. Prices go up into the millions, but 2 million is usually tops.

A majority of the homes sold today, Mr. Zimmern told us, are in the $400,000 to $600,000 range. For $500,000, say, you could expect to get at least 4 or 5 bedrooms, 2 1/2 to 5 baths, formal living and dining rooms as well as a den and a game room, and at least a 2-car garage. Many of the houses will have maid's quarters and a pool. You can expect at least 4,000 to 5,000 square feet of living area and plenty of landscaping on the grounds.

With prices like that, it is hard for young families to move into the villages. Most of the ones with young children moved here some years ago, when prices may have been relatively high but not as astronomical as they are now. And, in fact, the school-age population of the villages is decreasing even as the overall population grows slowly.

Still, the unifying force for this part of Houston is the school system. The Memorial Villages are part of a larger part of northwest Houston known as the Spring Branch–Memorial area and its boundaries are roughly the boundaries of the Spring Branch Independent School District. Back in the fifties, when Houston was really beginning to expand, a deal was made whereby Spring Branch agreed not to incorporate, providing its school district remained independent of the Houston schools. Houston gobbled up everything else, but the six tiny villages obviously didn't go along with the deal. Today that Spring Branch–Memorial area has an estimated population of 270,000 and if it were its own city—as it could have been—it would be the sixth-largest in the state and rank fifty-seventh in the nation.

When David's family moved to Spring Branch, this was still "country," with farms and horses, rice fields west of Addicks dam, and all of the school system housed in a single building. Each of the students and their parents were welcomed personally by the superintendent, Dr. H. M. Landrum, who reigned in that post for thirty-five years. The only paved roads were the Hempstead and Katy highways, heading northwest and west from Houston.

Today Houston extends way beyond the old confines of Spring Branch and the school district has thirty-eight campuses and more than 32,000 students, making it one of the twelve largest in Texas. Throughout all this period of rapid growth, the Spring Branch Independent School District has remained the yardstick by which all other districts in the area are measured. Each year, it is one of the leading districts in the nation in the number of students designated as National Merit semifinalists and its students score exceptionally well on scholastic aptitude tests (SATs). In 1981, in fact, Spring Branch's students scored 446 on the verbal tests (22 points higher than the national mean score) and 499 on the mathematics tests (33 points higher than the national mean). More than 85 percent of the graduates of the six Spring Branch high schools continue on to college and a survey of the area's residents revealed that more than 88 percent had moved here at least partly because of the school district's reputation.

Spring Branch has never been satisfied with anything less than the best in physical plant facilities, either. In May 1981, voters overwhelmingly approved a $39.7 million bond issue to upgrade all of the already modern school facilities. The district has the state's first and largest instructional television program and the state's largest video cassette loan library. At each high school, students have access to more than 20,000 literary and resource volumes and more than 100 periodicals are kept on microfilm. An environmental science center has halls of zoology, earth science, oceanography, and mammals, all of them featuring natural specimens displayed in lifelike dioramas. An arboretum displays trees, shrubs, and other plant life native to Texas. An art center and museum houses a valuable collection of African, Asian, Pre-Columbian, and American artifacts and paintings. And the district's athletic facilities include a 15,000-seat football stadium with Astroturf playing surface, a 5,000-seat coliseum, and a natatorium.

The area's medical facilities are equally impressive. Four general hospitals—Spring Branch–Memorial (215 beds), Memorial City (500 beds), Sam Houston (208 beds), and Rosewood (200 beds)—offer some of the finest facilities in the area outside of the Texas Medical Center. In addition to twenty-four-hour emergency care at each of them, they offer many community outreach programs, including free hypertension clinics, Lamaze and childbirth education classes, and LPN and RN refresher courses. The Memorial City Radiation Therapy Center has high-energy X-ray capability and Spring Shadows Glen is a 136-bed comprehensive psychiatric hospital. Opening in 1983, too, was the Brennan Preventative Medicine Center, whose founder, Dr. R. O. Brennan, was also founder and chairman emeritus of the International Academy of Preventive Medicine.

Nor do the area's shopping facilities lag behind. We've already mentioned the trend-setting Galleria, which still draws many shoppers from this area. Now, however, residents of the Spring Branch–Memorial area have three major reasons to shop "at home"—Memorial Shopping City, Town and Country Village, and, just opened in 1983, the Town and Country Mall. This last one is a stunning $155 million complex with name department stores such as Neiman-Marcus and Joske's plus 155 specialty shops. The three-story climate-controlled mall features a "gothic-inspired" ceiling of translucent contemporary fabric stretched taut over the length of the facility and the goal, says the developer, is to create "a grand nineteenth century European arcade . . . a public meeting place, a great room of limitless dimensions."

Fine schools and houses have always been a tradition of the Memorial and Spring Branch area. Quality shopping facilities have been around for some time, too. The most drastic change of the past decade, however, has been the increase in business construction in this part of Houston. While the population increased by 55 percent between 1970 and 1980, the amount of office space increased by 965 percent and total employment in the area increased by 313 percent. Commuting to downtown Houston will soon be relegated to the history books if it hasn't been already.

So intense has the development been along the Katy Freeway that it is now known as the Energy Corridor. Among the oil companies that have moved their headquarters or divisions here are AMAX Petroleum, Ashand Oil, Exxon Chemical Americas, Gulf Oil Chemicals, Chevron Oil, Dow Chemical, Getty Oil, Natomas Oil, Shell Oil Company, Shell Research, Superior Oil, and Welex. Amoco Production Company, Arco Oil and Gas, and Conoco currently have buildings under construction.

With all this hustle and bustle going on everywhere, it's all the more important to know that you can live your home life in an atmosphere of peace and quiet. That is what the Memorial Villages offer. First-rate schools, offices, and shopping facilities are just minutes away, but within the tranquil confines of the Memorial Villages you can still relax to the music of crickets and the evening dance of the fireflies.

FRIENDSWOOD

POPULATION: 10,699
NO. OF CRIMES: 290
CRIME RATE: 2,710.5 per 100,000

Friendswood, the only permanent Quaker settlement in Texas, is today a pleasant suburb located 25 miles southeast of downtown Houston. A major stream, Clear Creek, and four tributaries—Magnolia, Mary's, Chigger, and Cowart creeks—assure a plentiful supply of woods throughout the area.

Frank Brown, the town's founder, was impressed by the virgin pines and rolling banks and called this area the promised land of his dreams. He named the city Friendswood from the Bible verse (John 15:14), "Ye are my friends if ye do whatever I command you." A replica of his home on Mary's Creek is now the Heritage Museum in Friendswood.

Friendswood remained a small Quaker community until the end of World War II. The area was noted for its fig and satsuma orchards and a fig canning plant was one of the town's major industries. Two of the largest oil fields in Texas, the Hastings Oil Field and the Friendswood Field, surrounded the town. Then, in the sixties, came the NASA Space Center in nearby Clear Creek, just 20 minutes away. Friendswood, now blossoming as a shaded suburban town, welcomed astronauts and space engineers as its new residents. Astronaut Deak

Slayton and Jack Lousma, commander of the Columbia 3 space shuttle, are among the spacemen who call Friendswood home while on terra firma.

Friendswood occupies the northwest tip of Galveston County, at its convergence with Harris and Brazoria counties. This southern location makes it a convenient commute not only to NASA's Space Center, but also to Pasadena, Pearland, and other communities east and south of Houston. For those who are interested in water sports, Galveston, Freeport, and the Gulf of Mexico are just short distances away, and Galveston Bay is even closer. Boating is popular along Clear Creek and downstream in Clear Lake.

Friendswood's public school system is generally considered the second best in this area, behind only Clear Lake. Its Pegasus Program offers individualized reading advancement and the Friendswood school system continues to be chosen as a statewide model for grades 4 and 5 individualized instruction. A large number of its graduates continue their education in college.

The Friendswood public school system consists of a primary school (K–2), an elementary school (3–5), a junior high (6–8), and a high school (9–12). A Lutheran school and a Montessori school are among the private educational facilities in town. In the area are two junior colleges—Alvin Junior College and San Jacinto College South—and the Clear Lake extension of the University of Houston.

Medical facilities include Clear Lake Hospital in adjacent Webster, several local clinics, a convalescent center, and ambulance service. In private practice locally are seven physicians and surgeons, twelve dentists, three chiropractors, an optometrist, an osteopath, and a psychotherapist.

In our comparison year of 1980, Friendswood had no murders or rapes, 2 robberies, and 12 aggravated assaults. Property crime consisted of 117 burglaries, 136 larceny-thefts, and 23 motor vehicle thefts. This placed Friendswood below U.S. rural levels of crime in all categories of violent crime and just above U.S. rural levels in the categories of property crime. The total number of crimes increased in 1981, then fell in 1982 below 1980 levels.

The lower-priced homes in Friendswood are mostly in the 50s. The average price range is from the 90s up to $450,000, with two or three over the $1 million mark. Homes are generally new to eighteen years old. Older than that and you have one of the historic Quaker homes.

Three major price groupings in town are from $50,000 to $70,000, from $90,000 to $140,000, and from $160,000 to $300,000. The lower range will get you a house with 1,550 to 1,700 square feet of living area. The middle range: 2,000 to 2,400 square feet. And the higher range: 2,600 to 3,200 square feet.

In the $50,000 to $70,000 range, you could get 3 or 4 bedrooms, 2 baths, living room, den, and a country kitchen (that is, a kitchen with an eat-in area). Some will have a formal dining room as well as the country kitchen, while others will have a dining area as an extension of a large den. You would get central heat and air-conditioning and an attic but no basement. In one area, the lots are

60 × 120, but now there are no lots less than 90 feet wide and many of these houses are on 1/2- or 1-acre lots.

In the $90,000 to $140,000 range, you would get 3 or 4 bedrooms (sometimes even 5) and either both a formal living room and dining room or a living area and a game room. You would have a 2- or 3-car garage, an indoor utility room, and a lot of at least 3/4 acre and perhaps 1 acre. Some homes in this price range have individual swimming pools; others have an area pool that services the local subdivision.

Most of these homes are ranches and in some subdivisions you can keep a horse. To get a wooded lot on a creek, you will pay from $25,000 to $60,000 just for the land.

Your total tax bill in Friendswood—county, city, school, drainage district, *everything*—will run about $700 to $800 a year for a house in the $50,000 to $60,000 range; about $1,400 to $1,600 for a $125,000 house; and approximately $4,000 for a house valued at $200,000.

One thing you do want to look into carefully is the water supply and drainage of your property. This is low-lying country, just above sea level, with a high water table. At the time of our visit, the town was constructing new bridges and taking steps to prevent flooding. There had been a flood in 1979, but that was a rather special situation. A hurricane decided to hover over the Friendswood area and the result was the largest rainfall ever recorded in the United States—43 inches in a twenty-four-hour period.

Barring another hurricane, this is a pleasant community that offers you more house and more land for your money than you will find in most areas of metropolitan Houston. Move here and both the attractions of the city and the delights of the ocean will be at your fingertips.

WEST UNIVERSITY PLACE

POPULATION: 11,973
NO. OF CRIMES: 419
CRIME RATE: 3,499.3 per 100,000

Long before the Spring Branch–Memorial Villages ever existed, there were the fashionable southwestern suburbs (and separately incorporated communities) of West University Place, Bellaire, and Southside Place. Not that long ago, they were the western fringes of development in the Houston area. Today they seem incredibly and conveniently close-in to downtown Houston.

West University Place was incorporated in 1925. It is the nearest to downtown Houston of the three adjacent incorporated communities. It is also right next door (by Houston and Texas standards) to some of the most notable Houston institutions.

The "university" in the town's name, for example, alludes to Rice University, generally considered to be the Southwest's most prestigious academic center. It maintains a low profile, but Rice is often listed as the nation's third-ranking engineering and science school, behind MIT and CIT. Its liberal arts college also enjoys an enviable reputation and it boasts the nation's first college of space science. The campus, profusely shaded by live oak trees, is a lovely Mediterranean adaptation of an Ivy League school, and the surrounding neighborhoods—including West University Place—continue the serene old-school atmosphere.

The eastern border of the campus is tree-shaded South Main and Houston's museum and park district. Here you will find the Warwick, Houston's gracious European-style hostelry, and the Museum of Fine Arts, Contemporary Arts Museum, Houston Museum of Natural Science, Burke Baker Planetarium, and Hermann Park. The park has facilities for horseback riding, golf, and tennis, a children's train, a fishing pond, an ancient Korean pavilion, extensive rose gardens, and the Houston zoo (where you can see, among other things, a vampire bat colony). Miller Outdoor Theater has free summer opera, ballet, symphony, and Broadway performances.

Also in the immediate area is the Texas Medical Center, which makes Houston one of the nation's foremost medical centers behind Boston and Rochester, Minnesota. There are more than two dozen separate facilities in the complex, including medical, dental, and nursing schools, a graduate school of biomedical sciences, nine hospitals, clinics, and medical research and rehabilitation institutions.

All of this is in your backyard, you might say, when you live in West University Place. The village itself is almost entirely residential, zoned for single family dwellings. Zoning also prohibits more than one family living on a single lot, operating a business in a residence, and occupancy of a residence by more than two persons not related by blood, adoption, or marriage.

The village maintains its own water and sewage disposal plants, and provides police, fire, and ambulance service. Recreational facilities include a community center, a municipally owned swimming pool (heated in the winter), and a number of parks, with facilities for racquetball, tennis, weightlifting, and games. A branch of the Harris County Library is located in town.

One of the outstanding aspects of West University Place is its vast array of services for senior citizens. At a White House Conference on Aging, the town's program was used as an example of a successful one that does not rely on federal funds but rather on volunteer community action. A brochure available at city hall lists the services, among them home health care, emergency care, the lending of hospital equipment, home calls by student nurses, and assistance in filing Medicare claims. Volunteers help with transportation, shopping and errands, light housekeeping, and minor home repairs. Daily telephone calls at a specified time can be arranged for friendship and security. Screening is provided for health-care sitters, maids, repairmen, and yard workers. University students and others will often provide assistance of various sorts in exchange for room and board. The Meals on Wheels program is active here and a variety of activities are conducted at the Community Center and at the Southwestern Senior Center.

West University Place has more crime than we usually feel comfortable with in a Safe Place, but it does qualify with an overall rate of less than 4,000 crimes per 100,000 population. You also have to take into account its centralized location. It has higher crime than our other Safe Places in the Houston area, all of which are located farther out, but it compares very well with Houston itself and with the overall crime rates for U.S. metropolitan areas.

To be certain, we checked the city's 1981 and 1982 crime rates just before press time. In 1981, the overall crime rate went right up to the 4,000 mark, but in 1982 it returned back down. Moreover, in our comparison year of 1980, West University Place had 2 murders and 2 rapes. In both succeeding years, there was just 1 murder and 1 rape, placing the community at rural levels for those crimes.

Upon request, the city's police will provide a security analysis of your home and fire department officials will provide a safety check. The police also offer a House Watch program when you are away from your home and participate in Operation ID.

Helen Gorman, of Abel Realty, told us of houses on the market ranging in price from $87,000 to more than $550,000. The prices get higher, she said, the farther east you go (toward Rice University and downtown Houston).

The choicest area in town, Helen told us, is the Pemberton subdivision between Kirby Drive and Wake Forest. The houses there cost between $350,000 and $550,000, depending on their size and on the extent of renovation. (These are older homes mainly, with nice touches such as hardwood floors, high ceilings, and molding.) You would get at least 3 bedrooms and 2 baths and up to 5 bedrooms and 3 baths. Most have had central heat and air-conditioning added and have a formal living room and dining room as well as a family room. They sit on lots that are 65 × 120 or larger, usually with plenty of large trees, and some have swimming pools.

At the low end of the price range, she had a 2-bedroom, 1-bath house on the west end of town listed at $87,000. It had a living room and dining room and the bedrooms were small. The lot size was 50 × 100. Helen estimated that you would have to spend another $20,000 to $30,000 on renovation. Another house —this one in the center of town with 3 bedrooms and 1 bath—had a modernized bath and kitchen as well as central heat and air and was listed for $89,900.

While West University Place is basically a community of detached single-family homes, the perimeter streets that mark its boundaries do have some high-quality town houses. In most of the developments on Bellaire Boulevard, a 2-bedroom, 2½-bath town house with brick exterior will cost $200,000. Some older units with stucco exteriors go for $150,000.

Taxes, with a homestead exemption, would run about $900 for a house valued at $150,000.

If you are working downtown or on the near west side of Houston, West University Place allows you easy access without the long traffic jams you face from farther out. All the educational, medical, cultural, and recreational facilities of the South Main area of Houston are available for your enjoyment, making this a pleasant way to enjoy Houston without the hassle of fighting the crowds.

DEER PARK

POPULATION: 22,550
NO. OF CRIMES: 324
CRIME RATE: 1,436.8 per 100,000

Houston likes to boast that it wasn't located on the ocean, so it brought the ocean to Houston. That's a reference to the Houston Ship Channel, which established Houston as a leading port and made the modern metropolis possible. Fifty miles long, 400 feet wide, and dredged to a depth of 40 feet, it is used by more than 5,000 oceangoing ships each year, transporting oil, grain, chemicals, and a multitude of cargo to and from all parts of the world. Because of it, Houston was able to surpass Galveston as an industrial port and today the Port of Houston ranks as the nation's largest port in foreign trade tonnage and its third-largest (after New York and New Orleans) in total tonnage.

The course of the Houston Ship Channel is Buffalo Bayou and from the turning basin in Houston to the point where the bayou empties into Galveston Bay, the channel is lined by one of the most impressive arrays of industrial might in America. Oil refineries, rubber and steel plants, grain elevators, loading docks, petrochemical complexes, paper mills, and much more light up the skies at night. Exxon's Baytown Refinery is the largest in the world.

These banks are also among the most historical spots in the state. At San Jacinto, the Texas army under General Sam Houston defeated a much larger Mexican army on April 21, 1836, effectively establishing the Republic of Texas. The site is marked by an impressive 570-foot-high limestone monument topped by a lone star, the state's symbol, with a museum in its base and elevator rides to an observation tower at the top.

Crossing the Houston Ship Channel just north of San Jacinto Battleground is the Lynchburg Ferry, in operation since 1824 and the oldest operating ferry in Texas. Also near the grounds is the battleship *Texas.* A veteran of both world wars, it was the flagship in the 1944 D-Day invasion commanded by Gen. Dwight D. Eisenhower, a native of Texas. It is the last survivor of the dreadnought class and is open today to tourists.

In addition to the industrial might and the historical sites, this is *Urban Cowboy* country. The movie was shot on location at Gilley's Club in Pasadena, next door to our Safe Place of Deer Park. With a capacity of 5,500, Gilley's was billed as the largest nightclub in the world, a title now claimed by Billy Bob's Texas in Fort Worth.

For all the industrial workers employed in the plants lining the ship channel, as well as their foremen and managers, Deer Park offers a haven from the crime that typifies the metropolitan area. It is located on the south side of the channel, bordered by Pasadena on the west and La Porte on the east. The city boundaries extend to the San Jacinto Monument and within the city limits are such industrial giants as the huge Shell Oil refinery, Rohm & Haas, Diamond Shamrock, Lubrizol, and Union Carbide. Such a wealth of industrial residents is an obvious plus to the city's tax base. The twenty major taxpayers account for more than 60 percent of the city's total assessed valuation. The Deer Park Independent School District has total assessed valuation in excess of $1.5 billion and carries a Moody's credit rating of Aa.

The residential neighborhoods of Deer Park house the families of workers in the many industrial facilities along the Houston Ship Channel and at the nearby Bayport industrial development. Laid out in tract form on the prairies, the older and less expensive neighborhoods are to the north, the newer and more affluent neighborhoods to the south.

In the older neighborhoods, you will find mostly 3-bedroom, 2-bath ranches that sell in the high 60s to the 80s. While many of these homes have formal dining rooms, they also generally have one living area. Central air and heat, wall-to-wall carpeting, and 2-car garages are the rule and the average lot size is around 65 × 120.

The newer homes start at $100,000 and range up to $200,000 in price. With 2,100 to 2,200 square feet of living area, they have 3 or 4 bedrooms and are mostly custom-built, so that they come in a variety of architectural styles.

Deer Park's school district consists of seven elementary schools, three junior highs, and one high school with two campuses. The new $7 million south campus follows a modern mall concept and has two gymnasiums, an indoor swimming pool, vocational shops, eight tennis courts, and a well-equipped library. A Baptist school is also located in town.

In terms of crime, Deer Park ranks as the second safest Texas community with a population of 10,000 or more, in our comparison year of 1980. Only the West Texas plains town of Andrews was safer among the 152 communities. This crime rate rose only slightly in 1981 and 1982.

In our comparison year of 1980, Deer Park had 1 murder, 1 rape, 11 robberies, and 7 aggravated assaults. Property crime consisted of 152 burglaries, 94 larceny-thefts, and 58 motor vehicle thefts. This placed the city below U.S. rural crime levels in all categories except robbery and motor vehicle theft and in those categories it remained way below U.S. metropolitan crime levels.

With its central location in the industrial belt, its fine schools and pleasant homes, Deer Park is a good place to raise families and to partake of the energy boom that has made this area so prosperous.

DALLAS/FORT WORTH METROPLEX

Dallas and Fort Worth have been rivals for so long that it seems a bit strange to have them cooperating closely, as they have been lately in boosting the combined metropolitan region as the Southwest Metroplex. Plenty of Texas-style ribbing still takes place between them, but it is all good-natured and focuses on the contrasting images the cities like to display. It's hard for any real antagonism or resentment to build when *both* cities are enjoying a trend of growth and prosperity that makes most parts of the nation envious.

In size, Dallas is clearly the larger of the two. City populations are roughly 1 million for Dallas, 400,000 for Fort Worth. Their respective metropolitan areas have populations of roughly 2 million and 1 million. The total area population of 3 million makes it slightly larger than even the Houston metropolitan area. Dallas is the nation's seventh-largest city and the Metroplex is the nation's eighth largest metropolitan area.

While the population of the Metroplex region grew by 25 percent during the decade of the seventies, that actually is less than the rate of growth of many other Sunbelt centers—Houston, for example, which gained 45 percent during the same period. Metroplex boosters see this as a plus and refer to their rate as one of "steady, absorbable population growth."

In terms of the mix of the region's economy, there seems to be widespread agreement that the Dallas/Fort Worth area has a healthier economic climate than Houston. The reason why can be given in one word: diversification. The dominance of the oil industry in Houston means that both its booms and its busts are exaggerated, depending on the current fortunes of the oil industry. Here, the pattern of economic growth is more even.

We don't mean to shatter any preconceptions formed by watching J. R. Ewing at work on TV's "Dallas." Oil *is* important here and has been the major contributor to the boom aspects of the seventies. But the largest proportion of employment is in the high tech area, with a fifth of the labor force involved in research and development, instruments and controls, consumer electronics, computers, aerospace, and robotics.

In fact, the Dallas/Fort Worth Metroplex has the nation's third highest concentration of headquarters of corporations with a million dollars or more in assets. Only New York and Chicago have more. The area also has the second largest concentration of life insurance company headquarters in the United States—about 260, all total. This is the leading banking and financial center of the South as well.

During the late seventies and early eighties, the Metroplex led the nation in growth of retail sales. It is also a major distribution hub for the nation, with a territory for the dispersal of goods and services that is second in population in the United States only to Chicago's. Playing a key part in its role as a market center is the world's largest single-site merchandise mart, the Dallas Market Center. This is the nation's largest gift and home furnishing market, the major U.S. fashion center outside New York City, and one of the world's largest international cotton markets. Dallas is also one of the three top convention and exposition centers in the country, with about 2,000 of them a year.

This is a pretty amazing record for two cities that are landlocked—no ocean, not even a navigable river. In years past, those were usually prerequisites for growth, but oil, cattle, agriculture, and an aggressive business community all overcame that geophysical handicap. Then, in the sixties, the leaders of Fort Worth and Dallas took stock of their opportunities. In earlier eras, all roads had led to Rome; then London had been built by the sailing ship, New York by steamships, and Chicago by railroads. No city, however, had yet reached greatness by aviation. These leaders determined that the Metroplex would use aviation as *its* tool and the result was the Dallas/Fort Worth (or DFW) Airport.

Located halfway between the two cities, DFW Airport is the nation's largest in size—roughly as big in land area as Manhattan. In less than ten years, it has become the nation's fifth-busiest airport in terms of passengers handled and ranks fourth in scheduled aircraft operations. Direct and nonstop service is available to over 190 destinations around the nation and the world. American Airlines makes its headquarters here and both American and Delta use DFW as a key hub.

Impressive as that is, the airport's potential has only been scratched. Just four of DFW's thirteen projected terminal buildings exist today and it is expected that the greatest growth will be in air cargo. Metroplex leaders say that the day will come when DFW handles more cargo than the nation's largest seaport and given their record of accomplishment, this is not a claim to be taken lightly.

While these are business-oriented cities, all is not work—even here. The Sunbelt lifestyle emphasizes outdoor activities and the Metroplex is no exception. Water sports are popular, with more than fifty-five lakes within a 100-mile radius. The Metroplex is known as the saddle horse capital of the nation, with more than 100 riding clubs, polo matches, the largest youth horse show in the nation, and one of the top three quarter horse shows in the world. Golfers have more than sixty courses to choose from, including famed Preston Trail Golf Club in Dallas and the Colonial Country Club in Fort Worth.

Spectator sports are followed passionately here, too. In addition to the Dallas Cowboys, there's the Texas Rangers in professional baseball and the NBA's Mavericks. The U.S. Open Golf Championship has been held in both cities, the PGA Championship has been held in Dallas twice, and annual tournaments in the area include the Byron Nelson Golf Classic, the Colonial National Invitational, and the Mary Kay Golf Classic. This is the site of the grand finale tournament of the pro tennis tour and headquarters for the World Championship Tennis tournament. Rodeos take place almost all year long and intercollegiate sports are provided by the Cotton Bowl New Year's classic, Southern Methodist University in Dallas, and Texas Christian University in Fort Worth.

With all this going for the Metroplex, it should come as no surprise to learn that some 350 companies move here each year. In a 1977 study, Atlanta was the preferred destination for corporations planning a move to the Sunbelt. A new study, in 1981, showed Dallas/Fort Worth in the lead.

This study, conducted by the Center for Policy Studies at the University of Texas at Dallas, asked company executives in the Northeast, Midwest, and California to rank six fast-growing Sunbelt areas with respect to overall business climates. The Dallas/Fort Worth area placed first, followed (in descending order) by North Carolina's Research Triangle, Atlanta, Denver, Houston, and the Silicon Valley area of California.

The Dallas/Fort Worth area was given particularly good marks in regard to housing costs, business costs, and quality of schools. The relatively low cost of living, indeed, has been confirmed by the Bureau of Labor Statistics Comparative Cost of Living Survey. Living at a higher budget level will cost you $30,771 in Dallas, the study found, and $41,306 in Boston, $34,198 in Chicago, $34,124 in Los Angeles, and $42,736 in New York.

On the other hand, the responding executives said, the Metroplex's chief drawbacks were its extreme summer heat, large-city problems such as traffic, distance from other major markets, and higher labor and business costs than elsewhere in the South. Having hit the Metroplex in the middle of the summer during our Safe Places trip, we certainly can attest to the validity of the first two reservations.

The corporations and the people still keep coming, some despite the heat, others because of it and their aversion to cold winters. And if you're one of those headed for the Metroplex, we have several choice landing spots to offer you.

DALLAS AREA

Dallas has always boosted itself as the cultural center of Texas, rather more Eastern and formal in its ways than the rest of the state. For our part, we've always found Houston to be a more exciting city to visit, but in all fairness we must point out that the Houston–Dallas rivalry is second in the state only to the University of Texas–Texas A&M competition and half of your writing team (David) was born and raised in Houston.

Two things we will concede to Dallas: It has great hotels and great restaurants. We've had occasion to visit the city several times in recent years when David's brother Danny was living there and were always pleased with our accommodations and our gastronomic excursions. On the Safe Places trip, we treated ourselves to the ultramodern Loew's Anatole Dallas, with its spectacular atrium lobby and banners, and to one of its resident restaurants, the Plum Blossom, which has left its mark on us as one of the finest Chinese restaurants between the two coasts.

The city's culinary distinctions extend to the cafeteria level. Granted, cafeterias are a specialty of the South and of Texas in particular. But with the Highland Park Cafeteria in the posh Dallas suburb, the cafeteria line becomes an art form—and an extremely popular one. We *never* go to Dallas without at least one to-hell-with-moderation lunch there and if we're driving we never leave town without an ice cooler full of as many Highland Park leftovers as we can pack in.

Given Dallas' popularity, we wanted to pick a number of suburbs for this book, just as we did in Houston. That was not to be. Dallas itself has one of the highest crime rates of any big city in the United States—in our comparison year of 1980, only Boston was worse off among cities with a population of 500,000 or more. This crime spree, moreover, extends to the suburbs. Most of them are nowhere as bad off as the city, but as our Dallas Area Crime Chart (page 363) shows, they tend to be much too high to qualify for this book.

We were particularly disappointed that we could not include two of the city's nicest suburbs. Highland Park enjoys a national reputation as the well-heeled home of the Dallas elite and it *is* one of the most pleasant suburbs we have seen around the country. But its crime rate consistently runs between 4,000 and 5,000 crimes per 100,000 population. University Park, Highland Park's neighbor and the home of Southern Methodist University, is less affluent but just as delightful a neighborhood. But it, too, had a crime rate of just over 4,000 at the time of our visit.

Then we started driving around to the suburbs that *did* qualify as Safe Places. They were all located farther out, where the prairies are being cut up into tract developments, and we were despondent by the time we ran through the first three. We couldn't imagine putting the book together without including a suburb of Dallas. Yet we also couldn't imagine directing a business executive who was being transferred here to one of these spots.

We won't make any friends in these communities by doing this, but to give you an idea of what we encountered, we're going to read directly from the notes we took as we investigated the Dallas area for you.

"Coppell—tract developments on the prairie and woods along Denton Creek. Miles of roads of developments being built along Sandy Lake Road. No town, no character, ugly power lines, and airport close by."

"Rowlett—a cut above Coppell, but not much. More country being cut into tract homes. One nice development is Toler Bay area."

"Wilmer—the *worst* dump. Small frame houses that are not kept up—junky cars in front, lawns unmowed, unpainted. A few equally run-down businesses."

That was where we stood as we drove on to our last potential Safe Place. We were *not* in a happy frame of mind. That last possibility, DeSoto, may not be our favorite community in this book, but after making that loop around Dallas —from Coppell in the northwest to Rowlett in the northeast and Wilmer in the southeast—it was almost like being let loose on Fifth Avenue.

A postscript about University Park. Before going to press, we were able to take a quick peek at the 1981 and 1982 crime statistics for Texas and we're keeping our fingers crossed. In 1980, University Park's crime rate had been 4,009.1—just above our cutoff point of 4,000 crimes per 100,000 population—and we were afraid that this would increase still more in future years. Well, it did jump up in 1981, to 4,265.5. But in 1982 it dropped to 3,603.6. That's a three-year average of 3,959.4 and just 3.2 percent higher than DeSoto's three-year average of 3,837.4. We had no way of foreseeing this at the time of our visit, of course, but we're going to keep an eye on University Park's future crime rates for further editions of this book. University Park is a settled and pleasant community, built around the attractive Georgian-style campus of Southern

Methodist University. *If* its crime rate remains low enough, it would be our suburb of choice in the Dallas metropolitan area.

DE SOTO

POPULATION: 15,566
NO. OF CRIMES: 548
CRIME RATE: 3,520.5 per 100,000

DeSoto boasts the second-highest per capita income of any community in Dallas County, but it bears little resemblance to front runner Highland Park. There is no display of affluence here. The town achieves its ranking because there are no pockets of poverty to drive down the per capita figures. DeSoto is middle-class through and through, strongly oriented toward family life, the churches, and the schools.

Downtown Dallas is a half hour to the north via Interstate 35, which forms the eastern border of DeSoto. About a quarter of DeSoto's workers commute to jobs downtown and the rest are employed locally or in other suburban locations. Just north of town is Interstate 20/635, which loops around Dallas and makes the entire Metroplex area readily accessible to residents of DeSoto.

DALLAS AREA Crime Chart

	Crime Rate	Murder	Rape	Robbery	Aggravated Assault	Burglary	Larceny —Theft	Motor Vehicle Theft
United States								
U.S. Total	5,899.9	10.2	36.4	243.5	290.6	1,668.2	3,156.3	494.6
U.S. Metropolitan Areas	6,757.6	11.5	43.4	319.0	328.3	1,911.8	3,534.9	608.8
U.S. Rural Areas	2,290.4	7.5	15.5	22.5	136.9	830.2	1,143.9	133.9
Regional Crime Centers								
Addison	12,119.6	0	18.0	54.0	342.2	2,827.3	7,779.6	1,098.5
Carrollton	8,615.5	7.4	40.9	74.3	204.4	2,683.5	5,129.2	475.7
Dallas	11,777.5	35.4	124.5	553.6	695.3	3,347.7	6,151.7	869.2
Farmers Branch	7,108.6	0	12.1	104.7	88.6	1,876.8	4,522.9	503.4
Grand Prairie	8,572.7	19.6	65.9	129.0	340.6	2,141.8	5,013.8	862.0
Irving	7,453.8	3.6	30.1	94.9	243.6	1,879.4	4,602.7	599.4
Safe Place								
DeSoto	3,520.5	0	0	38.5	45.0	1,092.1	2,139.3	205.6

With only a quarter of the town's 24 square miles developed and only two industrial parks located within the city limits, DeSoto is also making a bid for additional development. Outside of the school system and the city, the largest local employer at the present time is K-mart and small plants in town produce limousines, athletic uniforms, prefabricated modular buildings, sinks and tubs, and ceiling fans.

In addition to local stores and shops, DeSoto is just a few minutes away from Red Bird Mall, one of the largest shopping centers in the Dallas/Fort Worth Metroplex. Medical facilities include local doctors and dentists, two nursing homes, and two counseling centers. Surgical and emergency services are 6 minutes away at the new facilities of Charlton Methodist Hospital, with Midway Park General Hospital also now under construction near DeSoto's eastern boundary. City recreational facilities include two swimming pools, four parks, lighted tennis courts, eighteen ball fields, and a skating rink. More than seventy organizations are active in the community, providing a wide variety of activities and projects in which you can get involved.

DeSoto's public school system consists of a high school (grades 9–12), a junior high (7–8), an intermediate school (5–6), and three elementary schools (K–4). About 42 percent of the teaching staff have graduate degrees. DeSoto's students are very competitive, whether it's in regard to SAT scores, marching band competition, or the state championship baseball team. Since 1977, DeSoto's students have won more National DECA competitive events than students from any other high school in America. During that period, DeSoto has also had twelve state DECA winners.

In addition to the public schools, DeSoto has nine child care centers and private schools.

DeSoto is one of the few communities we have found around the country that make a point of their low crime rates in promotional literature. In our comparison year of 1980, there were no murders or rapes, 6 robberies, and 7 aggravated assaults. Property crime consisted of 170 burglaries, 333 larceny-thefts, and 32 motor vehicle thefts. This placed DeSoto below U.S. rural crime levels in three of the categories. In the other four categories, DeSoto ranked above U.S. rural rates but still far below U.S. metropolitan rates and especially far below Dallas crime rates.

Since we had access to 1981 and 1982 data just before press time, we checked the town's record for those two years. The year 1981 was a bad one, with the crime rate rising to 4,233.6 per 100,000, but it came back down to 3,758.2 in 1982. The three-year average for the crime rate was 3,837.4. That's not as good as we would like and doesn't compare well with our Safe Places in most other metropolitan areas, but it's about as good as you will find in the Dallas area.

DeSoto's residential subdivisions range from uninspired tract developments to rustic areas of custom-built homes on wooded lots. A number of creeks meander through the town and some of the choicest locations are naturally the ones with creek frontage.

At Harwell Realtors, the Century 21 affiliate in DeSoto, Sue Slonina told us that most houses are in the $75,000 to $85,000 range, with very few under $60,000. In this range, you could get an all-brick ranch with 3 bedrooms, 2 baths, central air and heat, a 2-car attached garage, and carpeting throughout the house. Most have an eat-in kitchen, a formal living room, a den, and a fireplace. Sometimes there is also a game room or formal dining room.

Older houses—those built, say, ten years ago—are more likely to have a formal living room and dining room, since those features were more popular then. Because of unstable soil conditions, you won't find basements and there are few 2-story houses. Lots average 90 × 120 in size.

A new 4-bedroom house, Sue told us, will sell in the $85,000 to $90,000 range. The two highest-priced developments are Mantlebrook and South Meadows and in Mantlebrook the price can go up to $210,000. These houses have features such as game rooms, wet bars, and swimming pools.

With its strong emphasis on schools and community activities, DeSoto is a good place to raise a family. And with its convenient location to freeways, all of the pleasures and opportunities of the Metroplex become readily accessible—when you want it.

FORT WORTH AREA

Amon Carter, Fort Worth's legendary newspaper publisher, coined the phrase describing Fort Worth as "where the West begins." The other side of the coin is that Dallas, 35 miles east, is where the East "peters out."

The description is so appropriate that it's hard to believe it originated so recently. The country west of Fort Worth *looks* western, compared to the greener and more agriculturally productive lands east and south of Dallas. Fort Worth was the last major stop in Texas for cowboys headed north on the Chisholm Trail and they made the most of the opportunity for a little fun to break up the long trail ride. Even today the city maintains a western informality that is in contrast with the more formal ways of Dallas.

The Fort Worth stockyards are still in use, though only about 250,000 cattle a year are sold there now, compared to several million annually in the twenties. The Cowtown Rodeo is a major stop on the rodeo circuit and Billy Bob's Texas is the largest honky-tonk in the world, featuring the biggest names in country music and crowds of 6,000 inside the joint. (It set Merle Haggard back a pretty penny when he ordered a round of drinks for everyone, on him.) We couldn't leave the city without paying a visit to Ryon's, one of its many western stores and sometimes called the L. L. Bean of cowboy gear. Festivals and annual events like the Chisholm Trail Round-Up keep the western spirit alive.

While Fort Worth loves to celebrate its laid-back western style and call itself Cowtown, it also has its modern and sophisticated aspects. The building boom downtown has placed Fort Worth among the top ten U.S. cities in new construction. Every four years, the Van Cliburn piano competition attracts pianists from all over the world. Aviation giants such as General Dynamics and Bell Helicopter, and computer-age giants such as the Tandy Corporation/Radio Shack, call it home. And the Fort Worth Water Garden, downtown, is a dazzling array of concrete-terraced water gardens designed by Philip Johnson and John Burgee.

Most of all, though, there are the museums. Fort Worth has one of the most

FORT WORTH AREA Crime Chart

	Crime Rate	Murder	Rape	Robbery	Aggravated Assault	Burglary	Larceny —Theft	Motor Vehicle Theft
United States								
U.S. Total	5,899.9	10.2	36.4	243.5	290.6	1,668.2	3,156.3	494.6
U.S. Metropolitan Areas	6,757.6	11.5	43.4	319.0	328.3	1,911.8	3,534.9	608.8
U.S. Rural Areas	2,290.4	7.5	15.5	22.5	136.9	830.2	1,143.9	133.9
Regional Crime Centers								
Arlington	7,035.7	4.3	44.7	121.6	329.4	1,570.0	4,486.6	539.1
Euless	7,003.8	8.3	20.8	108.4	166.8	1,550.8	4,556.6	592.0
Fort Worth	12,671.7	27.7	88.3	597.4	513.0	3,928.0	6,634.5	888.5
Hurst	7,698.2	9.5	6.4	133.5	162.2	1,351.4	5,644.1	391.1
Safe Place								
Westover Hills	3,097.3	0	0	147.5	147.5	590.0	2,064.9	147.5

impressive arrays of art museums in the nation. The Amon Carter Museum of Western Art is another Philip Johnson structure, housing a major portion of the works of Frederic Remington and Charles M. Russell, as well as selections by Winslow Homer, Georgia O'Keeffe, and others. The Kimbell Art Museum, the last building Louis Kahn designed before his death and considered by many to be his masterpiece, features eighteenth-century British portraits and late European Renaissance art. Goya, El Greco, Ribera, Murillo, Rubens, Van Dyck, Cuyp, Monet, and Cézanne are found in its collections. And the Fort Worth Art Museum is devoted to twentieth-century works by Picasso, Rothko, and others.

Some cow town!

WESTOVER HILLS

POPULATION: 678
NO. OF CRIMES: 21
CRIME RATE: 3,097.3 per 100,000

Westover Hills is the sort of exclusive haven you might expect to find in Houston or Dallas. Yet here it is in Fort Worth, boasting the highest median household income of any community in Texas. In 1980 that came to $75,000+, while Highland Park in Dallas had a median household income of "just" $36,910. Of course, the population here is fewer than 1,000, while Highland Park has nearly 9,000 residents and when you get that large you're bound to get some poor folks who'll drive your average down.

In Westover Hills, you don't have that worry. Your neighbors are the "old money" families of Fort Worth—the Carters, the Johnsons, the Basses (the City Center complex downtown was built by Bass Enterprises), the families that started the early department stores, the city's bank presidents. Westover Hills is so exclusive, in fact, that the rumor persists that "you have to be voted in" before you can move into town.

The setting is lovely. Westover Hills *is* hilly, at least by comparison with the flat plains everywhere else in this part of the country. The homes are impressive and come in a variety of architectural styles and with plenty of landscaped land about them. Interstate 30 is just a couple of blocks south of the community and offers quick access to the museum district and to downtown Fort Worth.

Small it may be, but Westover Hills was incorporated in 1937 and has its own police department, fire department, garbage collection, and other public works. When we talked to a police officer, he assured us that the force provides twenty-four-hour surveillance in the compact area, but that many residents also have their own private guards. It's that kind of place.

In our comparison year of 1980, Fort Worth's crime rate was even higher than Dallas' rate (see our Fort Worth Area Crime Chart, page 366). Westover Hills, on the other hand, had no murders or rapes, 1 robbery, and 1 aggravated assault. Property crime consisted of just 4 burglaries, 14 larceny-thefts, and 1 motor vehicle theft. This placed the community below U.S. rural crime levels in three of the categories, and just above it—but still below metropolitan levels—in the others. But 1980 was a bad year for Westover Hills. In 1981, the crime rate decreased to 2,654.9 crimes per 100,000 population and in 1982 it dropped still further to 1,769.9. In 1982 the only crimes were 3 burglaries, 7 larceny-thefts, and 2 motor vehicle thefts.

At Helen Painter & Co., realtors, Sales Manager Sylvia Ashley told us that you can't usually get into Westover Hills for a price under $500,000. In the newer section of town, prices supposedly start at $300,000, but try and find a listing in that range. In fact, multiple listings in any range are rare. Most Westover Hills residents sell their homes very quietly, through an exclusive listing with a discreet broker or by word of mouth in their circle of friends and business associates.

One house that had been listed at $750,000 was about to be sold, with the closing date approaching. This was an older (twenty-five to thirty years) French Provincial home on Westover Drive, one of the most prestigious addresses. The kitchen needed refurbishing, but otherwise the home was elegant. It had about 3,500 square feet of living area and was situated on a lot of about 3/4 acre, with a rear view of wooded fields.

The first floor of this château-style house had the formal living room and dining room, a large family room, and the eat-in kitchen area. Downstairs was a game room and 3-car garage. Upstairs, one wing had the servants' quarters and the other had 3 large bedrooms, each with its private bath. As Ms. Ashley said, however, no mere listing of the rooms could convey the elegance of the home.

In the newer area near the Shady Oaks Country Club, another house was listed at $575,000. This one was more of a sprawling Texas-style ranch, with 4 bedrooms and 3 baths.

For truly elegant living, Westover Hills is without a doubt *the* place to call your home in the Metroplex area.

SAN ANTONIO AREA

San Antonio is nearly everyone's favorite Texas city and we are no exceptions. Its attractive blend of the state's Spanish, Mexican, and Anglo-American influences makes San Antonio truly one of the distinctive and most charming cities of America.

San Antonio has one of the most beautiful downtowns anywhere, for in the midst of the skyscrapers meanders the Venice-canal-like San Antonio River, with foot trails, landscaped tropical foliage and flowering shrubs, restaurants and gift shops lining the banks for several miles. You can take a ride in one of the river taxis, or gondolas, enjoy a riverside art show, and watch a play at a theater where the stage lies opposite the river from the audience. During Fiesta San Antonio in April, there are glittering torchlit float parades down the river. Nearby La Villita is a re-created adobe Mexican village of a century ago, and the Spanish Governor's Palace and patio was the seat of government when Texas was a province of New Spain.

The Alamo, or Misión San Antonio de Valero, is famous as the Cradle of Texas Liberty—where William Travis, Jim Bowie, Davy Crockett, and other Texas heroes fought the Mexican army to their death. Misión San José, with its delicately carved rose window, is considered by many to be the most beautiful Spanish mission in the United States. Three other Spanish missions found in San Antonio are Misión Concepción (said to be the oldest unrestored church in the United States), Misión Espada (with the sole remaining Spanish aqueduct in the United States), and Misión San Juan Capistrano.

San Antonio has much more as well: America's second largest zoo at Brackenridge Park; two outstanding museums, McNay Art Institute and the San Antonio Museum of Art; the Hertzberg Circus Collection, the largest collection of circusiana in the world; the Institute of Texas Cultures, with its exhibits and programs relating to more than two dozen ethnic, racial, and cultural groups prominent in Texas history; the Buckhorn Saloon, sporting one of the world's finest animal horn collections; historic Menger Hotel, with the bar where Teddy Roosevelt is said to have assembled his Rough Riders; and the Retama Polo Center, host to the U.S. Polo Association's United States Open. And that's just a sampling.

San Antonio has long been the center of Tex-Mex cuisine, music, and culture. Now it's also the center of a growing spirit of political and economic cooperation between the Mexican and Anglo components of the Texas population. The Alamo city itself is almost evenly divided between the two population groups and with the election of Henry Cisneros, San Antonio became the first major city in the United States to have a Hispanic mayor. Cisneros is a strong advocate of free-enterprise economic growth and he is supported by groups such as the Mexican-American Unity Council. While MAUC started as a War on Poverty effort, its president, Juan Patlan, now sees private development as the best way to alleviate poverty. "I used to be a strong advocate of government just giving people whatever they needed," Patlan says. "But I know now that doesn't work. It creates dependence and destroys personal pride. Productive jobs are the only answer."

While the military remains the single most powerful element in the city's economy, it is not as dominant as in the past. But with five major installations, San Antonio remains the largest military complex in the United States outside Washington, D.C.

Tourism remains the second most important industry, as it has been for some time, and San Antonio hosts more than 600 conventions a year. Food products and health care are other important pillars of the economy. But the new kid in town is the electronics and high technology industry. *Dun's Review* recently named San Antonio one of the three cities in the United States at the forefront of high tech expansion.

Although it has grown to be the ninth largest city in the United States, San Antonio is particularly cognizant of the problems as well as the advantages of growth. It doesn't want or intend to lose the special qualities that make it unique among Texas cities. As Scott Bennett wrote in a recent portrait, "What Texans are witnessing in San Antonio likely is not the birth of a world-class city with accompanying problems like, say, New York, Los Angeles, or even Dallas or Houston, but, rather, the creation of a dynamic jewel of a city on a par with the likes of San Francisco, Boston, Seattle, or San Diego. Many believe these are the cities of the future. They're fast becoming the homes of America's postindustrial technological revolution—they are cities that work."

HOLLYWOOD PARK

POPULATION: 3,231
NO. OF CRIMES: 30
CRIME RATE: 928.5 per 100,000

When the first residents moved to the area that is now Hollywood Park, this must have been true country. Even today, it is at the edge of development on San Antonio's north side. Hollywood Park offers ready access to San Antonio along with rustic homesites shaded by live oaks, set in the Texas Hill Country.

The eastern boundary of the compact town is U.S. 281, San Pedro Avenue. This takes you north to the Hill Country towns of Blanco and Johnson City and south (in just a couple of miles) to San Antonio International Airport and Interstate 410, the loop around the city. Passing in an east–west direction just north of Hollywood Park is another loop road, Ll604. It offers quick, uncongested connections to the interstates that take you to Austin or El Paso.

Hollywood Park was incorporated in 1955 and is populated largely by a cross-section of professionals—lawyers, teachers, doctors, businessmen, and others. The city government provides the usual services of police and fire protection, paved streets and lighting, recreational services, and garbage and trash pickups.

But with virtually no businesses, it is hard to describe this as a small town. It's more like an incorporated extended subdivision, where the common concern is the protection of the homes and their value.

The Hollywood Park Homeowners Association is the major organization in town, along with the volunteer firemen. The firemen's ladies auxiliary, women's club, garden club, and bowling league are also active. Much of the social life takes place, too, around the recreation facilities—the city swimming pool and the tennis courts and picnic grounds at Voigt Recreation Center.

Ample shopping facilities are located south along San Pedro (U.S. 281). Just a few blocks south of Hollywood Park is Brook Hollow Shopping Center and at the intersection of San Pedro and Interstate 410 are two regional malls. Central Park Mall has about ninety shops, including Dillard's, Beall's, and Sears. North Star Mall has 145 stores, including Joske's, Foley's, and Frost.

In Bexar County (pronounced BÁ-yer, like the aspirin), the public schools are divided into fifteen districts. Hollywood Park is in the North East Independent School District (ISD) and its students go to Winston Churchill High School, Eisenhower Middle School, or Hidden Forest Elementary School. Hidden Forest is located just a short distance southwest of Hollywood Park's city limits and the other two schools are further south on Blanco Road.

As a general rule, the best school districts seem to be in the northeast quadrant of Bexar County—grading them by the percentage of students continuing on to college or the amount of expenditures per pupil. Only the military school districts of Fort Sam Houston and Randolph Field have more college-bound students than North East, and Alamo Heights also ranks at about the same level.

SAN ANTONIO AREA Crime Chart

	Crime Rate	Murder	Rape	Robbery	Aggravated Assault	Burglary	Larceny —Theft	Motor Vehicle Theft
United States								
U.S. Total	5,899.9	10.2	36.4	243.5	290.6	1,668.2	3,156.3	494.6
U.S. Metropolitan Areas	6,757.6	11.5	43.4	319.0	328.3	1,911.8	3,534.9	608.8
U.S. Rural Areas	2,290.4	7.5	15.5	22.5	136.9	830.2	1,143.9	133.9
Regional Crime Centers								
Balcones Heights	20,014.0	0	35.1	315.5	0	1,962.8	15,843.0	1,857.7
San Antonio	7,343.8	20.8	45.9	221.1	253.4	2,255.7	3,962.7	584.2
Safe Place								
Hollywood Park	928.5	0	0	31.0	0	247.6	588.1	61.9

Nearby colleges include Trinity University, south in the Brackenridge Park area, and the University of Texas at San Antonio, located due west along Loop 1604.

Medical facilities are extensive in San Antonio and a list of hospitals can be obtained from the North San Antonio Chamber of Commerce. Northeast Baptist Hospital and Park North General Hospital are located north of the interstate loop and the huge South Texas Medical Center is located in the northwest quadrant of the metropolitan area. In the immediate vicinity of Hollywood Park, however, is the San Pedro Minor Emergency Clinic, at 14327 San Pedro. It offers general medical care, prompt treatment for minor emergencies, health maintenance services, and follow-up care.

Churches in the area represent the Methodist, Catholic, Church of Christ, Baptist, Presbyterian, Lutheran, and Episcopal faiths.

At city hall, we had pleasant talks with Rosamund Adair, the city secretary, and Charlie Hoover, city treasurer. Mr. Hoover told us that Hollywood Park taxes are based on 100 percent evaluation, with updating every year or whenever a house is sold. The total tax you would have paid at the time of our visit (July 1982) would have been as follows, per $100 of evaluation:

$ .55	Hollywood Park
.92	North East Independent School District
.8466	Bexar County
$2.3166	

The Bexar County tax bill consists of these separate items:

.0716	Road and flood district
.02	Edwards Water
.05	Junior College
.390	Hospital
.31	County
.0050	Road District No. 4

The fire department, Mr. Hoover told us, consists of four paid members plus about thirty volunteers. The paid force operates between 7 A.M. and 6 P.M. and the volunteers take over at night and on weekends.

The police force consists of six full-time patrolmen, two investigators, a warrant officer, three relief or part-time officers, and a reserve force of eight. The police operate twenty-four hours a day, maintain high visibility, and patrol along irregular routes. Along with its few access roads, this gives Hollywood Park pretty intense coverage. The homeowners' association also organizes a crime watch program, with sector chiefs for ten separate districts in the small and compact city.

San Antonio itself has a much lower crime rate than Houston, Dallas, or Fort Worth, but it is still higher than the U.S. crime rate for metropolitan areas (see our San Antonio Area Crime Chart, page 370). Hollywood Park, in contrast, had a very low rate in our comparison year of 1980—just 928.5 crimes per 100,000 population.

That year there were no murders, rapes, or aggravated assaults, and just 1 robbery. Property crime consisted of 8 burglaries, 19 larceny-thefts, and 2 motor vehicle thefts. This placed Hollywood Park below U.S. rural crime levels in all categories except robbery, where the one incident and small population base resulted in a rate above rural levels but still way below metropolitan levels.

In 1981 and 1982 the crime rate increased to 1,733.2 and 1,826.1 per 100,000, respectively, but those figures are still quite low—especially for a Sunbelt metropolitan region.

For housing information, we talked with Lynn Hicks of the Deanie Owens Company, the Better Homes and Gardens affiliate in the area. Lynn told us that the range of housing in Hollywood Park extends from $90,000 to $250,000.

In the 90s, you would get one of the older ranch-style homes which were built in the fifties and early sixties. You would probably need to update the kitchen and bath areas and install new carpeting. In this price range you would probably get 3 bedrooms, 2 baths, formal living and dining rooms, and a 2-car garage, on a 1/2-acre lot. Most of the kitchens have a breakfast area and some of the houses have added on a family room over the years. All have central heat and the newer ones have central air.

The most expensive homes are along Canada Verde, which borders Canyon Creek Country Club. A house on this street had recently sold for $237,000. It had 4 bedrooms, 3 baths, central heat and air, formal living and dining rooms, family room, inside utility room, and a 2-car garage. The lot was between 1/2 and 1 acre in size and the house had close to 3,000 square feet of living area. In a house such as this, you also get all the new appliances and amenities that the older homes don't have.

San Antonio, with its colorful mix of cultures, steady sunshine, and low cost of living, is popular with retirees and young families alike. Hollywood Park offers you a way of enjoying easy access both to the city and to the abundant recreational pleasures of the surrounding Texas Hill Country.

TEXAS HILL COUNTRY

The countryside west of San Antonio and Austin is one of the most popular vacation and recreational areas of Texas. Known generally as the Texas Hill Country, it consists of charming, rolling countryside teeming with white-tailed deer and wild turkey, and blanketed with bluebonnets and Indian blankets in the spring. Cattle, sheep, and goat ranches alternate with orchards of peaches, apples, plums, and pears. The upland areas are wooded with cedar (juniper), mesquite, and about six different varieties of oak, including the prevalent live oak. In the lowlands are stands of elm, hackberry, cottonwood, sycamore, willow, and pecan trees. There are bubbling cascades on the rivers and streams, shady pools beneath towering cypress trees.

Water sports are popular especially in the chain of lakes formed along the Travis River west of Austin. Towns such as Wimberley, Bandera, and Kerrville are noted for their dude ranches and resorts, arts and crafts shops, youth camps, and retirement homes. Everywhere there are caverns to explore, old forts and Spanish missions to search for, and tales of lost silver mines and buried treasure to fuel the imagination.

This is exceptionally healthy country, designated by a Rockefeller Foundation survey as the healthiest section of the United States and highly recommended for people suffering from asthma, arthritis, heart trouble, sinus, and hay fever.

Job opportunities are limited by the rural and small town nature of the area, but with its healthy climate, multitude of recreational opportunities, and low cost of living, this area has to be one of the best-kept secrets among retirees. In this book, we are concentrating on Safe Places in the nation's major metropolitan areas, but we could not forget the Hill Country town that we first spotlighted in the original *Safe Places.*

FREDERICKSBURG

POPULATION: 6,412
NO. OF CRIMES: 119
CRIME RATE: 1,855.9 per 100,000

In the 1840s thousands of German refugees fled religious and political oppression in their fatherland and sought a new life in the United States. Many of them entered Texas through Galveston and the then-bustling port of Indianola, also known as Carlshaven. Fighting cholera, lack of food, poverty, and inadequate transportation, these immigrants nevertheless made the trek to central Texas, where a colonization grant had been obtained. So extreme were the dangers of the trip across the Atlantic and then through Texas that of 7,400 leaving Germany, only about 2,800 survived to 1847.

New Braunfels was founded by these Germans in 1845 and the following year Fredericksburg was established by some of the colony's members, under the auspices of the Society for the Protection of German Immigrants in Texas, or *Adelsverein.* Under the leadership of Baron Ottfried Hans von Meusebach, who took the name of John O. Meusebach when he settled in Fredericksburg, the settlers signed a treaty with the Comanche Indians—a significant breakthrough in peaceful relations with the Indians on the frontier.

Through the years, Fredericksburg has retained both its German and its pioneer atmosphere and customs. Music and dancing are ever-popular, with country singers like Johnny Duncan performing locally, *Sängerfeste,* or song festivals, and German bands offering an opportunity to dance to waltzes, schottisches, *Ländler,* and "Herr Schmidts." The German heritage is reflected in the *Schützenfeste,* or marksmen's tourneys, the *Oktoberfest,* the *Kinderfest,* and various other "fests" throughout the year. (Around here you don't jog in a marathon, you join the International Walkfest, and the Volkssportverein Friedrichsburg sponsors a Swimfest.) The western heritage is reflected in the rodeos, the Garretson Calf Prospect Show, the Gillespie County Fair (oldest in Texas), the horse shows, and the barbecue cookouts and chili cookoffs.

Sometimes the German and frontier heritages intermingle in a unique way. One example is that of the Easter fires. There is a possibility that a similar custom was observed in some parts of Germany, but it began in Fredericksburg when children would inquire about Indian smoke signals seen in the distance. Trying to calm their children, mothers would tell them that it was the Easter rabbit cooking eggs and preparing dyes in large caldrons with which to paint them. Today the children of the community reenact the scene with a floral ballet and pageant, a hundred of them in rabbit costumes portraying Indian life and dances, their human sacrifices, the signing of the peace treaty, and finally their conversion to Christianity.

TEXAS HILL COUNTRY Crime Chart

	Crime Rate	Murder	Rape	Robbery	Aggravated Assault	Burglary	Larceny —Theft	Motor Vehicle Theft
United States								
U.S. Total	5,899.9	10.2	36.4	243.5	290.6	1,668.2	3,156.3	494.6
U.S. Metropolitan Areas	6,757.6	11.5	43.4	319.0	328.3	1,911.8	3,534.9	608.8
U.S. Rural Areas	2,290.4	7.5	15.5	22.5	136.9	830.2	1,143.9	133.9
Regional Crime Center								
Austin	8,754.8	12.5	69.0	197.4	222.8	2,101.2	5,695.0	456.9
Safe Place								
Fredericksburg	1,855.9	0	0	15.6	46.8	421.1	1,294.4	78.0

Fredericksburg was exceptionally safe when we first included it in *Safe Places* and we were delighted to see that the town hasn't changed in the past decade. In our comparison year of 1980, there were no murders or rapes, 1 robbery, and 3 aggravated assaults. Property crime consisted of 27 burglaries, 83 larceny-thefts, and 5 motor vehicle thefts. This placed Fredericksburg below U.S. rural crime levels in all categories except larceny-theft, where it was just above rural levels. In 1981 the crime rate stayed about the same and in 1982 it dropped considerably from this already-low level.

Most of your day-to-day shopping needs can be met in town and in recent years Fredericksburg has also become a center for art, antique, gift, and specialty shops. With the completion of Interstate 10 (it comes within 22 miles of Fredericksburg), the shopping malls of San Antonio are a quick 70 miles to the southeast.

That same interstate can get you to the huge South Texas Medical Center in San Antonio, but Fredericksburg itself has a modern 61-bed hospital, four clinics, eleven physicians and surgeons, and eight dentists.

The public school system consists of three elementary schools, a junior high, and a high school. St. Mary's Elementary School, a Roman Catholic school, also provides instruction from kindergarten through grade 8.

Recreational facilities include nearby LBJ State Park and Lady Bird City

Park, three public swimming pools, a 9-hole golf course, and numerous tennis courts. An exceptionally wide variety of service clubs and other organizations are active in town and a profusion of annual events and festivals will keep you busy all year long.

Richard Sechrist and Ruth Welgehausen of Hahn Ranch Realty were most helpful in providing information about housing costs. Although you can sometimes find a small 1-bedroom house for as low as $25,000, they told us that most sales start at the $70,000 to $75,000 level. For that price, you would get a 3-bedroom, 2-bath ranch with a combination kitchen and dining area, a combination living room and den with fireplace, and a 2-car garage. It would be on a city lot (anywhere from 75 × 130 to 100 × 200) and taxes would run between $500 and $600.

You would pay between $150,000 and $200,000 for a custom house with 4 bedrooms, 2½ baths, all the built-ins, and a landscaped yard. They had such a house available for $189,000. It was a 2-story house and the 100 × 200 lot had creek frontage. Taxes were $1,186 a year.

Town homes (mostly with 3 bedrooms) are available for $100,000 to $135,000. Some are built on nearby hills with views overlooking the town and have swimming pool and tennis court facilities.

A 75 × 125 lot in the older part of town would cost you $6,000 to $8,000. A 100 × 125 lot in a nicely treed area of a new subdivision can run as high as $15,000.

We asked Mr. Sechrist about ranch property and he said that smaller parcels (under 100 acres) will usually cost between $1,800 and $4,000 an acre, depending on how close to town they are, and larger parcels (over 100 acres) will cost between $1,500 and $3,000 an acre. He had a 31-acre tract with road frontage and water available for $4,255 an acre. One ranch of 944 acres was available for $2,000 an acre. And another one with 161 acres had a nice house and a creek, and was selling for $759,000.

Fredericksburg has always been a friendly town and perhaps that is why, when you travel east from the center of town, the cross streets are Adams, Llano, Lincoln, Washington, Elk, Lee, Columbus, Olive, Mesquite, and Eagle. Combine the first letter of each name and it spells "All Welcome." Or, as you're more likely to hear it put around here, "*Willkommen!*" Traveling in another direction, the message is "Come Back." Many do.

TEXAS "WEST OF THE PECOS"

"West of the Pecos." To a Texan, the term signifies the westernmost protrusion of his vast state, the part that juts out because of the "big bend" made by the Rio Grande. And it signifies something more: the Old West, the last frontier, cowboy country, where bandit raids were common well into the twentieth century. A land still barely tamed, at least in its physical aspect, with plenty of wide-open spaces where the only sounds you'll hear will be the trot of your horse, the swift departure of a startled herd of antelope, the howl of the coyote at night.

The land is as rugged as you will find anywhere in the Southwest, a mingling of the southernmost extension of the Rockies with the Chihuahuan desert surroundings more common to Mexico than to the United States. Two legendary rivers mark its western and eastern boundaries: the Rio Grande and the Pecos. Irrigation dams along their lengths have reduced their flow to a trickle of their former capacity, but to the pioneers they were formidable obstacles to be reckoned with.

Spanish explorers were the first white men in the area—Cabeza de Vaca and his three companions in 1535, others following them. Apaches and Comanches swept through the region for decades, plundering cattle from the relatively settled areas of Chihuahua, Mexico. (It is estimated that they drove off over 10,000 head of livestock in 1846 alone.) In addition to the Comanche War Trail, trails of another sort were appearing west of the Pecos in the 1800s. The Chihuahua Trail connected Chihuahua with San Antonio and Indianola, then a bustling port on the Gulf of Mexico; first opened in 1839, by 1848 the trail carried considerably more traffic than the better-publicized Santa Fe Trail. The Overland Trail was also known as the Emigrant Trail and was a popular route for hordes of would-be millionaires during the Gold Rush days. Extending from San Antonio to San Diego, it skirted the south edge of the Davis Mountains in this region. And twice a week the stagecoaches came whipping through along the Butterfield Mail Route, opened in 1858.

After the Mexican War, the army established a series of posts in the country west of the Pecos, attempting to protect the few brave settlers and the travelers along the trails. These forts were located at springs not only to guarantee themselves a plentiful supply of water, but also to deny the Indians access to the little water available in this arid country. The Comanches were finally defeated in 1874–75 and the Mescalero Apaches, under Chief Victorio, were defeated in 1880. When Alsate, another Apache chief, died in the Chisos Mountains in 1882, Indian troubles here were over. But as cattlemen started moving their herds into the country and the railroads began transporting new settlers, rustlers and bandits took up where the Indians had left off. We were well into the twentieth century before the frontier west of the Pecos was actually tamed.

Big Bend National Park, located in this region, is one of our lesser-known but most striking national parks. The Rio Grande, which forms 107 miles of park boundary, has carved out the Santa Elena, Mariscal, and Boquillas canyons. The Chisos (Ghost) Mountains dominate the center of the park and you can camp outside or in lodgings at an elevation of 5,400 feet. Trail rides take you to spectacular vistas of the desert, plains, and distant mountain ranges in Mexico, thousands of feet below and miles beyond you.

The country north of Big Bend is dominated by the Davis Mountains, a rough country of deep canyons and springs. Mount Livermore has an elevation of 8,382 feet and east of it there is no higher point in the United States. The higher slopes of these mountains are wooded with pine, oak, and black cherry and roaming throughout are black- and white-tailed deer, bear, mountain lion, antelope, wolves, and coyotes. At the lower altitudes are cattle ranches, with a few apple orchards.

Between the Davis Mountains and Big Bend National Park is our Safe Place of Alpine, the seat of Brewster County, the largest county in Texas. The expanses surrounding Alpine in all directions are the wide-open spaces you've heard about in countless tales of the Old West. Just *how* wide-open they are can be illustrated with one set of statistics. In all of Brewster County outside of Alpine there are just 2,108 people. Yet this one county, alone, is larger in size than the combined states of Connecticut and Rhode Island! So if you really want to "get away from it all," read on!

ALPINE

POPULATION: 5,465
NO. OF CRIMES: 118
CRIME RATE: 2,159.2 per 100,000

Located in high desert-mountain country, at an elevation of 4,481 feet, Alpine has always been a cow town. It retains that cow town look today and its business life has always been dominated by ranchers.

As H. T. Fletcher wrote in the Diamond Jubilee edition of the *Alpine Avalanche* in 1962, "Among famous West Texas cowtowns were Abilene, San Angelo, Lubbock, Amarillo, Midland, Marfa, and Alpine. In most of them the farmer has taken the place of the cowboy and the jingle of spurs is seldom heard. The High Plains country is largely given over to farming, and in the Midland and San Angelo areas, the stockman is fighting a losing fight with the cotton farmer. But it is scarcely probable that farming will ever seriously threaten the supremacy of ranching in Brewster County or spoil Alpine's charm as a 'cowtown.' "

The ranches raise Highland Hereford cattle, sheep, and goats. It may not look as if there's much grass in the expanses around Alpine, but it is mostly grama—a highly nourishing grass and better than the water-filled grass along the coast. Ranches in the Big Bend country tend to be large, with an average size of nearly 19,000 acres, and income from hunting rights also adds to the economy. Hunters take mule deer, pronghorn antelope, and upland game birds.

Tourism has played an increasing role in the economy since the opening of Big Bend National Park in 1944. Alpine is one of the two main routes followed by tourists from the populated eastern portions of the state, en route to Big Bend country, the Davis Mountains area, Carlsbad Caverns, and the El Paso–Juarez area. Taking that into consideration, the number of tourist-related businesses seems to be minimal, with room for future expansion. There are six motels and a few places like the Apache Trading Post in town and five more lodges in the Big Bend area.

In town, Sul Ross State University is the main employer and, with its 1,500 students, a major business market. The city and school system, the telephone company, and various state offices also are major local employers. Otherwise, employment opportunities are limited, with just a few small local industries, such as Alpine Barite (drilling mud), Big Bend Coca Cola, Woodward Ranch (jewelry), and Baily Fluorspar (fluorspar ores).

Alpine's mountain-type climate is a delight, especially to persons fleeing the hot and humid lowlands farther east in Texas. The low relative humidity (averaging about 50 percent annually), high elevation (4,433 feet), and abundance of sunshine (averaging about 75 percent of the total possible) are a winning combination. Alpine is protected from the worst northers—the cold air masses that move southward across the plains in winter. The ones that do come bring rapid drops in daytime temperatures from late fall to early spring, but these cold spells are of relatively short duration, rarely lasting more than thirty-six to forty-eight hours.

In January the mean daily temperatures range from a minimum of 33.7 degrees to a maximum of 58.2 degrees. The corresponding figures in July are 65.2 degrees and 89.2 degrees. Snow falls occasionally during the winter months, but usually it is light and remains on the ground just a short time. On average, there are just about sixty-three days a year when the temperature goes below 32 degrees and just two times a year when it stays below freezing all day long. The growing season averages 223 days and the usual frost-free period lasts from the very end of March to the beginning of November.

Shopping facilities are available in town for most daily needs, but for your specialized needs you must go to the Midland-Odessa area (about 150 miles) or to El Paso (220 miles, 120 of them by interstate). Schools consist of an elementary school, a junior high, and a high school, and a small Catholic elementary school is also located in town. Medical facilities consist of a 52-bed hospital, four clinics, a rest home, nine physicians, and two dentists. Ambulance service is available. Communications include cable TV, a radio station, and a local weekly newspaper. Alpine has Amtrak railroad passenger service and eight stops a day by Trailways. The municipal airport has a lighted 6,000-foot hard-surface runway, but the nearest scheduled passenger connections are at Midland-Odessa and El Paso.

Recreational facilities in town include two public parks, two public and six private swimming pools, a 9-hole golf course, a movie theater, and fourteen tennis courts (six lighted). There are also lighted football and baseball fields, a community center, an outdoor theater, a senior citizens center, a gun club (rifle, pistol, trap), and the activities at the university. The chamber of commerce lists artists, craftsmen, and galleries in a brochure, *The Arts in Alpine.*

Particularly popular in this cow town is the rodeo. It should be, for the National Intercollegiate Rodeo Association was originally formed in the halls of Sul Ross and the Sul Ross rodeo teams have brought home over 100 trophies.

The university can claim as alumni such all-time greats as Harley May, past president of the Rodeo Cowboy's Association and a World Champion Cowboy.

The crime rate is low in Alpine and lower still in surrounding Brewster County. In our comparison year of 1980, Alpine (including Sul Ross) had 1

WEST TEXAS Crime Chart

	Crime Rate	Murder	Rape	Robbery	Aggravated Assault	Burglary	Larceny —Theft	Motor Vehicle Theft
United States								
U.S. Total	5,899.9	10.2	36.4	243.5	290.6	1,668.2	3,156.3	494.6
U.S. Metropolitan Areas	6,757.6	11.5	43.4	319.0	328.3	1,911.8	3,534.9	608.8
U.S. Rural Areas	2,290.4	7.5	15.5	22.5	136.9	830.2	1,143.9	133.9
Regional Crime Center								
El Paso	6,366.4	12.7	51.3	194.8	402.5	1,474.2	3,675.2	555.8
Safe Places								
Alpine	2,159.2	*18.3	*18.3	0	109.8	914.9	1,024.7	73.2
Brewster County	948.8	0	0	47.4*	94.9	94.9	664.1	47.4

*Statistical distortion resulting from 1 incident in a small population base.

murder, 1 rape, no robberies, and 6 aggravated assaults. Property crime consisted of 50 burglaries, 56 larceny-thefts, and 4 motor vehicle thefts. This placed Alpine below U.S. rural crime levels in most categories and just above rural levels in burglary.

Alpine police have a five-man force and three radio-equipped cars. The county has thirty-six peace officers, twenty-five radio-equipped cars, and two radio-equipped airplanes. While they have a lot of territory to cover, that comes to an extremely high ratio of one peace officer per 185 residents.

Richard D. Allen, of Allen Realty, told us that most housing starts in the 40s. When you find something lower, at say $30,000, it is an older 2-bedroom, 1-bath house that needs a lot of work. He had two such houses in the past few months and both were sold within a week of their listing.

Most 2-bedroom, 1-bath houses that are not as tightly cramped will sell in the 40s. A 3-bedroom, 2-bath house would likely sell somewhere between $45,000 and the upper 50s.

Mr. Allen told us that there is a builder in town who is constructing *new* houses at $30 a square foot. One house had just been completed on a 58 × 138 lot. It had 3 bedrooms, 1 bath, and a 1-car garage. The bedrooms were small, but it was very well insulated and the house was a good value at $36,500.

Larger houses—not new—also average $30 a square foot. One with 2,000 square feet would therefore cost around $60,000. One or two houses were available for around $70,000, but most seemed to be in the 50s and 60s.

Mr. Allen told us about a subdivision located in the hills about 5 to 8 miles northwest of Alpine. Sunny Glen Estates has beautiful houses, some of adobe construction, others in contemporary cedar styles. These are located on a minimum of 5 acres. While a few parcels are still available for under $2,000 an acre, most run $2,550 to $3,850 an acre. Perhaps 75 percent of the tracts have been sold, but not all of them have been built on yet. Some owners are waiting to retire there or for mortgage rates to come down.

The average lot size in Alpine is around 70 × 138, with a price range of $3,500 to $7,500. In one high area near the university, with plenty of trees, a 140 × 140 lot sold for around $15,000. Outside city limits, with no city water or sewage, you can get a 1-acre lot for $5,500, and 7-acre tracts for $2,000 to $2,500 an acre.

We asked about ranch property and Mr. Allen said that very little ranch property comes on the market. He had several sections available within 12 miles of town at about $500 an acre (a section is 640 acres), but it's rare to have a ranch of 5,000+ acres come on the market. One popular area for smaller parcels, at $100 to $500 an acre, is in the Terlingua area west of Big Bend.

As you explore this land west of the Pecos, taking in its sights, you'll notice some peculiar customs. As you meet cars passing in the opposite direction, the driver of that other car will probably give you a friendly wave even if he doesn't know you (and he probably won't). Overtake an automobile or pickup going the same direction as you and he's likely to drive onto the shoulder of the highway, just to give you better clearance for passing. Meet someone on the sidewalk of one of the towns and a "howdy," with a tip of the hat, will greet you.

Such respect and friendliness is contagious and you'll find yourself responding the same way. Indeed, folks here are about the friendliest and most courteous we have run into anywhere and we hope there never is a large enough influx of population to change that way of life. It's rather nice the way it is.

Where to get further information:

State

State Department of Highways, Travel and Information Division, P.O. Box 5064, Austin, TX 78763.

Taxpayers' Rights, Remedies, Responsibilities! is a guide to the property tax system in Texas. From: State Property Tax Board, P.O. Box 15900, Austin, TX 78761.

Regional

Houston Area: Greater Houston Convention and Visitors Council, 1522 Main Street, Houston, TX 77002. Houston Chamber of Commerce, Attention: Publications, 1100 Milam Building, 25th Floor, Houston, TX 77002, has a *Newcomer's Packet* available for $11.

Dallas/Fort Worth Metroplex: The best source of business information on the Dallas/Fort Worth area is the North Texas Commission, Administration Building, Box 61246, Dallas/Fort Worth Airport, TX 75261.

Dallas Chamber of Commerce, 1507 Pacific Avenue, Dallas, TX 75201; ask for a list of their publications or send $5.00 for their *Newcomer's Packet.*

Fort Worth Chamber of Commerce, 700 Throckmorton Street, Fort Worth, TX 76102.

San Antonio Area: San Antonio Convention and Visitors Bureau, P.O. Box 2277, San Antonio, TX 78298. Greater San Antonio Area Chamber of Commerce, P.O. Box 1628, San Antonio, TX 78296. North San Antonio Chamber of Commerce, 7400 Blanco No. 130, San Antonio, TX 78216.

Local

Memorial Villages: Spring Branch–Memorial Chamber of Commerce, 9235 Katy Freeway, Suite 102, Houston, TX 77024. For the *Spring Branch Schools Prospectus and Map:* Spring Branch Independent School District, 955 Campbell Road, Houston, TX 77024.

Friendswood: Friendswood Chamber of Commerce, P.O. Box 11, Friendswood, TX 77546. Office of Public Information, Friendswood Independent School District, 302 Laurel, Friendswood, TX 77546. Friendswood City Hall, 109 Willowick, Friendswood, TX 77546.

West University Place: City of West University Place, 3800 University Boulevard, Houston, TX 77005. Senior Services of West University Place, 6104 Auden, Houston, TX 77005.

Deer Park: Deer Park Chamber of Commerce, 1605 Center Street, P.O. Box 153, Deer Park, TX 77536.

DeSoto: DeSoto Chamber of Commerce, P.O. Box 100, DeSoto, TX 75115. *Direct Line* is an informative newsletter published quarterly by the DeSoto Independent School District, 200 E. Belt Line Road, DeSoto, TX 75115.

Hollywood Park: Town of Hollywood Park, 2 Mecca Drive at San Pedro, San Antonio, TX 78232. North East Independent School District, 10333 Broadway, San Antonio, TX 78217.

Fredericksburg: Fredericksburg Chamber of Commerce, 112 W. Main, P.O. Box 506, Fredericksburg, TX 78624.

Alpine: Alpine Chamber of Commerce, 106 N. 3rd Street, P.O. Box 209, Alpine, TX 79830.

Utah

Utah is the Western state with a difference, and the difference is the Mormon Church—the Church of Jesus Christ of Latter-Day Saints (LDS).

Seeking a safe haven from persecution, Brigham Young brought his followers to the Utah wilderness and founded Salt Lake City in 1847. Before his death thirty years later, he directed the founding of over 350 Mormon communities in the West, but Salt Lake City always remained the church's religious and cultural capital. About two thirds of Utah's population today are Mormons; all others are referred to here as gentiles.

Agriculture, the original industry, is still important to the state's economy but has been eclipsed by the growth of manufacturing. Present-day Utah has some 1,800 manufacturing firms and among them are giants such as U.S. Steel, Kennecott Copper, Elmco, Thiokol Chemical, Hercules, Boeing, California Oil, Litton, and Sperry Rand. Major industries include the smelting and refining of nonferrous metals, missile production, petroleum refining, steel and pipe making, machinery, printing and publishing, the fabrication of metal products, and food processing and products.

Mining has been a bulwark of the economy since the 1860s. In order of their value, Utah's most important minerals today are petroleum, copper, coal, gold, natural gas, sand and gravel, silver, zinc, salt, stone, lime, and lead. Indeed, all useful minerals, with the single exception of tin, are found in the state.

Utah's topography is tremendously varied and likewise the climate. In just 12 miles, from the north end of Utah Lake to the high Wasatch Mountains southeast of Salt Lake City, the average annual rainfall increases from less than 11 inches to nearly 60 inches. Small wonder, then, that the state boasts over 700 species of wildlife and 3,000 species of plants.

About half of Utah is part of the Colorado Plateau. Extremely rugged, this is the area renowned for its brilliant coloring and fantastic assortment of rock formations, carved into limestone and sandstone. Many of these areas are preserved as national and state parks and monuments. The average elevation in this region is 5,000 to 6,000 feet, with valleys and peaks ranging from 3,000 to

13,000 feet. Our Safe Place of Cedar City is located in this region in the southwest corner of Utah.

Another third of the state consists of the area known as the Great Basin. Here you'll find landlocked Great Salt Lake, the bulk of the state's agricultural production and manufacturing, and 75 percent of the state's population. They are concentrated along the eastern border of the Great Basin, which is also the western base of the towering Wasatch Mountains. Our Safe Place of Provo is located here.

The remainder of the state is the Rocky Mountain region—the north–south Wasatch Mountains range and east–west Uinta Mountains range. The Wasatch is one of the most rugged mountain ranges in America, provides most of the water used in the state, and divides Utah into an arid eastern zone and an arid western zone. Our Safe Place of Logan is found in the very northern part of the state, at the base of the mountains.

With such a wide assortment of topography and climates, Utah is an outdoors paradise. In addition to five national parks, it boasts eight national forests, seven national monuments, two national recreation areas, one national historic site, forty-three state parks, and more than 450 improved campgrounds.

How does Utah's unique religious orientation affect the subject of this book—crime and safety? Since Mormons are a very traditional people and adhere to a strict moral code, we would expect to find a better climate for law and order here. At the same time, it *is* a rambunctious Western state, in the midst of a part of the country noted for its exceptionally high levels of crime. Which influence would predominate?

UTAH Crime Chart

	Crime Rate	Murder	Rape	Robbery	Aggravated Assault	Burglary	Larceny —Theft	Motor Vehicle Theft
United States								
U.S. Total	5,899.9	10.2	36.4	243.5	290.6	1,668.2	3,156.3	494.6
U.S. Metropolitan Areas	6,757.6	11.5	43.4	319.0	328.3	1,911.8	3,534.9	608.8
U.S. Rural Areas	2,290.4	7.5	15.5	22.5	136.9	830.2	1,143.9	133.9
Regional Crime Centers								
Midvale	11,132.8	0	0	166.0	517.6	2,392.6	7,382.8	673.8
Murray	10,785.7	0	23.6	133.8	141.7	1,909.1	7,971.2	606.2
Ogden	11,129.0	9.3	77.6	172.2	423.6	2,256.2	7,460.7	729.3
Salt Lake City	11,710.3	9.8	85.9	324.0	274.9	3,174.5	7,017.2	824.0
South Salt Lake	19,500.3	9.5	133.5	400.5	238.4	4,910.8	12,138.8	1,668.7
Safe Places								
Cedar City	3,258.5	7.1	21.4	7.1	114.3	535.9	2,401.0	171.5
Logan	2,884.2	0	0	7.4	167.5	372.1	2,232.9	104.2
Provo	3,567.2	0	2.7	23.0	86.5	591.8	2,648.4	214.8

When we checked the statistics, neither side had won a clear victory. But that, in itself, makes Utah unique in comparison with other Western states like Arizona, Nevada, Oregon, and Washington, where the criminals have won a clear-cut victory. Of the twenty-one communities in Utah with a population of 10,000 or more, eight qualified as Safe Places, thirteen did not. That's the highest proportion of Safe Places you will find in the West.

But when they're bad out here, they're *real* bad. As our Utah Crime Chart (page 383) reveals, five Utah cities—including the Mormon and state capital of Salt Lake City—have crime rates higher than you'll find in New York City or Washington, D.C. South Salt Lake's crime rate is nearly *double* the rate of those two Eastern cities! So you can't take your personal safety for granted and the importance of our Safe Places should not be minimized even here in the Mormons' land of milk and honey.

CEDAR CITY

POPULATION: 13,994
NO. OF CRIMES: 456
CRIME RATE: 3,258.5 per 100,000

Cedar City is a remarkable town for its size. Set in the midst of spectacular scenery, it hosts an internationally renowned Shakespearean festival each year—so good it was filmed by the British Broadcasting Corporation (BBC) in 1981. Publications as varied as *Esquire, Mountainwest Magazine,* and *Small Town U.S.A.* have featured it, with *Mountainwest* picking it as one of eight Western communities that are "a good place to live and raise children."

Like most Utah towns, Cedar City is clean and well-maintained. It straddles Interstate 15, with Las Vegas 175 miles to the southwest and Salt Lake City 265 miles north. Mountains tower over it to the east and desert views dominate the landscape to the west.

Retirees who like four seasons, meaning snow in the winter, like Cedar City. Those who want to get away completely from snow head instead for St. George, 44 miles down the Interstate and 2,600 feet lower in elevation. The altitude here is 5,500 feet, and temperatures range from an average of 32 degrees in the winter to 70 degrees in the summer. Nights are almost always cool, even in the summer.

Cedar City is a hub for a number of government agencies, including the Federal Aviation Agency, U.S. Forest Service, and Bureau of Land Management. Some manufacturing plants are also located here. Cullman Products manufactures all of its sleeping bags here and Hallmark Cards' Cedar Products manufactures the racks for their cards here. The town is actively seeking additional industry and points to its location on the Interstate route between Southern California and Denver, its airport, equipped to handle commercial and business jets, and its location on the main line of the Union Pacific Railroad between Salt Lake City and Los Angeles.

While the nearest bright lights of a big city are those in Las Vegas, 175 miles away, that doesn't mean you are isolated if you live here. Residents enjoy the rugged, remote setting even as they keep in touch with the rest of the world through four Salt Lake City television stations, cable TV, four commercial radio stations, a regional daily newspaper, two statewide daily newspapers, and a weekly county newspaper.

Medical facilities include the services of more than twenty-five physicians, mostly specialists, and the 73-bed Valley View Medical Center. Schools consist of a high school (9–12), middle school (6–8), and four elementary schools. Southern Utah State College is a four-year liberal arts college which dates back to 1897, located on a beautiful 80-acre campus. With an enrollment of about 2,000, it offers bachelor degrees in thirty-one major fields of study, plus preprofessional and vocational/technical training in a number of areas. Churches include the Mormons, who have twenty-six Wards in four Stakes of the church here, plus congregations of the Baptist, Presbyterian, Church of Christ, Catholic, Assembly of God, Lutheran, Jehovah's Witnesses, and Episcopal churches.

Without a doubt, the town's most famous activity each year is its Utah Shakespearean Festival, which completed its twenty-first season in 1982. Three of the Bard's works are presented during each seven-week season, which begins in mid-July. The program for the 1983 season consisted of *The Two Gentlemen of Verona, The Merchant of Venice,* and *Henry V.*

Performances take place in an authentically styled theater on the college campus. It retains as much Tudor styling as possible while maintaining convenience and comfort for a modern audience and no seat in the theater is more than nine rows from the stage. Plans for the festival's third decade include an entire village of Tudor shops that will be open all year.

Each night's performance is just the main attraction. There are also literary and production seminars, backstage tours, a Bard's banquet and special opening night events, art festivals, and—before each night's performance—a green show featuring Elizabethan dancing, madrigal and lute singing, Punch and Judy shows, and readings of Elizabethan sonnets.

In a 1982 interview in Cedar City's *Iron County Record,* founding director Fred C. Adams explained how the festival evolved over the years.

"We conceived the festival twenty-one years ago," he said, "as an opportunity to acquaint Southwest audiences with the works of Shakespeare and at the same time provide opportunities for young actors to perform. Gradually this concept has enlarged, until now in our twenty-first year we are working toward professionalism in all areas of the festival; and, in addition to southern Utah people, we have audiences from all over the world and a festival company selected from nearly 1,000 applicants each season. That's quite a change."

Another summer program that we found most interesting was the selection of specialized courses offered by Southern Utah State College. They ranged from dutch oven cooking to classes in the writing of local history and the roots of the

English language. Relive the Old West was a series of workshops on activities such as bread making, butter churning, pioneer dancing, story-telling, and basketry. And most interesting of all were the workshops on Pioneer Survival Crafts. These included quilting and sewing, wood stove safety and firewood lore, cabin crafts, meat cutting and slaughtering/curing/smoking, food preservation, self-defense, home security, leather crafts, and soap making.

Switching from pioneer survival to modern-day survival, let's take a look at Cedar City's crime rate. In our comparison year of 1980, there were 1 murder, 3 rapes, 1 robbery, and 16 aggravated assaults. Property crime consisted of 75 burglaries, 336 larceny-thefts, and 24 motor vehicle thefts. This placed the city below U.S. rural levels of crime in four categories, slightly above rural levels of rape and motor vehicle theft, and between rural and metropolitan levels of larceny-theft.

On housing costs, Clayton Frehner of Corry Realty, a Century 21 affiliate in Cedar City, was most helpful. Houses in this area are built very well, he said, with excellent insulation in the walls and ceilings. Double-pane windows are common, and some houses have triple panes. Most houses now are all-electric, with some powered by solar energy. While some have central air-conditioning, more houses use "swamp coolers"—fans that distribute water-cooled air around the house. As long as there isn't much humidity, they work fine and around here there are only three or four days a year when the temperature rises above 100 degrees.

At the lower end of the price scale, there are some homes that were built in the 1950s with about 900 square feet of living area. They now sell for between $45,000 and $50,000.

Newer homes at the bottom of the price scale have about 1,100 square feet plus basement, with a 2-car carport, fireplace in the living room, 3 bedrooms, 1¾ baths, and an informal dining area off the kitchen. These are often rambler-type homes and sell in the range of $61,000 to $65,000.

Older homes were mostly brick. But with rising costs, most homes built since about 1973 have been frame with brick decoration. The city requires lot frontage of 90 feet and most lots run 110 to 120 feet deep.

The more expensive homes will be found in developments west of the Interstate. Some sell for more than $200,000, but most are around $150,000. They are situated on larger lots—usually 100 × 175 (about one third of an acre).

For $150,000, you could get a 2-story house or a house with one story plus finished basement—close to 4,000 square feet of living area. People finish off their basements because they are easy to dig and they double the amount of living space. They're also cheaper. You can finish off a basement around here for $10 to $12 per square foot, while something on the main level would cost $40 to $42 per square foot. A house in this price range would probably have 2 upstairs bedrooms, family room with fireplace, living room with fireplace, finished basement with 2 bedrooms, formal dining room, and an eat-in kitchen.

Two of the more popular areas are Cedar Knolls in the southwest part of town, where a lot costs $15,000 or $16,000 and a house runs $80,000 to $85,000 (including the land) and the Cove development in the northwest part of town, where lots run $12,000 to $13,000 and the houses between $65,000 and $70,000. On the hill, lots run $14,000 to $20,000 and the total cost of a house could reach $150,000.

And above the city, in the mountains, is Cedar Highlands. Lots of about 1 acre cost $18,000 and almost every one has a view. The elevation here is around 7,500 to 8,000 feet, so you'll get plenty of snow—sometimes 12 to 18 inches at a time—but not as much as the really heavy snow at the top of the mountains.

Beyond the mountains, to the east, are the parks and monuments that have made this part of Utah known as Color Country—a wonderland described in the December 1980 *National Geographic* as "a more fantastically beautiful—and infinitely varied—country than in any other like-size area on earth." Of the many notable attractions, two that topped our list to see—because we'd never been in Southwest Utah before—were Zion National Park and Bryce Canyon National Park. We had our favorites, as you will too, with Holly and Melissa favoring Zion and David equally partial toward Bryce Canyon.

Zion is an oasis of green as the Virgin River cuts through the massive, rugged badlands of Kolob Terrace. Here you're on the bottom looking up, inspired by landmarks such as the Great White Throne, Towers of the Virgin, the Three Patriarchs, and Angels' Landing. You follow the river—by car, on foot, or horseback—as its canyon rises up more than 2,000 feet and narrows at times to less than 100 feet across.

At Bryce Canyon, on the other hand, you're at the top looking down. You pass through forests of ponderosa pine, spruce, fir, and aspen, until suddenly you find yourself at one of the dozen horseshoe-shaped amphitheaters carved by erosion of the pink cliffs of the Paunsaugunt Plateau. Below you is a dazzling forest of a far different sort—a fantasyland of free-standing spires, pinnacles, and minarets, hundreds of them, thousands it seems like, their bewildering array of reds and oranges and pinks mixing with the deep green of the forests and the equally vivid blue of the clear sky to stun you into awed silence.

Ebeneezer Bryce, the Mormon settler whose name lives on in the park's name, had the final word on Bryce Canyon: "A hell of a place to lose a cow!"

Both parks are open the year around and from a home base in Cedar City you can enjoy them in all the seasons, take in the skiing at Brian Head's 11,000-foot elevations, try snowmobiling through Cedar Breaks National Monument, and otherwise lose yourself in enjoyment of the natural wonders at your doorstep. It's a world you cannot match anywhere else in *this* world.

LOGAN

POPULATION: 26,871
NO. OF CRIMES: 775
CRIME RATE: 2,884.2 per 100,000

We entered Utah at its northeastern tip, arriving from Wyoming. One of our first sights in the state was Bear Lake, where the waters are so dazzlingly blue that they make the sky seem pale in comparison. Taking U.S. 89, we crossed over the Wasatch Range and soon found ourselves going down, down, down for more than 30 miles until we reached Logan. This was Logan Canyon, one of the most beautiful canyon roadways we have seen in the West. The gushing waters of the Logan River are always close at hand; picnic spots and campgrounds abound and hiking paths beckon you to take the time to see some fossils or some caves eroded out of limestone or the Jardine Juniper. At age 3,500 (give or take a few years), it is believed to be the oldest living thing in Utah.

Logan itself is an exceptionally clean and sparkling city, even by Utah and Mormon standards. It is the principal commercial and cultural center of this far-northern part of the state and the presence of Utah State University makes it an educational center as well, with more than 10,000 students enrolled here. Visible for miles around are the landmarks of the city's "skyline"—the Mormon Temple, with its twin gray towers, and the bell tower of USU's Old Main building.

Beyond Logan to the north, south, and west is the Cache Valley. Lush and green, it is populated by neat and prosperous-appearing farms. In this idyllic setting you can understand why the early settlers gave names like Providence and Paradise to their farming communities. They obviously felt that this part of the world had been divinely blessed.

Agriculture remains the keystone of the Cache County economy and the main source of income. Dairying is particularly important, and the celebration known as Black and White Days in nearby Richmond honors the Holstein dairy cow. Farmers here say their Holsteins are "not only contented, but slightly conceited."

Five cheese factories, including the world's largest Swiss cheese factory, are located in the valley. Tours are available. Other food processing industries include condensed milk plants, flour milling, food baking, the production of animal foods, a cannery owned by Del Monte Packing Company, and a meat-packing plant.

In recent years, Logan's economy has become more diversified with the addition of various manufacturing enterprises. Today mobile homes, pianos, women's clothes, and farm machinery are all manufactured here.

Medical facilities include Logan Regional Hospital. Shopping facilities are concentrated in the downtown area and at 400 North and 1300 North Main.

Logan has a four-season climate. Its altitude is 4,526 feet and the average growing season is 165 days. In January the average maximum temperature is 33.8 degrees, the average minimum temperature 15.4 degrees. In July these are 88.2 degrees and 54.1 degrees. Winters are usually cold but not severe. The valley is blanketed with snow in the winter months, but most of the snow is found in the mountains. Spring is the wettest season of the year and nearly 40 percent of the total annual precipitation falls in March, April, and May. Summer usually arrives rather abruptly in the early part of June. Humidity is relatively low in the daytime and prolonged heat spells are rare. Nights are cool. And autumn is crisp and cool, with the first frosts usually arriving rather early, before mid-October.

A number of festivals and activities will keep you busy throughout the year. Black powder shoots and mountainman contests are featured in the Cache Valley Mountainman Rendezvous. Rodeos, Pioneer Days celebrations, the Festival of the American West, the Great West Fair, mock Indian battles, the Dairy Festival Princess Pageant, a Threshing Bee and Antique Show, a raspberry harvest celebration, and the main event of the year, the Cache County Fair, celebrate the region's Western and agricultural roots. In addition there are marathons, art exhibitions, the 4th of July fireworks display in the USU stadium, golf tournaments, sidewalk bazaars, and USU's Homecoming Days to keep you busy.

One of the most interesting attractions is the Hardware Ranch, in the midst of Wasatch National Forest. Up to 650 wild elk congregate here in the winter for a free "handout"—stored hay, carried to them on Hardware Meadow by horse-drawn sleds. When snow covering is adequate, free sled rides are available. Otherwise you can watch the feeding from the Visitor Center area.

Logan's crime rate is the lowest of any Utah community of 10,000 or more. In our comparison year of 1980, there were no murders, no rapes, 2 robberies, and 45 aggravated assaults. Property crime consisted of 100 burglaries, 600 larceny-thefts, and 28 motor vehicle thefts. This placed Logan below U.S. rural crime levels in all categories except aggravated assault and larceny-theft, and in those categories it still remained way below U.S. metropolitan levels.

Sandy Pitkin of Gold Key Realty told us that older, small homes with 2 or 3 bedrooms and 1 bath cost in the vicinity of $45,000. The more expensive homes are generally in the $100,000 to $140,000 range, though there are a half dozen, perhaps, selling for around $230,000 and up to $500,000 in the county.

As an example of a house on the market for a higher price, she told us of a house on the Logan River. It had 1,650 square feet of living area on the main floor, but a finished loft area added 200 to 300 square feet. The house had 5 bedrooms, 3 baths, a hot tub, living room, family room, and a very large kitchen with a dining area. It sits on a standard 1/4 acre city lot, with a 2-car garage with opener. Taxes are $700 a year.

Town house condominiums, Sandy told us, are available in the city from $35,000. That would be for a 2-bedroom, 1-bath unit, with monthly maintenance of $15 to $20. The most expensive ones are priced at about $120,000, and have 3 or 4 bedrooms and 2 or 2 1/2 baths.

Building lots range from $13,000 to $30,000. Size doesn't vary that much—from 1/3 to 1/4 acre in size, usually—so location is the key factor in the price.

Outside Logan, 1-acre homesites cost $20,000 to $30,000. From 1 acre you jump to 10-acre or 40-acre parcels of land.

A check of the newspaper's classified ads resulted in some interesting listings:

• For $89,500: A 2-story house with 4 bedrooms and 1½ baths.

• For $109,000: A three-year-old English Tudor with 4 bedrooms and a sun deck, on a landscaped river lot with a garden and shade trees.

• For $95,500: A builder's 6-bedroom executive house, with 3 baths, family room, game room, air-conditioning, 2 fireplaces, and a 2-car garage.

• For $150,000: A 10-acre "farmette" with a 3-bedroom house and outbuildings.

• For $197,000: "One of Logan's most prestigious homes," with 3 bedrooms, 2½ baths, elegant formal dining room, 3 fireplaces, and a Cliffside Drive view lot.

• And for $450,000: A 300-acre gravity sprinkler dairy farm, available on contract terms.

That's quite a range of choices with which to entice you to this beautiful corner of the world. A lovely university town . . . towering mountains with rushing streams and scenic canyon drives . . . and a fertile, prosperous valley. If that sounds like an unbeatable combination to you, it's time you check out Logan, the Wasatch Mountains, and Cache Valley.

PROVO

POPULATION: 74,007
NO. OF CRIMES: 2,640
CRIME RATE: 3,567.2 per 100,000

Our largest Safe Place in the United States is this bustling city, the West's major steel center and the home of the nation's largest private university and largest 4th of July celebration.

Provo was established originally because of cattle rustlers. The rustlers were Ute Indians who helped themselves to the beef left grazing in the meadows of Utah Valley by the Mormon pioneers, when they settled down in Salt Lake City. To protect the grazing grounds, Brigham Young decided to build a fort. Soon Fort Utah was overflowing with settlers and the town began to grow outside its protective gates.

A major change in the town took place during World War II, when the government's Office of Production Management had the U.S. Steel Corporation draw up plans for an extensive steel operation. The result was the Geneva works of U.S. Steel, just outside Provo's city limits. It is the largest steelworks west of Chicago and one of the most modern plants in the nation. In good times it employs more than 5,000 workers, but at the time of our visit—during the 1982 economic slump—there were layoffs of up to 1,500 employees.

After U.S. Steel, the major employer is the Signetics Corporation, with 1,500 workers. Inside Provo are seventy-eight manufacturing plants. Steel and steel byproducts are joined by products such as women's, girl's, and infant wear (Jolene Company, Mini World, Carlisle Manufacturing), doors, glass, and paint

(Jones Paint & Glass), computers (Billings Computer Corporation), and handguns (North American Manufacturing). Salt Lake City is just 43 miles north on Interstate 15, so there is considerable commuting between the various cities of Utah Valley as well.

Major sources of nonmanufacturing employment are Brigham Young University, Utah Valley Hospital, the Provo school district, Utah Technical College, Mountain Bell Telephone, the city government, Sears, Eyring Research (research and development), the Denver & Rio Grande Railroad, and Albertsons (food services).

The central role of the Mormon church in Provo becomes evident when we note that Brigham Young University—a Mormon institution—employs more people than U.S. Steel and with more than 27,000 students is the largest private university in the nation. Founded in 1875, it offers 130 different bachelor's degrees as well as 115 master's and 56 doctorate degrees. Its MBA program and engineering school are especially prominent and athletically it ranks fourth in the nation in total sports competition.

Provo's second outstanding educational institution is Utah Technical College, a two-year vocational/technical institution with more than thirty majors, from accounting to welding. It enrolls more than 4,000 students and its graduates enjoy the highest placement record of any school in the nation.

Also enjoying a reputation for excellence is the public school system, with numerous elementary schools, junior high schools, and two high schools. The Mormon emphasis on education has given Utah the highest educational level of any state in the United States and nowhere is this more true than in Provo.

No survey of Provo is complete, of course, without mention of Donny and Marie Osmond. Though their entertainment careers are currently in somewhat of an eclipse, except for commercials, there's no doubt they gave more publicity to Provo in recent years than anyone else. That is so, even though their Osmond Studios and Osmond Entertainment Center are actually located across town boundaries in Orem. This is considered one of the finest television production facilities in the country and no visit to Provo/Orem is complete without a tour.

The Mormon influence. It is evident in the stability and productivity of the work force. It is evident in the educational level and attainments of the community. And it's evident in the exceptionally low crime rate for a community of this size.

In 1974, when David wrote *America's 50 Safest Cities,* Provo was right up there in the Top 10 out of all the nation's cities with a population of 50,000 or more. And it's still safe, as is evident from its selection in this book. Swen C. Nielsen, Provo's Chief of Police, makes the religious connection explicit.

"While we, in the police department, would be pleased to take credit for the low crime rate in our community," he told us, "we must nevertheless attribute that to the commitment and adherence to the law by an overwhelming preponderance of the citizens who live here. The community is comprised of a highly homogeneous population, a high percentage of which are members of the Mormon church."

For real estate information, we talked with Kaye Morris, a sales associate of Osmond Real Estate. (Donny and Marie's father, George, was in real estate long before they became stars.) Kaye told us that prices for most sales begin in the high 60s or the 70s and go up from there. As everywhere, you pay for a view. Provo is situated at the base of the Wasatch Mountains and extends to Utah Lake, so the finest views are up the hills and slopes of north Provo. In the Hill area and Grandview area, the developments have names such as Sherwood Hills, Indian Hills, and Oak Hills. There are also some nice and expensive neighborhoods at the other end of town, below Interstate 15, along the Provo River.

For $70,000, you could get a 3-bedroom house on an 80 × 100 or 100 × 100 city lot. It would probably have 1¾ baths, living room, fireplace, kitchen with dining area, a full unfinished basement, and a double garage or carport. There would be 1,200 to 1,400 square feet of living area and most people convert their basements into bedrooms or family rooms.

To get 4 bedrooms and a formal dining room, you're talking about a larger rambler or a 2-story house. The range for these is from $100,000 to $160,000.

For $129,900, for example, Osmond had a listing for a 2-story colonial in north Provo, built with lots of oak and extra features. It had 3 bedrooms, 2½ baths, and a full basement.

But the listing that really caught our eye was down in Provo's prestigious Riverbottom development. Exuding old English charm, this was an elegant Tudor priced at $189,500. Its extras included an exceptional master bedroom suite, balcony, Jacuzzi, hardwood floors, a backyard designed for entertainment, central vacuum, burglar alarm, and intercom.

Some typical tax assessments we noted: $418 for a house valued at $60,000, $475 for $66,000, $992 for $100,000, $988 for $129,000, and $733 for a twenty-year-old house valued at $130,000. (Here, as elsewhere, newer homes tend to be assessed at a higher rate than older homes.)

Located at an elevation of 4,540 feet, Provo—like most of northern Utah—has a definite four-season climate. In January, the average minimum temperature is 19 degrees, the average maximum 36 degrees. In July those figures are 63 degrees for the minimum and 91 degrees for the maximum.

Leading into the mountains from Provo is the scenic canyon of the Provo River, described as America's most heavily fished trout stream. Nine miles up the canyon is Robert Redford's Sundance, a year-round family resort featuring skiing in the winter and hiking and horseback riding in the summer. A few more miles brings you to 600-foot Bridal Veil Falls and one of the depots of the Heber Creeper—a steam railroad that chugs along 18 miles east to Heber City. Also at the falls is the steepest aerial tramway in the world.

In the mountains, barely an hour from Provo, are some of the most famous and popular ski resorts in America and year-round resort centers such as the historic silver mining town of Park City. But all of this is in your backyard. The added dimension of your Provo location is that it places you smack in the middle of the West's most famous attractions. Within a 400-mile radius are the Tetons and Yellowstone in Wyoming, Idaho's Sun Valley, Las Vegas, the Grand Canyon, all the canyonlands of southern Utah, and the Rocky Mountain resorts of Aspen and Vail in Colorado. All of this is yours within a day's drive when you make Provo the Safe Place for you.

Where to get further information:

State

Utah Travel Council, Council Hall/Capitol Hill, Salt Lake City, UT 84114. *Travel Utah* is updated monthly from May through October, *Skiing Utah* the remainder of the year; both are available from Utah Holiday Publishing Co., P.O. Box 985, Salt Lake City, UT 84110. *Utah Holiday,* a monthly magazine, is available from the same address at $14.70 a year.

Regional

Color Country, P.O. Box 220, Cedar City, UT 84720.
Bridgerland Tourist Council, 52 West 2nd North, Logan, UT 84321.
Mountainland, 160 E. Center Street, Provo, UT 84061.

Local

Cedar City: Cedar City Chamber of Commerce, 286 N. Main, P.O. Box 220, Cedar City, UT 84720. Utah Shakespearean Festival, Cedar City, UT 84720. Southern Utah State College, Cedar City, UT 84720. Superintendent, Bryce Canyon National Park, Bryce Canyon, UT 84717. Superintendent, Zion National Park, Springdale, UT 84767.

Logan: Cache Chamber of Commerce, 52 West 200 North, Logan, UT 84321. For information on cheese factory tours: Cache Valley Dairy Association, Smithfield, UT 84335. For a map ($1.00): Wasatch-Cache National Forest, 125 S. State Street, Salt Lake City, UT 84138.

Provo: Provo Chamber of Commerce, 10 East 300 North, Provo, UT 84601.

Vermont

Mountain vistas await you in all corners of this compact state—stunning vistas that cause you to catch your breath, whatever the color of the season's covering: the lush green of summer, the yellows and reds of autumn, or winter's snowy whites.

Famous for its natural beauty, the Green Mountain State is an ever-popular destination for tourists, especially those with a strong interest in photography. Think of Vermont and you picture pristine villages, country inns, rolling farmlands nestled between mountain ranges, auctions, antiques, covered bridges, maple syrup, cheese, skiing . . . and so much more.

If you love skiing, by the way, you'll find some thirty-two alpine ski areas here and an average of more than 200 inches of snow a year. Campers and hikers have the Appalachian and Long trails, Green Mountain National Forest, and sixty-three state parks and forests. Water enthusiasts can take their pick of more than 400 freshwater lakes and reservoirs, led by Lake Champlain with its 250 miles of shoreline in Vermont.

For all its rural flavor, though, Vermont has many more residents employed in manufacturing industries than in agriculture. It also leads the nation in production of marble, granite, and asbestos.

Vermont is one of the last places most people would associate with any kind of crime, save perhaps an occasional theft of a cow. Granted, this isn't Boston or New York when it comes to crime rates, but you'd be surprised—at least we were—how much looks can deceive. And size. Take for example, a tranquil hamlet like Peru, population 312. Crimes of violence are blessedly rare, but it's a different matter for burglary. There were 7 in 1980, 14 the next year. When you adjust for population, that's a crime *rate* per 100,000 of 2,243.6 and 4,487.2 those two years—way above the burglary rate for the nation's metropolitan areas!

Another problem for us was the difficulty of obtaining reliable crime statistics for Vermont communities. In our comparison year of 1980, the FBI published crime information for only two towns in the state, and both of them—Colchester and South Burlington—did not qualify as Safe Places by our strict standards.

Vermont is one of the few states that do not compile crime statistics on a statewide level. You must get the information from each local jurisdiction—no small task. Few local police departments will give out Top Secret information like the number of crimes (that's the way they seem to conceive of it) without prior clearance from the chief. And the chief either doesn't want to give out that information or really doesn't have it (you'd be surprised how many small town departments keep no compilations for past years or immediately pack them away in a dingy basement where they can't ever be retrieved). Other chiefs seem never to be available to see you, or the sergeant they put in charge of statistics is off on vacation or getting a haircut . . . Well, you get the picture.

But that's not all. In many Vermont communities, the state police handle some cases and a local constable or police department the others. And in some of them there's still a third authority to take into consideration, if the sheriff of that county is active. You must get statistics from all of them in order to have an accurate picture and you have to make certain the various sets of statistics are not overlapping.

In short, Vermont is a decentralized mess when it comes to crime statistics. And as difficult as that made our task of finding a Safe Place, we have to cry hallelujah! At a time when every snoop is trying to enter us in his computer memory bank and the biggest snoops are trying to forge a national identification card, can you imagine the problems they'll face when they try to wheedle some information out of these heirs of the Green Mountain Boys? Actually, your two snoopy authors can't think of a better reason to move here, and especially since we *were* able to surmount the obstacles and find you an enchanting Safe Place second to none.

DORSET

POPULATION: 1,648
NO. OF CRIMES: 36
CRIME RATE: 2,184.5 per 100,000

This picturesque village has a number of "firsts" to its credit. It was here, at the Dorset Conventions of 1776, that Vermont first declared its independence. In 1785, the first marble quarry in North America began operations on nearby Mount Aeolus. And the Dorset Field Club claims that its 9-hole golf course is the oldest in the country (though there is another claimant to that honor).

Artists and writers have made Dorset their home for years. At the Dorset Playhouse, a professional troupe performs during the summer and amateur townspeople take over during the rest of the year. The Southern Vermont Art Center is located nearby.

Dorset is also a popular summer retreat for Albany-area families and for retirees migrating north each year to escape the Florida humidity. It is home

VERMONT Crime Chart

	Crime Rate	Murder	Rape	Robbery	Aggravated Assault	Burglary	Larceny —Theft	Motor Vehicle Theft
United States								
U.S. Total	5,899.9	10.2	36.4	243.5	290.6	1,668.2	3,156.3	494.6
U.S. Metropolitan Areas	6,757.6	11.5	43.4	319.0	328.3	1,911.8	3,534.9	608.8
U.S. Rural Areas	2,290.4	7.5	15.5	22.5	136.9	830.2	1,143.9	133.9
Regional Crime Center								
South Burlington	9,126.6	0	46.8	177.7	46.8	1,112.8	7,069.4	673.3
Safe Place								
Dorset	2,184.5	0	0	0	121.4	849.5	1,152.9	60.7

year-round to professionals and tradesmen, to people employed in Manchester (6 miles east) and at local ski areas.

Surrounded by 3,000-foot mountains, Dorset is not disturbed by much hustle and bustle of any kind. You can go to Manchester for that. Here you'll just find lovely homes and a few businesses and community centers—Pelter's Market (established in 1860) and the Williams store, Factory Point National Bank, the Dorset Historical Society Museum and the town library, a hardware store, and at least three inns: Village Auberge, the Barrows House, and the Dorset Inn on the village green, advertising "fine food, drink, lodging since 1796."

Batten Kill is a renowned trout-fishing stream and in Manchester the Orvis Company—maker of fishing gear—operates the Museum of American Fly Fishing, with displays of the rods of Presidents Hoover and Eisenhower, Hemingway, Andrew Carnegie, and other famous fishermen. For skiers, there are three major attractions in the area: Bromley, Stratton, and Magic mountains. At Bromley, you can climb by chairlift 5,750 feet up the mountainside to an elevation of 3,260 feet, take in the view of five states, and return, if you wish, on the 4,060-foot alpine slide, where you control the speed and braking on your small plastic sled.

Dorset has an elementary school and the private Long Trail School in town; bus service to the high school in Manchester is provided. Town taxes are low, since there is no high school or police force (state police and two constables have jurisdiction). There is no town sewage, either; everyone has his own septic system.

Crimes of violence are virtually nonexistent here—2 aggravated assaults in 1980. There were also 14 burglaries, 19 larceny-thefts, and 1 motor vehicle theft. Dorset's crime rate was below that for U.S. rural areas in all categories except burglary and larceny-theft and there it was barely above rural rates. In 1981, it was above rural rates only in the number of burglaries.

Local housing reflects the ready availability of marble: the main area of the village has marble sidewalks and many old homes rest on marble foundations.

Slate roofs are also popular in the area, since slate is mined right over the border in New York State.

By far the most spectacular marble edifice in the area is the Old Stone House, which was the first or second all-marble house in the country. It was on the market for $475,000 at the time of our visit. The main residence has 12 major rooms (8 bedrooms, 6 baths). Also on the 26 acres are extensive landscaped gardens linked by marble walks, a hillside pergola, a teahouse with terrace beside the reflecting pool and fountain, several garages (one with a second-floor apartment), a frame cottage, a 2-room frame cabin, a barn, and a pistol range.

We discussed real estate with the Snare Associates' very knowledgeable Marjorie Snare Chapman. She told us that from time to time you'll find something on the market for under $100,000, but usually it's higher. A 1-acre lot will cost $20,000; if you buy a 10-acre parcel, you may pay $5,000–$6,000 per acre. New suburban-type houses (not too plentiful around here) will cost $135,000 or so. And the nineteenth-century houses on the village green would probably sell for $150,000 to $175,000 if any were for sale, which there weren't at the time of our visit. Usually you will find about thirty properties on the market in Dorset.

For $135,000, Ms. Chapman had a large country house available with slightly over 8 acres and a 2-story barn. Among its 13 rooms were 7 bedrooms and 3½ baths, and yes, the kitchen needed modernization. Taxes were approximately $1,000 a year.

Whether you get your inspiration from an easel or on the golf course, from landing a feisty brook trout or careening down a perilous alpine slope, Dorset is ideally located to make your life rewarding all year long.

Where to get further information:

State

For a state highway map and a wide variety of tourist literature (state your interests): Vermont Travel Division, 61 Elm Street, Montpelier, VT 05602.

New England Vacation Center, 630 Fifth Avenue, New York, NY 10020.

Vermont Life (61 Elm Street, Montpelier, VT 05602) is probably the best-known state magazine east of Arizona.

For information on hiking trails, including the Long Trail: Green Mountain Club, P.O. Box 889, 43 State Street, Montpelier, VT 05602.

For information on farm vacations and maple-sugar houses open to the public: Department of Agriculture, Dept. SS, Montpelier, VT 05602.

Town

For information on the Manchester area, write to the Manchester-and-the-Mountains Chamber of Commerce, P.O. Box 928, Manchester Center, VT 05255.

Virginia

The present and the past are friends and allies, not enemies, in the Old Dominion. Virginia can be thoroughly modern when it wants to be—this is no backwater period piece, wrapped in a time warp—but Virginians have a special skill at blending tradition and innovation to produce a genuinely civilized pace of life.

Virginia played such a critical role in the early and middle periods of the nation's life that it is impossible to imagine what the history books would resemble without its contributions. Those contributions began with the first permanent English settlement in the New World, at Jamestown, and subsequent landmarks included the first legislative assembly in the colonies and the first armed rebellion against the government (Bacon's Rebellion, in 1676). Virginia gave us Patrick Henry's stirring patriotic oratory, Thomas Jefferson's Declaration of Independence, George Washington's critical leadership, James Madison's Constitution, and George Mason's Bill of Rights. A century later, fully half of the fighting in the War Between the States would take place on the soil of Robert E. Lee's proud commonwealth.

Geographically, Virginia ranges from the coastal plains of the Tidewater region, to the forests and tobacco farms of the rolling Piedmont Plateau, and on farther westward to strikingly beautiful mountain ranges and valleys. Modern industries are scattered throughout the state; apple orchards add their blossoms and fruit to the natural beauty of the Shenandoah Valley; shipbuilding and naval operations dominate the Norfolk area; marine industries and sports prevail along the ocean and the shores of Chesapeake Bay; and in northern Virginia, alas, the obese bureaucracy of the federal government has overflowed its central habitat in Washington, D.C., spilling over to the southern side of the Potomac.

Two of our Safe Places in Virginia remain the same ones we chose for our original *Safe Places*, published in 1972. Leesburg, hub of the aristocratic hunt country of Loudoun County, is now also a suburb of Washington, D.C. Lexington is a historical and architectural gem nestled in the Valley of Virginia. It would be fruitless to attempt to find more charming towns than these two, so we didn't even try. For those of us who love the ocean, however, there's a special allure to the Eastern Shore of Virginia and Maryland, and so this time we added one of our favorite haunts in that part of the state, picturesque Chincoteague.

VIRGINIA'S EASTERN SHORE

Virginia's Eastern Shore is that narrow band of land east of Chesapeake Bay and comprising the bulk of Virginia's Atlantic Ocean frontage. To the north is Maryland's Eastern Shore, and to the south—on the opposite side of the mouth of Chesapeake Bay—are Norfolk and Virginia Beach, connected by an engineering marvel, the 17.6-mile Chesapeake Bay Bridge-Tunnel.

The first English settlers arrived here in 1614 and they kept the Indian name Accawmacke ("land beyond the waters"). Messages from the crown were sent to "our faithful subjects of ye Colonie of Virginia and the Kingdom of Accawmacke," and the earliest continuous court records in America will be found here, dating from 1632.

Important industries include agriculture (the Irish potato and other vegetables), seafood, tourism, and poultry. We passed the giant processing plants of Holly Farms and Perdue Foods at night and they were ablaze with light as they turned out their thousands of chickens for the supermarkets of America.

EASTERN VIRGINIA Crime Chart

	Crime Rate	Murder	Rape	Robbery	Aggravated Assault	Burglary	Larceny —Theft	Motor Vehicle Theft
United States								
U.S. Total	5,899.9	10.2	36.4	243.5	290.6	1,668.2	3,156.3	494.6
U.S. Metropolitan Areas	6,757.6	11.5	43.4	319.0	328.3	1,911.8	3,534.9	608.8
U.S. Rural Areas	2,290.4	7.5	15.5	22.5	136.9	830.2	1,143.9	133.9
Regional Crime Center								
Norfolk	7,577.7	13.5	42.0	380.6	377.6	1,975.8	4,420.2	368.2
Safe Place								
Chincoteague	1,295.8	0	56.3*	0	0	225.4	957.7	56.3

*Statistical distortion resulting from 1 incident in a low population base.

Eastern Shore architecture is unique, with varying roof levels and two or more chimneys in the old houses. The roofs are mostly of the A-type, with small dormer windows on the front and back. A house with four different roof levels is referred to as "big house, little house, colonnade, and kitchen."

There are no large towns or cities on the Eastern Shore; instead you'll find quaint villages and towns that take you back in history. Accomac, Eastville, and Onancock are "musts" for history buffs. Wachapreague is a sport fishing center. On Tangier Island, there are no automobiles and the natives still speak in an Old English accent. But our favorite place of all is found on one of the barrier islands that protect the mainland from the enticements and the fury of the ocean . . .

CHINCOTEAGUE

POPULATION: 1,775
NO. OF CRIMES: 23
CRIME RATE: 1,295.8 per 100,000

Memo to: Steven Spielberg
From: David and Holly Franke
Subject: Have discovered perfect location for next film follow-up to Jaws, Raiders, *and* E.T. *Suggest a classic monster-from-the-deep horror flick set in isolated hamlet, on island connected to mainland by causeway. NASA space station nearby, with rocket launches and huge radar dishes. Coast Guard station. Lighthouse. Oyster, clam, fishing boats everywhere. Desolate lovers' lanes aplenty. Fog rolling in over the moors. Eccentric old salts walking the streets and lounging on the docks. Old community theater where teenage kids can congregate to watch* Jaws *as the real monster slinks in. Carnival grounds on edge of town where younger kids can be terrorized next.*
Title: THE MONSTER OYSTER THAT ATE CHINCOTEAGUE!

Mr. Spielberg may feel he has better subjects than a monster oyster for his next movie, but we seriously doubt he could dream up a better locale for one than this real-life fishing village on Virginia's Atlantic coast. Farther north in Maryland and Delaware, the summer resorts of Ocean City and Rehoboth Beach have been developed beyond recognition to satisfy the craving of Washingtonians for sand, sun, and surf. Here, however, time has pretty much stood still. There used to be an old hotel in town with a cozy dark bar on the ground floor, sort of a combination fisherman's watering hole and old English pub. It's gone now, but everything else remains surprisingly the same as we remember it from nearly twenty years ago.

Chincoteague (pronounced "Ching-co-TÉEG") has everything going for it that we pointed out to Mr. Spielberg and more. Chincoteague Island is protected from the Atlantic, in all but the worst storms, by adjoining Assateague Island. And Assateague Island is now preserved in its natural state as Chincoteague National Wildlife Refuge on the Virginia side of the state border, and on the Maryland side as Assateague Island National Seashore.

The two islands, Chincoteague and Assateague, are a bird lover's paradise, with 262 species listed in Refuge literature. More than 15,000 snow geese winter here. You don't have to be a knowledgeable bird-watcher to enjoy the show, however. We were lullabied to sleep at night and gently awakened the next morning by a chorus of chirps and cackles. We were constantly stopping to ooh! and aah! at one of the graceful beauties in the marshes by the side of the road or to chuckle at the sight of a cattle egret hitchhiking on the back of one of the wild ponies grazing by the road.

Ah yes, the wild ponies of Chincoteague. Ever since Marguerite Henry wrote *Misty of Chincoteague*, they have been the islands' most famous residents. Although they don't run at the sight of humans, they are nonetheless wild since they maintain themselves in all seasons without any assistance from man. Stunted by the low nutrition of salt marsh grasses, they are somewhat smaller in size than a "normal" horse, resembling a Welsh pony but larger and more graceful than a Shetland.

Scholarship now suggests that the Chincoteague ponies first arrived here when early colonists sought to avoid the tax levies that were placed on livestock on the mainland. We prefer the romantic legend that says they are the descendants of mine horses that survived the shipwreck of a sixteenth-century Spanish galleon. At any rate, the main tourist event of the year takes place on the last Wednesday and Thursday of July, when the horses are rounded up and the excess foals are sold at auction.

If you love "wild" beaches, uncluttered by motels and amusement stands, take the paved road from Chincoteague into the wildlife refuge. It ends at the beach, where you can enjoy 10 miles of unspoiled surf.

If fishing is your sport, this mid-Atlantic coast is hard to beat. Surfcasters aim for channel bass, black drum, rock, whiting, shad, white perch, and gray trout. The bays, coves, channels, sloughs, and narrows are filled with them too, as well as clams and the famous Chincoteague oysters. The largest clam packer in the world is located on Chincoteague and its delicious catch supplies the Howard Johnson's chain of restaurants—one of only two reasons we sometimes weaken and pull over for lunch at one of them. (We're convinced that Howard Johnson's *trains* its waitresses to be irritatingly slow and virtually invisible. Nevertheless, the other reason for stopping, since you asked, is its grilled hot dogs. Just take plenty of maps and reading material inside to pore over while your hunger builds for HoJo's fried clam strips or grilled hot dogs.)

Chincoteague has something for every visitor—motels, a colonial inn with no telephone or TV, rental houses, mobile-home parks, campgrounds. And when you decide to stay awhile longer, you'll find town houses available as well as single-family houses. Never say never, but we don't expect to see big developments anywhere on the island, since everyone—within town limits or outside—is forced to rely on individual septic tanks. There's also a height restriction to 2½ stories.

At Island Property Enterprises, friendly Floyd Mason, Jr., talked to us about Chincoteague and gave us its current lists of houses and building lots for sale. The houses ranged in price from $25,000 to $160,000 and taxes were even lower than the local crime rate.

For $37,500 you could get a 14 × 70 mobile home with 3 bedrooms, covered patio, and wood-burning fireplace. It was on a 51 × 100 lot, with annual taxes of $82.55.

Just $75,000 would get you a waterfront home on South Main Street. From there you could look west to dramatic sunsets over Chincoteague Bay, and north to track the fishing fleet entering and leaving the harbor. With 2 bedrooms, a sleeping alcove, and den, it sits on a 42 × 242 lot. Annual taxes: just $223.44.

The most expensive house on the market, at $160,000, was a new waterfront retreat with a cathedral-ceilinged great room, 3 bedrooms, 2 1/2 baths, hardwood floors, 2 fireplaces, library, 2-zone central air-conditioning, porch, large deck, private dock, and 165 feet of natural deep water frontage.

Mullberry Square offers 2-bedroom town houses with central air-conditioning and plenty of extras, beginning at $48,500.

As for building lots, they ranged in price from $23,000 to $40,000 for waterfront parcels, from $10,000 to $18,500 for water-view/water-access lots, and from $8,000 to $15,000 for residential lots. Two mobile-home lots were also available for $12,000 each.

The crime rate in Chincoteague is exceptionally low at 1,295.8 per 100,000. The actual number of crimes in our comparison year of 1980 came to 23. The town ranked below U.S. rural crime rates in all categories except rape, where an unusual occurrence of a single incident resulted in a statistically high rate for a small town like this. There were no other crimes of violence in 1980 and in 1981 the only crime of violence was 1 aggravated assault.

If you love water, water everywhere, from frothy surf beaches to misty wetlands, if you're looking for a respite from worldly pressures where there's always time to listen to the birds or to watch the gulls circle overhead and swoop down for a catch, then look into that special place the Indians described as the "beautiful land across the water." They called it Chincoteague.

NORTHERN VIRGINIA

The black migration to the North and the civil rights movement of the fifties and sixties resulted in vast demographic changes not only in Washington, D.C., but also in the surrounding areas of Virginia and Maryland. As Washington became a mostly black city and more particularly as the Washington public schools became virtually all black in enrollment, the white population of the capital city responded with its own mass exodus to the suburbs. Small and medium-sized towns became major suburban cities, all in just a few years.

Then came the vast expansion of the federal government during the Kennedy, Johnson, and subsequent administrations. The stately old columned buildings in central Washington that housed government bureaus became much too small to handle the new hordes of civil servants. Field offices, often entire departments of the government, moved to the suburbs.

The old political boundaries remain, of course, but any map that would portray Washington, D.C.—that is, the federal government—as an economic entity would have to include not only the District of Columbia, but also most of Montgomery and Prince Georges counties in Maryland, as well as Arlington and

Fairfax counties in Virginia, along with their independent cities of Alexandria, Falls Church, and Fairfax.

The fact that the federal government is (to put it mildly) a growth industry explains the economic prosperity of this entire area. If you don't work for the government, you're probably employed by some group that deals with the government (such as the countless lobbies that have enjoyed comparable growth rates). And if you're not employed in either of those categories, you're probably engaged in a service business where most of your customers or clients *are* so employed. The end result: secure, sizable salaries and incomes all around, low levels of unemployment and poverty, and exceptionally high per capita income levels for the area. Nobody complains about this around here, of course. Why should they when we privately employed taxpayers around the country are stuck with the tab?

AREAS WITH HIGHEST PER CAPITA INCOME IN THE UNITED STATES
(1980 Census)

COUNTY OR CITY	1979 PER CAPITA INCOME
Bristol Bay Census Area, Alaska	$14,948
FALLS CHURCH, VIRGINIA	12,885
Alpine County, California	12,861
Juneau Census Area, Alaska	12,757
ARLINGTON COUNTY, VIRGINIA	12,565
Marin County, California	12,525
MONTGOMERY COUNTY, MARYLAND	12,339
ALEXANDRIA, VIRGINIA	12,209
Pitkin County, Colorado	12,054
Valdez-Cordova Census Area, Alaska	11,642
FAIRFAX COUNTY, VIRGINIA	11,551
Anchorage Census Area, Alaska	11,366
North Slope Census Area, Alaska	11,006
New York County, New York	10,889
Johnson County, Kansas	10,885

The 1980 census proved the point beyond a doubt. Of the fifteen areas in the United States with the highest 1979 per capita income, five were in suburban Virginia and Maryland.

Actually, the situation is even more pronounced than that. Five of the top fifteen places were in Alaska. But Alaska is an anomaly. The cost of living is exceptionally high there, largely because of its isolation, and as a result exceptionally high salaries are required to lure workers there. If we omit the Alaskan locations, *fully one half—five out of ten—of the most prosperous areas of the United States are suburbs of Washington, D.C.*

Unfortunately, along with Washington's spillover population has come Washington's high crime rate.

Overall, the District of Columbia's crime rate is roughly on the same level as New York City's. Both are very high, although those of Boston, Dallas, Phoenix, Detroit, and San Francisco are even worse, and Cleveland's crime rate is also slightly higher than Washington's (see Appendix I, page 435). Washington has more murder and rape than New York, while New York has more burglaries and many more motor vehicle thefts, but overall the two cities are comparable.

NORTHERN VIRGINIA Crime Chart

	Crime Rate	Murder	Rape	Robbery	Aggravated Assault	Burglary	Larceny —Theft	Motor Vehicle Theft
United States								
U.S. Total	5,899.9	10.2	36.4	243.5	290.6	1,668.2	3,156.3	494.6
U.S. Metropolitan Areas	6,757.6	11.5	43.4	319.0	328.3	1,911.8	3,534.9	608.8
U.S. Rural Areas	2,290.4	7.5	15.5	22.5	136.9	830.2	1,143.9	133.9
Regional Crime Centers								
Alexandria	9,291.1	67.8	60.1	511.5	315.8	2,525.7	5,250.1	621.0
Arlington County	6,275.3	5.9	36.7	246.4	185.5	1,408.9	3,965.9	426.0
Fairfax	7,782.4	15.5	15.5	72.2	87.7	1,444.0	5,606.0	541.5
Fairfax County	4,859.1	3.5	17.1	87.1	68.9	1,124.6	3,272.9	285.0
Falls Church	7,052.0	0	0	157.6	42.0	1,429.3	5,160.3	262.7
Washington, D.C.	10,022.8	31.5	69.1	1,400.6	509.4	2,560.0	4,890.8	561.7
Safe Place								
Leesburg (1980)	3,877.0	0	0	23.9	35.9	502.6	3,087.2	227.4
(1981)	3,063.3	0	0	23.9	23.9	382.9	2,429.1	203.4

In the Virginia suburbs, as our Northern Virginia Crime Chart (above) illustrates, Alexandria has an overall crime rate that is almost as high as Washington's. Then there's a jump down in the crime rate to the still high levels of Fairfax (the city), Falls Church, and Arlington County. Of all the close-in suburban areas, Fairfax County has the best record, but even its crime rate is still way too high to be a Safe Place.

Unfortunately, statistics for Arlington and Fairfax counties are not broken down by individual communities, except for the independent cities listed in our crime chart and the Fairfax towns of Herndon and Vienna, which also do not qualify as Safe Places. This forced us to go beyond the close-in suburbs in our effort to find a Safe Place for you in northern Virginia.

The result, Leesburg, is an exceptionally pleasant community and many people believe it well worth the extra commuting time. We just wanted you to understand why there are no other Safe Places closer to Washington on the

Virginia side of the Potomac. They don't exist, or if they do exist, their separate statistics confirming this are not available and, at best, they are surrounded by a sea of crime.

LEESBURG

POPULATION: 8,357
NO. OF CRIMES: 324
CRIME RATE: 3,877.0 per 100,000

When we first picked Leesburg as a Safe Place in 1972, we described it as "a picturesque rural town just 36 miles from the White House, in a Virginia county famous for its early American homes and estates, its horse shows and fox hunts, and other reminders of its colorful history."

And we noted that "Loudoun County was President Madison's refuge in 1812 as the British sacked Washington; today it is the refuge of other citizens as Washington again comes under siege, this time by the criminal element."

A decade has passed since we wrote those words and we're happy to report that they still apply. Leesburg is not as rural as it was in 1972, since the population has almost doubled, but careful restrictions on the growth have maintained the central town's eighteenth-century flavor.

The crime rate has increased, too, unfortunately but probably inevitably. Still, the crime rates of the nation's metropolitan areas have also increased, so that Leesburg is still relatively safe in comparison with them. We admit we were somewhat worried about the 1980 crime rate—Leesburg barely qualified as a Safe Place, since we require a rate of less than 4,000 crimes per 100,000 and it came in that year at 3,877. Then, however, the 1981 statistics arrived and Leesburg's rate dropped more than 20 percent, to 3,063.3 per 100,000. *That*'s a trend in the right direction!

In 1980, Leesburg had 2 robberies, 3 aggravated assaults, 42 burglaries, 258 larceny-thefts, and 19 motor vehicle thefts. In 1981, this dropped to 2 robberies, 2 aggravated assaults, 32 burglaries, 203 larceny-thefts, and 17 motor vehicle thefts. There were no murders or rapes during those two years. Thus, both years Leesburg placed below U.S. rural crime rates in all categories except robbery, larceny-theft, and motor vehicle theft. And in those categories it placed well below metropolitan levels. Especially significant to us was the below-rural burglary rate both years, which is quite unusual for an affluent suburb in a high-crime metropolitan region.

Most of surrounding Loudoun County also seems to have remained quite safe. The exception is the charming village of Middleburg, which has high rates of property crime. This may be traced to Middleburg's large number of business establishments, its popularity with tourists, and its location on one of the most popular routes from Washington to the mountains.

Leesburg itself has so many historical and architectural attractions that we can merely suggest you drop in for the exhibits and film at the Loudoun County

Museum and Tourist Information Center at 16 West Loudoun Street, then take the Walk Around Leesburg tour and see places like the courthouse square, where James Monroe presided as a justice of the peace and Patrick Henry pleaded in court for a client.

Scattered throughout Loudoun County are such historic residences as Belmont Plantation, built by the Lee family and said to have been Madison's headquarters during the War of 1812, when the British burned Washington; Dodona Manor, the former home of General George C. Marshall, chief of staff during World War II and author of the Marshall Plan; Rokeby, where the Constitution, Declaration of Independence, and other important documents were kept while the British were in Washington; Oatlands, a late Georgian mansion now deeded to the National Trust for Historic Preservation; Oak Hill, President Monroe's home, a classic porticoed house in Federal style; and Morven Park, a Greek Revival mansion built in the 1780s on a 1,200-acre estate. Morven Park and Oatlands are open to the public; the others are private residences today, but you can view them from the highways and visit some of them during Historic Garden Week in the spring.

Then there are the old inns, such as the Laurel Brigade Inn in Leesburg (where Lafayette has preceded you as a guest) and the Red Fox Inn at Middleburg, said to be the second oldest operating inn in America. You can take a ride, too, on the last remaining ferry on the Potomac—tiny White's Ferry, operating where Generals Jeb Stuart and Robert E. Lee crossed with their armies in the invasion of Maryland during the War Between the States. There's been some kind of ferry here since the 1700s and you can relax as you cross, watching fishermen in their boats and couples gliding by in canoes.

Elevations in the county, by the way, range from 180 to 1,900 feet above sea level. Summers can be hot; winters are cold but not severe, with an average snowfall of 23.0 inches annually.

At the House of Lords Realty, Robert Welch showed us what had recently sold in the town and in the county. For $49,950, you could have bought a 3-bedroom, 1½-bath condominium town house, with a 16 × 12 living room, 10 × 8 dining room, 8 × 8 kitchen, 5 × 5 utility room, 10 × 15 master bedroom, and front porch. Town and county taxes were $455 a year.

At $152,500, the most expensive recent sale was a beautifully restored Victorian frame house, with cherry cabinets, high ceilings, and spacious rooms. It had 3 or 4 bedrooms, 3 full baths, 15 × 15 living room, 14 × 15 dining room, 14 × 16 kitchen, fireplaces in the living room and dining room, front and rear porches, and a full basement, all on a 10,000-square-foot lot. Taxes were $1,400.

A "typical suburban" sale was a 4-bedroom, 2½-bath colonial brick and frame house for $100,000. Four years old, it had a 15 × 12 living room, 12 × 12 dining room, 12 × 12 kitchen, 17 × 12 family room, and a 17 × 13 master bedroom. It was on a 10,000-square-foot lot.

And if you wanted to live out in the rolling countryside, you could have bought this property for $99,500: a 100-year-old 2-story house in excellent condition, on 5 acres with a barn, garage, fruit trees, and stream. It had a 15 × 17 kitchen, 10.7 × 17 living room, 13.2 × 17 family room, 6 × 8 pantry, 1 full bath, and 3 bedrooms with the largest 11 × 17. Near the village of Lovettsville, it was also just ten minutes from the Amtrak commuter train to Washington.

That commuter train makes stops locally at Harpers Ferry, West Virginia, and Brunswick and Point of Rocks, Maryland, from 5:30 to 7:43 A.M. Commuter buses are also available from Leesburg and the Sterling Park area of the county, but most people commute by automobile. Downtown Washington is 36 miles east and suburban destinations are closer.

Leesburg and Loudoun County offer you that access to the Washington area along with an unspoiled eighteenth-century ambience and rural Virginia charm. All it takes is one visit to convince you that this is a combination you'll find hard to match elsewhere in northern Virginia.

SHENANDOAH VALLEY

Virginia's fabled Shenandoah Valley is one of the scenic attractions of the eastern United States, a storybook land of prosperous farms and apple orchards ringed by the Blue Ridge Mountains on the east and the Shenandoah and Allegheny ranges to the west. It is also one of the most fought-over pieces of real estate in the country. Stonewall Jackson's famous Valley Campaign took place up and down this corridor and one diarist who lived through the War Between the States counted the town of Winchester changing hands seventy-two times.

SHENANDOAH–BLUE RIDGE Crime Chart

	Crime Rate	Murder	Rape	Robbery	Aggravated Assault	Burglary	Larceny —Theft	Motor Vehicle Theft
United States								
U.S. Total	5,899.9	10.2	36.4	243.5	290.6	1,668.2	3,156.3	494.6
U.S. Metropolitan Areas	6,757.6	11.5	43.4	319.0	328.3	1,911.8	3,534.9	608.8
U.S. Rural Areas	2,290.4	7.5	15.5	22.5	136.9	830.2	1,143.9	133.9
Regional Crime Center								
Roanoke	10,275.1	16.9	31.9	225.0	245.9	2,694.5	6,551.0	509.8
Safe Place								
Lexington (1980)	3,167.9	0	0	27.4	54.9	754.3	2,235.3	96.0
(1981)	2,262.7	0	0	27.4	27.4	411.4	1,741.6	54.9

The valley can be viewed either along its Shenandoah River bottomlands, taking Interstate 81, or from above on the more leisurely parkways atop the Blue Ridge Mountains. For 105 miles, starting due west of Washington, D.C., the parkway is known as Skyline Drive and is part of Shenandoah National Park. It continues south an additional 469 miles through Virginia and North Carolina as the Blue Ridge Parkway, ending at Great Smoky Mountains National Park.

Vistas of farms and fields await you from countless scenic turnoffs along the parkways, as well as breathtaking seasonal displays of rhododendron, azalea, and dogwood.

By and large, the valley is populated with towns and villages that are peaceful in fact as well as appearance. Crime is not a major concern here. True, as our Shenandoah–Blue Ridge Crime Chart shows (page 407), the major city of western Virginia, Roanoke, has an overall crime rate slightly higher than you'll find in Washington and New York City. Elsewhere, however, there's a succession of smaller—and safer—communities.

So, for a pleasant change, our difficulty was not in finding a Safe Place but in choosing among numerous possibilities. Our ultimate choice, Lexington, was picked therefore not out of desperation but because it offers opportunities and qualities that ranked it at the top of the class.

LEXINGTON

POPULATION: 7,292
NO. OF CRIMES: 231
CRIME RATE: 3,167.9 per 100,000

In the southern reaches of the Shenandoah Valley is a community of historical significance and architectural delights. Lexington, county seat of Rockbridge County, is the final resting place of the South's two most notable heroes, Robert E. Lee and Thomas J. (Stonewall) Jackson. It is home to two small men's colleges of national repute, Virginia Military Institute and Washington and Lee University. Walking through their campuses and along the streets and byways of downtown Lexington is like walking into the past, with eighteenth- and nineteenth-century homes, churches, and business structures gracing the shaded lanes. Classical Revival is the principal architectural style of the historic buildings, but there are excellent examples too of Greek Revival, Federal, Gothic Revival, and Italianate construction both in the city and in the country houses scattered throughout the Virginia countryside.

Central to the community's history are the two campuses. Washington and Lee, with its majestic white-columned buildings, is the oldest university off the Atlantic seaboard and fifth oldest in the nation. In 1798 George Washington put it on a sound financial footing with the largest gift up to that time to any American educational institution. After the War Between the States, Robert E. Lee assumed the presidency of the college, broadening and improving the curriculum during his administration.

Virginia Military Institute is known as the West Point of the South, and is regarded as one of the best military schools in the nation. Its distinctive Gothic architecture is now protected as a national historic landmark. Among its famous alumni are explorer Richard E. Byrd, General George S. Patton, and General George C. Marshall.

Elevations in the valley around Lexington range from 1,000 to 1,500 feet above sea level and from 3,500 to 4,000 feet in the nearby mountains. Temperatures average 35 degrees in January, 75 degrees in July. Precipitation is about 40 inches annually. Humidity is so low in this area, it's not even listed. Annual snowfall is about 20 inches. All in all, it's a delightful alpine climate.

In our comparison year of 1980, Lexington had no murders or rapes, 2 robberies, 4 aggravated assaults, 55 burglaries, 163 larceny-thefts, and 7 motor vehicle thefts. This placed Lexington below U.S. rural crime rates in all categories except robbery and larceny-theft. The same pattern held the following year, except that the total number of crimes decreased by more than 28 percent. In 1981, Lexington had a crime rate of just 2,262.7 per 100,000, with no murders or rapes, 2 robberies, 2 aggravated assaults, 30 burglaries, 127 larceny-thefts, and 4 motor vehicle thefts.

We talked with James and Greg Mays, of Mays Real Estate, about housing costs in this idyllic community. They told us that Lexington is a popular new home for people leaving the Washington, D.C., area, for retirees, and even for commuters to Roanoke, almost 50 miles south by Interstate 81. They warned that unless you are retired or bring your work with you, Lexington can be "a wonderful place to live but a hard place to earn a living."

Lexington has no condominiums and the apartments are at a premium because college students fill that market. With single-family residences, the old historic homes are popular but have liabilities as well—they are hard to heat, their kitchens are old, and their wiring usually needs to be updated. You can get a nice historic property at prices that start in the 30s and 40s, however. Also popular are "farmettes," which offer you "more lawn than you need to mow" yet not enough to farm.

For $100,000, you can get a splendid house in this area. The most expensive one in town in recent years went for $179,000—it was someone's dream house on the golf course.

You could get a nice subdivision home for $74,900. One in particular had 1,880 square feet, sat on 1.24 acres, and was located in a subdivision with well water, septic, and underground wiring. Five years old, it had 4 bedrooms and 2 baths.

As an example of the type of estate available at a good price (by city standards), the Mayses showed us a brochure for Alphin Manor, on the market at the time of our visit (July 1982) for $180,000, with annual taxes of $400. Originally built around 1850, it lies on the western side of the Shenandoah Valley on a 13.7-acre tract which is mostly in open, rolling pasture, fenced well for horses, with some wooded acreage.

The home has over 4,000 square feet of living area, consisting of wide center halls on each floor, 5 bedrooms, 2½ baths, large living room, sitting room, dining room, fully equipped eat-in kitchen, and den, with fireplaces throughout. Outside, the pitted tin roof and eave brackets suggest an Italianate house, but the double-portico Doric porch and pedimented doorways are Greek Revival.

The brickwork is very fine Flemish bond on all sides except the south, where it is common bond.

The barn, equipped with electricity and water, has 4 stalls, tack room, 4 garage bays, and a hayloft. Also on the property is a detached greenhouse and a frame storage building.

Looking for an escape from the rat race? For a town with an active community life and civic pride? For a climate that is moderate, yet having four distinct seasons? Lexington offers you all that and more. In Lexington, the charm and grace of previous centuries and the convenience of your own day merge to offer you one of the most attractive living communities in the eastern mountains of America.

Where to get further information:

State

Virginia State Travel Service, 6 N. 6th Street, Richmond, VA 23219. Virginia Department of Highways and Transportation, 1401 E. Broad Street, Richmond, VA 23219. Travel Development Department, Virginia State Chamber of Commerce, 611 E. Franklin Street, Richmond, VA 23219.

Regions

Virginia's Eastern Shore: Eastern Shore of Virginia Chamber of Commerce, Inc., Accomac, VA 23301.

Shenandoah Valley: Shenandoah Valley Travel Association, P.O. Box 488, New Market, VA 22844.

Towns

Chincoteague: Chincoteague Chamber of Commerce, Chincoteague Island, VA 23336. Real estate listings and map from Island Property Enterprises, Inc., P.O. Box 2, Chincoteague, VA 23336. The U.S. Fish and Wildlife Service, Chincoteague National Wildlife Refuge, P.O. Box 62, Chincoteague, VA 23336 has brochures on the refuge and its birds, animals, ponies, and visitor programs. National Park Service, Assateague Island National Seashore, Route 2, Box 294, Berlin, MD 21811. The Chincoteague-Assateague Fishing & Recreation Map was available locally for $2.00 at the time of our visit; it is published by Alexandria Drafting Co., 6440 General Green Way, Alexandria, VA 22312. Also available locally is an interesting booklet, *The Complete Stranger's Introductory Guide to Chincoteague Island,* by Robin di Meglio (conceived by Bernie S. Shepherd).

Leesburg: Loudoun County Chamber of Commerce, 109 E. Market Street, Leesburg, VA 22075. Loudoun Museum and Information Center, 16 W. Loudoun Street, Leesburg, VA 22075. Ask in particular for the *Loudoun County Information and Buyers Guide* and *A Walk Around Leesburg.*

Lexington: Lexington-Rockbridge County Chamber of Commerce, 107 E.

Washington Street, Lexington, VA 24450. Superintendent, Shenandoah National Park, Luray, VA 22835. Blue Ridge Parkway Association, P.O. Box 475, Asheville, NC 28802. Superintendent, Blue Ridge Parkway, 700 Northwestern Bank Building, Asheville, NC 28801.

Washington

Washington is one of our most diverse and interesting states. Occupying the northwest tip of the forty-eight contiguous states, it has everything from rocky coastline to inland plains, from rain forests to desert.

Farthest west is the Pacific coastline, with a seafood industry that ranks in size only behind California and Massachusetts. Salmon is the most famous of the 200 species of fish and shellfish caught in its rivers and along its coast and processed in Washington's ports.

Rising above the Pacific waters is the Coast Range of mountains, with heights of up to almost 8,000 feet in Olympic National Park, where you'll find glacier-capped peaks, alpine meadows with the nation's largest remaining herds of Roosevelt elk, and moss-draped forests that get 150 to 200 inches of rain a year.

North and east of the Olympic Mountains is Puget Sound, where 2,000 miles of shoreline and more than 300 islands create a water-sports paradise. In the lowlands surrounding the sound are most of the state's major cities, including Seattle and Tacoma, and the major concentrations of industry—aircraft factories, oil refineries, canning plants, lumber mills, and pulp and paper plants.

Towering above the surrounding countryside in a north–south band is the Cascade Range, the American Alps. Rising as high as the 14,410 feet of Mount Rainier, they are home to North Cascades National Park and Mount Rainier National Park and divide the state into two distinct climatic regions—a mild coastal climate to the west and the harsher continental climate to the east. Forestry, wood products, and tourism are major industries here.

East of the Cascades is the great interior basin of the Northwest—a land of orchards, agricultural expanses, rolling wheatfields, and western plains carpeted with sagebrush. Washington produces more apples than any other state and is also a leader in other orchard fruits, vegetables, and wheat. Beef cattle are raised in the center of the state, while dairy cattle predominate in the northeast and west.

One of the highlights of our Safe Places trip—and *the* highlight of the trip for Melissa—was our trek to a decidedly unsafe spot, Mount St. Helens. The volcano that erupted on May 18, 1980, had been a favorite topic of curiosity and study in Melissa's second grade class at Melrose School and it was simply unthinkable that we should be so close and pass it by. As it turned out, we were all awed by the object of our attentions.

As we turned east off Interstate 5 onto Route 503, we stopped at a tourist center to pick up some dramatic posters and a few booklets for Melissa (she also charmed the attendant out of a cellophane bag of volcanic ash, which would be necessary to prove to the skeptical boys in Melissa's class that she had really been there). East of Yale the road narrowed but was still paved and maintained by the state. Then we entered Gifford Pinchot National Forest and got our first up-close views, which inspired us to drive ever closer. A forest ranger office supplied us with maps of forest roads, which we proceeded to follow even as they got narrower, became unpaved, and were rimmed by cliffs that seemed to drop hundreds of feet without so much as a guard rail. We got as close as 3 miles from Mount St. Helens and were photographing the spectacular countryside and its volcanic cone when some angry gods decided to belch up a few puffs of white smoke. We got out of there a lot faster than we took in arriving.

SEATTLE AREA

Seattle, with all its hills, lakes, sounds, and inlets, has many fine residential areas offering superb views and homes of high architectural quality. Imagine a rambling contemporary residence utilizing stone and shingles and exposed beams, a natural setting of forest and rocks shielding you from neighbors, a colorful variety of shrubs and flowers arranged erratically in terraces Japanese-style, a broad expanse of lawn leading down to your lakeside boathouse, and a view of the Olympic Mountains or Mount Rainier off in the distance—and you have Puget Sound living at its best.

There are other essential ingredients, of course, if you are to lead the good life in a metropolitan area—and Seattle has them. The people, shopping facilities, fine restaurants and nightclubs, cultural activity, and easy access to outdoor recreation are all important considerations.

The people in Seattle reflect the trades of the Northwest—loggers who have moved to the city in search of better jobs, fishermen plying the productive waters of the northern Pacific, engineers and technicians of the aerospace industry. There are enough of them here (nearly 1/2 million people, all told, just inside city limits) so that you'll find others sharing your interests and the activities and clubs and services satisfying those interests. The people here are not involved in a continuous cultural game of one-upmanship with New York, after the manner of the San Franciscan, whose every other word is "cosmopolitan." They are friendly and courteous in the small town manner. And they love the outdoors, taking full advantage of their gorgeous setting between the waters and the mountains.

Unfortunately, somebody let more than a few snakes (human variety) into

SEATTLE AREA Crime Chart

	Crime Rate	Murder	Rape	Robbery	Aggravated Assault	Burglary	Larceny —Theft	Motor Vehicle Theft
United States								
U.S. Total	5,899.9	10.2	36.4	243.5	290.6	1,668.2	3,156.3	494.6
U.S. Metropolitan Areas	6,757.6	11.5	43.4	319.0	328.3	1,911.8	3,534.9	608.8
U.S. Rural Areas	2,290.4	7.5	15.5	22.5	136.9	830.2	1,143.9	133.9
Regional Crime Centers								
Auburn	10,414.7	0	54.3	120.2	158.9	2,240.3	7,093.0	748.1
Des Moines	10,278.8	14.1	98.6	183.0	140.8	2,562.7	6,336.2	943.4
Everett	11,325.2	7.3	49.5	231.0	526.1	2,597.6	7,037.5	876.2
Kent	12,020.2	12.9	86.3	163.9	232.9	2,760.3	8,022.1	741.8
Lynnwood	10,070.0	4.6	22.9	155.5	379.6	2,442.0	6,365.8	699.7
Marysville	10,747.4	0	0	98.6	453.6	1,636.8	8,085.2	473.3
Renton	11,722.8	6.7	63.5	130.4	287.6	2,434.9	7,806.3	993.3
Seattle	10,834.4	12.8	104.1	458.0	482.4	2,801.4	6,197.0	778.6
Tacoma	10,446.5	8.2	104.4	358.0	420.0	3,237.8	5,752.7	565.5
Tukwila	44,475.5	0	195.8	643.4	727.3	4,783.2	36,139.9	1,986.0
Safe Place								
Clyde Hill	3,935.5	0	0	62.0	0	1,704.4	2,138.2	31.0

this paradise. We mentioned in our introduction that it was especially difficult finding Safe Places in the south and west. Here it was almost impossible.

Washington had the seventh highest crime rate of the fifty states during our comparison year of 1980 and of its thirty-six communities with a population of 10,000 or more, only one—Pullman—qualified as a Safe Place. (Pullman is a university town and shipping center for the wheat-producing Palouse Hills of eastern Washington.) Usually, then, we look for smaller communities that are safe. Here, however, we had trouble finding *any* place of any size that would qualify as a Safe Place.

As our Seattle Area Crime Chart shows (above), there is no lack of crime centers. We listed only the cities and towns with a crime rate of more than 10,000 crimes per 100,000 population; that's roughly the crime level of New York City and Washington, D.C. There were ten such communities here. One of them, Tukwila, really has our curiosity aroused. Its population is only 3,575, but its crime *rate* comes to a stratospheric level of 44,475.5 crimes per 100,000 population. If we can get our publisher interested in a book on Dangerous Places, we'll engage the services of an armored car and report back to you on just what makes Tukwila tick (besides time bombs).

We did manage to find a couple of Safe Places around Tacoma and several more farther north and east in Snohomish County. We wanted a community that was close-in to Seattle, however, and finally found one on the eastern shore of Lake Washington. It has more crime than we like (we're sure its residents share that view), but it *does* qualify as a Safe Place and certainly compares favorably with most of the communities in this area. And its other qualities also make it a truly delightful find.

CLYDE HILL

POPULATION: 3,227
NO. OF CRIMES: 127
CRIME RATE: 3,935.5 per 100,000

Lake Washington constitutes the eastern border of Seattle. On the lake's eastern shore—the side opposite Seattle—is a cluster of suburban communities. The largest of these is Bellevue, which has grown to the point where it is a city in its own right. Two bridges connect the two shores of the 32-mile-long lake.

One of the small communities on the eastern shore of the lake is Clyde Hill. While it is generally thought of as a neighborhood of Bellevue, it was incorporated as a town in 1953 when local residents decided they must act to keep the area from being commercialized. This was particularly a threat along the eastern approach to the Lake Washington Floating Bridge.

As a result of that decision to incorporate, Clyde Hill has remained a residential community of shaded, lovely homes, many of them situated on hills that afford views of the lake and the Seattle skyline. One spot is zoned agricultural, so it can have horses, and there are two gas stations in town. Other than that, this is a community of single-family homes.

We had a delightful talk with Ruth Saari, the town clerk, who told us that most lots in town are about 20,000 square feet (roughly 1/2 acre) in size. Town government consists of a mayor and a five-member council, all volunteers; there is a six-member police department and a one-man street department. Clyde Hill contracts with Bellevue for fire protection, water, and sewage. An engineer and an attorney serve the town on a retainer basis.

Mrs. Saari gave us some copies of *Clyde Hill Views*, a newsletter for residents containing municipal news and thoughtful columns by the mayor and police chief. We've encountered many town newsletters around the country and this one impressed us as perhaps the best we've seen. The emphasis in each issue on crime prevention speaks well for the community's determination to remain a Safe Place.

In our comparison year of 1980, Clyde Hill barely met our qualifications for a Safe Place. Its overall crime rate was 3,935.5 crimes per 100,000 population and our cutoff point was 4,000. But "in the past two years," according to Mayor Dwayne A. Richards, "we have had a dramatic decrease in our crime statistics."

Even in 1980, Clyde Hill was the safest town in the immediate area and one of the safest in the whole Puget Sound metropolitan region, as our Seattle Area Crime Chart (page 414) shows. This was particularly true with crimes of violence, since there were no murders, rapes, or aggravated assaults, and just 2 robberies. In property crime, there were 55 burglaries, 69 larceny-thefts, and 1 motor vehicle theft.

In the town's newsletter, Police Chief Kenneth Weinstein has mentioned some of the ways in which his department is trying to cut the crime rate. Among them:

• *Police visibility:* "Common sense tells us that if a uniformed police officer in a marked police car is present, it is highly unlikely that a criminal act will occur at his location . . . It is our department's intention to create in the mind of the criminal the constant presence of police as a deterrent." (Ruth Saari told us that the town was in the process of buying its third cruiser—not bad for a place with fewer than 4,000 residents.)

• *Vacation watch:* "Notify us if you intend to be gone for more than twenty-four hours by filling out a short form with pertinent information at the Police Department in the Town Hall. During your absence patrol officers will make every effort to increase surveillance of your home . . ."

• *Home surveys:* "I will gladly conduct a physical security survey of your residence and with it provide suggestions on how to reduce your vulnerability to crime."

• *Citizen involvement:* "The first step in organizing a neighborhood house watch is to get a group of your neighbors together who are interested in mutual protection against burglary. These neighbors agree to watch out for one another's homes and report unusual incidents to the police, as they are aware of who belongs in the neighborhood. In addition to agreeing to assist each other, they also agree to collectively meet with us for training, which is not all that time consuming. In some instances, these training sessions have been expanded at the request of participants to seminars on rape prevention, personal safety, robbery, and shoplifting. There is no cost for this program; we provide the technical assistance . . . With the revival of community spirit and self-help, our citizens are discovering that minding someone else's business can indeed pay off."

We also liked the chief's insistence that parents have the primary responsibility in preventing juvenile crime. "We police are here to offer protection, assistance, and guidance," he told those parents. "We are not bent on prosecution or on frightening people into obeying the law. The Clyde Hill Police Department is more concerned with the discovery and rectification of any situation that might develop into a criminal act, particularly where juveniles are concerned."

For information on housing costs, we checked with the Coldwell Banker office in Bellevue. "Clyde Hill is one of the areas that most people want," we were told.

Houses in Clyde Hill range from just under $100,000 to $300,000 and sometimes a house as high as $500,000 comes on the market. Most, however, are at the lower price levels. Under $125,000 you'll find the older and smaller homes—say, twenty or twenty-five years old and with 3 bedrooms and 1½ baths. There would usually be a living room and small dining room, but not necessarily a family room. In this price range, you might have a carport, or a 1-car garage, or even a 2-car garage—there's quite a variety available.

Starting at around $115,000, the houses will be perhaps twelve to fifteen years old. At $150,000 and up, you get 4 bedrooms. And for $174,000, Coldwell Banker could offer an eight-year-old 2-story house in a traditional style, with 4 bedrooms, 3 baths, living room, family room, eat-in kitchen, and 2-car garage. In all, there was about 2,500 square feet of living area.

Adjacent Bellevue offers some of the most attractive shopping malls and stores you could ask for and one of the nation's most interesting big cities is just across Lake Washington. The Cascades, Puget Sound, the Olympic rain forests, and the Pacific coast are all readily accessible. Whatever your interests may be, few places can offer you better opportunities to fulfill them in beautiful physical surroundings.

Where to get further information:

State

Tourism Development Division, Department of Commerce and Economic Development, General Administration Building, Olympia, WA 98504.

Regional

Seattle–King County Convention and Visitors Bureau, 1815 Seventh Avenue, Seattle, WA 98101. Bellevue Chamber of Commerce, 550 106th Street N.E., Bellevue, WA 98004.

Local

Town Hall, Town of Clyde Hill, Bellevue, WA 98004.

West Virginia

When the War Between the States erupted in 1861, the twenty-six western counties of Virginia were already angry at Richmond. For decades, they felt, they had been overtaxed, shortchanged in services, and underrepresented in the state legislature. Slaves were counted as part of the population for voting weight and there were few slaves in these western counties. So after Virginia seceded from the United States, West Virginia seceded from Virginia.

WEST VIRGINIA'S EASTERN PANHANDLE Crime Chart

	Crime Rate	Murder	Rape	Robbery	Aggravated Assault	Burglary	Larceny —Theft	Motor Vehicle Theft
United States								
U.S. Total	5,899.9	10.2	36.4	243.5	290.6	1,668.2	3,156.3	494.6
U.S. Metropolitan Areas	6,757.6	11.5	43.4	319.0	328.3	1,911.8	3,534.9	608.8
U.S. Rural Areas	2,290.4	7.5	15.5	22.5	136.9	830.2	1,143.9	133.9
Regional Crime Centers								
Frederick, Md.	8,977.8	3.6	21.8	18.1	834.6	1,506.0	6,078.3	333.9
Harpers Ferry, W.Va.	9,929.1	0	0	236.4*	472.8	5,673.8	2,364.1	1,182.0
Safe Place								
Shepherdstown, W.Va. (1980)	2,624.2	0	0	55.8*	167.5	781.7	1,563.4	55.8
(1981)	1,114.8	0	0	0	55.7	167.2	891.9	0

* A statistical aberration caused by low population and crime numbers.

Today's economy is dominated by manufacturing and mining, with agriculture a distant third. Iron and steel mills are found in the northern panhandle of the state, glass and chemicals are also major industries, and coal mining is important almost everywhere in the state. West Virginia's eastern panhandle, where our Safe Place is located, is the main fruit-growing region.

Tourism is also growing in importance, as residents of the Eastern United States discover the state's scenic treasures. In a word, those treasures are its mountains. West Virginia's nickname is the Mountain State, its motto *Montani*

Semper Liberi ("Mountaineers Are Always Free"). With an average altitude of 1,500 feet, this is the highest state east of the Mississippi.

West Virginia began to be settled by Europeans around 1732, with a flow of Scotch-Irish and German pioneers from Pennsylvania and Maryland. Our Safe Place was one of their first settlements.

SHEPHERDSTOWN

POPULATION: 1,791
NO. OF CRIMES: 47
CRIME RATE: 2,624.2 per 100,000

Located in the eastern panhandle of West Virginia, on the banks of the Potomac River, Shepherdstown is the oldest continuously settled town in the state. It was chartered as Mecklenburg in 1762 and its name changed to Shepherdstown in 1798.

Shepherdstown has many firsts to its credit within West Virginia—the first printing press (1790), the first newspaper *(The Potomac Guardian,* 1790), and the first book published in the state, *The Christian Panoply* (1797). That book is now on display in the public library, formerly the Old Market House, which was built in 1800. You can also see the world's oldest (1739) and perhaps largest (40 feet in diameter) waterwheel, which operated Thomas Shepherd's gristmill.

It was in Shepherdstown, too, that James Rumsey gave the first public demonstration of the steamboat in 1787. He died four years later, though, and his achievement was all but forgotten because of the rival claims of John Fitch and Robert Fulton's later commercial success with the *Clermont.*

Letters in the Library of Congress even reveal that George Washington seriously considered Shepherdstown as the site of the nation's capital.

Two centuries after its founding, Shepherdstown still retains the feel of an eighteenth-century town. German Street, the main street, has patches of brick sidewalk remaining in areas and is lined with handsome brick colonial and Federal homes and buildings. Even the name of the town's weekly newspaper captures the spirit of the place in a delightful way: It's the *Spirit of Jefferson Farmer's Advocate.*

Shepherdstown's crime rate is yet another delight—delightfully low. In our comparison year of 1980, there were no murders or rapes, 1 robbery, 3 aggravated assaults, 14 burglaries, 28 larceny-thefts, and 1 motor vehicle theft. That placed the town below U.S. rural crime rates in all categories except aggravated assault, larceny-theft, and robbery, where the one incident—and the town's small population—resulted in a statistical aberration.

The following year, moreover, Shepherdstown's crime rate dropped by more than 57 percent. With just 1 aggravated assault, 3 burglaries, and 16 larceny-thefts, its overall crime rate dropped to 1,114.8 per 100,000 population and it placed below U.S. rural crime rates in all categories. *That*'s progress!

Today's Shepherdstown also enjoys the cultural leavening that results from the presence of Shepherd College, established in 1871. Its more than 3,000 students pursue programs that lead to liberal arts, business, and education degrees. Its Millbrook Center for the Performing and Visual Arts is host to the forty-piece Millbrook Center Chamber Orchestra, comprised of professional musicians residing in the tri-state area.

Annual events in the Shepherdstown area include the House and Garden Tour, the Horse Show at Morgans Grove Park in July, the Mountain Heritage Arts and Crafts Festival and Old Tyme Christmas at Harpers Ferry, and the Jefferson County Fair in Charles Town. Hiking and biking are popular along the C&O Canal that follows the Potomac. Harpers Ferry National Historic Park is just a few miles away and the attractions in Charles Town, the Jefferson County seat, include the restored Opera House and year-round nighttime thoroughbred racing. To top it all off, Shepherdstown has two restaurants that have achieved a strong regional reputation, the Bavarian Inn and the Yellow Brick Bank.

With attractions like these, you can understand why more and more people have been "discovering" Shepherdstown in recent years. At Shepherdstown Realty, we had a delightful talk with Mary Lowe and Linda Spunich. Mary's husband was born and raised in Shepherdstown, but she came from Washington, D.C. "The transition to a small rural town took some getting used to," she admitted, "but I think it's well worth it."

Since both Washington and Baltimore are about 70 miles distant, we were surprised when Mary and Linda told us that more and more new residents commute to jobs in those two areas. "They don't mind the distance," we were told, and if you're going to downtown Washington you can catch the Amtrak commuter trains from Harpers Ferry.

Another source of growing population is the college itself, as students decide to stay here or move back after they are married and starting a family. Maryland teachers also like to live here because of the lower real estate prices and much lower taxes. (On a $100,000 house, you'd pay only about $536 a year.) In recent years, the presence of Secret Service agents in town were a favorite topic of conversation, as Mrs. Walter Mondale visited friends here and presidential aides moved to the area.

At the time of our visit (September 1982), houses on the market ranged in price from $33,000 to $225,000. The 50s and 60s make up the best-selling range, we were told. Some houses are available on a rental basis ($350 to $450 a month) and there are a few 2-bedroom apartments renting for $275. Shepherdstown has no condominiums.

Recently sold for $72,000 was a 2-story white frame country-style home, located on two city lots. It had been rewired, insulated, and modernized in its plumbing and kitchen. There were 3 bedrooms, a living room, a dining room, and a screened porch.

More typical of the newer homes was a Cape Cod on 1 acre with river access. The first floor had 2 bedrooms, a small kitchen, dining room, living room, and bath. Two bedrooms and a full bath were on the second floor and the unfinished basement had a hearth for a wood stove. Its asking price was $79,900.

Five miles out of town was Scrabble, a late Victorian farmhouse on 11-plus acres with Potomac River access. It had nice features such as a winding staircase, plus 2 new baths, but needed partial renovation. A large bank barn and several other outbuildings were also on the property, which had dropped in price from $94,500 to $89,500.

And if you have the money, you will get much more here than in the built-up suburbs or neighborhoods of Washington and Baltimore. For example, a completely restored town house in the Georgetown tradition was available in Old Town Shepherdstown for $179,000. It had 3 large bedrooms, 2 baths, a handcrafted kitchen with French doors to the patio, fireplace, plus a private yard and parking area.

The most expensive listing, at $225,000, was for an old inn—the Potomac Lodge—now used as a private home. Its 7 acres of land included water frontage, a Potomac view, a 20 × 40 L-shaped pool, and city water, sewage, and septic. The 2-story stone and frame house had 6 rooms, a huge central hall, and a bath on the first floor, 8 rooms and 3 baths on the second floor, 8 fireplaces, and hardwood floors.

With all its attractions and special features, it is clear that Shepherdstown is no ordinary small rural town. It offers eighteenth-century charm, reasonably priced housing, and for many people, just the right combination of seclusion from—and accessibility to—the Washington and Baltimore metropolitan regions.

We suspect, indeed, that Shepherdstown is just beginning to be discovered by people escaping those two cities. A move here today should prove to be an even wiser choice tomorrow, as real estate values climb and you continue to reap the psychic benefits of life in this delightful haven on the banks of the Potomac.

Where to get further information:

State

Travel Development Program, Governor's Office of Economic and Community Development, State Capitol, Charleston, WV 25305. Materials may also be ordered by telephoning 800/624-9110. *Wonderful West Virginia,* a monthly magazine, is available for $7.00 a year from the Information and Education Division, Department of Natural Resources, State Capitol, Charleston, WV 25305.

Regional

Eastern Gateway Travel Council, West Virginia Information Center, Harpers Ferry, WV 25425. *Cumberland Valley Revue* is a monthly guide to the region, available for $12.00 a year or $1.00 per single copy from Bayer Enterprises, Inc., P.O. Box 2032, Hagerstown, MD 21740.

Local

Jefferson County Chamber of Commerce, P.O. Box 430, Charles Town, WV 25414. For information on the House and Garden Tour: Shenandoah-Potomac Garden Club, P.O. Box 40, Shepherdstown, WV 25443. For their information sheet on the town and housing lists: Shepherdstown Realty, Inc., P.O. Box 550, Shepherdstown, WV 25443.

Wisconsin

America's Dairyland produces 19 *billion* pounds of milk a year, which constitutes about 17 percent of the nation's total. Wisconsin cheese is in demand throughout the United States, as is its sausage and beer. Wisconsin also leads the nation in production of hay and in the canning of fresh vegetables.

For all that, agriculture still takes third place in the state's economy. Tourism is second and in commanding lead is manufacturing—metalworking, machinery and equipment, paper and paper products, auto assembly, shipbuilding, and much more.

Wisconsin is mostly rolling plains, broken by 14,000 lakes and 1,500 streams and bordered on three of its four sides by Lake Michigan, Lake Superior, and the Mississippi River. Apostle Islands National Lakeshore on Lake Superior, the Door Peninsula that juts out into Lake Michigan, and the rugged southwest corner of the state are just some of the state's scenic attractions. In its geography and flavor, Wisconsin is part New England (the Door Peninsula), part Midwestern prairies, part North Woods, and part Mississippi River Valley. And along with this mélange, the state is a mecca for fishing, hunting, winter sports, and camping.

The one part of Wisconsin we haven't mentioned yet is also one of its most interesting aspects—the big city that beer made famous, an ethnic mosaic on the shores of Lake Michigan and one of America's best-kept urban secrets, Milwaukee.

MILWAUKEE AREA

Beer is its most famous product, but the breweries employ only 2 percent of the work force. Much more important in that respect is the manufacturing of major machinery, with giants like Allis-Chalmers, Allen Bradley, Briggs Stratton, and A. O. Smith leading the way in making this one of the industrial centers of the nation. Milwaukee ranks eighth in manufacturing and is the nation's third largest user of steel.

Milwaukee is also a significant cultural center and has an exceptionally large number of museums for a city of its size. Its city parks, particularly along the lakeshore, are among the nation's finest. Milwaukee enjoys a reputation as a clean, progressive, hardworking, and honest city. It's the only major Northern city with an AAA rating in regard to borrowing and the city closest to it is Indianapolis, with a mere A rating. Even Milwaukee's crime rate is quite low for a big city; of the twenty-three U.S. cities with a population of 500,000 or more, only Indianapolis and Philadelphia have lower crime. And they aren't nearly as interesting.

Chief among the things that make Milwaukee interesting is its ethnic heritage. As the saying goes, Germans and Milwaukee go together like beer and brats (bratwurst to you outsiders), but you can just as easily feast on Polish kielbasa, Bohemian sausage, or Chinese pressed duck. All told, some sixty-five ethnic groups make their mark felt in the city. This is reflected in the neighborhoods, in the churches (Roman Catholics and Lutherans predominate), in the restaurants, and in the festivals—Volksfest, Festa Italiana, Irish Fest, Polish Fest, Oktoberfest, Fiesta Mexicana, and more.

Our stay in Milwaukee, brief as it was, was also one of the more pleasant stops on our harried cross-country trip. Our room at the Milwaukee River Hilton Inn was clean, nicely furnished, spacious for the money, and offered a peaceful view of the river; its restaurant also served excellent seafood luncheons. And for some traditional Milwaukee *Gemütlichkeit*, we feasted on schnitzel and enjoyed the Old World atmosphere of Karl Ratzsch's. One of Milwaukee's famous German restaurants, it displays truly spectacular collections of cut glass and steins. It was like dining in a museum where everyone was having a lot of fun.

We've referred to Milwaukee's crime rate once already. While it is *relatively* low for a major city, it is still above U.S. average rates for most categories. So the situation here is good only by comparison with most other big cities.

The same is true for Milwaukee's suburbs. While most of them do not qualify as Safe Places, the situation still could be worse. Take, for example, the suburb of Glendale, which has the area's worst overall crime rate (see our Milwaukee Area Crime Chart, page 425). Even there we discover that what boosts Glendale's overall crime rate so high is a phenomenally high rate of larceny-theft —roughly three times the rate for U.S. metropolitan areas! In part, this can be blamed on the location within Glendale of the huge Bay Shore Shopping Center. But other cities and suburbs have giant shopping centers without larceny rates that zoom that high. It is clear from the figures for Milwaukee, Glendale, and our Safe Place, that larceny-theft is the highest-crime category for the Milwaukee area. To which we're sure many will join us in saying, "Too bad, but better that than murder or rape or robbery."

Milwaukee, like most of the northeastern cities, *does* have a number of suburbs with quite low crime rates. Our Safe Place of Whitefish Bay is one of the nicest among them. But while it is a comfortable middle-class to upper-middle-class suburb, it is not the poshest of Milwaukee's suburbs by far. One interesting way to judge that was a comparative study we received from Head & Seemann

MILWAUKEE AREA Crime Chart

	Crime Rate	Murder	Rape	Robbery	Aggravated Assault	Burglary	Larceny —Theft	Motor Vehicle Theft
United States								
U.S. Total	5,899.9	10.2	36.4	243.5	290.6	1,668.2	3,156.3	494.6
U.S. Metropolitan Areas	6,757.6	11.5	43.4	319.0	328.3	1,911.8	3,534.9	608.8
U.S. Rural Areas	2,290.4	7.5	15.5	22.5	136.9	830.2	1,143.9	133.9
Regional Crime Centers								
Glendale	11,729.5	0	14.4	151.6	72.2	628.0	10,516.8	346.5
Milwaukee	6,538.8	11.7	33.6	283.4	193.6	1,520.6	3,901.0	595.1
Safe Place								
Whitefish Bay	2,462.9	0	0	26.8	26.8	287.8	2,081.4	40.2

Realtors, listing the price ranges for the "greatest selection" of houses in various communities. In the north shore area, Whitefish Bay and Shorewood both had a range of "greatest selection" from $70,000 to $130,000. It was comparable in Thiensville ($80,000 to $120,000) and higher in Fox Point ($90,000 to $140,000), Bayside ($100,000 to $150,000), Mequon ($100,000 to $170,000), and above all River Hills ($150,000 to $225,000), where most areas are zoned for a minimum of 5 acres. West of Milwaukee, Brookfield ($70,000 to $150,000) and Elm Grove ($100,000 to $160,000) were comparably priced. And while there certainly are some nice suburbs to the south and southwest, they tend to be less affluent or to have a narrower price range of housing.

WHITEFISH BAY

POPULATION: 14,942
NO. OF CRIMES: 368
CRIME RATE: 2,462.9 per 100,000

Whitefish Bay is tucked away on the north shore—the Gold Coast—of Lake Michigan, between Shorewood and Fox Point. It's an exceptionally convenient location, with downtown Milwaukee just 7 miles and fifteen minutes away. You can take either Interstate 43 or North Lake Drive and you won't face the traffic congestion that exists in other areas.

We were quite favorably impressed by Whitefish Bay. It is an older-style suburb that has aged well, with neatly manicured streets lined by 2-story homes with peaked roofs that sit on narrow, wooded lots. The houses are predominantly brick and often finished with stone trim. As a general rule, the closer you get to the lakeshore, the larger they are. The most prized locations are on the lake side of North Lake Drive.

This is primarily a residential community of single-family homes, with just a few apartment buildings, a complex of 2-bedroom town houses, and one block of luxury condominiums. There is no industry and local businesses—fine retail shops, a theater, and professional offices—are centered on Silver Spring Drive. Bay Shore Mall, with large department stores, is conveniently located just west of town.

Whitefish Bay High School blends nicely into the town, too. It is a 3-story brick structure with white stone trim and a central tower that gives it more of the appearance of an Ivy League college. Two other high schools are located in Whitefish Bay and serve the surrounding area as well—Dominican, with its Spanish architecture, and the University School of Milwaukee (nursery through grade 12), with traditional architecture.

Schools are very important to the residents of Whitefish Bay. They start here with a very popular four-year-old junior kindergarten. The elementary schools are so conveniently located that all children walk to school and there are no buses. Whitefish Bay's public school system is considered to be one of the best in the Midwest, with excellent library facilities, and 85 percent of the high school's graduates go to college—the highest percentage in the Milwaukee area.

At the local office of Head & Seemann, Realtors, on North Port Washington Road, we had pleasant and informative talks with Ralph P. Knoernschild and Larry Poll. Mr. Knoernschild has been a trustee of the village of Whitefish Bay for twenty-eight years and he told us that "its people are willing to pay the extra dollar for good police protection and fire protection." The police provide house checks while you are away on vacation and just recently started a Neighborhood Watch program. Overnight parking on the streets is prohibited and this allows the police to keep a close check on who is parked in front of whose house. By providing license plate numbers to the police, you can obtain three-day parking permits for visitors and seasonal permits for children in college who have come home for the summer.

Mr. Knoernschild told us that Whitefish Bay isn't interested in county government and prefers to provide its own city services. In the winter, he said, "Even the sidewalks are plowed before you get up to go to work in the morning." (Hear that, Washington? Hear that, Indianapolis? *That*'s the way to handle Old Man Winter!) Mr. Knoernschild also explained why you won't find any inner-city decay in Whitefish Bay. For many years the village had a program whereby it bought any delapidated old buildings, razed them, and then sold the property. They figured they would make it up in the long term with increased tax revenues. Now there's nothing left to be razed.

Mr. Knoernschild and Mr. Poll both noted the advantages of a built-up older suburb—and the fact that it sometimes takes a little time to appreciate, if you're used to spaced-out lawns with lots of crabgrass to keep you busy in the summer. Mr. Knoernschild noted that because there are sidewalks everywhere and children can use them for bicycling, in effect the entire town becomes a playground. In fact, bicycle safety is a major program of the police department, with contests for the kids and awards for good bicycling practices.

Mr. Poll and his wife were both raised in the western suburbs of Milwaukee, so they were used to acreage. When it came time for them to buy a house, though, they looked for the most home for their money—and that was in Whitefish Bay. Larry noted that some of the older homes don't have all the amenities of those in newer suburban developments; they may have just a one-car garage, for example, because when they were built most families didn't have more than one car. But people very soon get to like the aura of a lakefront community.

Even during the slow market of the past few years, Larry told us, there was a steady demand for homes in Whitefish Bay. And because it is a younger community, mainly families with children, most of the older homes have already been renovated at least once. Along with the renovation you retain all the character and charm of an older home, such as center-hall layouts and details like fine wood molding and high ceilings.

All homes in this area have basements. Almost everything is 2-story because of the narrow lot sizes—usually 40 or 45 × 125. It is difficult to find a house with a family room until you get in the $90,000 range and unusual to have 2 full baths for less than $100,000. Taxes are lower than in Milwaukee or Shorewood. Houses are assessed at 42 percent of market value; taxes would come to $1,321 for an assessment of $50,000 or $2,600 for an assessment of $100,000.

At the time of our visit (September 1982), there were a dozen homes on the market for under $70,000. These were small, with 2 or 3 bedrooms and no more than 1,000 to 1,100 square feet of living area.

You won't find a decent selection of 4-bedroom, 2-bath homes until you get to the $120,000–$125,000 range. These would usually have about 2,300 square feet, with a living room, family room, and formal dining room. But this is a rock-bottom price range and the selection increases along with the price.

Cumberland is one of the nicest streets in the village and houses there range from $130,000 to $250,000. It is unusual to find a Lake Drive home for less than $225,000 and the baronial ones will sell for $450,000. There are no flooding problems in Whitefish Bay, we were told. There have been some problems with bluff erosion, but engineers have now rebuilt the bluffs.

As we drove around Whitefish Bay, we noticed an attractive stone English Tudor on a corner lot on Cumberland. It was selling for $169,000 and had 5 bedrooms and 3½ baths, including a third-floor bedroom and bath. Among the 9 rooms in this 1931 house were a 22 × 16 living room, 14 × 11 family room with paneled bookcases, 22 × 15 rec room, 15 × 12 dining room, 11 × 11 kitchen, and 22 × 13 master bedroom. There was also a 2-car detached garage, the lot was 51 × 110, and taxes were $3,781.

"Lots of people change suburbs as their income increases," Larry Poll told us, "but in Whitefish Bay people often want to change houses within the community rather than move away."

With its first-rate schools, attractive neighborhoods, lakeshore frontage, and convenient location, it is easy indeed to see how living in Whitefish Bay could become a habit you don't want to break.

Where to get further information:

State

Wisconsin Division of Tourism, Department of Development, 123 W. Washington Avenue, P.O. Box 7606, Madison, WI 53707.

Regional

Greater Milwaukee Convention and Visitors Bureau, 756 N. Milwaukee Street, Milwaukee, WI 53202. *Head & Seemann's Guide to Better Serve the Transferee* ($3.00) is an excellent guide to Milwaukee-area communities: Head & Seemann, Realtors, 6000 N. Port Washington Road, Milwaukee, WI 53217.

Local

Village of Whitefish Bay, 5300 N. Marlborough Drive, Whitefish Bay, WI 53217 publishes an *Official News Letter* for residents.

Wyoming

If you are looking for the wide-open spaces and don't care too much for city life, consider Wyoming. In many ways, it is the archetypical Western state, where the cowboy tradition remains most genuinely intact. Texas has always been too big and diversified to be regarded solely as a Western state. California long ago became overcivilized. Most of Arizona has been taken over by Yankees and Californians, and Coloradans worry that they are becoming a colony of Texas. Every Western state in the contiguous United States has at least one metropolis that serves as its economic and cultural center—except Wyoming. Its largest city, Casper, has just about 51,000 people, while its state capital, Cheyenne, has only 47,000. Indeed, the entire state—almost twenty times the size of Connecticut—has a population of less than 1/2 million. In Wyoming, big game outnumber the people. The cattle and sheep outnumber the people. With only five human beings per square mile, you *know* the jackrabbits outnumber the people.

The tourist usually associates Wyoming with Yellowstone and Grand Teton National Parks, but actually they are an exception to the usual Wyoming vista. The country around Yellowstone and the Tetons is lush and green; nearly all the rest of the state is semiarid mountain, plains, and desert country more reminiscent of the Southwest. Spruce and fir forests blanket the Yellowstone-Teton country; sagebrush is more the rule in the rest of the state. What all the sections of this state have in common, though, is a ruggedness—both a ruggedness of terrain and a ruggedness in the spirit of the people who survive in that terrain.

In two areas, conservation and women's rights, Wyoming has an impressive array of "firsts" to its credit. In conservation, Wyoming had the nation's (and the world's) first national park, Yellowstone, the first national monument, Devil's Tower, the first national forest, Shoshone, and the first preserve for the protection of a wild, free species of big game animal, the National Elk Refuge. In women's rights, Wyoming was the first state to grant the vote to women—in fact, it did so in 1869, while it was still a territory. It also had the first woman justice of the peace, the first women jurors, and the first woman governor. Not without reason is one of its nicknames the Equality State. (Its other is the Cowboy State.)

Wyoming provides more than half of all the oil produced in the Rocky Mountain states, making oil the state's major industry. Wyoming also has the largest coal reserves of any state in the United States. Tourism, agriculture, and livestock are other major industries. Wyoming has more than a million cattle and more than a million sheep, placing the state third behind Texas and California in the production of wool.

In the past, Wyoming has always been a favorite stop for us on trips west. On this Safe Places trip, we added a new booster of the state's charms with Melissa. In Grand Teton National Park, she fell in love with her horse Bandit on her first trail ride, as we circled the Moose Ponds and rode along the shores of jewel-like Jenny Lake. The trip down the Snake River was too tame, she complained, but it did give her a chance to make a new friend of a companion on the float, Elena Grinberg. But Yellowstone was even more of a child's delight: peering literally over the top of Yellowstone Falls, from the vantage point of a rock ledge, as it crashes down more than 300 feet straight below you to the accompaniment of a constant, thunderous roar; the moose, elk, and bison grazing peacefully as you drive by; and above all, the fascinating thermal display presented by the colorful paint pots, fumaroles, and geysers. When the explorer John Colter discovered this region in 1807, he nicknamed it Colter's Hell, but to the awestruck eyes of a seven-year-old it was a touch of heaven as well, and we promised—again and again and again—to return as soon as fortune allowed.

BUFFALO

POPULATION: 3,853
NO. OF CRIMES: 139
CRIME RATE: 3,607.6 per 100,000

While the Oregon Trail and other immigrant routes passed through the southern part of what would become the state of Wyoming, the northeast corner of that future state remained a hunting stronghold of the Sioux and the Crow. White men knew better than to venture into the lands between the Big Horn Mountains and the Black Hills to their east.

Then came the discovery of gold in Montana, way out west beyond Yellowstone. Starting in 1863, John M. Bozeman and others began using the eastern slope of the Big Horns as a wagon route for freighting supplies from the Missouri River country to the Montana gold camps. The Indians mightily resented this intrusion on their hunting grounds, of course, and every freighting party was met with attacks by them. Then, in 1866, Fort Phil Kearney was established near what is now the little town of Story, Wyoming. Set in the middle of 600 miles of wild Indian country, Fort Kearney, during its little more than two years of existence, was the site of more Indian battles and hostilities than probably any other army post in the history of the Western frontier. There were fifty-one encounters in its first six and a half months alone.

Some years later, in 1878, Fort McKinney was established a few miles south of where Fort Kearney had stood. Various businesses of trade and entertainment began to cluster nearby on the banks of the Clear Fork of the Powder River, later known as Clear Creek. Soldiers apparently liked to part with their pay there and the community grew and prospered. Johnson County was organized in 1879 and the next year saw the opening of the Occidental Hotel and the naming of the new community, now a county seat, as Buffalo. Contrary to what you might expect, it was not named after the bison that roamed the countryside but after Buffalo, New York. It had been decided to name the town by placing suggested names on slips of paper and depositing them in a hat on the Occidental's bar. The one drawn happened to be that of Will Hart, formerly of Buffalo, New York. And so Buffalo avoided being named Pollock or Absaraka—some other suggestions.

Buffalo was a typical frontier town, with both its bawdy and its civilizing influences. It was famous for its saloons, dance halls, and painted ladies, as they were called. Competition was stiff and one madam was so enterprising, we are told, as to order 100 roller skates to aid the drunken cowboys as they chased her gals. On the other hand, Buffalo had its substantial citizens, its churches, and its literary clubs and social affairs. The Occidental Hotel, which served as a social center in the town's early days, has been rebuilt and renovated several times, but it remains today on the original site. It was made famous by Owen Wister in his novel, *The Virginian*, the prototype of the Western as a form of fiction. You may remember it as the spot where the Virginian got his man.

By far the most famous episode in Buffalo's frontier history was the Johnson County cattlemen's war, also known as the Johnson County invasion. The story is far too complicated to go into here, but it remains the classic tale of big cattlemen versus small cattlemen and homesteaders, complete with a special train chartered by the big cattlemen, full of gunmen brought in from Texas. "The Johnson County cattle war," wrote Mrs. D. F. Baber in *The Longest Rope*, "marks the dividing line between the old West, under the rule of the big cattle kings, and the new West of the pioneer homesteader."

As Buffalo grew, people of many different nationalities came to call it home. The English and the Scots were the first to come, for London and Edinburgh capital was behind many of the huge cattle empires. Sheep ranching brought in Irish and some Portuguese. Then in 1914, with the onset of World War I, Basques arrived on the scene—they were experienced as shepherds, of course, and the mountains here resembled the ones they left behind. During World War II, the Chicago, Burlington & Quincy—which runs from Omaha to Billings—brought in Danes with the railroad's spur line to Buffalo (since discontinued), using them to irrigate and farm railroad lands. Thus, the Danish Lutheran church in Buffalo. Some Swedes came here as loggers and lumbermen and in Sheridan, with its coal mines, there is a concentration of peoples of Slavic background.

Buffalo today still retains much of its Western charm. There it is, a picturesque little town of fewer than 4,000 people, spread out in a basin with the Big

WYOMING Crime Chart

	Crime Rate	Murder	Rape	Robbery	Aggravated Assault	Burglary	Larceny —Theft	Motor Vehicle Theft
United States								
U.S. Total	5,899.9	10.2	36.4	243.5	290.6	1,668.2	3,156.3	494.6
U.S. Metropolitan Areas	6,757.6	11.5	43.4	319.0	328.3	1,911.8	3,534.9	608.8
U.S. Rural Areas	2,290.4	7.5	15.5	22.5	136.9	830.2	1,143.9	133.9
Regional Crime Centers								
Gillette	8,626.8	0	57.7	107.2	263.9	1,468.0	6,152.6	577.3
Rawlins	7,697.0	8.7	52.2	60.9	644.3	1,018.7	5,363.5	548.5
Rock Springs	11,614.7	25.8	30.9	195.7	1,504.0	2,044.8	6,901.9	911.7
Safe Place								
Buffalo	3,607.6	0	0	0	129.8	519.1	2,803.0	155.7

Horn Mountains soaring in the background. Its Main Street is crooked and for good reason. It originally was a buffalo and cow trail and when the first freight wagons came through this country, they followed the buffalo path and its ford across Clear Creek. And when the first buildings were erected, the logical site was along the trail.

Tourism, agriculture, cattle and sheep production, and petroleum all have important roles in Buffalo's economy. There are many producing wells in the southern part of Johnson County, near the Teapot Dome oil field, and they pay a good percentage of the taxes that maintain the county. Mountain streams and reservoirs supply the irrigation water for grain and forage crops, which in turn support the county's livestock economy. Cattle, sheep, wool, oil, and lumber are the main commodities sold for export. Johnson County also has rich, thick veins of subbituminous coal and it was for this reason that Reynolds Mining Corporation built its aluminum plant a few miles north of Buffalo at Lake DeSmet.

Medical facilities consist of a 35-bed hospital, a clinic, a nursing home, and six doctors and three dentists. For shopping, Buffalo is the trade center for Johnson County. Sheridan is the regional trading center for this section of Wyoming and Montana and for more sophisticated shopping needs, Billings, Montana, is 170 miles away.

Buffalo's elevation is 4,645 feet and the peaks of the Big Horn Mountains just west of town rise to 13,165 feet. Its climate is that of northern mountain country, with four distinct seasons. The city lies in a cuplike depression at the foot of the mountains, which protects it from the winds. Buffalo is almost always a few degrees cooler than the surrounding area in the summer and not quite as cold in the winter. The average annual snowfall is 44 inches.

Crimes of violence are relatively rare in Buffalo. In our comparison year of 1980, there were no murders, rapes, or robberies, and just 5 aggravated assaults. Property crime consisted of 20 burglaries, 108 larceny-thefts, and 6 motor vehicle thefts. This placed Buffalo below U.S. rural crime rates in all categories except larceny-theft and motor vehicle theft, and in those categories it was still way below U.S. metropolitan levels.

Buffalo had been one of the towns in our 1972 book, *Safe Places,* and Betsy Kirven, executive director of the chamber of commerce, told us that they had received "a great deal of written responses to your book, and from time to time still get a letter or phone call referring to your book. An interesting fact that I noted about these calls and letters is that in many of the cases, the request came to us from someone who had been a recent victim of a crime (or crimes) and just felt that they couldn't bear to be victimized again."

Ms. Kirven added that "most of the residents of Buffalo believe that this community is still the best place to raise our children. I have composed a list of all the clubs and organizations in the community and I was *surprised* at the number of activities going on in this small community!" Her list was indeed impressive, with eight pages listing business organizations, youth groups, agricultural groups, hospital and nursing home associations, miscellaneous clubs, garden and music clubs, social groups, fraternal organizations, senior citizen groups, extension clubs, dance clubs, political organizations, sports clubs, and church activity groups. Annual events sponsored by the community include the Johnson County Fair and Rodeo and the Autumn Festival, featuring Basque folk dancing, live entertainment, and food and crafts booths.

Richard Frankovic, of Frankovic Realty, told us that houses and ranches range in price from $30,000 to several million dollars. The majority of the houses are in the $50,000 to $80,000 range and the average price in 1982 was $66,800.

For that average price, you could expect to get a 3-bedroom, 2-bath ranch on an average-sized city lot of 8,000 square feet. It would have either a living room and family room or a living room and a formal dining room—though formal dining rooms are not that common out here. It would have a 2-car garage, and may or may not have a basement.

As for taxes, he noted that "we're one of the lowest tax towns" in the area and that 1982 taxes on a home listed at $68,500 came to $228.78 with the Wyoming homestead exemption.

For $185,000, you could get a 1976 contemporary with shingle roof, native rock, and cedar exterior, on 5 acres that include a barn, dog kennels, and horse corrals. The house had 1,920 square feet of living area on the main floor, plus 1,200 square feet of finished daylight basement. It had 3 bedrooms up, 2 bedrooms down, living room, formal dining room, family room, rec room, 2 fireplaces, breakfast nook, 3¾ baths, and a 2-car attached garage. Taxes on this property were $382.76 with the Wyoming homestead exemption.

Mr. Frankovic added that he had three houses like that out in the countryside, all in the same price range.

Buffalo has a good number of apartments, he told us, and the rent for a 2-bedroom unit would be in the $300 to $325 range. Luxury 3-bedroom apartments with fireplace and garage would run $450 to $500.

The Old West wasn't so long ago here in Buffalo. Today you can explore and relive that exciting past, even while you take advantage of all the modern conveniences that Buffalo has to offer. Just one visit and we think you'll agree that Buffalo is Western living at its best.

Where to get further information:

State

Wyoming Travel Commission, Cheyenne, WY 82002. Wyoming has some of the finest travel literature available in the country today and we particularly recommend the exquisitely produced booklet, *Wyoming . . . excites your senses!* and four self-guided tours, to the northern, central, southern, and western parts of the state.

Regional

Sheridan County Chamber of Commerce, P.O. Box 707, Sheridan, WY 82801. Big Horn National Forest, c/o Regional Forester, U.S. Forest Service, 11177 W. Eighth Avenue, P.O. Box 25127, Lakewood, CO 80225.

Local

Buffalo Chamber of Commerce, 55 N. Main Street, P.O. Box 927, Buffalo, WY 82834.

APPENDIX I

CRIME RATES—U.S. Cities with a Population Over 500,000

(Ranked highest to lowest on basis of 1980 statistics. "Crime Rate" refers to number of crimes per 100,000 population.)

Rank/City	Population	Crime Rate
1 Boston	562,582	13,465.6
2 Dallas	900,104	11,777.5
3 Phoenix	772,884	11,453.6
4 Detroit	1,197,325	10,642.1
5 San Francisco	674,150	10,446.4
6 New York	7,035,348	10,094.0
7 Cleveland	572,657	10,058.7
8 Washington	635,233	10,022.8
9 Los Angeles	2,952,511	9,952.1
10 Columbus	562,416	9,843.6
11 Baltimore	784,554	9,776.8
12 New Orleans	557,761	9,605.4
13 Houston	1,619,644	8,886.3
14 San Jose	628,106	8,252.0
15 San Diego	874,826	8,059.4
16 Jacksonville	542,795	7,901.7
17 Memphis	644,957	7,895.3
18 Honolulu	762,020	7,574.4
19 San Antonio	788,049	7,343.8
20 Chicago	2,986,419	6,583.4
21 Milwaukee	633,845	6,538.8
22 Philadelphia	1,681,175	6,016.3
23 Indianapolis	698,753	5,326.6

APPENDIX II

STATE CRIME RATES

(Ranked highest to lowest on basis of 1980 statistics. "Crime Rate" refers to number of crimes per 100,000 population.)

Rank/State	Crime Rate	Rank/State	Crime Rate
1 Nevada	8,854.0	26 Kansas	5,378.8
2 Florida	8,402.0	27 Illinois	5,275.3
3 Arizona	8,170.8	28 Oklahoma	5,052.9
4 California	7,833.1	29 Montana	5,024.5
5 Hawaii	7,482.3	30 Vermont	4,988.5
6 Colorado	7,333.5	31 Wyoming	4,986.4
7 Washington	6,915.0	32 Alabama	4,933.6
8 New York	6,911.6	33 Indiana	4,930.4
9 Delaware	6,776.6	34 Minnesota	4,799.5
10 Oregon	6,686.9	35 Wisconsin	4,798.6
11 Michigan	6,675.9	36 Idaho	4,782.2
12 Maryland	6,630.1	37 Iowa	4,746.7
13 New Jersey	6,401.3	38 New Hampshire	4,679.6
14 Alaska	6,210.0	39 North Carolina	4,640.5
15 Texas	6,143.0	40 Virginia	4,620.0
16 Massachusetts	6,079.1	41 Tennessee	4,497.9
17 New Mexico	5,979.0	42 Maine	4,367.6
18 Rhode Island	5,932.6	43 Nebraska	4,305.2
19 Connecticut	5,881.7	44 Arkansas	3,811.1
20 Utah	5,880.6	45 Pennsylvania	3,736.3
21 Georgia	5,603.7	46 Kentucky	3,433.7
22 Louisiana	5,453.7	47 Mississippi	3,417.2
23 South Carolina	5,439.2	48 South Dakota	3,243.2
24 Missouri	5,433.1	49 North Dakota	2,963.7
25 Ohio	5,431.4	50 West Virginia	2,551.6

Index

(Page numbers in italics refer to crime charts; page numbers in **boldface** refer to main text for town)